# Evelyn Waugh

## The Early Years 1903–1939

# Evelyn Waugh

## The Early Years 1903–1939

*Martin Stannard*

J. M. Dent & Sons Ltd
London   Melbourne

First published 1986
© Martin Stannard 1986

This book is set in Ehrhardt by Input Typesetting Ltd, London SW19 8DR
Printed in Great Britain by Mackays of Chatham Ltd, for
J. M. Dent & Sons Ltd
Aldine House, 33 Welbeck Street, London W1M 8LX

**British Library Cataloguing in Publication Data**
Stannard, Martin, *1947–*
 Evelyn Waugh.
 The early years: 1903–1939
 1. Waugh, Evelyn——Biography 2. Novelists,
 English——20th century——Biography
 I. Title
 823'.912  PR6045.A97Z

ISBN 0–460–04632–2

# Contents

# List of plates

[vi]

# TO DEL

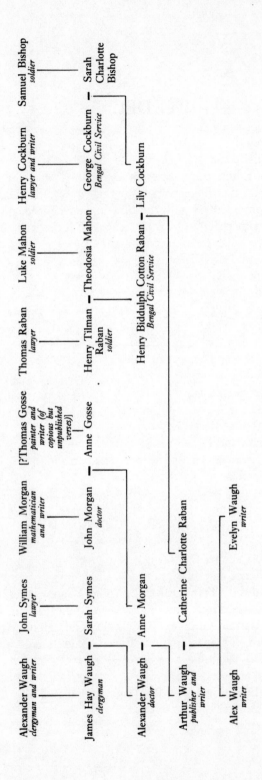

Evelyn Waugh's ancestry

Samuel Bishop
*soldier*

Sarah
Charlotte
Bishop

Henry Cockburn
*lawyer and writer*

George Cockburn
*Bengal Civil Service*

Lily Cockburn

Luke Mahon
*soldier*

Theodosia Mahon

Thomas Raban
*lawyer*

Henry Tilman
Raban
*soldier*

Henry Biddulph Cotton Raban
*Bengal Civil Service*

[?Thomas Gosse
*painter and
writer (of
copious but
unpublished
verses)*]

Anne Gosse

William Morgan
*mathematician
and writer*

John Morgan
*doctor*

John Symes
*lawyer*

Sarah Symes

Anne Morgan

Catherine Charlotte Raban

Evelyn Waugh
*writer*

Alexander Waugh
*clergyman and writer*

James Hay Waugh
*clergyman*

Alexander Waugh
*doctor*

Arthur Waugh
*publisher and
writer*

Alex Waugh
*writer*

# ACKNOWLEDGMENTS

It would require a separate small volume to cite all those who have helped me to produce this biography. Let me begin, then, by begging the forgiveness of those *not* mentioned.

First on my list must come the Leverhulme Trust and the Department of English, University of Edinburgh, for my three years as Leverhulme Research Fellow there; second, the Department of English at the University of Leicester. The first provided me with the time and space to begin the book; the second offered both relief from some teaching duties and professional support to allow me to finish the work. My sister, Josephine Stannard, typed much of the first draft and Sylvia Garfield, Ann Gregson, the late Ann Sowter and Patricia Taylor of the Leicester English Department office have given invaluable service with their excellent secretarial help on my behalf.

A few brave spirits read the whole or part of the typescript and offered useful suggestions and corrections: Mark Amory, Professor Bernard Bergonzi, Professor Robert Murray Davis, Dr Kelvin Everest, Professor David Lodge, Joy Rutter, Rick Rylance and Dr Nigel Wood. Three others combined this work with proof-reading: my tireless editor, Malcolm Gerratt, Peter Hargreaves (who also helped with the index) and Sharon Ouditt. Marie-Claire Uhart compiled the General Index.

For lengthy formal interviews I must thank Sir Harold Acton, Gillon Aitken, the late Sir John and Penelope, Lady Betjeman, Sir William Deedes, Sir Alexander Glen, Graham Greene, Hon. Jonathan Guinness, Hon. Mrs G. Heathcoat Amory, the late Christopher Hollis, the late Lord Kinross, Lady Pansy Lamb, Lady Dorothy Lygon, Lady Diana Mosley, Hon. Mrs Evelyn Nightingale, Anthony Powell, Peter Quennell, Dr Elisabeth Stopp, Christopher Sykes, Mr F. B. Walker, the late Alec Waugh and the late Douglas Woodruff.

The rest are most conveniently thanked under separate headings. Additional correspondence and discussion: the Marchioness of Bath (Daphne Fielding), Baron Bradwell (Tom Driberg), Dudley Carew, the late Claud Cockburn, Michael Davie, Hon. Mrs Gabriel Dru, John Ellison, Dr Donat Gallagher, the late Alastair Graham, Rev. Colin Gill, Hon. Mrs Bridget Grant, Basil Handford, Thomas Ingram, Rev. Gerald Irvine, Adam Low, Lord Moyne, Benedict Nightingale, Gaston Palewski, Professor Wallace Robson, Stephen Wall and Auberon Waugh. Libraries: the staffs of the BBC Script Library; the BBC Written Archive Centre; the Bodleian; the British Library; Cambridge University Library; Edinburgh University Library; the Harry Ransom Humanities Research Center, University of Texas at Austin;

ACKNOWLEDGMENTS

Leicester University Library. Publishers and editors of earlier work by myself: Routledge and Kegan Paul for permission to quote from *Evelyn Waugh: The Critical Heritage* (1984) and the editors of *Essays in Criticism*.

Thanks are also due to the following for permission to quote extracts from the works of Evelyn Waugh:

*The Letters of Evelyn Waugh*: The Trustees of the Estate of Laura Waugh, reprinted by permission of A. D. Peters & Co. Ltd; Ticknor & Fields, a Houghton Mifflin Company; text © the Estate of Laura Waugh 1980; Introduction and compilation © Mark Amory 1980.

*The Diaries of Evelyn Waugh*; *The Essays, Articles and Reviews of Evelyn Waugh*; *Men at Arms*: The Trustees of the Estate of Laura Waugh, reprinted by permission of A. D. Peters & Co. Ltd; Little, Brown & Co., Inc.

*Edmund Campion*; *Robbery Under Law*; published articles not contained in *The Essays, Articles and Reviews of Evelyn Waugh*; unpublished letters, manuscripts and broadcasts: The Trustees of the Estate of Laura Waugh, reprinted by permission of A. D. Peters & Co. Ltd.

*Black Mischief*; *A Handful of Dust*; *Vile Bodies*: The Trustees of the Evelyn Waugh Settlement, reprinted by permission of A. D. Peters & Co. Ltd; Little, Brown & Co., Inc.

*Decline and Fall*; *Labels*; *Ninety-Two Days*; *Remote People*; *Rossetti*; *Waugh in Abyssinia*; *Work Suspended*: The Trustees of the Evelyn Waugh Settlement, reprinted by permission of A. D. Peters & Co. Ltd.

# Abbreviations and note on references

Unpublished letters are given full references; those published by Mark Amory in 1980 are alluded to by '*Letters*, p . . .'. The date and recipient of these letters is made clear in the text. For convenience I have cited quotations from the Penguin Books editions of Waugh's fiction. Full reference to date and place of first publication appears in the Bibliography. For the travel books, biographies and *ALL*, page references are given to the first edition. Place of publication (for all works) is London unless otherwise stated. Where Waugh's journalism or reviews of his book have been reprinted, cross-references to *EAR* and *CH* are added. Letters between Waugh and his agent are cross-referred to Robert Murray David's *Catalogue* of the HRC Archive, Texas. The contractions used in the footnotes are explained below.

## *Abbreviations*

| | |
|---|---|
| *ALL* | Evelyn Waugh, *A Little Learning. The First Volume of an Autobiography* (Chapman & Hall, 1964) |
| ALS, nd, np | Autograph letter, signed, no date, no place (i.e. no address) |
| BBCSL | BBC Script Library |
| *Catalogue* | *A Catalogue of the Evelyn Waugh Archive at the Humanities Research Center, The University of Texas at Austin,* ed. Robert Murray Davis (Troy, New York, Whitston Publishing Company, 1981) |
| *CH* | *Evelyn Waugh. The Critical Heritage,* ed. Martin Stannard (Routledge, 1984) |
| *C Her* | *Catholic Herald* |
| *CL* | *Country Life* |
| *CSM* | *Christian Science Monitor* |
| CUL | Cambridge University Library |
| *Diaries* | *The Diaries of Evelyn Waugh,* ed. Michael Davie (Weidenfeld & Nicolson, 1976) |
| *DE* | *Daily Express* |
| *DR* | *Dublin Review* |
| *DS* | *Daily Sketch* |
| *DT* | *Daily Telegraph* |
| *EAR* | *The Essays, Articles and Reviews of Evelyn Waugh,* ed. Donat Gallagher (Methuen, 1983) |

| | |
|---|---|
| *EN* | *Evening News* |
| *ES* | *Evening Standard* |
| *EWAHW* | *Evelyn Waugh and His World*, ed. David Pryce-Jones (Weidenfeld & Nicolson, 1973) |
| *FR* | *Fortnightly Review* |
| HRC | Henry Ransom Humanities Research Center, University of Texas at Austin |
| *HB* | *Harper's Bazaar* |
| *JB* | *John Bull* |
| *L&L* | *Life & Letters* |
| *LCM* | *Lancing College Magazine* |
| *Letters* | *The Letters of Evelyn Waugh*, ed. Mark Amory (Weidenfeld & Nicolson, 1980) |
| *MBE* | Alec Waugh, *My Brother Evelyn and Other Profiles* (Cassell, 1967) |
| *MP* | *Morning Post* |
| MS | Manuscript |
| *N&A* | *Nation & Atheneum* |
| *ND* | *Night and Day* |
| *NPMM* | *Nash's Pall Mall Magazine* |
| *NS* | *New Statesman* |
| *NYHTBR* | *New York Herald Tribune Book Review* |
| *NYTBR* | *New York Times Book Review* |
| *OMR* | Arthur Waugh, *One Man's Road, Being a Picture of Life in a Passing Generation* (Chapman & Hall, 1931) |
| *OFR* | *Oxford Fortnightly Review* |
| *SD* | *Sunday Dispatch* |
| *SR* | *Sunday Referee* |
| *S. Tel.* | *Sunday Telegraph* |
| *ST* | *Sunday Times* |
| Sykes | Christopher Sykes, *Evelyn Waugh. A Biography* (Collins, 1975) |
| TS | Typescript |
| *TEYOAW* | Alec Waugh, *The Early Years of Alec Waugh* (Cassell, 1962) |
| *TLS* | *Times Literary Supplement* |
| *Writers* | Julian Jebb's interview with Waugh printed as 'Evelyn Waugh' in *Writers at Work* (Secker & Warburg, 1968), pp. 105–114 |

# *Preface*

The first, and until now the only, extensive study of Evelyn Waugh's life and work was published by Christopher Sykes under the title *Evelyn Waugh. A Biography*. In his Preface he states that 'I describe this is as *a* and not *the* biography of Evelyn Waugh because the great quantity of documentary material on which this book is based suggests to me that other biographical studies could and perhaps should be written' (p. ix). This in itself emphasises the need for a fuller portrait.

The quantity of available research material has continued to increase: Michael Davie's almost complete text of the *Diaries* (1976), Mark Amory's *Letters* (1980), Professor Davis's vast *Catalogue* of the Waugh archive in Texas (1981), Donat Gallagher's *Essays, Articles and Reviews* (1983) and my own *Critical Heritage* (1984). During the last decade many new memoirs by and biographies of Waugh's friends have appeared, Anthony Powell's *To Keep the Ball Rolling* being perhaps the most important of them. And these are only the published sources relating to Waugh's life. There are thousands of 'documents' – letters, manuscripts, broadcasts, interviews, short fiction and journalism – which remain out of print. Mark Amory's substantial volume contained but a fifth of the correspondence at his disposal. I have, then, been able to draw upon a wide range of unpublished material.

The most avid Waugh fanatics might throw up their hands in despair at this news. Is there not quite enough on the market already without another book on the man ? Do we *need* another biography? I believe we do. The result of all this research has been to call into question not only the accuracy of Sykes's work but also many of its personal and literary judgements.

We must be grateful to Christopher Sykes for his pioneering efforts, writing, as he was, before many of his sources were published and annotated. I owe a particular debt to him for his generously offering two lengthy interviews and I hope, given his disclaimer, that he will not consider it an act of ingratitude that I should write a different kind of book, offering a different image of Waugh and trying, as far as I am able, to set the record straight. Sykes was a close friend of Waugh and as such had an intimate insight into his subject's character which it would be impertinent for an outsider to imitate. As a friend and co-religionist, though, Sykes had a fastidious discretion which often needlessly veiled information that was even then common knowledge. Almost nothing, for instance, is said of Waugh's sexual relationships before his re-marriage in 1937 and the account of the collapse of the first marriage is biased and, it would seem, misinformed.

For the reclamation of a more accurate narrative of that collapse I must thank Waugh's first wife for the honesty and courage to talk about these events after maintaining so long a silence. Mrs Nightingale (as she now is) has never defamed Waugh and, despite her own misgivings about the marriage, has remained staunchly loyal and reticent, never shirking responsibility for the break-up. It remains an agonising memory for her and, if any other impression is conveyed by the text (which I hope it is not), that is entirely my responsibility.

There is ultimately no better source for the biographer than the first-hand account and in this respect I have been unusually fortunate in the good will of Waugh's friends and acquaintances. The book draws on lengthy interviews – with, among others, Sir Harold Acton, Sir John and Penelope Betjeman, Graham Greene, Christopher Hollis, Lord Kinross, Lady Dorothy Lygon, Lady Diana Mosley and Alec Waugh – and tries to collate these personal impressions with the enormous range of scholarly evidence now available. It attempts something which no other biographical study of Waugh has done: to forge a relationship between the crucial events of Waugh's life and his developing aesthetic. His public image was largely self-constructed. As a form of defence he often pretended during his early career that he was not serious about writing. My argument suggests that, while for many years he did not want to be a writer and despised the egotism of the self-consciously *avant-garde*, he was nevertheless a serious artist from 1929 and quite capable of defending his position when threatened. I see Waugh as a brilliant but awkward, isolated, and neurotic man, with many intimate friends and few lovers, almost frightened but with dauntless bravado, a scintillating manic depressive, not 'possessed' as Belloc suggested, but dispossessed, alienated.

No biographer could 'capture' so evasive a character and I have not attempted to do so. The facts, wherever possible, should be allowed to speak for themselves and I have tried not to bully the reader into restrictive interpretations. I hope I have avoided the amateur psychoanalysis Waugh loathed in contemporary fiction and biography. But even in naming one's subject one suggests an uncomfortable authorial 'attitude' of patronage/approval/disapproval. Auberon Waugh, reviewing Sykes's biography, explained that he had once considered writing his father's life himself. The task was abandoned, he said, because he could settle on no satisfactory title for someone so close. Should it be 'Evelyn', or 'Mr Waugh', or 'Waugh', or 'my father' or 'papa'?[1] A similar problem arises here. I have, for convenience and clarity, generally settled on 'Evelyn' for the early years and 'Waugh' for the period of adulthood. This connotes no more than a literary device.

[1] Auberon Waugh, *Books & Bookmen*, October 1975, 7.

# Prologue

When Evelyn Waugh's *Diaries* were published in 1976 the reviewers were, by turns, perplexed, outraged and amused. There was much talk of warts; Frederic Raphael saw in these jottings a 'portrait of the artist as a bad man'.[1] The book met with a critical reception which, although frequently inane, was entirely in keeping with the sort of press to which Waugh had become inured thoughout his life. Even beyond the grave, and in a document not intended for publication, he could still shock his public.

At the end of his life Waugh remained an enigma: malicious yet capable of extraordinary kindness, a selfish Christian, a cultured and articulate aesthete for whom British painting had been in relentless decline since Augustus Egg. He wanted nothing to do with the modern world and, as he said in his autobiographical novel *The Ordeal of Gilbert Pinfold* (1957), his strongest tastes were negative. He abhorred 'plastics, Picasso, sunbathing and jazz'.[2] He despised the telephone. For years he refused to have a radio; television was insufferable. He dressed expensively, often in outrageously loud cloth, and in premature old age sported a Victorian ear trumpet which he would raise when talking and lower when spoken to. He caused scenes and insulted friends; his children were brought up with love but strict formality. He was, in the conventional sense of the word, a 'snob'. The signs on the gates of his country houses were lucidly snubbing: 'Entrance Interdite Aux Promeneurs'; 'No Admittance On Business'. But it was not always so. He wrote of Pinfold that he 'gave nothing away'.[3] In early manhood Waugh had given everything away and had lived to regret it. His squirearchical isolation resulted, at least in part, from a determination never to repeat those mistakes.

Waugh cultivated eccentricity in others and himself as a last refuge of liberty, diversity and privacy. The fraternal ideals of socialism he saw as a miserable humanist delusion. The corporate state represented to him an attack on the irreducible individuality of the soul. He was deeply sceptical of man's capacity for altruism in a secular world. His own cruelty constantly reminded him of the

1. Frederic Raphael, *ST*, 5 September, 1976, 27.
2. *Pinfold*, p. 14.
3. *Ibid.*, p. 9.

need for its control by the laws of his faith. Christopher Sykes, his friend and biographer, noted that Waugh's life was coloured by a 'sleepless sense of story-telling'.[4] But if this sense of the absurd brought laughter to his friendships and generated the riotous black comedy of his writings, it also brought Waugh less welcome gifts: fear of failure and a crushing, paranoic boredom. The conflict between his public and his private life was never satisfactorily resolved. He loathed following the crowd, yet simultaneously, he wanted to be popular. A profound modesty and a weakness for panache were constantly at loggerheads.

At the outset of his career Waugh had no ambition to emulate Joyce or Lawrence. Necessity, not vocation, drove him to literature. But his success, as both artist and self-publicist, began early and never faltered. By the end, his position as a senior figure of British letters he found supremely satisfying and mildly embarrassing. He was his own most mordant critic without ever falling prey to false modesty. Today he is accepted as one of the finest prose writers of the century. His entire fictional opus and most of his biographical and travel writing is still in print twenty years after his death. Many disliked the man and the causes he apparently espoused; none could deny his prodigious talent.

Waugh's behaviour was mischievously provocative; the repertoire of offensive and startling tricks was designed to fence off a private world from the intrusive eye of the Age of the Common Man. It worked. A successful libel action followed Nancy Spain's attempt to interview him without invitation in 1957. None dared disturb him again. The BBC considered it a considerable 'scoop' when in 1960 he agreed to be cross-questioned by John Freeman on his 'Face to Face' programme. This trial by television has long since taken its place in the catalogue of Waugh anecdotes. Freeman was noted for his relentless probing of sensitive memories and had secured lasting fame by reducing Gilbert Harding to tears while raking about in his childhood. Waugh came prepared.

Soberly dressed, a carnation in his buttonhole, with the inevitable cigar and a quizzical glare of amused condescension, he answered all the questions designed to reveal psychological instability with devastating brevity. When pushed for details, he mixed fantasy and truth at just the right pitch of levity to confuse and deflate his inquisitor. At last, somewhat desperate, Freeman managed to pin Waugh to a definite statement. The novelist agreed that the best he could hope for was that people should ignore him. 'You like that when it happens, do you?' 'Yes.' 'Why are you appearing in this programme?' 'Poverty,' came the reply. 'We've both been hired to talk in this deliriously happy way.'[5]

Waugh was consistently modest about his achievements. Chaos and madness, he thought, were never far from anyone's door and vanity, particularly artistic vanity, for ever eager to admit them. The sense of the profound absurdity of the

4. Sykes, p. 163.
5. 'Face to Face', recorded 18 June, 1960; transmitted 26 June, 1960; BBCSL.

human condition lay at the heart of his vision and, while relishing its comic potential, he did not exempt himself from its terrors. He was, temperamentally, an anarchist. As Christopher Hollis once remarked: 'He liked life to be full of disturbance.'[6] Opposed to this, his intellectual temper was that of an Augustinian Roman Catholic. Much of his adult life was spent defending the structure and discipline of Christian civilisation. The latter, strangely, allowed of the former. His writing was an anarchic defence of order, at first similar in form to that of some of the *avant garde* in France and America, but profoundly different in its implications.

The cross-references in modern French theses between his work and that of Sartre and Camus would have made him chuckle. Someone once remarked to Waugh that he must have been influenced by F. Scott Fitzgerald. In fact, he did not read *The Great Gatsby* until later in life. He abhorred the self-important manifestoes of the *avant garde*. The tiny span of individual existence, when examined beyond the context of Christianity, seemed, to the mature Waugh, plainly unreasonable. He accepted the benefits of contemporary literary techniques which eschewed sentimentality but refused to accord any importance to the 'quest for identity' upon which Aldous Huxley and Virginia Woolf concentrated their attention. His work offers a sustained critique of the humanist values of such writers. For most of his career as a novelist, Catholicism represented the only 'identity'.

As in his art, so in his life. In early manhood he was swept along, at times in a hallucinatory daze, despair following on disappointment. Later he exercised a degree of control by inventing protective masks, the 'eccentric don' and 'testy colonel' of *Pinfold*. Increasingly he felt persecuted, an alien sensitive spirit in a crumbling civilisation. The *Diaries* adequately demonstrate the encroachment of paranoia. He always believed himself safe behind the 'massive defences of . . . the borderline of sanity',[7] but at one point the don and the colonel became himself and, temporarily, he went mad.

In his first full-length work, a biography of Rossetti, Waugh stated: 'Taking him simply as a character for a story-book, his life is one of intense interest; but it is necessary first to clear away the traces of legend that hang about him.'[8] The encrustation of legends that surrounds Waugh's life has often distorted our understanding of the man. He was perfectly successful in excluding the journalists and thesis writers. But it is only through an understanding of, and sympathy with, the 'story-book' element which he deliberately injected into existence that we can begin to tell his story.

6. Christopher Hollis, 'Introductory Memoir' to John St John, *To The War With Waugh* (Leo Cooper Ltd, 1973), p. v.
7. *Work Suspended* , p. 120.
8. *Rossetti*, p. 12.

He told part of it himself. Waugh's last book was the first volume of his autobiography, *A Little Learning* (1964). His brother, Alec, and his father, Arthur, had already published reminiscences; Arthur's he found dull, Alec's painfully intimate. The massive revisions of Waugh's manuscript suggest that he found the public reconstruction of his own life unusually difficult. His imagination instinctively 'fictionalised' and this technique was not appropriate. In addition there was the problem of privacy, maintaining a decorous reserve. For years he had lambasted the amateur psychoanalysis of contemporary memoirs and fiction. He had no wish to confess. Writing had always been 'something external to himself'[9]. In the early 'sixties, though, he found himself needing to reveal more of his personal affairs than ever before. He had to devise an approach which would both deflect the Freudians and tell the truth.

The result, most reviewers agreed, was brilliantly successful. We are accurately informed of the details of his early life and his own analysis of the crucial relationships is perceptive. It is the unenviable task of any biographer of Waugh to re-trace the ground covered by his subject's own succinct and often self-lacerating narrative of those first twenty-one years. But if it is unlikely that there will ever be a better account of that period, one can, at least, construct a fuller one. For all its honesty, it is a biased book.

Certain minor distortions are concealed by the rhetoric of its taut prose. The relationship with his father and brother was more awkward than he suggests. The picture of untroubled felicity in childhood reflects more Waugh's determination to allow the psychologists no room for manoeuvre than his absolute honesty. The degradations and homosexual affairs of Oxford are largely omitted in favour of a 'Brideshead' picture of the university. Generally there is an unacknowledged predisposition towards his mother's opinions and family. Looking back at his feckless youth he is impatient and dismissive of his failings. The classically precise use of language, ornately archaic at times, reflects a pervasive irony. Waugh succeeds in maintaining his privacy (as does Graham Greene in *Ways of Escape*) by treating his younger self as another character. This was, in one sense, Basil Seal quietly riding again round those strange tracks of his childhood and adolescence lost for ever but to a failing memory. Ultimately he leaves us with a mystery rather than an explanation.

Memory, as he knew too well, reconstructs the past. *A Little Learning* is a dangerous thing in this respect. Modesty forbade presenting himself as an ebullient and amusing companion; a prickly sense of social and religious distinction betrays a certain distaste for his humble and Protestant origins. He regrets the strength of his animosity towards his father and C. R. M. F. Cruttwell but cannot disguise it. When the book was published, angry letters of protest appeared in the press defending his Oxford tutor. Set alongside other contemporary accounts

9. *Pinfold*, p. 10.

its areas of fictionalised subjectivity begin to emerge. There was no deliberate distortion. But the material he omits or merely sketches in can be as interesting as that which he emphasises. *A Little Learning* dealt with much that he would rather have forgotten. Occasionally he forgets to remember, or at least pretends to do so.

# I

# *Ancestral Voices*

Turning left off Fortune Green Road into Hillfield Road, West Hampstead, one ascends a slow gradient between terraces of three-storey Victorian villas. They are modest houses, gabled, red brick, hiding their third floors in basements or in the roof space at the rear. A tiny patch of land divides them from the footpath; thirty yards of garden at the back afford some privacy. After a quarter of a mile or so the road stops dead: a bank of grass, some trees, a bench. On the right up a steep flight of concrete steps is No. 11.

Today (1986) it is divided into four flats, the concrete is chipped and the sloping front garden a waste of tangled grass and shrubs. In the early autumn of 1903, Arthur and Catherine Waugh had lived there for eight years and it was as neat as a bandbox. Five years earlier artisan lodgers had been common in Hampstead. By the turn of the century, thanks to the land-company estates, the petit-bourgeoisie had colonised the area. Hillfield and Aldred Road had stood alone at first, comfortable homes at a respectful distance from the gentry on Hampstead heights. By today's standards they are substantial: three rooms on each of the two main floors and an attic overlooking the garden. In 1903 a single family occupied the space now used by four.

Then, as now, it was a quiet, unpretentious street; Arthur and 'Kay' were a quiet, unpretentious couple, well-to-do but not wealthy. Their first son, Alec, had been born in the house five and a half years earlier. Arthur earned about £600 a year and belonged to a London club, the National. He knew many celebrated writers. But he had no urgent ambition to leave this unfashionable address; it suited their needs and income. Each morning he would set off for work in a silk hat; each evening he would return to draw pictures of battles for Alec. In the summer, father and son played single-wicket cricket in the narrow garden. There was a maid and a nanny. Catherine was heavily pregnant. Everyone, it seems, was contented and especially Alec whose most earnest hope was that his mother should produce a wicket-keeper. English Literature has reason to be grateful for her failure in this respect.

Evelyn Arthur St John Waugh was born in this house on 28th October, 1903. His parents were well pleased with their baby, though Arthur had been hoping for a girl. Alec's initial enthusiasm was short-lived. A boisterously athletic infant, he had converted the nursery, until then entirely his domain, into a cricket pitch where he played a complicated game of his own invention. By bouncing a tennis ball from the wall he could bat to his own bowling. The chairs were fielders; he added and subtracted runs according to each shot. For hours at a time the house resounded to quiet thuds of the ball. It was a serious business and the baby interfered with it. Evelyn's cot now occupied a corner of the room and Alec was required to restrict the ferocity of his sport. He still played and generously adjudged himself 'out' when the ball landed on the net which protected his new brother. But it was not the same. There had been an invasion of territorial rights.

At that time Hillfield Road still maintained an air of rural seclusion. From the bow windows of the nursery Alec remembered a clear view over the street to South London and the Surrey Hills. He could make out the dome of the Crystal Palace and the Great Wheel of the Earl's Court Exhibition. The Finchley Road, just to the north, was little more than a country thoroughfare, with isolated mansions in secluded gardens. Buses were horse-drawn. When the family returned to Paddington from their summer holidays in the West Country a barefoot man would follow the cab to the house in the hope of a tip for helping with the luggage. There was no telephone or electricity; gas lit the hall and stairs, lamps the main rooms; candles stood on the mantelshelf.[1] In the summer Arthur and Catherine could take their tea under the willow-tree undisturbed by the dull moan of traffic noise which now invades every suburban garden.

Arthur was then thirty-seven and had been married for ten years. A little under two years earlier, he had been appointed to the managing directorship of Chapman and Hall, the publishers. A complex character, he was nervous and asthmatic, modest but not shy, a rigorously efficient man of business. Often likened to Pickwick, he had a blustering, amiable ebullience, a 'theatrical' personality which never disguised deep-rooted insecurity. Important domestic decisions would be rushed into impulsively and all debate on the matter thereafter closed. He detested discussion – a characteristic which Evelyn in later life found intolerable.

Catherine, on the other hand, seemed immune from neuroses. Her even, rather unimaginative temperament held the home together with tact and patience. She was a small, tight-knit woman, practical and impervious to panic. She accommodated herself to her husband's occasional eccentricities and, negotiating the rapids of potential argument, steered the family into clear water again. They complemented each other well and Arthur was devoted to her. Inevitably she found herself at odds with him over several issues and, in particular, Evelyn's education. But she would make her point and then allow her partner his way. Entirely satisfied with their own company and that of their family and close friends, they would never entertain hordes of professional acquaintances as did Arthur's cousin, Edmund Gosse. W. W. Jacobs, the short-story writer, and his family became part of their inner circle. But the shrieks and bitter, tempestuous separations of that

1. Cf. *TEYOAW*, pp. 12–14.

household were foreign to the Waughs. For Catherine and Arthur marriage had largely represented an escape from an unsatisfactory childhood; their home was a haven of domestic security, a symbol of their deliverance from confusion and oppression.

Towards the end of his life, with many misgivings as to his ability for the task, Arthur completed his autobiography, *One Man's Road* (1931). It was typical of him in this *mélange* of astute analysis and sentimental reflection that he should deal so generously with his father. Alec's and Evelyn's accounts[2] are more candid. Alexander Waugh (1840–1906) was aggressive, on occasions to the point of sadism. He was a successful country doctor. In the spring of 1865 he moved to Somerset and took up a practice centred in Midsomer Norton, then a picturesque village. As a gold medallist at Bristol Medical School, and later at Barts, a prosperous future was predicted for him but he chose not to specialise, preferring certain eminence in a small world to the vagaries of stronger competition. The decisive factor was his devotion to country life; he was 'a sportsman to the core'.[3] At Radley he had been a successful oarsman, footballer and runner. Later he devoted his spare time to shooting. 'From his first days as a medical student', Arthur wrote, 'my father had regarded the shooting season as the compensating reward of a year's struggle with sickness and death.'[4] Arthur was his eldest son; weak-chested and timorous, he was something of a disappointment to his aggressively masculine father.

Alexander's wife, Annie (née Morgan), was sensitive and delicate. She spent much time reclining on a chaise longue teaching Arthur the sentimental Victorian ballads which framed her fantasies. Water-colour painting and the manufacture of salmon-flies occupied her more industrious moments. There was a strain of unspoken sadness in her life. She, too, had married to escape – in this case the religious tyranny of a home dominated by the Plymouth Brethren. But she had escaped only to find herself subject to another form of despotism. Her husband's moods were unpredictable.

Alexander's public image was one of stern good humour. Patients would eagerly anticipate visits from this robust good fellow in his smartly turned out dog-cart. He was widely respected and word spread, when specialists came down from London, that he was unusually well-qualified for a country doctor. The village felt safe in his hands and the practice prospered. But at home he would without warning plunge into thunderous tempers. The household would quiver and cower, waiting nervously for the storm to pass. 'My father', Alec wrote, 'was born on August 24 and my grandmother during the previous weeks was terrified lest her confinement should interfere with her husband's first day of partridge shooting.'[5]

2. Cf. *ibid.*, pp. 7–8 and *ALL*, pp. 21–3.
3. *OMR*, p. 7.
4. *Ibid.*, p. 66.
5. *TEYOAW*, p. 7.

This was typical. Evelyn Waugh knew neither of these grandparents but, loyal to his mother's distaste for Alexander, records a macabre incident: 'It is related that once when he was sitting opposite my grandmother in the carriage, a wasp settled on her forehead. He leant forward and with the ivory top of his cane carefully crushed it there, so that she was stung.'[6]

Arthur had inherited his mother's neurotic sensitivity to suggestion and it was heightened by these emotional upheavals. He heard the servants' lurid country gossip of murder and burglary and, locked alone in the nursery at the top of the stairs, succumbed each night to paroxysms of terror. He could not sleep and his father's cure for insomnia was simple. He designed a course of physical experiments to improve the boy's nerve and moral character. Alexander sat Arthur on a rocking-horse and reared it violently back and forth; he perched him on a high narrow mantelshelf; he sent him down alone in the dark to the smoking room to kiss his gun case.

The inevitable result was that Arthur throughout his life suffered agonies of apprehension over the most trifling things. Like Evelyn, as an adult he could shrug off physical danger or pain but, unlike him, his imagination would constantly race ahead of events and suggest a multitude of possible calamities. Arthur had always to know exactly where Catherine was; if she were half an hour late from a visit to the country he would become restive. He was a fussy, petulant man when presented with threats to his domestic equilibrium.

Catherine never disguised to her sons her dislike of their paternal grandfather, and her mother-in-law's bird-like timidity made her impatient. She had endured many years of their authority over her future husband during a long courtship. Memories of Alexander's rages interspersed by theatrical and patronising displays of affection still rankled late in her life. But it was Alexander's immediate family who suffered more. Arthur had a younger brother, Alick, and three sisters, Connie, Trissie and Elsie, who were later to exercise an important influence over Evelyn's childhood.

Alick, physically the stronger of the two sons, was beaten ferociously by his father. Not surprisingly, he soon 'manifested a roving disposition'[7] and passed into the *Britannia* as a naval cadet just before he was thirteen. Two years later he was a midshipman aboard *The Iron Duke*. From his mother he had inherited a talent for water-colour painting and his illustrated logs were vividly remembered by those who served with him. He married in Hobart and brought his wife back to Midsomer Norton where a son, Eric, was born in 1900. But only three months later Alick contracted malaria in the Solomon Islands and by the autumn was dead. As he lay feverish and hopeless of recovery in Midsomer Norton he perhaps consoled himself with the thought that at least his wife and child would be cared

6. *ALL*, p. 22.
7. *OMR*, p. 110.

for. The plan had been that she should remain with the Waughs. Alexander thought otherwise. The distressed widow was promptly packed off back to Tasmania, taking with her, as his parting gift, bills for the funeral expenses and an unpaid tailoring account.

Connie, Trissie and Elsie were hardly more fortunate, though none in later life would utter a word of disrespect for her father. His harsh tongue would frequently reduce at least one of them to tears during family meals, forcing an abrupt withdrawal from the dining room. All remained maiden ladies and devoted themselves to his service for the rest of his life. And Alexander was not the only dominant male they had to contend with. It was a family riddled with blustering patriarchs. Alexander's father, James Hay Waugh, still exerted considerable influence in Arthur's youth. He was the Rector of Corsley, a Somerset village four miles from Frome. The Rectory, scene of Alexander's youth, represented a shrine of family feeling.

As a boy Arthur would usually be taken there for a month's summer holiday while his parents escaped to Weymouth or Scotland. It was an experience which generated mixed feelings. The children, all baptised by their grandfather, were a little afraid of him. He brooded over the family with a dour benevolence which had some warmth and a great deal of authority in it. Arthur remembered him best standing ready to receive guests in his doorway, 'his long white beard blown in the wind, and his arms open to lift down the youngest first'.[8] He was the head of the house and demanded the respect due to that office.

Corsley was literally the repository of family tradition. The house contained the portraits and books of their ancestors, and, in an inlaid cabinet, their curious heirlooms. It was a place of romance for Arthur and one in which sternly to reflect on the privilege of inheritance. Dour nineteenth-century faces loomed from the canvases in the dining room where, on special occasions, the family silver would be unwrapped and dinner served with elaborate ceremony. The glass of the cabinet protected an unauthenticated lock of Wordsworth's hair, miniatures, silver buttons and a seventeenth-century love-letter. He was taught pride in his family but was perhaps a little intimidated by the responsibility. Overhanging everything, especially in the person and rhetoric of his grandfather, was the omnipresence of death.

The portraits, silver and *memento mori* were inherited by Alexander and installed at Midsomer Norton. To them he added a collection of medical curiosities; his children contributed tourist trophies (from Alick's travels) and a clutter of furniture and draperies. Evelyn and Alec spent delightful summer holidays in the house under the care of their bustling maiden aunts. The place was a treasure trove of the odd and macabre. A stuffed monkey grinned down from a case above the bath, all but its teeth disappearing from view as the steam condensed on the

8. *OMR*, p. 59.

glass; there was a phial of 'white blood' from one of Alexander's terminally anaemic patients. In this mid-Victorian atmosphere the young Evelyn was perfectly happy. It had the stamp of distinct personalities upon it. It was full of strange and delicious smells, 'the still airs of gas and oil and mould and fruit'.[9] There were stables where his aunts kept a pony and trap and where for years the family brougham decayed. It compared very favourably in his active imagination with the sterile and odourless new house in London which his father had bought.

Evelyn, like Arthur, was deeply impressed by the social position of these ancestors. But, unlike his father, he experienced only exhilaration in contemplating the variety and dignity of their lives. He grew up with a profound sense of his gentility. His father's relatives included the painter, Holman Hunt, as well as a pharmacist to Queen Victoria and a mathematician turned insurance wizard who retired in the nineteenth century on two thousand a year. There had been a patrimony from a corn merchant of £150,000. The rest were strongly rooted in the professional classes as lawyers, divines and doctors. They were a clever family and from an early age Evelyn sensed that he was clever too. They had escaped 'trade' several generations earlier. A Little Learning scarcely conveys this childhood pride, only the arrogance into which it grew at school. The Midsomer Norton house is remembered as an adventure playground, nothing more. The collections become 'bric-a-brac', the silver 'Sheffield plate'; the portraits, he emphasises, were by 'nameless artists'. He was not ashamed of his love for the place but, reviewed objectively, it had no intrinsic aesthetic merit. Looking back, his father's family seemed a rather dismal procession of nonentities.

*

A Little Learning notes four great-great-grandfathers, three from his father's side. One of these was Alexander (1754–1827), James Hay's father. Waugh's remarks about him are ultimately disparaging. Two zealous clergymen with a taste for panegyric constructed an arid and almost unreadable biography of the man.[10] Even from this, Waugh admits, we can discern 'an admirable and entirely likeable character'[11] but he could not warm towards him. This is odd because, like Waugh, Alexander had had to make his own way in the world, and even stranger because his great-great-grandfather was more like Evelyn as a boy than anyone else in the male line. The correspondence goes unremarked.

Alexander's qualities extended far beyond an amicable nature. He was not eccentric like James Hay, or aggressive like Arthur's father or timid like Arthur.

---

9.  *ALL*, p. 47.
10. Rev. James Hay and Rev. Henry Belfrage, DD, *A Memoir of the Reverend Alexander Waugh, DD* (Hamilton, Adams & Co., 1830). James Hay Waugh, Rev. Alexander's son, Waugh's great-grandfather, was named after the co-author, a close family friend from Kinross.
11. *ALL*, p. 5.

He was a bright little boy with an eager curiosity, 'the leader of all frolics',[12] yet unusually pious, given to secret prayer. It could almost be a description of Evelyn's early boyhood except that Alexander did not have his descendant's advantage of a cultured professional background. He was a country lad from a family who had, for at least four generations, been tenant farmers in Berwickshire.

By the standards of working people in those days they were comfortably situated. Their savings sent him to Earlstoun Grammar School where he received a solid grounding in the Classics and his parents continued to support him through thirteen years of study as he progressed through school and the universities of Edinburgh and Aberdeen. It was a considerable sacrifice for farming folk with no scholarly tradition but his academic successes were repayment enough. At Edinburgh he excelled in moral philosophy under the influence of William Ferguson; at the Divinity Hall of the Burgher Church of Scotland he studied under John Brown.

He was no dreary pedagogue. Fellow students at Aberdeen, where he eventually took his MA, remembered his 'exuberant flow of animal spirits'.[13] And, at the end of it all, he had the courage and modesty to express doubts as to his vocation. He was trained for the ministry of the Secession Church. For most of his professional life he was based at the Wells Street Church in London, although Scotland remained his abiding love, and he ensured that his sons were educated under the then more liberal and democratic system of his homeland.

He was a reformer, a founder member of The Dissenters Grammar School at Mill Hill and the London Missionary Society; he established the *Evangelical Magazine* and acted as a genial and benevolent spiritual guide to the Scots community in London. Carlyle remembered him with respect. His influence stretched far beyond the narrow bounds of his calling and attracted people of all religious persuasions. In the London of the late eighteenth and early nineteenth century a popular preacher enjoyed the prestige and influence of a politician. He agitated for the abolition of slavery and travelled widely. Wherever he preached in Britain he was met with crowded congregations and in 1815 Aberdeen awarded him an honorary DD. It was a distinguished career for a minister of a small and, until his time, relatively obscure denomination.

When he died[14] at seventy-six the enormous cortège at his funeral testified to his popularity.[15] Dr Waugh was a considerable personality. How was it, then, that

---

12. Cf. *Alexander Waugh, An Earlstoan* [sic] *Grammar School Boy*, a pamphlet (Galashiels, 1946).
13. *Ibid.*
14. 14 December, 1827.
15. The funeral was on 22 December, 1827. The hearse was followed by forty-two mourning coaches, thirteen private carriages and an immense concourse of people. The procession stretched for over half a mile. The service at Bunhill Fields was conducted by Rowland Hill and Edward Irving, two of the more celebrated preachers of their day, representing markedly different schools of thought.

Waugh could state that his great-great-grandfather 'never sought to move outside his own community' and that he was merely 'a prominent man in an obscure world' whose talents were praised only by those refusing, or incapable of, close scrutiny?[16] Protestants, and especially Dissenters, met with little sympathy from Waugh in later life. His traditionalist Catholicism presumed intellectual ineptitude in anyone who repudiated the Church. Free Churchmen had seemed absurd to him from early manhood and Alexander's earnest humanism placed him firmly beyond the pale.

Dr Waugh was a generous, unbigoted man. Despite his own commitment to the Secession Church he reviewed quite calmly the prospect of two of his sons becoming Anglican clergymen. One of them, Alexander (1795–1824), had been sent to Glasgow University where he had won the prize in moral philosophy. His doubts were complex and he consulted his father who, far from being offended, expressed sympathy and left the matter to conscience: ' . . . Should the conclusion [you reach] be different from my views', he wrote, 'I shall not respect you the less, but very carefully aid and assist you to the utmost of my power.'[17] In the end Alexander happily joined the Secession and was given the ministry of Miles Lane Church, London, in 1819. For approximately four years the Waughs were an even more powerful force in the Scots Church of the metropolis. Dr Waugh was delighted to have his boy beside him; there was an air of enthusiasm inspired by the re-inforcement of principle in the younger generation. But the son was weak-voiced and delicate. His father had once, rather naïvely, packed him off to the seaside in the belief that learning to preach above the thunder of the waves would strengthen his vocal cords. It did not. He died in his thirtieth year[18] after a long illness. Alexander's other sons (including, at this time, James Hay) were in business. Now there was no-one to continue the family tradition. It was a fundamental shock to the old man and one from which he never quite recovered. He died three years later and with him there went from the family a combination of unworldly enthusiasm and natural piety which only re-emerged with Evelyn Waugh. Alexander had been the only one of his children in any way like him.

Waugh mistakenly suggests that there were only four sons, [19] presumably because only four are easily traceable. Two have already been mentioned: Alexander and James Hay. Two others were Thomas and George. Of Thomas we know little other than that he was a Master of the Merchant Taylor's Company in 1849, but George secured fame in more than one way. Dr Waugh had married a Scotswoman, Mary Neill, and her brother, John, had amassed a considerable fortune as a corn merchant in Surrey Street, Strand. Being childless, he left the

16. *ALL*, p. 8.
17. *Ibid.*, p. 15.
18. 2 August, 1824.
19. Cf. *ALL*, p. 7. There were six sons and four daughters.

entire amount, £150,000, in trust to his nephews and nieces and, during his lifetime, contributed substantially to the upkeep of Dr Waugh's household. This was the legacy which helped maintain the Waughs in the upper middle classes for three generations until it finally ended with Arthur.

George received £30,000 of it[20] and set himself up as a fashionable pharmacist with a large house in Queensborough Terrace, Kensington, and a country villa in Leatherhead. Always known as 'Dr' Waugh he had, in fact, no right to the title, never having qualified in medicine. *A Little Learning* suggests the opposite, presenting George as a trained doctor of impeccable social qualifications.[21] In fact he was a high-class quack and an assiduous social climber. There was little communication with Thomas because he was 'in trade'. George moved easily through the elegant circles he sought and crowned his escape from his father's simple life by becoming Druggist to Queen Victoria. The fashionable world flocked to him for their salts and potions.

Perhaps even more important to his self-esteem were his eight daughters[22] – Mary, Fanny, Margaret, Emily, Eve, Isobel, Edith and Alice. They were known as the 'eight beautiful Waugh sisters', and represented the perfect ornament to their father's prestige. He guarded them with possessive pride and showed them off as they bobbed round the guests with sugar plums or entertained at the piano. 'From dawn to dusk', he would proclaim, 'this brave instrument is never silent. Day after day, hour after hour, my eight daughters pound the ivory keys.'[23] Like Podsnap, he had bought a large slice of the world and insisted on forcing it down everyone's throat. As his fortune grew steadily, so his status changed on the girls' marriage certificates from 'Chymist' to 'Gentleman' and handsome dowries were arranged. In the end he owned blocks of property in and around Regent Street.

This prosperous, and somewhat preposterous, gentleman might have been quickly forgotten had it not happened that three of his daughters made most unlikely (and to him, distressing) marriages. Thomas Woolner, a sculptor in the Pre-Raphaelite Brotherhood, first invaded the respectable sanctuary in pursuit of Alice. He introduced the painter, Holman Hunt, who courted Fanny. Both were eventually successful and, two years after Fanny's death, Hunt married her younger sister Edith in defiance of the Deceased Wife's Sister Act. George Waugh was not pleased when, less than a year after the ceremony, Hunt took Fanny, seven months pregnant, on a perilous journey to Egypt. After their departure Woolner tactlessly let it slip that Hunt had always been known as 'The Maniac' and George Waugh raved about the house cursing the Land of the Pharaohs. One can only guess at what he might have said had he realised that

20. Cf. Diana Holman Hunt, *My Grandfather, His Wives and Loves* (Hamish Hamilton, 1969), p. 27.
21. Cf. *ALL*, p. 7.
22. Waugh mistakenly says 'three' in *ALL*, p. 7. George Waugh also had two sons.
23. *My Grandfather, op. cit.*, p. 23.

Hunt and Fanny's trip had been delayed, not by her father's splutterings about disease in the Levant, but by blackmail. Annie Miller, a former model and lover, also seven months pregnant by Hunt, was negotiating a high price for their love-letters. And after all, the worthy chemist was proved right: Fanny died in Florence after an excruciating confinement.[24]

This, then, was Evelyn Waugh's connection with the Pre-Raphaelites. Throughout his life they exerted a powerful fascination. The lurid anarchy of their adventures was a constant delight; their revolutionary aesthetic satisfied his sense of artistic propriety. He was avid for information, particularly about Hunt whom he considered 'the only pre-Raphaelite'.[25] It was one of the few subjects which, in later years, could rouse him to enthusiasm. His first book was a biography of Rossetti. Towards the end of his life he longed to write a life of Hunt. The latter was not a blood relation, being only son-in-law of James Hay's brother, but Waugh took pride in the connection. The painter stood out for him from a dull line of respectable, self-important conformity.

There was an element of truth in Waugh's prejudice. As has been noted, patriarchs dominated the family. Dr Waugh was constantly invoked as a household god to his great-grandchild, Arthur, by James Hay. Arthur, in his turn, passed on sentimentally heroic visions of his forebears to his own children. In this, his almost aggressive desire for harmony within the family got the better of his rigorous honesty. Towards the end of *One Man's Road*, though, the truth inevitably leaks out. The picture he paints there of the male line of his maternal forebears is grim indeed. His mother's sufferings remained a poignant memory.

\*

The line begins with a likeable fellow, William Morgan (1750–1833), whom Waugh mentions in *A Little Learning* as one of his traceable great-great-grand-parents. His portrait and miniature were familiar to Waugh from Midsomer Norton and for some reason he singles Morgan out from his father's family as the only man of distinction. In fact, very little is known of him save that he trained as a physician, became a mathematician and ended wealthy. As co-founder and actuary of the Equitable Insurance Company he had conceived the brilliant idea, then quite original, of drawing up a statistical analysis of mortality upon which the company's policies could be based. It was he who retired on two thousand a year. He was astute and kindly and revolutionised the insurance trade but his claims to fame seem no higher than the Reverend Alexander's. *A Little Learning* uses William as a stick with which to beat the unworldly, but equally clever and more widely celebrated, divine. '[Alexander] would not, I think, have shone in the company of my two other notable forebears, William Morgan and Henry

24. Cf. *Ibid.*, pp. 249–52.
25. *Diaries*, 14 November, 1925, p. 233.

Cockburn.'[26] What Waugh seems to mean by this was that the humble clergyman did not move in the same social circles. His chief complaint about Alexander is that 'he adopted armorial bearings to which it is scarcely conceivable that he had any right'.[27]

William's son, John, followed his father's first career and became a doctor. Waugh omits him from *A Little Learning* but he was a significant figure and one whose religious obsession directly impinged on Arthur's life. John rose to eminence at Guy's Hospital as one of Britain's earliest ophthalmic surgeons. His colleagues remembered him as supremely efficient but dour and unapproachable, lacking the flair of the great men of medicine. This was a generous estimate of his character if Arthur's account is to be believed. John Morgan was a profoundly dreary man.

He prospered nevertheless and maintained a general practice in Finsbury Square and a large country house in Tottenham. It was in Tottenham that Arthur's mother spent her infancy after John's marriage to Anne Gosse in 1831. She too was dreary. Both were Plymouth Brethren. It was a bleak household, all pleasure crushed. By 1847 Anne Morgan was a widow with seven children and the situation worsened. She sold up the Tottenham house and returned to Poole, her home town. For the children, years of exile followed here and at other homes in Clifton and Wales. Their misery was further deepened by the *eminence grise* of the patriarch who considered it his responsibility to guard the moral welfare of this fatherless family. To death, displacement and diminution of income had been added the frequent appearances of Anne's cousin, Philip Henry Gosse.

Philip Henry is now infamous as a protagonist of *Father and Son* (1907), the autobiography of his son, Edmund. Philip was a distinguished naturalist of the Devon coast. But he was also a Plymouth Brother and the two occupations, in the dawn of Victorian science, were mutually incompatible. An intelligent and meticulous observer, he also believed in a Divine Plan. Palaeontology was the problem and, in particular, Darwin's interpretation of it. Unable to accept the theory of evolution by natural selection and incapable of ignoring the existence of fossils of creatures clearly extinct, he arrived at a stunningly idiotic explanation: God must have inserted the fossils in the rocks during the Creation. Why, he was not sure. It was a mystery.

Such arguments cut little ice with the scientific community reading Lyell and Darwin. Perhaps to compensate for his failure in the large world, he imposed his authority on the small one of his cousin's family. On entering Anne's house he would sonorously enquire whether they were prepared for the Second Coming. It was eagerly anticipated by him several times a year. After cursory greetings, he and Anne would settle themselves to the task of calculating the exact date from Holy Scripture. The day would come and pass. Some error would then be

26. *ALL*, p. 8.
27. *Ibid.*, p. 8.

discovered in the figures and they would begin again with unabated vigour. Arthur's mother remembered his knock on the door with a shiver. So did her brothers and sisters.

There were four daughters and three sons. The boys managed to escape to train for their professions. The eldest was working in the office of the insurance company founded by his paternal grandfather; the other two went to Bristol Medical School. But Annie and the other girls were stuck. There was nothing for them to do but to submit to an endless series of chapel services and lectures. Arthur found it distasteful to think of his mother and her three gentle sisters being treated to coloured magic lantern slides illustrating the internal diseases of habitual drunkards. His own enthusiasm for life raged against such a lack of sensitivity.

At Bristol, Annie's brothers befriended Arthur's father and brought him home to Clifton in the vacations where he met Annie. Alexander was a bright, energetic young man with a substantial allowance from John Neill's patrimony and she eagerly accepted his proposal of marriage, beside herself with excitement until she could set up independently in Midsomer Norton. Arthur remembered with tenderness the many hours of his childhood during which she had amused him with her water-colours, cut-outs and drawings.[28] As the distance grew between

28. Evelyn Waugh appears to be mistaken about one of his great-great-grandfathers. In *ALL* (pp. 13–14) he states that Anne Gosse, Annie's mother, was the daughter of Thomas Gosse (1765–1844), the itinerant miniature painter and father of Philip Henry. That would mean that Anne Gosse was Philip Henry's sister and Arthur Waugh states clearly in *OMR* that Philip Henry was Anne's 'first cousin' (p. 12). Thomas had four children: William (b. 1808), Philip Henry (b. 1810), Elizabeth (b. 1813) and Thomas (b. 1816). There is no record of his having a daughter named 'Anne'. Frederick J. Stopp's file in Cambridge University Library contains a family tree constructed with Waugh's help. On it Stopp wrote: 'Waugh has in library three portraits of famous great-grandfathers [*sic*] Henry Cockburn, Alexander Waugh, Wm Morgan.' No mention is made of Thomas Gosse. The family tree noticeably peters out at the parentage of Anne Gosse. Thomas Gosse *was* the father of Philip Henry and the grandfather of Edmund Gosse. Waugh appears to have derived his dramatic account of Thomas's life in *ALL* from Raymond Lister's *Thomas Gosse. A Biographical Sketch of an Itinerant Miniature Painter of the Early Eighteenth Century* (Cambridge, Linton, 1953) and from Edmund Gosse's *The Life of Philip Henry Gosse* (Kegan Paul, 1890). Waugh infers in *ALL* that his artistic talents might derive from Thomas who was, it seems, only the brother of his great-great-grandfather. The name of Waugh's forebear remains obscure. Seven children of William and Elizabeth Gosse (Thomas's parents) are recorded: Susanna (b. 1750); Anne Lyne (b. 1752); Henry (b. 1754); William (b. 1756); Sarah (b. 1763); Thomas (b. 1765) and John (b. 1767). There were apparently eleven brothers in the family and three sisters. Waugh's great-great-grandfather could be Henry, William, John or any one of the seven untraceables. Cf. also Douglas Wertheimer, *Notes and Queries* (January 1976), 8: 'In *A Memorial ... of Emily Gosse*, pp. 59–60, Philip Gosse recorded his sincerest feelings of gratitude for unexpected kindnesses of Mrs Anne Morgan, the Clifton cousin, and this was repeated in *Life* (p. 270). ... John Morgan, FLS (1797–1847), was a respected surgeon at Guy's Hospital who married Anne Gosse of Poole. He attended Philip's father, Thomas, during his last illness in 1844, and Mrs Thomas Gosse was present at John Morgan's funeral. ...'

herself and her husband she quietly poured her store of affection into the heart of her eldest son. Never able to forget her own despair in the grip of the Brethren, she refused to take Arthur to church before he could appreciate the service. This led in turn to his flexible religious opinions which are implicitly mocked in *A Little Learning*. Waugh spared no sympathy for the complex emotional tensions out of which his father's character had grown.

Religious difference was an addition to the catalogue of Arthur and Evelyn's incompatibilities rather than its origin. In *A Little Learning* Waugh states bluntly that he 'never saw [Arthur] as anything but old, indeed as decrepit'.[29] The next chapter will deal with Arthur's direct influence on his son's childhood. But we can only understand Arthur's eccentric enthusiasm and his bitter disappointment at Evelyn's rejection of intimacy in the context of Arthur's childhood experiences. His father was a bully and his mother's sensitivity had been raped first by the Brethren and then by her husband. Like Evelyn, Arthur felt closer to his mother and determined that his married life and his relationship with his children would be profoundly different. Ironically, he saw himself as a progressive; not 'old' and 'decrepit', but a revolutionary subverting domestic despotism.

*One Man's Road* offers the best testimony to this exuberant self-deception:

> We meant so well in the beginning, but it was an impossible undertaking. We saw the limitation of the Victorian home; the autocracy of the armchair; the lack of confidence between father and son; the insincere cover-up of the facts of life; the secret whispers, shrugs, and lifted eyebrows. We distrusted it all. We read our Ibsen, and sat spellbound at the feet of Miss Elizabeth Robins, as Hilda Wangel[30] demanded her castle-on-the-table, or announced the younger generation knocking on the door. And we protested that our children should 'live their lives out after their own fashion' . . . and that we would share every yard of the way with them, knowing exactly what they wanted, and recognising their right to their own personalities, their own ambitions and goals. We would be young with the young.[31]

How differently it turned out.

*

It is doubtful whether Catherine shared her husband's enthusiasm or ideology. She was in no sense an Ibsenite heroine. In comparison with Arthur's, her background had had a less dramatic effect on her emotional life. Little is known

---

29. *ALL*, p. 63.
30. Ellida Wangel, second wife of a country doctor in Ibsen's *The Lady from the Sea* (1889). As the son of a despotic country doctor himself, Arthur may have found this play particularly apposite.
31. *OMR*, pp. 373–4.

of Catherine's family. Her mother, Lily, was a Cockburn, grand-daughter of Lord Henry Cockburn of Cockpen (1779–1854), the eminent Edinburgh lawyer and writer still revered for his *Memorials Of His Time* (1856). He, like another of Evelyn's great-great-grandparents, Alexander, took passionate delight in the Scottish countryside. In emulation of Scott's Abbotsford, but on a smaller scale, he built a castellated Gothic mansion, Bonaly Tower, in the seclusion of his beloved Pentland Hills[32] and from here he would stride off for long, solitary walks. Henry became a law lord. His father ended as Baron of the Scottish Court of the Exchequer and his uncle was Henry Dundas, Lord Melville, the uncompromising Tory dictator of Edinburgh during the late eighteenth and early nineteenth centuries. But Henry Cockburn loathed the 'ferocious bitterness and systematic zeal'[33] of repressive Tory policy and soon defected to the Whigs. It was a brave move.

So tight was Tory control over Edinburgh affairs when Henry was a young man that open acknowledgement of more liberal views inevitably resulted in poor business for a lawyer. He was a reformer who had considerable sympathy with the 1789 French Revolution in its early days. As he grew older a dislike of mob politics modified his radical ideas but a fierce intolerance of social injustice remained with him throughout. He was a sensitive man, alive to the plight of working people, who would often fight their causes in the courts. Until his time Scottish colliers were slaves, the property of mine-owners. He changed that and his successful defence of Helen MacDougal, common-law wife of Burke in the body-snatching trials, won him a certain notoriety as an advocate.

But his talents were not confined to the Bar. He was keenly interested in literature and painting and was, again like Alexander Waugh, the co-founder of a school, Edinburgh Academy. He wrote for the *Edinburgh Review;* Sir Walter Scott was a friend, although a strong political opponent; he was co-founder of the Commercial Bank and Rector of Glasgow University. Genial and astute, he was at the same time mildly eccentric. As Judge Cockburn, this tall, ungainly man with his misshapen hat and ugly boots, was often to be found in winter careering along pavement slides and playing snowballs. The boys of the Academy held him in the highest respect. He was a powerful orator and an impressive leader. Yet every July he would appear in the playground distributing invitations to a strawberries and cream tea at a shop in Queen Street.

Edinburgh commemorates him as a grand figure with a street, a hotel and a statue, though he will be best remembered for his own written records. Lord Cockburn lived through an era of massive social transformation from aristocracy to industry, from political despotism to the infancy of pervasive democracy. As a

32. During the Second World War, Evelyn Waugh was sent there on a Company Commanders' Course; cf. *ALL*, p. 11.
33. Lord Henry Cockburn, *Memorials of his Time* (Edinburgh, A. & C. Black, 1856), p. 72.

[ 19 ]

judge he was in a particularly fortunate position to observe the changes and comment upon them. His *Memorials* and *Circuit Journeys* (1888) are literary works of lasting quality. *Memorials*, in particular, is a notable achievement, written in a lucid, succinct prose uncommon in the mid-nineteenth century. Its polite ridicule of civilised life is never cruel or aloof, but dryly ironical and accurate in its aim. It is the only literary work of permanent value to have been produced by Waugh's family before Evelyn began writing. Alec's novels have not withstood the test of time. Arthur's publications have become interesting period-pieces. Arthur was a sensitive critic, within his own terms, but he lacked the imagination and intellect to escape the sentiment of his childhood and a strictly conventional concept of literary form. He was clever but Cockburn was brilliant. This lawyer's subversive humour with its poignant sense of the absurd descended not only to Evelyn Waugh but also to Waugh's cousin, Claud Cockburn.

Most of Catherine's male antecedents were not writers but soldiers or civil servants who spent many years in India. Consequently they are difficult to trace and remain shadowy figures. Two of Lord Henry's brothers founded Cockburn's Port in Oporto. One of his sons, Francis Jeffrey, experimented with gunpowder as a boy by pouring it down a horn into the kitchen furnace and blew off his right forearm. He became a judge in India and a bizarrely punctilious Christian. Claud Cockburn briefly describes this strange man, his grandfather, in his autobiography.[34] But the information is scrappy and anecdotal and it is impossible to piece together a picture of a continuous development as we can with Arthur's family.

The lack of any cohesive chain of connection could be seen as important in itself to Catherine. Her grandmother had remarried and there were step-children under the name of Devenish. Catherine's father, Henry Biddulph Cotton Raban, grew up in the care of his father's sisters. He died prematurely and Catherine's mother re-married a parson, creating yet another 'second family' of step-sons and step-daughters. From that point they were constantly on the move and Catherine felt unsettled. The houses of her grandmother and mother had been crowded and their internal relationships confused. When Arthur emerged as a suitor she was eager to establish a family which she could call her own. Her mother had been brought up to be idle; Catherine was industrious and practical. She taught herself the arts of housekeeping and prided herself on keeping house efficiently. Like Annie Waugh, she had suffered as a child from strict religious conformity although it is doubtful whether her repression at home had been as

34. Claud Cockburn, *I, Claud* . . . (Harmondsworth, Penguin Books, pp. 19–23). Originally published in three volumes: *In Time of Trouble* (Rupert Hart-Davis, 1956); *Crossing the Line* (MacGibbon & Kee, 1958); *View from the West* (MacGibbon & Kee, 1961). Francis Jeffrey Cockburn dissuaded the Indian Civil Service from employing his son, Claud's father, on the grounds that he had lost his faith. Claud's father is referred to in Waugh's *Diaries* as 'China Harry'.

acute as Arthur's. He describes her family as a refreshing influence, a vital, rather boisterous entourage. Evelyn also liked visiting his Raban grandparents and their house stuffed with Indian mementoes. Like Midsomer Norton, it seemed pleasantly exotic to the boy. But Catherine was a fundamentally different character from her husband and son. Quiet and purposeful, she perhaps felt uneasy amid the strained loyalties of a household containing much younger half-brothers and half-sisters.

*

Her relationship with Arthur took root early, before his last term at Sherborne when the Rabans moved to a nearby village. He would lend her his books and they would spend contented days reading and walking. He soon discovered that she preferred novels to poetry, his own great passion. The latter she read dutifully but her cooler, more analytical mind could not submerge itself in Browning or Tennyson. Arthur for some years wrote and published verse. He aspired to being a librettist in the vein of W. S. Gilbert. Catherine admired but could not share his enthusiasm.

In many respects she was, comparatively, almost deliberately, philistine in her shy, stubborn, matter-of-fact ways. Alec Waugh has even described his mother as 'distrustful of the written word'. After the disastrous collapse of Evelyn's first marriage in 1929 she said more than once: 'If it hadn't been for [Evelyn Gardner] he might have designed lovely furniture.' Alec would protest, 'But think of the books he's written.' 'I know, Alec dear, I know,' she would say; 'but furniture is so useful; besides he would have been happier designing furniture.'[35]

In a family as consciously 'literary' as the Waughs, it seems an extraordinary position to adopt. All the men in her house were writers. Perhaps she had had enough of it and this was her quiet protest. Catherine contributed a stabilising influence of common sense to leaven the potentially volatile atmosphere in a home containing three powerful male temperaments. She was far from foolish (Evelyn always preferred her company to his father's) but she lacked passion and the ability emotionally to submit to the aesthetic impulse. Arthur and she were in most respects perfectly matched. They were a team and within the domestic security she provided he laboured to establish himself as a man of letters.

Crucial to this ambition was Edmund Gosse, the son of Philip Henry, and Arthur's distant cousin. Arthur venerated Edmund as a writer of exceptional talent and was proud of his kinship. Evelyn, from their first meeting, loathed the man and all he stood for. He saw Gosse as chief among the 'numerous, patronising literary elders who frequented our table'.[36] More than any other man, Gosse seems to have been responsible for Evelyn's distaste for the *literati*.

35. *MBE*, pp. 192–3.
36. 'General Conversation: Myself . . .', *NPMM*, March 1937, 8; *EAR*, pp. 190–2.

Gosse was, nevertheless, an important professional connection for Arthur and deference towards the author of *Father and Son* was understandable. There was a considerable age-gap between the men. When Arthur came down from Oxford with an undistinguished third in Greats, Gosse was a regal figure in the metropolitan literary world. Arthur felt nervous about making approaches. His record up to that point had been far from distinguished.

At Sherborne Arthur had led a miserable life, bullied for his 'ignoble athletic calibre', jeered at for being a 'swot'.[37] Lonely and asthmatic, he had at last secured some prestige in the Fifth Form by writing bitter lampoons of masters and unpopular pupils and, eventually, in the Sixth, by becoming editor of the school magazine and winning the English Verse Prize. At Oxford he had soon slipped back into anonymity. He lacked both the intellectual tenacity to excel in the classics and the physique of a sportsman and he succumbed to his lasting passion for drama. The opening of the New Theatre during his first term in February 1886 was the great event of his undergraduate life. He spent as much of his time there as his allowance would permit and, during vacations at Midsomer Norton, would throw himself fervently into amateur productions. Nevertheless, and by his own admission, he was always a looker-on. He never joined the OUDS,[38] fearful of the expense and of the elite it represented.

But he had one success – winning the Newdigate Prize Poem set on the unpromising subject of 'Gordon in Africa'. In those days the prize was held in high regard and, as now, the winning entry was automatically published. It was a start. When he came down his father did not rant about the profligacy of youth. He had, after all, encouraged his son away from his studies during the holidays to join him in various local melodramas and farces. Alexander was a clever, practical man who had never been to Oxbridge. Success might have angered him more as a threat to his intellectual autocracy. Arthur was humble in defeat and his father was feeling generous. The boy, he thought, should set to and find a position in the world of business. Arthur showed a strong inclination towards publishing and writing and his father, moderately wealthy, considered buying him a share in a publishing house. He did not consider it for long. He needed all he had for his own rather extravagant life-style and there was no reason, he felt, why Arthur should not make his own way. So Mrs Waugh wrote to Edmund Gosse enclosing a copy of 'Gordon in Africa'.

The letter Gosse returned still exists.[39] Its chill compliments held out little hope and when, a little later, he met Arthur he thought this wide-eyed young fellow unsuited to the daily routine of publishing or any other business. But, the kinship re-established, Gosse introduced him to Woolcot Balestier, a young

37. *OMR*, pp. 84–5.
38. Oxford University Dramatic Society.
39. See Sir Evan Charteris, *The Life and Letters of Edmund Gosse* (Heinemann, 1931).

American publisher who was later to become Kipling's brother-in-law. Arthur was delighted. Tennyson, Ibsen and Kipling were his literary idols and Balestier had secured rights to Kipling's works. Kipling was a 'revelation, a portent and a shock . . .' to Arthur; he was 'irresistible'.[40] In later life it seemed absurd to Arthur that the 'nineties should be epitomised in the public imagination by Wilde and a handful of decadents. This, after all, had been the period of his young manhood when Ibsen 'filled his drama with the tonic breeze of the moral idea and the naked gospel of cause and effect'.[41] It was the period, not only of *The Barrack Room Ballads*, but of Shaw and Pinero, of Henry James and Hardy and Yeats, a time of literary revolution for Arthur and many young men like him – renaissance, not *fin de siècle*. Nothing could have been less representative of the age, in his view, than the languorous pandiculations of Beardsley's drawings.

The 'nineties were for Arthur a period of intense industry. Although his daily schedule for Balestier's firm (the Lovell Company) was arduous, he also took on a commission in 1891 to write a life of Tennyson. When on 6th October, 1892 the great man died, the book was rushed to a conclusion and, with incredible alacrity by modern standards, published eight days later. Within three days it was in the hands of the reviewers and they received it warmly. Tennyson had been an undisputed leader of English poetry for more than half a century. Argument raged as to who might be a fitting successor to the Laureateship. The popular debate swept Arthur's biography through six editions. He had 'arrived' at last and plans could be made for marriage to Catherine.

His euphoria was short-lived. Even as the book was selling it became clear that Balestier's business was unsound. In February 1893 it went bankrupt and the ungenerous bailiffs (of the Curates Augmentation Society) took possession. The business was a total wreck and Arthur found himself facing a blank future once more. Catherine and he deferred the ceremony. Friends told them to marry and chance it but he loathed taking risks. He wanted to provide a secure future for her. Paramount among his virtues was a keen sense of responsibility to others. When the firm crashed Arthur was twenty-six, short of money and eager to be married. He had been courting Catherine for eight years. Yet as soon as the royalties from Heinemann were handed over he took the entire amount and distributed it in lieu of the unpaid salaries owed to Balestier's employees. It was a supremely noble action. He never saw a penny from that book.

Desperate but not despairing, he started again, writing round to various journals and newspapers for reviews. The reputation secured by the biography brought him work. He took anything he could get and was grateful for it, writing for *The Literary World* and *The Sun* and even literary gossip for New York's *The Critic*, an indulgence which he later admitted to be a painful prostitution of values. He

40.  *OMR*, p. 184.
41.  *Ibid.*, p. 183.

became a sub-editor on *The New Review* for which he secured the serial rights of W. W. Jacobs's early stories. And by the autumn he had enough of an income to consider marriage again. On 5th October, 1893 he and Catherine married and they established their first home over a dairy in Fitzjohn's Pavement on the Finchley Road.

It was a humble and insecure start for a couple who both came from solid middle-class families. Arthur's father seems only to have contributed a minimum of financial assistance; Catherine's mother and step-father had six other children to support. There was no large patrimony or dowry to set them up and Arthur's regular employment was by definition temporary. But they cared nothing for this. An independent unit at last, they delighted in their frugal and intimate life. Most of their evenings were spent alone together. Arthur would sometimes go off on Sunday afterncons to Edmund Gosse's literary *salons* in Delamere Terrace. Occasionally they would visit the Rhys's[42] or the Pawling's.[43] They did little else. Arthur was more often in the flat, writing his articles and reviews while his wife busied herself with domestic improvements. Marriage gave him new confidence. The security of their home was built round a mutual enthusiasm for his ultimate success.

Ironically, this came about by his being a contributor to the first number of *The Yellow Book*.[44] The two of them turned up at the inaugural dinner amid a scintillating galaxy of artistic figures – George Moore, Yeats, Lionel Johnson, Beardsley, Ernest Dowson, Ernest Rhys and Walter Sickert were there – and sat quietly talking to their friends. Arthur could never have guessed that the critics would later single out his contribution, an essay entitled 'Reticence in Literature', as the only piece worthy of praise. They howled at the decadence of the rest and heaped accolades upon him: 'a sane and manly, an instructed and well-written essay', said the *Academy*.[45] As a result he found himself, almost overnight, in a position of considerable eminence as a defender of the principles of literary tradition. Much of Evelyn Waugh's mature critical writing defends a similar aesthetic conservatism. In early manhood, though, his tastes were often aggressively modern. His father's approach condemned Arthur as one of the old men.

Success brought its problems. Arthur was a young man with a bright future and he had the opportunity to capitalise on his fame in one of two ways: he could either continue as a free-lance writer which would afford him enough spare time to write his poetry and drama; or he could establish himself in publishing and secure a more stable financial future. As usual, fears about what might happen,

42. Ernest Rhys, first Editor of Everyman's Library (Dent's). His wife became one of Catherine Waugh's close friends.
43. Sydney Pawling, who inherited a third share of Mudie's Library from his uncle Charles Edward Mudie and later joined the Board of Heinemann's.
44. 16 April, 1894.
45. Cf. *OMR*, p. 257.

especially since his marriage, prompted him to take the conventional course. After two years of the unstable life of an independent critic his 'native lack of enterprise'[46] prompted him to join Kegan Paul as a part-time adviser, and from this point his work was primarily concerned with the business rather than the writing of books. Throughout his life he continued to write large numbers of reviews and essays. The latter were later collected in *Reticence in Literature* (1915) and *Tradition and Change* (1919), both of which sold well. But he realised that the acceptance of the managerial post represented the death of any serious artistic aspiration.

With his increased income they were able to move from the dairy to Hillfield Road and there, in July 1898, Alec was born. A new phase was opening up. Arthur and Catherine began to feel settled and would rattle off together at weekends on long bicycle rides into the countryside round London. And so the first seven years of the marriage passed by easily in modest routine until, in 1901, Arthur was contacted by W.L. Courtenay, his old tutor from New College.

Courtenay was on the board of Chapman and Hall, a firm which since Dickens's death had been running into increasing difficulties. He had heard of Arthur's efficiency at Kegan Paul's and offered him the post of managing director with Chapman's at the precocious age of thirty-five. The job would restrict his literary activities even further but it was too good an offer to refuse. On 31st January, 1902 he attended his first board meeting and he remained with the firm for the rest of his working life. Without regret but with considerable resignation, he enlisted in the black-hatted army of commuters whose lives were regulated by office hours and train time-tables.

Chapman's in 1902 relied heavily on the Dickens copyrights and lost money on almost everything else. The offices in Henrietta Street were musty and inefficiently organised; there was a pervasive air of mistrust amongst the employees. When Arthur arrived they suspiciously guarded the secrets of their individual work for fear that, should anyone understand it, it might be removed. The general manager, Etheridge, was, according to Alec, lazy and incompetent. Etheridge attempted to discourage Arthur from 'miscellaneous publishing' and secretly swore that he would have this young puppy of a chief removed within a year. But Arthur had been employed to make changes and he was not to be deflected.

He was by nature a scrupulously honest man, modest, loyal and industrious, who brought a boyish enthusiasm to his work. He was shocked when he failed to find these qualities in other men of business, but not discouraged. A new director, he realised, especially a young one, is immediate prey to a multitude of sharp practitioners eager to exploit his inexperience. He decided, for instance, against the former practice of the firm, to encourage literary agents and was soon presented with a mountain of previously unsaleable manuscripts. This he politely

46. *Ibid.*, p. 277.

ignored, as he did the surliness and machiavellian tricks of the least reliable of his staff. Very quickly he impressed himself upon everyone as a kindly but efficient operator. With characteristic earnestness, he organised an office cricket team to restore team spirit. It worked; the experience of shared activity beyond office hours re-established mutual trust. Arthur was a shrewd judge of character. He soon noticed those who were prepared to offer foolish or selfish counsel. But no-one was sacked and, before long, no-one could even muster a serious grudge.

The house prospered, the list rapidly increased to include Wells, Bennett and Maugham; employment was secure. He subtly succeeded in combining traditional with new business practices. The firm retained its nineteenth-century air of domestic disorganisation. Until 1920 there was no telephonist and only one line to the director's secretary who was tucked away three floors above and separated from him by offices let out to other businesses; there was no waiting room. Authors coming for interview had to stand by a counter with booksellers' collectors and paper salesmen to be served by a misanthropic clerk who could remember Trollope in his hunting coat, banging his crop impatiently for service. The counting-house held other clerks perched over ledgers on their high stools. Yet behind everything Arthur exerted a benevolent and shrewd control.

His self-imposed routine was strenuous. By nine he was at his desk. By half-past the correspondence was sorted and he would visit each department to deal with the day's problems. At ten his secretary came to take dictation for an hour. Letters, whenever possible, were answered by return. Eleven o'clock saw the arrival of trade visitors – printers, paper makers, binders, artists – followed by literary agents. After lunch there would usually be a long discussion with one or other of his authors. Tea was at four, followed by the signing of the sheaf of morning letters. Often he would stay on in the evening to write a review. He never used office hours for personal work. Whenever his secretary typed up his articles he paid her at the proper rate per thousand words. When a Christmas bonus was decreed in 1919 after a particularly good balance sheet, he refused to take anything for himself. He never charged 'business lunches' to the firm. His loyalty endeared him not only to his subordinates but to other publishers.

Honesty and courtesy had been restored. Arthur's management transformed business from a scrambling egocentric tussle into an industrious routine. He worked and thought fast, but with Courtenay and the others maintained decorous relations. (Once Courtenay came into the office when Arthur was signing a letter to him. The old man read it through. 'Thank you,' he said. 'A very interesting letter. I shall not answer it but I shall take note of it.')[47] There were things 'not done'. Arthur disapproved of flamboyant advertising. The best-seller, he thought, should sell itself. The publisher's business was to issue a list and, perhaps, if he were sure of its quality, to send a book on to a literary friend in the hope that

47. *TEYOAW*, p. 151.

he might review it. Self-advertisement by authors was strongly discouraged. Arthur had eventually to accommodate himself to these changes but he never approved and Evelyn's blatant publicity-seeking in later years can only have been a disappointment. Publishing to him was a sober and gentlemanly occupation. He was there to sell books, not to tout them. He abjured the outrageous or provocative.

\*

By the time of Evelyn's birth, in 1903, Arthur was settled into a comfortable routine, earning a substantial salary. He was still nervous but no longer insecure. There had been no death in his immediate family other than his brother Alick's in 1900, and the Midsomer Norton household was just as he had left it. He felt curiously youthful until, in the year of his fortieth birthday (1906), his father died.

It might seem extraordinary that a middle-aged man should be devastated by the demise of a father by whom he had always been intimidated. Yet there was a deep well of affection in Arthur. Towards the end of Alexander's life they had become a little closer, sharing once again in amateur theatricals. But when the rumbustious doctor had visited his son in Hillfield Road he had left with the declaration that, although he considered it a happy home, a week of Arthur's son and dog would render him insane. Alec was an indulged child. Alexander could not accommodate himself to the easy-going domestic intimacy which precluded authoritarian discipline. Always the autocrat of the fireside, he maintained even in old age a gruff formality with his children.

Alexander's death represented more to Arthur than simply the loss of something which had always been there. It meant, in effect, the death of his youth. He felt himself to be suddenly older and determined from that point spiritually to regenerate himself through his sons. And there was another, more practical, aspect to the changed circumstances. The death meant a consolidation of financial security, for there was a small inheritance. His three sisters used their share to maintain the house in Midsomer Norton where they cared for their mother until her death fifteen months later. After this, tended by Self, the old manservant, they remained in the house, three lively maiden aunts, running Bible and literacy classes for children and miners, providing a holiday home for Alec and Evelyn, and living a life of blameless, mildly eccentric beneficence, pillars of the village community as their father had been before them. But it was the end of a family tradition of 'gentility'. The inheritance was the final instalment of John Neill's legacy, given so many years ago to Dr Alexander Waugh's children. From this point there was no unearned income and Evelyn's family was once again in 'trade'.

Arthur took his money gratefully. Alec's indoor cricket was already beginning to wreck the best room in Hillfield Road. As the tennis ball knocked holes in the nursery's plaster there was some concern for Evelyn's safety. They needed more space.

Three reasons had prompted their original choice of Hampstead. Both Catherine and Arthur wanted an environment which, within their means, would approximate to the rural setting of their childhood; they wanted to be near their friends the Pawlings; and lastly, but most importantly, Hampstead had a reputedly healthy climate which it was thought might help Arthur's asthma. They did not want to leave the area and could now afford to choose something more in keeping with their original intention. One morning they went to look over the fields being developed below the northern corner of the Heath and, with his usual impetuosity, before evening Arthur had decided on the site for their new home.

It was on a quiet country road just below the carriage entrance of the Manor House in the village of North End. The site did not maintain this air of rural seclusion for long. As Evelyn suggests in *A Little Learning*, Arthur could have had small reason for complaint when in the following years the surrounding fields were swallowed by streets. He had been, after all, one of the first exploiters of the countryside. The house, situated just beneath the crest, was romantically named 'Underhill' after a road in Midsomer Norton. Eventually, a number was forced upon it by the Post Office and its address altered from North End to Golders Green.

Arthur, though, never relinquished his initial enthusiasm for the place. Almost every day during the summer of its construction he would hurry home from work to visit the site. Impatient and excited, he and Catherine crawled under planks, stepped out the rooms, and discussed modifications with the builder. They did away with the normal suburban drawing-room, installing in its place a library which with typical modesty was named the 'book-room'. Here there was an inglenook; bookshelves, wainscotting and a pannelled ceiling, all in dark oak, faked antiquity. This was Arthur's province. Catherine had a drawing-room to herself at the top of the first flight of stairs. The boys were given a large, sunny day-nursery down the corridor from this, looking out onto the back garden and the adjacent kitchen garden of the Manor House. At night they moved up one floor to a room overlooking the road.

Today the house has lost part of its original rear elevation to an extension and is converted into flats; a black iron fire-escape scars the back wall. It is barely recognisable from Arthur's photograph. Cracked and decrepit, it appears somehow withered and reduced. The land on either side has been sold off. To the right a smaller villa has squeezed in; to the left an unpaved drive leads down to a series of ramshackle garages and a 'crash repairer's'. Disembowelled cars now litter the area where the Waughs' garden was laid out decoratively with lawns and bowers and the family posed self-consciously for photographs in the setting of their new prosperity.

This, then, was the home in which Evelyn was first conscious of his surroundings. He was nearly four when they moved in September 1907. But almost as soon as he was old enough to share family life it was disrupted. Alec had been away for his summer holiday in Midsomer Norton while Underhill was being built. Within three weeks of his return he was despatched to preparatory school, Fernden, near Haslemere, and for the next sixteen years he and Evelyn spent little time in each other's company. More things divided them than geographical separation. Even at this stage it was apparent that they were radically different in temperament. Alec was growing into a sturdy, athletic child, boisterous and a little slovenly. Arthur relished his company, reading aloud to him or teaching him the finer points of spin bowling. Evelyn could not share in the surrogate religion of Lords and Wisden. Frightened by his brother's forcefulness, he preferred the company of his mother. Quieter and more fastidious than Alec, with a sunny, friendly nature, he would unpredictably dissolve into tears, and at nine years old Alec had no time for such girlish nonsense.

The five-year age-gap represented a substantial barrier between them until Evelyn was a young man at Oxford. Even then, their intimacy was short-lived. It is hard to imagine how two brothers, both of whom became famous novelists and both of whom shared an affectionate home, could grow up as strangers. But that is precisely what happened.

# II
# *A Little Learning: 1907–1921*

In his autobiography Evelyn Waugh describes North End Road in 1907 as a dusty track winding up to the village of North End; at the bottom of the hill, he says, Golders Green was a grassy cross-roads. This is a romantic image. Golders Green tube station had been opened that year and had already spawned new development. North End itself, though, remained relatively untouched.

Pavlova lived from 1912 to 1931 in the elegant Ivy House a hundred yards or so up from Underhill. Blake had once visited a weatherboarded cottage in the woods behind the Manor House; Leigh Hunt, Keats and Constable had lived on the Heath nearby. Arthur Waugh had settled into a select retreat from London which had pleasant associations with artistic life. The new house was exactly what he wanted.

For a short while Underhill was the only new house in the village and the community was not dissimilar to Midsomer Norton. The pattern of life remained feudal: deference was due to the local gentry – Miss Hoare of North End House and another maiden lady at North End Manor. It was from the latter despotic spinster that Arthur had purchased two plots of land and, later, the kitchen garden. Communications from her were restricted to business matters and vitriolic letters of complaint concerning the trespasses of young Evelyn into her property, usually to retrieve a ball. Miss Hoare was less formidable, a cheerful country woman in her plain clothes and large boots who nevertheless maintained a discernible sense of her social position.

When the Waughs arrived she called on them in her carriage. She and Catherine took upon themselves the responsibility for a primitive form of social service. Down the hill a little there was a row of workmen's cottages, 'The Terrace'. This was Catherine's particular province. In addition, she and Miss Hoare shared the care of slum families in a part of Shoreditch. It was a patrician concept of community service later largely usurped by the Welfare State but one which vividly characterises the rural aspect of the village at the time. In Midsomer Norton the Waugh aunts were fulfilling much the same function with their Bible and literacy classes.

The contemporary photographs of Underhill suggest a false impression of its size. Arthur's statement that it 'was never any more than a very ordinary little suburban villa'[1] is accurate. Its isolation at first lent it an air of massiveness but in truth it was a moderate, rather ugly, detached family residence. Arthur spoke reverently of its 'timbers' with the affection of a captain for his ship.

Shortly after moving in he celebrated it in print: 'I look out of my window as I write, across the tulips and the wall-flowers; and away to the north-west, steadily spreading in my direction, I see the fresh white walls and red roofs of Hampstead Garden Suburb – surely a land of promise. . . . The days will not be long, I fear, before the meadow set with willows, behind my little garden, will hear the sound of the bricklayer's trowel. Yet how can I grudge the Garden Suburb its steady growth, since I have myself watched every new house in it from foundation to roof-tree, and walked its ways of pleasantness from spring to mid-winter?'[2] He never did grudge it. It was, he felt, every Englishman's right to build his own house and he was instinct with the ideology of Metroland.

Underhill was his cottage and his castle, and his pride in it never wavered. As a young man, Evelyn came to see this exuberant worship as ludicrous, and with some reason. He disliked the house simply on the grounds that it was aesthetically hideous, a shameful object of his father's adulation. In July 1907 the Hampstead and Highgate tube stations had opened and with them came the estate agents. Golders Green quickly took on the appearance of a gold-rush town: a sea of churned mud; a confusion of builders' carts and scaffolding; hoardings proclaiming new branches of chain stores. And once it had started, nothing could stop it. The workmen's cottages disappeared; every available space became valuable building land. In the end, only the Heath prevented the ugliness and conformity from spreading further. It was a source of deep regret for Catherine.

Catherine, it seems, felt the loss of a genuine rural life more deeply than Arthur. Both had grown up in the country but Arthur could accommodate himself to or ignore metropolitan life. To his wife, London was a place of exile and the thousands of villas an invasion of privacy. She never went into town if she could help it. Before her mother had re-married Catherine had lived at Shirehampton in the care of two maiden great-aunts and a great-uncle. She wistfully reviewed her early girlhood there as an idyll of family life with its solid domestic security rooted in a daily round of practical tasks. At Underhill she tried to re-create that security for her own family.

As Evelyn toddled round the garden, his mother would constantly be at work there: planting, pruning, weeding. For hours at a stretch she could be found in her wash-leather gloves, busy about the kitchen garden or instructing the man who came in once a week to mow and dig. The wasteland of mud and builders' rubble surrounding Underhill had been rapidly and efficiently cultivated. The garden was neat, well-organised, with nothing that did not fulfil a practical

1. *OMR*, p. 322.
2. 'An Englishman's Castle', *Reticence in Literature* (J. G. Wilson, 1915), p. 200.

purpose. Peas grew over the ornamental arch; flowers were planted only in those beds not needed for fruit or vegetables. She was an unusual woman for her time. Arthur was hopelessly impractical; all minor repairs to the fabric of the property were done by her. Evelyn remembered her: ' . . . always busy with her hands, sewing, making jam, bathing and clipping her poodle . . . , and with hammer and screwdriver hanging shelves and building rabbit hutches from packing cases.'[3] The comfortable atmosphere of his infancy was largely due to her influence.

Such descriptions in *A Little Learning* are suffused with an unmistakable aura of devotion. Evelyn felt safe with this reticent, entirely dependable woman. Her deceptively severe approach did nothing to disguise a total absorption in her sons' welfare. She would not fuss over them and brooked no nonsense. But they always knew to whom they could turn in a crisis. Her great virtue was the entire predictability of her reactions. Evelyn never found this frustratingly unemotional; he was temperamentally drawn towards such consistency and his appreciation of it only deepened with the years. By the same token, he became suspicious of his father's histrionic enthusiasm and his assumption of intimacy by right of parenthood.

The importance of this division in Waugh's affections as a child can scarcely be over-stressed. It not only darkened his young manhood but also, when he began writing, helped to colour his attitude to a whole generation. His diary often expresses sorrowful confusion at his inability to communicate with, even to be pleasant to, his father. Neither Evelyn nor Arthur was ever quite sure what had gone wrong.

It is a common enough experience that in a household containing two sons with a considerable age-gap between them, the younger should cling to the affections of his mother, while the father indulges himself in shared pursuits with the elder. Alec, by rapid stages, was evolving as a distinct personality. When Arthur began to make approaches to Evelyn as he grew up, encouraging him to join with himself and Alec in their various interests, two things seem to have occurred: Evelyn felt at first intimidated, then upset by the rough-and-tumble of masculine society, and Alec resented the intrusion which subverted his intimacy with his father. The elder boy was impatient with and often unpleasant to his brother and Evelyn apparently felt, from first becoming conscious of the situation, that there was something of a conspiracy between his father and Alec to make him appear foolish.

This is nothing extraordinary. What is remarkable is that Evelyn's sense of persecution should persist throughout his adolescence, changing in character and intensity, but never leaving him entirely. When he was sixteen he arrived at an evening party wearing a tail coat. 'It was my father's coat,' he said, 'then it was Alec's; now it is mine. In fact it has come down from generation to generation

3. *ALL*, p. 32.

of them that hate me.'⁴ Of course it was a joke, but one which parodied a genuine sense of rejection. In his various memoirs Alec reveals that he had considered Evelyn a nuisance and had wasted no time in telling him so. The difficulties were compounded by Arthur's blatant favouritism towards his elder son. Evelyn was fastidious and rather effeminate at first. He loathed cricket, which rivalled Christianity as a staff of life for his father and brother. In the dining room there was a high-backed chair presented to Catherine by her husband on the condition that she should carve the meat. Whenever threatened with discipline by Arthur or Alec, Evelyn would dive into the seat claiming sanctuary. Arthur preferred the more 'masculine' bluntness of his first-born.

This in itself is curious when we remember how Arthur had suffered at the hands of his own father and found solace in his mother's company. *One Man's Road* is a sad and confused book. It unwittingly tells the story of a man apologising for his weakness and inadequacy when his chief delight in life has been to live a surrogate youth through his sons. It is both morbidly modest and arrogant. Underhill represented to him, in physical form, the beginning of this surrogate life. He always maintained a schoolboy worship of physical prowess; he never discarded the sentimental ideals of team spirit and loyalty to the establishment. Evelyn's lack of enthusiasm for the very things which had made his own schooldays a misery affronted his enthusiasm for success within a conventional framework. Arthur seemed unaware of the inconsistencies in his argument, inconsistencies best illustrated by his attitude to his sons' education.

Alec was sent to Fernden in September 1907. The school was just beginning; there were only eight boys in the first term. Arthur chose it because the co-founder had been a contemporary of his at Oxford (they 'talked the same language'⁵) and because there was an excellent field for games. 'Fernden', he writes, 'was bound to succeed.'⁶

Alec's health, despite his athleticism, had been precarious in the nursery, yet he was sent to an establishment quite unparalleled for its Spartan rigour. He writes of it sourly in his memoirs but none of his sufferings appears to have been understood by Arthur. Instead he talks effusively of how the school's 'sons learnt to be good sportsmen and men of honour',⁷ the annual paters' match and Alec's natural 'break from the off'. It is quite obvious that the masters knew little or nothing about teaching. They considered Alec a brilliant pupil, likely to win a Winchester scholarship, when even Arthur realised that ' . . . like all the Waughs, he lacked that essential accuracy, without which there can be no real success in the classics.'⁸

4. Cf. *MBE*, p. 165.
5. *OMR*, p. 328.
6. *Ibid.*, p. 328.
7. *Ibid.*, p. 328.
8. *Ibid.*, p. 328.

Either they were fools or they were flattering him in order to maintain custom. However one interprets the matter, it might have made any father apprehensive as to the wisdom of leaving his son in their hands. None of this occurred to Arthur. He was neither selfish nor callous nor foolish; he was a highly-principled and intelligent man. But he was easily impressed by anything that set itself up as an establishment and purported to represent the values of his youth. His delight in watching the progress of his boy through school obliterated any qualitative assessment of the school's value to the boy. Exactly the same impulsive spirit governed the choice of Evelyn's public school some years later. It was something which his younger son found impossible to forgive.

Alec never blamed his father for the miseries of Fernden. He had been an indulged child who, as a result of the special attention accorded him by Arthur, had developed an exaggerated idea of his own importance, a 'superiority complex', as he calls it.[9] His table manners had been neglected and he had become fussy about his food. At Fernden there was a rule that everything – lumps of fat and gristle included – had to be eaten. Once, overcome with nausea after a helping of sago pudding, he had vomited into the plate. The headmaster, unperturbed, had insisted that the boy should finish his dessert. But resentment towards Arthur was out of the question. He was Alec's favourite companion. If there was anything wrong, Alec believed it to be the fault of the school. The two issues remained separate and in retrospect he was ruefully grateful to the place for cutting him down to size; it helped him to fit more easily into public school. At the time he regarded it as a form of endurance test designed to strengthen his 'manhood'.

During the holidays he would proudly regale Evelyn with horrific tales of school discipline. The younger brother listened with a mixture of awe and terror. Three more years were to elapse before Evelyn was sent to school. He approached the prospect with some trepidation. Everything seemed calculated to make him fearful of the masculine aggression which inevitably awaited him beyond the gates of his home. Between 1907 and 1910 he was taught the 'three Rs' by his mother in the company of Stella Rhys, the daughter of Ernest (first editor of Everyman's Library). It was cosy but frighteningly tame in contrast to Alec's catalogue of rough treatment.

There was a fundamental difference between the home environment of Alec and Evelyn's infancies. Until Arthur had secured the managing directorship of Chapman and Hall's in the year before Evelyn's birth, he had only worked part-time in London. His free-lance journalism had been written at home and Alec had grown up with his father a familiar figure around the Hillfield Road house during the day. It had afforded them both opportunities to develop an unusual intimacy. By 1906 Arthur's entire working day was spent in the Henrietta Street office and Evelyn's earliest memories of him were of an ominous stranger looming

9. *MBE*, p. 164.

into the nursery in the early evenings. The click of his latch-key in the front door signalled Evelyn's imprisonment, as he was hurried up to bed. His father, rather than appearing as he did to Alec as a partner to Catherine, seemed a gross intruder, a usurper of his mother's affection. Arthur would come upstairs to make overtures of friendship but they were coolly received. Evelyn, as has been said, always regarded him as an old man. The house was permeated by the smell of Himrod's Asthma Cure, burnt every evening, and Arthur's violent fits of coughing on winter mornings seemed to epitomise his decrepitude. The firmly established relationship between father and elder son only made matters worse. In a sense, Evelyn felt that he had never really belonged to the family group.

'Firmly established relationship' rather understates the case; Arthur worshipped Alec. The new life represented by his son's beginning school was eagerly antici-pated as an antidote to the lethargy he feared might result from regular office work; it would ' . . . banish the phantom of approaching middle-age'.[10] Ultimately he was forced to admit the vanity of this dream but in 1907 it occupied his whole attention. During term he would write long, entertaining letters to Alec two or three times a week and in the holidays disappear with him to the cinema or cricket matches. The prospect of a second son at school and another set of vicarious experiences filled him with excitement and he did not have long to wait. In 1910, a month before his seventh birthday, Evelyn was sent to a local prepara-tory school as a day-boy.

'It was natural', Arthur wrote, 'that we should have sent him to Heath Mount School, on the summit of the hill above us; for the head master, J. S. G. Grenfell, was an old schoolfellow of mine at Sherborne, where he had indeed been more distinguished as the school wicket-keeper than in the classroom.'[11] The logic of this decision is, once again, nothing short of astounding but we may suspect that Catherine brought her influence to bear on the matter, ensuring that her more sensitive son should not endure the rigours of Fernden. Sending Evelyn to a local school meant that she could keep him at home. The evidence indicates that she disliked the idea of his being a boarder, even at public school.

The question of Evelyn's education was one of the few things which provoked open disagreement between herself and her husband. When the time came, in 1914, to think about moving Evelyn to Fernden to prepare for public school entrance, Arthur, fearing financial collapse during the war, abandoned the idea. This can only have delighted Catherine and Evelyn, ensuring, as it did, their unbroken intimacy for three more years. Yet, reflecting on this in his autobi-ography, Evelyn betrays a hint of disappointment. 'Had I gone to one of the preparatory schools which cram for scholarships at Eton or Winchester', he

10. *OMR*, p. 325.
11. *Ibid.*, pp. 329–30.

remarks, 'I might conceivably have won one.'[12] It became a matter of considerable regret to him that he had been denied his fair chance at a 'leading school'. Once again, he thought, he had been discriminated against.

Heath Mount, nevertheless, appears to have been a sensible choice. Every morning Arthur would accompany Evelyn there as it lay on his route to Hampstead tube station. 'During these walks,' Evelyn wrote in an article in 1962, 'I began to know him and enjoy his company.'[13] It was not a statement repeated in *A Little Learning* but it seems probable that this first opportunity for close companionship went a long way towards closing the gap that had grown between them. Arthur's melodramatic nature seized the chance of a captive audience to construct an entertainment each morning. The twenty minutes together were filled with accounts of flamboyant characters who had lived in the area. Every turning held some significance; highwaymen, rebels, fraudulent railway speculators, poets and painters began to people the landscape along with wholly fictitious creatures of Arthur's creation. For the first time there was a point of contact between father and son which, if it did not inspire awe in Evelyn, at least assured him that his parent was no-one to fear. Arthur was always amicable and well-intentioned.

Evelyn's attitude to school, though, was a great disappointment to him. 'Nothing could have been more different', Arthur noted, 'than the fashion in which the two brothers lived through their school-days. Alike at his preparatory and public schools, Alec was up to his neck in the life of the place, so keen on competition that he allowed house rivalry to freeze into a positive hatred of his opponents. Evelyn, on the other hand, took the routine of the school, its games and amusements, in a sort of negligent stride. He did what was required of him . . . ; but he did it all without relish or genuine interest.'[14] The preference for his elder son is perfectly plain. Detailed accounts of the most trivial incidents concerning Alec are recorded with delight; Evelyn's scholastic achievements, far superior to his brother's, are briefly summarised but not especially recommended to the reader's attention. One senses a hint of disapproval, or, at least, of despairing incomprehension, in his descriptions of Evelyn; the boy never fitted into any pattern of behaviour recognisable from his own experience.

As Evelyn veered from a preternatural seriousness and piety through boredom towards Bohemianism Arthur found himself at each stage quite at a loss as to how to deal with him. As we shall see, Alec's behaviour was just as much calculated to outrage his father's Victorian ideals. Arthur could forgive mistakes. It was Evelyn's *attitude* that was wrong. Like Dickens, his literary hero, Arthur abhorred world-weary indifference and this was a pose Evelyn later adopted in the home to combat his father's embarrassing exuberance. Evelyn lacked the

12. *ALL*, p. 86.
13. 'My Father', *S Tel*, 2 December, 1962, 4–5.
14. *OMR*, p. 333.

humility as a child to ask for forgiveness from Arthur even though he could be deeply wounded by invoking the displeasure of his mother or nanny. His father saw this refusal of intimacy, this obstinate determination to go his own way, as a gross display of 'hubris'. It was painful to him. He had, after all, been a waster himself at university, but his contrition before his own father had effected a reunion. He must have longed for Evelyn to climb down and appeal to him, as a friend, for help.

'In later life,' Alec wrote, 'Evelyn may have given the impression of being heartless; he was often snubbing, he could be cruel. But basically he was gentle, warm and tender. He was very like his father, and his father's own emotionalism put him on his guard. He must have often thought, I could become like this. I mustn't let myself become like this.'[15] The seeds of this feeling were sown early. His mother's reticence and thoroughness seemed preferable to his father's impetuosity. Evelyn was a punctilious little boy, acutely conscious of his body, embarrassed by physical contact. He preferred not to be cuddled and mauled and played cricket with. He set a high price on modesty and yet simultaneously he was, like Alec, ambitious. It was a volatile combination of characteristics: on the one hand gentle, shy, studious, and pious; on the other, aggressive and stubborn in the face of what he took to be unfair discrimination. The artist and mystic in his nature were always at war with the younger son demanding power and loving panache.

Even before he went to school he displayed a precocious talent for organisation. He had three particular friends – Jean, Philippa and Maxwell Fleming. These and others he directed in nursery theatricals, coaching the company through a play he had written. Later (1912), the Flemings formed the nucleus of his 'Pistol Troop', marshalled to defend the Realm against possible attack from Germans and Jews. A field between Underhill and the Manor House, used as a repository for builders' materials, supplied an exciting terrain for the game and a clay heap in which elaborate provisions were stored.

But it did not stop there. As early as this there were discernible elements of that thoroughgoing, professional approach which was to obsess him later when, if he could not do a thing excellently, he would rather abandon it. A 'Pistol Troop Magazine' was produced with himself as editor and articles from schoolmasters, clergymen and other adults. It was typed by Arthur's secretary and bound in full morocco. It still exists. Waugh's own contribution, a short story, 'Multa Pecunia', occupies the first six pages. Arthur looked on with a mixture of pride and misgiving at the driving force of this proud, serious, sharp-eyed boy. It had not been his way as a child. On one occasion he gave a garden party. Most of the guests having disappeared from the lawn, he traced them to the day-nursery. Evelyn was holding their attention with an impassioned speech about the injustices of what

15. *MBE*, p. 166.

is now called male chauvinism and the need to secure votes for women before the next General Election.

*

In July of 1911 Arthur and Catherine travelled with Alec to Sherborne where the boy was to be presented for a scholarship examination. Alec's failure in this in no way clouded the expedition's 'four days of sheer delight'[16] for Arthur. He lunched on the dais and reminisced with the masters and boys. Returned to the scene of so much discomfort in his own childhood, he was consumed with excitement at the prospect of his son becoming part of the school's tradition. Arthur's loyalty to the place was extraordinary, even by the standards of his day. 'During the next four years', he wrote, 'I must have been the youngest man of my age in London, all my thoughts and interests were absorbed in my two school-boys. I might almost be said to have lived at Sherborne in my imagination. . . .'[17] Evelyn had been at Heath Mount for less than a year when this change took place; once again his brother inhabited a higher, inaccessible world. Alec's initiation into the hallowed cloisters of Sherborne cemented his exclusive relationship with Arthur and further isolated Evelyn.

From the first day Alec loved his school. He plunged into its competitive world with fierce ambition. Arthur and Catherine would frequently catch a train on Friday nights to spend the week-end there, leaving Evelyn behind. One wonders if Catherine was quite as entranced as her husband with Alec's tales of house politics and his chances of 'colours', but she was a loyal companion and doubtless enjoyed the break from London. Even during the holidays the school was not forgotten. A constant stream of Alec's friends came to stay, much to Arthur's delight. Evelyn must have felt more than a little estranged. His reaction, his father said, was to approach school in an entirely different fashion. Until his last year at public school he invited no-one home. 'I think [my father] lacked that sense of identity which he felt with my brother in both his triumphs and scrapes,' he wrote. 'I did not want to confuse my home with my school life.'[18]

Home life during his period at Heath Mount (September 1910 – Easter 1917) was simple and conventional. It would be entirely wrong to imply that by this stage Evelyn had formed a positive dislike of his father; he was simply much closer to his mother and his nurse, Lucy, and found Arthur's and Alec's world exclusive and confusing. But it is perhaps significant that he began his diary at the age of seven just after Alec's departure for Sherborne. 'Daddy is a Publisher', he wrote in the first entry, 'he goes to Chapman and Hall office it looks a offely dull place. I am just going to Church.'[19]

16. *OMR*, p. 332.
17. *Ibid.*, p. 332.
18. 'My Father', *op. cit.*, 4.
19. *Diaries*, p. 5.

There were few aesthetic pleasures in the monotonous round of a six-day week at school and when, during 1910, his parents started taking Evelyn with them to St Jude's in Hampstead Garden Suburb he relished the services and made no complaint. The vicar, Basil Bourchier, was celebrated for his flamboyant pulpit manner. He improvised festivals and was later satirised in A. S. M. Hutchinson's *If Winter Comes* (1921) as the Rev. Boom Bagshaw. Arthur, as a young man, had suffered a period of religious uncertainty but was by 1910 content to share regular church attendance with Catherine. Bourchier's approach appealed to his sense of the dramatic; it was an entertainment. Evelyn's interest, though, gradually moved beyond the pleasures of simple diversion. The ornaments of Bourchier's Anglo-Catholicism exerted an elementary aesthetic appeal.

It was the one taste from which Catherine actively discouraged Evelyn. On holiday with her in Brighton during a half-term in 1915 Evelyn noted in his journal: 'In the evening we went to church. We struck a horribly low one. I was the only person who crossed myself and bowed to the altar.'[20] With this in mind it might seem easier to understand his sense of association (in *A Little Learning*) with the little boy (Catherine's father) caught by his aunts concealing a rosary. In fact, Evelyn's aunts actively encouraged him. As a twelve-year-old he constructed a small shrine in his bedroom at Underhill at which he lit incense. When he told his aunts of this they ' . . . instantly promised to make me a frontal. Aunt Elsie is going to give me a crucifix when I'm confirmed and Aunt Trissie has given me two sweet brass bowls to fill with flowers.'[21]

Despite the sincerity of his devotion there is an unmistakable element in all this of his treating it as a hobby. He was fascinated by the paraphernalia of ritual and avidly assembled his bits and pieces with the concentration most bright little boys bring to stamp-collecting or train-spotting. Evelyn Waugh was never a serious candidate for the priesthood. At school he joined with the others in ragging the feebler masters, and his mother, Alec recalls, once rebuked Evelyn for his quick and spiteful tongue. It was, she said, his 'besetting sin'. He agreed but, much to Catherine's amazement, replied by asking her whether she was aware of her own fundamental failing. ' "No, Evelyn," she said, "what is it?" The answer came straight back: "A lack of faith in Catholic doctrine." '[22] Throughout his life there seemed no contradiction to him between the assertion of faith and personal failure perfectly to emulate Christian principles. The two were quite separate issues; there was no question, he thought, of hypocrisy.

The earliest diaries (1911–1916), brief and disjointed, provide no evidence of precocious talent. But divided as they are into 'chapters' and 'volumes' (a 'chapter' usually no more than a paragraph), they testify to his awareness of the vocabulary

20. *Ibid.*, p. 8.
21. *Ibid.*, Easter Term, 1916; aged 12, p. 9.
22. *MBE*, p. 167.

of literary life. In the Waugh household it was impossible to escape the world of books. Costing, binding, advertising, the arrival of new manuscripts, the problems with authors – all this formed the daily conversation at table and it only increased in intensity when Alec became an active part of it a few years later. As a young man, Evelyn found it oppressive and wished to turn his artistic talents in an entirely different direction. But at school he was keen to follow the tradition.

In 1910 he wrote his first 'novel', *The Curse of the Horse Race*, a cautionary tale illustrating the moral laxity of betting (probably derivative of similar stories told by Lucy, a devout Calvinist). In 1916 he edited *The Cynic* at Heath Mount, a magazine of his own invention, to which he contributed a story, various articles and a short play. 1916 also saw the writing of a long poem in three 'cantos' about Purgatory, using the metre of *Hiawatha*. He called it *The World To Come*. A family friend had a few copies privately printed and bound and it can still be seen in the British Library. It was an ambitious project for a twelve-year-old and moderately successful, although Waugh expressed nothing but embarrassed contempt for it as an adult. At Heath Mount, he had wanted nothing more than to be a clergyman, an ambition which did not leave him entirely until his mid-twenties.

Arthur was a direct influence on the literary preferences of his children. In the soft ruby glow of the book-room lamps he would read aloud to his sons and any of their friends who cared to stay. He loved an audience. Even his cautious younger boy sat spellbound by the performances. The repertoire was large and various – Victorian melodramas from Arthur's youth, Shakespeare, Dickens, Thackeray, Trollope, Browning and Tennyson – and always acted with vigour and conviction. What might have been an absurdly embarrassing pantomime to Evelyn's critical eye became, in the form of an entertainment, the broad basis for a liberal education. He remained grateful for it. Towards the end of his life he remarked that, where the reading of poetry was concerned, he had ' . . . never heard [Arthur] excelled except by Sir John Gielgud'.[23]

The early diaries make no mention of these cosy evenings, probably because they imperceptibly became absorbed into the daily routine as Evelyn grew up. Entries are confined to school news, infrequent journeys and, on one occasion during 1912, an extraordinarily calm and brief note about an operation for appendicitis. Almost nothing is said of the latter although Waugh described the incident in some detail in *A Little Learning*. He had been strapped down, chloroformed and cut open on the kitchen table. Sent away to convalesce, he had experienced his first intense pangs of alienation. He seems from his earliest days to have inherited his father's stoical approach to physical pain. (Arthur, late in life, made no fuss about having all his teeth extracted without anaesthetic.)

Away from home he was a tough little character. The diary records several victorious scraps. Cecil Beaton was a contemporary pupil at Heath Mount and

23. 'My Father', *op. cit.*, 4.

remembered Waugh vividly with his 'diabolical stare'[24] as the leader of the school bullies. Pugnacious and vainglorious at Heath Mount, he enjoyed his small world of power before returning to the home where he could exert little influence. Waugh never denied Beaton's charges. Indeed, in a review of his book he seemed positively to relish the memory, impishly correcting him on a point of fact. The tortures did not, apparently, include bending Beaton's arms back to front, but the frequent insertion of pins into his body.[25]

Equally unpleasant, and indirectly connected, are the attitudes to the working classes which he recorded as a child. It is difficult to say where he imbibed such impressions. Certainly his mother had no aversion to the poor and Arthur was mildness personified. But like Alec, possibly as a result of the undivided attention of one parent, he seems to have developed a 'superiority complex'. In his scratchy little record we find phrases like 'street cads' and 'vile Southend trippers'; he corrects the use of 'ladies', when describing the womenfolk, to 'females'. His extreme sensitivity to anything gross or ugly could cause him to over-react and to retreat into a precious, elemental snobbery. Waugh's enemies believe that these concepts remained with him throughout adult life. This is nonsense. Looking back on his schoolboy diaries Waugh was appalled by their 'consistent caddish-ness', barely able to recognise the individual depicted. He was an awkward child whose blustering self-assertion and tantrums were interspersed with equally unpredictable withdrawals into hurt silence. His mother was rarely certain that she understood him; Arthur was utterly baffled. Both worried as to how things would turn out.

\*

The last eight terms of Evelyn's preparatory school life (September 1914 – April 1917) fell during the First World War, but the national disaster had little immediate effect on the steady routine of his life. During the hot and lazy summer of 1914 Arthur and Alec had picked up hints at cricket matches that conflict was imminent. When war was declared in August, no-one was unduly perturbed. Most expected victory by Christmas. Middle-class Englishmen had a complacent sense of the superiority of their nation. None guessed that their security was to be permanently wrecked. That summer was the last of its kind for Arthur and Alec.

The fighting remained a distant and abstract problem for the Waughs for almost a year. Arthur was too old to enlist, his sons too young. Life at Underhill continued to flow in its regular channel for Evelyn. At Heath Mount the boys subscribed to buy a watch for a master leaving for the Army. The presentation

24.  Cecil Beaton, *The Wandering Years. Diaries: 1922–1939* (Weidenfeld and Nicolson, 1961), p. 173.
25.  'Footlights and Chandeliers', *Spectator*, 21 July, 1961, 96.

was emotional and patriotic, many of the pupils turning their heads to hide the tears. Evelyn, unaffected by the scene, simply recorded that he 'felt rather sorry now I used to rag him so'.[26] He joined the scouts and raised a school patrol; during the summer of 1915 he acted as a messenger in the War Office, constantly passing Kitchener's door, never invited in.

A large proportion of the staff of Chapman and Hall were men in middle life. Arthur was thus able to maintain a skeleton staff throughout the war. He went to his office each day as he had been doing for twelve years and book production was largely unaffected. But as soon as Alec returned to Sherborne in September it became apparent that radical change had occurred. The upper part of the school was massively depopulated by the flood of recruits for various Officer Training Corps. Seventeen was the minimum age for enlistment in 1914 and few were immune to the fervour of nationalism which then gripped the country. Alec, at sixteen, found himself suddenly a senior pupil, projected into positions of responsibility he might never have achieved, under normal circumstances, two years later.

A natural leader, he survived the pressures and, with competition reduced, won various honours. Despite the war, Alec's successes made this one of Arthur's happiest years. He rejoiced at his son's claiming the English Verse Prize and thus following the family tradition. But far outstripping this in his estimation came Alec's permanent position in the First Eleven. So impatient was he to hear of Alec's performances that he insisted on the scores being telegraphed to Underhill. His jubilation verged on sublimity when one of these missives announced that the House Cup had been won, largely due to his boy's long innings. Quotations from Kipling sprang easily to his lips. ' "Once in a while" ', he said to himself, ' "we can finish in style." '[27]

In fact, Alec did not finish in style but disgrace. Although not actually expelled, he was asked to leave at the end of the summer term, 1915. 'Fifty years ago', he wrote, ' . . . a conspiracy of silence shrouded the main moral of school life. Today the danger is recognized with frankness; and I wonder how many ex-public school boys would deny that at some point in their schooldays they indulged in homosexual practices; practices that had no lasting effect, that they instantly abandoned on finding themselves in an adult, heterosexual world. I was not the immaculate exception, and I had the bad luck to be found out.'[28] Certain masters, outraged at his not being expelled, and further irritated by his lack of humility, encouraged their pupils to boycott his company. The idea caught on and although it was impossible to enforce it rigorously as Alec was an important figure in so

26.  *Diaries*, Christmas Term, 1914; aged 11, p. 8.
27.  *OMR*, p. 348.
28.  *TEYOAW*, p. 63.

many sports teams, he spent that last term largely in solitary confinement. None of his prizes was publicly presented.

It was a bitter blow to Arthur but he resigned himself to the situation and never indulged in recrimination. Nothing is said of the matter in his autobiography. Evelyn heard about it for the first time from his brother's published account in 1962; one wonders whether even Catherine was informed of the details. It seems unlikely. Alec had for some time been impatient to abandon school and join the army. Leaving when he did in itself drew no attention to possible scandal and Arthur went out of his way to keep things quiet. In September of 1915 Alec joined the Inns of Court OTC and, after preliminary training at Lincoln's Inn, was sent to Berkhamsted. Here he regularly visited an old acquaintance of the Waughs, W. W. Jacobs and his family. They lived in a large house, Beechcroft, on the outskirts of the town. Barbara Jacobs, the daughter of this tempestuous union, was then only fifteen-and-a-half, a small, attractive, elfin figure, sensitive and shy. She and Alec became close companions. Her younger sister, Luned, later became a friend of Evelyn's and provided him with a primitive sexual experience. His only contact with girls by 1915 had been with one Muriel during his convalescence from the appendicitis operation. In a deserted school for girls by the mud flats of the Thames estuary, cold and alienated, they had shared a mutual display of private parts.

Alec was allowed home only from lunch-time on Saturdays until Sunday evening and Arthur was beginning to realise how close he might be to losing his beloved boy for ever. Each week the newspapers' casualty lists grew to more ominous proportions. Already several family friends had died in France. Arthur would travel to Euston to meet the Berkhamsted train in order to savour every moment of Alec's company. At home they would sit quietly in the book-room together reading poetry, isolated from the rest of the family and wrapped in a reticent, masculine sorrow. In the face of possible death the circumstances of Alec's leaving Sherborne seemed of little consequence to either of them.

As a boy of twelve, Evelyn can have had little conception of the serious nature of these events but he must have been aware of the nervous atmosphere in the house. Alec was even further at a distance, ensconced in the world of men, but this time his younger brother did not resent it. Evelyn, from his earliest years, admired men of action. Of all his juvenile toys he prized the soldiers most. Alec's enlistment rendered their past squabbles insignificant. To Evelyn, the war represented adventure and a legitimate outlet for his belligerence. During September of 1915 the family experienced the first air-raid on Hampstead. 'Alec woke me up in the night at about 11 o'clock', Evelyn noted, 'saying the Zeps had come. We came downstairs and the special constable was rushing about yelling "Lights Out" and telling us the Zeppelin was right overhead. We heard two bombs and then the Parliament Hill guns were going and the Zep went away in their smoke cloud to do some baby-killing elswear [*sic*].'[29] Such raids were fairly frequent, the new building work on the Heath Extension being mistaken for the hangars of Hendon aerodrome. The family would ritually collect in the book-room on these occasions for a midnight meal. Evelyn found the whole business highly invigorating. His brother's direct involvement in the fighting provoked undiluted admiration.

Direct involvement, however, was a long time coming for Alec and his own feelings were confused by his annoyance over the scandal at Sherborne. His affection for the school never wavered. What irritated him was the institution's hypocritical public image to which he had, in a sense, been sacrificed. Ever since the trials of Oscar Wilde there had been a public hypersensitivity to the whole issue of homosexuality which coloured any mention of the slightest transgression. Alec, wounded by the injustice of the situation, determined to discuss it openly in a novel about school life. With the energy of a man who knows that he might be dead in two months, he began work shortly after Christmas, 1915. Seven and a half weeks later the book was finished. He was only seventeen but the work inaugurated a long career as a novelist. *The Loom of Youth* became a 'best-seller'. He had to wait forty years before another of his novels, *Island in the Sun*, achieved comparable popularity.

'Popularity' is not quite the right word; 'notoriety' comes closer to the truth. Even Arthur was unhappy with it. Sections of manuscript were posted to him as Alec completed them and, while pleasantly surprised at Alec's literary facility, he was doubtful about the content. In his autobiography Arthur deals generously with the book, saying that he had only asked Alec to amend the description of a particular master which was potentially libellous before acceptance by Chapman's could be considered. This Alec refused to do. His obstinacy over the matter must have relieved his father.

*One Man's Road* professes shock at the novel's reception but Arthur was an astute publisher. He cannot have been unaware that the subject was likely to stimulate controversy. Other firms, at any rate, saw the danger. The manuscript was returned several times until Alec, in a fit of temper, refused to send it out again. Frustration piled on frustration. In the early part of 1916 the minimum age for officers was raised to eighteen and Alec was posted to a coastal defence force in the meantime. Through Arthur's agency he was relieved of this duty and allowed to return to Hampstead to study for the Sandhurst entrance exams. On 24th August he passed into the Royal Military College where he met Thomas Seccombe, an instructor and an old family friend. Seccombe opened his house to Alec and, on discovering that he had written a novel, read it and passed it on to Grant Richards. Richards agreed to bring the novel out provided that Seccombe

29. *Diaries*, 1915; aged 11, p. 8.

contributed an introduction. No objections were raised and shortly afterwards proofs began arriving at Sandhurst.

It was a long and complex path from Seccombe's initial interest to the book's eventual appearance. The best part of a year had elapsed by the time *The Loom* was released on 20th July, 1917. By that time Alec had finished his machine-gun course and passed out of the RMC. There was a favourable review in the *Times Literary Supplement* that week and Arthur telegraphed his congratulations to Grantham where his son was waiting for an overseas posting. Late the next night Catherine and he were disturbed by some gravel flung up at their window. It was Alec. He was to travel to France in the morning.

There was no sleep at Underhill that night as the family padded nervously about, conscious that this might be their last reunion. Arthur returned to a dismal house a few hours after the painful journey to Victoria Station to see his boy off. Evelyn was back for the summer after his first term at public school, despondent and, perhaps, a little resentful. His brother's book had radically altered the course of his own career.

\*

For some years Evelyn's name had been down for Sherborne's School House. He was due to go there in September 1916. But Arthur, sensitive to the possibility of repercussions from Alec's *roman à clef*, requested an interview with the Head Master to clarify the position. *The Loom*, he explained, would not certainly be published but, if it were, would Evelyn still be acceptable as a pupil? They met for lunch in Nowell Smith's London club and, although Arthur writes of the discussion as an amicable exchange of views, it was in all probability extremely awkward.

Arthur's devotion to the school and reverence for the 'Chief' were beyond dispute. Yet his elder son had very nearly been sacked for homosexuality and had now sat down to write a novel to justify his actions. Were the book to receive any popularity, Sherborne's name would inevitably be sullied. Nowell Smith might well have been astounded at Arthur's audacity in sending another son to him. The father's hopeful and sincere countenance perhaps allayed strong feeling. Smith might even have felt sorry for him. Clearly the school was a governing passion in Arthur's life and he wanted his younger boy to follow the family tradition. But there was no room for compromise. Quite apart from any question of retaliation, Evelyn's own position in a school where his brother had become a public enemy would be insufferable. From all points of view, Smith explained, it would be better if Mr Waugh looked elsewhere.

The decision was more of an embarrassing disappointment than a shock. Above all, it was an inconvenience. Evelyn would have to stay on at Heath Mount while they decided what to do with him. At nearly thirteen he had already outgrown the place and was fretting about its being like a kindergarten. Earlier in the year he had been confirmed at St Jude's and his absorption with religion was becoming greater with every month.

During August, 1916, in the only detailed record of a week of Evelyn's life in the early diaries, there is an account of a holiday with his mother at Westcliff-on-Sea. The curious assortment of interests reveals something of the contradictions in the boy. Coupled with his piety and delight in church architecture there are signs of the adolescent aggression which formed so strong a part of Alec's character. Evelyn disliked competitive sport but loved swimming in as heavy a sea as he could find: 'It was rougher than ever. . . . The waves were simply lovely.'[30] Several references are made to 'sketching', indicating that his preoccupation with graphic art had already taken root. The gambling instinct is there, too, in the form of 'a most enthralling slot [machine]'.[31] Penny arcades fascinated him throughout his time at public school, to be replaced later by casinos. Unlike Arthur, he liked taking risks, financial or physical.

Arthur was aware that the rapidly-expanding interests of his younger son could only be hampered by more time at Heath Mount. It was a difficult period for everyone. With Alec just off to Sandhurst, his posting to the Front had been deferred, but only for a few months and its inevitability hung over Arthur as a perpetual source of anxiety. Catherine had joined the St John's Ambulance Brigade and much of her time was now spent out of the house. War-time economies had caused the *Daily Telegraph* in 1914 to dismiss its freelance writers and Arthur had lost the £50–£60 a month from a twice-weekly review column he had written for several years. The depression felt by a country which had spent over two years fighting and could still see no end to it had begun, by slow degrees, to infect the atmosphere of Underhill. Everything Arthur had sought to establish seemed to be dissolving and the question of Evelyn's next school, important as it was, had to take its place alongside a multitude of other equally urgent concerns.

Catherine wanted Evelyn to go to a London day-school – Westminster, St Paul's or the University College School in Hampstead. But this time Arthur was not to be deflected. It would have seemed unnatural and unhealthy to him not to send Evelyn away to complete his education. With such short notice, though, the choice was restricted and, characteristically, he rushed into a decision and stuck to it. Lancing College was selected, chiefly because Arthur considered that it would prove a test of the sincerity of Evelyn's piety. One of the Woodard schools, Lancing had been founded to inculcate High Church principles and was largely populated by the sons of Anglican clergymen. It sounded dull and Evelyn was offended. Quite unjustly, he considered Lancing an inferior establishment. In his autobiography, over forty years later, he struggled to be fair to his father's

30. *Ibid.*, 14 August, 1916, p. 10.
31. *Ibid.*, 15 August, 1916, p. 11.

decision but the fury remained, the bitterness and sense of abandonment: ' . . . with a minimum of deliberation', he notes, '[my father's] choice fell on Lancing, which he had never seen and with which he had no associations.'[32] It is a particularly acid comment on a man whose obsessive interest in Shirburnian lore had coloured Evelyn's earliest memories.

The emotional problems involved in the change were exacerbated by Arthur's impatient desire to hurry everything to a conclusion. Although it was not the universal practice then to send children to school at the beginning of the autumn term, it was usual. But, the place secured, Arthur refused to wait until September, probably considering that they had delayed long enough already.

On 9th May, 1917, a damp and overcast day, he travelled to Lancing with Evelyn. It was a miserable journey prefacing two years of despondent loneliness for the boy. Arthur hastily made his escape, leaving Evelyn in the care of his House Master, 'Dick' Harris. Sitting alone at the table reserved for 'new men' with a book Harris had given him, Evelyn soon discovered that his enforced solitude was unlikely to be relieved for several weeks. New pupils were discouraged from associating with older boys during their first term. Only one other lad joined him at the table and they did not immediately take to each other. 'Every public school boy worth his salt', Arthur declaimed in *One Man's Road*, 'believes that his own years at school were lived in the golden age of the place's history. . . .'[33] His younger son would not have agreed.

*

In the Freeman interview Waugh attempted to deflect any enquiry into his early unhappiness at Lancing. He pretended that he could not remember making any statement about his misery there. But Freeman had done his homework. In an earlier radio broadcast (November 1953) the following dialogue had been recorded:

> 'And were you happy at school?'
> 'No – no fault of the school's, I think I shouldn't have been happy at any school.'
> 'Why were you unhappy?'
> 'Hated the boys so.'
> 'You didn't like them at all – I mean they had nothing in common with you?'
> 'No, I didn't discover it in the years I was there.'
> 'All the boys – did you really hate all the boys in the school?'
> 'I didn't hate them, I just didn't like their company about the place.'[34]

32. *ALL*, p. 96.
33. *OMR*, p. 78.
34. 'Frankly Speaking', 16 November, 1953, BBCSL, p. 12.

This is, of course, facetious. Like so many of Waugh's accounts of his own experience (especially in the *Diaries*), one aspect of the truth has been caricatured. It was not how he remembered things but how he chose to recall them in public; it was more entertaining and illustrative and, more importantly, it gave less of himself away. His time at Lancing contained moments of abject despair and periods of elation. But his description in the broadcast touches on something fundamental and continuous in his attitude to Lancing. It would, as he said, have applied to any school.

Although he came to enjoy the company of selected friends, he was not at first convivial. In this he was entirely the opposite of his father and brother. Team spirit meant nothing to him, not because he was from the outset an iconoclast, but because he had an aversion to crowds and to the sensation of being swept along merely as a constituent part of the mass. Lancing, unfortunately, was peculiarly well adapted to aggravate Waugh's sensitivity on this point. It represented a considerably milder regimen than he would have experienced at Sherborne but it lacked that school's geographical good fortune of being an organic part of a county town. Lancing's grim isolation was in those days complete.

Very little existed for the boys beyond the life of the school; contact with the outside world, beyond letters and the occasional visit, was lost almost entirely during term. A gaunt flint structure, built high on the Downs on massive terraces cut into the chalk, Lancing College is dominated by an immense Victorian Gothic chapel. It was a difficult place to reach or to leave. In 1917, the nearest houses were in Shoreham, then a run-down village on the coast between Brighton and Worthing providing no form of diversion. Evelyn found himself imprisoned in a crowd. There was no escape for several terms, other than into his own thoughts and fantasies and there were very few boys in the school, even later, to whom he could turn for intellectual companionship.

During the first two years he kept a diary in which the frequent black days were marked by a border of chains surrounding the page. This document, referred to in *A Little Learning*, no longer exists. As an older and more arrogant schoolboy Waugh certainly mutilated his personal record in order to excise 'dangerous' material and we may well suspect that similar motives explain the disappearance of his earliest diaries at Lancing. He eventually took up the position in the school which he had occupied at Heath Mount as a pugnacious leader. It would have been disastrous for any diary of his to have been found to contain signs of abject weakness and homesickness. The public façade of strength was his only defence against nagging self-doubt. He was constantly anxious that he might fall from favour and back into the miserable condition of his first terms.

The relative luxury of Evelyn's Hampstead life had barely been interrupted by attendance at Heath Mount. He had never been subjected to rigorous discipline or any severe reduction of home comforts. At Lancing the boys slept in stone dormitories beneath open windows. Bedclothes were kept to a minimum. At 6.30

am, after nights when it was sometimes difficult to sleep for the draught, the boys had to rise and take a cold bath. The rules of the school were complex, especially regarding dress and access to the various parts of the grounds. Any infringement was punished with the cane and beatings were often severe. Younger pupils were not allowed beyond bounds unless accompanied by an adult. The only female with whom Evelyn had any contact during his early terms was the matron of his house, formerly nanny to the Head Master's children. But by far the worst privation was the diminishing supply of food. By 1917 war restrictions were severe and public school cuisine was reduced to tiny and repulsive portions. It was Evelyn's first experience of hunger.

The structured formality of the school did not in itself depress him. He had looked forward to public school as an inevitable step in the process of maturity and keenly anticipated taking his place alongside Alec in the world of men. He would have been ashamed of being a day-boy all his life and, although intimidated by the severity of Lancing, he learnt its code quickly and abided by it. His primary concern as a new boy was to keep out of everyone's way. He was 'morbidly afraid of being in any way conspicuous'[35] but was, unfortunately, unsuccessful in this attempted self-effacement.

The very fact of arrival at such an unusual time in the year drew attention to him. He would be pointed out as a curiosity and then ignored. The fastidious habits acquired through living so long beneath the eye of his mother became an object of ridicule. He would recoil at the undignified exposure of the doorless latrines. The loss of privacy was painful; he loathed the sheer physical imminence of this crowd of loud-mouthed youths. And overt piety only worsened his reputation. Each night the boys would kneel by their beds to pay tribute to the Almighty and the chamber pot. To most, prayer was a cursory duty; but long after they had risen Evelyn would still be deep in his worship. He was not liked but he did not, as he would have said, repine. He bravely endured, living for letters and holidays, an awkward, clever little boy who kept his nose clean and his opinions to himself.

His sole companion at this stage was Roger Fulford, now well-known as a historian and biographer. He had been the other new pupil on that first dismal May afternoon. Both had been placed in Head's House, a privilege for which an extra fee was paid and which conferred honour on its boys though no tangible benefit. The honour resided in having the Head Master, Canon Bowlby, in peripatetic attendance. Fulford's account of his schooldays draws attention to Waugh's low opinion of the place. 'I should not talk so much about Lancing,' Waugh remarked to Fulford when he arrived as an undergraduate at Oxford. 'If you weren't at Eton or Harrow or Winchester or Rugby no-one minds much

35. *ALL*, p. 109.

where you were.'[36] The perfectionist in him reacted later against association with something which he considered to be of the second rank. This was not crass snobbery. Bowlby himself, a former house-master at Eton, according to Waugh left no doubt in the minds of his pupils that Eton was superior.

Waugh, though, appears to have reacted to this idea far more strongly than Fulford. The latter's descriptions suggest that Bowlby was 'a great Headmaster' leading a staff of gifted men. *A Little Learning* gives us a picture of Bowlby as a limping bishop manqué with no serious interest in education. At Eton, Waugh says, Bowlby was a figure of fun and, for the duration of the war, his staff largely consisted of a ramshackle collection of temporary replacements. Things were certainly shabby until the Armistice, but Waugh implies that the run-down aspect of the place in his first four terms was merely a grosser manifestation of its innate inferiority. He objected because he felt it was trying, through its network of rules and its private language, to ape more famous establishments.

Dudley Carew, another contemporary, agreed that 'there was somehow an impression that the school was pretending to be what it was not'[37] but he was so heavily influenced by Waugh's opinions that we may doubt the absolute independence of his remarks. Even Carew was shocked by what he considered the gross distortions of Evelyn's autobiography. The book had provoked irate responses in the newspapers from loyal Old Boys. Waugh always saw things in a different, more lurid, light from others. Lancing was tough and more than a little down-at-heel when he first arrived but it was well-run and maintained a substantial reputation. Waugh's refusal to recognise its qualities reflects both his early difficulties in the school and that sense of persecution mentioned earlier. It was difficult for him to see the place as anything other than a stop-gap result of his father's indecision.

*

In fact the account of Lancing in *A Little Learning* is not supported by Waugh's contemporary record. When the *Diaries* resume in September 1919 we do not find a catalogue of derisive commentary on the school. School, as an institution which separated him from home, certainly aggravated a growing emotional instability and frequently depressed and bored him, but it would have been the same had he been sent to a more eminent establishment. The very first entry emphasises this:

> Alec once said that he kept his life in 'watertight compartments'. It is very true; here I am flung suddenly into an entirely different world,

36. *EWAHW*, p. 16.
37. Dudley Carew, *A Fragment of Friendship* (Everest Books Ltd, 1974), p. 38.

different friends, and different mode of life. All the comforts of home are gone but one doesn't really miss them much.[38]

He never forgot his first Ascension Day holiday. At Lancing the boys were given the day off to roam or go out with relatives until evening chapel. On that 13th May, 1917, having been there only four days, no-one came for him and there was no fellow to share the free time. He even misunderstood the alteration to lunching arrangements and could get nothing to eat. Isolated, hungry and depressed he had shambled round the grounds in the gusting rain, longing for evening to put an end to his humiliation. To some degree, that dreadful day epitomised in his memory the atmosphere of Lancing. But there was never any question of deliberate intellectual isolation until his last term. He threw himself determinedly into the internal competition of the school; he craved success, if anything, more fervently than had his father and brother.

Arthur's description of Evelyn's taking everything 'in a sort of negligent stride' reflects only that image of himself which Evelyn wished to project as a form of defence. He even thirsted for prominence in athletics and was infuriated at his inability to excel, and thus to gain power, in this area of school activity. 'I am afraid there is little chance of my getting a place in the five-mile team', he noted in January 1920, 'none of House colours.'[39] And, a little later: 'I should like to have gone for a training run but I mustn't train too palpably as it is only too probable that I shan't get a place at all.'[40] When his House won the football cup in the following February he recorded the victory with breathless enthusiasm: 'It really is too wonderful . . . God, it's too good to be true.'[41] This appears to be the sort of partisan rivalry which Arthur had relished during Alec's Sherborne days. Why, then, was there not the same shared excitement between father and younger son?

Alec's and Evelyn's motives were different. Evelyn had no love of sport, fair play or team spirit; there was no belief on his part in the quasi-ethical public school concept of a healthy body and a healthy mind. He was looking the other way when the decisive goal was scored in the football cup and had complained bitterly in his diary about compulsory attendance at the match. He had not wanted to be present because it was commonly held that Head's House would suffer ignominious defeat. His jubilation was an outburst of delight at the disconcertion of the authorities. Waugh would rarely exert himself for anything other than personal gain. His ambition for his House was a thinly disguised vehicle for his overweening desire to be an outstanding member of a superior group. The phrase 'a bad loser' barely describes him at this stage. There was an obsessive fear of

38. *Diaries*, 23 September, 1919, p. 19.
39. *Ibid.*, 27 January, 1920, p. 52.
40. *Ibid.*, 30 January, 1920, p. 54.
41. *Ibid.*, 19 February, 1920, p. 59.

public humiliation that pushed him to acts of capricious malice as a schoolboy, despite his own shame at what he was doing.

He never lost a feeling of preternatural vulnerability to ill-fortune. 'I seem to miss everything by a hair's breadth', he wrote in September, 1919, 'first my house colours and now this [library privileges]. I expect when I die, I shall miss getting into heaven by just one place and the golden gates will clang to in my face.'[42] Yet this sense of persecution did not evoke empathy with the persecuted. He was entirely pragmatic. Success ensured greater control over one's immediate circumstances, deflected potential attack. In order to render oneself less vulnerable, one must make others more so. He once unfairly forced himself into the lead in a race and noted afterwards: 'I am beginning to believe that there must be some malignant fate that makes me foul. I never think of the man behind at all. I spend all my attention on trying to get in front of the man in front.'[43] This remained a lifelong ambition.

These trivial references to his athletic performance epitomise Waugh's intense self-consciousness as a schoolboy. They stand out from a diary which reflects a mixture of abnormal intellectual maturity and the typical traumas of adolescence. But the arrogance, and often the fatuous pomposity, of this early document show quite clearly that Waugh considered his generation a unique product of historical circumstance. It was something which preoccupied him throughout his later years at Lancing and for some time afterwards. His father was always emphasising how much more advanced the new generation was: 'I wonder if we really are going to produce any great men', Evelyn asked himself in 1919, 'or if we will fizzle out into mediocrity. We certainly seem more precocious if that is at all a good sign.'[44] By 1921 he was in no doubt:

> The more I see of Lancing the more convinced I become that our generation . . . was a very exceptional one. One day I must try and work out the many influences which contributed to this. I think that if I do I shall find that the war is directly responsible for most of us. . . .[45]

*

The war, of course, had directly impinged on life at Lancing and affected his family. In 1917 Alec's then imminent posting had caused him to rush through the writing of *The Loom of Youth*. When eventually published it had generated such an outcry that the author was removed from Sherborne's roll of Old Boys. (Arthur then nobly removed his own name.) Alec, in his absence at the Front, had unwittingly become the champion of rebellious youth, the hero of those

42. *Ibid.*, 28 September, p. 21.
43. *Ibid.*, 19 March, p. 121.
44. *Ibid.*, 10 October, 1919, p. 27.
45. *Ibid.*, 11 February, 1921, p. 112.

critical of the public school spirit in which the war was being fought. He was posted missing during Evelyn's Easter holiday in 1918. While his parents waited for news, Underhill was deluged with sympathetic correspondence from his readers. A telegram eventually arrived, picked from the mass of fan-mail, stating that Alec was a prisoner at Mainz. It was nine months before they saw him again.

Evelyn remembered the Christmas holidays of 1918 as the best of his life. The war was over, Alec was back, and money was being spent freely again. Arthur had published his second collection of essays, *Tradition and Change*, that December and prefaced it with a dedicatory letter to Evelyn. It indicates that the predominant concern was now with change rather than tradition. It speaks of Evelyn's attempts at cubist painting decorating the walls of his bedroom and appeals to an ideal of domestic harmony in danger of disintegration. At just fourteen Evelyn had published an article, 'In Defence of Cubism', in *Drawing and Design*,[46] lucidly, if simply, defending abstract art. His father must have seen this as an unmistakable warning that a precocious and aggressive new generation was not only knocking on but knocking down his door.

Arthur's essays, often quoted now as examples of the critical intransigence which greeted the imagist poets, berate Gertrude Stein, Eliot and Pound for their apparent rejection of metre and melody. He was hopelessly 'out of date'. Until he lost the job on the *Telegraph* in 1914 he had reviewed only novels and biographies in his column and had not even heard of Edward Marsh's volumes of *Georgian Poetry*. Everything was moving too fast for him. The war appeared to have caused fundamental shifts in artistic and social attitudes. Alec was publishing radical articles on the rights of the young; even little Evelyn had set up as a defendant of modern painting. He felt for the first time that he had been left behind and that this dislocation between the generations was fundamentally dangerous. When Evelyn sent him an essay on 'Romance' in October 1919, he was intensely irritated by its satirical approach.

Earlier in the same year, on 29th July, Alec had married Barbara Jacobs. He had become engaged to her during a fortnight's leave from the front in February 1918, and now had to redeem his promise. Because of the housing shortage they had had to furnish two rooms in Underhill and live in awkward proximity with his parents. When Evelyn came home for his Christmas holidays there was another domestic unit on the premises.

He didn't object. Barbara had already been living in the house for some months while attending London University and Evelyn had grown close to her. During his holidays they would often go off together to the theatre, galleries or cinema. Like her mother she was a feminist. It was she who instructed Evelyn about *avant-garde* painting. Thanks to her, 'Vorticism' and 'Futurism' became familiar words and gave him an intellectual advantage at school. During his first two years

46. *Drawing and Design*, Vol. 6, No. 31 (November 1917), 9.

at Lancing he visited Berkhamsted for regular holidays and there met Luned, Barbara's younger sister. It was Luned who provided him with his second 'sexual' experience and, though they never kissed, there was an unspoken, adolescent attraction. An ill-defined game was played at Beechcroft for the crowd of children in the house. The lights would be switched off. The object was to crawl through people's legs to the other side of the room. Evelyn and Luned always suggested the game and found each other quickly. Under the cover of darkness, they rolled on the floor clasped in an ecstatic embrace. When the lights came on they glanced at each other with furtive intimacy. It went no further than that but he never forgot her. The Jacobs became an extension of the Waugh family.

There was no obvious friction at Underhill as a result of the double ménage, except that Alec became increasingly morose. In January 1920 he had taken a part-time post as a reader with Chapman's and, after the war, the routine of office life grated on his nerves. But, there was a more profound anxiety: the marriage was, and remained, unconsummated and he suffered agonies of guilt about how to resolve the problem.

Inevitably it ended in separation and divorce and, despite Barbara's sunny nature, the awkwardness between them must have disturbed other members of the family. In the early days of the marriage Evelyn was proud of his famous brother. He fought another boy at school in defence of Alec's reputation and when Alec and Barbara came to visit him at Lancing in October 1919 he saw them, in his monastic isolation, as enviably glamorous figures. But, as it slowly became obvious something was wrong, their case represented yet more evidence for his theory that the war had caused irreparable damage to the younger generation. Had it not been for the vanity and the sentimental follies that had precipitated and sustained hostilities, Alec and Barbara might never have married.

*

The war, physically and emotionally, left an indelible stamp on Evelyn's intellectual development. He was determined not to be taken in by the 'imperialist trash about discipline and the capacity for leading'[47] which had for so long been regarded as the great product of a public school education. But as an intensely ambitious boy this left him with the problem of how best to react against the system while not destroying his career. The Officer Training Corps, subject only to mild 'military' discipline (defaulters' parades), became an obvious target. Evelyn loathed the 'Corps maniacs' among his fellows; 'the discomfort of uniform and the revolting touch of cleaning materials'[48] appalled his aesthetic sense.

He became the infamous leader within Head's House of a series of elaborate 'rags' designed to make the Corps appear ridiculous. At first these simply entailed

47. *Diaries*, 1 February, 1920, p. 55.
48. *Ibid.*, 6 February, 1920, p. 56.

deliberate awkwardness; rifles were dropped, the platoon would have to fall in several times before they satisfied procedural rules of smartness. Then came refinements. One boot would be scrupulously polished and the other left filthy. On a defaulters' parade in 1920: 'Fulford wore running shorts, tweed coat with huge sprigs of holly, and socks (with suspenders), and corps boots. I wore running things and a great coat and a woollen muffler.'[49] Their house-master, Woodard, was displeased.

When Evelyn went to see him to ask if he might resign from the Corps he was told quite firmly that such action would destroy any chance of his becoming House-captain. Woodard could do nothing directly to reprimand him but must have realised that this ultimatum would strike a nerve: 'I do want to be House-captain, chiefly because I know father wants it very much and because I want other distinctions like editor of the magazine and president of the literary society for which one has to be one.'[50] He capitulated without delay, staging a final grand 'rag' in an attempt to save face.

The competition for Platoons' House Shield was the culmination of the year's activities in the Corps. The winning House traditionally stampeded with the trophy through the other dormitories on a 'jerry run'. Waugh planned to win it and then conduct a funereal procession as a mark of disrespect. The diary records his absurd speech to the assembled men of Head's House and an equally ridiculous message which he sent round to his platoon on the day: 'It is more than ever vitally necessary', it read, 'for the honour and self-respect of the House, that we should win the Platoons Shield; we have the House's promise and are confident. Trust in God and stand steady in the ranks.'[51]

Evelyn had a definite 'presence' as a mob-orator. He was at the time only head of the dormitory, a junior position, yet everyone followed his leadership. For a week the entire House had blancoed and polished, and thumbed discarded manuals. In the event, they only came third. Waugh's parting gesture of derision had failed and shortly afterwards, with rather bad grace, he took the first step on the ladder of conventional success by becoming House-captain. 'Limited Bolshevism'[52] had to be his motto and from this point it was severely limited by his ambition.

The flouting of military authority had been the only outlet for deeper discontents. The Corps represented to Waugh a gross manifestation of outmoded ideals which should have been smashed for ever by the fiasco of the Great War. But in itself it was trivial, an unworthy object of attack. He was more seriously occupied by two, largely opposed, ideals personified by Francis Crease and J. F.

49. *Ibid.*, 11 October, 1920, p. 106.
50. *Ibid.*, 11 March, 1921, p. 116.
51. *Ibid.*, 18 March, 1921, pp. 119–21.
52. *Ibid.*, 9 March, 1921, p. 116.

Roxburgh, whom he described as his 'two mentors' in *A Little Learning*. They represented, respectively, the aesthetic life and the panache of the man of the world. Waugh never resolved the conflict of interests which they offered. It was the struggle to maintain a balance between these mutually antipathetic world-views that caused him in his twenties both to cultivate the aristocracy and to camouflage the sincerity of his artistic purpose.

\*

His early interest in sketching had combined with the passion for ecclesiastical artifacts to produce an absorbing hobby: the study of book illumination (the decoration of borders and initials) and script. During Evelyn's first year at Lancing Arthur had taken his fourteen-year-old boy to visit Edward Johnston, the scribe, then a prominent member of the 'Ditchling Colony'.[53] Over forty years later Waugh still relished the encounter:

> [He] took me into his work-room, . . . took a turkey quill and cut it into a chisel pointed pen. Then, to show how it was used, he wrote a few words for me in what is now called his 'foundational' hand. I treasure that piece of writing. But still more I treasure the memory of the experience of seeing those swift, precise, vermillion strokes coming to life. It was a moment of revelation. . . . It was the awe and exhilaration of the presence of genius.[54]

Evelyn's subsequent attempts at emulation had drawn the attention of his second House-master, E. B. Gordon. Waugh could never decide whether he liked Gordon (the 'Pussy-Foot' of the *Diaries*), but there is no doubt that this energetic young master helped and encouraged his pupil greatly. He owned a small printing press which Waugh, rapidly becoming a passionate bibliophile, helped to maintain and operate. It was Gordon who first introduced Waugh to Crease.

For some time a strange, solitary figure had been noticed sitting in the side aisles during Sunday evening chapel services. No-one seemed to know who he was. Then, after a vigorous scrap in the boxing ring one day, Evelyn received a message to go and be 'shown off' to an illuminator friend of Gordon's. The boy arrived hot and exhausted to find this same mysterious man. He was examining an illustrated missal with which Waugh had recently won first prize in the College's art exhibition. It was an incongruous scene: Waugh red-faced in sporting strip; Crease in fine tweeds and an elegant silk tie. Waugh was just sixteen; Crease middle-aged. Delicate, almost effeminate, soft-spoken and neurotic. The

53. A group of artist-craftsmen, of whom Johnston and his pupil, Eric Gill, were the most important members, moved to the then remote village of Ditchling, in Sussex.
54. 'The Hand of the Master', *Spectator*, 24 July, 1959, 108, 110; review of Priscilla Johnston's *Edward Johnston* (1959); *EAR*, pp. 536–7.

artist sat uncomfortably amongst the canes and lists of the master's office. Evelyn was uncertain what to make of him. But he soon discovered in Crease a ruthless aesthetic objectivity which he came to cherish. 'He was most contemptuous over my script', he noted at the time, 'but praised the illumination. Apparently if one is ever going to do good work one has to give one's whole life to it. I suppose this is really true of everything.'[55]

The meeting had taken place during the last days of the autumn term, 1919, and the diary references during the Christmas holiday are noticeable for their frivolity. There was a continual round of theatres, dances, exhibitions, cinemas and minor flirtations. He went to dancing lessons and took the whole business very seriously. His father read him the first two chapters of his autobiography which had temporarily been abandoned and Evelyn thought it good. Arthur and he were as close as they were ever to be. During the following months Crease, quite unconsciously, helped to force a gap between parent and child which was never successfully to be bridged again.

Evelyn was a dilettante in search of a cause. During that November he had helped to found a Dilettanti Society. At the instigation of his old House-master, Dick Harris, he, Hugh Molson, Fulford, Carew and others had set about devising the constitution of a debating group for the Fifth Form which was excluded from speaking in the closed shop of the official Sixth Form Society. Artistic, literary, political, and dramatic groups evolved, each with its own chairman and secretary. Papers were given, followed by an informal discussion, and the scheme had become an outstanding success. Applications had flooded in, often from people Evelyn found quite unsuitable. He had been elected chairman of the Art Group and his qualifications for the post were certainly impressive for a boy of sixteen. Apart from his published essay on Cubism and first prizes for 'illuminated prayers' in two Lancing competitions, he was also designing book jackets for Chapman's and eagerly awaiting his guineas in the post. The first paper he had given was on 'Book Illustration and Decoration'. But up to this point there had been no-one to guide his taste. Crease's rigorous standards, indeed his whole way of life, represented for nearly a year a teasing alternative 'system' to that of Lancing or Underhill.

The 'system' was a word Evelyn borrowed from Crease to describe the forces of authority massed against the individual. In the Spring term of 1920 a series of weekly visits was sanctioned by the school for lessons in script. Crease lived six miles away across open, windswept downland at Lychpole Farm, but neither distance nor bad weather deterred Evelyn from running or walking over. Sometimes he would get a lift on Gordon's motor bike. 'Owing to my visits to Crease,' he wrote in February, 'Thursday has become the best day of the week by far. I believe he is beginning to take a real interest in my work. . . . The best part is

55. *Diaries*, 16 December, 1919, p. 44.

when work is put away and we have tea in his beautiful blue and white china. It is such a relief to get into refined surroundings.'[56]

It is no coincidence that this was the term that saw the flowering of his overt 'Bolshevism', the hatred of the Corps, the impatience with Lancing's 'traditions', which he considered 'ridiculous in so modern a school'.[57]

In November 1919 he had been outraged after a school debate by those in authority who exploited the rules for their own success. 'If I was one of "the unkillable children of the very poor"', he noted, 'I am sure I should be a raving revolutionary.'[58] His violent reaction to injustice, however, was carefully controlled. As a Fifth Former he fought to have the official debating society opened and was invited to speak 'on the paper', a considerable compliment. When President himself in the Sixth, he promptly closed it again.

Blatantly Machiavellian in his House politics, Evelyn was nevertheless depressed by the process of achieving success. The tranquil isolation of Lychpole with its single-minded dedication to the arts, its handleless Crown Derby cups and civilised conversation, came to represent a harbour from the rough seas into which ambition constantly pushed him. 'I see the only way to get any pleasure out of life here is to cut oneself off as much as possible from the tide of events,' he recorded. 'I have tried plunging in and trying to enjoy the cold water but it was no good. Crease's life is about the best after all.'[59]

By the Easter holidays of 1920 he regarded Crease as his only close friend and invited him to stay at Underhill. Evelyn's parents were assiduously polite and paid all expenses. But Arthur, with his hearty derision of 'aesthetes', must have found the man a strange, and possibly suspicious, companion for his son. The boy had never brought any of his schoolfellows home. Suddenly he had arrived with an effeminate bachelor of distinctly homosexual appearance. Arthur said nothing. It was rather Crease's comment on Arthur that widened the breach between father and son: ' "Charming, entirely charming, and acting all the time." ' When Evelyn asked his mother for her opinion she 'confirmed this judgment. My eyes were opened and I saw him, whom I had grown up to accept in complete simplicity, as he must have appeared to others.'[60]

Those holidays saw a significant change. Crease had helped Evelyn to rationalise his distaste for the literary bun-fights he was dragged into during the holidays, the play-readings and the tea parties at the Rhys' house which Arthur relished. The diary in the Sixth bitterly records his father being 'incorrigibly theatrical as usual'.[61] 'The extraordinary thing', he wrote, 'is that the more I see

56. *Diaries*, 4 February, 1920, p. 55.
57. *Ibid.*, 8 February, 1920, p. 56.
58. *Ibid.*, 9 November, 1919, p. 36.
59. *Ibid.*, 9 February, 1920.
60. *ALL*, p. 69.
61. *Diaries*, 2 April, 1921, p. 123.

through my Father the more I appreciate Mother. I always think I am discovering some new trait in his character and find that she knew it long ago. She is a very wonderful woman.'[62] Evelyn was so nervous of appearing foolish that he rejected his father on the grounds that he was a public embarrassment. The knowledge that others might find Arthur silly came as a shock. The extraordinary thing is that Evelyn had no sympathy for a histrionic temperament.

Everyone who knew Evelyn agreed that he too was acting all the time. The theatricality of father and son, though, was different in kind – Arthur's springing from a sentimental desire to colour life into a romantic image, Evelyn's from a mischievous urge to kick a response from dull conformity. Unlike his father he did not believe in the 'naked gospel of cause and effect'. Even as a boy, as his Lancing debate speeches reveal, he saw human behaviour as arbitrary, often pointless or perverse, and he suffered from a manic-depressive boredom. Taken to its logical extreme, this state of anarchic confusion in which he rejected everything but art eventually led him away from his father, religion and even from Crease. For the next decade he remained in a constant state of flux, furiously espousing new modes of life and bitterly thrown down by each disappointment. The one thing that remained constant was his mockery of weakness and an obsessive desire to avoid exploitation.

Few at Lancing can have guessed at his neurotic instability. To each friend he presented a slightly different brave face but there was no-one in whom he felt he could confide. His proud and independent spirit, even in failure, was the secret of his later success in the school. Fulford admits to having been a little afraid of the cutting edge of Evelyn's intellect; Carew doted slavishly on his every word and preserved as many essays, poems and letters as he could find; Hugh Molson was erratic, politically ambitious and lacking in aesthetic sensitivity. Evelyn's closest friends in the Sixth (Longe and Hale), as so often later, were clever and studious, fundamentally estranged from his volcanic temperament. At the height of his success in school, Waugh felt more isolated than ever.

In allowing himself to be taken up by Crease, though, Evelyn had largely dissociated himself from the career structure of Lancing. When Roxburgh first met the mincing little craftsman he had greeted him derisively: 'The sage of Lychpole, I presume.' Evelyn thought that Gordon was becoming jealous. Friends were refused permission to visit the farm, though both Carew and Molson were eventually taken there. It was not seen as a suitably masculine endeavour. But Evelyn remained loyal to his artistic mentor. During the rest of each week after his visit, he would spend most of his free time in the library reading widely, drawing and practising calligraphy. The award of 'library privileges' in February 1920 had been an enormous relief, allowing easy access to that vaulted, tranquil

62. *Ibid.*, 23 April, 1921, p. 125.

refuge in the evenings. It became, for the rest of his time at Lancing, a spiritual home.

When Crease went away during May of 1920 Evelyn continued to visit Lychpole and work quietly with materials left out for him. One day there he broke a quill knife and wrote to apologise. Crease's reply came as a radical shock. He was furious at the boy's interference with property which had been put away in a drawer. The letter had been scribbled in haste. Soon, another arrived apologising for his outburst; the knife had been a particular favourite, antique, exquisite, without which he felt he could never do good work again. It was in retrospect a trivial incident. But it was enough to destroy their intimacy. Evelyn felt betrayed and once again thrust alone among strangers.

From that point he began to look back towards the school for some system to order his existence; the number of visits to Lychpole decreased as he began to lose faith in it as an aesthetic refuge. A ferocious pragmatism began to characterise the entries in his diary. More worldly concerns pressed on him. There was work to be done for his School Certificate; he had to begin thinking of Oxford. During that summer he learnt that he had passed all seven subjects with credit and, when he returned in September, he had just been taken by Arthur on an excursion to the University. He had never seen anything so beautiful. Placed in the Upper Sixth, he suddenly became conscious that there would probably be only one more complete year at Lancing. Crease was away for nine months. By the time he returned in July 1921 the spell was broken and Roxburgh's influence was predominant.

*

J. F. Roxburgh, later the first Headmaster of Stowe School, had returned to Lancing in September 1919 with a distinguished war record. A brilliant classical scholar, tall, elegantly dressed, he soon became the dominant personality of Lancing. His performance in debates was polished and incisive. There was a ruthless humour in his judgment; Canon Bowlby's laborious puns were openly parodied in Roxburgh's classes. His air of effortless superiority attracted Evelyn. The curriculum of the Sixth allowed the boy to drop French, Greek and Maths (always his weakest subject) and to concentrate on History with a little English and Latin. His social position in the House was automatically raised and he began, in emulation of Roxburgh, to desire authority and distinction, to cut a figure in the school.

He upholstered his desk in blue leather and set two brass candlesticks upon it. He joined 'J. F.''s modern play-reading group (Shaw, Pinero, Galsworthy) and the Shakespeare Society. He studied librarianship in preparation for promotion and began for the first time actively to consider a literary career. But the closer he drew to Roxburgh, and the more he came to appreciate the man's flamboyant individualism, the more the school itself began to pale by comparison. Intense boredom set in, verging on the despair of his first two years. The revolutionary and the aesthete of the Fifth Form were only shallowly buried and he continued to attack Lancing's institutions and values, though in a more sophisticated and conventional fashion.

In debates he would support outrageous causes in the guise of *enfant terrible*, playful yet relentlessly ingenious in argument. In September of 1920, for example, he opposed the motion that 'This House deplores the disrespect for age by modern youth'. The entire speech is transcribed in his diary, a clear reflection of his pride at this first showing as a Sixth Former. It is vitriolic, cruelly pertinent, and in it we see for the first time that phrase 'the old men', so often repeated in his advocacy of the younger generation during the next decade. These 'grotesque, decaying old men, with the supreme arrogance of the impotent' had had their war and made the young men fight it. 'No generation has ever wreaked such disasters as the last,' he bellowed at his audience. 'After numerous small indiscretions it had its fling of a war which has left the civilised world pauperised, ravaged, shaken to its foundations.'[63] As an advocate of youth politics he was abrasive and entertaining and it was in this role that he steadily rose to eminence in the school.

During the Christmas holidays of 1920 Evelyn made his first serious attempt at a novel, a study of a man with two characters by his brother. The diary dried up almost entirely for two months as he concentrated on his fiction. But it was hard work and he found it unpleasant. By 10th January it was abandoned and the aborted fragments handed over to his disciple, Dudley Carew.

Carew, also an aspirant writer, by this time had a second novel in draft. Everything was submitted to Evelyn for criticism and his remarks bear a strong resemblance to judgements expressed nine years later as an established reviewer:

(1) Avoid any conversations on general subjects.... General conversations may only be allowed when they show character.
(2) ... Don't be slack about grammar ...
(4) Don't put down thoughts at such length. Directly suggest – be subtle, leave something to us readers.
(5) *Keep cutting out* – motto for all artists ...[64]

For Carew this relationship made the period 1920–1921 one of intense delight and rapid intellectual development.

Evelyn marked Carew's volume of Victorian verse, singling out Housman, Middleton, Belloc, Dowson, and Symons. They both drew and painted and strode off for long walks discussing religion and philosophy. There was never any doubt as to who was the master and who the pupil. Carew, the son of a clergyman, was

63. *Ibid.*, 25–30 September, 1920, pp. 102–4.
64. Carew, *A Fragment, op. cit.*, pp. 18–19.

astounded to learn that Evelyn had ceased to be a Christian in the Sixth Form but he dragged along lamely in the argument, intrigued and intimidated. For Evelyn their conversations were little more than an opportunity to bounce ideas off a blank wall. It was a necessary but ultimately frustrating process, for Carew's adulation grew to embarrassing proportions. As a schoolboy Evelyn sometimes wondered whether his intellectual superiority was evidence of artistic genius but he remained unsure and his friend was unable to judge.

The Spring term of 1921 saw great changes. Evelyn stopped ragging the Corps, as we have seen, in return for authority. He became a junior sacristan in chapel. He (unsuccessfully) entered poems for *Public School Verse* and jotted down ideas for the Prize Poem. His life was an unhappy compromise. He was by nature rebellious and discursive, with a taste for the absurd and grotesque. He was a romantic turned pragmatist. 'You must keep your nose down in the mud', he told Carew, 'once you look up, or even forward, you're done. If I thought enough about this I should go mad, you've got to concentrate on your next step and never look beyond.'[65]

The diary for 1921 is full of such statements – thoughts of suicide, agonies of persecution – and, of course, they are no more than adolescent pretensions. They represent frustrated ambition rather than genuine despair but his need to frame this in terms of the highest drama is significant. Where his intellect saw life as a tedious chain of disappointments, his imagination refused to accept this, constructing fantasies to puncture boredom. What has been interpreted as malicious distortion in the *Diaries* was often no more than a game Waugh played by himself, injecting that 'story book element' into a mundane existence. His cruelty and inconsistency in relationships were frequently no more than an invitation to engage in this game of fictionalising. If people cowered at the onslaught he could not respect them. He wanted them to engage with him and fight the mock battle. He preferred his friends to be stronger than himself and there was none stronger at Lancing.

Floundering in self-pity and confused by his intellectual superiority, he buried his aesthetic sensitivity beneath the need to press ahead with his nose in the mud towards a conventionally successful school career. The previous June, Gordon had been reading Arnold Lunn's *Loose Ends* to them and from this – via the notes on Pope's *Essay on Man*, Leibniz, and casual reading about the eighteenth-century Enlightenment – he eventually came to lose his faith, or to admit that it had died, in June of 1921. With typical inventiveness Waugh described his apostasy in terms of a scene involving Tom Driberg. Nothing of the sort happened; there was no dramatic conversion. Agnosticism became just another facet of his lack of faith in everything.

That June he was occupied with a satirical play about public-school spirit,

65. *Ibid.*, p. 32.

*Conversion*, intended to up-stage his brother's novel. Divided into three acts, the first represented school 'as our maiden aunts believe it to be'; the second, 'as some of our novelists represent it' (a parody of *The Loom*); and the third, 'as we all know it really is'. The Head Master sat through the House production and then generously allowed it to be presented to the entire school. Carew devoured it avidly as another product of Evelyn's genius; the masters and Arthur (who came down to see it) reviewed this expression of 'hubris' with tolerant amusement at its ingenuity. Evelyn himself evinced little enthusiasm. He was cheered by its success but it was just another score in his, now thinly disguised, sport with the authorities.

The school 'as we all know it really is' is a scene of unrelieved tedium. The hero, Townsend, is a rebel blackmailed into conformity, and the narrative of *Conversion* is clearly laced with autobiographical allusion. At the beginning of the term Evelyn had been made House-captain. In July he was appointed Editor of the Magazine and President of the Debating Society. He had won the Scarlyn Essay Prize and next term, much to Arthur's delight, carried off the English Verse Prize. But none of this pleased Evelyn. Woodard had offered the magazine to more conventional candidates first; Molson with his delight in political chicanery had packed the house with Waugh's friends for the Debating Society election. 'I am burdened with failure this term', he noted, 'when I have been most successful really. Everything I have has come to me shop-soiled and second-hand.'[66] It is the tail-coat story again.

He was playing the establishment at its own game and winning, but a neurotic perfectionism denied him satisfaction. There was something missing from his life and he could not at the time identify it as the aesthetic enthusiasm he had shared with Crease and since rejected. He read Bergson and thought through large numbers of trivial propositions concerning the relativity of all things. He composed pompous suicide notes and passed away the time in vague reveries about Oxford or Paris. But since Crease there had been no intimate friend. He felt himself to be liked but not respected. People found him a little crazy, a spectacular entertainment they could not quite understand.

\*

The next term, September-December 1921, was his last. He had passed his Higher Certificate and come back for an intensive period of work prior to sitting for an Oxford scholarship. During the holidays he had become aware of the rift between Barbara and Alec and his disaffection with his father had reached new heights. His chief solace over the last year of home visits had been frequent attendance, often with Barbara, at *The Beggar's Opera*. Its Bohemian atmosphere and lurid Macheath could raise him to enthusiasm where almost everything else

66. *Diaries*, 24 July, 1921, p. 132.

failed. Overt belligerence was once again showing itself. He bought the stick which he toted everywhere in Oxford until it was lost one drunken night, 'English oak, about as formidable and heavy as a rifle, with a large knob and a leather thong'.[67] Was this the manifestation of his frustration and his desire to smash up the stolidity of the world that surrounded him?

Back at school in the dignified History scholarship set, he became supercilious and awkward in authority. Maintaining discipline had always been a problem. He had earlier tried to run his dormitory on democratic lines but the boys had interpreted laxity as weakness. No-one, he determined, would take advantage of him again and he played a role as disciplinarian fundamentally unsuited to his nature. The editorship of the Magazine alone provided privacy and mental stimulation. He disliked scholarship, applying himself to it by an effort of will, but his journalism was done energetically and thoroughly. His editorials were to be his intellectual stick. In the light of these, it is not surprising that Woodard, a humourless clergyman, looked on him as an unhealthy influence.

When Woodard had requested moderation in return for the captaincy of the House, Evelyn had 'got going on the God tradition [the Prefect system] and the war gap and our generation'.[68] The master had listened but insisted on his own terms. Charge of the magazine was Evelyn's chance for revenge and his two editorials represented a revolution in the history of that pedestrian publication.

The first (November 1921) was ironically entitled 'The Community Spirit'. It very obviously broke from tradition by being written in the form of a short story. A foreigner, enamoured of 'the community spirit of three hundred friends', is gradually informed by the narrator that, through differences of House grouping, age, and the hierarchy of achievement, loneliness and frustration are the lot of the public school boy. It was a direct assault upon the school's principles of comradeship.

The second, 'The Youngest Generation' (December 1921), took as its subject his obsession with the 'war gap' – the division of an age by the Great War into three quite separate 'generations':

> The men of Rupert Brooke's generation are broken. Narcissus-like, they stood for an instant amazedly aware of their own beauty; the war, which the old men made, has left them tired and embittered. What will the young men of 1922 be? They will be, above all things, clear-sighted, they will have no use for phrases or shadows. In the nineteenth century the old men saw visions and the young men dreamed dreams. The youngest generation are going to be very hard and analytical and unsympathetic, but they are going to aim at things as they are – and they will not call their aim 'Truth'. ... The young men of the nineties subsisted

67. *Ibid.*, 8 September, 1921, p. 138.
68. *Ibid.*, 31 March, 1921.

on their emotion, and their painting and their poetry thrills with it . . .; middle-aged observers will find it hard to see the soul in the youngest generation.

But they will have – and this is their justification – a very full sense of humour. . . . They will watch themselves with, probably, greater egotism than did the young men of the nineties, but it will be with a cynical smile and often with a laugh.

It is a queer world that the old men have left them and they will have few ideals and illusions when they 'get to feeling old'. They will not be a happy generation.[69]

Waugh described this in *A Little Learning* as 'a preposterous manifesto of disillusionment'.[70] It was another intellectual pose resulting from the boredom of having outgrown school life, but it was also an astonishingly accurate prediction of attitudes he seriously espoused several years later.

Evelyn, with Carew, Molson, Fulford and others had earlier in the term founded the 'Corpse Club' for 'those who were weary of life'. As the presiding dignitary, Evelyn was the 'Undertaker'. They addressed each other on mourning notepaper and wore a black tassel in the lapel. All this, if rebellious, was done with a sense of fun. But it was not an attitude selected at random. The 'old men' and 'Rupert Brooke's generation' were clearly personified for Evelyn by his father and brother. His appreciation of Roxburgh's panache and Crease's aesthetic fastidiousness offered alternative systems. He loathed the sentimental, the substitute, the second-rate, and the editorial is an astute analysis of his own need to develop an aesthetic which would allow a realistic appraisal of the tawdry modern world while at the same time maintaining dissociation from it.

During this term Evelyn engaged in a voluminous correspondence with his father concerning plans for the immediate future. In his autobiography Waugh blames Arthur for sending him up to Oxford in the by-term (January), but the complaint is unfair. Arthur patiently and generously replied to his son's many requests which changed weekly with his mood, and in the end refused to enter into further discussion. Evelyn in fact suggested at one point that he wanted to go up as soon as possible. A similar discrepancy exists in his complaints about Hertford College. He always maintained that he only chose such a dull place because it offered more scholarship money. The diary reveals that his History master advised Evelyn to apply there because he was more likely to achieve prominence and to be given attention in a smaller college. There was no thought in his mind then that the place was inferior. When he first arrived he was perfectly

69. *Lancing College Magazine*, December 1921, 85.
70. *ALL*, p. 138.

happy. It was a characteristic trait that he always needed someone to blame for his own mistakes. He needed, as Peter Quennell once remarked, 'aunt Sallies'.[71]

He travelled to Oxford with Hugh Molson on 5th December, 1921 for the examinations and revelled in the General Paper. In this he wrote extensively on Symons' life of Beardsley, the Pre-Raphaelites and Rupert Brooke. Later he found that he could cope easily with the Latin, French and History and he enjoyed the *viva*. For three more days he sauntered round the city, already in love with the place. On the ninth he went back to London where he dined with his brother and a woman whose relationship to Alec appeared intimate. Evelyn was shocked, not distressed, by her presence. Alec represented that cosmopolitan world he hoped soon to share. Uncertain of his prospects of success but relieved that it was all over, he returned to Lancing in amiable mood. He was happier than he had been for months. Whatever happened, at least he would soon be finished with school.

The first news of his scholarship arrived by telephone. In the *Diaries* a quite different stage is set with Evelyn arriving at the breakfast table to find two congratulatory letters. He seems to have visualised everything in symbolic terms, almost unconsciously transforming the indignities of reality. But with the Senior History Scholarship assured, maintaining dignity was no longer a problem. He could afford to relax and the urge to prove himself in public temporarily subsided. The achievement spoke for itself. He moved about the school, unsentimentally glad to leave, for the first time at ease. He played musical chairs with the boys of his dormitory and chatted with the masters. Woodard and he said their cursory goodbyes, mutual dislike tempered only slightly by good manners; the Head discoursed affably on philosophy and politics.

Waugh kept a letter from Roxburgh all his life. Written after that first editorial, it contained a remarkable compliment. If Waugh used his gifts wisely, it said, he would do more than anyone to shape the course of his generation. Now, at last, the promised triumphs were in view. He experienced for the first time since his arrival at Lancing a certain tranquillity. 'I am sure I have left at the right time', the last entry of the Lancing diary reads, ' – as early as possible and with success.'[72]

71. Interview with Peter Quennell, Spring 1979.
72. *Diaries*, 16 December, 1921, p. 154.

# III
## *Oxford: 1922–1924*

Waugh's career at Oxford is now infamous. Christopher Sykes's biography conveys the idea of this period as a continual round of roistering drunkenness, vomitings, homosexual encounters. Certainly this was the image of his undergraduate life Waugh publicised. He remains a legend at the University. In 1975 there was a 'Vile Bodies Dining Club' centred on the Union at which the participants were expected to arrive in costume to re-live the swashbuckling iconoclasm of their hero. Waugh has become an archetype of the reckless, sophisticated undergraduate, moody and brilliantly amusing, lunging at authority; the man who, despite all efforts to grind him down, achieves greater success than any of his dreary tutors or industrious contemporaries. He is warmly remembered as a modern Hamlet. But this is only part of the story.

When he arrived at Hertford College in January 1922 there was small choice of rooms, most of the better ones having already been taken by the October entry. He found himself poked away up a stair in the oldest building overlooking New College Lane and above the Junior Common Room Buttery with its clattering plates and cooking smells. He felt none of the resentment expressed in *A Little Learning* about being sent up in the by-term. At Lancing he had found himself pressured into an unpleasant public image by the structure of authority. At home he was uncomfortable amid the cloying sentimentality of his father's house and the patronage of Arthur's and Alec's literary friends. He was glad to get away. His Oxford rooms were decorated with Lovat Fraser prints and the finely-bound volumes which he had saved so hard to buy as a boy. He bought himself a bicycle, started smoking a pipe and explored the local countryside. He kept up with his Lancing friends and wrote back to the school, thirsting for news of the old place.

Oxford released the warm, ebullient side of his nature. When he described, six years later, the blameless existence of Paul Pennyfeather in *Decline and Fall* he must have been thinking to a certain extent of the quiet, conventional routine of his first two terms. 'I am enjoying life here very well', he wrote to Tom Driberg on 13th February:

> I do no work here and never go to Chapel. As I am too bad to play soccer for Hertford I have joined a local hockey club with Southwell [another Lancing man] which is quite a joke. There is a pleasant old world violence about the game which appeals to me strongly.

> Yesterday I heard [Dean] Inge preach at the University Church. Very witty and scholarly. Just what one wants at Oxford. Oxford is not quite itself but the aged war-worn hero type is beginning to go down. It ought to be right again by the time you come up. I am well pleased with Hertford. At first I thought I could not be happy outside New College but there are [sic] really an extremely pleasant set of men here. The buildings are pretty beastly.
>
> I went to a wine [drinks party] with Hill [his former Head of House at Lancing] last night. He got pretty tight. I was cheery. . . . It was very pleasant.[1]

The aggression remained but it had mellowed. There was a good deal of Pennyfeather in him.

No diaries exist for the period of Waugh's undergraduate career. They only resume late in June 1924 with an account of the last night of his last term. It seems that he mutilated his personal records, as earlier, to conceal 'dangerous' material, but the morbid introspection of Lancing had disappeared. He no longer felt the spiritual and intellectual isolation of his schooldays. The conflict of interests represented by Crease and Roxburgh was beginning to resolve itself. In the easy atmosphere of Oxford he began for the first time to relax. Roxburgh's letters now seem stilted and academic. Waugh very soon wrote to Driberg describing the schoolmaster as thoroughly second-rate. Crease, however, was reinstated in his admiration: 'a wider outlook', he wrote to Carew in March, 'has given me a far larger realisation of Crease's designs, I am convinced now that that man is a really great artist. Before I hung my admiration on his character and did not understand his work fully.'[2]

His opinions were to change yet again during the next autumn when he came into contact with Harold Acton and his sophisticated circle of Etonians, but Waugh's first two terms represented a quiet and unambitious period of emotional release. He made his maiden speech at the Union on 8th February, opposing the motion that 'This House Would Welcome Prohibition'; he trotted off happily to a Problem Club at Brasenose; he studied hard for his History Previous (preliminary examination), struggled with an entry for the Newdigate Prize Poem and was elected Secretary to the Hertford College Debating Society.

Waugh did not regard his scholarship as a commitment to spending long hours in the Bodleian but as a reward for a period of uncomfortable industry at school. The legend of F.E. Smith still predominated in the University. A man with talent, Waugh thought, could spend three years in comfortable dissipation and then sit up with black coffee for three weeks before Finals and walk out with a First. It was a myth which proved disappointing to many talented men of that generation.

1. *Letters*, p. 7.
2. *Letters*, p. 8.

Waugh and Anthony Powell both left with bad Thirds; John Betjeman was sent down for failing an examination (normally a formality) in Divinity.

This careless attitude to scholarship engendered the now infamous acrimony between Waugh and his tutor. Ultimately there was undisguised hatred between them, as there had been between Waugh and Woodard at school, but there is no detrimental reference to C. R. M. F. Cruttwell in the enthusiastic letters of those early days. The two highlights of his first term, he told Driberg, were the discovery of the perfect cigarette (imported Egyptian) and his purchase of the Ricardi Press's *Rupert Brooke*: 'I cannot possibly afford it but sufficient for the day is the beauty thereof. I am having [it] bound – after much hesitation between levant moroccos, calfs, pigskins and Morris papers – in full vellum, bevelled boards, absolutely untooled anywhere. I think this is perhaps most appropriate to him.'[3]

The interest in Rupert Brooke should not go unremarked. Driberg thought in retrospect that the last sentence contained a sexual pun which he had not noticed at the time and he is probably right. One of the important factors contributing to the sense of release Waugh felt was the loss of sexual inhibition. The Lancing diaries and later letters reveal quite clearly that he had felt strong homosexual urges which had been repressed. The farewell school editorial, lampooning Brooke, had been a pose. He was, in fact, passionately drawn to the male Narcissus figure and the ideal of unswerving friendship Brooke represented. Looking through a memoir of Brooke in the previous November he had noted: 'I felt very envious reading, particularly the parts about Rugby and friendship. I do honestly think that that is something that went out of the world in 1914, at least for one generation.'[4]

It was an opinion generated by the multiple neuroses of his schooldays. At Lancing his prudish, meticulous nature could be shocked, even in the Sixth Form, by the boys 'talking filth', or by a ribald music-hall turn. But at Oxford that sense of depressing isolation disappeared almost at once. It no longer mattered that he was (like his father) short and of indifferent athletic calibre; as the Senior History Scholar, he found himself in a position of easy eminence which carried nothing of the strain of exerting discipline or cutting a public figure. He revelled in the teaching of 'dons of real erudition'; homosexuality was not uncommon and was talked of openly. The whole atmosphere of the University came as an enormous relief to him, although on first arriving he had to roam from college to college to dig up old school acquaintances.

When settled, he made friends easily and, in particular, formed a close homosexual relationship with a brilliant, shy Wykehamist, Richard Pares. Waugh considered him 'abnormally clever' and so he was. For the first two terms Waugh was devoted to this gentle scholar. Even after leaving Oxford, when their paths

3.  Unpublished ALS to Tom Driberg, 'Prid. Cal. Mart.', MCMXXII, from Hertford College.
4.  *Diaries*, 22 November, 1921, p. 147.

had irrevocably divided, he remembered him warmly. Bathed in the tranquil light of this first sincere emotional attachment, Waugh forgot his neuroses. 'Life here is very beautiful', he wrote to Driberg. 'Mayonnaise and punts and cider cups all day long. One loses all ambition to be an intellectual. I am reduced to writing light verse for the "Isis" [undergraduate magazine] and taking politics seriously.'[5] And to Carew: 'I am still content to lead my solitary and quiet life here. I have enough friends to keep me from being lonely and not enough to bother me. I do a little work and dream a lot. I have exactly threepence in my pocket and my cheques are worth only the twopenny stamp on them – but one muddles along.'[6]

When he returned to Underhill in the Easter vacation, separation from this idyllic life drove him to the verge of melancholy mania. His father's and brother's absorption in what seemed to Waugh a second-rate literary world frustrated and bored him. Only Driberg's correspondence alleviated depression:

> After Oxford London, and particularly Suburbia, is quite indescribably dreary and your letter came as a welcome interruption to the long back-chat of literary cliques. There are rumours that The Times Literary Supplement is going to cease, that Katherine Mansfield is not going to die after all, that J. C. Squire has taken seriously to drink at last. . . . I enjoyed last term immeasurably and left Oxford with regret and a pocket-book of unpaid bills. I did no work and do not propose to do any next term so I am trying to learn a little during the vac. – I have Schools [exams] next term. Between whiles I read *Alice in Wonderland*. It is an excellent book I think.[7]

His distaste for Mansfield and Squire, and the delight in Carroll, are important landmarks in Waugh's developing taste. At the age of sixteen he had written a parody of Mansfield's style in a remarkable paper, 'The Twilight of Language', presented to the Dilettante Society. Dudley Carew, whose intelligence Waugh always found to be clouded by an effusive emotionalism, was negotiating to join the London world of Georgian *littérateurs* and, shortly afterwards, having failed to secure an Oxford scholarship, worked for Squire on the *London Mercury*. It was probably Pares who demanded that *Alice* be taken seriously. He wrote an ingenious disquisition on the meaning of the word 'runcible' for the undergraduate press and was passionately devoted to the book. These influences stayed with Waugh. He used 'Runcible' as the surname for the heroine of *Vile Bodies* (1930) and quoted from *Alice Through the Looking Glass* in the novel's epigraph; *Decline and Fall* (1928) contains a thinly-disguised satirical portrait of Squire.

5. *Letters*, p. 10.
6. *Ibid.*, p. 11.
7. *Ibid.*, p. 9.

Early in 1922 his tastes were loosely governed by an immediate aesthetic response to ingenuity and luxury – Beardsley, Lovat Fraser, fine bindings – but there was always another side to him that admired strength and a tough objectivity in art and which delighted in madness and violence. He was for many years more interested in Webster than Shakespeare, and more intrigued by philosophical discussion than the watery half-truths of the contemporary English literary scene.

This derision for his father's world caused relations between them to deteriorate even further. But there were more particular emotional strains for Arthur. It was a difficult period for him and he could have done without his dismissive younger son returning bored and penniless. Evelyn, it will be remembered, had lunched with Alec and a strange woman in London after the Scholarship examinations. At the time Evelyn had wondered whether she might be his brother's mistress. She was, and Christmas 1921 had proved to be the breaking-point of Barbara and Alec's marriage.

Since the spring of 1921 both partners had realised that their unconsummated union must end. They had already lived apart for weeks at a time, she at Underhill, he down at their new bungalow in Ditchling. Christmas had been spent together in Hampstead, living the lie of convivial family life. Alec was tense and irritable. As a sportsman he had asserted his virility but the knowledge that he could not, in his words, 'make his wife a woman' was a source of profound depression. He was too ashamed to consult a doctor. His affair was with an experienced woman, about to leave for India and a 'safe' marriage. Her valedictory indulgence cured the young man of his sexual problems but created others. There was no chance of the relationship continuing but it represented an open admission of the failure of his marriage. In January there had been a formal separation, Barbara returning to Ditchling, Alec remaining in Hampstead. All this had occurred precisely at the time Evelyn had gone up to Oxford.

The prospect of divorce was radically shocking to the family, and particularly to the maiden aunts in Midsomer Norton. Underhill was deluged with impassioned correspondence from Alec's relatives imploring him to think again. He was made to feel guilty at abandoning his pretty and affectionate wife to a life of rural solitude. Much as he loved her, there seemed to be no other sensible course for them both.

Alec's relations with Arthur were further complicated by friction at work. Alec found his employment as a reader at Chapman's profoundly tedious after the drama of the war. Moreover, both father and son had begun to realise when they worked together that their attraction was that of opposites. Temperamentally, Alec was closer to his mother. He had an exact and careful mind. When certain issues in the office demanded discussion, Arthur, with his policy of instant decision, dismissed them abruptly. Back at Underhill he wanted to forget the business of the day; Alec felt the need to hammer out unresolved problems.

Arthur's impatience with both his sons at this period was understandable. After the growing prosperity of Chapman's during the early years of his directorship, the firm was again showing signs of financial instability. And this critical period, once again, corresponded with Evelyn's years in the Sixth and Oxford. The Dickens copyright ran out in 1920. The balance sheet for 1921 showed a diminished profit; next year's was worse and in 1923 it was clear that the ordinary shareholders would suffer. Every year there was a public meeting at which Arthur had to stand up and account for the year's business. He loathed these occasions and faced the one for 1924 with particular trepidation. Trouble could be expected. There were certain careerists determined to force change and they succeeded. Too polite to mention any of this in his autobiography, Arthur was nevertheless deeply upset by the filibustering tactics of one of his colleagues.

There was a young man, J. L. Bale, head of the technical department before the war, who had returned confident and aggressive. Arthur felt uneasy with him. He did not fit comfortably into the older man's concept of the gentleman publisher with his unkempt hair and careless manners. He had not been to public school; he had not been an officer. At the shareholders' meeting his brother-in-law, an engineer, vilified Arthur for slack management. A survey had shown that technical books had accounted for most of the firm's meagre profits. Bale was put up for election and, along with Alec, voted onto the board. At the next meeting in 1925 the engineer appeared again, this time with a total stranger. The balance sheet had not improved. Once again he was on his feet, hectoring and vehement. He had just the man with him to pull the firm out of its difficulties. R. E. Neale was introduced. He was another engineer and with impeccable qualifications. It was again argued that Chapman's should concentrate on the side of their business that was making money; that they should elect Neale rather than the affable Truslove. The shareholders were swayed by the oratory, Neale accepted; Truslove, an old friend of Arthur's, was abandoned.

Bale must have had foreknowledge of this surprise attack. He had effectively colluded with others outside the firm in a plot against one of his fellow directors. The courteous system of mutual respect inculcated by Arthur had been forcibly breached. He could, of course, recognise the validity of their arguments but their methods appalled him and largely spoilt his remaining years in publishing.

Ironically, Neale turned out to be one of Arthur's closer associates and served also to secure the firm's stability by bringing in an important novelist – Evelyn Waugh. When *Decline and Fall* was submitted in 1928 the board was divided in its opinions. Neale had the casting vote and, having enjoyed the book enormously, gave his approval. It is arguable that Waugh owed his literary career to the technical department. But that was six years ahead. In 1922 he had no intention whatever of becoming an author.

When he returned for that first Easter vacation, feckless and exuberant, he found the household saddened and apprehensive. Carew and Molson came over to visit him and they went off to the Alhambra music hall. But even this brief diversion was spoilt. Carew had just left Lancing. He wanted to pour out his soul to Evelyn and had written several times from school asking for advice about his future. He had never shared Evelyn's intimacy with Molson and they made an awkward trio.

Carew was devoted to Arthur and relished the cricket gossip and literary anecdotes. One term of Oxford had left Waugh openly antagonistic to this aspect of Underhill life. Carew remembers him, on other occasions, heaving audible sighs across the dinner table as Arthur related stories about Edmund Gosse. He had heard the tale, he would interrupt, not once but many times. Arthur's benevolent countenance would break into a smile of strained tolerance and the subject would be changed. The atmosphere was uneasy. 'I hardly know how I shall live through the next ten days . . .', Waugh wrote to Driberg towards the end of the holiday. 'The Beggar's Opera is my only comfort. I am oppressed with an unfinished Newdigate and numberless books of history.'[8]

Earlier that holiday he had travelled down to Ditchling to spend a few days with Barbara. He missed her company in the house although he appears to have accepted the separation with equanimity. He had, after all, suspected for some time that Alec and she would ultimately be divorced. But there was no-one now left at Underhill with whom he could plunge into London for elaborate shopping expeditions or visits to teashops and cinemas. His mother was usually occupied. Alec had his own circle of friends, largely drawn from their father's generation, with a shared fanaticism for rugby and cricket. Waugh was delighted to escape to Sussex.

The visit could not have been one of unclouded happiness. Only three months later Barbara came up to London to announce, much to Alec's relief, that she had found another man and wanted to re-marry. The divorce, already under way, reached the courts in January 1923 when a decree of annulment was granted. Evelyn must have suspected that this was probably the last time he would see his sister-in-law and that indeed proved to be the case. He might conceivably have met Alec's replacement, a nephew of Edward Johnston, the scribe who had had such a profound effect on his own early life. Barbara would have enquired how Alec was faring. It was an open secret that he was already involved in another affair. The situation bristled with potential embarrassments and was made all the more awkward by Evelyn's proximity to his old school. Most of his Lancing friends had returned for the summer term and he wanted to visit them. But he was convinced that people would have nothing but sour memories of him after his 'quite insufferable' behaviour of the last term. 'Love to Lancing', he wrote to Driberg on returning to Underhill. 'I was staying quite near it last week – Ditchling – and thought of coming over but was afraid I should not be welcome.'[9]

8. Unpublished ALS to Tom Driberg, nd [Easter, 1922], from 145 North End Road, London.
9. *Letters*, p. 9.

Carew had taken over the magazine and had written to him in March asking for advice and a poem. Waugh had supplied the poem – an objective reflection on the Corpse Club which is pictured twelve years on to have grown out of all proportion in the lore of the school – but he was chary of offering moral direction. 'I feel a prig now giving advice', he wrote:

> My former counsels of imperfection were largely wanton taunts. . . . I am learning this that one can't fit people's characters about. Each one is a design and must be completed in its own way. The great and only mistake in design is that it becomes conventional. . . . you were made to be charming so keep on being charming but be honest and reserved too. Be as profligate as you like but don't be a pimp – don't be mean. Don't be selfconscious. Don't be too efficient or romantic. Do things because you want to whatever others say but don't do things because others tell you not to. You force me to be a Polonius at eighteen. Well for Christs sake don't be a Laertes. There is one thing more. I don't want the Waugh spirit to go on at Lancing even if it could. It rose pretty suddenly except in the House in healthy Bolshevism. I did really influence Lancing for more than a term – let it die too. . . . Let Woodard & people think, 'Well, his influence has proved as superficial as his nasty character.' We know & one or two others. Let it rest at that. . . . If anyone thinks fit to defend me don't print it. But I can't think that they will. I imagine that I am pretty well disliked now – as good God I deserved to be. I am changing pretty hard and I think for the better but I am not changing in my interest for Lancing & all of you.[10]

Returning to Oxford after the frustrations of that first Easter vacation, the sense of release was, if anything, even greater than on first arrival. At Hertford his particular friend was Terence Greenidge whom Sir Harold Acton described to the present author as 'Very mad. A dear, charming loony.' Greenidge was a kleptomaniac, hoarding little stores of stolen property in various nests about the college and periodically inspecting them. While people talked to him he would search about his feet, collecting scraps of rubbish to stuff in his pockets. Waugh recalls how he would pop out from his room and constantly close a gate the college servants needed open so that in the end a guard had to be posted.

Greenidge was unpredictable in a mild, almost infantile fashion – intelligent yet incapable of serious concentration on any of his various interests. He settled on each with a devouring passion, only to be distracted by some other whim. At Oxford he was a successful athlete and a devotee of the cinema, Kant and Dostoievsky. He was largely responsible for Waugh's own fascination with the silent screen as a new art form and was the director of an eminently forgettable

10. *Letters*, p. 8.

amateur film in which Waugh played the Dean of Balliol, 'The Scarlet Woman' (1924). After going down, the actor Tony Bushell, a Hertford contemporary, secured Greenidge small parts in Olivier's early films. He published some poetry under the pseudonym of 'A Master of Arts', wrote novels and filmscripts and in 1930 a book, *Degenerate Oxford?*, which Waugh reviewed as favourably as he could.[11]

Greenidge was an intellectual butterfly inclined to the left in politics. But Waugh remained friends with him to the end. There was an air of innocent bravado about Greenidge's actions; he demanded protection. He represented a type to whom Waugh was perennially attracted in the early years – bright, whimsical, child-like, undemanding and affectionate. Waugh felt safe with Terence, delighting in the streak of madness. And he was arguably Waugh's only friend in the University who was received with equal warmth at Underhill. Arthur and Catherine were both fond of him. Alec Waugh, when the present author asked about Greenidge's later life, remarked rather sadly, 'He just fell apart'.

It was in Greenidge's rooms, during his first term, that Waugh was introduced to the President of the Union, and the editor of the *Isis*. Alec's now infamous novel was by 1922 standard secret reading of every public schoolboy. Douglas Woodruff had heard that the younger brother had come up and that he was a Conservative. At that time the Liberal contingent (supporting the coalition government) represented the majority in the debating chamber and Woodruff, looking for Tory support, made Waugh a teller, the first step in a Union career.

At Lancing Waugh had been an outstanding speaker both for his precocious grasp of a subject and his impassioned delivery. He shocked his audience into admiration and made them laugh. Oxford was less easily impressed. In the company of such capable orators as Woodruff and Christopher Hollis, Waugh's belligerent incoherence was smiled away. He was entertaining and always anticipated with some relish but no-one took him seriously as a candidate for Union honours. Waugh offered his speeches almost as music-hall turns, arguing anything for the sake of an intellectual brawl. His ostensible political position was violently right-wing, yet on one occasion he insisted that he was the only 'man in the street' among the arrogant intellectuals of Oxford. Whenever a specifically political motion was to be debated he would not speak. Politics, the world of Hugh Molson, he found sterile and academic; a motion on the sanity of Hamlet he considered far more intriguing.

There can be little doubt, though, that he was disappointed by his failure to

11. *FR*, March 1930, 423–4. Waugh also reviewed Greenidge's novel, *Tinpot Country* (Fortune Press, 1937) in *ND*, 21 October, 1937, 28–9. Despite Waugh's distaste for the novel's communistical thesis, he remained loyal to his friend even here. Waugh was willing to advertise the book by reviewing it although he clearly found it incompetent. The problem is resolved by the reviewer's withholding judgement and merely offering an account of the plot.

impress. While many of his later friends consciously ignored the Union, Waugh maintained his connection with this political world until he went down. In February 1924 a report stated that 'Of the old speakers . . . perhaps the best was Mr Waugh . . . who made a speech of more than usual charm and penetration in support of doctrines less than usually absurd.'[12] 'I was not chagrined by lack of success', he wrote in *A Little Learning*.[13] But this was, perhaps, not quite true. As at school, he was secretly and ardently ambitious, never able to be entirely serious, yet unhappy in the role of buffoon. Why else should he have entered himself for the Union elections in June 1923? The results, however, reflected the hopeless nature of his aspirations. Hollis was elected President with three hundred and nine votes; Waugh came last with twenty-five.

It was through the Union that Waugh first met Christopher Hollis and they remained friends until Waugh's death. In later life they were country neighbours, fellow converts to Catholicism. At Oxford they pottered from pub to pub with Greenidge and other members of the 'Hertford underworld'. Woodruff, always rather serious and a 'cradle Catholic', disapproved of Waugh's influence. As a result of the drinking and his duties as President, Hollis, a talented writer and politician, was yet another of Evelyn's acquaintances to get a Third in Final Schools. Woodruff went down in the summer of 1922 to become a lecturer in History at Sheffield but his mother lived in Oxford and he returned every Thursday night to witness with dismay what seemed to him the relentless decline of his companions. He hardly knew Waugh at this stage but was to prove an important friend to him in the 'thirties when he became first a staff member of *The Times* and later, Editor of the Catholic periodical the *Tablet*.

As with many undergraduates, the effects of alcohol proved a revelation to Waugh. 'Do let me most seriously advise you to take to drink', he wrote to Driberg in the summer of 1922. 'There is nothing like the aesthetic pleasure of being drunk and if you do it in the right way you can avoid being ill next day. That is the greatest thing Oxford has to teach.'[14] The painful self-consciousness of his schooldays was lost in a hazy sense of well-being and conviviality. Only one thing irritated him now: the quite reasonable demands of his tutor that, as Senior History Scholar, he should do some work. After a freshers' 'blind' at the end of the Summer term this abrupt and schoolmasterly don summoned his pupil and politely informed him that such reckless behaviour would have to stop. It was a friendly warning but Waugh had developed an immoderate revulsion for the man. Cruttwell was blunt and caustic with recalcitrant students. The delicacy and reserve Waugh had come to expect of Oxford manners had been obliterated by years of trench warfare. Instead of apologising Waugh became, in his own

12. 'The Union', *Cherwell*, 23 February, 1924, 115.
13. *ALL*, p. 182.
14. *Letters*, p. 10.

words, 'fatuously haughty', stating that he cared nothing for his reputation in college, furious that this common little man should attempt to correct him. From that point an undisguised hatred existed between the two. Waugh did a bare minimum of work to prevent rustication; his tutor, at one point in 1923, refused to see him at all, leaving Waugh with no formal teaching other than the lectures he never attended. Both appear to have been satisfied with the arrangement.

The man in question was the now infamous C. R. M. F. Cruttwell, Dean, Tutor and Lecturer in Modern History at Hertford College. Waugh's initial distaste for him was tenderly nurtured into a fantasy of disgust. It is often impossible to understand why Waugh took such a violent dislike to certain people. Friends called it 'teasing'; others who knew him less well found such behaviour vindictive. A general explanation of such perversity does, however, suggest itself, beyond the statement which so many of his cronies repeat that he was 'a bit mad'.

Waugh was a perfectionist; his dislike of 'all things uncomely and broken' was not merely an abstract aesthetic ideal but a governing passion. He loathed ugliness with a fervour that only an aesthete disappointed by his own appearance can achieve. As a young man with his mop of auburn hair, penetrating blue eyes and elfin ears Waugh was charming and attractive. But he was not conventionally handsome and only five foot five. Maintaining dignity from this inferior elevation always struck him as a problem. Throughout his life he was acutely conscious of remarks about his physique. At Oxford he was unable to decide whether to capitalise on his faun-like appearance and play the Shakespearian fool or to appear in the guise of a serious artist. Playing the fool left him largely immune from attack (other than from bores like Cruttwell) but left unsatisfied those nagging sensations that he had, as he once said in a letter to Carew, 'a touch of genius'.

His friendship was reserved for those who were perceptive enough to penetrate these masks of frivolity and aggression. His rudeness and inconsistency, often to those he loved, was an invitation to a test of strength. He greatly admired those who refused to be disconcerted. If anyone cowered or moralised before Waugh's onslaught he was lost. He would truck in, eyes bulging, for the kill. In later life, as he candidly admitted in *Pinfold*, the game occasionally got out of hand. A bad bottle of wine or an impertinent stranger could rouse him to violent aggression. It took him some years to learn that he was irredeemably shockable.

Oxford saw a different, even less stable character, who had not yet developed an obsession with qualitative standards and who found a flawed beauty in the incoherence of experience. Everything was comic material to him. The most mundane incidents and characters were worked up into a fantastic network of private jokes. And in this atmosphere, the mild, eccentric Greenidge was the perfect companion. It was Terence who invented the *soubriquets* for various acquaintances – 'Hotlunch' for Molson, who complained of cold midday meals, 'Philbrick the Flagellant' for a harmless Brasenose man (F. A. Philbrick) who spoke at the Union. It was Waugh who was blamed for them. Anthony Powell remembers an occasion when the subject of whipping occurred in a film and the undergraduate audience started to chant Philbrick's name. At a party shortly afterwards, the man and a friend laid in wait for a befuddled Evelyn and beat him up. Fooling, he quickly learnt, did not always provide immunity from attack.

The feud with Cruttwell, however, was no game. Waugh lost no opportunity to abuse him. Unsigned articles in the *Isis* proved an excellent vehicle for mockery. 'Belated congratulations to the Dean of Hertford on his recent bowling successes. The following headline has been suggested to us: "Crutters collects Considerable Kudos in County Cricket. *Macte virtute esto*, 'Googly Dean' "'.[15] To accuse a man of success at cricket was a powerful insult. But he went further.

The *Isis* was, until Waugh's arrival, a staid, rather hearty undergraduate journal. It ran a series of regular articles, 'Isis Idol', which normally eulogised 'successful' men – Presidents of the Union, members of the OUDS, captains of the various University teams. Waugh's two subjects immediately broke with this tradition: Harold Acton, a notorious aesthete much despised by the sporting fraternity, and Cruttwell.

It was, of course, unheard of for an undergraduate to evaluate the career of a don and Waugh ingeniously disguises his satire beneath the complex syntax of what is, ostensibly, a paean of praise. The googly Dean's face shines from the centre of the page, neither old nor young, displaying bad teeth within an unfortunate smile. The man's name is mentioned only once in the text and then at the very end and in full – Charles Robert Mowbray Frazer Cruttwell. His intellectual powers are indirectly attributed to 'a dose of pungent hops in him'. Cruttwell clearly represented the antithesis of Waugh's ideal man: 'a badger-like figure, clad in ancient tail-coat and lop-sided white tie . . . suffering plodders gladly . . . an olive branch which looks and talks like a bludgeon' who 'doggedly changes his ground in defence of superstition and prejudice'.[16] In describing him in *A Little Learning* as 'a wreck of the war' Waugh completes the analogy. He allied his tutor with 'the old men' and 'Rupert Brooke's generation'. These were associated in his mind with muddled thinking, the pastoral follies of the Georgian poets; with the 'supreme arrogance of impotence', they were responsible for the Great War and the subsequently confused standards of the 'youngest generation'.

At this stage, of course, there was an element of pose in his criticisms, and of sheer malice. Waugh thrived on animosity. Cruttwell and he simply despised each other from the outset and Waugh never forgave him. In every novel up to *Scoop* (1938) he used his tutor's name for an ignominious minor character. The short story 'Mr Loveday's Little Outing' was originally entitled 'Mr Cruttwell's Little

15. 'Heard in the High', *Isis*, 24 May, 1923, 6.
16. 'Isis Idol', No. 596, 'C. R. M. F. Cruttwell, M.A., Dean, Tutor and Lecturer in Modern History, Hertford College', *Isis*, 5 March, 1924, 7.

Outing' and Waugh only made the alteration for the 1936 eponymous collection[17] at the insistence of his publishers. When, in 1935, Cruttwell lost the traditionally safe Conservative seat of Oxford University to A. P. Herbert, Waugh was jubilant.

Poor Cruttwell apparently suffered agonies of apprehension with the announcement of each new novel, wondering in what guise he would be lampooned next. Perhaps Waugh's acute sensitivity had identified a streak of madness in him unnoticed by others – the man, after all, died insane in an asylum. But it is equally probable that Evelyn contributed to his disintegration. Waugh was, even as an undergraduate, a formidable and elusive enemy. Christopher Hollis lived near Cruttwell in later life and recalled nothing remarkable about him. A. L. Rowse remembers him as a tough-minded military historian with 'a tongue like a rasp' but 'a good heart'.[18] Like Waugh, Cruttwell played up his eccentricities and had an uncharitable sense of humour. His copper nose and idiosyncratic language led Richard Pares to include Cruttwell in his Carrollian mythology as the 'Dong with the luminous nose'. In his youth father Cruttwell had been a brilliant scholar: a double First and Fellow of All Souls before the First War; he became an authority on the political history of the Rhineland. But to Waugh and his new set of friends he was a nonentity. 'He was just a don,' Hollis told the present author, 'just a don.'[19]

Hollis had first come up to Balliol from Eton as Brackenbury History Scholar in October 1920, four terms, but effectively only one year, ahead of Waugh. His own memoir, *The Seven Ages* (1974), recalls how he arrived an agnostic and left a Catholic; how, paradoxically, Waugh was the only one of his friends vigorously to protest at his reception into the Roman Church. Much of their time together, as has been said, would be spent in down-at-heel public houses with Greenidge and P. F. Machin, a Lancing friend, 'mouthing Kant into a pint glass'.[20] Waugh, all his friends agree, had even during this phase of muscular agnosticism, a profoundly religious temperament and would spend hours analysing the arguments of believers if only, ultimately, to dismiss them. But although his friend's conversion failed to generate radical change in Evelyn, the importance for him of Hollis's Etonian connections can scarcely be over-estimated.

Hollis had been at school with Harold Acton and his brother, William, Henry Yorke ('Green', the novelist), Anthony Powell, George Orwell, Brian Howard, Billy Clonmore, Alan Clutton-Brock, Cyril Connolly, John Lehmann, Robert Byron, Robert Gathorne-Hardy, Ian Fleming and Oliver Messel. It was an Eton generation of extraordinary talent and precocity. When Acton came up in October

17. *Mr Loveday's Little Outing and Other Sad Stories* (Chapman & Hall, 1936). Even the substituted name was that of a 'war-worn hero type', formerly one of Arthur Waugh's fellow directors at Chapman and Hall.
18. A. L. Rowse, *A Man of the Thirties* (Weidenfeld and Nicolson, 1979), p. 160.
19. Interview with Christopher Hollis, 27 November, 1976.
20. *Diaries*, 18 April, 1925, p. 208.

1922 Waugh immediately recognised in him something for which he had been thirsting since the days of the Dilettanti Society. Here at last were combined the panache of Roxburgh and the aestheticism of Crease; an aggressive, charming, rigorous intellect and a fervent dedication to the arts.

So much has been written of the Eton of 1920–2 that it would be superfluous to repeat it. Cyril Connolly's 'A Georgian Boyhood' in *Enemies of Promise* (1938), Sir Harold Acton's *Memoirs of an Aesthete* (1948) and Anthony Powell's *Infants of the Spring* (1976) offer excellent accounts. All are more accurate and perceptive, it should be noted, than Martin Green's *Children of the Sun* (1977), a theoretical treatise suggesting that Acton and Howard were the protagonists of a 'cultural thesis' termed 'dandy-aesthete'. In 1978, when the present author interviewed Sir Harold, he was moved to a near apoplexy of rage at the very mention of Green's book.

Acton and Howard were the prime movers of The Eton Society of the Arts, which included most of those mentioned above with the notable exceptions of Connolly and Orwell. It was a more sophisticated version of Waugh's 'Dilletanti', similarly including aspiring writers, painters and designers, and had been inaugurated similarly, in opposition to the hearty public-school ethos founded on games-worship. Acton was a notorious anti-athlete, although his brother William and Brian Howard attempted later, and unsuccessfully, to inhabit both the sporting and the aesthetic fraternities. William Acton painted with considerable skill in the style of Diaghilev posters and won a first prize when Roger Fry came down to judge an exhibition; Powell drew excellent imitations of Lovat Fraser; Howard and Acton banged the drum of the modernist movement in poetry – Eliot, Edith Sitwell and Pound.

Waugh soon realised that the work of the Eton group was immeasurably more erudite and adult than his own amateurish fumblings at Lancing. Acton had published poetry in *The Spectator* and *The New Witness;* Howard in O. R. Orage's *New Age.* Aldous Huxley had at one time been their schoolmaster. Just before coming up to Oxford, both had edited *The Eton Candle*, an *avant-garde* magazine representative of the Society's work, and Huxley and Sacheverell Sitwell had contributed poems. Edith Sitwell had earlier written to Howard: 'There can be not the slightest doubt that your gifts and promise are exceedingly remarkable. You are undoubtedly what is known as "a born writer".'[21] Acton had repeatedly attended Diaghilev's 1918 season at the London Coliseum, awe-struck by the innovative fusion of music, dance and design. Through his father, he had met Rebecca West and Firbank. By the time he arrived at Christ Church he was a formidable connoisseur by undergraduate standards. Inevitably, he found Greenidge immature. In contrast, Waugh's aggressive enthusiasm for the arts

---

21.   Marie-Jacqueline Lancaster, *Brian Howard: Portrait of a Failure* (Blond, 1968).

immediately appealed and a friendship was cemented which survived until the novelist's death.

Tall, with precise and perfect manners, Acton seemed to have stepped straight from the world of Henry James. His father was a wealthy art dealer, his mother from the Chicago plutocracy. Acton's childhood had been spent in Chicago and Florence. In Italy they lived in a splendid palace, La Pietra, itself a work of art. The chief concern of Arthur Acton had always been to embellish his home with fine furniture, sculpture and paintings, to landscape its neglected gardens, transforming it into a shrine to Renaissance dexterity. Bernard Berenson, the foremost authority on Renaissance art, was a neighbour and frequent visitor. Acton knew the Baroque and Rococo as familiar domestic styles and spoke of them with affection. It came, for Waugh, as a body blow to any lingering affection he could feel for Golders Green. Underhill became an embarrassment.

By January 1923 Acton had already begun organising the publication of a new undergraduate magazine, the *Oxford Broom*, designed to make a clean sweep of the complacent sentimentality he saw in *Isis* and the *Cherwell*. The *Isis* had been the established journal for thirty years. It paid its contributors and supported the 'establishment'. The *Cherwell* was new and more lighthearted but essentially frivolous. Acton was determined to break into the market with an aggressive paper to provide a platform for those seriously interested in the arts. Through the critical success of *The Eton Candle* he and Howard had become acquainted with the Sitwells. Through Edith Sitwell the intellectual connections extended tenuously to Gertrude Stein, Joyce and Picasso. Most of his contemporaries, governed in their tastes by representational painting and the shallow emotionalism of the Georgian literary hierarchy, knew of these peculiar expatriates as little more than names whose very mention would provoke laughter. Acton determined to change all that.

The effect of his campaign for modernism in the University was restricted to a small and loosely-organised band of sympathisers centred on the Etonian set. Others gravitated cautiously towards them – notably Peter Quennell and John Sutro. But all varied widely in the degree to which they supported it. There was never a 'movement' as with the socialist poets of the 'thirties and each, eventually, carved his own niche in the artistic or academic world. Oliver Messel became a distinguished stage designer, William Acton a portrait painter, Connolly a novelist, critic, and author of *pensées*, Clutton-Brock a professor of archaeology, Byron a travel writer and Byzantinist, Sutro a film producer, Quennell a historian, poet and critic, and, of course, Powell and Yorke novelists.

Paradoxically, Waugh was the only ardent disciple. In later life his attacks on the abstraction and presumption of the *avant-garde* marked him out as a staid traditionalist. But his first novel was dedicated to Acton 'in homage and affection' and, certainly up to 1928, this extraordinary Florentine Etonian largely moulded Waugh's developing aesthetic. Picasso and the Gestalt psychologists, Roger Fry's criticism, Edith Sitwell's and Eliot's poetry defined for him the language of reaction against his father's world of cricket and domesticated literature.

The *Broom* was launched in February 1923, clothed in garish orange. Waugh provided an aggressive cover design for the second issue in harsh, twisted black images but contributed nothing to the literary content until June when he published a short story (never re-published), 'Anthony, Who Sought Things That Were Lost'.[22]

It is a strange piece in the stylised prose of the King James Bible, set in the imaginary kingdom of St Romeiro, presumably some time in the future; a mixture of Wildean fairy-tale allegory and Websterian cruelty, it methodically debunks romantic love. During a revolution the handsome Count Anthony is imprisoned and his betrothed, the 'fair and gentle' Lady Elizabeth, chooses to share his captivity. After a delicious consummation the lustre of their youth fades in the dungeon and the animal requirements of survival re-assert themselves. Lady Elizabeth, bargaining for release, seduces the pock-marked turnkey in front of Anthony who is too weak to resist. The agony of his humiliation rouses him to a final act of strength. He strangles her by kneeling on the chain shackling his wrists. The turnkey, discovering the death of his own hope, locks the door again, never to return.

The hero, we are told, is called 'Anthony, Who Sought Things That Were Lost' 'Because he seemed always to be seeking in the future for what had gone before'. The story, setting aside the school editorial and one light piece for the *Isis* a month earlier, represents Waugh's first 'serious' published fiction. He had for some time delighted in the macabre and in his role of anti-romantic. But there is a certain intensity here, an element of bitterness which suggests that there is more to the tale than the ingenuity of the *poseur*. It possibly reflects his feelings at the breakdown of his relationship with Richard Pares. Waugh's reputation in the 'thirties rested on his being an oblique, impersonal writer. It is surprising to find that at several points in his life he attempted to exorcise depression through literary composition.

Sir Harold remembers Pares as quiet and donnish. With his mop of fair hair and sharp blue eyes Pares had that pronounced Pre-Raphaelite beauty to which Evelyn was always attracted. They were devoted to one another; it was a homosexual romance. It is far from certain, however, that this love was ever physically expressed. Sir Harold believes it to be unlikely. It is too easy in an age of Gay Liberation to misinterpret the male domain that Oxford represented in the 'twenties. 'Homosexual' friendships were the norm because women were rarely admitted to the life of the University. Female students bicycled in and out to lectures from the *purdah* of their colleges discreetly immured beyond the city

22. 'Anthony, Who Sought Things That Were Lost', *Oxford Broom*, June 1923, 14–20.

centre. An unembarrassed delight existed in the exclusiveness of male company and, inevitably, intimate friendships developed. Among Waugh's Oxford acquaintances there were, of course, men who were and who remained homosexual in the full sense that the word now implies – including Howard and Byron. And Waugh undoubtedly moved further towards this more fantastic world of extroverts and 'prancers' in his last year. But there is every reason to suppose that his relationship with Pares was idyllically platonic.

It was through his involvement with the Etonian set that Waugh had become a member of the Hypocrites' Club. This now infamous institution was founded in reaction to the staid and gentlemanly formality of the Union, the Carlton and Liberal Clubs. Originally it catered for serious, rather hearty Trinity men in beer-stained corduroys who shoved ha'pennies, played darts and talked philosophy. Located over a bicycle shop at 34 St Aldates, its rooms were reached up a dingy staircase which reeked by day and night of frying onions.

The main function of the place had always been as a drinking shop but with the incursion of the more worldly Etonians its whole character changed. It became the centre of Bohemian life. Tom Driberg describes it in his memoirs as unashamedly homosexual, the scene of frequent and (to him) delicious orgies. But this is inaccurate. Certainly there were those whose affection for each other was publicly demonstrated. Howard, very soon relinquishing his role as serious poet, joined the Bullingdon, hunted, and frequently concluded the evening in the bed of a pretty equestrian. (His affectations are clearly drawn in Ambrose Silk of *Put Out More Flags* (1942) and Anthony Blanche of *Brideshead Revisited* (1945).) But for most it was merely a place to get drunk.

There was a piano at which Byron would hammer out favourites from his repertoire of Victorian songs. Mark Ogilvy-Grant contributed Border ballads and David Plunket Greene, Harlem blues. The obese twenty-year-old Peter Ruffer would sit regularly at the instrument, lachrymose and desperate, hymning the decay of his youth. Brown-papered walls were set off by Byron's and Messel's innovative frescoes. As the evenings wore on the atmosphere would become frenetic and superficially aggressive. Any formal 'constitution' that ever existed dissolved in beer and high spirits. On one drunken night Waugh was elected Secretary but he never found any duties to perform. Another occasion, in his last year, saw him banished for a time for smashing up the few shabby remnants of furniture with his stick. The authorities, and in particular F. F. ('Sligger') Urquhart, Dean of Balliol, reviewed the club with undisguised horror and waited for an excuse, not long in coming, to close it down.

Pares, a Balliol scholar, was one of those earmarked by Sligger for a distinguished career. (Although not a portrait, there is much of Urquhart in Anthony Powell's characterisation of Sillery in his series of novels, *A Dance to the Music of Time*.) Urquhart was an academic manipulator and diplomatist. Each summer he would travel to the Continent with selected undergraduates for reading parties. To find Pares and Hollis contaminated by the revelry of such disreputable figures as Waugh and Acton was intolerable. As a Catholic he felt his moral sense offended; as an intellectual entrepreneur his sphere of influence invaded.

But he need not have feared for Pares. It was the world of the Hypocrites which effectively separated him from Waugh. Pares could not share in the rebellion against academic authority and, more important, found it impossible to consume large quantities of strong drink. The latter was an enormous disappointment to Waugh. As he mellowed into intimacy, Pares would remain aloof and diffident, mildly shocked at his companion's beery *alter ego*. The wilful abnegation of intellect never appealed to Pares. He was brilliant, rather pedantically left-wing, essentially serious. Acton never found much in common with him. The door into the fantasy world of inebriation meant only an invitation to sickness and headaches for Pares and, much to the distress of both, he and Waugh began to take divergent paths.

Pares's track led him, under Sligger's guidance, to a double First and a Fellowship at All Souls. He eventually became a Professor of History at Edinburgh and died tragically early from muscular sclerosis. With Waugh as a constant companion he had contributed regular short stories to the *Cherwell* and promoted ingenious debates on Edward Lear. But as Waugh thundered down the road which his friend could see leading only to self-destruction, Pares had to stop, let him go, and return to the scholastic framework he loved and understood. It was a wise decision. Pares, like Anthony in the story, was looking for historical continuity. Waugh had no intention of 'seeking in the future for what had gone before'. He didn't know what he was seeking but, as the second Lancing editorial shows, he was determined that it should be different from the world of the 'old men' and 'Rupert Brooke's generation'. Pares became a friend and colleague of Cruttwell. In the end Waugh only escaped suicidal dypsomania by the narrowest of margins because, much to his surprise and even annoyance, he discovered a prodigious literary talent.

The description of this broken relationship would seem to support the assumption that Waugh led an entirely feckless life at Oxford. But the stories of his drunken exploits, repeated with such relish by himself and others, account only for that half of his nature which loved iconoclasm. One smiles at his chanting 'The Dean of Balliol sleeps with men' beneath Sligger's windows and the placing of a stuffed dog in Hertford quad to impute bestiality to Cruttwell. Looking at the *Isis* and *Cherwell* one finds that, under his influence, a tone of belligerent, if thinly-disguised, mockery had crept in. The *Isis* became peppered with bogus advertisements for insurance schemes (against examination failure and fines) and college courses. In the 'Heard in the High' column (7th March, 1923), for instance, a regular feature formerly devoted to witty remarks by passing rowing blues, we see ' "Manners Makyth Man". Take the correspondence course. New

College. Every man we turn out is typical of Comfort and Dignity.'[23] Also: 'The World the Flesh and the Devil. Come and resist them at Mansfield', and an advertisement quoted from the *Oxford Chronicle:* 'Lodger, to share Bedroom with elderly widow'. But all this rather infantile baiting of respectability is counter-pointed by one of Waugh's drawings (signed 'Scaramel') entitled 'At the Sign of the Unicorn. Mr Harold Acton (Editor of the *Oxford Broom*), The Last of The Poets'. Acting as sub-editor for *Isis* he had not only lightened its tone but had carried the fight for *avant-garde* literature into the very camp of the Philistine. Four numbers earlier the magazine had noted the appearance of the *Broom* in a brief and patronising review. Waugh, committed to the cause, could not allow it to rest there.

The exact nature of his interest in Acton's ideas is best described by himself in the other 'Isis Idol' article:

> When Mr Acton came up to Oxford, he found the University, as far as literature was concerned, in a very sad way. There was the grim pipe-smoking *intelligentsia* who lived in Wellington Square, ran the 'Ordinary' and despised almost everything; there were a few ornamental and tiresome folk who were proud of having read Mallarmé and there was the *Oxford Outlook* under the care of Mr Scaife[24] and Mr Murray[25] and Mr Hollis. With the 'Broom' high spirits entered into this foetid atmosphere.[26]

As usual, Waugh has over-stated the case for dramatic effect. F. W. Bateson, for instance, the founder editor of *Essays in Criticism*, recognised himself as one of the grim pipe-smokers and he and Acton respected each other. Bateson always held Eliot's critical essays, *The Sacred Wood* (1920), in high esteem and sympath-ised with Acton's battle to establish him as a major poet. The 'Ordinary' was a literary society at which Graham Greene, an exact contemporary of Waugh's (1922–5), gave papers on the English poets. He and Scaife later co-edited the *Oxford Outlook*. Greene and Waugh, who were to become friends in 1937, did not move in the same circles at the University but that did not signal Greene's antagonism to modernism. His first book was a volume of modernist poetry.

23. 'Manners Makyth Man' was one of Arthur Waugh's favourite sayings, repeated in *OMR*, p. 371. This jibe at the New College motto, almost certainly from Evelyn's pen, must also represent a criticism of his father.
24. C. H. O. Scaife, Liberal President of the Union, Trinity Term, 1924, a well-known 'Georgian' poet and performer of folk-song and dance. Graham Greene later co-edited the *Oxford Outlook* with him. Waugh as Union reporter for *Isis* constantly criticised Scaife during his presidency.
25. Basil Murray, son of Gilbert, the Oxford critic: partial model for Basil Seal in *Black Mischief* and other stories.
26. 'Isis Idol. Harold Acton', *Isis*, 20 February, 1924, 7.

Waugh's account, though, is largely accurate. C. S. Lewis and J. R. R. Tolkien, then young dons, must be added to the list of those who were, and continued to be, opposed to formal experiment in the arts. The conflict between the two camps was advertised in their dress and habitat. Acton painted his rooms in Meadow Building lemon yellow and filled them with Victoriana. He could be seen titupping down the High in mauve trousers so voluminous (he 'invented' Oxford bags) that they appeared almost to be a pleated skirt. Lewis, in reaction, clapped on a greasy macintosh and dilapidated hat to proclaim his normality. Eliot was 'bilge' in Lewis's view and he always loathed the 'pansy aesthetes' who promoted such work. Under Tolkien's influence the Oxford English Faculty was purged of all modernist (or even Victorian) taint. Until recently, literary study there stopped at 1832.

The *Broom* only survived for four numbers, the last (delayed) one being printed in conjunction with the *Cherwell* in February 1924. But it had served its purpose in generating a controversy which established Acton as a principal figure in the artistic life of the University. On first arrival he had been forced to barricade himself in his rooms to prevent assault from a group of outraged athletes, an incident amusingly expanded in *Brideshead*. But during 1924 he was invited with Peter Quennell to edit the 'official' annual printing of undergraduate verse, *Oxford Poetry*. And by 1925, after Waugh had gone down, Acton was a recognisable 'star' in the galaxy of student talent, accepted by both the sporting and artistic fraternities. The battles in the columns of the *Isis* against the denigrators of Chekhov and Eliot had been largely won. Considerable numbers attended Acton's lectures on 'Early Victorian Art' at the Newman Society. In 1925 he invited Edith Sitwell and Gertrude Stein to speak there and both were rapturously received.

In all this, Waugh was the disciple, Acton the arbiter of taste, the man who seemed more than anyone marked for literary fame. Waugh's interest in Victorian and Renaissance art, Firbank and Eliot, his loathing of Wilde and the fatuous languor of the 'nineties all derived directly from Acton. This extraordinary Etonian gave Waugh an intellectually respectable argument against the swains and swinging rhymes, the 'olde-worlde' obsessions with rusticity, the sentimental claptrap of the Georgians.

Yet, in his own right, Waugh was a famous undergraduate. When Anthony Powell came up to Balliol in 1924 and asked who were the 'amusing' figures, Waugh's name was immediately mentioned. Meeting with no great success at the Union, he had turned to that other traditional channel for the ambitious undergraduate – student journalism. *A Little Learning* dismisses these activities lightly. In fact, from his third term he was continually working for one paper or another. Autumn 1922 saw him as a manager and Union reporter for the Conservative Carlton Club's *Oxford Fortnightly Review*. That collapsed in December and by January he was Acton's chief support in launching the *Broom*. During the summer John Sutro, backed by an eccentric plutocrat, revived the defunct *Cherwell*. With editorial offices in Godstowe (a village nearby – Hollis became the editor), this re-vamped paper fast established itself as the mouthpiece of the Bohemian aesthetes and their friends. Acton, Waugh, Byron, Quennell and Pares all contributed. Then in the spring of 1924 Waugh worked as a sub-editor on the *Isis*. His last term he gave up to frenetic preparation for Final Schools. It was something he always regretted.

Waugh has described himself as lazy and particularly so at Oxford. Cruttwell would have agreed. But although Waugh squandered little time on history, he must have spent many hours each week sweating for his various journals. As sub-editor or 'manager' he was able to assist Acton and lampoon the authorities. When in February 1924 the Proctors inexplicably banned Sir Harold's projected '1840 Exhibition' Waugh took up the cudgels in the *Isis* and soundly battered the thick skulls of the philistines. He had worked himself, quite deliberately, into a powerful position. Never one to shy from self-advertisement, Waugh used his influence in Oxford journalism to provide an easy market for his own contributions to Acton's campaign – short stories and, much more important, drawings.

Apart from 'Anthony', Waugh's literary work at this stage gives small indication of talent. Five other pieces appeared in the *Cherwell* during the autumn of 1923 when Sutro was trying to revive it. One story, reprinted in 1925, carried a new sub-title: 'A Tale of Blood and Alcohol in an Oxford College' and this will serve to categorise three of them. They are populated by corrupt and lunatic dons, flamboyant aristocrats, and oblivious college servants. The central figure is usually a quiet, sophisticated student, bored by politics and intellectually superior to the Bullingdon hearties. They are tales of revenge, dreams of violence, flippantly Marlovian. Another describes a meeting between various men whose lives have been racked by a vamp. It is all immature, clever and amusing but to Waugh the stories were never more than provocative space-fillers. He seems to have spent the summer of 1923 stockpiling odd pieces of fiction and drawings to help Sutro's enterprise. He had no pretensions to literary genius. The art work was a different matter.

As a graphic artist Waugh was decidedly serious. With characteristic modesty *A Little Learning* states that, although he did not imagine himself 'a Titian or a Velasquez', his ambition was ' . . . to draw, decorate, design and illustrate. I worked with the brush and was entirely happy in my employment of it, as I was not when reading or writing.'[27] In his scholarship examination he had drawn on his knowledge of the Pre-Raphaelites and Beardsley.[28] His Lancing drawings had been influenced by Beardsley and Lovat Fraser. From Crease he had imbibed a passion for the intricate design of script and the decoration of initials and borders.

27. *ALL*, p. 190.
28. Cf. Chapter II, p. 66 above.

As we have seen, his first Oxford term saw his return to a powerful appreciation of Crease's work. Under Acton's influence all this changed.

During the first term of that new friendship, autumn 1922, Waugh invited Crease down to Oxford and engineered a meeting with Acton. Waugh had moved to elegant rooms, and decorated them with his finely-bound volumes, Fraser prints and examples of Crease's work. He was proud of his early mentor and wanted to show him off. Sir Harold, unfortunately, was not impressed: 'Crease was a very gentle, mild little calligrapher, who did delicate drawings; a charming, old-fashioned, modest craftsman. He was an entirely sexless little man, rather lady-like, neat and clean-shaven who had this *passion* for design. At Lancing he was the only person who had any appreciation of the arts. But, of course, with us at Oxford he didn't shine at all – just a local talent.'[29] In the harsh atmosphere of Lancing, Waugh had believed Crease's small sun of aesthetic enthusiasm to be the centre of the universe. Post-impressionism, Marinetti and Wyndham Lewis were names to be bandied about in precocious school essays but they were not part of his experience. Acton's familiarity with the Paris school and Roger Fry's writings meant that he could only look on Crease with good-mannered tolerance. It was all too English and parochial for his Latin tastes.

After this Waugh altered his approach. Cartoons of bored undergraduates began to appear, followed during the next term by more vigorous exhibits. Two styles predominated: the perfect drawing of complex outlines (such as he used to illustrate *Decline and Fall*) and the modern, angular designs of the pen and ink sketches and woodcuts. One is cool, dispassionate, totally without moral commitment; the other vital, distorted and intense, demanding attention. In a travel book, *Labels* (1930), describing a Paris exhibition, Waugh later defined the aesthetic problem he was exploring here:

> Picabia and Ernst hung cheek by jowl; these two abstract pictures, the one so defiant and chaotic, probing with such fierce intensity into every crevice and convolution of negation, the other so delicately poised, so impossibly tidy, discarding so austerely every accident, however agree-able, that could tempt disorder, seemed between them to typify the continual conflict of modern society.[30]

Waugh was committed to the idea of being an artist and was well-read in aesthetic theory. Throughout his time at Oxford he continued to design book jackets for Chapman's and contributed prints to the *London Mercury* and the short-lived *Golden Hind*. He took lessons in wood engraving and in drawing from the nude and exhibited twice at the Oxford Arts Club annual exhibition, receiving elaborate praise. In 1924 he was one of six undergraduates on the club's Hanging

29. Interview with Sir Harold Acton, 19 November, 1978.
30. *Labels*, p. 20.

Committee. Even a cursory examination of the *Isis* or *Cherwell* will reveal the extent of his artistic influence. He designed covers and numerous column headings repeated in every issue, some of which were still in use up to the Second World War. There was a series of extraordinary cartoons, 'The Seven Deadly Sins', in gashes of black and white, facetiously depicting violence and debauchery by the inverted standards of the youngest generation. The sins are: 'The intolerable wickedness of him who drinks alone'; 'The horrid sacrilege of those that ill-treat books'; 'The wanton way of those that corrupt the very young'; 'The hideous habit of marrying negroes'; 'That grim act parricide'; 'That dull, old sin, adultery'; 'The grave discourtesy of such a man as will beat his host's servant'.

These cartoons clearly reflect his tongue-in-cheek flirtation with that cosmopolitan world he had begun to covet. There were no 'servants' at Underhill other than a maid and, earlier, a nanny. Waugh did not come from a world where the women married negroes or adultery had become hackneyed. But there had begun at Lancing a life-long pre-occupation with the concept of the 'man of the world'. He never quite gave up the ambition to become one, believing that, were he to achieve this condition of educated indifference, he might be content. To his credit, indifference was never more than a pose. Pessimistic to the point of bitterness on occasions, often desperate, a manic depressive in youth, he was never cynical. Behind the mordant criticism there lay an indestructible sense of humour and the child-like romantic personality which charmed his friends. Like his father, he was a passionate man.

He was best known at Oxford for his love of life. He relished the flamboyant eccentricities and excesses of his wealthy companions. Hubert Duggan, according to Waugh, was permanently drunk. The epitome of a Restoration rake, he kept a string of hunters at the University and each night travelled to London for the cafés and night clubs. In the small hours he would scale Balliol's walls to his first-floor rooms. Bribes for his scout's silence apparently ran to several hundreds of pounds. Robert Byron would attack any enthusiasm or enemy with vigour, bursting into rooms and quarrelling violently with everyone. Waugh and he on many occasions nearly came to blows. Brian Howard, outrageously homosexual, was still dangerous, immature, 'Mad, bad and dangerous to know', as Waugh said, but perversely fascinating. 'I think he became mad and bad', Sir Harold remarked to the present author, 'in the sense that he would let anyone down . . . and if he could get away man or woman from the person they were fond of, he would do so. He was completely amoral.' Peter Quennell was sent down for having spent the night with a woman in his rooms. At the Hypocrites' (motto: 'Water is best'), parties raged with women smuggled in from London. Alec, a bachelor again, came down on several occasions and for the first time he and Evelyn began to enjoy each other's company. In *The Fatal Gift* (1973) he recalled an odd scene during one of these visits.

At the end of the Christmas vacation, early in 1924, Alec had taken Evelyn to the Cave of Harmony, a night-club in Charlotte Street run by Elsa Lanchester and Harold Scott. It was later to prove a frequent rendezvous for Evelyn and friends. That night, however, Alec introduced him to Joyce Fagan, who expressed a wish to attend an Oxford 'blind'. Women were strictly forbidden from college premises after dark; Miss Fagan had not been serious when she had mentioned it. But Evelyn pounced on the idea. 'You could dress up as a man,' he said and promptly arranged a party for her in King Edward Street. No-one believed it would come to anything but Evelyn would never retract. Keeping promises and maintaining dignity often led him into dangerous escapades.

Alec suggested that Evelyn would respect her for taking up his dare and he was right. The girl was clothed in voluminous plus-fours, a loose roll-neck jumper, and a cap to hide her hair. The latter was plastered with brilliantine which caked hideously on the back of her neck. She was introduced as a jockey and all went well until a raid by the Proctor and his 'bulldogs'. Giving her name as Terence Greenidge in a lowered voice, she escaped undetected. 'I felt', wrote Alec, 'that it implied some criticism of the contemporary *mores* that so repellent an object could pass as a man.'[31]

The comment points up an essential difference in attitudes between the brothers. Alec, with his ascendant literary reputation and his rugger on Saturdays, found the exhibitionist homosexuality, so prominent in that group, immature and essentially distasteful. Evelyn was at that time passing through an overtly homosexual phase. After Pares had drifted from him, Waugh had taken up with Alastair Graham and was, once again, passionately devoted.

Graham was a small man, quiet, whimsical, gentle but, Sir Harold added, 'very active; full of guts and invention'. Like Waugh he took no interest in his studies and left without a degree. But the friendship was to continue beyond Oxford for several years and, indirectly, resulted in Waugh's turning to a literary career. Graham, like Greenidge, had a child-like warmth and earnestness.

Waugh was at this stage a keen propagandist of the honesty and cruelty of the child's vision of the world. Dean Inge, the popular preacher who had impressed him during those first two terms, had come to speak at the Union in December of 1922. Inge had attacked modern art as a 'return to the nursery'. Waugh, now under Acton's aegis, could not let that pass. In the *Isis* he developed a 'Children's Corner' by 'Aunt Ermentrude' and drew cartoons to accompany it. The Oxford University Railway Club (founded by Sutro early in 1923) also had a flavour of the nursery about it. Beneath the swagger of dining on the Edinburgh-Penzance Express lay the undisguised delight of a game. The evening dress and speeches,

31. Cf. Alec Waugh, *The Fatal Gift* (W. H. Allen, 1973; Book Club Edition, 1974), pp. 7–12. Alec Waugh ambiguously dates this at 'the end of the Christmas vac.', 1924, ten months prior to his brother's *viva voce* in September. (Waugh's *viva* was actually in July 1924.) In his brother's account of the party, Waugh is clearly still an undergraduate. The date of the party, therefore, was probably January 1924.

the toasts and formality, were not the manners that made men of their fathers. ('Manners makyth man', the motto of Arthur's college, was doubtless a phrase used by him to correct his disrespectful younger son.) The whole concept of 'manhood' had been found wanting and rejected. As a generation they felt isolated, inebriated by the freedom from imitation, reckless because they knew that this holiday from responsibility could not last.

Waugh, in an *Isis* editorial, 'Wittenburg and Oxford' (14 February, 1924), argued that Hamlet was a faithful portrait of undergraduate uncertainty. 'We also know', he wrote later, 'that when there is a war the fighting people at least have moments of really intense enjoyment and really intense misery – both things which one wants at our age. . . . there is just no chance of any of us being able to earn a living, or at least a living decent enough to allow any sort of excitement or depravity. Here we are with bills, over-fastidious tastes, and a completely hopeless future. What can we do but long for a war or a revolution?'[32]

Waugh certainly had bills. Credit was easily obtained and he ran accounts at numerous shops. Under the influence of his wealthier companions his taste for excellence was rarely hindered by common sense. He dressed neatly and expensively. His soft tweed suits, his shirts and shoes were hand-made. There were Charvet silk ties, fine wines, cigars and Turkish cigarettes. The University meant, for Waugh, an education of the senses. His father's nagging reminders about living beyond one's means served only to irritate him to further extravagance.

During his last year he inevitably reached a point where creditors' demands could no longer be ignored. A private auction was held of his more valuable books and pictures. He tried to pass it off as a light-hearted affair. But the memory of this ignoble necessity rankled for several years, providing a crucial incident in his first sustained attempt at fiction, *The Balance*, in 1926. A passionate bibliophile, he cherished his collection of beautiful books and, deprived of them, he vacated his elegant rooms for the most sombre accommodation Hertford could provide. His cronies – Hollis, Acton, Byron, Quennell and others – would gather there for a parsimonious luncheon of bread, cheese and beer, ostentatiously described as 'offal'.

The group was a volatile mixture. Acton, who disliked beer, sat primly with a glass of water. Byron would roar out xenophobic prejudice. But they respected each other's differences and, strangely, the snobbery of money or 'background' seemed irrelevant. Instead there was instituted a snobbery of talent, of individualism. Friendship was based on a mutual appreciation of the arts but, equally firmly, on each person's not being like his neighbour. Acton's rejection of the 'greenery-yallery-Grosvenor-Gallery' ethos of the 'nineties, he told the present author, was a reaction against the affectations of artistic and social exclusivism. It was the wearing of green carnations and velveteens, and the association of all

32. *Isis*, 12 March, 1924, 10.

that was affected and false in art that he loathed as a form of social snobbery. It was 'a thing one revolted against if you felt *really* that the arts had sunk rather low and needed revival. . . . Firbank's . . . was a voice which, in spite of the language, parodied just that. It's the last gasp of the 1890s but he's laughing at them all the time.'

Waugh's Oxford generation has been described by Martin Green in terms of 'aesthetes' and 'dandies' but their mockery of pose with pose has been sadly misinterpreted by those desperate for generic terminology. Whether it were Waugh with his dapper, slightly comic, blue tweed suit and stick or Acton with his 'bags' and megaphonic poetry recitals, each aggressively played a part and was conscious of his role. Waugh's cartoons frequently pictured the debauches of satyrs or the tortured urban man's strap-hanging absurdity of the Underground, telephones, pipes, and suburban architecture. The fight was against conformity, affectation and sentiment; the pose almost arbitrary so long as it were entertaining.

During the autumn term of 1923 Waugh had requested his father's permission to leave Oxford. He had wanted to go to Paris and apply himself seriously to the study of art. Arthur had refused. It was, he very reasonably insisted, only sensible to finish the degree first. Evelyn, irritated at his parent's dingy pragmatism, must at the same time have experienced a secret satisfaction. He could now argue that he remained at the University under duress. 'I perversely regarded [the decision]', he wrote, 'as a *laissez passer* to a life of pure pleasure.'[33] For the first two terms of that year his hedonism ran unchecked. After Easter, however, he experienced the teasing and potentially embarrassing doubt that his father might have had a point.

When 'progged' at the King Edward Street party he had said glumly to Alec: 'Crutters will be pleased. It will be extra ammunition for the final showdown.'[34] He was right. And, although in the summer term he locked himself away with his books, he had small hope of academic success. The Birkenhead-black coffee method failed to repair the ravages of the last two years. Trying to be clever in Final Schools, he knew all the time that he was making a fool of himself.

The *Diaries* begin again in a melancholy tone with a description of his final 'blind':

> At twelve o'clock, so far as I at all clearly remember, I was in the room of poor Michael Leroy-Beaulieu in Balliol. Much of the evening he had spent in tears because Peter [Quennell] had frightened him by breaking a plate. There was a prodigious crowd and everything quite insufferably hot. After 12 there were only left the Balliol people and a few incapable drunks. Piers Synott was put to bed. Benoit and Patrick Balfour let me out of Richard [Pares]'s window by a string a little before 1 o'clock. I

33. *ALL*, p. 175
34. *The Fatal Gift*, p. 11.

returned over New Quad water closets, to the great detriment of my clothes, for a few hours sleep.[35]

The next morning (21st June) he caught the London train and arrived home to find 'my parents surprisingly agreeable'.[36] The Balliol party had been arranged to bid him a spectacular farewell; Waugh had found it oppressive. On the train he had dined with 'poor Brian Howard'. Even this exotic specimen now seemed reduced and dishevelled by the encroachment of the real world. Oxford had begun to pall and London rushing at them up the line held small promise of adventure. Waugh was sullen and depressed.

In London he spent most of his time with Alastair Graham, visiting galleries, theatres and cinemas. But Alastair had arranged to attend a school of architecture and intended to winter abroad. In a few months Evelyn knew he would be alone again. He was touchy and petulant. Dudley Carew had long since joined J. C. Squire's camp on the *Mercury* and was publishing a novel which turned out, rather irritatingly, to be tolerably good. Most of his Oxford friends would be returning to the University in the autumn or seemed already to be set on brilliant careers. He alone appeared to have a hopeless future and he resented the relative poverty which would inevitably prevent his sharing the world of those he loved. Accepting charity appalled his reckless generosity; the anonymity of Hampstead appeared to be swallowing him again.

In reaction he began his first novel, *The Temple at Thatch*. His first day at Underhill was spent thinking out the plot. A month later he began it. But it was an academic exercise. All the time he strained towards the world of the artist-craftsman. At the Empire Exhibition he and Alastair visited the Palace of Art: 'The William Morris [room] was the best . . .', he noted. 'I saw sculpture and desired with all my heart to be a sculptor and then I saw jewels and wanted to be a jeweller and then I saw all manner of preposterous things being made in the Palace of Industry and I wanted to devote my life to that too.'[37] The determination to commit himself to craftsmanship was powerful and sincere but constantly hampered by financial embarrassment and a feckless desire to do everything. His bank refused further overdrafts. His father, appalled at his son's extravagance, continued his allowance but constantly fretted about the situation. Evelyn doggedly went on spending.

The date for his *viva voce* in Oxford was set for 29th July. The week before he had begun the filming of 'The Scarlet Woman', a Hypocrites' project which remained incomplete for over a year. Greenidge had set several films under way and this one, written by Waugh, was shot mainly in Oxford, on Hampstead Heath,

35. *Diaries*, 21 June, 1924, p. 161.
36. *Ibid.*, 21 June, 1924, p. 161.
37. *Ibid.*, 30 June, 1924, p. 164.

and in the back garden at Underhill. Arthur relished the whole thing and became thoroughly absorbed by it, constantly popping out of the house to offer advice and refreshment. The cast included many of Waugh's close friends – Lord Elmley, Sutro, Greenidge, Alec, and Elsa Lanchester.[38]

For an undergraduate project it was a tolerable success. While helping to edit the *Isis* in the spring term Waugh had written several film reviews for the paper. These display a keen interest in cinematic technique (montage, cross-cutting). 'The real charm of the cinema', he wrote, 'is in the momentary pictures and situations which appear.'[39] This flickering series of images presented a fascinating new art form and, much as he disliked acting, he was as enthusiastic as Greenidge about learning the aesthetic language of the cinema. The film was another aspect of that attack on Sligger Urquhart's intellectual and religious orthodoxy, a satirical tale of the Dean's unsuccessful attempt to convert the Prince of Wales to Roman Catholicism.[40] But Waugh was dissatisfied. Despite his exertions in a lop-sided white wig as the Dean of Balliol, this 'ecclesiastical melodrama' was to him little more than another student rag which belonged to a life he effectively no longer shared.

The return to Oxford was purgatorial. Alastair and he shared a leaking caravan in the grounds of the Abingdon Arms at Beckley, a small village nearby. The pub had been the scene of many a drinking party. The old squire, the farm hands and the landlady were established friends. But everything was darkened by the approaching shadow of failure. The *viva* was a formality. 'I telegraphed to my parents', he recorded, 'to inform them of my certain third and returned much dispirited to Beckley.'[41] Waugh never received a degree. He would have needed to return for another term in order to complete the statutory nine terms' residence. With the poor result his scholarship was revoked. There seemed little point in prolonging the farce in order to put letters after his name. Cruttwell dropped him a note expressing 'disappointment' to ensure that the ignominy had been noted.

38. Waugh can claim to have 'discovered' Miss Lanchester, later the wife of Charles Laughton, for the screen. He knew her from the Cave of Harmony and secured her services by paying for her meals.
39. *Isis*, 23 January, 1924, 5.
40. Terence Greenidge wrote: '*The Scarlet Woman* was made mainly in the summer of 1924, in Vacation. The capitalists (£5 each) were myself, my brother John . . . , John Sutro and Evelyn Waugh. Evelyn wrote the story, which concerned an attempt by the Pope to convert England to Roman Catholicism by influencing the Prince of Wales (Edward VIII, as he subsequently became) through the Dean of Balliol College, Mr Urquhart, who was, in fact, a Roman Catholic and a snob. The intrigue was finally foiled by the Prince falling in love with a cabaret singer, of Evangelical principles.' ALS to Charles Linck, 19 November, 1961; reproduced Linck, p. 107. Cf. also *Diaries*, p. 169, n. 4 and *ALL*, pp. 209–10.
41. *Diaries*, 29 July, 1924, p. 172.

Evelyn did not go home. Instead, he and Alastair packed up quickly and headed for Ireland. It did little to enliven them. Waugh, unable to share his friend's enthusiasm for landscape, trudged blackly about in the rain and flies. He was relieved to return to the land of draught bitter but this meant also returning to the company of the fractious Mrs Graham. Her country house, Barford House in Warwickshire, was often to prove a haven for Waugh during the following years. There was an attic, formerly the 'cutting-out' room of a lady's maid, furnished only with a table, chair and limbless dressmaker's dummy, where he often went to write. But 'Mrs G.', or 'The Queen Mother' as she is sometimes called in the *Diaries*, was an irascible lady, neurotic about her son's welfare. Waugh used her as the model for Lady Circumference in *Decline and Fall* but what was amusing in fiction proved difficult in fact. She clamorously insisted that he dissuade Alastair from the projected visit to Africa. There was nothing he could do. Had he been able to retain his friend's company, Evelyn would have done it. Alastair was his lover and, although this was not the end of the friendship, it was the end of the affair. Mrs Graham's insistence on his influence made the inevitable parting all the more painful.

Back in London by September he determined to take stock of his situation and, at last, to do something definite about his future. The date of Alastair's embarkation, the 18th, he knew would mark a watershed in his life. He found himself in a semi-comatose state, wasting entire days in cinemas, filling time to drug the sense of impending loss. *The Temple* limped on but he knew that it was dull. So he arranged that the 18th should also begin his new career and signed on for a course of instruction at Heatherley's Art School in Newman Street. On the 13th, perhaps auspiciously, Alastair was received into the Roman Church, and two days later they paid a final visit to Oxford together. There, Alastair bought Waugh a Bible and himself a breviary. But religion was now a barrier between them. Alastair was due to meet Fr Martindale for communion.

Waugh no longer felt comfortable in Oxford. This was, he felt, a valedictory tour of the sordid old haunts. The Hypocrites' premises, long shut down by the authorities, were occupied by David Plunket Greene; Evelyn could only hate the place now for its 'discomfort and its associations'.[42] Everything appeared jaded and devoid of fantasy. Alastair wanted to stay on and loyalty to him alone kept Waugh there.

On the day of his friend's departure, Waugh dissipated his sorrow by arranging the luggage and relatives. But he was 'not allowed' to go to the boat with Alastair, presumably to defer the anguish of actually seeing him leave England. That evening he wrote a mournful entry in his diary: 'After he went, feeling more than a little disconsolate, I wandered about London all day. . . . The most important thing I have forgotten – I went almost immediately after luncheon to examine

42. *Ibid.*, 16 September, 1924, pp. 178–9.

Heatherley's. There are things about it that I find most forbidding. . . . However I expect that it will serve.'[43]

43. *Ibid.*, 18 September, 1924, p. 179.

# IV
# Poverty and Obscurity:
# 1924–1927

'Today', Waugh noted in his diary for 19th September, 'my life of poverty, chastity and obedience commences . . .'.[1] He can have had little faith in such optimism. He carried away from Oxford a craving for luxury, and this projected asceticism was never more than a hopeless ideal. Heatherley's had depressed him at first inspection. With its palette sign and earnest students it seemed only distantly related to that Bohemian delight in creative work he idealised. But he felt obliged to try the place out. His parents were anxious about his extravagance and aimlessness and he knew, as well as anyone, that the imposition of a rigorous routine was necessary if he were ever to become an artist.

The next Monday he forced himself to Newman Street but found little there to cheer him. The *Diaries* of the period revert to the detail of his schoolboy records – introspective, alienated, spiteful, tinged with melancholy scepticism, enlivened only by his love of the absurd. Frustration bred sneering criticism of the second-rate: 'The whole place is full of girls,' he wrote of Heatherley's, ' – underbred houris most of them in gaudy overalls; they draw very badly and get much in the way of the youths who seem to be all of them bent upon making commercial careers for themselves by illustrating *Punch* or advertising things. It does not seem to me likely that I shall find any pals among them.'[2] He didn't. A fellow student remembered him as red-faced, awkward and aloof. Virulent class-consciousness seethes beneath the surface of the diary entries. Having associated with the rich he felt he belonged with them. This was not something peculiar to Waugh. John Betjeman experienced a similar sensation when he was sent down to the monasticism of schoolmastering, though his cheerful temperament accommodated the change more easily. Waugh's reaction was less stable. There is an underlying neurosis in his comments, a controlled terror that Oxford might not prove a prelude to but the conclusion of a dream.

Until four o'clock each day he would sit glumly in the downstairs studio drawing from the nude. Fixed hours exhausted him and he immediately broke from the vow of poverty to enliven his day by lunching at the expensive Previtali. After only a week, obedience went the same way and he began taking time off. Alec

1.  *Diaries*, 19 September, 1924, p. 179.
2.  *Ibid.*, 22 September, 1924, p. 180.

had a pleasant bachelor flat at 22 Earl's Terrace, plenty of money and a sparkling social life. Evelyn, having lost his independence, was forced once again into permanent residence at Underhill. Alastair was in Africa, most of his friends were back at Oxford. There was no spare cash beyond a basic allowance doled out by a reproving father. To Evelyn's jaundiced gaze, Arthur's apparent niggardliness was ungentlemanly. Moderation had never appealed to Waugh, compromise appalled. He had friends or enemies, few 'acquaintances'; he wanted to love or to hate absolutely, to live in the world reflected by his drawings of violent black and white or cool dissociation. Yet nothing was possible without money, and toiling back and forth in the tube each day from Golders Green he perhaps saw himself as a lurid caricature of his own urban cartoons. Games were invented to dispel the monotony. He would hide pennies on his way back from the station, sixpences on one drunken evening. It provided some small diversion to see how many of them were left next morning. Much to his amazement, none was ever removed. Nothing, it seemed, could provoke the unpredictable in his life.

At Hampstead in July, just before he began filming 'The Scarlet Woman' with Greenidge, he had launched enthusiastically into his novel. It was his first sustained attempt at fiction since the aborted schoolboy story more than three years earlier. With the inevitable disaster of his *viva* looming scarcely more than a week ahead, there had been a note of defiance, even of desperation in the project. Carew was making his way on the *London Mercury*, Acton had published two volumes of poetry and was firmly established on a literary career; Hollis was abroad on a round-the-world debating tour. Waugh, alone of the young Oxford artists and critics, seemed threatened by failure. He was determined not to allow Cruttwell victory. *The Temple at Thatch* was to be his riposte.

It concerned 'an undergraduate who inherited a property of which nothing was left except an eighteenth-century classical folly where he set up house and ... practised black magic'.[3] But the subject itself was a 'folly', redundant and incongruous beyond the sunlit towers and quadrangles which had protected the internal logic of his dream life. The talent which had sustained those 'amusing' undergraduate tales of blood and alcohol proved to be little more than a talent for shocking the immature. Where dress, food, wine and a technical knowledge of aesthetics and sex were concerned Waugh had emerged from Oxford an articulate adult. In many respects, though, he remained a child. Worse still, as far as his writing was concerned, he was a spoilt child.

He pouted at the strictures of his London life which thrust timetables, careers and respectability upon him. If that drab regularity represented the 'real world' then he could do without it. He wanted to write as he drew, spontaneously creating a world of pure imagination. The discovery that literary composition required discipline and sheer hard work was enough of a deterrent. The novel

3.  *ALL*, p. 223.

limped along, a thin, rather dreary thing, for nearly a year, but as early as September 1924 he had noted: 'Still at work on *The Temple*. A suspicion settles on me that it will never be finished.'[4] It never was. Some years of emotional agony needed to pass before he could believe that the world did not owe him a living. But it was this period which taught him the rules of suffering, and allowed him the objectivity and discipline to harness his brilliant imagination. Had he been born to one of those independent incomes he so coveted, he might never have written anything of lasting value.

\*

After the publication of *A Little Learning* (1964) Waugh found great difficulty in beginning the second volume of his autobiography. By his death only five sheets of heavily-scored manuscript had been completed describing his relationship with Alec in the early 'twenties:

> ... I can with confidence record the extraordinary indulgence which my brother showed me then and later. He has left his own account of those years. He has a far sharper memory than I. But the picture he presents of his London life is far different from what I remember. He writes of himself as straitened in means and humdrum [?] in experience. To me and to my friends he was flush of money, generous and socially promiscuous. ... Alec was now on his own living in an agreeable flat between Kensington High Street and Edwardes Square. He had not repeated the great success of his first novel, *The Loom of Youth*, but was quietly settled in the profession of letters.
> ... He emphasises Saturday afternoon winter journeys by tube to the outer suburbs for games of football; summer afternoons on the cricket field with forgotten writers. I saw little of that part of his life. To me he was someone who owned Havelock Ellis's *Studies in the Psychology of Sex* in which I lubriciously browsed, as a host who introduced me to the best restaurants of London, on whom I sponged, bringing my friends to his flat and, when short of money, sleeping on his floor until the tubes opened when I would at dawn sway home to Hampstead in crumpled evening-dress among the navvies setting out for their day's work. My brother had his books bound by Rivière his shirts made at Hawes and Curtis. He was not an ostentatious dandy – indeed neither he nor I was built on the right model for that – but he was judicious in his expenditure and was already accumulating a large and heterogeneous collection of cronies, drawn from the stage, from journalism and literature who have stood by him through life. I have seldom shared his taste either in friends or in women. My heart sinks when a new acquaintance introduces himself as a friend of Alec's. But

4. *Diaries*, 7 September, 1924, p. 177.

in the years of my poverty and obscurity I was constantly at his table. Once I even played cricket for a side of his and to the manifest disapproval of our fellows knocked up a few runs in unorthodox costume and entire absence of style.[5]

In fact, it was Alec who first tempted Evelyn away from his orderly life. One Sunday in October he took him to lunch with E. S. P. Haynes and this apparently innocuous engagement turned out to mark the beginning of his younger brother's relentless decline during the next two years.

Haynes was an old family friend, a frequent visitor to Underhill. He used often to break his regular Sunday walk there for a glass of port or beer. As a lawyer with an established family practice and as a man of letters he fitted comfortably into the professional and literary life of the house. But he was markedly different from its other visitors for he was an eccentric of the first order.

Evelyn relished his company. Stories about him were rife. To save the long trek between office and lavatory he kept a chamber pot in his rooms in Lincoln's Inn. In the middle of a conference he had been known quite suddenly to turn his back on a female client and use the vessel. His enormous girth was supported from the shoulders by means of a patent truss. At his stucco-fronted four-storey house in St John's Wood Park he had evolved a rigid domestic routine and kept early hours. Even here, though, his erratic personality left its mark. As he shambled about the place, one fly-button invariably undone, he left a trail of miscellaneous jumble to be cleared up by his wife. At his end of the table he sat surrounded by a fantastic array of condiments – small jars, bottles, tins of chutney, garlic, sauces, charcoal biscuits. Although he was of Arthur Waugh's generation, he showed little of that gentleman's quiet respectability. He had always been closer to Alec and remained a valued friend for more than thirty years. The end came in characteristic style. In 1948 he was struck off the Roll by the Solicitors' Disciplinary Committee for irregular accounting, the result of carelessness, not deceit. Shortly after Christmas in 1950, while warming himself before the gas fire in his bedroom, his shirt tails caught alight. He died from pneumonia subsequent to first-degree burns.

Through Alec, Evelyn came to consider Haynes a friend. As an authority on divorce and marriage laws, he was retained by Waugh in 1929. That business was conducted with typical informality: ' . . . he gave me', Waugh recorded later, 'more in oysters and hock during its transaction than he charged me in fees. He was the most remarkable of solicitors; a man who actually enjoyed the company of literary men of all ages and reputations. A second Watts-Dunton, the reader will ask? Not a second Watts-Dunton. Haynes did not seek to restrain the

5.   MS of *A Little Hope*; HRC.

pleasures of his clients; however extravagant he applauded and promoted them.'[6]
Alec has described Haynes as 'Rabelaisian in his conversation and behaviour. . . .
He never did anything for effect, that was his great charm. He was of a piece.
He "did what came naturally". Having evolved a pattern that was congenial to
himself, he observed it rigidly.'[7]

This combination of individualism and industry appealed strongly to Evelyn,
perhaps because it brought together the Crease and Roxburgh alternatives.
Haynes was eccentric and untidy, not because he was a dim, ineffective little
man, but because he concentrated all his energies on those things he considered
important. By the end of his life he had written some thirty books, both *belles lettres*
and standard legal texts. Rupert Brooke, Edward Thomas, Belloc, Beerbohm and
Wells had attended his table regularly. Evelyn himself was later to join the list of
illustrious dinner guests. Even at that first luncheon he was not deceived by the
man's shabby appearance.

Haynes did not seem one of the 'old men'. There was something enviable
about the ruthless, child-like egotism with which he pursued his pleasures, something ageless and charming in his aggressive wit and extravagance. The three of
them drank a bottle each of vintage burgundy and followed this with two varieties
of port and tumblers of 1870 brandy. By the time the young art student came to
leave the house he was in his words 'far from sober'. 'My next clear memory',
Waugh recorded, 'is being found at dinner-time in the Long Bar of the Trocadero
by Tony [Bushell] and a friend of his called Bill Silk. . . . With Tony and the
man Silk, who appeared to be a good fellow, deeply devoted to Tony, I dined at
the Previtali and drank chartreuse at the Café Royal until it closed. Then much
the worse for drink we went to Elsa's cabaret where I bought a bottle of whisky.'[8]

Isolated from Oxford, Waugh had, as he suggested, latched on to Alec's friends
in London. Tony Bushell was one of his few acquaintances who shared both
circles. An old Hertford contemporary, Bushell was by 1924 a prosperous actor
on the popular London stage. He was a strikingly handsome young man with a
theatrical manner, but he became neither vain nor exclusive in his new success
and remained a close friend of Evelyn's during his years of anonymity.

The Cave of Harmony night-club in Soho, to which Alec had introduced
Evelyn earlier in the year, was run by Elsa Lanchester and Harold Scott. It was
the centre of the Bohemian acting world where cabarets and *avant-garde* plays
would be performed and where customers danced and (illegally) drank the night
away. Elsa, Tony and Bill are recurrent figures in Waugh's diary for 1924–7. Silk
was an actor-manager; Elsa soon became famous as a film star and wife of Charles

6. 'Lesson of The Master', *ST*, 27 May, 1956; *EAR* [in version reprinted in *Atlantic*, September
   1956], pp. 515–18.
7. *MBE*, pp. 232–3.
8. *Diaries*, 29 October, 1924, p. 183.

Laughton. The glamorous theatrical set attracted other wealthy young people: Viola Garvin who was engaged to Dudley Carew and was Literary Editor of the *Observer*, daughter of its Editor; Elizabeth Ponsonby who was proclaimed by the press as a leader of the Bright Young People; Carew, now making a name for himself in the Squirearchy, re-emerged in Waugh's life.

Against these pleasures of the flesh Evelyn had to set his serious concern to become an artist-craftsman. Adrian Stokes, another Oxford friend, was then in London. With him, Waugh could tranquilly pursue those abstract discussions of aesthetics which intrigued him. Stokes later became famous as a philosopher of art. In the autumn of 1924, he was probably writing his *Thread of Ariadne* (1925), a book which, arguing against the inadequacy of 'absolute' statements, bears close resemblance to Evelyn's own thinking at the time. Waugh attended private views and allowed himself and his drawings to be exhibited to D. S. McColl, a friend of Arthur's and Keeper of the Wallace Collection. He drew bookplates and ruminated in his diary about the 'vision of form'.[9] But all the time there was the irritating sensation that everyone else appeared to be having a good time while he showed no signs of ever being able to join them on an equal footing.

At the beginning of October his father had given him eighty pounds to pay off the more pressing of his debtors. The obligation to accept it outraged Waugh's dignity. Underhill seemed drab and claustrophobic, invaded as it now was by Arthur's wireless. Most important, he realised that he was making no artistic progress at Heatherley's. His technical skill improved but his talent was inadequate to fulfil his ambition. In matters of artistic competence he was acutely self-critical. His perfectionism would not evade the issue even though it left him without a career. Several drunken days had followed the visit to Haynes. Shortly afterwards he came 'to the conclusion that it is not possible to lead a gay life and draw well'.[10] Accepting painfully that he would never draw well, he chose the gay life.

The 28th October, 1924 was Waugh's twenty-first birthday. On that day, he noted, 'I became a man and put away childish things.'[11] But he didn't and hadn't. Jean and Philippa Fleming, his childhood companions from the Pistol Troop, gave him an exquisite silver snuff box. In those last days of wilful Oxonian extravagance, waiting for his *viva*, he had bought himself a valuable cameo ring. These two objects were often pawned over the next two years to support his excesses. By early November the lure of Oxford had snared him again and his aesthetic seclusion was broken.

\*

9. *Ibid.*, 29 October, 1924, p. 185.
10. *Ibid.*, 29 October, 1924, p. 183.
11. *Ibid.*, 29 October, 1924, p. 182.

Oxford in 1924–5 was changing beyond recognition. Harold Acton had left his Meadow Building rooms for a quieter set in Oriel Street where there was no space for his vast collection of early Victorian *bric-à-brac*. The Jazz Age had arrived and Acton didn't like it. Undergraduates motored noisily from college to college for drinking parties and roared down to London at eighty miles an hour. Harlem Blues and Gershwin echoed from the Gothic casements. Flappers abounded. A new smart set was in the ascendant, led by the young dons – Roy Harrod at Christ Church and Maurice Bowra at Wadham. In Beaumont Street each Sunday morning, 'Colonel' Kolkhorst (called 'Colonel' because he was so unlike one) held sherry parties for the artistically inclined.

It was at one of these that Waugh first got to know Anthony Powell and, probably, Betjeman. Kolkhorst was a University Reader in Spanish and Portuguese and reputed owner of the Lisbon tramway system. 'Batty' Billy Clonmore is credited with 'discovering' this delightful eccentric and Betjeman popularised his passion for the values and traditions of the 'nineties. Bowra, with his sharp, epigrammatic mind disliked the affection his bright young men felt for the Colonel. 'Pity old Kolkhorst has a touch of the tar brush,' he would croon at dinner parties.[12] Everyone enjoyed the antagonism of the dons fishing for talent. Oxford, for those with money and no inclination to study, was faster and more exuberant than ever.

Waugh's first return visit to the University was significantly on a Monday when he should have been at Heatherley's. John Sutro had invited him down for a luncheon party and kept his arrival a close secret. It had not taken long for Evelyn's brash undergraduate self-confidence to wear thin. He was nervous about this attempt to re-capture the past, trusting no-one to maintain affection for him as soon as he was out of sight. But he need not have worried. His emergence from the suburbs was a triumph.

Acton, Mark Ogilvie-Grant, Hugh Lygon, Byron and Pares attended the luncheon in his honour. Later he found Greenidge, Powell, Quennell, Molson, Gyles Isham (the OUDS star) and Desmond Harmsworth and drank himself insensible in his new happiness, so that he had to stay the night. By Friday he was back for a week-end of parties. 'Never have I seen so many men being sick together or being so infernally dangerous,' he recorded. 'They threw about chairs and soda water syphons and lavatory seats. Only one man was seriously injured.' It was during this week-end that he first met Hollis's brother, Roger, 'a good bottle man' (later head of British Intelligence, MI5) and 'a freshman called Yorke'.[13] Henry Yorke was to become one of his dearest friends.

Waugh did not share Acton's distaste for the rowdy party atmosphere of Oxford. It was a welcome relief from the monotony of his Hampstead life. But there is a

12. Interview with Sir John Betjeman, 10 February, 1979.
13. *Diaries*, 18 November, 1924, p. 188.

marked distance in his comments about the flying syphons and toilet seats. He engaged with equal ferocity in the drinking but now he invariably ended in melancholy detachment. It solved nothing. Next week he was back at Heatherley's and paying regular visits to the National Gallery 'discovering' Velasquez, Rubens and Poussin. Reason pleaded for rectitude; appetite craved sensation and drew him back repeatedly into his 'vastly expensive career of alcohol'.[14]

In late November he was in Oxford again, continuously drunk for three days. 'On Wednesday I was sober. . . . Next day I lunched with Hugh [Lygon] and drank with him all afternoon and sallied out with him fighting drunk at tea time when we drank at the New Reform until dinner. I dined with Terence and then went to Hertford to see the film but was too drunk to stand and went away and drank with poor Hamerton at some clubs and pubs until he was sick. I went to the Hypocrites and then with Harding to a dance in the Town Hall. Next day feeling deathly ill I returned to London having spent two months' wages. I had to dine with Richard Greene in company with Alec, Julia Strachey,[15] Olivia Greene and Elizabeth Russell.'[16] Clearly he could not go on living this phantasmagoric life. Alcohol only temporarily obscured his despair at failing as an artist. Quite apart from the physical and mental debilitation involved, he could not afford it. He needed a change of tack and the group at that dinner party were soon to form the nucleus of a new life.

Shortly after his return to London he wrote to Harold Acton:

> I was sad that I saw so little of you in Oxford. It seemed impossible ever to find you alone. There is so much that we might have discussed.
>
> I have practically decided that it is impossible to draw in London between tube journeys and telephone calls and am seriously considering going to live in Sussex with a man called James Guthrie who has a printing press where he is making books from copper plates. . . . I am almost sure that you would dismiss him as 'arty' but quite sure that you would be wrong because he is doing quite sincerely what all the other 'arty' people are pretending to do.[17]

Waugh went down to see the Pear Tree Press on 19th December. Guthrie he had already met in London and found 'sweet and modest';[18] in Flansham (near Bognor) he was impressed by the 'obvious creative exuberance'[19] of the whole family. But the printing methods saddened him when he found the whole process

---

14. *Ibid.*, 8 December, 1924, p. 189.
15. Later a novelist; daughter of Oliver and niece of Lytton Strachey, the biographer.
16. *Diaries*, 8 December, 1924, p. 190.
17. *Letters*, p. 19.
18. *Diaries*, 15 December, 1924, p. 191.
19. *Ibid.*, 19 December, 1924, p. 192.

to be 'directly dependent on trade photography'[20]. He scoured the village and Bognor looking for lodgings. In the end, though, deciding against becoming Guthrie's pupil, he returned, hopeless, to London. It was another defeat. Arthur Waugh had already paid the premium for Waugh's apprenticeship and Guthrie refused to refund it.

Before the visit Waugh had applied to Truman and Knightley's, the scholastic agents, for a post as a private schoolmaster. Guthrie had been his last hope of securing the aesthetic life, the dedicated world of the hand-craftsman. Somehow he had to rectify his appalling financial position. Fiscal independence was essential if he were to maintain self-respect. There was nothing for it. He sat down and wrote numerous letters to headmasters detailing his *curriculum vitae*. With his inglorious defeat in Schools and no degree it was not impressive. Only two replied. One of them was a Mr Banks from Arnold House, a Welsh school in Denbighshire.

In early January, Banks came up to London to interview him. Waugh found him lugubrious and dim, 'a tall old man with stupid eyes'.[21] According to the account in *A Little Learning* only one question was asked. Did he possess a dinner jacket? It was a necessary garment in which to entertain the wealthier parents. He did. The post was secured at £160 a year. Term began in a little over a fortnight. Banks was desperate and Evelyn must have been aware of the fact. It was a dismal prospect. Waugh lacked all vocation for teaching. He was to exile himself for a pittance he could not afford to refuse. And there were additional complications. During December he had fallen in love. Christmas had been miserable. It seemed to him that some malignant fate had organised things so that Christmas week saw the dissolution of his few romances – Luned Jacobs, Richard, Alastair. Now there was every chance of it happening again. No sooner had he become infatuated with Olivia Plunket Greene than he was forced to separate from her.

Waugh had in effect fallen in love with the entire Greene family. David (nearly seven feet tall) and Richard he had known at Oxford, where the first had introduced black American jazz and the second had taken over the Hypocrites' old rooms and acted, on occasions, as Harold Acton's bodyguard. On New Year's Day Evelyn was introduced to their mother, 'Lady' Gwen. The *rapport* was instantaneous. She was a gentle, elegant Bohemian, the daughter of the musician Hubert Parry, the niece (by marriage) of the theologian Baron von Hügel, the separated wife of the Irish singer, Harry Plunket Greene. Her elder sister had married Arthur Ponsonby, an early aristocratic convert to the Labour Party, and their children, Matthew and Elizabeth, were both friends of Waugh's from the rich and fast set which gathered at the 'Cave' and other night clubs.

20. *Ibid.*, 19 December, 1924, p. 192.
21. *Ibid.*, 5 January, 1925, p. 195.

Olivia was a curious girl. From her mother she had inherited a profoundly religious temperament. But at the same time, with her cousin Elizabeth, she was a prominent member of the Bright Young People – a heavy drinker in the tempestuous round of parties that became fashionable in the mid-twenties. As with Evelyn, alcohol drove her towards manic depression, long melancholy periods of introversion when she withdrew completely from her friends. She was, in Alec's words, 'the last person equipped to restore his self-confidence and self-esteem'.[22]

There were many complex reasons for this. As they themselves failed, after many hours of deep discussion, to unearth the roots of a fundamental incompatibility which saddened both, it would be presumptuous to offer answers. But certain difficulties can be isolated. Alec has noted that Olivia was 'pretty, gracious and well-mannered. She was not negative, since on several points she held strong opinions; but she was profoundly indifferent to the forces that activate most creative lives. She was without personal ambition, and could not understand the hold ambition takes on others. . . . Evelyn must have known that no public success of his would enhance her opinion of him. . . . She was a profound depressant. . . . Olivia invariably diminished Evelyn's self-esteem, not willingly, not consciously: she was basically good-natured, but through her indifference to his problems.'[23] Evelyn, at this time, was torn between the desire to become an artist of some sort and the need to make money. He needed support and encouragement and, although she told him that he was a great artist, her passionless self-containment, her lack of enthusiasm, her rigid common sense, depressed him unutterably. He knew, after all, that her high estimate of his ability as a graphic artist was a misjudgement and felt that in all probability her belief in him was no more than a display of loyalty.

More important, perhaps, there was a distinct sexual awkwardness between them which was only exacerbated by the intimacy of their conversation. Both clearly had problems in this direction. Olivia ended her life unmarried, a *réligieuse* living alone with her mother and practising an idiosyncratic brand of Catholicism. Evelyn, for many years, found it difficult to move from friendship to physical intimacy with women. Away from Oxford, he was beginning to re-discover girls but he was hopelessly inexperienced. Five years later a diary entry records a conversation with Nancy Mitford in which he attempted to explain 'sexual shyness in men'.[24] He became obsessed with the idea that women did not find him attractive. It seemed obvious to Waugh that Olivia was more than half in love with Tony Bushell. The contrast between that Byronic young actor and himself seemed painfully obvious.

22.  *MBE*, p. 177.
23.  *Ibid.*, pp. 177–8.
24.  *Diaries*, 18 June, 1930, p. 316.

That was bad, but the prospect of isolation in darkest Wales was worse. The week-end before his departure had been very expensive. Alastair had returned from Africa and together they had visited Oxford. In London on the following day he had guzzled alcohol to forget the immediate future. But 'I could not get drunk try as I might and was very rude to Olivia who was too drunk to mind'.[25] Next day the attempt was successful. Raving with drink, Waugh, Bushell and Silk went round to Greene's house in Hanover Terrace and hammered on the door at half past midnight. 'At least,' he recorded, 'Tony and I called. Bill lost his way between the taxi and the door and was never seen again.'[26] Waugh refused to leave until Olivia had knelt and apologised for the previous evening. She refused. Waugh broke a gramophone record.

Olivia took no offence. Evelyn's occasional descents into the irrational were part of his attraction for her. On his last days in London they were close friends again. Penitent and sorrowful, he had spent all the money he needed to travel to Denbighshire in that final blind and had pawned the ring and snuff box to buy the ticket. The incident clearly made a strong impression on him. It was translated into the pathetic farce of the scene in *A Handful of Dust* (1934) where Tony Last and Jock Grant-Menzies pester Brenda. Olivia's intimacy only deepened his depression at leaving her. 'I went to bed', he says, 'feeling more desolate than I had felt since the embarkation of Alastair.'[27]

*

His arrival at the school was not auspicious. His bag was packed with the fragments of his Oxford life – drawing equipment, abortive notes for the *Temple*, Frazer's *Golden Bough, Alice in Wonderland*. On the train he had been required to supervise a boisterous group of Arnold House pupils also travelling from Euston. As at Lancing, he disliked being the instrument of discipline. He sat glumly amongst the rabble as they stuffed themselves with sweetmeats. By the time they had arrived at Llanddulas, a tiny windswept town between Rhyl and Colwyn Bay, the children had realised the vulnerability of their new master. There was one taxi. Instead of walking with the boys to the school he clambered in quickly, eager for solitude and dignity. But before he could escape, a chorus of voices pleaded with him to take the cases. He hesitated, uncertain as to the correct response. Immediately he found himself inundated with bags, burying him and obscuring the windows. As the tiny car strained up the drive to the school, the headmaster's wife was waiting to greet him. Waugh struggled ingloriously from beneath the mountain of hand-luggage to shake her hand. She was not impressed. The boys, Mrs Banks informed him, should have carried their own cases. He

25.  *Ibid.*, 20 January, 1925, p. 198.
26.  *Ibid.*, 20 January, 1925, p. 199.
27.  *Ibid.*, 21 January, 1925, p. 199.

should have known that. *They* certainly did. And there was another thing. A curious telegram had arrived. She could not understand it. It was from Hugh Lygon and John Sutro: 'On, Evelyn, on'.

Waugh had never met anyone like Mrs Banks before. Later, he says in *A Little Learning*, he was frequently to encounter her type in remote corners of the Empire, 'the memsahib boss of distant communities of English exiles'.[28] The simile was appropriate. Waugh felt like a criminal transported to an outpost of civilisation. Wales, in his diary, takes on the barbarous extravagance of unmapped Africa: 'Everyone in Wales has black spittle and whenever he meets you says "*borra-da*" and spits. I was frightened at first but after a time I became accustomed to it.'[29] Waugh casts himself as the central *naïf* in this sustaining fiction. Once he noted: 'This story is not really quite true but I have recounted it in so many letters that I have begun to believe it.'[30] There is a remarkable textual correspondence between his letters and diaries at this time, not because he copied one from the other but because to fictionalise his purgatory was his only relief.

At the heart of this misery was Mrs Banks and her rigid propriety. Her husband turned out to be an amiable, modest, inefficient fellow whose chief responsibility appears to have been in the hiring of staff. That done, Mrs Banks assumed command and with alarming efficiency organised the daily routine. It was she who reprimanded laxity. Waugh was not her idea of a suitable assistant master. After his inglorious entrance and that odd telegram she eyed him with suspicion. Above all, she demanded respect for the reputation of the school. It must have been obvious from the outset that their shy, rather sullen, new man despised the place.

Arnold House is now famous as the inspiration for Llanabba Castle in *Decline and Fall* (1928) but there was small resemblance between them. 'It is not really', he admitted in a letter to Harold Acton, ' . . . a bad school as schools go but it is a sorry waste of time & energy.'[31] Instead of hating himself for the profligacy which had necessitated his defection from the arts, he hated the school. Other letters and the diary transformed it into a grotesque joke. Writing to his mother after the first week he said:

> There is a sea and a railway and a quarry which periodically startles me with the most terrific cannonades. There are three pitch-pine stair cases, the floors are covered with very highly polished linoleum. The house is on a hill with the perplexing result that one goes in at one door, climbs two storeys & then on looking out of a window finds that one is on the ground floor again.

28. *ALL*, p. 221.
29. *Diaries*, 25 January, 1925, p. 201.
30. *Ibid.*, 14 May, 1925, p. 211.
31. *Letters*, p. 22.

There is one sad thing. After all our trouble & expense I find that I shall not be required to wear either football or gym shoes. Do you think the shop would change them for some brown crepe soled shoes? If they will I [shall] send them back.

So far I have had nothing to do but preside at a sausage tea and say grace for it. It is the most curiously run school that I ever heard of. No time tables nor syllabuses nor nothing. Banks just wanders into the common room & says 'There are some boys in that classroom. I think they are the First or perhaps the Fourth. Will someone go & teach them Maths or Latin or something' and someone goes and I go on making a wood engraving. Perhaps it will be more highly organised later in the term.[32]

It was. Mrs Banks saw to that. Acton sent him his new book of poems, *An Indian Ass*. Waugh replied wearily:

... you cannot imagine what a time I am having. There is a woeful imposition called a 'week on duty' which has at last fallen to my turn. It means that from eight in the morning until eight at night one has literally no minute to spare in which to read a post card or visit a *cabinet*. From eight at night until ten I sit with a blue pencil correcting history essays. Last night a boy had written 'at this time it was reported that James II gave birth to a son but others supposed that it was conveyed to his bed in a hot water bottle'.[33]

Neither did he escape supervising games. Through an almost perfect ignorance of the laws of sport, he was demoted to refereeing the ten-year-olds.

The school was quite ordinary. It was Waugh who was strange. When he first arrived he was introduced to the Head Boy, Derek Verschoyle, and made an immediate impact. Instead of the neat suit, collar and tie which camouflaged most masters, Waugh clad himself in baggy plus-fours and tweed jacket; over the collar of a roll-necked jumper sprouted half an inch of checked shirt. From Monday to Friday this was his regular uniform. Mrs Banks thought it scruffy. Waugh owned a suit for dining at the headmaster's table and Sunday church. But during the week he refused to conform. To cheer himself during term he ordered hand-made shoes and cases of wine. Outlandish dress was another small gesture of defiance.

Llanabba Castle is a fantastic establishment with Gothic castellations and a staff of lunatics, criminals and bores. Arnold House was a plain, gabled late-Victorian building, a respectable preparatory school with the normal crop of dull masters. Waugh lived with two of them, Chaplin and Gordon, in the Sanatorium,

32. *Ibid.*, pp. 21–2.
33. *Ibid.*, 18 February, 1925, p. 23.

a small house set apart up a precipitous path. With these and others he visited hotels in the neighbouring towns for occasional dinners and, despite the *Diaries'* lurid condemnations of most of his fellow teachers on first meeting, they came to form a cheerful *coterie*. As at Lancing, Evelyn delighted in leading others astray. Normally quiet pedagogues found themselves in his company blind drunk in Rhyl. But such excursions were rare. With melancholy irony he wrote to Acton: 'I am growing a moustache and learning to smoke a pipe and ride a horse and altogether quite becoming a man.'[34]

His mind was awash with self-pity. The same letter states: 'I got very drunk all alone a little time back and was sick among some gooseberry bushes.'[35] Even that was a fiction. Certainly he was drunk and sick but in the company of people he could not bear to describe to his elegant friend. Isolated from the prestigious golden circles of London and Oxford, he felt alienated and neglected. The one bright spot of his day was the distribution of the post. More than once he was subjected to rebukes from Mrs Banks for rummaging through the mail before it had been sorted.

The 'wood engraving' mentioned earlier had been for Olivia. He pined for her, saw her as the symbol of everything from which he was exiled. But she did not reciprocate his passion. Her infrequent letters were 'chatty and impersonal'.[36] Waugh had perhaps believed that the job would provide a subsistence wage for minimal effort, and time, peace and seclusion in which to write and draw his way back into artistic recognition. Before leaving he had been tinkering with his novel and engrossed in the *Discourses* of Sir Joshua Reynolds. Now there was no time even to think. Acton's book of poems further irritated Waugh's baulked ambition. He had an idea for a book about Silenus ' – very English and sentimental – ' he told Acton, 'A Falstaff forever babbling o' green fields. . . .'.[37] But he knew that, in these conditions, it would never be written. 'Most of [the poems]', he wrote to Acton, 'I had heard before and they brought back many memories of a life infinitely remote. I still like the Lament for Adonis by far the best, . . .'[38]

There is something faintly absurd in this small, disconsolate man drifting about the junior football pitch in plus fours, all the time thinking of himself as unjustly ousted from the Bacchic train. It is difficult to feel sympathy and he spares little for himself in *A Little Learning*. But his despair was genuine enough. Back in Hampstead for the Easter vacation the diary reveals the first signs of that chronic insomnia which was to plague him for the rest of his life.

Once again, there was a problem of dignity. If he could not do a thing well

34.  *Ibid.*, pp. 23–4.
35.  *Ibid.*, p. 23.
36.  *Diaries*, 2 March, 1925, p. 203.
37.  *Letters*, p. 23. This idea for a 'book about Silenus' perhaps became *Noah; Or The Future of Intoxication*; cf. p. 129.
38.  *Ibid.*, p. 23.

then he would rather not do it at all. If he was not built on elegant lines then he would dress as a golfer or bookmaker rather than appear as an inferior imitation of Harold Acton. If people were going to laugh at him, and he felt neurotically susceptible to mockery, then they would laugh on his terms. He would baffle derision by his own self-mockery. And by the same token, if his career was in ruins he often felt at this time that the only defence was to ruin it further. There was an element of death-wish in his behaviour.

He was spoilt and petulant, angry at the world for not heaping honour upon him. Success seemed to come so effortlessly to his friends. He was blind to the self-discipline and industry of men like Acton, Byron, Quennell and Pares. Everyone knew that he had as much talent as they. Money, he decided, was the key factor; money and social position. If he had been wealthy he too would have been making his mark in the arts by now. But he was blocked, barred, discriminated against by the ignominious requirement of scraping a few pennies together. Underhill came to represent everything that was holding him back.

Released from Wales for Easter, he pub-crawled with Matthew Ponsonby from central London to Golders Green and back again. In Oxford Street, both were arrested for being drunk and disorderly and incarcerated overnight. Matthew's father, Under Secretary of State for Foreign Affairs, came and bailed his son out but left Waugh there. It was the same old story.

Waugh went to Lundy Island for a holiday with the Greene family, Terence and others. The Greenes had rented a disused lighthouse. It promised to be a refreshing, tranquil time amongst those he loved. In the event, Olivia was cool and distant. Tortured conversations long into the night only brought him to the unavoidable conclusion that she was sexually indifferent to him. 'When everyone had gone to bed Olivia and I sat in the dark until nearly 4 and I became sentimental and no doubt tedious, but she bore it with much kindness.'[39] The drunken excesses of his companions left him unmoved, distant and awkward. Somehow he always seemed to be an outsider but he could not cure himself of love for Olivia and the 'insistent sorrows of unrequited love'[40] sent him to bed in melancholy chastity. The vacation ended with a visit to Barford House and, inevitably, Oxford. Even Alastair was now committed to the world of arts and crafts. He had become a pupil of Newdigate at the Shakespeare Head Press, Stratford-upon-Avon. Most days he had to leave Waugh to pursue his apprenticeship. But together they visited the Max Beerbohm exhibition in London. Waugh found it 'quite marvellous',[41] though he seemed further away than ever from that ideal aesthetic life. He had to return to Denbighshire.

*

39. *Diaries*, 15 April, 1925, p. 207.
40. *Ibid.*, 15 April, 1925, p. 207.
41. *Ibid.*, 1 May, 1925, p. 210.

The misery of his return was lightened a little by the arrival of a new master. The man, a Mr Young, was an unrepentant pæderast. If the *Diaries* are to be believed he had been expelled from Wellington, sent down from Oxford, and forced to resign his commission in the army. Three schools had sacked him for sodomy. Yet he continued to secure posts because no headmaster ever dared admit in a reference that he had employed so manifest a degenerate. Young was the 'original' of Captain Grimes in *Decline and Fall*. In this case, the model was in some respects more colourful than the fiction it generated. Waugh found in Young a mild antidote to the monotonous respectability of Arnold House. They spent many evenings in the Fairview, the local pub, while the older man rambled through fantasies of sleeping youths. All too soon, though, this fantasy paled into another aspect of Waugh's paranoic boredom.

It was probably at the beginning of this term (summer 1925) that he sent the early chapters of *The Temple* to Acton requesting constructive criticism. At the same time he applied for another job. Alec had told him that Charles Scott Moncrieff, the translator of Proust, was looking for a secretary in Pisa. Suddenly things seemed marginally brighter. He began working on a new book and in a rare moment of inspiration ploughed into it enthusiastically. His excitement derived from a technical innovation: making the first chapter a 'cinema film'.[42] Early in June, Alec wrote to say that Moncrieff would take Evelyn. He stopped work on the novel, gave in his notice and for the first time for nearly a year, relaxed. He neglected his diary. In the long hot days of June he dreamed of his future Italian life. With the promise of this Renaissance ideal he pottered about the school, bathing after dinner from the secluded beach, even taking an affectionate interest in his pupils. Then, equally suddenly, his plans collapsed.

Acton sent back a polite but chilling commentary on *The Temple*. 'Too English for my exotic taste. Too much nid-nodding over port.'[43] A letter from Alec followed this. He had misunderstood Moncrieff. He didn't want Evelyn after all. 'I think the proprietor [Banks] would be quite unwilling to take me back even if I wanted to return,' Waugh recorded. 'I can hardly expect my poor father to give me any more money. The phrase "the end of the tether" besets me with unshakable persistence all the time.'[44]

At the beginning of term, sunk in 'Julian apathy', he had debated the 'simple paradoxes of suicide and achievement'[45] and thought about buying a revolver from Young. Self-pity had temporarily been obliterated by optimism. Now, with

42. *Ibid.*, 28 May, 1925, p. 212.
43. *ALL*, p. 228.
44. *Diaries*, 1 July, 1925, p. 213.
45. *Ibid.*, 5 May, 1925, p. 211. One line has been omitted from the original hardback printed version of this entry, making nonsense of the crucial last two sentences. Instead of 'which come in by . . . Young, the new' read: 'which I bought last week at Blackwell's. In the meantime I debate the simple. . . .'

the future even blacker than before, suicide seemed more than ever attractive. At least he could do that with dignity. Over the preceding months he had begun to turn to philosophy for answers, discussing Kant with Greenidge on Lundy, reading a book of Bertrand Russell's essays. Bergson had intrigued him since his schooldays. He convinced himself that he was taking the objective view. Self-destruction, he thought, under his present circumstances, would be neither folly nor cowardice; it was the only logical alternative to a life of misery beyond his control.

His friend's judgement on *The Temple* had been perfectly fair. He took the exercise book which Acton had returned and cremated it ceremoniously in the school boiler. Then, one night in early July[46] he walked down to the deserted beach and undressed. He had already prepared his valedictory note, a quotation from Euripides, taking the trouble to verify it from the school text. This he left with the pile of clothes and struck out defiantly into the dark water.

We shall never know how serious was his intention to kill himself. He did not know himself. As it happened, this grand gesture ended, like everything else in his life then, in ignominious defeat. He swam into a shoal of jellyfish and was stung back to reason. Returning, shamefaced and shivering to the shore, he tore up the pretentious Greek tag. He had, of course, brought no towel. Drying himself as best he could, he clambered damply into his clothes and walked back to the school.

There is no mention of Acton's letter, the destruction of the novel or the attempted suicide in the *Diaries*. He could not bear to record such ostentatious stupidity. *A Little Learning* concludes with the dishevelled figure walking back from the shore, climbing 'the sharp hill that led to all the years ahead'.[47] It was a symbolic moment and is described as such; fatuous despair was rejected and a new determination began slowly to take root.

The few manuscript sheets of *A Little Hope* begin:

> The steep, shady track which led from the beach to the cottage where Mr Vanhomrigh[48] quartered his assistant masters, glistened in the moon-light. It might have been one of those magical ascents which used sometimes to appear in Christmas pantomimes. I was unaware of change. There was no sense of exhilaration, merely the glum knowledge that I had made an ass of myself. My prospects were as empty, my character as feckless as before my encounter with the jelly-fish. I had nevertheless unknowingly passed a climacteric. After that night every-thing about me began by small degrees to ameliorate.
>
> I had given my notice and did not ask to withdraw it. I was finished

46. Probably 1 or 2 July, 1925.
47. *ALL*, p. 230.
48. Waugh's pseudonym for Mr Banks.

with schools, I thought, and in the confidence of early release even the school became more tolerable. Moreover a friend appeared. R. M. Dawkins held the chair of Modern Greek at Oxford. . . . He was a much loved, learned, fidgety, humorous bachelor who would have passed as a contemporary and companion of Edward Lear. He possessed a large old-fashioned house near the school; in fact he owned the school and let it to Mr Vanhomrigh. He had for a time provided an aegis for the Hypocrites Club. I had not known him well. Now, when he came home for the long vacation, he appeared as a rescuer sent to me in the desert of that green country.

Professor Dawkins was a man of almost boundless tolerance but he did not take to Captain Grimes.[49] To me and to another young master [Gordon] he offered open-handed hospitality and comradeship. He was on purely formal terms with the headmaster and I think my frequent requests to dine with her landlord were a further cause of vexation to Mrs Vanhomrigh. With this refuge always available I spent the last weeks of that summer term on the fringe of euphoria.

The end of that term found me in a state of joy which increased to ecstasy as the long journey to London came to its end. Most of my salary was already committed to the payment of personal loans and of tradesmen but I had a few pounds in hand and few qualms about the future. London was all. It was a town where I had spent little time in my holidays from school and vacations from Oxford had been mostly rural. But now London seemed alight and alive with variety. More than this it seemed a lovable place, dignified and beautiful, with its own inalienable character. The love was short-lived. In a few years I saw it distended, despoiled and reduced to insignificant uniformity.[50]

Waugh, even in his old age, could not resist a final dig at the snooty Mrs Banks. Whenever anyone tried to put him down (and at this stage it sometimes seemed that almost everyone was engaged in a conspiracy to do this) he fought snobbery with snobbery. Any rebuke was construed as impertinence.

The *Diaries* do not entirely support this description of Waugh's last weeks at the school. 'For myself', he noted on 10th July, 'I have a heart of lead and nerves of fire and can see no hope of anything ever happening.'[51] Young's confessions and Dawkins's hospitality lifted his spirits only marginally. The excitement he remembered was in getting away from the place to find Alec at the Ritz, Bushell in his dressing room and the Greenes in their new house in Sumner Place. He wrote round to the directors of art galleries and the editors of art magazines but none offered work. Back in London he began spending again – a new suit, visits

49. Waugh's pseudonym for Young.
50. MS of 'A Little Hope'; HRC.
51. *Diaries*, 10 July, 1925, p. 214.

to the Café Royal and various theatres. Pirandello's *Henry IV* ('an intriguing mixture of Bergson and melodrama')[52] and Chekhov's *Cherry Orchard* ('a perfectly marvellous play')[53] refreshed his taste for the arts. Life was better, some of the old enthusiasm had returned, but he was far from euphoric. Alastair and Claud Cockburn were on holiday in Germany, Tony was famous and wealthy, Richard Greene was blithely immured in his love for Elizabeth Russell. More than ever, his friends' happiness contrasted bitterly with his own. On 16th August he recorded: 'I was tired and ill at ease, as I usually am with Olivia, and my father's jollity seemed more than usually depressing.'[54] The diary was written up in the small hours of sleepless nights.

The last-noted entry begins: 'I have got the Aston Clinton job'. With Alastair away, Waugh's social life had concentrated on the Greenes. He had, as he has said, effectively become part of the family. Richard was then a music master at a cramming establishment near Aylesbury and had suggested that Waugh apply for a post there. Greene was also suffering a depressive phase. The Russell parents refused their consent for his marriage to Elizabeth because of his own penury. If both he and Waugh were forced to live in purgatory, it would be more amusing to endure it together. Waugh held out little hope: ' . . . I have no doubt', he wrote, 'that it will fall through like everything else.'[55] But it didn't. His idealised vision of a life as an artist-craftsman was as far distant as ever but at least he had a job for September.

At this point his misanthropy began to drain away. Alastair was back and, much to Mrs Graham's annoyance, guaranteed Waugh's overdraft. They visited Barford and Beckley together and drove over to meet his cousin, Claud Cockburn, at Tring. Aston Clinton had the added advantage of being within easy reach of the Cockburns' house, Oxford and London. There was no danger of enforced isolation and with the promise of some sort of social life Waugh became less neurotic. During that peaceful summer he felt that he had turned a corner and could look back with equanimity at the disasters of the past. He was quite deliberately striving towards an objective view – attending Mass with Alastair, reading his way into Bergson and Plato, and, more important, writing again.

The 'novel' which had begun as a 'cinema film' was knocked into shape as a long, *avant-garde* short story. 'I have finished my story', he noted on 26th August, 'which I have called *The Balance* and took it to be typed. It is odd but, I think, quite good.'[56] Christopher Sykes states that it was, in fact, rather bad. That is unfair. The tale, of course, lacks the accomplished touch of Waugh's later stories and he himself thought it second-rate. It has never been reprinted. But, at the

52. *Ibid.*, 1 August, 1925, p. 215.
53. *Ibid.*, 7 August, 1925, p. 216.
54. *Ibid.*, 16 August, 1925, p. 216.
55. *Ibid.*, 13 August, 1925, p. 216.
56. *Ibid.*, 26 August, 1925, p. 218.

lowest estimate, it is an arresting piece of experimental writing and was recognised as such when it appeared. From a biographical viewpoint it is even more intriguing. As his first sustained attempt at fiction, written during a protracted period of misfortune, completed less than two months after the aborted suicide, it represents an effort (as earlier with 'Anthony') to rationalise his disordered life through artistic expression.

\*

*The Balance* draws heavily on personal experience. It is the only piece of Waugh's fiction which included the Oxford book auction, the Art School setting or the attempted suicide. Other details – the carelessness of the heroine for the hero's love, the failure as an artist, the pretentious valedictory Latin note and the apparent indifference of his Oxford cronies – can leave us in no doubt. Waugh was summing up his life here.

The 'balance' concerned is 'the balance between appetite and reason'. A bold experiment in narrative technique, the story is for the most part written as a scenario for a silent film about the characters involved. Large captions indicating place, time, and occasionally, dialogue, break up the page and shift the scenes. The characters speak a great deal but this is, presumably, not heard by the audience. Gladys and Ada (a cook and a parlourmaid) and someone 'with a Cambridge accent' sit in the stalls offering bemused or arrogantly 'arty' comments: 'These Bo'emians don't 'alf carry on, eh, Gladys?' or 'It is curious the way that they can never make their heroes and heroines talk like ladies and gentlemen – particularly in moments of emotion.' The film, the second of four sections, ends with Adam Doure's (the hero's) death by suicide in an Oxford hotel bedroom and the audience leaves uttering banalities. But there follows a 'Conclusion' in lucid analytical prose, in which Adam revives from his coma and remembers vomiting ingloriously over the balcony during the night, despite all efforts to hold down his poison.

He takes stock of the situation and recalls an incident when, as a child, he had fallen from a chair balanced precariously at a great height:

> Later he learned to regard these periods between his fall and the dismayed advent of help from below, as the first promptings towards that struggle for detachment in which he had not, without almost frantic endeavour, finally acknowledged defeat in the bedroom of the Oxford hotel.
>
> The first phase of detachment had passed and had been succeeded by one of methodical investigation. Almost simultaneously with his acceptance of continued existence had come the conception of pain – vaguely at first as of a melody played by another to which his senses were only fitfully attentive, but gradually taking shape as the tangible objects about him gained in reality, until at length it appeared as a

concrete thing, external but intimately attached to himself. Like the pursuit of quicksilver with a spoon, Adam was able to chase it about the walls of his consciousness until at length he drove it into a corner in which he could examine it at his leisure. Still lying perfectly still, with his limbs half embracing the wooden legs of the chair, Adam was able, by concentrating his attention on each part of his body in turn, to exclude the disordered sensations to which his fall had given rise and trace the several constituents of the bulk of pain down their vibrating channels to their sources in his various physical injuries.[57]

The metaphorical parallel between Waugh's and Adam's new position of detachment is self-explanatory. As Adam walks along the 'towing path away from Oxford' he thinks abstractedly of his fellow guests in the hotel that morning:

All around him a macabre dance of shadows had reeled and flickered, and in and out of it Adam had picked his way, conscious only of one insistent need, percolating through to him from the world outside, of immediate escape from the scene upon which this bodiless harlequinade was played, into a third dimension beyond it.[58]

It is a dangerous and largely futile business attempting to correlate an author's life with incidents in his fiction. Waugh suffered greatly in later years from misguided critics searching for models of his fictional characters. He always insisted, quite rightly, that the good writer created and transformed, never transcribed. But *The Balance* is, perhaps, the most significant exception to this rule in his *opus*. Indeed, it alluded to autobiographical secrets (such as the attempted suicide) not revealed until the publication of *A Little Learning* (1964). Quite apart from any aesthetic consideration of the story's technical merit, one of the reasons for his refusal to reprint it must have been the embarrassing intimacy of its subject-matter. It gave too much of himself away. There is a great deal of the young Waugh in Adam Doure and the author's friends must have recognised the correspondence. All the evidence points to the fact that his hero's vision of the world as a 'bodiless harlequinade' and his resulting 'struggle for detachment' were Waugh's own.

The third section, 'Conclusion', ends with a dialogue between Adam and his reflection as he leans over a bridge after the destruction of the suicide note. He has found no secret, it appears, only 'bodily strength' in the discovery of the true nature of 'the balance', that necessary state of mental equilibrium in a phantasmagoric and unreliable world. Unlike the Romantic and Victorian

57. Evelyn Waugh, 'The Balance. A Yarn of the Good Old Days of Broad Trousers and High-Necked Jumpers', *Georgian Stories 1926*, ed. Alec Waugh (Chapman & Hall, 1926), p. 286.
58. *Ibid.*, p. 287.

dilemmas, this is not seen as a balance between 'life and death', but between 'appetite and reason' in which 'the reason remains constant' (but largely ineffectual) and 'the appetite varies'. The implicit difficulty in this realisation is that appetite has no absolute value as a directing principle; its object achieved, it either ceases to exist or is re-directed and re-defined. Even the appetite for death 'is appeased by sleep and the passing of time'. There is no 'reason', no 'honour to be observed to friends', no 'interpenetration, so that you cannot depart without bearing away with you something that is part of another'. Even Adam's art is only 'the appetite to live – to preserve in the shapes of things the personality whose dissolution you foresee inevitably'. And in the end 'circumstance decides', not the individual. The paradox suggested by this vision is of man simultaneously isolated ('no interpenetration') and left without individual identity.

For the artist seeking to depict this dilemma the problem of his own subjectivity generates further complications; he must somehow detach himself from the life he describes while at the same time suggesting that detachment in all but the most superficial respects is impossible. This led to Waugh's use of the film scenario here and largely governed the more subtle stylistic detachment, the apparent comic indifference, of his early novels. They are not flippant, as so many reviewers presumed; quite the reverse.

He became a serious writer as much interested in stylistic innovation as Joyce or Gertrude Stein. He was even concerned with the identical aesthetic problem of developing a new form of literary expression which banished the author's intrusive voice. But there is an essential difference between Waugh and the 'serious' *avant-garde*. Behind all their experiments lies the assumption that there exists a reality, disjointed and cacophonous, but a reality waiting to be described in all its complexity. In *The Balance*, indeed in all Waugh's later work, this assumption is challenged. Circumstance decides but, however accurately observed, these constituent events are not 'truth', merely an accurate description of falsehood. Neither man's actions, nor his words, can embody an empirical truth. Circumstance alone decides and, at this stage (1925–6), circumstance is seen as the inadvertent product of collective action.

The last section is entitled 'Continuation', the implication being that no conclusion is possible, that the individual, swept along by circumstance, can exert little influence over his condition. The scene is the elegant luncheon table of a country house. The hostess, mother of one of Adam's Oxford friends, has invited all the bright young people of her son's set. They sit about gossiping. Adam has not been invited. He flickers briefly in the conversation and then is extinguished. They pass on to the next trivial issue. Imogen Quest, the heroine, wants desperately to meet a man who is 'short and dirty with masses of hair'. Throughout the brief interlude there are constant references to the guests smoking at table – something Waugh, with his fastidious manners, found repulsive. The hostess thinks the scene charming and '*chic*'. Waugh offers no authorial comment but the implication is clear enough. He is mocking them. There is a scarcely suppressed rage at their treatment of Adam, a bitter resentment that his 'reality', his complex psychological and moral 'being', is no more to them than a shadow in a piece of amusing tattle.

At the root of many of Evelyn's complex emotional difficulties, surely, there lay this obsessive fear of enforced anonymity. What happened to Adam must never happen to him. He would *not* be absorbed into the crowd. In the *Diaries* of the period we see: 'This morning a letter from Richard [Greene] telling me that the Greene family are quarrelling with me. I just don't mind. This sort of thing has happened before so often that it has ceased to shock me. I shall have to regard all my friendships as things of three to six months. It makes everything easier.'[59]

*

On 24th September, 1925, Richard and Elizabeth drove Waugh down to Aston Clinton. All three were deeply depressed. After a miserable meal in the school and a quick drink at the Bell (the local inn), Liza returned to London with the car, leaving the men stranded in 'a house of echoing and ill-lit passages and frightful common-room'.[60] In his unhappiness he again saw a perfectly normal private school through a fish-eye lens. Hyperbolic adjectives loom from the page of his diary. The pupils, unremarkable slow learners from wealthy homes, became to Waugh 'the mad boys'; 'There is a boy I like the look of,' he notes, '. . . who is not mad but diseased'.[61] Translated this probably meant 'quite intelligent but spotty'.

The headmaster, Dr Crawford, was a mild man with liberal notions of discipline. Waugh had been employed to teach English, History and Art with subsidiary games and shooting. In general it was an easier regimen than Arnold House with smaller classes, more free time and no Mrs Banks to complain about his clothes or inefficiency. But he could not like it. Aston Clinton was a nondescript linear development on the way to Aylesbury. There was nothing to do there but dine and drink at the pub. The single virtue of the place was that it was not in Wales. With lifts from friends, or lengthy bus excursions he could reach Oxford, London or Tring.

This was to be the pattern of Waugh's life for the next seventeen months. His diary entry shortly after arriving was typical: 'Richard and I went up to London, in spite of an attempt by Crawford and the cavalry officer to keep us at Clinton.'[62] The 'cavalry officer' was another master, Captain Hyde-Upward. Waugh found

---

59.  *Diaries*, 18 May, 1925, p. 212.
60.  *Ibid.*, 24 September, 1925, p. 224.
61.  *Ibid.*, 26 September, 1925, p. 224.
62.  *Ibid.*, 8 October, 1925, p. 226.

none of Young's sympathetic extravagance in this military gentleman. The Captain believed in efficiency and discipline. His one endearing lapse was to polish and clean out his pipe while standing naked at his bedroom window. But in public he worked actively and unsuccessfully to frustrate the plans for escape of his two young colleagues.

During that visit to London Waugh met Elizabeth Ponsonby for the first time. 'Two years ago, or less even,' he recorded, 'I suppose I should have been rather thrilled by her.'[63] He was thrilled by her, nevertheless. Elizabeth was beautiful, rich and vivacious. For more than a year Waugh was considerably infatuated and tried on several occasions to prosecute an affair. It never came to anything but it served to consolidate his unhappy alliance with the Bright Young People. The next two years were to be his *Vile Bodies* period of frenetic movement and smart parties. The desperate energy of his search for sensation directly contradicts the philosophical message of *The Balance*. The story had described an ideal of detachment which he was unable to apply. His analytical mind proposed but appetite disposed.

Most week-ends and often during the week he would be driven to Oxford, returning late and exhausted for a few hours' sleep before his classes the next morning. Parties of his friends came over in expensive cars, sometimes forming impromptu rugby squads to play the school team. He was living beyond his means and the rich visitors had small concern for his penury. On one occasion that November, after a large meal and drinks at the Bell, they rolled off into the night leaving Richard and Waugh with a massive bill. Depression and that nagging sense of persecution, of being used and forgotten, crept back. On his twenty-second birthday, after a dreary day's teaching and the receipt of a few nondescript presents he wrote: 'I think that I should have been incredulous last year or the year before if I had been told how this birthday was to be spent.'[64]

A few days later Matthew Ponsonby and some friends arrived and drove him to the Spread Eagle at Thame, a favourite haunt of Oxford undergraduates. Fothergill, the benign host of this famous pub and restaurant, once marked John Betjeman's bill: 'Less £6 for extravagance'.[65] It was there that Betjeman, about to become a teacher himself, once met Waugh and was told that he would never laugh so much as he would as a schoolmaster. But, as Waugh noted in *A Little Learning*, 'in my case there was no happiness; merely hilarity'.[66] The food was good but Evelyn was worried: 'Matthew is trying to exclude me from the independent party at dinner tomorrow night and put me on to Chris [Hollis]. We do not

---

63. *Ibid.*, 8 October, 1925, p. 226.
64. *Ibid.*, 28 October, 1925, p. 230.
65. Interview with Sir John Betjeman, 10 February, 1979.
66. *ALL*, p. 225. Sir John told me that this remark was made at the Spread Eagle; Waugh says it was made at Betjeman's 'place of bondage'.

like each other, I am afraid.'[67] As a defence against insecurity, he wanted more than anything to be accepted by the smart set and the difficulties with Ponsonby hindered this ambition.

He did not attend Ponsonby's Oxford dinner. He was in Oxford that week-end and was eventually invited. But he refused, his pride outraged at not being a principal guest. Greenidge was shooting the last part of 'The Scarlet Woman' in the garden of a house up the Woodstock Road. Waugh ambled up to play his part but disliked the people there. A taxi was called for one of the scenes. He jumped into it and drove off. The evening was spent avoiding those he thought had snubbed him. Seeing Liza Greene's party in the Cornmarket he scuttled into the bar of the Clarendon. They had spotted him and followed. Waugh, having drunk himself into a heightened condition of persecution mania, attempted to make his escape through a window. He fell and sprained his ankle badly.

Had he not hurt himself in this ridiculous incident, Waugh might never have become a writer. The injury deferred his immediate return to Aston Clinton. The next day he hobbled about in Greenidge's film. It was cold and his ankle was beginning to swell badly. That night Richard and Elizabeth drove him back to London and deposited him at Underhill where he spent three days on 'a sofa in my father's frightful house'.[68]

His parents ministered to him sympathetically; his friends called with presents. But marooned in Golders Green he felt miserable and isolated. Richard and Elizabeth appeared 'remote from me behind an impenetrable wall of happiness'.[69] In unhappy contrast, the world seemed to be showering Richard with its bounty – an inheritance, a new job as music master at Lancing and, at last, permission to marry. He was to leave the school at the end of term.

For want of anything better to do, Waugh began to browse amongst his father's books. He found himself attracted by the melancholy of the Pre-Raphaelites and quickly became immersed in their writings. 'I want to write a book about them', he recorded.[70] Liza Greene drove him down to Aston Clinton where he again propped himself on a sofa and continued his obsessive reading:

> The Pre-Raphaelites still absorb me. I think I can say without affectation that during this last week I have lived with them night and day. Early in the morning with Holman Hunt – the only Pre-Raphaelite – untiring, fearless, conscientious. Later in the day with Millais – never with *him* but with my biography of him – a modish Lytton Strachey biography. How he shines through Holman Hunt's loyal pictures of him. Later, when firelight and rum and loneliness have done their worst, with

67. *Diaries*, 6 November, 1925, p. 232.
68. *Ibid.*, p. 232. Davie reads: 'delightful house'.
69. *Ibid.*, 6 November, 1925, p. 233.
70. *Ibid.*, 6 November, 1925, p. 233.

Rossetti, soaked in chloral and Philip Marston's 'Why is he not some great exiled king, that we might give our lives in trying to restore him to his kingdom?'[71]

Copious notes were made, but with the return of health and the resumption of his duties, Waugh's natural dilettantism got the better of him. The book was not begun. Nothing more was done about his interest in the Brotherhood for eight months. Term ended with a general sense of fatigue and continued fiscal instability.

*

Christmas Day and Boxing Day were not spent at Underhill but at Alec's flat. John Rothenstein, later Director of the Tate Gallery, was there and Audrey, the daughter of the *littérateur*, E. V. Lucas. Six years later Waugh was to have an affair with her. She was an old family friend. But he showed little interest in 1925. He had planned to visit Paris with Bill Silk and could not wait to escape. By 27th December they were booked into a cheap hotel near the Louvre.

The alliance with Silk was uneasy. He was a homosexual, infatuated with Tony Bushell, a generous, agreeable fellow who spent money liberally on friends. The Parisian visit meant only an opportunity for debauchery for him. Waugh had other ideas, preferring food, wine and galleries to the *quartier Latin*. On one occasion he accompanied Silk to a male brothel and wrote up an account – no doubt grossly exaggerated – in his diary. There is an element of false worldliness in his descriptions of negroes and pretty boys which probably disguises a fastidious distaste for such exoticism. He felt that he ought to be impervious to shock but somehow he never was. Pretending to himself that the price was 'prohibitive' and that Bill's haggling had grown too tedious, he ran away. 'This morning', he noted the next day, 'Bill still sleeping off his excesses, I went to the Louvre.'[72] In those cool corridors, alone with Poussin and Mantegna, he was supremely happy.

This routine continued until the end of the month. Silk would be out until late in the brothels; Waugh would retire early and then spend the morning examining the city's art treasures in peaceful seclusion. Silk would not usually be up by the time Waugh returned at midday. Afternoons and evenings they shared in cafés and restaurants exploring the more innocuous sensual pleasures of French *cuisine*. They came back to London on New Year's Day and so inspired was Waugh by what he had seen that he even went back to Heatherley's for a day. 'It was odd', he remarked, 'to see the same people still drawing away there after all that has happened since I was last there.'[73] He never returned.

71. *Ibid.*, 14 November, 1925, p. 233.
72. *Ibid.*, 29 December, 1925, p. 240.
73. *Ibid.*, 5 January, 1926, p. 241.

The rest of the holiday was mostly spent with Alastair at Barford House and Oxford. The Paris trip seems to have settled Waugh into contemplative mood. He bought some books, 'including T. S. Eliot's poems which seem to me marvellously good but very hard to understand. There is a most impressive flavour of the major prophets about them.'[74] Back in London Gwen Greene lent him the original letters sent to her by her uncle, Baron von Hügel, expounding the 'modernist' Catholic position.[75] At Barford Waugh attended Mass with Alastair, as he had on several other occasions.

Perhaps to lessen the blow of his defection to Lancing, Richard Greene had bought Waugh a motor-bicycle. Now that Elizabeth would no longer be motoring down to see Richard, Waugh would be deprived of access to a car. The gift was a thoughtful gesture. Without transport, Evelyn might well have succumbed to the despair he had felt in Wales. Such generosity from a friend points up the distortions generated by Waugh's sense of persecution. His feelings of rejection were usually ill-founded. Those close to him cared for Evelyn almost as they would have for a child. Beneath the brusque exterior they recognised a man peculiarly vulnerable to misfortune, a man of great, unfulfilled talent. They looked out for him.

The machine added a new dimension to the extravagance of his public character. The *Oxford Fortnightly Review* recorded a dramatic entrance in early February: 'Evelyn Waugh made a perilous but successful journey to Oxford the week before last on Queensbury, his new motor-bicycle, and a few were privileged to watch him, leather-coated and leather-helmeted, pushing it along the Corn in a gallant but blasphemous effort to shame [it] into some sort of activity.'[76] The paper was edited by Frank Pakenham, later Lord Longford, at this time a distant friend. Waugh was not forgotten. He had developed into a fantastic, almost fictional, character and he encouraged this mythical image. He would burst upon the continuing social life of Oxford or London from his exile and, equally suddenly, disappear. His less intimate acquaintances remembered him for his eccentricity, not, as with Acton or Byron, for his talent. It was a most unsatisfactory situation for a man of Waugh's ambition and only served to confirm his vision of society as a ghostly harlequinade without depth or continuity. Whatever pleasure he derived from his friends was always counterbalanced by the fact that he

74. *Ibid.*, 11 January, 1926, p. 242. The remark seems to suggest that Waugh was reading Eliot for the first time in 1926, an extraordinary revelation considering the close relationship with Acton at Oxford. He had, of course, *heard* Acton reading *The Waste Land* but possibly never bothered to buy the text. It is more likely, however, that he is referring to those early poems – 'Prufrock', 'Portrait of a Lady', 'Rhapsody on a Windy Night', 'Sweeny among the Nightingales' etc. – re-printed for the first time in 1925 in *Poems: 1909–1925* (Faber and Gwyer).
75. Gwen Plunket Greene edited these letters for publication in 1928 under the title: *Letters from Baron Von Hügel to a Niece*. It quickly became a popular work of Catholic apologetics.
76. *OFR*, 9 February, 1926, 42.

would inevitably have to wobble back, wind-blasted and slightly absurd, to the unrelenting mundanity of Aston Clinton.

Despite this frenetic travelling, 1926 saw the beginnings of withdrawal and consolidation. The spoilt child, pouting at misfortune, had been replaced by an altogether more likeable character. His diary and letters adopt a quieter, more controlled vocabulary. He began to see so many of his generation destroying themselves that he seems to have made a conscious decision not to be subsumed in their nihilistic hedonism. In March Acton wrote to him telling of his brother William's 'accident'. Waugh replied in avuncular fashion: 'Please tell him how sorry I am. It must be a terrible worry for you. I hear various accounts of the circumstances of this fall – all rather disturbing.'[77] William had fallen from a window into Peckwater Quad while drinking ether and alcohol. Later in his life there were several attempts at suicide. Evelyn now felt at a considerable distance from that deserted Welsh beach.

He even began to take some interest in his job. In *A Little Learning* he depicts himself as an unpopular schoolmaster at Arnold House, sad and isolated. Derek Verschoyle, in direct contradiction, remembers that Waugh was warmly regarded: 'In matters of academic studies he adopted a policy of live-and-let-live. It could not be said that he made any great formal effort to teach. On the other hand, if any child showed curiosity on any specific point he attempted to satisfy it and sometimes succeeded. To those who were at the top of the senior form he extended a degree of tolerance which permitted the study of French novels not on any curriculum during what were in theory history lessons.'[78] This attitude persisted at Aston Clinton.

'At first the boys despised me,' he wrote in 1937, 'but I bought a motor bicycle and from that moment was the idol of the school. I bribed them to behave well by letting them take down the engine.'[79] No mention is made of this in the *Diaries*. It was typical of the man to presume himself unlikeable. The young were not fooled by his mask of severity. He always felt awkward with children and was quite incapable of sentimental patronage, but he seems in his youth to have had a sympathetic understanding for their buoyant naïvety. Perhaps the boys at Aston Clinton recognised this in him.

In the convivial atmosphere of his second school he was able to respond more openly. Two pupils, Charles and Edmund, become recurrent figures in his diary. There was some element, it appears, of homosexual attraction, but his affection for them seems to have been platonic. He shared their games and small adventures; he invited them and their friends for tea. Every evening he would go up to the

77. Unpublished ALS to Harold Acton, nd, np [probably from Aston Clinton, about 7 March, 1926].
78. Sykes, p. 60.
79. 'General Conversation: Myself', *NPMM*, March 1937, 10; *EAR*, pp. 190–2.

dormitory to say good-night. If, through the frustrations of his private life, he spoke sharply to any of his charges, he suffered remorse at having assaulted their simple trust.

Waugh, of course, nagged himself for slipping too easily into the character of the polite schoolmaster. He ran the Literary Society and invited Alec down to address it. He worked on the school magazine and designed its cover. Crawford had given him a sitting room over the stables which he furnished cheaply. He was becoming comfortable and he despised himself for it. But he needed this period of relaxation. When he went up to London to see Olivia in March he found her 'packing bottles in a bedroom littered with stockings and newspaper. Fatter and larger generally, unable to talk of much except herself and that in an impersonal and incoherent way. I sat on her bed for some time trying to talk to her with my heart sinking and sinking. . . .'[80]

He had had enough of it. The Oxford parties rolling over to Aston Clinton in cars full of Charleston records, Olivia's obsession with drink and jazz and negroes, William's 'fall' – everything was going too fast. A certain prudishness caused him to withdraw from anarchy. His friends were becoming uncontrolled and dangerous; it was different in kind from the limited Bolshevism he practised. At the end of term Young came down from Wales for a visit 'and was rather a bore – drunk all the time. He seduced a garage boy in the hedge.' The entry is marked, not 'April 1st', but 'All Fools' Day'.[81]

Returning to London for the Easter holiday he could only bear the city for two days. Alastair had gone to Constantinople and Waugh also craved escape. Penury limited choice but what he did was in many ways extraordinary. He no longer sought the release of Bohemian drinking bouts and parties. Instead, he mounted his motor-bike and cruised peacefully down to his maiden aunts' house in Midsomer Norton. 'Since then', he recorded, 'I have read out-of-date novels in shabby easy chairs and listened to my aunts' condemnation of everything they know nothing about.'[82] The comment is not derogatory. This escape into parochialism was the perfect antidote to the rational anarchy of urban life. In the capital there were rumours of a General Strike.

Waugh had no interest in the Strike's political aspect. He saw it only as a potentially exciting event posing intriguing philosophical problems:

> I have begun to think whether perhaps April 1926 may not in time rank with July 1914 for the staging of house parties in sociological novels. I suppose the desire to merge one's individual destiny in forces outside oneself, which seems to me deeply rooted in most people and shows itself in social service and mysticism and in some manner in debauchery,

80. *Diaries*, 15 March, 1926, p. 249.
81. *Ibid.*, p. 250.
82. *Ibid.*, 12 April, 1926.

is really only a consciousness that this is already the real mechanism of life which requires so much concentration to perceive that one wishes to objectify it in more immediate (and themselves subordinate) forces. How badly I write when there is no audience to arrange my thoughts for.[83]

The analysis is clumsy but nonetheless interesting. Waugh's notion that 'individual destiny' was not the private business of the individual, that it was an integral part of 'forces outside oneself' was later to form an essential tenet of his aesthetic and religious principles. The 'quest for identity' at the heart of so many contemporary novels seemed to him to be essentially trivial because of its subjective partiality. Inventing linguistic tricks to describe the multiple sensations of consciousness did not, to his mind, represent 'objectivity'. It merely confounded issues by concentrating attention on the relative viewpoints of single characters.

'Claud [Cockburn] lent me a novel by Virginia Woolf which I refuse to believe is good', he had noted in September 1925.[84] It did not matter to him what Mrs Dalloway or Molly Bloom thought. The only important issue was the way in which the individual related to the overall pattern. Even in those reckless, agnostic days, when mysticism could be lumped together with social service and debauchery as futile grapplings at the wrong end of the philosophical stick, the assumption of an inherent pattern and order in the universe lay securely behind his thinking.

At this stage he had not the slightest idea of the form that universal order might take. He merely experienced the negative pleasure of seeing inadequate versions of it debunked. One inadequate version was political ideology, which he saw as complacent on the right, and an absurd surrogate religion on the left. He stayed in the country for a restorative three weeks visiting friends. On the day of his return to Hampstead, 1st May, the miners came out and the General Strike began.

Five days later he accompanied Alec to Limehouse 'where, with the same rigid orthodoxy which sends him to Jermyn Street for his shirts and Paris for his fornication, he enrolled himself as a special constable'.[85] A shiver of panic and outrage ran through the wealthier classes when faced with massive industrial action. The Russian Revolution and its subsequent holocaust had occurred only nine years before. Volunteer forces for essential services were grossly oversubscribed at the rallying call to save the nation. Evelyn could scarcely have cared less. 'Yesterday I went to a meeting in Hyde Park where very revolutionary stuff went down frightfully well', he wrote on 3rd May, 'much talk of shooting'.[86]

83. *Ibid.*, 18 April, 1926.
84. *Ibid.*, 28 September, 1925, p. 225. The novel was probably *Mrs Dalloway* (Hogarth Press, 1925).
85. *Ibid.*, 11 May, 1926, p. 252.
86. *Ibid.*, 3 May, 1926, p. 252.

After going to the recruitment centre with Alec, Waugh drove back to Aston Clinton for the beginning of term. Due to the disruption of transport hardly anyone was there. Three days later only fifteen boys had arrived. There was little to do and 'to escape boredom under a colour of duty'[87] he decided to return to London and sign up as a volunteer himself. Crawford saw through this uncharacteristic display of patriotism but felt obliged to release him. As it turned out, Waugh had very little fun from his adventure. For two days he was shunted about, first as a police despatch rider and then a special constable, without ever being given a specific task. He was appalled by the hopeless confusion of arrangements. On his second day the strike was called off. Twenty-four hours later he was back at the school.

That summer term was to prove a turning-point in Waugh's life. He settled back into the easy routine, sometimes not leaving Aston Clinton at all during the week. The weather was generally fine. He happily read *Wind in the Willows* to Edmund. Alastair, having rented a house at East Hendred to get away from his mother, came over for a long week-end on 16th July. On the Sunday, tired by two days of heavy drinking, they drove to Windsor for a quiet dinner. Alastair was still persevering with his apprenticeship at the Shakespeare Head Press and suggested that Evelyn might like to write something for him to print. The idea appealed to Waugh. He dug out those old notes on the Pre-Raphaelites and set to work.

The result, never reprinted, was: *P.R.B.: An Essay on the Pre-Raphaelite Brotherhood 1847–1854*. 'I think it is quite good,' he noted. 'I got it done in four and a half days, in between correcting exam papers.'[88] One of his pupils typed it up and when he returned for the summer holiday five days later he showed the piece to his father. Arthur was delighted. *The Balance* could hardly have assured him of his son's stability; *P.R.B.* was much more in the vein of his own mellow contributions to literary periodicals. When it was eventually printed, he proudly inscribed copies with 'this bibliographical rarity from . . . the author's father'[89] and gave them as Christmas presents. His wayward son was at last showing some signs of self-discipline.

*

Evelyn's prospects did seem marginally brighter. After finishing *The Balance* during the previous August he had sent it to Leonard Woolf at the Hogarth Press. It was soon returned. During the autumn he had unsuccessfully tried various publishers. Then, apparently, he relinquished the struggle and forgot about it. In the spring of 1926, however, Alec was compiling contributions for an anthology

87. *Ibid.*, 11 May, 1926, p. 253.
88. *Ibid.*, 24 July, 1926, p. 257.
89. A copy, inscribed thus, is held in the HRC.

of short stories. The *Georgian Stories* volumes were Chapman and Hall's prose equivalent of Edward Marsh's extremely successful series, *Georgian Poetry*. That year Alec was the editor. He liked Evelyn's piece and agreed to include it for publication the following October. Financial reward was minimal as most of the contributions were reprints but it meant that his work would appear alongside that of Coppard, Gerhardi, Huxley, O'Flaherty, and Gertrude Stein. It was a considerable *coup* for an unknown writer. Strangely, there is no mention of this success in the *Diaries* until the book appeared in print over six months later. Even then, his cursory remarks reveal small concern for its reception.

Alec's offer was too good to refuse but Evelyn may well have felt that it stemmed from charity. This was not the case but, as in his last term at Lancing, he perhaps felt that success was coming to him shop-soiled and second-hand. Possibly Adam Doure's neurotic strugglings for 'detachment' and the story's pretentious linguistic experiments now seemed jejune and embarrassingly intimate. Anyway, he had no intention of spending his life in the family trade of writing. Literary composition up to this time had been for his own amusement or for therapy. He did not feel drawn to it as a means of artistic expression. He was not looking for any breakthrough into the profession of letters.

That summer he spent almost entirely in Alastair's company, first with Mrs Graham on a holiday in Scotland, then with Richard and Elizabeth touring France. Both expeditions were unsatisfactory. 'The Queen Mother' spent most of her time working herself into fits of temper. She had not much cared for Evelyn's joining them and ended by accusing him of consistent rudeness to her. His intimacy with Alastair was an affront to her belligerent maternal authority. But the journey took Evelyn to Edinburgh and York for the first time, both of which he loved. More importantly, it provided experience which he was later to use in his war trilogy and *Brideshead Revisited* (1945) – details of Scottish country house life and a visit to Alastair's old nurse. Waugh admitted to Mrs Graham's being the model for Lady Circumference but in many respects her relationship with Alastair seems to be more subtly reflected in that between Lady Marchmain and Sebastian Flyte. Certainly, the character of Sebastian was drawn heavily from Waugh's knowledge of Alastair.

After three weeks of bickering Waugh must have relished the prospect of France. Alastair and he took a train to Paris but relations between them were strained to breaking point. 'I did not see much of Alastair', Waugh recorded, 'nor did I want to. He is so ignorant about Paris and French. This surprised me. I think I have seen too much of Alastair lately.'[90]

Two other Oxford friends – Hugh Lygon and his elder brother – were in the city. Waugh preferred to spend his day with them, dining and visiting Luna Park. (The latter clearly made an impression, the image of its Great Wheel featuring

90. *Diaries*, 25 August, 1926, p. 263.

prominently in Otto Silenus's speech towards the end of *Decline and Fall*.) Alastair and he parted company and Waugh made his way alone to Tours where he joined Richard and Elizabeth. There they hired a car and engaged in a vigorous cultural tour of the chateaux in the Loire Valley. But Waugh's curiosity was quickly exhausted. Even Chartres Cathedral, a building he came later to venerate as an architectural masterpiece, evoked little enthusiasm. He was more interested in re-reading I. A. Richards's *Principles of Literary Criticism*. He disliked being a tourist in crowded public rooms. When he tried driving a car for the first time he ran over a dog. The car journey back to Le Havre was uncomfortable. Poverty necessitated his taking a second class passage across the Channel, sleeping in the vehicle. Altogether it was a miserable holiday.

Back in London he spent ten days fiercely engaging in the social life he had abandoned. He went for the first time to see the Blackbirds, a negro revue enjoying enormous success in London. He dined with Bill Silk and attended a lesbian party. But it was tame by comparison with his earlier excesses and he did not wish to repeat them: ' . . . they are to be my last days of this sort of life', he wrote on 22nd September, ' – or so I am determined. My mother has given me £150 to pay my debts, and with next term I am resolved to attempt again a life of sobriety, chastity and obedience. On a surer foundation this time I think.'[91]

*

His second campaign against intemperance was undertaken with determination. When he visited Oxford early in October to have his diaries for the year bound by Maltby's, he took with him a wallet full of five-pound notes. The tailors and restaurants did not tempt him. He marched from shop to shop repaying astonished tradesmen and drove abruptly back to Aston Clinton. When he travelled to London during that week it was to order a smart suit and to join the Times Book Club. Alastair was sending him proofs of *P.R.B.*; Chapman's had paid for *The Balance*. For the first time for several years his bank account was in credit. His vanity scourged, he was more prepared to adopt the moderate aims of a literary schoolmaster.

In keeping with this, towards the end of October he wrote to Kegan Paul, the publishers of a series of short books, *Today and Tomorrow*. Waugh offered them one on *Noah; Or The Future of Intoxication*, possibly based on the idea he had mentioned earlier to Acton of 'a book about Silenus'. To his amazement they agreed to the proposition, although no contract was entered into.

He started writing enthusiastically in a 'mannered and literary'[92] style. But by December he was recording: 'I have had an idea or two for finishing *Noah* but lack the energy to put them into form. . . . I have had a lot of work to do lately

---

91. *Ibid.*, 22 September, 1926, p. 265.
92. *Ibid.*, 10 November, 1926, p. 270.

besides *Noah*, which drags along somehow and I am very tired . . . I am tired of words and want a holiday badly when I shall read and write nothing but just see things and try to draw a little.'[93] Alastair, having finished *P.R.B.*, had abandoned printing for the Diplomatic Service and had gone to live in Athens. When the end of term came Crawford gave Waugh his usual £40 and, after haggling, added £10 more. It was just enough to get Evelyn to Greece.

*

*Noah* was rushed to a conclusion in Hampstead and dispatched to Kegan's. On Christmas Eve he embarked on the most ambitious adventure of his life so far. He took a train to Marseilles then boarded the *Patris II*, cruising eastwards through the Mediterranean. 'I sit all day either in the spray on deck or the heat below', he wrote, 'and doze and read *The Varieties of Religious Experience*[94] and attempt drawings for a book I intend doing to be called the Annals of Constitutional Monarchy.'[95] That 'book' was never written. Possibly the title was just a private joke to cheer his jaded spirits. For the tranquil seclusion he had sought seemed no nearer than at Aston Clinton. The boat was overheated and overcrowded. He was pestered by cheery shipboard acquaintances. One American's conversation he found 'vulgar and boastful and blasphemous'.[96] The use of that last adjective and his reading matter suggest that he was beginning to enquire seriously into mysticism as an alternative means of escape into that 'third dimension' beyond the harlequinade. Von Hügel's letters must have interested him.

Athens did little to relieve his depression. It was not the antique curiosity he had hoped for but brashly cosmopolitan. Alastair lived in a modern flat with Leonard Bower, an Attaché at the British Embassy. The walls smelt of plaster and the talk reeked of homosexuality: 'The flat is usually full of dreadful Dago youths . . . with blue chins and greasy clothes who sleep with the English colony for 25 drachmas a night.'[97] The image of the seedy, expatriate world, like Luna Park, became branded on his memory. It was seventeen years before he transformed it into the *ménage* of Sebastian and Kurt, re-located in Fez, for the Moroccan scenes of *Brideshead*.

Alastair was the perfect host. He drove Evelyn to the tourist sites in the diplomatic car, bought him dinners and introduced him to his friends. But Evelyn was all the time morose. He felt estranged. Alastair's life was no longer his. They were bound to each other now only by loyalty to the past. It took just seven days before Waugh, 'overwhelmed by claustrophobia',[98] set out alone on a circuitous

93. *Ibid.*, 6 December, 1926, p. 272.
94. William James's book (1902) deals with the psychology of conversion.
95. *Diaries*, 26 December, 1926, p. 273.
96. *Ibid.*, 26 December, 1926, p. 273.
97. *Ibid.*, 1 January, 1927, p. 275.
98. *Ibid.*, 5 January, 1927, p. 276.

route home. 'I am afraid I have inherited overmuch of my father's homely sentiments,' he recorded. 'The truth is that I do not really like being abroad much. I want to see as much as I can during this holiday and from February shut myself up in the British Isles.'[99]

Alastair filled a flask with brandy, supplied toilet paper and razor blades for Evelyn's journey, took him to Piraeus, and drove off. It was a stormy afternoon and a melancholy one for Waugh. The boat for Patros and Delphi did not leave for five hours. 'I walked about in the mud of Piraeus for a little, sorry that the Athenian adventure had been such a failure.'[100] In his bag he carried Alastair's parting gift, a lovely but worm-eaten ikon. Perhaps he saw it as symbolic. His departure marked the end of a wrong turning in his life: he now knew beyond doubt that he was not homosexual.

From Olympia he sailed to Corfu 'in a vile ship called the *Yperoke*, . . . travelling second class in barely conceivable discomfort'.[101] Two hours there gave him enough local colour to provide a situation for Margot's villa in *Decline and Fall*. There was a delightful aura of luxury about the island. But he could not stop. Resources were low. He moved on to Brindisi and caught a train to Rome where he mooched about contentedly for three days with a guide-book. In his eagerness to see the city he overspent and was forced into the embarrassing necessity of cabling to his father for money. An excruciating two-day rail journey without a couchette to Paris and London concluded his journey. Resources, by this time, consisted of ten francs and a bottle of Vichy water. On 15th January he arrived at Underhill, exhausted, dirty and starving to find his father in bed with influenza and a letter from Kegan's refusing *Noah*.

His 'tether' was considerably longer than it used to be. The refusal was 'rather a blow as I was counting on the money for it', but not a disaster; 'perhaps it is a good thing. I was not pleased with it.'[102] He spent two mornings reviving his spirits at the Royal Academy's Flemish exhibition, had a quiet week at home and then returned to school.

A new, rather timid, master, a Mr Attwell, had arrived. At first sight of him Waugh despaired. A dull teetotaller was not his idea of a companion so he initiated a playfully malicious campaign of subversion. The corruption of Attwell became his chief diversion. Most evenings he would take him down to the Bell and pay for the drinks. After three weeks he succeeded in making the poor man sick. Attwell had been prone to engage Waugh in tedious conversations about education. He was cured of that and, with the barriers of formality breached, they became friends.

99. *Ibid.*, 4 January, 1927, p. 276.
100. *Ibid.*, 5 January, 1927, p. 276.
101. *Labels* (1930), p. 156.
102. *Diaries*, 24 January, 1927, p. 280.

Another new arrival was also to prove significant. Waugh first describes this replacement matron as 'admirable'. She was attractive and, as she had known some of Evelyn's friends, willing to give him preferential treatment. Little perquisites of food were slipped his way. Evelyn, unfortunately, mistook kindness for encouragement. On 19th February he and Attwell adjourned to the Bell with the usual consequences and, rolling back, encountered the matron. Waugh later told his friends that he had tried to 'seduce her in French'. Probably he did little more than to racket around and make a few lewd suggestions. But it was enough. The next day she went to the headmaster to file a complaint. The *Diaries* complete the story:

> Most of the last days have been profitless. A man wrote to me from Oxford offering to pay me 10 guineas for a story to put in a book he edits called *The New Decameron*. . . .
>
> Next Thursday I am to visit a Father Underhill about being a parson. Last night I was very drunk. How odd those two sentences seem together.
>
> About five minutes after I wrote the last sentence, while Attwell and I were sitting over the fire laughing at our drunkenness of the night before, Crawford suddenly arrived and sacked us both, me on the spot, Attwell to leave at the end of the term. Apparently that matron has been making trouble. . . . I packed hurriedly . . . and slipped away feeling rather like a housemaid who has been caught stealing gloves. I rang up my parents to apprise them of my coming, and dined in a very sorrowful household.[103]

*

Abruptly and ingloriously his second phase of attempted rectitude was in ruins. He could not bear to tell his mother the truth, informing her instead that he had been dismissed for drunkenness. The next day, in a moment of despair, he recorded: 'It seems to me the time has arrived to set about being a man of letters.'[104] But he was not serious.

The *Decameron* request had come from Michael Sadleir who, like G. B. Stern, had recognised the originality of *The Balance*.[105] During the following week Waugh spent two days writing a 'story about a duke' for him. Again there is no mention in the *Diaries* of its publication. It appeared later in the year as 'The Tutor's Tale. A House of Gentlefolks',[106] an amusing and macabre account of a young man, recently sent down from Oxford, who is engaged as a tutor to an adolescent

103. *Ibid.*, 20 February, 1927, p. 281.
104. *Ibid.*, 21 February, 1927, p. 281.
105. Cf. *MBE*, p. 179.
106. *The New Decameron: The Fifth Day*, ed. Hugh Chesterman (Oxford, Basil Blackwell, 1927), pp. 101–16. Sykes mistakenly suggests that 'it may be presumed . . . it was not published' (p. 72).

and supposedly lunatic Marquess. The latter (family name: 'Stayle') is ultimately revealed as the only sane person in the household, trapped by dotty relations and prevented from contacting the outside world. There is some excellent, unmannered writing and Waugh's ear for dialogue is precise. It is, nevertheless, an occasional piece, more in the vein of his Oxford stories than *The Balance* or the fiction that was to follow. There was nothing here to promise prosperity.

He was beginning to drift again. The day after finishing 'The Tutor's Tale' he kept his appointment with Father Underhill who, quite rightly, dismissed Evelyn's vocation to the Church as frivolous. He left the ecclesiastical tea table for dinner at Carew's flat in Ladbroke Grove. There he met his friend's fiancée, Viola Garvin. As reviews editor of the *Observer*, she was to prove a useful literary contact. 'We went later', he records, 'to the Blackbirds and called on Florence Mills and other niggers and negresses in their dressing-rooms. Then to a night club called Victor's to see another nigger – Leslie Hutchinson.'[107] Lesley Hutchinson, the pianist and singer, was the lover of Zena Naylor and a possible model for 'Chokey' in *Decline and Fall*. Waugh disliked this association with Jazz Age black Americans; he had no ear for music, he felt superior to coloured people. But the fashionable world had taken them up and he was too uncertain of himself to disregard the fashionable world.

The entry is a typical record of his life until the early summer. With no direction or ambition, he was back in the vortex of over-drinking and over-spending. Sylvia Gosse, the artist and daughter of Edmund, was showing an interest in him but he could not reciprocate her affection. She was twenty-two years his senior. Harold Acton had returned from Paris and taken an elegant flat in John Street, Adelphi. Oliver Messel gave elaborate parties at his studio in St John's Wood. Sacheverell Sitwell, whom he now came to know better, had published *Southern Baroque Art* (1924) and his *German Baroque Art* (1927) was about to appear. Waugh lived in one room in his father's house, an unemployed private schoolmaster with no money, lover or prospects. But he would not release his hold on this brilliant world; he would not be forgotten.

A series of temporary jobs followed. In early March he joined the staff of a state school in Notting Hill as a replacement for five weeks. The indignity and instability of his position resulted, predictably, in neurotic class-consciousness: 'The school in Notting Hill is quite awful. All the masters drop their aitches and spit in the fire and scratch their genitals. The boys have close-cropped heads and steel-rimmed spectacles wound about with worsted. They pick their noses and scream at each other in a cockney accent.'[108] He was just round the corner from Carew's flat and used often to stay there overnight. The social life it represented was a bitter contrast.

*

107. *Diaries*, 28 February, 1927, p. 281.
108. *Ibid.*, 7 March, 1927, p. 282.

On 7th April he recorded:

> The job in Holland Park[109] is over but it does not seem at all difficult
> to earn a living. I am in some doubt at the moment whether to go on
> the *Express* or write a biography that Duckworth show some interest in.
> I have been to such a lot of parties and spent such a lot of money. I
> have met such a nice girl called Evelyn Gardner and renewed friendship
> with Peter Quennell and Robert Byron.[110]

Quite suddenly his career seems to have taken a new turn. But the blithe self-
confidence of the diary is a little deceptive. National newspapers regularly engaged
young graduates to work 'on space' at less than union rates. It was an equable
arrangement. The newspapers hoped for the occasional 'discovery'; the young
men acquired experience. The temporary contract would usually be terminated
after a few weeks. Waugh knew perfectly well that little hope lay in that direction
and, moreover, he did not want to write the book. His optimism arose mainly
from the meeting with Evelyn Gardner.

She-Evelyn, as she became known, fulfilled his highest expectations. She was
pretty, unaffected, vivacious with an enthusiastic, child-like nature. At the same
time she was an intelligent, well-bred 'modern' young lady with cropped hair and
literary aspirations of her own. When he first encountered her (probably at a
party in Carew's flat), she and Pansy Pakenham both had rooms in a bed-and-
breakfast house in Ebury Street. Pansy was Frank Pakenham's sister and involved
in an affair with the painter, Henry Lamb. A little later, much to the distress of
their parents, the two debutantes shared a flat together. It was a brave move for
unmarried women in those days. Waugh admired their independence. The Iris
Storm archetype described first by Michael Arlen in *The Green Hat* (1924) had
always fascinated him. There was much of it in Olivia but she was morose and
unapproachable. She-Evelyn's bright, open personality attracted him powerfully
by contrast and before long it became clear that the feeling was mutual.

The offer from Duckworth's had come about through Anthony Powell. After
coming down from Oxford the previous summer, Powell had taken a junior post
in the publishing house with a view to buying into a partnership later. Gerald
Duckworth (now infamous as the relative who fumbled with the young Virginia
Woolf) was in 1927 a sprightly, garrulous middle-aged man, interested in putting
money into 'young Oxford'. Powell was a useful contact. Harold Acton and the
Sitwells were already on Duckworth's list. Powell's job was partly to encourage
talented writers from his generation – Yorke (Green), Connolly, Byron – to join
them.

He had not known Waugh well at Oxford but they met again during a particu-

109. Holland Park is next door to Notting Hill Gate.
110. *Diaries*, 7 April, 1927, p. 284.

[ 134 ]

larly dreary period in Powell's life, early in 1927, and became close friends. Evelyn would take him back to Underhill for cold suppers. 'On these pleasant North End Road evenings, Arthur Waugh would tell literary anecdotes at the dinner-table; Mrs Waugh (whose quiet exterior suggested much inner firmness of purpose) scarcely speaking at all, slipping out at the first opportunity. When the company moved from the dining room Arthur Waugh might continue to chat for a minute or two, then also retire, probably to work. Waugh and I would sit and talk. I usually stayed until nearly midnight, when a last bus could be caught to the neighbourhood of Piccadilly.'[111] Powell was then living amid the prostitutes of Shepherd's Market, where he was later to place the young hero of *A Dance to the Music of Time*.

At some stage Waugh showed him *P.R.B.* The slim volume (25 pages) was passed to Gerald Duckworth who thought it admirable. The centenary of Rossetti's birth was due the next year. Waugh, always with an eye for the main chance, suggested that he might write a biography to coincide with this. Duckworth agreed, as did Tom Balston, Powell's immediate superior. But Waugh did not enter into a contract at this stage. He would see how the *Express* job worked out first before committing himself to such labour.

Waugh was quite happy careering about the metropolis to accidents and parties for the gossip column of the paper. He met another delightful girl, Inez Holden, also on the *Express*, a torrential talker and excellent company. (Later she too became a writer and a close friend of Orwell; it was Waugh who introduced her to Powell.) Evelyn was in higher spirits than he had been since Oxford. But by the end of the fifth week it was clear that he was not to be a 'discovery'. Only one piece written by him was ever published, and there was a rumour that he stole the story from another paper. Rather grudgingly, he accepted Duckworth's commission. Against normal practice, they offered an advance of £50 to this unknown author. Arthur Waugh shook his head gloomily: 'Balston will never see that book', he muttered. 'I suppose I shall have to make it good.'[112]

Certainly Waugh found it difficult to begin and his comment in the Julian Jebb interview that he 'rushed off and rushed it off'[113] is inaccurate. The money had been spent in a week and the size of the task depressed him. After being sacked from the *Express* at the end of his sixth week, he took a month's holiday. His parents had disappeared on the Blue Train for a holiday in Nîmes, leaving him alone in the house with a substantial sum to meet expenses. He had bought high-quality, monogrammed foolscap sheets. But he could not settle to writing. He left London for a week of country house life then returned for Alec's farewell

111. *To Keep the Ball Rolling. The Memoirs of Anthony Powell*, Vol. II, *Messengers of Day* (Heinemann, 1978), p. 21.
112. *MBE*, p. 180.
113. *Writers*, p. 108.

cocktail party. Alec was off to see a woman in Tahiti. At this gathering, Evelyn met Brendan Bracken for the first time, later the 'model' for Rex Mottram in *Brideshead*. 'I feel awkward with men like that', he later confided to his brother, 'but I wonder if he wouldn't be right for Olivia. Vulgar but not common.'[114] Waugh was still not cured of his unrequited love for her. Much of the pain in that relationship was transferred to his description of Julia, Mottram's lover, in the novel.

On the spur of the moment, Waugh decided to accompany Alec who planned to spend a few days in Nîmes with his parents, *en route* to Marseilles. It was a rare period of intimacy for the brothers, and their last evening in the *Vieux Port* supplied yet more material for *Decline and Fall*. 'Saw Alec off . . .', he noted, 'after amusing evening beginning decorously at Basso's with caviare and Meursault and ending less creditably in the slums. A street called the Rue Ventomargy is said to be the toughest in Europe.'[115] All the details found their way into the fiction. It was a formative experience in his worldly brother's company, and possibly the first time Evelyn had slept with a woman.

With Alec gone, he took the train to Les Baux to spend five more days with his parents. They remembered it as one of the happiest times they had spent with him. Evelyn was relaxed and convivial. The awkwardness between himself and Arthur dropped away temporarily and, refreshed and exhilarated, Waugh returned to London and the empty house. Very little of the money was left. There was now no escape from that blank paper. 'After a month's holiday', he recorded tersely on 1st July, 1927, 'I have settled down to work on the Rossetti book.'[116]

114.  *MBE*, p. 182.
115.  *Diaries*, 1 July, 1927, p. 285.
116.  *Ibid.*, 1 July, 1927, p. 284.

# V

# *The Claim of Youth: 1927–1929*

'I have finished about 12,000 words of the book on Rossetti without much real difficulty', he noted three weeks later. 'I think it will be fairly amusing.'[1] But London was full of distractions. Alastair had returned from Greece; Olivia, morbid and depressed, began to occupy too much of his time. Worse still, her melancholy was affecting him. He understood his own weakness now. If the book were ever to be finished, he would need to retreat somewhere and concentrate his energies. It was a pattern he found necessary throughout his literary career.

The Abingdon Arms was the obvious choice. This small village pub north of Oxford had been a second home to himself and to Alastair as undergraduates. He knew the landlady and the regulars and could secure a cheap room there without difficulty. If he needed other company, Barford House was within easy reach and Francis Crease was now living nearby at Marston. 'I came here', he recorded in Beckley on 23rd August, 'rather suddenly ten days ago. . . . ':

> Since then I have been happier and felt much better than I have for months. I go into Oxford most days to work in the Union Library. It is very quiet and nice without all those gawky young men. I have written 40,000 words of my book and sent them off to be typed and feel easier in my mind about it. . . . Beckley is much altered . . . .The central figure nowadays seems to be a scorbutic baronet called Wilfred Moon.[2] He keeps arriving in a rather smart car . . . and stands drinks all round and makes jokes. He is just the sort of man whom Chris [Hollis] and I would have adored four years ago. I must say I find him rather a bore when I want to work. Besides I have lost the capacity for swilling down pint after pint of watery beer.[3]

The romance of Oxford had at last faded. A year later Waugh noted in a review: 'Mr Douglas . . . has now resolutely turned his back on the idiosyncrasies of his fellow men for the abiding delights of scholarship and imagination.'[4] Waugh had

1. *Diaries*, 22 July, 1927, p. 285.
2. The 4th Baronet; later ADC to the Governer of Fiji.
3. *Diaries*, 23 August, 1927, pp. 286–7.
4. 'Turning Over New Leaves', *Vogue*, 17 October, 1928, 59; review (amongst others) of Norman Douglas, *In the Beginning* (Chatto and Windus, 1928); *EAR*, pp. 40–3.

a similar objective in 1927. He often went to call on Crease whom he found 'particularly charming and witty in a way I had forgotten'.[5] He was reading copiously in the field of biography and art criticism. The aesthetic life seemed at last to be within his grasp.

As always, though, peaceful routine was at odds with his impatient temperament. The day after that diary entry he was writing: 'Today and for the last two days I have done no work. I feel somehow that with those first three chapters my work at Beckley is over and I must go somewhere else.'[6] The colophons of the pre-war novels testify to the same restlessness. He worked quickly, against the threat of that tide of boredom which would inevitably overpower him after a couple of weeks. Then he would move on. From Beckley he went to Barford for three days but could do nothing under the 'high tension'[7] of Mrs Graham's tantrums. Forced back to Underhill he found himself even less able to write: 'How I detest this house and how ill I feel in it. The whole place volleys and thunders with traffic. I can't sleep or work. . . . Mother is away at Midsomer Norton where Aunt Trissie is dying. The telephone bell is continually ringing, my father scampering up and down stairs, Gaspard [the family poodle] barking, the gardener rolling the gravel under the window and all the time the traffic. Another week of this will drive me mad.'[8]

In the middle of that entry there is the brief but significant note: 'I reviewed the books and have begun a comic novel.' Alec Waugh suggests in his memoirs that his brother began *Decline and Fall* to raise money for his marriage to Evelyn Gardner. Certainly he continued it for that reason. But its genesis appears to have pre-dated this motive. He seems to have started it for his own amusement, as light relief from the biography and review work for the *Bookman*. It is no coincidence, surely, that the same night, unable to sleep, he had sat up reading through his Lancing diaries. *Decline and Fall* contains strong elements of autobiography. In many respects it was a comic version of *The Balance*.

Money was short. He made a little by selling his review books at half-price but he could not allow himself to luxuriate in the belief that he was really beginning the life of a leisured *littérateur*. All the time he was actively seeking more regular employment. Fortunately for literature, he was refused by another headmaster and left with nothing much to do but write. He interviewed Hall Caine[9] and May Morris[10] and through September and October continued to move between various households – Barford House, the Bell at Aston Clinton, and Underhill. The last reference to the biography (in the *Diaries*) concerns the visit to Miss Morris on

5.   *Diaries*, 23 August, 1927, p. 287.
6.   *Ibid.*, 24 August, 1927, p. 287.
7.   *Ibid.*, 26 August, 1927, p. 288.
8.   *Ibid.*, 3 September, 1927, p. 289.
9.   Novelist (1853 – 1931); friend of Rossetti.
10.   The daughter of Jane, William Morris's wife.

6th October. The account of this appears towards the end of the Rossetti manuscript. We can assume, then, that Waugh had finished it by the end of the month, probably before.

In late September he was already writing to Powell at Duckworth's enclosing the four line-diagrams demonstrating the 'rhythmic unity' of Rossetti's composition. By this time he had become deeply involved with the work: 'I have made three failures at The Question and am not sure it is right yet. I like The Wedding of St George much the best.'[11] The book was published in the spring of 1928. When one reviewer stated that 'Mr Waugh evidently values that part of his book in which he confounds the modern school of art criticism',[12] he was most certainly correct.

The 'school' referred to was that of Bloomsbury, and in particular, Clive Bell and Roger Fry. The Hogarth Press had produced a series of essays, three of which – E. M. Forster's *Anonymity*, Hubert Waley's *The Revival of Aesthetics*, and Fry's *The Artist and Psycho-Analysis* – had intrigued Waugh. He addressed their arguments directly in his book. Fry and Waley argued for a concept of 'significant form' in defence of abstract art and what they said came very close to thoughts Waugh had himself expressed in the *Diaries* and in that precocious schoolboy article, 'In Defence of Cubism'. The representational aspect of a painting, Bloomsbury suggested, was irrelevant. What mattered was the underlying structure, the 'rhythmic unity' (to use Waugh's phrase) of the forms depicted. Waugh largely agreed with this. In his book he talks of 'the pellucid excellencies of Picasso'.[13] He was not then the artistic conservative he was to become; quite the reverse. But Rossetti presented a problem.

'Approached from this standpoint', he wrote, 'Rossetti with all his "temperament" and "inspiration", is nothing but a melancholy old fraud. If art is restricted to the splendid succession of European painting and to such works of negro sculpture as may be held to have some kinship with it, Rossetti is not "a real artist"[14] either in achievement or intention. The last thing he wished to do was to express the necessary relation of forms.'[15] Aesthetic discussion was one of the few things about which Waugh was consistently serious. And the Rossetti paradox was particularly tantalising because, as he progressed with his study he began to see himself reflected in the artist's character.

Waugh describes his subject as:

the baffled and very tragic figure of an artist born into an age devoid

11. Unpublished ALS to Anthony Powell [late September 1927], from Barford House, Warwick.
12. 'Reader's Reports', *L & L*, July 1928, 141–2.
13. *Rossetti*, p. 14.
14. Fry's term in *The Artist and Psycho-Analysis*.
15. *Rossetti*, p. 223.

of artistic standards; a man of the South, sensual, indolent, and richly versatile, exiled in the narrow, scrambling, specialised life of a Northern city; [16] a mystic without a creed; a Catholic without the discipline or consolation of the Church; a life between the rocks and the high road, like the scrub of a Southern hillside, sombre, aromatic, and impenetrable.[17]

The quotation could serve as an epigraph to this volume. It describes no-one more accurately than the young Evelyn Waugh. This most English of Englishmen leant, temperamentally, to the warmth and exuberance of the Mediterranean. Northern Europe he came to associate with desiccated Protestant rationalism. Italy was the home of his heroes – Acton, Firbank, Norman Douglas – and of Sacheverell Sitwell's extravagant baroque. Waugh's later allegiance to Rome had more emotion in it than he cared to admit.

The resemblances between Waugh's portrait of Rossetti and Waugh himself were extraordinary to the point of being prophetic. In later years both became addicted to heavy doses of chloral and alchohol in an effort to combat insomnia and suffered equally from bouts of persecution mania; both continued deep platonic relationships with other men's wives. (A final and irrelevant coincidence is that they both died on Easter Day.) In 1927 Waugh clearly recognised a kindred spirit in his subject. He notes the artist's insensitivity to music and to the beauties of landscape, a business-like attitude to the sale of his art, a love of intrigue, his truculence and inconsistency. In almost every particular Waugh shared his tastes and disabilities. Both author and subject were influenced by fathers who were professional literary men; both had sensible, less erratic brothers; both were deeply disappointed in love. Catherine Waugh was small and slim but, with this one qualification, her son might have been describing her when he wrote: 'Mrs Rossetti was practical, sympathetic, devoted, an excellent housekeeper, pious, possessed of great rectitude and considerable learning, of ample and matronly appearance.'[18] Other possible comparisons riddle the book. The biography was in many respects a reflective portrait. Rossetti's was a parallel case and he used him to rationalise his own discontents.

His ultimate assessment of Rossetti's 'failure' is particularly interesting in this respect:

> It is not so much that as a man he was a bad man – mere lawless wickedness has frequently been the concomitant of the highest genius

16. The Southern/Northern vocabulary had been borrowed from Fry's *Flemish Art, A Critical Survey* (Chatto & Windus, 1927), a book Waugh had been reading while preparing *Rossetti*. Cf. *Diaries*, 24 August, 1927, p. 288: 'Lent Crease Roger Fry's *Flemish Art*.'
17. *Rossetti*, pp. 13–14.
18. *Ibid.*, p. 16.

– but there was fatally lacking in him that *essential rectitude* that underlies the serenity of all really great art. The sort of unhappiness that beset him was not the sort of unhappiness that does beset a great artist; all his brooding about magic and suicide are symptomatic not so much of genius as of mediocrity. There is a spiritual inadequacy, a sense of ill-organisation about all he did.[19]

The personal association he felt for his subject had, surely, a great deal to do with this judgement. Speaking of his own failure as a graphic artist in the interview with Jebb he stated that 'I failed as I had neither the talent nor the application – I didn't have the moral qualities'.[20] The discipline of writing this book was Waugh's attempt to rectify 'ill-organisation'. The years of immaturity – of *The Temple* and *The Balance* and 'brooding about . . . suicide' – were behind him. He now felt that he was in a position to avoid Rossetti's mistakes.

Waugh's main interests still lay in the field of arts and crafts. During the composition of the biography he wrote a preface for a privately printed edition of Crease's designs. In this he warmly praises Crease for 'the emancipation of the essential structure of design from its accidental resemblances' ('significant form' versus representation again) and states that only one man 'could suitably have undertaken to write a preface for this collection of temperate and exalted designs; that is John Ruskin'.[21]

Waugh envied the Pre-Raphaelites' inter-disciplinary approach as painters, scribes, decorators, architects and printers; above all as craftsmen modestly eschewing individual indulgence for the reputation of 'The Shop'. The highest aesthetic achievement in his view was to produce work both 'temperate and exalted'. Rossetti, with his ' "temperament" and "inspiration" ', did not fit happily into this placid, workmanlike approach. That was his essential failing. Yet he presented a powerful example of the spontaneous imagination.

According to Waugh, composition was not, for Rossetti, the result of a conscious mental process relating various 'forms'; 'shapes rose within him' and he wanted to express them in paint. That was all there was to it and Waugh could not avoid sympathy with this approach. It was the way his own imagination operated. Somehow, he suggests, we shall have to combine both notions if we are ever to develop a satisfactory theory of the creative process. In the manuscript he wrote: ' . . . it is probable that in the future a comprehensive aesthetic may be based on [the investigations of the Gestalt psychologists], and that we shall be able to regard the artist quite simply as one in whom states of mind are translated directly

19.  *Ibid.*, pp. 226–7.
20.  *Writers*, p. 108.
21.  *Thirty-Four Decorative Designs By Francis Crease* (M. R. Mowbray, 1927). Sixty copies were 'printed for private circulation'. Waugh's preface, pp. v–viii, was written at Barford House, 1–3 October, 1927.

into visible forms.'[22] The printed version is more cautious: 'It is not possible', he says, 'in the present state of psychology, to produce this as a brand-new, cast-iron system of aesthetics'; the psychological approach has, he says, 'certain obvious inadequacies'.[23] He did not know the answer but it was essential for him to tackle the problem. Until he had clarified the issues, he would not be in a position seriously to attempt creative work of his own.

Like Rossetti, Waugh felt he had been born into an age devoid of contemporary 'masters'. Virginia Woolf and Huxley left him largely unmoved; contemporary painting, having lost its initial attraction of aggressive vitality, was receding into the incomprehensible. The artist, he began to believe, must not only translate but communicate. One attitude he now firmly rejected. 'To the muddled Victorian mind', he says, 'it seemed vaguely suitable that the artist should be melancholy, morbid, uncontrolled, and generally slightly deranged.'[24] Waugh's book insists that this 'romance of decay' must be abandoned. The description exactly fits Waugh's earlier temperamental instability. He no longer felt himself subject to it or to the need to express emotional anarchy in art. But this left him in something of an aesthetic void.

The books he used in preparing *Rossetti* were heavily scored and annotated. Exasperated comments at slovenly thinking block the margins: 'Hunt still does not distinguish between *artistic sincerity* and the sincerity of believing faithfully in the truth of the events and emotions portrayed. I use "emotions portrayed" deliberately not in the sense of the aesthetic emotion implicit in the work but the ordinary human emotions of pity etc. likely to be excited through the obvious associations wt. the incident illustrated.'[25] He found it stimulating to knock logical impurities from Hunt's assumptions, but in the end it was a dispiriting, negative business because he had not yet found an art form through which to express himself. Somehow, he knew, he must combine Rossetti's passion with Fry's intellectual austerity. His emotions consistently directed him towards drawing and painting but he lacked enough talent to achieve the high standards his perfectionism demanded. His intellect allowed him to write well but he did not enjoy it. The last words of the *Rossetti* manuscript are subscribed: 'The End. Thank God.'

One last piece of marginalia should be noted. Waugh underlined Hunt's: 'I argued that the appeal we made could be strengthened by adopting the knowledge which human penetration had acquired' and wrote beside it: 'Hunt is essentially

22. MS, pp. 2–3; HRC.
23. *Rossetti*, p. 3.
24. *Ibid.*, p. 226.
25. In Holman Hunt's two-volume *Pre-Raphaelitism and the Pre-Raphaelite Brotherhood* (Chapman and Hall, 1913), Vol. 2, p. 62. Waugh's copy was the second edition, signed and dated 'Aston Clinton November 1927'. It is part of his library now kept at the HRC.

Victorian, Rossetti definitely not.'[26] This is a value judgement in favour of Rossetti. In the Jebb interview Waugh stated: 'An artist must be a reactionary. He has to stand out against the tenor of his age and not go flopping along; he must offer some little opposition. Even the great Victorian artists were all anti-Victorian, despite the pressures to conform.'[27] Throughout his adult life, the Victorian consciousness was characterised for Waugh by its futile belief in 'progress'. Even in 1927 he disliked Hunt's assumption that 'knowledge' and 'human penetration' represented qualitative improvement. It was, he thought, the characteristic fallacy of those 'fathers' and 'old men' who had been responsible for the war.

All this had been demolished in the Lancing editorial and his attack on the fallacies of Victorian humanism continued unabated all his life. But if he could not accept Hunt's humanist aesthetic – that art should be seen as a function of 'human penetration' and thus act as an extension of the dominant moral values of society – Waugh began to find something in Hunt which the erratic Rossetti lacked. Rossetti he viewed as a latter-day Romantic promoting a heroic and anarchic individualism; Hunt, he suggests, saw the individual as a fragment of a larger process. As an argument about Romanticism in general it is facile but the terms in which he sets out the problem throw an interesting light on Waugh's own assumptions.

The affinity between Waugh and Rossetti stretched to seeing in the latter's historical period problems of cultural development:

> There was something wrong with a generation which flocked ... to giggle at General Tom Thumb, while Haydon was dying of neglected vanity. Indeed the transition from aristocracy to industrialism came very near to crushing out English Art altogether; the present generation is confronted by the incalculable consequences of the transition from industrialism to democracy.[28]

Waugh had little time for the 'romantic' either in Rossetti's age or his own:

> Among the Victorians, and ... among most modern people too, there were two main attitudes to the rest of the universe. There was the breezy, common-sense attitude to life typified by Millais as 'one damned thing after another', and there was the solemn perception of process, typified by Holman Hunt, an attitude which saw the earth as part of a vast astronomical system, and man's life as a brief phase of its decay, and any individual life as infinitesimally small and unimportant except as an inseparable part of the whole – a system that appeared comforting or terrifying as the observer was a Tennyson or a Stevenson. Most

26. *Ibid.*, p. 104.
27. *Writers*, p. 113.
28. *Rossetti*, p. 22.

intelligent men took this attitude when they took the trouble to think about it, and based the normal activities of their life upon the first assumption. The romantic outlook sees life as a series of glowing and unrelated systems, in which the component parts are explicable and true only in terms of themselves; in which the stars are just as big and as near as they look, and '*rien n'est vrai que le pittoresque*'.[29]

The passage is vital to any attempt to describe this complex transitional phase in Waugh's life. It clearly indicates a movement away from the despairing austerity of *The Balance*. Human experience remained an incomprehensible series of shifting façades. An 'intelligent man' would 'base the normal activities' of his life on the assumption that there was no sense to be made of it. But this was now seen as an unsatisfactory philosophical approach. It represented nothing more than self-defensive pragmatism. And at this point Waugh parts company with Rossetti and aligns himself with 'the mystical . . . habit of mind', 'the solemn perception of process'. The quotation takes us back to the earlier stages of his intellectual development – to the 'objectivity' espoused in the Lancing editorial, and to the arguments of *The Balance* which circle round the insignificance of individual action. In this Adam moves beyond the 'bodiless harlequinade' in which it could be said that 'the component parts are explicable and true only in terms of themselves', and into a 'third dimension beyond it'. In 1926 this escape from absurdity represented little more than sceptical dissociation. By 1927 Waugh was beginning to see himself much more as 'a mystic without a creed; a Catholic without the discipline or consolation of the Church'.

Clarifying the issue, however, did nothing to resolve his mental confusion for, marooned in fashionable agnosticism, he remained the bright young man clubbing his elders' simplistic beliefs while having nothing with which to replace them. *Rossetti* offers intriguing clues as to the theological direction his mind would take less than three years later. At this stage, though, his arguments were little more than absorbing intellectual exercise. He was young; he was in love; he had just written a book. He was not, as he later became, frightened and disgusted by the inconsistency of human behaviour. The potential terrors of a godless, uncontrolled universe could still be defused by art and by a sense of humour. Both offered solace, temporary resolution of conflict. In both he could lose himself in protective fantasy. It is no coincidence that his committed struggles with aesthetic paradoxes correspond so closely with theological argument. Art was, in a sense, his surrogate religion in the desert of rationalism. It was insufficient; it did not satisfy those longings for ultimate order. But, like so many of his generation, he derived a powerful sense of excitement from nervous instability and he was not prepared to exchange indiscipline for the 'consolation' of formal belief. He looked on himself as a buccaneer, an opportunist, ready for anything.

29.  *Ibid.*, p. 52.

His work on the Pre-Raphaelites revived other old enthusiasms. He refused to regard the biography as the inauguration of a literary career. 'As you know', he wrote to Harold Acton in April 1928, 'I am not proud of the book. I think it has some eloquent phrases but there are few pages I can read without a shiver at some place or other.'[30] He did not want to spend his life in such uncongenial employment. Instead, he decided on one more concerted effort to return to the world of the hand-craftsman.

\*

In October 1927 Anthony Powell was attending a course at Holborn Polytechnic. As part of his training as a publisher Duckworth's required him to study printing technique and several evenings a week he would go to classes in Southampton Row. After Powell had acted as intermediary in Waugh's preliminary negotiations with his firm, the business was now largely in the hands of his superior, Tom Balston. Powell had neither seen nor heard from Waugh for several months until, one night in October, he caught sight of someone hurrying down the corridor towards him. It was Evelyn.

Both expressed astonishment at meeting in such odd circumstances. Powell was intrigued. What on earth was Waugh doing there? How was the book going? Waugh seemed deeply pre-occupied. His answers were brief. 'Carpentry ... Tolstoy and all that.'[31] Modesty forbade reference to his studies as 'cabinet-making' but there could be no doubt that he was deeply committed to them. During the day he planed boards and drew projections; the evenings were spent learning wood carving. Significantly, it was only the carving that failed to intrigue him. He revelled in the workmanlike discipline of his studies and was perfectly happy in once again having the tools of a trade at his disposal. The school (properly named the Central School of Arts and Crafts) had been founded in 1896, a product of the Art Workers' Guild. It drew its inspiration from Ruskin, Morris and Philip Webb, all characters who figure in *Rossetti*. In his small way he saw himself as emulating the Pre-Raphaelite ideal. He always remembered this period with wistful affection.

This new concentration and stability had much to do with Evelyn Gardner. During that autumn their relationship had progressed slowly towards intimacy. She-Evelyn's flat-mate, Pansy Pakenham, was in love with the painter Henry Lamb. At the time he was seeking divorce from his long-estranged wife in order to marry Pansy. The four of them made a happy *coterie* around which other friends circulated. Alec Waugh found the girls a remarkable couple and introduced Powell, who was later to marry Pansy's sister, Violet. Nancy Mitford, who

30. ALS to Harold Acton [27 April, 1928], from 10 Hill St, Poole [Henry Lamb's house]; *Letters*, p. 27.
31. Anthony Powell, *Messengers of Day, op. cit.*, p. 62.

in Waugh's middle years was to become one of his *confidantes*, was then Evelyn Gardner's closest friend. Together with Quennell and Connolly (both then reviewing for the *New Statesman*), Byron, Acton, Stokes, Henry Yorke (who wrote as Henry Green), Sacheverell Sitwell and others, they could be said to have formed the nucleus of an alternative Bloomsbury.

It was never, of course, a 'movement' but a loosely connected social group of clever, largely young people (Lamb was much older than the rest) soon to be taken up by the society magazines. Many of them were the children of aristocratic families. Their light-hearted rejection of the values of their parents attracted the popular press and the scorn of the socialists. Few took them seriously. But, despite their superficial frivolity, there was here a nucleus of real talent. Any list of the more important English novelists who emerged during the period following the Great War would include Waugh, Henry Green and Anthony Powell.

The carpentry continued until mid-December. Henry Lamb offered to introduce Waugh to Romney Green, a cabinet-maker with a workshop at Christchurch near Bournemouth. It was Waugh's serious intention, should Green accept him as a pupil, quietly to continue his apprenticeship and then to set up as a craftsman. On the 14th he and Lamb were to travel down to Christchurch. Terms were agreed and a premium paid. He was due to take up residence in January.

The only unfavourable aspect of the job was the enforced separation from Evelyn Gardner. He was by now deeply in love with her. But he had little confidence in his own attractions. She was considering emigration to Canada; he was about to move permanently out of town. Unless some positive steps were taken he would lose her. So two days before the projected interview, he took her out to dinner at the Ritz and, rather desperately, suggested that they should marry and 'see how it goes'.[32] It was an unfortunate phrase in a proposal, suggesting as it did that he was not entirely serious. In all probability it was a ham-fisted stab at *savoir-faire*. But she never forgot it.

As he perhaps expected, she gave an inconclusive answer. It had been sprung on her rather suddenly and in unflattering terms. There were obvious practical objections. Her mother, Lady Burghclere, was a strident aristocrat who demanded consultation on all matters regarding her daughter's future. She-Evelyn had always felt intimidated by her. Waugh had neither money nor social position. Lady Burghclere was bound to object. Young men had proposed and been disposed of in the recent past. She-Evelyn was bewildered by this unexpected turn of events. She needed time to think it over. That night she left him with a promise to phone the next day and give a definite decision.

Waugh's mind was suddenly aflame with a range of new possibilities. He rallied support by telephoning Pansy for advice, knowing full well that, as soon as she

32. Michael Davie's account, *Diaries*, p. 305. In her interview with me, 26 April, 1986, she confirmed that, although Waugh did not use 'those words', he used 'words to that effect'.

Some of Evelyn Waugh's ancestors: three great-great-grandfathers,
Alexander Waugh DD (top left), William Morgan FRS (top right), Lord
Cockburn (bottom left); Waugh's great-grandfather, Rev. James Hay Waugh,
Rector of Corsley (bottom right)

Some of Evelyn Waugh's distant relations connected with the Pre-Raphaelite Brotherhood: left, Edith Hunt, née Waugh, by William Holman Hunt; centre, Alice Woolner, née Waugh, by Arthur Hughes, 1864; right, Fanny Hunt, née Waugh, by William Holman Hunt, 1866

Family group, 1870: in the centre are Alexander (Evelyn Waugh's paternal grandfather), Alick (in naval uniform), Annie (Alexander's wife) and Arthur, flanked by Arthur's three sisters, Connie, Trissie and Elsie

11 Hillfield Road, West Hampstead, the house in which Evelyn Waugh was born. The first-floor window looked out from his nursery towards South London and the Surrey hills (photographed by the author in 1986)

Family group, about 1904; left to right: Catherine, Evelyn, Arthur and Alec Waugh

Evelyn Waugh and his mother, about 1908

Arthur and Catherine Waugh about 1917, the year Evelyn Waugh went to Lancing

Detail from a Lancing photograph showing Evelyn Waugh, about 1921

Alec Waugh during the First World War

Evelyn Waugh at Oxford, about 1923

Evelyn Waugh's cover for Harold Acton's
*Oxford Broom*, February 1924

Wood engraving by Evelyn Waugh,
August 1923

THE TRAGICAL DEATH OF Mr WILL. HUSKISSON    SEPT. MDCCCXXX.

The drawing with which Evelyn Waugh won the Oxford Art Club Exhibition,
1924. It is dedicated 'To Mr John Sutro'

Harold Acton by Pruna, 1925

Villa La Pietra, the
Actons' house in
Tuscany

Arthur, Catherine and Alec Waugh at
Underhill, 145 North End Road,
1909. Evelyn Waugh was five at the
time. Later he was very conscious of
how unfavourably Underhill
compared with houses such as
La Pietra

The famous, much-misdated photograph of Evelyn Waugh on Magdalen Bridge, Oxford, not when he was an undergraduate but on one of his flying visits in 1925 while schoolteaching at Aston Clinton, near Tring. He sent the photograph on a postcard to his mother from Aston Clinton on 20th February, 1925

Evelyn Waugh's holiday on Lundy Island, Easter 1925. The group includes, standing left to right, Richard, Olivia, Gwen and David Plunket Greene, Terence Greenidge and Elizabeth Russell. Evelyn Waugh is seated

returned to the flat, She-Evelyn would consult her. If he could win Pansy over to his side there would be considerable hope for success. But he need not have bothered. Lady Pansy was in no doubt that it was a good match. He went on to see Olivia, then home to Underhill and a sleepless night. In the morning Evelyn called him and accepted. He went off to Southampton Row as usual but found it impossible to work. His plans would have to be altered.

It is at this point that a six-month gap appears in his diary, probably as the result of Waugh's subsequent mutilation of the record. He was in high, romantic spirits, the buccaneer supreme. All references to Evelyn Gardner were at some point methodically expunged as an embarrassing reminder of failure. The best account of this crucial period in his life appears, rather unexpectedly, in a light magazine article in 1937. 'My next plan', he wrote after a summary of his teaching career,

> was to be a carpenter. . . . Those were delightful days, under the tuition of a brilliant and completely speechless little cabinet-maker who could explain nothing and demonstrate everything. To see him cutting concealed dovetails gave me the thrill which, I suppose, others get from seeing their favourite batsman at the wicket or bullfighter in the ring. It was a charming class too. . . . It soon became apparent, however, that it would be many years before I should qualify for a wage, and then for a few shillings a week. That did not worry me, but I had an inclination to get married, so I looked for more remunerative work. Some dreary weeks followed during which, though I cannot claim to have trudged the streets without food, I certainly made a great many fruitless and rather humiliating calls on prospective employers. Dickens held it against his parents that they tried to force him into a blacking factory instead of letting him write. The last firm at which I solicited a job was engaged, among other things, in the manufacture of blacking. I pleaded desperately. If I wasn't employed there I should be driven to Literature. But the manager was relentless. It was no use my thinking of blacking. That was not for the likes of me. I had better make up my mind and settle down to the humble rut which fate had ordained for me. I must write a book.[33]

The piece, of course, distorts for comic effect. But there is no doubt about one thing: he did not want to write for a living. *Rossetti* was not considered by him as a work of 'literature'. It was an adjunct to the craftsman's life, a work, like Fry's or 'Sachy' Sitwell's, elucidating the aesthetic principles of craftsmanship. He suffered, he says in that article, from 'an almost fanatical aversion from pens, ink or paper', and continued to do so for many years. Nothing was further from his intentions than to follow his father and brother into the family trade of letters.

33. 'General Conversation: Myself . . .', *op. cit.*, *NPMM*, March 1937, 10; *EAR*, pp. 190–2.

He wished neither to compete as a critic with Arthur nor as a popular novelist with Alec. 'I held out until I was twenty-four', he wrote, ' . . . then I was sucked under.'[34]

During that autumn he had treated Anthony Powell to a private reading of the fragment of his 'comic novel'. Only ten thousand words had been written under the title of *Picaresque: or the Making of an Englishman*. They had sat alone together after one of those quiet Underhill dinners and laughed loudly over the handwritten sheets. Towards Christmas Powell asked Waugh what he had done with the fiction. 'I've burnt it,' he replied. [35]

This, as we shall see, may well have been true. But, probably in January 1928, a similar reading was repeated, this time with Dudley Carew. By then there were some fifty pages. Composition was dilatory. He did not apply himself seriously to it until prospective employers had refused him. In any case, he admitted to Carew, the subject was probably too outrageous to be acceptable for publication.

About this time he wrote to Harold Acton: 'I spend most of my day in the Institute of Surgery with my leg in an electric oven. *Rossetti* will be out soon. The novel does not get on. I should so much value your opinion on whether I am to finish it.'[36] He still could not take himself seriously as a novelist. The cool reception of *The Temple* had rendered him nervously uncertain about his powers as an imaginative writer. On literary matters he deferred absolutely to Acton's judgement.

In February he scrawled a note to Patrick Balfour (later Lord Kinross) whom he had met again with Cyril Connolly in their shared flat. Balfour worked as a gossip columnist for the *Daily Sketch* and wrote much of Lady Eleanor Smith's social chatter for the *Sunday Dispatch*. He had mentioned Evelyn's forthcoming biography. 'Thank you so much for the advertisement', Waugh wrote. 'As soon as I see any hope from my window in the Slough of Despond I will let you know. As a matter of fact I think there will be an elopement quite soon.'[37] The Hon. Evelyn Gardner was not only the daughter of Lady Burghclere but the niece of Lord Carnarvon (discoverer of Tutankhamen's tomb). She would be the subject of hot gossip for Balfour when she married a penniless writer-schoolmaster. Waugh was quite prepared to give him advance warning in return for publicity. He did exactly the same thing, much to the chagrin of his second fiancée, when he married again in 1937.

The 'elopement' did not in fact take place for several months. She-Evelyn had

---

34. *Ibid.*; *EAR*, p. 190.
35. *Messengers of Day, op. cit.*, p. 22.
36. *Letters*, p. 25. We do not know what was wrong with Waugh's leg, unless it was the recurrent weakness resulting from the weeks during which he was strapped down and immobilised as a child for the convalescence from his appendicitis operation.
37. *Ibid.*, p. 26. *EWAHW* incorrectly states (p. 185) that 'the last sentence refers to the end of his first marriage'. It clearly refers to the beginning of it.

spent Christmas with the Waughs at Underhill and had struck up an immediate *rapport* with her future mother-in-law. It was the first Christmas Waugh had enjoyed since school. His fiancée was clearly devoted to him. Afterwards, she wrote to Catherine thanking her 'for the happiest Christmas I have ever had'. 'Somehow,' she continued, 'I thought that you wouldn't be pleased, because Evelyn is such an exceptional person and I know how proud you are of him. I hope that I shall be able to make him happy. I think that when one loves someone as much as I love Evelyn, one is terrified of disappointing them.'[38] Any idea that she was superficial, scheming or careless about the marriage is entirely false. She was as deeply committed to it as Waugh. Whatever went wrong was an equally bitter shock to her.

There was no elopement after that Christmas but there were changes. If the couple were ever to have enough money to set up house something had to be done about that novel. Pansy and She-Evelyn were both trying to write. Henry Lamb, now secretly engaged to Pansy, had a house in Poole, Dorset.[39] So Pansy and the two Evelyns moved down for a working holiday to a neighbouring village, Wimborne. The girls took rooms in a boarding house there; Waugh stayed two miles away in Colehill's village pub, the Barley Mow, and for the first time set seriously about the business of becoming a 'man of letters'. There he dealt with the final negotiations concerning *Rossetti* and with publication of an article on the painter for the *Fortnightly Review;* and there he finished *Decline and Fall*. He even corresponded with the BBC suggesting a talk on Rossetti to mark the centenary.

The novel did not have its ultimate title then and neither did *Rossetti*. The latter was originally to have been called *Last Born of Eve;* the former *Untoward Incidents*, a phrase, he reminded Powell in a letter, ' ... used by the D⸍ of Wellington in commenting on the destruction of the Turkish fleet in time of peace at Navarino. It seems to set the right tone of mildly censorious detachment.'[40] It was nearly finished by the time he received his advance copy of *Rossetti*.

This arrived at the pub in early April. Waugh was in high spirits, delighted with its appearance, eagerly organising the inscribed cards for presentation copies. Lady Burghclere, he insisted, was not to get a 'with love' one, but one marked 'with kind regards'.[41] There was a distinct awkwardness between them already which he had earlier attempted to placate by calling on her in full morning dress. She had not been impressed. As an aristocratic widow in 'reduced circumstances' with a marked intolerance towards the *bourgeoisie*, she wanted her daughter to marry into money and position. Lancing College, schoolmastering and a vague

---

38.   Unpublished ALS from Evelyn Gardner to Catherine Waugh [January 1928?].
39.   10 Hill Street, Poole.
40.   Unpublished ALS to Anthony Powell, nd [April 1928], from the Barley Mow, near Wimborne, Dorset.
41.   *Letters*, p. 26.

promise of royalties did not excite her interest. It was an embarrassment for Waugh but he cared little for her opinions. His self-confidence had never been greater. This literary business seemed rather easy when he put his mind to it. 'I am thinking out a story about a religious maniac molested by a tramp. Called "Advent" ', he wrote to Powell, avid for business.[42] It was never written. The religious maniac found his way into *Decline and Fall*.

When the novel was completed in late April Waugh went on to stay with the girls and Henry Lamb 'who is painting my portrait and delivering illuminating discourses to me on Cézanne'.[43] (The picture – of Waugh poised with pipe and pen over writing paper – is now lost, only a photograph of it remaining.) After two months of industry his life had changed beyond recognition. He returned to London triumphant.

*Rossetti* was a *succès d'éstime*. It was well received when it appeared in late April. Waugh's was the first of several works celebrating the centenary and it was given considerable space in most of the prestigious literary columns. Among others, Roy Campbell reviewed it for *Nation and Athenaeum*, Edward Shanks for the *London Mercury*, John Drinkwater for the *Telegraph*, J. C. Squire for the *Observer*, and Osbert Lancaster, an old friend from Kolkhorst's salon, for the *Isis*. The *Times Literary Supplement* gave it a front-page spread. Everyone was pleased with it. The soundness of the aesthetic analysis, the obvious knowledge of the practical techniques of painting, the terse humour in description and the appearance of scholarship in quietly correcting Marillier's authoritative catalogue – all this provided a stout framework upon which the author could hang the few flamboyantly cheap rags of hearsay.

It was the custom then (by no means defunct today) to write long review articles on the subject rather than the book. The work itself could almost be ignored as loquacious critics used it as a vehicle for their own ideas. But Waugh was pleased with the publicity. Only two pieces excited his anger: one by the anonymous reviewer in the *TLS*, the other by Peter Quennell in the *New Statesman*.

The *TLS* had misconstrued Waugh's gender. He sat down immediately to scribble a mordant reply. Dudley Carew and his wife Anthea were staying at Underhill at the time, just returned from their honeymoon. When they came down for breakfast they discovered Waugh sitting at a writing desk in a recess in the dining room. Though his back was to them he was visibly furious. The letter was published the following week: 'Your reviewer refers to me throughout as "Miss Waugh". My Christian name, I know, is occasionally regarded by people of limited social experience as belonging exclusively to one or other sex; but it is unnecessary to go further into my book than the paragraph placed charitably inside the wrapper for the guidance of unleisured critics, to find my name with

42. *Ibid.*, p. 26; *Letters* reads 'murdered' for 'molested'.
43. *Ibid.*, p. 27.

the correct prefix of "Mr".' He had never liked his effeminate Christian name. (Alec Waugh has suggested that his brother adopted an aggressively 'masculine' attitude to dispel potential mockery on these grounds.) Now, in the most important review of his first book, he saw himself as held up to public ridicule. No-one else gave it a second thought. Waugh's letter seethes with a sense of outraged sexual identity. He never forgot the slight.

The quarrel with Quennell was a different, and more serious, matter. It perhaps marks the beginning of a process of disaffection which ended with Quennell becoming a perpetual butt of Waugh's malicious humour. In the 'twenties and 'thirties it was a common practice for authors to direct their books towards friends who were reviewers. Waugh referred unapologetically to this literary freemasonry in *Rossetti*. In 1928 he had few friends capable of offering this sort of assistance. Quennell was one of them. Waugh expected support and was affronted by its conspicuous absence. Acton wrote to Waugh congratulating him strongly on the book and adding that Quennell had attempted to discourage this favourable opinion. Phrases in the review like 'we could have been spared Mr Waugh's lengthy analysis of Rossetti's pictures' and 'His treatment is consequently a little sparse and curtailed' angered Waugh and his circle. On 14th May, amazed at their reaction, Quennell wrote to apologise. The letter is preserved, along with others, in the back of the bound manuscript Waugh kept in his library. 'I am sorry to think', Quennell said, 'that the Other Evelyn can be in a white heat of indignation.'[44] Miss Gardner defended her fiancé's reputation vigorously.

Quennell's lukewarm response stood out awkwardly against a chorus of otherwise unanimous praise. The whole notion of biography as a literary form had become a contentious critical issue since Lytton Strachey's *Eminent Victorians* (1918). The reviewers were pleased to note Waugh's awareness of the new problems and responsibilities attaching to this literary form. Indeed Waugh discusses them at some length in the book. The old-fashioned biography, he suggests, often represented little more than a turgid two-volume eulogy. The new style could too easily slip into guesswork and scepticism. As Roy Campbell put it: 'It is the most perfect instrument that has yet been invented to enable the mediocre to patronise the great.'[45] Waugh addressed this problem too:

> No doubt ... with the years, we shall once more learn to assist with our fathers' decorum at the lying-in-state of our great men;.... Meanwhile we must keep our tongue in our cheek, must we not, for fear it should loll out and reveal the idiot? We have discovered a jollier way of honouring the dead. The corpse has become a marionette. With bells

44.  ALS from Peter Quennell, 14 May, 1927 from 189 High Holborn, W., included in *Rossetti* MS, HRC; *CH*, p. 71.
45.  Roy Campbell, *N & A*, 19 May, 1928, 212; *CH*, pp. 71–4.

> on its fingers and wires on its toes it is jigged about to a 'period dance'
> of our own piping . . . [46]

Campbell, like most other critics, considered that Waugh had avoided the traps and produced a 'life of Rossetti which is both lively and reliable'.

The manuscript certainly supports Waugh's statement that it was written quickly. It is studded with grammatical inaccuracies and contradictions. The footnotes which appear in the book were originally just blocks of supporting information wedged awkwardly between parentheses and probably represent the work of Duckworth's reader. Waugh's process of composition in the early days was not, as Powell has suggested, to 'write all his books straight off, then make one fair-copy for the publisher, which was not . . . typed.'[47] He wrote in sections, sending them off to the typist as they were completed. Single pages might be re-written. He was far too lazy to make an entire fair-copy. It was the typescript which he used as 'rough draft'. He worked on this with a craftsman's precision, pruning and re-phrasing.

Critics have occasionally glanced at his early manuscripts (now in Texas) and, finding them relatively 'clean', presumed, quite erroneously, that Waugh spent little time editing his own work. The typescripts of these, except for part of *Vile Bodies*, no longer exist. It is only through the tedious business of collating the manuscripts with the first editions that his scrupulous attention to detail is revealed. As his writing matured the differences between the two decrease. But for *Rossetti* and *Decline and Fall* they are substantial.

We need not bother with textual variants when they concern grammatical details. Waugh wrote rapidly and carelessly and, despite his energetic defence of the purity of the English Language in later years, had a shaky grasp of its finer details in his youth. He relied on the typist to correct spelling and punctuation. Much more interesting are the large-scale alterations.

In *Rossetti*, for example, he has clearly spent much time re-writing the aesthetic arguments. Originally, the discussions about Fry and Waley and 'significant form' appeared near the beginning. This has been carefully expanded, re-phrased and divided into two sections, the bulk of it appearing as a concluding chapter: 'What Is Wrong With Rossetti?' At another point we can see that he did not quite deserve the accolades received for avoiding gossip biography. Describing Elizabeth Siddal's 'suicide' he wrote: 'A story of Rossetti's movements on that night has been widely reported and widely believed . . .; there is probably no-one now living who could personally be hurt by its repetition but in the absence of any trustworthy source, it is no doubt best left unpublished.' In the printed text this has been replaced by two theoretical and extremely dramatic reconstructions. The

46. *Rossetti*, p. 12.
47. *Messengers of Day, op. cit.*, p. 22.

change may be interpreted as more evidence of Waugh's determination not to fulfil the role of obsequious obiturist. But we may suspect mixed motives. He was not simply being commendably honest. He was well aware that there was no 'trustworthy source' and deliberately elaborated unfounded rumour in order to add colour and dash to Rossetti's life.

It is a small point but an important one for it illustrates two crucial aspects of Waugh's writing. Firstly, that whenever he tackled biography or travel writing, he always approached these from the point of view of the imaginative writer, the novelist, rather than that of the mere compiler of facts. And secondly, that with this particular book he found himself in something of a dilemma.

The idea of making his subject 'jig about' to a 'period dance' was abhorrent to him. Most of the corrections concern the deletion of his personal opinions; objectivity was all. 'Interpretation' is often rigorously excised unless supported by evidence or argued on the ground of a tenable system of aesthetics. This was the book which he needed to establish his reputation as a 'man of letters'. But he also wanted it to attract attention and thus needed the colourful anecdotes. If it were to have gone unnoticed, he might have been doomed again to schoolmastering. More importantly, it might have resulted in an indefinite delay of his marriage. No wonder that She-Evelyn was incensed by Quennell's indifferent review.

Fortunately, the favourable reception of the biography meant that Evelyn now commanded literary respect. Patrick Balfour and Tom Driberg could legitimately advertise his name in their gossip columns. Duckworth's were keen to follow up the success of their young discovery with the novel he was promising. Despite his unwillingness to write fiction, Waugh enjoyed working on *Decline and Fall* after the labour of *Rossetti*. He knew it was good. The future was far from secure but it held more promise than ever before, and on this basis the two Evelyns plunged into matrimony.

\*

Waugh's *Diaries* resume with two brief fragments: 22nd June–25th July and 4th October–24th November, 1928.[48] He probably left these sections intact because they reveal nothing intimate yet deal with crucial developments in his career. The first describes the marriage, the second concerns the period immediately after the publication of *Decline and Fall*.

Waugh's own description of the wedding and related events is flippant. Anthony Powell's memoirs note that it was characteristic of parents during this period to disapprove of their children marrying early. Many couples in the 'society' world were prevented from marrying on the grounds of age where none of the traditional objections as to money, morals or status could be raised. Explanations for this

48. *Diaries*, pp. 294–301. The printed version does not indicate the break between them.

obstructive attitude vary. But, inevitably, the psychological effect of the Great War cannot be ignored. It was difficult, even ten years later, for many who had been directly involved in its social upheaval to lose the habit of pessimism. There was a distrust of anything pretending to stability and continuity and, as a result, an even greater distrust of romantic, impetuous decision.

The children of the wealthy often responded to this morbid caution with hedonism. Their reckless drinking and impulsive liaisons, their fast cars and parties partly represented a refusal to grow up and join the grey pragmatic world of their elders. Most, like Evelyn, quickly abandoned this wilful childishness but there was another 'war problem' for them to face. The enormous casualties had left a surplus of eligible females and an extraordinarily unbalanced society with few young married couples. 'When young men and girls of my own vintage married,' Powell has remarked, 'that was like a departure in social patterns; . . . there was no continuous sequence.'[49]

These two factors – the romantic rejection of caution and the adventure of young marriage in a society consisting almost exclusively of older couples – were undeniably important to Waugh. The 'old men' appeared to him to live in perpetual fear of disaster. Arthur's timidity and prudence, he thought, epitomised the whole debilitating psychological process. He refused to be cowed. Where Arthur had waited years for Catherine until he could guarantee financial security, Evelyn married at the first glimmerings of income, delighting in the risk.

The *Diaries* try to disguise enthusiasm by being affectedly casual about crucial events: 'Evelyn and I began to go to Dulwich to see the pictures there', he wrote on 22nd June, 'but got bored waiting for the right bus so we went instead to the vicar-general's office and bought a marriage licence.'[50] Here he is the dispassionate observer recording inconsequential action. Five days later the ceremony is noted with a similar austerity:

> Evelyn and I were married at St Paul's, Portman Square, at 12 o'clock. A woman was typewriting on the altar. Harold [Acton] best man. Robert Byron gave away the bride, Alec and Pansy the witnesses. Evelyn wore a new black and yellow jumper suit with scarf. Went to the 500 Club and drank champagne cocktails under the suspicious eyes of Winifred Mackintosh and Prince George of Russia. From there to luncheon at Boulestin. Very good luncheon. Then to Paddington and by train to Beckley.[51]

In fact, no one was typing on the altar. The vicar was typing his Sunday sermon in the vestry.

49. *Messengers of Day*, *op. cit.*, p. 31.
50. *Diaries*, 22 June, 1928, p. 294.
51. *Ibid.*, 27 June, 1928, p. 295.

According to Acton's *Memoirs*, the bride was so overcome 'that she could scarcely bring herself to whisper the words "I do". It was a pretty sight.' Acton had paid for the wedding breakfast: 'We were all very gay. It was June, sunny and warm, and we shared visions of love in a cottage. . . . Ephemeral though it was, I cannot forget the smile of the radiant faun.'[52]

None of this is suggested by Waugh's account. Was he trying to keep his emotions in 'water-tight compartments' by pretending to himself that he had not succumbed to enthusiasm, the besetting sin of the Victorians? The two Evelyns did not want a traditional marriage with its orgy of sentimentality. Even if they could have afforded it, it would not have been permitted by Lady Burghclere. The clandestine ceremony was conducted with an air of naughtiness: the children were escaping parental control. Arthur and Catherine Waugh were not invited.

Evelyn was not a 'romantic' in the strict historical/cultural sense; but he fitted our debased contemporary understanding of the word exactly. He positively glowed with pride at his wedding. He longed for permanent commitment and was passionately devoted to his new wife. The ultimate annulment was granted by the Church on the grounds that neither party had participated in this ceremony seriously. In Catholic terms that seemed perfectly obvious. But there can be little doubt, despite the diary entries, that both anticipated a long and happy life together.

*

The shoestring honeymoon at Beckley lasted just nine days. It was to be their only time alone together for nearly three months. On their return they had to face penury and homelessness. They also had to face Lady Burghclere. Waugh broke the news to her by letter. The reply was blunt. She was, she said, 'quite inexpressibly pained'.[53] Shortly afterwards the marriage was recorded briefly in *The Times*. Two days later he attended a formal interview with her. There is no record (in the *Diaries*) of what passed. It was a difficult period made worse by a continuing series of problems with *Decline and Fall*. 'Lady B' had a hand in them too.

'How Duckworth's lost Waugh' became one of the most widely repeated stories in publishing. Tom Balston did much to propagate it in his later years. It was widely believed until recently that Gerald Duckworth refused Evelyn's first novel (in Balston's absence) on the grounds of obscenity. Like many good anecdotes this was a *mélange* of truth and fiction.[54] Balston was not in fact absent. But in this particularly delicate case his superior had decided to oversee the business personally.

---

52. Harold Acton, *Memoirs of an Aesthete* (Methuen, 1948), p. 202.
53. *Diaries*, 27 June, 1928, p. 295.
54. Cf. Anthony Powell's *Messengers of Day, op. cit.*, pp. 102–5.

It was delicate because Duckworth was distantly related to Lady Burghclere.[55] She had made it known that she thought the match between her daughter and Waugh unsuitable. A crusty, old-fashioned bachelor he supported the family in the matter. He was further shocked by this young adventurer's licentious prose. Publishers were extremely cautious about potential lawsuits in the 'twenties, Duckworth particularly so. *Lady Chatterley's Lover* had landed Lawrence in the courts in 1928 and the case had set a precedent. A prim form of censorship was universally exercised.

In its original form *Decline and Fall* was certainly lubricious by contemporary standards. The manuscript, for instance, suggests an overt homosexual relationship between Captain Grimes and the boy Clutterbuck. There are references to Peter Pastmaster's prettiness and to his attractiveness to Margot's lovers. Incest, 'the forgotten vices of adolescence', a 'knocking shop' and the suggestion that the Welsh 'mate freely with the sheep' crop up. No publisher would have accepted it without changes. Waugh fully realised that limitations would be imposed on this sort of undergraduate ribaldry. He had, after all, grown up in a family of publishers and he had no objection to toning down his impish private entertainment to make a marketable product. Indeed, it was financially essential for him that it be printed and as soon as possible. Writing was, and remained, a business to him.

He waited patiently for the document to come back with the inevitable emendations. But when, eventually, it was returned he was appalled by the cuts on which Duckworth insisted. Anything vaguely suggestive of sex had to go. All 'indelicate' words (such as 'lavatory') were altered. Pencil marks ran everywhere. Duckworth even found obscenity in the debagging of Paul Pennyfeather during the first chapter. Waugh was outraged and, not knowing quite how to react, turned to his literary mentor, Harold Acton. Acton advised his friend to stand fast and not allow this castration of his satire. Duckworth would not budge. So, rather unwillingly, Waugh took his manuscript three doors down Henrietta Street to his father's firm.

Waugh had not wanted to do business with Chapman and Hall. He longed for complete independence of family interests. There was the whole irritating and recurrent question of success coming to him 'shop-soiled and second-hand' through the influence of friends and relations. But the matter was urgent. There was no time to hawk the book elsewhere. Even so, it was a close-run thing. Arthur was absent; the board was divided; as noted earlier, the casting vote in favour of accepting the book was made by R. E. Neale, head of the technical department.

It often happens that an author, refusing the alterations required by one

55. She was the sister of Lady Margaret Duckworth, wife of Sir George Duckworth, Gerald Duckworth's brother.

publisher, accepts them from another. Waugh was no exception. His diary during that hectic period after the honeymoon records: '... hard at work on the proofs of *Decline and Fall*. Chapman's *not* an easy firm to deal with.'[56] Collation of the manuscript with the first edition reveals that Arthur demanded changes only slightly less rigorous than Duckworth's. The debagging remained, but all sexual references had to be converted into innuendo; the lavatories became water jugs or boiler-rooms. Most of the cuts came, rather sadly, in Grimes's conversation. ' "I like drink and sex" ' ended as ' "I like drink and a bit of fun" '; ' "I've never been really attracted by women" ' limped into print as: ' "Women are an enigma," said Grimes, "as far as Grimes is concerned." ' It was annoying, but Waugh eventually had the last word. Many of the original readings were restored in the 1962 Uniform Edition.

The difficulties with Chapman's were compounded by the fact that during much of those two months after Beckley the two Evelyns had to live at Underhill while looking for a flat. There was little time for house-hunting amid the confusion of proof-reading and the skirmishes with Lady Burghclere. In addition, Waugh was drawing book jackets and, as soon as the proofs were done, began work on two new books – a biography of John Wesley and a detective thriller. London was staggering under an oppressive heat-wave. The young couple had a hectic social calendar. The first months of their marriage were, by any standards, disjointed and exhausting.

It was probably not until September that Waugh secured a cheap, first-floor flat: 17a Canonbury Square, in the then unfashionable area of Islington. It was a small, five-room apartment, rather dusty and drab at first, with a communal laundry room in the basement (though She-Evelyn remained ignorant of its existence). But the sitting room and main bedroom overlooked the spacious, well-proportioned nineteenth-century square with its trees and lawns. Waugh saw immediately that the place had potential. With the same energy he had concentrated on his nascent career, he threw himself into the task of converting the flat to his own taste.

He scoured local shops for odd bits of furniture which he would carry off to repair and restore. He quickly worked his way through every aspect of interior decoration. Nothing was left untouched. Sir Harold Acton has affectionate memories of him at this time 'squatted on the floor, deeply pre-occupied, surrounded by confetti-like pools of ... bright little stamps which he would stick in elaborate patterns on an ugly old coal-scuttle, his hair all tousled and his fingers dabbled in glue. Later he would give the object a coating of varnish, endowing it with the *patina* of a Sir Joshua Reynolds. He devoted infinite care to such arts and crafts.' 'The atmosphere', he remarks, 'was that of a sparkling nursery.'[57]

56. *Diaries*, 27 June, 1928, p. 295.
57. *Memoirs of an Aesthete, op. cit.*, p. 204.

The image of child-like simplicity and devotion is one which recurs in several accounts of the Waughs' Islington household. Nancy Mitford remembered them wheeling their few possessions to the flat on a hand-cart with the enthusiasm of two little boys. She-Evelyn had the gift of organising the most humble artefacts into a home. Wedding presents from their rich friends (none from Lady Burgh-clere) provided a few fine complementary objects – a painting, a cut-glass chandelier centre-piece to sit on the tiny dining table. At very little expense they ended with an elegant, unostentatious apartment. People felt at home there and from the outset Canonbury Square became a regular venue for their friends. They made an attractive couple.

The unconventional nature of this secret marriage was in itself a delight to many – a deliciously irresponsible attachment between a redundant schoolmaster with one dim biography to his credit and an attractive, titled young lady forging a career for herself in fashionable journalism. They personified the vitality of the younger generation, 'full of guts and invention'. With She-Evelyn's 'Eton Crop' hairstyle they even looked similar. But beneath the warmth and gentle manners lay an unmistakable severity of purpose. They were a pair, a small smart unit ready to do battle with all-comers in defence of the Rights of Youth. During their first days in the flat Waugh worked at *Wesley* while his wife ploughed on with a novel of her own (never finished). *Decline and Fall* had been published on 18th September and was reviewed well. The world, at last, seemed to want them and they were not going to allow it to forget their presence.

Another myth about Waugh's first novel suggests that it was an immediate best-seller. The critics, many of them Arthur's friends in the trade, were certainly impressed. It was considered a great compliment to receive attention in Arnold Bennett's prestigious *Evening Standard* column. A favourable notice there was supposed to sell an entire impression in twenty-four hours. Arthur had taken the precaution of writing to the great man, drawing his attention to the book. And Bennett responded generously: 'A genuinely new humorist', he wrote, 'has presented himself in the person of Evelyn Waugh, whose *Decline and Fall* is an uncompromising and brilliantly malicious satire, which in my opinion comes near to being quite first rate. . . . I say without reserve that this novel delighted me.'[58]

Waugh was equally delighted with the review. He began nervously to watch the weekly sales figures. Could Bennett make him a rich man? Unfortunately not. Sales doubled but it was only from (approximately) 200 a week to 400. By October 1929 it had just reached its fourth impression. It was a publishing gambit then to make each printing small, about 2,000 copies in Chapman's case. A best-seller could then be advertised dramatically as 'Now in sixth impression' within a couple of months. *Decline and Fall* was not in that category. It sold only steadily for the

58.  *ES*, 11 October, 1928, 5; *CH*, p. 82.

first year until the enormous success of *Vile Bodies* (1930). From then on it earned Waugh a substantial annual royalty cheque for the rest of his life.

Two things, however, dampened Waugh's elation at the novel's warm reception. His wife fell seriously ill and Harold Acton, in contrast to his own literary good fortune, had published a novel and been mercilessly panned by reviewers. *Humdrum* had appeared in the same month as *Decline*. Acton did not care for his own novel, admitting later that it had been a mistake ever to attempt fiction. But he was, nevertheless, wounded by Cyril Connolly's notice in the *New Statesman*.

Connolly, a mutual friend, took the opportunity to review the two books in a disparaging comparison. 'As a satire,' Connolly wrote, '*Decline and Fall* seems to possess every virtue which [*Humdrum*] lacks. . . . *Humdrum* reads like a painstaking attempt to satirise modern life by a Chinaman who has been reading *Punch*, and the result is a catalogue of offences in the style of Becker's *Gallus* or a second-rate Roman satirist in a third-rate modern crib.'[59] For a long time at Eton and Oxford Connolly had lived in the shadow of Acton's literary reputation. This was his chance to assert himself. But in a sense it was a ruthless kick at a fallen man. In that letter of generous congratulation on *Rossetti* Acton had remarked to Evelyn: 'I am quite sad when I think of the utter miscarriage of my poems. . . .' His career as an imaginative writer was in ruins.

Waugh, deeply loyal, did his best to cheer him. But he had other problems:

> You must forgive me for not having written before to tell you how much I like *Humdrum*. On my return from your delightful luncheon party[60] I found Evelyn laid up with an attack of 'flu' which became acute the next day and most worrying – her temperature up to 104 degrees and a little delirious. I had to spend most of the night sitting up with her and have been unable to attend to things. . . . In these difficult circumstances I read *Humdrum* and found the greatest delight in it. As I said at luncheon I do feel it is rather a popularised Barry Jackson *Cornelian*[61] – Harold Acton for the masses but this, of course is all in its favour from the financial point of view which I imagine is important to you as to me. But as a light novel I think it is by far the most amusing book since Firbank.[62]

She-Evelyn's illness, which turned out to be a bad case of German measles, could scarcely have come at a worse moment.

59. *NS*, 3 November, 1928, 126; *CH*, pp. 85–7.
60. At the Savile Club, 8 October, 1928. Reggie Turner (the novelist and friend of Oscar Wilde) and Raymond Mortimer (who had reviewed *Decline and Fall* favourably) were there. Waugh found Mortimer affected and pretentious. Cf. *Diaries*, p. 297.
61. *Cornelian* was one of Acton's volumes of poetry.
62. Unpublished ALS to Harold Acton, nd [probably 11–12 October, 1928], from 17a Canonbury Square, Islington N1.

*Decline and Fall* was just out and, thanks to Waugh's agent, editors were for the first time requesting articles. An old family friend, A. D. Peters, had been Alec's literary agent for some years. Peters had frequently visited Underhill and remembered Evelyn only as a soft-spoken young man who refused to enter into intellectual debate. Nothing was a greater surprise to him than to find that this modest exterior concealed an abrasive literary talent. But, impressed by the precocious skill of the novel, he invited Waugh at once to become a client. Waugh accepted and it was a decision he never regretted. Peters remained his agent until the end. Before the publication of *Decline* Peters had been canvassing newspapers and magazines without success. Suddenly he was landing Waugh with more work than he could handle. She-Evelyn occupied his whole attention and a nurse had to be called in to care for her during the day.

They had only been in their new home for a few weeks, then, before once again their privacy was invaded. 'The last three weeks have been very distracting', he wrote to Acton at the end of October, 'with Evelyn in bed and my flat in the possession of nurses and doctors. We have got away at last and are staying in my brother-in-law's house in the downs near Marlborough in great peace and luxury.'[63] (This contains more exaggeration. She-Evelyn's old nanny came to look after her during the day and the doctor called *once*.) Alathea, his wife's elder sister, had married Geoffrey Fry and it was at their home, Oare House, that Waugh wrote his first piece of popular journalism.

Earlier he had suggested to Peters that ' . . . it would be so nice if we could persuade them [newspaper editors] that I personify the English youth move-ment'.[64] Waugh had a nose for business. Youth was news and he rightly thought that he could add spice to the tedious arguments about wayward behaviour which clotted the correspondence columns. The chief advocates of the new freedom – Beverley Nichols and Godfrey Winn – were not noted for their scintillating grasp of the issues. Alec had frequently, but decorously, joined the debate with Dean Inge and the *ancien régime* on the opposition bench. The *Evening Standard* took up Waugh's suggestion and his article succeeded in turning discussion into controversy.

It was printed three months later as 'The Claim of Youth or Too Young at Forty. Youth Calls to the Peter Pans of Middle-Age Who Block the Way'. The War, he insisted, was at the root of the problem. After the Armistice senior professional positions had been occupied by young officers. The system of gradual succession to seniority had been upset. Now the way was blocked:

> by the phalanx of the Indestructible Forties. A fine, healthy lot, these
> ex-captains and majors work by day, dance by night, golf on Sundays,

63. *Letters*, p. 29.
64. *Ibid.*, p. 30.

nothing is too much for them and nothing is going to move them for another 30 years. How they laugh and slap their thighs and hoot the horns of their little two-seater cars. . . . 'But,' I shall be asked, 'if these plump old soldiers whom we have so long looked upon as "modern" are not the younger generation, what is the younger generation like?' In reply I can mention five writers . . . who seem to me to sum up the aspirations and prejudices of my generation. These are, first, Harold Acton, poet and novelist; Mr Robert Byron, the art critic; Mr Christopher Hollis, the Catholic apologist; Mr Peter Quennell, poet and literary critic; and Mr Adrian Stokes, philosopher.[65]

It was designed to be provocative. Controversy, he realised early, was publicity and he revelled in it. 'The surprising and rather humiliating result', he wrote in a follow-up piece, 'was a small crop of intemperate letters of protest written by elderly people from obscure addresses. Some even threatening whippings and kickings followed me to the obscurity of my own address.'[66] Waugh encouraged outraged reaction by tongue-in-cheek literary intemperance. He was engaged on a campaign of self-advertisement which succeeded admirably. The trick was to keep one's name constantly before the public. Arthur didn't like it.

There was, in fact, small danger of Waugh's being forgotten so long as Driberg and Balfour were gossip columnists. They often referred to his social life, emphasising his youth and intellectual versatility. When *Decline and Fall* was published they were quick to spot a few instances of malicious portraiture. Chapman's had insisted, in addition to the cuts, that Waugh preface his novel with a disclaimer: 'I hope that my publishers are wrong when they say that this is a shocking novelette. I did not mean it to be when I wrote it. . . . Still less is it a book with a purpose. In fact I have never met anyone at all like any of the characters. . . . Please bear in mind throughout that IT IS MEANT TO BE FUNNY.' But his friends knew the truth.

Grimes was clearly based on Young from Arnold House, and there were other distinctly recognisable figures: 'David Lennox' as Cecil Beaton, 'Jack Spire' of the *'London Hercules'* as J. C. Squire of the *Mercury*. No-one minded these caustic little lampoons. But good taste drew the line at using a near-identical version of someone's name when the character was patently homosexual. Clearly the 'Martin Gaythorn-Brodie' and 'Kevin Saunderson' of the first impression were Eddie Gaythorn-Hardy and Gavin Henderson. Robert Byron wrote to Waugh angrily about the matter. For the third impression the last two names were changed to 'Hon. Miles Malpractice' and 'Lord Parakeet'. Lady Ottoline Morrell's solicitors (and Chapman's) clearly missed a visual joke at her expense in the illustration of

---

65. *ES*, 22 January, 1929, 7; *EAR*, pp. 45–70.
66. 'Matter-of-Fact Mothers of the New Age', *ES*, 8 April, 1929, 7.

the Marseilles street scene. Prominent above one of the brothels hangs the sign 'Chez Ottoline'.

Waugh cared little about this aspect of his work. Later in his career he complained bitterly about accusations of direct portraiture. But in this instance there was no denying it. He did not care because the characters involved were mere decorations, briefly observed. On 7th April he had written to Powell: 'The novel will be finished in a week. I will send it to you as soon as it is typed and then want to revise it very thoroughly and enlarge it a bit. I think at present it shows signs of being a bit short. . . . I am sure I could write any novel in the world on two postcards.'[67] The manuscript contains numerous insertions. Several expand Philbrick's crazy autobiography; one is the house-party scene at King's Thursday in which much of the specific social satire and dubious nomenclature occurs. These were just, in Grimes's words, 'a bit of fun'. They had nothing to do with the essence of the novel.

*

Identifying that 'essence' is particularly difficult. Peter Fleming, brother of Ian (creator of James Bond), and later a friend, reviewed it for the *Isis:* 'The outline of the plot is indicated by the author's cover design, which shows the bust of a not very inspiring young man in the clothes of an undergraduate, a bridegroom, a convict and a clergyman. In the Prelude . . . Paul Pennyfeather, an essentially dim undergraduate, falls in with the members of an aristocratic club . . . they deprive (him) of his clothes, and his college sends him down for indecent behaviour. After becoming a master at a fantastically bad school in Wales . . . , he falls in love with the fabulously wealthy and politely depraved mother of one of his pupils, but is arrested on the eve of his wedding for dabbling unwittingly in the White Slave Traffic – the main source of his fiancée's revenue. His placid career in prison is cut short by the intervention of the Home Secretary, who has become the *mari complaisant* of his late betrothed, and the Epilogue leaves Paul studying theology at his old college, while the sound of the Bollinger Club keeping up its old traditions drifts discordantly through the window. *Decline and Fall* is a very good satire of the irresponsible variety: the mixture of fantasy and reality is judged to a nicety, and the author by keeping a straight face throughout, heightens the effect of his wit by contrast. He should, however, avoid the temptation to be smart by dabbling in personalities.'[68]

This is as good a resumé of the plot as one could wish and Fleming's approach was typical of the book's critical reception. Ralph Straus (on the Board of Chapman's) echoed the general feeling that it was a brilliant exercise in facetious

67. *Letters*, p. 26.
68. *Isis*, 17 October, 1928.

humour: ' . . . it *is* uproariously funny, far too funny to be anything else.'[69] And this has remained the consensus opinion. Any book which makes one roar with laughter cannot be 'serious'.

Waugh's attitude to writing only seemed to confirm this. Asked in interview in 1953 whether he wished in his novels to convey original thoughts or a 'message', he replied: 'No, I wish to make a pleasant object. I think a work of art is something exterior to oneself, it's the making of something whether it's a bed-table or a book.'[70] Readers took his disclaimer at face value. *Decline and Fall* was clearly an entertainment rather than 'a book with a purpose'. In contrast with Huxley's six hundred pages of turgidly high-brow satire in *Point Counter Point* (1928), its freshness and lucidity were a welcome relief. Is there more to it than this?

This is not the place for a lengthy critical discussion. But certain points should not be forgotten. Restricted to the flat during the early days of his wife's illness, he had been reading Virginia Woolf's *Orlando* and wrote to Acton saying that he was 'transported' by it, ' . . . tho' I regretted the slight Clive Bell self-consciousness – the references to the fact of the book she is writing being a book'.[71] One of the chief problems confronting him as a young author was that of conveying experience objectively. A brief examination of his Oxford correspondence with Carew reveals a serious preoccupation with experiments in literary form which would serve this end. At Lancing Carew had written a novel and sent it to him for criticism. What he had failed to appreciate, Waugh thought, was the need 'to bring home thoughts by actions and incidents. Don't make everything said. This is the inestimable value of the Cinema to novelists. . . . Make things happen. . . . Whatever the temptation, for God's sake don't bring characters on simply to draw their characters and make them talk. Fit them into a design.'[72]

Approaching literature from the viewpoint of the visual artist, 'design', the subjugation of the individual parts to an overall pattern, a rhythmic unity, was the predominant issue. Complaints that the characterisation of his early work is shallow miss the point. In concentrating on the collective, rather than the individual, tragedy of his characters he was making a deliberate aesthetic decision to move away from the subjective and 'romantic' towards the objective and 'classical' – and particularly towards the 'mystical habit of mind'.

'Tragedy', of course, is too strong a word to apply to *Decline and Fall*. At this stage he delights in the inconsequential misfortune of Pennyfeather's career and humour is used as a further device to keep an emotional distance between the hero and the reader. At one point the narrator ingenuously apologises for disappointing us with this technique: 'the whole of this book', he says, 'is really

69. *Bystander*, 31 October, 1928, 260.
70. 'Frankly Speaking', 16 November, 1953; BBCSL.
71. *Letters*, p. 29.
72. *Ibid.*, p. 2.

an account of the mysterious disappearance of Paul Pennyfeather, so that readers must not complain if the shadow which took his name does not amply fill the important part of hero for which he was originally cast'.[73] Paul became the prototype of the central *naif* in all Waugh's pre-war novels, a mirror upon which experience is reflected, a man of few emotional reactions, exploited and controlled by a corrupt world. It was the old satirical device used by Fielding and Voltaire. But as he wrote *Decline and Fall* Waugh was all the time experimenting with and adapting that type, consciously moving towards a vision of the world which was subtly different from that of *Tom Jones* or *Candide*.

In this respect, the manuscript offers us an intriguing detective story. We have noted how Waugh told Powell that he had burnt the early section read aloud at Underhill. What he omitted to mention was that he had only destroyed what had already been replaced by something else. Deleted chapter numbers suggest that there must have been two short chapters at the beginning (presumably the piece Powell saw) which were re-written into the tighter form of the 'Prelude'.[74]

Waugh's concept of his hero underwent constant revision. That re-written section is not called 'Prelude' in the manuscript but 'Prologue. Almer [*sic*] Mater.' All the evidence indicates that, far from wishing Paul to 'disappear' into the pallid nonentity he became, Waugh originally intended to write an amusing *éducation sentimentale* novel, a comic equivalent to *The Balance*, in which Paul moved through experience to knowledge. In the early chapters he is allowed to react. His ' "God damn and blast them all to hell" ' on leaving Oxford is scarcely in keeping with a man who later finds seven years penal servitude 'rather a blow'. His 'disappearance' developed into a parody of the sort of self-knowledge, the movement into 'a third dimension' achieved by Adam Doure. From the initial idea of a simple, honest, and therefore exploited, fellow Waugh changes Paul into a puppet figure, 'like one of the wire toys which street vendors dangle from trays'.[75] The manuscript, for instance, at first read: 'Ten days before the wedding Paul moved into . . . the Ritz and devoted himself seriously to shopping.' This has been altered to: 'Ten days before the wedding Paul moved into . . . the Ritz and Margot devoted herself seriously to shopping.'[76] There are several similar corrections obliterating his decisions and opinions.

Everything Pennyfeather does later in the novel is seen to be the result of manipulation by external forces. One large deletion in the manuscript strongly suggests that Waugh originally thought of the book, not as a social satire (the

73. *Decline and Fall*, p. 122.
74. The whole section which now begins 'Part 1. Chapter One. Vocation' (Paul's interview with his guardian), from ' "Sent down . . . " ' to 'Office of Works' is a one-page insertion. The next section, now beneath an asterisk break, is on a separate sheet and headed 'Chapter Three [deleted] One. Paul Finds a Career'.
75. *Decline and Fall*, p. 135.
76. *Ibid.*, p. 150.

house party scenes were, after all, 'padding'), but as a humorous philosophical puzzle about the problems of identity. The deletion occurs after the hero has been sent to prison and represents the beginning of a new chapter: 'Paul's Meditations. (This Chapter May Be Omitted on the First Reading)'. The deleted section is extraordinarily out of keeping with the rest of the book:

> Who am I? I am Paul Pennyfeather. For all I know there may be a hundred other people with the same name. I did not choose my name. The name Pennyfeather was preordained for me centuries ago; the name Paul was chosen by my mother because she had an uncle Paul who had been kind to her as a child. Why was he called Paul? Perhaps for the same reason. What do I mean when I say I am Paul Pennyfeather? A chain of consequences so obscurely connected and of such remote origins that it is impossible to trace what I mean. Here I am called D.4.12. That means that for twenty-two hours out of twenty-four I can be found in the twelfth cell of the fourth landing of block D. D.4.12 is the creature of order and purpose. Paul Pennyfeather is the creature of chaos.
>
> This is not quite true. D.4.12 has only extension in space: Paul Pennyfeather has continuity in time. How does continuity in time suggest itself to the imagination? In the form of a series of positions in space, Paul Pennyfeather at Scone, at Llanabba, at King's Thursday etc. That is to say that Paul Pennyfeather is a series of which D.4.12 is an expression. Sometimes I am a part and sometimes a whole. It is very perplexing. Explain the position D.4.12 in the series, Paul Pennyfeather. Why am I here?[77]

The rest of the sheet is blank. It was not used in any form in the novel. Why? The reason seems obvious. It is boring. It was amateur philosophy, not art, and too close to the 'conversation and biology'[78] he abhorred in Huxley. In terms of the aesthetic elucidated in *Rossetti* it is too 'intellectual'; it tells the reader what the novel is about rather than constructing a metaphorical 'impression'. He had fallen into the trap of didacticism and in struggling for objectivity lost it altogether. Paul's voice here was too close to Waugh's own.

Even so, it is important to notice that Waugh conceived of Pennyfeather's history in terms of a philosophical dialogue. Whether spelt out or not in the terms used in 'Paul's Meditations', the novel remains a metaphorical enquiry, albeit a light-hearted one, into the struggle for identity, of man as part of a 'chain of consequences so obscurely connected', of time, space, continuity and 'position' in the chaos.

The references to these questions which remain in the printed text deal with

77. MS of *Decline and Fall*, p. 104; HRC.
78. *Diaries*, 7 October, pp. 296–7.

precisely the same ideas only they are presented in terms of their relation to specific incidents rather than as abstract speculation. Paul, for instance, finds an unexpected freedom of spirit in solitary confinement 'relieved from the smallest consideration of time'.[79] We are led to suspect the man who allows his intellect totally to govern his actions through the characters of Silenus, Lucas-Dockery and Maltravers. Life presents its own metaphors for 'reality'; Waugh considered it the business of the artist to perceive these and give them order. It is a structural rather than a 'picturesque' approach. What the characters say is relative and often immaterial; there is no question of a Huxleyan 'dialogue'. The patterns and shapes which they take as they group and re-group are more important than the story of any individual's development. It is, like *The Balance*, a discussion of 'circumstance' but, with his improved personal fortunes, Waugh's ideas on the matter had shifted towards optimism.

In *The Balance* circumstance 'decides'. There is nothing the individual can do to control it because it is the accidental product of collective action. In *Decline and Fall* there is an element of choice. Otto Silenus directs a long speech about 'Life' to Paul. It is, he says, like the wheel in Luna Park: ' . . . a great disc of polished wood that revolves quickly. At first you sit down and watch the others. They are all trying to sit on the wheel, and they keep getting flung off, and that makes them laugh.' Paul, rather sadly, does not think this sounds much like life.

> Oh, but it is, though. You see, the nearer you can get to the hub of the wheel the slower it is moving and the easier it is to stay on. . . . Of course at the very centre there's a point completely at rest, if only one could find it. . . . Lots of people just enjoy scrambling on and being whisked off and scrambling on again. How they all shriek and giggle! Then there are others, like Margot [Metroland], who sit as far out as they can and hold on for dear life and enjoy that. But the whole point about the wheel is that you needn't get on it at all, if you don't want to. . . . Now you're a person who was clearly meant to stay in the seats. . . . It's all right for Margot, who can cling on, and for me, at the centre, but you're static. Instead of this absurd division into sexes they ought to class people as static and dynamic.[80]

This static/dynamic classification is at the very root of Waugh's philosophical approach and needs some explanation.

Waugh had a pugnacious, ambitious spirit. He disliked weakness and would often exploit it for amusement or as a means of furthering his own ends. There was a streak of mild sadism in him. But it was only mild. He enjoyed the struggle, the competition of life, and was intolerant of those who backed away from it. At

79. *Decline and Fall*, p. 170.
80. *Ibid.*, pp. 208–9.

the same time he was gifted with a sensitive, contemplative intelligence, and was acutely self-critical. Mixed incongruously with his aggression, and perhaps partially responsible for it, was a nervous uncertainty which saw persecution and failure round every corner. As an artist he was exorbitantly modest; as a man he had little faith in his own attractions. Waugh was his own perpetual assailant. In a sense, he did not much like himself and the ascetic and the hedonist were always at odds in the mental battle to rationalise or obliterate the unpleasant fact of his physical existence. For many years he failed to come to terms with the conflict between the ideals represented by Roxburgh and Crease. Should he aspire to the life of a man of the world or to that of the retiring artist-craftsman? His early reading in philosophy went some way towards resolving the paradox.

We know from the letters and diaries that Waugh first began reading Bergson during June 1921 at Lancing. At the time he was producing his satirical play, *Conversion*. His life then appeared to be running along the smooth rails of school success. As a recently-converted agnostic he was more interested then in Leibniz and Kant and their arguments against the existence of God. Oxford was only six months away and he was collecting most of the available school prizes. Bergson's abstract notions of 'memory' and 'potential relativity' seemed of little importance. It was only after Oxford, when experience appeared to judder and flash like a badly edited cinema film, that he began to seek a broader notion of continuity in time and space. It was then that he turned back to the popular 'time-mind' philosophies of Bergson and Spengler and dabbled in mystical writings.

Waugh was not unusual in this. There were certain books of philosophy and anthropology which many undergraduates would have dipped into: Bergson's *Creative Evolution*, Spengler's *Decline of the West*, Frazer's *Golden Bough*. Waugh had looked at them all. But it is quite clear that Bergson and Spengler represented more than casual reading. They offered a vision of life which Waugh, and other similar creedless 'Catholics', found comforting. T. S. Eliot, for example, attended Bergson's lectures in Paris. By the late 'twenties Bergson was less fashionable (after Wyndham Lewis's assault on 'time-mind' theories in *Time and Western Man* (1927)), Spengler more so. Both appear to have been influential on Waugh. The Great War had destroyed for many people the traditional view of qualitative historical progress and continuity. In the cacophony of the modern world young people with 'the mystical habit of mind' found themselves in a spiritual desert, too intelligent to accept the Christianity which had supported brutal jingoism, half in love with the shabby reality of the post-war world because at least it represented a form of truth; yet nagged by the intimation of some cohesive principle behind it all. It was largely this which drove Auden and Isherwood to Berlin and socialism and Waugh and Eliot to religion and tradition. For the latter pair, Bergson and Spengler filled the gap between atheism and the re-adoption of Christianity.

Waugh's use of 'static' and 'dynamic' is taken directly from Bergson, and the general principles of the philosophy are summarised by Bertrand Russell in terms which bear obvious correspondence to *Decline and Fall:*

> ... The whole universe is the clash and conflict of two opposite motions: life, which climbs upward, and matter, which falls downward. Life is one great force, one vast vital impulse, given once for all from the beginning of the world, meeting the resistance of matter, struggling to break a way through matter, learning gradually to use matter by means of organisation; ... partly subdued by matter ... yet retaining always its capacity for free activity, struggling always to find new outlets, seeking always for greater liberty of movement amid the opposing walls of matter.[81]

This is surely an accurate description of Grimes's peculiar heroism.

In the manuscript Waugh first conceived of Grimes as an outrageous homosexual schoolmaster whose poverty allowed him to be bamboozled into engagement to the headmaster's dingy daughter. The first six chapters had originally constituted 'Book I' and been sent off to the typist together. At the end of this Grimes committed suicide by allowing himself to be decapitated by the Irish Mail as it thundered through Llanabba station. But in scrapping the incident and resurrecting him, Waugh developed Grimes into an unmistakably Bergsonian protagonist.

Towards the end of the novel a distinction is made between him and the 'static' characters:

> Lord Tangent was dead; Mr Prendergast was dead; the time would even come for Paul Pennyfeather; but Grimes, Paul at last realized, was of the immortals. He was a life force. ... engulfed in the dark mystery of Egdon Mire, he would rise again somewhere at some time, shaking from his limbs the musty integuments of the tomb.[82]

The point is laboured further with an extensive passage of mock-heroic prose linking Grimes with that world of fauns and satyrs which inhabited Waugh's woodcuts and cartoons. On the opposite page appears a line drawing (by Waugh) depicting the man triumphant in the skies astride a white charger and brandishing a banner inscribed 'Excelsior'. Bergson's was an unphilosophical philosophy deriding our analytical powers in favour of intuitive thought. Grimes's is undeniably a victory of instinct over intellect.

Waugh, of course, was telling the truth when he said that *Decline and Fall* was not a 'book with a purpose'. He was certainly not attempting a fictional realisation

81. *A History of Western Philosophy* (George Allen & Unwin, 1946), p. 820.
82. *Decline and Fall*, pp. 198–9.

of Bergsonian principles. But the most difficult aspect of all his pre-war novels is understanding their moral structure. So successful was he in developing an objective style that the novels often confuse readers. The normal questions – 'What does the author think?'; 'What is he trying to express?' – don't apply. You don't ask the cabinet-maker what he is trying to express in a bed-table. In very general terms, once Waugh had adopted Catholicism, the objects of his satire glare from the page. *Decline and Fall*, however, was the one novel written while he was still living in faithless optimism, confident and aggressive. Without the Bergsonian connection it appears as little more than a brilliant romp; with it, we find unmistakable form and structure.

The characters, for instance, divide neatly into two worlds representing on the one hand instinct, imagination, the 'life force', and on the other, intellect, dullness, 'matter'. Grimes assaults the modest conformity of the domestic life. To him it represents no more than 'the hideous lights of home and the voices of children'.[83] Philbrick's identity in the book relies on a series of mutually contradictory fantasies concocted to defraud others. Yet in the end, he, like Margot, succeeds where Pennyfeather, Potts, Lucas-Dockery and other pallid nonentities are controlled or killed. Unlike Waugh's later fiction, this is not a satire of man's helpless plight among the savages of civilisation but the reverse. Waugh is on the side of the life force here; he is backing the eccentrics, the confidence tricksters, the manipulators.

There is an element of facetious perversity in choosing a pæderast, a burglar and a nymphomaniac white slaver as the chief representatives of this vitality. But there is no mistaking where his sympathies lie. Commentators, interpreting the novel in the light of later work, have often presumed that the replacement of King's Thursday by the factory-house of concrete and vita-glass was a criticism of architectural barbarity. In fact, this seems unlikely. Waugh loathed domestic Tudor. If anything the description of the original mansion with its tangle of musty passages and its archaic facilities represented something which had to be swept away by the clarity and concision of modern thinking. In 1929 Waugh reviewed a translation of Le Corbusier's *Urbanisme* and found much to praise in its plan for future cities of concrete and glass.[84] Jack Spire's sentimental preservation campaign is scorned as typical of the muddled Victorian mind. Waugh takes the opportunity also to mock Silenus's machine-turned aesthetic but it is not a value judgement in favour of tradition or against Margot's desire for 'something clean and square'.[85]

All of this relates directly to the views expressed in *Rossetti*. There he proposes

---

83. *Ibid.*, p. 102.
84. 'Cities of the Future', *Observer*, 11 August, 1929; review of Le Corbusier, *The City of Tomorrow*, trans. Frederick Etchells (Rodker, 1929); *EAR*, pp. 63–5.
85. *Decline and Fall.*, p. 119.

two attitudes to life: the 'romantic' and the 'mystical'. The first broke experience up into separate pieces and examined them individually; life was just 'one damned thing after another'. The second saw 'process', form, pattern – 'duration', to use Bergson's term. The difference between the two was the difference (in the terms Spengler borrows from an ancient philosophical debate) between 'being' and 'becoming', intellect and intuition. Rossetti, Waugh thought, belonged to the second category. But unlike Grimes, he did not struggle 'to break a way through matter, learning gradually to use matter by means of organization'. Instead he succumbed and was ultimately dragged down by it. Prendergast's fate demonstrates how matter cannot be ignored; it attacks the individual unless attacked first. Dockery, whose romantic stolidity sees the universe as a composite of discernible facts, issues carpenters' tools to a homicidal maniac. All criminal activity, he believes, is the result of artistic frustration. He will not be dissuaded from his neat theory until Prendy is decapitated with a saw.

This hilarious twist might remind us of the conclusion of a later short story, 'Mr Loveday's Little Outing'. Even as a Catholic Waugh changed little in his approach. There was a temperamental sympathy for eccentrics, manipulators, men of the world and a compensating scorn for the fact-mongering rationalists. In much of his writing there is a conflict between those who understand the evanescence of the 'bodiless harlequinade' and adapt to exploit it, and those who are dupes to the essential 'romantic' folly that *rien n'est vrai que le pittoresque*. Beauty was not truth for Waugh and the intellectual beauty of a coherent system explaining the vagaries of behaviour was furthest of all from reality. Psychologists, sociologists, economists and politicians, with their vain faith in the power of reason, were no more than professional bores to him, barking in empty coverts while the fox, irrational but cunning, sported itself in a meadow downwind. Only the absolute truth he saw in Catholicism and the occasional splash of colour from man's eternal (and to him delicious) propensity for lunacy made life at all tolerable.

*Decline and Fall* can be read, not simply as nihilistic farce but as an exuberant, drunken challenge to Mammon. Let the world threaten us with its materialistic absurdities, its schools and prisons and barbarous aristocrats, Grimes (and, by implication, Waugh) as a life-force will survive. It is almost as though Pennyfeather represented what Waugh had most feared he might become – a failure at Oxford, easily contented with the routine of schoolmastering, a dupe to romantic passion and confidence tricksters, a drifter rather than an incisive force in the world. Paul's career at 'a small public school of ecclesiastical temper on the South Downs' clearly reflects Waugh's own. Pennyfeather's unambitious undergraduate life is similar to Evelyn's first two terms at Hertford.

Waugh was then constantly handing out pretentious advice to Carew as to how best to live his life. He was full of theories in those days. In practice he found himself to be shy with the opposite sex, romantic and self-conscious; he blundered into pomposity, over-reacting to imagined attacks; he became frightened and appalled at the marginal control he appeared to have over the circumstances which governed his life. That is not to say, of course, that Pennyfeather *is* Waugh. But Evelyn probably felt a closer association with him than might at first be apparent. Paul grows a 'cavalry moustache' to disguise himself on returning to Oxford. A few months after the publication of the novel, Lady Eleanor Smith reported of Waugh: 'His coming tour awakened a second idiosyncrasy – he is to grow a very hearty, terrific moustache.'[86]

\*

The moustache may have been a joke but the tour certainly was not. A. D. Peters had persuaded the line operating the *MY Stella Polaris* to allow free passage to Waugh and his wife in return for publicity about the ship in a subsequent travel book. They were due to leave in February 1929. She-Evelyn had recovered from her illness but her health was still fragile and the winter particularly severe. The trip was to be their first real honeymoon – a chance for her to regain her strength and for Waugh to collect material for a new novel. Both needed to recuperate.

During the autumn Waugh had been struggling to establish his reputation. He had written regular reviews of art books for Viola Garvin in the *Observer*, knocked out his piece on 'Youth' for the *Standard*, and prepared a series of light articles for *The Passing Show:* 'Careers for Our Sons'. Although it had not been a period of intense literary activity it had certainly been one of strain. *Decline and Fall* had been a constant source of anxiety as had his wife's health. Her convalescence had lasted until early November and money remained a problem. They could not have accepted the free passage had not her sister, Alathea, underwritten the incidental expenses.

With the New Year, however, their prospects improved. The *Standard* article appeared in January and provoked enough reaction to require a reply; the *Spectator* asked him to continue the argument. Both pieces appeared in April after he had left for the Mediterranean and display greater seriousness. 'Clearly', he says in the first, 'I had not made myself plain. I appear to have given the impression that youth was admirable . . . the one fundamental failing of the whole of the younger generation is their almost complete lack of qualitative standards.'[87] The second re-phrases the Lancing editorial, again dividing European society into three generations split by the war. But, he continues, 'the real and lasting injury to the younger generation was caused, not by danger, but by the pervading sense of inadequacy. Everything was a "substitute" for something else, and there was barely enough of even that.'[88]

Having taken up the cause of youth to gain a foothold in the popular press, he

86. *SD*, 3 February 1929, 4. The piece was probably written by Patrick Balfour.
87. 'Matter-of-Fact Mothers of the New Age', *ES*, 8 April, 1929, 7.
88. 'The War and the Younger Generation', *Spectator*, 13 April, 1929, 570–1; *EAR*, pp. 61–2.

wished quickly to abandon it. If he was to be misinterpreted as advocating shingled hair, free love and all the other absurdities which enraged elderly readers of the *Standard*, then he would have to set the record straight. He did not respect the 'intolerable tolerance' of the majority of young people. They had debased the word 'real' ('People no longer speak of "pearls" and "artificial pearls" but of "pearls" and "real pearls" '); they were not representative of that group of individual minds to which he had originally drawn attention. He lauds instead 'the unsystematic discipline' of the modern mother 'who aims at a very small family kept well in the background of a hygienic nursery'. The new generation should be 'hard' and 'unsympathetic' (qualities in Waugh's view), but not 'analytical'. It should oppose the cloying domestic confusion of the two previous ages and the undiscriminating standards of its own. At present he saw no sign of it developing a coherent system of aesthetic or moral standards to replace those it had rejected.

Waugh left England in February a rather serious young man. Balfour advertised his departure in terms calculated to excite the envy of *Daily Sketch* readers. Mr and Mrs Waugh, he noted,

> ... were about to spend the proceeds of *Decline and Fall* in a tour of Southeastern Europe and the Levant from Monte Carlo to the Crimea ... in ... the most luxurious boat in the whole Mediterranean. 'But the trip to Soviet Russia,' said Mr Waugh, 'will be on a Turkish cargo boat.' ... Mr Waugh is going to write a travel diary about the trip. ... But there is more to come: 'I am really going to concentrate on drawing during the voyage. ... I hope I can bring back enough sketches to hold an exhibition in June, and, if it is successful, abandon writing for painting.'[89]

His ambition to be a graphic artist died hard.

In fact the journey was not at all glamorous. The travel diary Waugh kept was later destroyed after serving its purpose as an *aide-mémoire* for *Labels* (1930). That book is the only record we have of the journey. There is no mention of his wife. To avoid the embarrassment of her presence he created a fictional couple, Geoffrey and Juliet 'presumably, from the endearments of their conversation and marked solicitude for each other's comforts, on their honeymoon ...'.[90] But there is no mistaking the identity of Mr and Mrs Waugh, despite the fact that they are described as strangers. 'The young man', he wrote, 'was small and pleasantly dressed and wore a slight, curly moustache.'[91]

*

89. 'Evelyn Waugh as Artist', *DS*, 30 January, 1929, 5.
90. *Labels*, p. 21.
91. *Ibid.*, p. 29.

*Labels* suggests that they flew to Paris (they did not: far too costly) and from there caught an inexpensive train to Monte Carlo. During the journey south the bitter winter refused to soften. The windows of the train were frosted over and She-Evelyn sat huddled and shivering in a fur coat. Clearly she was beginning to sicken again. Waugh took her temperature – it was 104°. Rather foolishly he persuaded her to drink *crème de menthe*. By nightfall she was feverish and he put her to bed in a *couchette*, a decision made difficult by the expense. There was no room for him. Next day they arrived in Monte Carlo to find it deep in snow. 'We walked from hotel to hotel', Mrs Nightingale wrote to the present author, 'because when they saw I looked ill they didn't want to take us in. Finally, we succeeded and Evelyn got a doctor. I *think* we were there two days.'[92]

The *Stella Polaris* took them from there via Naples and Haifa to Port Said. 'I knew I was ill', Mrs Nightingale says, 'because I spat blood. The journey was a nightmare. Evelyn went ashore at Haifa for the day and brought me back "a flower of the field". The ship got an Israeli [*sic*] nurse in who was hopeless and stayed till Port Said. There the head of the hospital insisted that I go ashore to the hospital. I was left on the stretcher for two days as they were afraid to move me. I was very well looked after at the hospital; the head doctor, I think, saved my life. This was when poor Pansy [Lamb] had a postcard from Evelyn saying that by the time she got it, I would probably be dead.'[93]

They had vainly hoped that the voyage would effect a recovery. On 6th March Waugh scribbled hastily to Harold Acton from Port Said:

> I should have written before but I have been so worried about Evelyn & with cabling bulletins to all our relatives that I have not written a letter since we started. You have probably heard how ill she has been. Double pneumonia critically ill for a fortnight.
>
> At last she is out of danger. Meanwhile of course our trip is broken, we shall be here for a month & all my work at a standstill. I hope now things are easier to start on a new novel. . . .
>
> Apart from everything else this illness has been frightfully expensive, so that we shall not be able to do any more travelling unless perhaps we go to Cyprus for a fortnight while Evelyn recuperates.[94]

Alathea Fry sent them £50 but ideas of Turkish cargo boats to Russia had now to be abandoned.

Alastair Graham, having returned to Athens with the Diplomatic Service, was his nearest friend. Christopher Sykes states that at this point Evelyn travelled to Cyprus to meet him and devotes a paragraph to excusing this 'odd' behaviour on

92. ALS from Mrs Evelyn Nightingale (née Gardner), 23 January, 1986.
93. *Ibid.*
94. *Letters*, p. 31.

the grounds that Waugh 'did not want to disappoint an old friend'.[95] In a letter to the present writer Alastair Graham clarified this misunderstanding: 'Christopher Sykes is mistaken', he wrote, 'in saying that we met in Cyprus. I was never there at the time. But I vividly remember receiving a pathetic cry for help from Port Said when Evelyn was ill in hospital and going over there to see if I could be of any use. . . .'[96] Waugh was desperate. He never forgot this spontaneous expression of loyalty.

Graham stayed for two days. Port Said had a salacious reputation. The two of them pottered disconsolately off in search of low-life 'local colour' for Waugh's proposed books only to find (as he told Acton) 'Two expensive & very dirty hotels, one brothel, a cinema & this awful club [the Union Club] where the shipping office clerks try to create an Ethel M. Dell garrison life by drinking endless "gin & tonic" & talking about "the old country" and "pukka sahibs" '.[97] The intolerable dullness of the place did nothing to distract him from worry. In those days he had no sympathy for the colonial mentality.

Waugh visited his wife in hospital and tried to read her P. G. Wodehouse but her fever rendered even these simple narratives unintelligible. When she was well enough to go out for drives they began to think of moving on. Cyprus was forsaken on the hearsay that it had no hotels fit to cater for an invalid. Instead they decided to head south – 'wherever, in fact,' he wrote to his father, 'I can persuade an hotel to give me advantageous terms in return for commendation in my book'.[98] By the end of March they were happily ensconced in the 'enormous and hideously expensive'[99] Mena House in the shadow of the pyramids a few miles from Cairo.[100]

It was a relatively contented time. Waugh was intensely relieved to escape from Port Said with its associations of illness. In the sunshine his wife steadily regained her strength. They were alone together at last without the interference of doctors or relations. Catastrophe averted, Waugh's impish humour returned and he could view his surroundings with that old delight in the exotic and absurd. 'There is a huge garden full of garish flowers & improbable insects – ', he wrote to Acton, 'all rather like the final scene of a Paris revue. The people range from exquisitely amusing Australian trippers with sun helmets & fly whisks to Cairo demi-mondaines in picture frocks – one with a pet monkey in silver harness which

---

95. Sykes, p. 92.
96. ALS from Alastair Graham to Martin Stannard, 10 June, 1977. Mrs Nightingale adds: 'I remember clearly saying that I would not go [to Cyprus] but thought it would be nice for Evelyn as he had been so bored in Port Said with nothing to do. I do not know who told Christopher Sykes of it. He *never* came to see me, even though I had asked Tony Powell to tell him I would see him' (ALS from Mrs Evelyn Nightingale, *op. cit.*).
97. *Letters*, p. 31.
98. *Ibid*, p. 31.
99. *Ibid.*, p. 32.
100. 'Mena House – Hotel Pyramid's. On their notepaper, a quantity of which Waugh removed, another hotel in the group is named as 'Shepheards', the title he used later that year for Rosa Lewis's 'Cavendish' in *Vile Bodies*.

sits & fleas its rump on the terrace.'[101] His mind at ease, the world was once again a Firbank novel.

She-Evelyn's uncle, Lord Carnarvon, had secured fame in 1923 as co-leader of the archaeological expedition in the Valley of the Kings. Waugh was keen to see what had been unearthed and was overwhelmed by its beauty: ' . . . the Tutankhamen discoveries', he informed Acton, 'are real works of art – of exquisite grace – just as fine as anything which has survived of Athenian art.'[102] He regarded the tour as an opportunity for aesthetic gluttony. At every stop he wanted to soak himself in each country's art treasures. Objects of purely historical importance held no interest – the Sphinx was 'a complete fraud, a shapeless lump of masonry. . . . We leave here on the 12th', he continued, '& go to Malta where I hear there are some fine churches and then to Constantinople for alas only two days. Then via Ragusa to Venice for another two days. It will just give me time I suppose to see some pictures. . . . Do please send us advice as to what to see in Venice in so short a time. Remember I know nothing of Venetian painting except for what I have seen in London & the Louvre.'[103]

This to Waugh was the very stuff of life. This was why he wanted to be rich. Money allowed the freedom to develop civilised tastes and to enjoy them in untramelled independence. Wealth made the difference, if used discriminatingly, between 'being' and 'becoming', static and dynamic. Unfortunately there was very little of it available to the young couple. They were substantially overdrawn before they even embarked on the *Ranchi* for Malta. There was no option but to travel second-class.

It was an overcrowded, uncomfortable journey with 'no place above or below', as he remarked in *Labels*, 'for a man who values silence'.[104] Before leaving, Waugh had written to the two leading hotels proposing the customary deal: free accommodation for a kind reference in the book. One, at least, he expected to refuse. On board he had been advised which was the better. Much to his surprise, representatives of both met him at the customs house. Undaunted, Waugh directed the man from the superior hotel to take charge of his luggage while the other angrily waved the letter in his face. 'A forgery,' Waugh explained coolly. 'I am afraid that you have been deluded by a palpable forgery.'[105] He loved winning; getting something for nothing through the exercise of mild duplicity gave him the greatest pleasure. And there was another stroke of good fortune in Malta: the *Stella Polaris* had docked on her second cruise. The remainder of their journey home would be *gratis*.

From Malta they sailed to Crete and Constantinople. Trying to impress his

101. *Letters*, pp. 32–3.
102. *Ibid.*, p. 33.
103. *Ibid*, p. 33.
104. *Labels*, p. 120.
105. *Ibid.*, p. 123.

readers in *Labels* he casually let it drop that he had dined at the Embassy: 'Osbert and Sacheverell Sitwell were there, combining the gay enthusiasm for the subtleties of Turkish rococo with unfathomable erudition about Byzantine archaeology and the scandals of Ottoman diplomacy.'[106] The situation had in fact been rather different. 'We saw Osbert and Sachie and Georgia Sitwell . . .', he informed Acton, 'but only for a brief and rather uneasy luncheon party at the Embassy.'[107] He was much happier a few days later in the light-hearted atmosphere of Athens with Alastair and Mark Ogilvy-Grant.

Mark was 'very sweet and skittish' and, according to Waugh, outrageous in his behaviour, 'relieved of the burden of keeping up appearances'.[108] Alastair disappeared periodically to decode telegrams at the Chancery. It was all great fun for Waugh. Very little time was spent on this second visit touring the sights. It was a delightful round of restaurants and night clubs and dinners on the ship. Perhaps his wife felt a little awkward in this overtly homosexual world. But if she did, he failed to notice. She was well again and the prospect of the return journey via Italy and Spain filled him with excitement.

In Venice he found Adrian Stokes and a city with so complex a cultural heritage that it defied his customary aesthetic generalisations. Ragusa (Dubrovnik) impressed him with its aristocratic, 'Catholic' aloofness, its fourteenth-century Venetian Gothic and sixteenth-century baroque. The stop at Barcelona provided the 'discovery' of the contemporary *art nouveau* architect, Gaudi, whose work displayed that 'inarticulate fantasy'[109] he found essential in all great art. By mid-April they were back in England and Waugh felt himself to be richly loaded with experience. Despite the debts and near disasters of the voyage, he was confident of his ability to set matters right with a few weeks' industry. The dream of abandoning authorship for painting had been destroyed by the various disruptions. On the way home he had had to spend his spare time writing articles and posting them to Peters. But few had met with success and he accepted the fact that there could now be no further delay before he attempted another novel.

He had written to Acton from Athens, pleased at his friends' concern, saying that they had received letters from (among others) John Heygate. A tall, lounging, mild-mannered man, always well-dressed, Heygate was an affable, attractive fellow. Waugh took to him immediately and Heygate became a frequent visitor to the flat. It was there that Anthony Powell met him and Powell and he remained friends for life. The Heygate-Waugh alliance, as we now know, was to end abruptly. In the letters he was soon to be characterised contemptuously as 'the Basement Boy'; in the fiction he became John Beaver.

*

106. *Ibid.*, p. 146.
107. Unpublished ALS to Harold Acton, nd [May 1929], on *Stella Polaris* notepaper.
108. *Letters*, p. 34.
109. *Labels*, p. 179.

The London Waugh returned to in the spring of 1929 was vibrant with contrast. As the *Stella Polaris* came into the Channel news reached the ship of the first day's count in the General Election. That election brought Labour into office. Under Ramsay Macdonald, it was promised, the poorer classes would receive their share of the cake. The rule of the rich was over.

At the same time, the capital was the scene of riotous social extravagance. With the advent of the gossip column, Society had become 'news'. The *ancien régime* maintained its stately gatherings in the mansions of Mayfair and Belgravia; their children, in the guise of Bright Young Things, racketed from party to party. Both were reported with great relish in the popular press. 'William Hickey' and 'Dragoman' provided fantasies of opulence for the less fortunate enduring the timetabled lives of Metroland. One might have expected an electorate radical enough to support Socialism to have reacted bitterly against the undisguised decadence of the wealthy. But, for the majority, the opposite was the case. That peculiarly British love of its ruling class was never seriously challenged until the 'fifties. In 1929, the fact that the antics of young Lords were written up alongside cookery tips and gardening calendars seemed revolution enough. Papers like the *Mail* and the *Express* projected an illusion of comradeship between the classes which helped maintain the status quo.

Although nothing fundamental had changed, everything appeared to be in a state of flux. There was not only a new government, but new functional artistic forms; chrome and pre-cast concrete seemed to bear the promise of a Brave New World. Architects vied with each other to design stations for the London Underground; *couturiers* no longer based the designs for their clothes on the need to disguise the human body. It was the period of short skirts and cloche hats, Eton crops and shingled hair. Girls lopped off coiling tresses which had formerly been a point of vanity; young men had long since refused to wear the frock coats and wing collars of their fathers. Sunbathing became a 'craze' and occasionally provoked near riots as gangs of moralists attempted to disrupt harmless, half-clothed folk at the Welsh Harp. The word 'craze' itself evokes much of the atmosphere of those times. Anything that was 'modern' was news; anything that was modern and indulged in by the rich and smart was especially good news.

People had grown tired of the war and its aftermath. Waugh's irreverence towards the hero-dominated society had articulated a predominant feeling amongst the younger generation. They were bored with this old albatross. For the last year the literary market had been saturated with war books and it was to continue in this vein beyond 1930. Christopher Isherwood later discussed the problem in *Lions and Shadows* (1938). Young men, he suggested, had experienced a sense of guilt and inadequacy at having missed the Test of Manhood. They had had enough of enforced gratitude. If those who were too young to have shared in the ordeal were prevented from joining the adult world on equal terms then they would make a virtue of their youth and use this as their weapon.

[ 177 ]

Waugh returned to an aggressively 'youthful' society. The cocktail and bottle parties had been invented; fashionable treasure hunts rampaged through department stores and across country; elaborate fancy-dress parties became so commonplace that even the gossip columns began to grow weary of this predictable scrambling for the unpredictable. An exasperated Arnold Bennett had entitled his unfavourable review of *Humdrum*: 'Being New At Any Cost', and the phrase conveniently summarises the attitude of the Bright Young Things. Their search for novelty even produced a superficial re-shuffling of social roles. Threatened by income tax and death duties, the young aristocracy pronounced itself eager to earn its living. Heirs apparent trained as journalists and sold motor cars; debs appeared behind the counters of expensive milliners. Henry Green during this period was working on the shop floor of his father's Birmingham factory from which experience he wrote *Living* (1929), the *avant-garde* novel Waugh thought a masterpiece. Green, like Frank Pakenham, Peter Quennell, Graham Greene, Claude Cockburn, Tom Driberg and Nancy Mitford, had socialist sympathies. Not all of Waugh's friends were right-wing.

There was a general feeling that the hypocrisy and class-consciousness of Edwardian society had been overturned by youth. Elderly hostesses were outraged by the arrival of uninvited guests and gatecrashing in every sense became something of a sport. All the old, artificial barriers appeared to be breachable. The Socialists had forced their way into Parliament; the wealthy had discarded false pride and taken to trade. Negro jazz singers hob-nobbed with the highest in the land and the notorious Mrs Meyrick ran a chain of illegal night clubs to send her son to Harrow on the profits. She was a typical eccentric of the period. No-one thought any the less of her for several stretches in prison. Her daughters married into the aristocracy. Rosa Lewis was another with her 'young men' and her extraordinary Cavendish Hotel [110] where 'a bottle of wine' was always champagne.

People with money, it appeared, were willing to try anything, and people without money were persuaded that they could easily acquire it. Amongst the smart young set, sex could be talked of openly. Havelock Ellis and dog-eared copies of *Ulysses* (smuggled from Paris) passed from hand to hand. The Labour victory had routed Sir William Joynson Hicks, a particularly prudish Home Secretary, but those eager to listen to the truth-tellers still found themselves baulked by the Obscene Publications Act. An exhibition of Lawrence's paintings (attended by Waugh) in July 1929 was closed down and the canvases confiscated; Radclyffe Hall's *The Well of Loneliness* had been suppressed by the year before and, like *Lady Chatterley*, was available only under the counter. Most young educated men and women were sceptical of those who set themselves up as the guardians of morality. And in the spiritual vacuum left by their devalued seers and churchmen they sometimes

110.   The book and television series, *The Duchess of Duke Street*, were based on her.

turned to dangerous or flamboyant substitutes. Aimée Semple Macpherson's ranting American evangelism attracted huge crowds. Astrology and black magic were re-examined. Among the more serious-minded, conversion to Catholicism increased as did the adoption of some form of radical political ideology. But many, and especially those to whom the logistics of survival were not a serious business, found nothing to fill that void except 'fun'. The parties became wilder, the drinking heavier, the divorce rate higher. Drug abuse (hashish, cocaine) was not unusual for the Bright Young People.

All this, of course, had not suddenly exploded in British society since Waugh's departure for the Mediterranean. Even so, returning to the London season after the painful experiences of the voyage, primed with aesthetic enthusiasm for Catholic culture and the great works of European art, he found the new Bohemianism irredeemably trivial. Association with the smart set flattered his self-esteem and he had fought long and hard for his place there. But he could no longer join in their games with enthusiasm. Crowds and mob hedonism distressed him.

His young wife, though, was understandably keen to taste a little irresponsible pleasure. If the cruise had been difficult for Waugh, it had been worse for her. With her health at last restored, and returned to the supporting framework of their wealthy friends, she wanted to dress up, go out and enjoy herself. For two months she had lived almost exclusively in Waugh's company or that of comparative strangers. He was (and remained) a demanding companion for anyone in perfect health. For an invalid, despite his assiduous attentions, it must have been a testing time. Some of the romantic enthusiasm which had led her into an impetuous marriage had inevitably died during that trip. During the year of their marriage she had suffered two serious illnesses and an operation. In order to collect material for his travel diary Waugh had often disappeared on solitary excursions. Now she wanted company.

*

Waugh had that novel to write. Christopher Sykes suggests that some of it had already been completed during the cruise. This is not necessarily the case. Possible confusion arises from a letter Waugh scrawled to his agent on the notepaper of a Cairo Hotel: 'I have asked Evelyn to send you as soon as they are typed the first ten thousand words of *Vile Bodies*, my new novel.'[111] It became Waugh's practice to remove quantities of hotel notepaper during his travels. In this case the address has been deleted and 'Abingdon Arms, Beckley, Oxon' inserted in its place. Clearly, it was written in England after his return and from the retreat he had used while working on *Rossetti*.

The two Evelyns' temporary separation was amicably arranged. He needed to be alone to complete the novel quickly. She wanted to enjoy London social life.

111.   Unpublished ALS to A. D. Peters, nd [about 26 June, 1929]; *Catalogue*, E106.

During June Waugh had left for Beckley, and to keep She-Evelyn company her closest friend, Nancy Mitford, had moved into the spare room in Canonbury Square. Heygate and the other unattached men of their circle could be relied upon, Waugh thought, to chaperone his wife through the visits to nightclubs and parties for the six weeks or so of his absence.

One of the smartest venues for the Bright Young People was the *Friendship*, an old sailing ship moored permanently at Charing Cross Pier. Crowds of up to five thousand would often assemble to watch the revels and marvel at the costumes. In late June, Bryan and Diana Guinness had hired it: 'It was a fancy-dress party,' said the *Bystander*, 'inspiration to be taken from Watteau, but nowadays all such routs seem to be seized upon not so much for fancy dressing as fancy undressing. There was a cosmopolitan and bohemian mixture of guests that included . . . the Hon. Nancy Mitford and the Hon. Mrs Evelyn Waugh whose husband has isolated himself in the country in an attempt to excel his first novel. . . .'[112] The girls were having a grand time with Heygate constantly in attendance. Hosts were for ever attempting to out-do one another with original themes for their extravaganzas and Heygate had firmly established himself as a leading figure by his 'Party Without End'. (Guests could arrive, leave and return as they wished, to be regaled with a variety of exotic sandwiches.) There seemed no limit to possible permutations: Mrs 'Syrie' Maugham's 'White Party' for stage people; Norman Hartnell's 'Circus Party' (to which Eleanor Smith took a pony); even a 'Second Childhood Party' at which people arrived in prams and baby clothing, the evening concluding with a car race round the square to the accompaniment of shouts and cat-calls and motor hooters.

Far away from all this in the silence of the Oxfordshire countryside Waugh was struggling with his book. He returned to London for the week-ends but, apart from his wife and Nancy, seemed always to miss the people he most wanted to meet. For some weeks he had not seen Harold Acton and, depressed about his work, he wrote to him from Beckley:

> I see your name often in the papers, reported as appearing at parties. I nearly came up again today for Bryan's party but I feel so chained to this novel. I am sure you will disapprove of it. It is a welter of sex and snobbery written simply in the hope of selling some copies. Then if it is [at] all a success I want to try and write something more serious. I have done half of it and hope to get it finished in another three weeks.[113]

He still could not convince himself that he was a novelist. The main problem, perhaps, apart from the uncongenial labour of composition, was that he lacked a subject. He could project fantasies of a disorientated modern world and mock its

112. *Bystander*, 3 July, 1929, 4–5.
113. *Letters*, p. 37.

insufficiency and contradictions. But he had no 'point of view', no moral position in his love-hate relationship with anarchy. He was intrigued by the linguistic experiments of Firbank, Henry Green and Hemingway and was trying to develop them further in his new work. But there was no object on which he could focus them. While he despaired at the vacuity of the London party world and its clamouring for novelty, he could not avoid a certain sympathy for its reckless hedonism. The first part of his book (described to Acton) was not the bitter satire it was to become. Corrections were made a few months later to transform its gently malicious tone. Quite suddenly he found his subject and 'point of view'. More correctly, it was forced upon him by events which nearly cost him his sanity.

During those weeks of seclusion in June and early July he had been working to a fixed routine. As each section was written, he would send it to his wife who would have it typed and passed on to Peters for his criticism. Shortly after he had written to Acton, a letter (dated 9th July) arrived from She-Evelyn which had nothing to do with the book. She was in a desperate confusion of happiness and misery. She had, she said, fallen in love with John Heygate and did not know what to do about it. She begged forgiveness, even help; emotionally, it seems, she had plunged beyond her depth.

Waugh was devastated. 'Evelyn's defection', he later wrote to his parents, 'was preceded by no kind of quarrel or estrangement. So far as I knew we were both serenely happy.'[114] The foundations of their trust had seemed to him deep and permanent. His first reaction was to think that his wife had lost her senses. It could not be true. There had to be a more reasonable explanation.

Abandoning the novel, he returned to London immediately. The situation was intensely embarrassing. Nancy Mitford was still in the flat though she knew nothing of the affair; his wife was racked with guilt and more than a little afraid. But she could only repeat what she had said in the letter. Heygate and she were not only 'in love' but lovers. Waugh was appalled but, in this desperate situation, prepared to simulate liberality. He had never been able to take sexual passion altogether seriously. Their relationship was too precious to be destroyed by hurt pride over a casual affair. If she would give up Heygate, he said, he would forget the whole business and they could go on as before. Out of loyalty to him, she agreed. It was the sensible, logical thing to do.

Waugh stayed in London for a fortnight and neglected his novel in an attempt to repair the marriage. Perhaps he thought that their difficulties had been caused by his too frequent neglect of her. Perhaps he had taken her undying love for granted and left her alone too often. In later years this was Catherine Waugh's explanation. She-Evelyn denies ever claiming (or even thinking) that she had felt neglected during her husband's absences. The marital problems were not so

114. *Ibid.*, p. 38.

simple and Waugh must have known this. Nevertheless, the experience had jolted him badly. Determined not to make the same mistake again, he embarked upon the round of party-going she had enjoyed with Heygate. Wherever she went, her husband was now always at her side.

Christopher Sykes suggests that this interlude was happy. It was not. 'We decided once more to try and "make a go" of our marriage', wrote Mrs Nightingale. 'The following fortnight was a very unhappy time with E. even saying that I was trying to poison him! He had been reading the early Agatha Christie's which we both enjoyed.'[115] The caption beneath a photograph of the couple in the *Bystander* was perhaps more perceptive than its author realised: 'The Hon. Mrs Evelyn Waugh and her husband attired for the "Tropical" party – ', it read, 'which was hot in more ways than one – on board the Friendship. The author of *Decline and Fall* looks somewhat scared, although there were no fierce Zulus on board.'[116] London was sweltering in a heat-wave. Waugh was irritable and nervous. Although the subject of Heygate had been dropped, neither was able to forget about him. She cannot have escaped the impression that she was being watched or, at least, guarded. Disguising their embarrassing secret made the situation all the more awkward. Waugh no doubt felt saddened that even his marriage was now 'shop soiled and second hand'. Compromise did not come easily to him.

The Waughs were reported at various parties during July. That was also the month of the now famous 'Bruno Hatte' hoax staged by Bryan Guinness and his friends. An exhibition of *avant-garde* paintings in the style of Picasso was faked with Tom Mitford, heavily disguised, and mumbling from a wheelchair in incoherent German, playing the part of this artistic 'discovery'. Waugh wrote the catalogue notes but no critics hailed a new genius in Herr Hatte. Everyone was anticipating the fashionable acceptance of the incomprehensible. Only a few of the public were taken in. Lytton Strachey bought a painting to please Diana Guinness, knowing perfectly well that it was a fake. Even so, Waugh must have seemed an enviable fellow. At twenty-five with two books behind him and a third in the pipeline, above all with his attractive wife and rich friends, he was depicted in the newspapers as the epitome of the smart young man. His public image was everything he had sought to make it. He must constantly have been aware of the gap between this and the reality: the new novel and the marriage were both in a bad way.

Experience warned him against sliding into self-pity and disorganisation, but it was impossible to work in these circumstances. *Vile Bodies* was promised for autumn publication. If it were a failure and he were to slip back into the role of dilettante unemployed schoolmaster, all hope would be lost. Persecution mania

115. ALS from Mrs Evelyn Nightingale, *op. cit.*
116. *Bystander*, 17 July, 1929, 178–9.

haunted him. Heygate, an old Etonian and a news editor in the newly formed BBC, was the youngest son of a baronet. Waugh felt that he held his position in 'Society' through force of talent. In his eyes, She-Evelyn's adultery was perhaps more than a personal affront; there was an element in it of the aristocracy closing ranks on a *parvenu*. Of course it was nothing of the sort. But he could never forget Golders Green.

What happened next is open to debate. Christopher Sykes says that after Waugh's fortnight of conscientious social activity to re-establish himself as his wife's husband, he left for Cheshire for five days on 26th July. There then follows a dramatic account (presumably deriving from Nancy Mitford) of She-Evelyn's being photographed at a party with Heygate after her promise never to see him again. They had met accidentally, says Sykes, but She-Evelyn feared repercussions. She then revealed to Nancy that she had never loved her husband. She had married only to escape parental oppression and now she regretted it.

The statement appears in the eyes of the official biographer to be damning evidence of callousness. He adds that Harold Acton and Pansy Pakenham both thought that her long illness had 'worked a change in her mind and feelings' and that the idea that she had never loved Evelyn was a retrospective delusion. (The passionate commitment to her fiancé expressed in that letter to Waugh's mother can leave no doubt about this.) Sykes's story concludes with Waugh's returning from Cheshire, shocked to find the flat empty, his wife's and Nancy's possessions removed. He was, we are told, forced into the humiliating expedient of seeking out the woman employed as a daily help to learn what had happened. The next day a letter arrived from his wife. It informed him that she was living with Heygate in his flat in Cornwall Gardens, South Kensington.[117] Mrs Nightingale recalls the chronology of events rather differently.

According to her, the fortnight in London was the period of Waugh's attempted reconciliation which concluded with *his* decision that they should divorce. Anthony Powell and Heygate were at the time on holiday together in Germany. It was at this point Waugh sent the telegram noted by Powell in his memoirs: 'Instruct Heygate return immediately Waugh.'[118] This was in effect a demand for Heygate to come and take She-Evelyn away. Lady Burghclere insisted that her daughter go to Venice to think things over. She-Evelyn and Heygate, both following instructions, accordingly found themselves during the next week still hundreds of miles apart. In Italy she heard from Heygate that he was waiting for her – so she returned at once and went to live temporarily with him in Cornwall Gardens. Shortly afterwards they moved into the Canonbury Square flat as the lease was in her name and Waugh wanted nothing more to do with the place. There was no shock desertion: the decision to separate had been taken by Waugh himself,

117. Cf. Sykes, pp. 93–5.
118. *Messengers of Day, op. cit.*, p. 128.

as his letters testify. The story about the daily help was probably a fiction. He would certainly not have been surprised to find the flat empty. Nancy had left, fearing scandal, as soon as she knew that the couple might separate. The shock was at standing alone in the place which, only three weeks earlier, had formed the focus of an apparently serene domestic life. Perhaps he had hoped that she would change her mind and be waiting repentantly for him. Now he knew that she had taken him at his word. There would be no going back.

She-Evelyn was frightened and ashamed. Her guilt at the pain she had caused left enduring scars which have often been opened by wounding public references to her desertion. In fact, given that events had gone too far for reclamation, she acted as honourably as she could. Catherine Waugh wanted her daughter-in-law to divorce Waugh, it being the 'proper' course in those days for the woman to act as plaintiff, no matter where the blame lay. (Diana Guinness divorced Bryan Guinness in 1934 at her father's insistence, despite the fact that it was she who was having an affair – with Oswald Mosley.) She-Evelyn refused this easy option and the salvation of her 'reputation'. It was her fault that the marriage had broken down and she was willing to admit it openly. As we shall see, she offered further evidence against herself in Waugh's defence four years later.

As a Catholic, Christopher Sykes is justified in his intolerance of adultery. The present writer has spoken to many of Waugh's contemporaries and, in general, the Catholics among them have adopted a similarly critical attitude towards Evelyn Gardner. Douglas Woodruff, for example, found her 'silly', a lightweight product of the Jazz Age. Sykes never met her, only coming into contact with Waugh some months after the separation. Many others, however, were shocked at his portrayal of her as a brittle philandress. Anthony Powell has remained her lifelong friend. Alec Waugh thought her irresistibly charming and intelligent. The late Lord Kinross (Patrick Balfour) agreed with this. The same question was put to them all: 'Do you think that, at least as far as she was concerned, the sexual side of the marriage was inadequate?' Most agreed that they had long believed this to be the case.

Waugh wrote a second article on marriage a year later, in August 1930. It has an oddly personal ring to it in the light of this evidence:

> Responsible people . . . say, 'You cannot lead a happy life unless your sex life is happy.' . . . It is not only nonsense, it is mischievous nonsense. It means that the moment a wife begins to detect imperfections in her husband she thinks her whole life is ruined. . . . By the present system of education the one thing that is hidden is the actual facts about sex; as a natural result [people] regard this as the most important thing of all. When they find that after some time of marriage sexual relations are not so absorbingly interesting as they had been led to suppose, they

think it is because they have made a mistake in their choice of mate. Then they get into the divorce courts.[119]

Was he speaking here of his own experience? We shall probably never know. Waugh refused ever to discuss the matter. His first wife is understandably reticent: 'Of course I meant what I said when I wrote to Mrs Waugh. But my marriage wasn't exactly warm. Evelyn was not an affectionate person. I was.'[120]

During August various further attempts at reconciliation were made by the two families but without success. Waugh was dissuaded from immediately seeking a divorce. A month of painful discussions passed. Then, on 3rd September Waugh filed a petition against his wife through E. S. P. Haynes and on the 9th was required to attend at the solicitor's office to serve it on her. The then barbaric divorce law also required the presence of Heygate and a professional informer to identify him as the 'co-respondent'. It was a brief and formal ceremony. Waugh never saw Heygate again. He met Mrs Heygate (as she became) on one further occasion, several years later.

119. 'Tell the Truth About Marriage', *JB*, 23 August, 1930; *EAR*, pp. 94–6.
120. Unpublished letter from Mrs Evelyn Nightingale (née Gardner) to Martin Stannard, February 1986.

# VI
## *Hunger for Permanence:*
## *1929–1930*

'There is practically no part of one that is not injured when a thing like this happens', Waugh wrote to Henry Yorke in September, 'but naturally vanity is one of the things one is most generally conscious of . . .'.[1] The public humiliation cut deeply. In an effort to cheer him, John Sutro took him out to dinner. It was not a success. Waugh sensed that the people in the restaurant were laughing at him.[2] During the tortured negotiations preceding the separation he had begun to drink fiercely and, as we have seen, developed a belladonna complex.[3] His terror of ridicule, largely buried since Lancing, had emerged more forcefully than ever.

Waugh's first reaction was to escape London. He went to stay with people he hardly knew – Liza Plunket Greene's brother and his wife – in Shere near Guildford. From there the embarrassing letters of explanation were written. He preferred to be beyond reach while relatives and friends absorbed the impact of the disaster:

> Dear Mother and Father,
> I asked Alec to tell you the sad & to me radically shocking news that Evelyn has gone to live with a man called Heygate. I am accordingly filing a petition for divorce.
> I am afraid that this will be a blow to you but I assure you not nearly as severe a blow as it is to me.
> I am staying here with Lady Vita Russell on my way to Bryan and Diana Guinness in Sussex. . . . My plans are vague about the flat etc.
> May I come and live with you sometimes?
> Love,
> Evelyn.[4]

To Acton he was more abrupt: 'A note to tell you. . . . That Evelyn has been pleased to make a cuckold of me. . . .'[5] Acton responded by return: 'Are you so

1. *Letters*, p. 40.
2. Sykes, p. 95.
3. Cf. also *MBE*, p. 191.
4. *Letters*, p. 38.
5. *Ibid.*, p. 38.

very male in your sense of possession? I am somewhat astounded by all the philandering I see around me. Or is it the fact of its being Heygate? Or is it due to quarrels and boredom?'[6] Perhaps Waugh was irritated by the tone of that first sentence. 'It is extraordinary', he wrote to Yorke, 'how homosexual people however kind & intelligent simply don't understand at all what one feels in this kind of case.'[7]

'No', he informed Acton:

> Evelyn's defection was preceded by no sort of quarrel or estrangement. Certainly the fact that she should have chosen a ramshackle oaf like Heygate adds a little to my distress but my reasons for divorce are simply that I cannot live with anyone who is avowedly in love with someone else.
>
> Everyone is talking so much nonsense on all sides of me about my affairs, that my wits reel. Evelyn's family & mine join in asking me to 'forgive' her whatever that may mean.
>
> I am escaping to Ireland for a weeks motor racing in the hope of finding an honourable grave.
>
> I have absolutely no plans for the future. Evelyn is to live on at Canonbury. Naturally I have done no work at all for two months.
>
> I did not know it was possible to be so miserable & live but I am told that this is a common experience.

The 'two months' here is probably a slip for 'two weeks'.[8] In the fortnight after the disaster he had moved from Shere to Sussex to Barford House where he was staying with Alastair. By mid-August he was in Belfast, possibly with Alastair and David Plunket Greene (an amateur racing driver), watching the screaming cars and registering an image which was to find expression in the novel when he

6. *Ibid.*, p. 39.
7. *Ibid.*, p. 40.
8. *Ibid.*, p. 38. The dating of this crucial letter is difficult. Amory, following the reference 'I have done no work for two months' suggests 'September? 1929', two months after the separation. On the other hand, the letter seems to be responding immediately to Acton's enquiry of 5 August. It would be odd to begin a letter with, 'No, . . .' two months after the question had been asked. Also, there is a letter from Waugh to Peters dated 15[?] August, 1929, from the Union Hotel, Belfast, enquiring about the market for a satirical account of the Belfast motor races. [*Catalogue*, E109, pp. 87–8.] It is possible, then, that the letter to Acton was written in early August and that 'two months' is a slip for 'two weeks'. The evidence against this is that it is written from Barford House. The only reference to this address during the months in question is in the Peters correspondence dated 9 and 16 November. By this time, though, Waugh was vigorously writing again and had been for over a month (*Vile Bodies* was finished by early October). It is much more likely that he paid an unrecorded visit to Barford House in August and went with Alastair Graham (and possibly David Plunket Greene) to the Belfast motor races.

returned to it. He did not resume writing for another month. For the moment work was out of the question. Frequent removal helped alleviate the pain.

A wide circle of close friends rallied to his support – Yorke, Sutro, Graham, the Plunket Greenes – but it was a new friend to whom he felt closest: Diana Guinness. Waugh had known her husband, Bryan, at Oxford and her sister, Nancy, had been part of the Canonbury Square inner circle. Alec Waugh remembered meeting Diana first at a party in the flat. She was eighteen, a stunning nordic beauty. This sharp-witted girl was about to marry into the Guinness millions. By any standards she was glamorous but she was also sympathetic. In Evelyn's distress, Bryan and Diana offered him amusement and affection.

There were various houses at their disposal: their own elegant town house in Buckingham Street, Pool Place on the Sussex coast, Knockmaroon the family seat near Dublin, Grosvenor House in London and a Paris flat. Waugh spent time in all of them over the coming months. Bryan was a quiet man with a passion for the drama. In Ireland he was deeply involved with the Abbey Theatre and its dramatists. Diana professed equal enthusiasm at first but soon tired of bad plays twice a week. Her autobiography suggests that from the early days of her marriage she found her husband a worthy but dull companion.[9] Waugh had much more of the irreverent wit which fired her enthusiasm. She became deeply fond of him. He fell in love with her.

Knockmaroon is a large Georgian house on the outskirts of Phoenix Park. Waugh travelled there from the races to be with Diana. His delight in her company raised his spirits. 'There was no hint of painful depression . . .',[10] she wrote. Both suffered the Abbey Theatre in a silent conspiracy of boredom. On one occasion Waugh met Yeats,[11] but he was more interested in Diana: 'Do you and Dig share my admiration for [her]?' he wrote to Yorke on his return. 'She seems to me the one encouraging figure in this generation – particularly now she is pregnant – a great germinating vat of potentiality like the vats I saw at their brewery.'[12] It was nine years before he attempted to depict in fiction the complexity of his feelings for her. More than anyone she helped to restore his pride.

He could only cope with his wife's defection by striking the marriage from the record. He mutilated his diary. The dedication of his travel book was, at She-Evelyn's instigation, to have been to Alec and Alastair. Instead, the honour went to Bryan and Diana, because, Alec believed, of the source of the original suggestion. When *Rossetti* was re-issued in 1931, the dedication to Evelyn Gardner was

9. Cf. Diana Mitford Mosley, *A Life of Contrasts* (Hamish Hamilton, 1977; reprinted Times Books, 1977), pp. 68–9: 'Robert Byron suggested [on the wedding day] we might meet in Cappadocia later in the year. "Oh yes," I cried, "we will. Let's all meet in Cappadocia *soon*." "I don't particularly want to go to Cappadocia," said Bryan drily.'
10. *Ibid.*, p. 75.
11. Interview with Lady Diana Mosley, 1 October, 1983.
12. *Letters*, p. 40. 'Dig' was Adelaide Yorke, Henry's wife.

dropped. Talking of her in an interview in 1962 he refused even to mention her name: 'I went through a form of marriage', he said, 'and travelled about Europe for some months with this consort.'[13] There is no mistaking the flavour of his words: 'cuckold'; 'form of marriage'; 'consort'. His friends soon learnt never to mention She-Evelyn's name in his presence. It was as though she had never existed.

*

While staying at Knockmaroon Waugh received an untimely request from the *Daily Mail* for an article on marriage. He did not hesitate. He was short of money and the public were beginning to forget his name. This was no time to be sentimental. Under Diana's influence he was beginning to regain his sense of black comedy. The subject, he told Peters, seemed 'mildly comical in my present circumstances'.[14] He could, just about, see the funny side of it. But when the article appeared, it made austere reading.

'Let the Marriage Ceremony Mean Something' reflects his mood immediately before returning to his novel:

> Marriage ... has always been a problem, and it is one that does seem to have become more perplexing in recent years. The root of the difficulty is this – that while all the evidence goes to prove that the advantages of marriage are temporary, the best advantages can only be gained from it if it is regarded as permanent.... Many reasonable and virtuous people ... have decided that indissoluble marriages are undesirable. This seems very plausible and straightforward but, like most American ideas of progress, it depends on the supposition that everything is simpler than it really is. The only real value of marriage to any two people is not so much the opportunity for each other's society which it provides as the illusion of permanence. In every age this idea of permanence must in a great number of cases have proved an illusion, but the force of social convention and religious feeling was strong enough to isolate these cases.[15]

The approach is perfectly in keeping with his later beliefs. As he had said to Alec on revealing that he intended to seek divorce, 'The trouble about the world today is that there's not enough religion in it. There's nothing to stop young people doing whatever they feel like doing at the moment.'[16]

13. *Writers*, p. 108.
14. ALS to A. D. Peters [late April, 1929], from Knockmaroon, Castleknock, Co. Dublin; *Letters*, p. 39. Amory suggests '[September? 1929]', but cf. *Catalogue*, E110, p. 88, where the same letter is dated about 25 August, 1929.
15. 'Let the Marriage Ceremony Mean Something', *DM*, 8 October, 1929, 12.
16. Quoted *MBE*, pp. 191–2.

Rather abruptly we find Waugh in this article on the side of 'social convention' and 'religious feeling'. The civil marriage ceremony is seen as 'obviously comic'. 'Under the present system', he says, 'we find the State attempting to usurp spiritual powers and endue the bare civil contract with the sanctity of the ecclesiastical ceremony it seeks to supplant.' He attacks the 'poverty of purely reasonable, contractual relationships' and foresees a 'revival of ecclesiastical marriages, not for the sake of the lilies and the organ . . . but for the sake of its sanctity'.[17]

Even so, Waugh was not a Christian when he wrote this. John Freeman suggested to him that it was unclear from *Vile Bodies* whether its author was 'almost a Catholic' when writing it. 'Not at all', came the reply. 'No, no, no, I was as near an atheist as one could be, I think, at that time.'[18] To some extent Waugh was teasing Freeman away from any fruitful line of enquiry. 'Atheist' was too strong a word; 'agnostic' comes closer to the truth. Waugh had never lost his interest in the 'mystical habit of mind' but at this stage remained sceptical of any formal system of belief. Late in 1929 he was drawn towards the stability and continuity of orthodoxy and was opposed to humanist ideologies of 'progress'. That word 'permanence' occurs with obsessive regularity in his article. But he remained unable to make that final leap of faith.

*

During September Henry Yorke received a letter from a hostelry in Devon.

> I . . . came here to make a last effort at finishing my novel. It has been infinitely difficult and is certainly the last time I shall try to make a book about sophisticated people. It all seems to shrivel up & rot internally and I am relying on a sort of cumulative futility for any effect it may have. . . .
>
> I had a harrowing time with my relatives & Evelyns. The only parents to take a sensible line were the basement boy [Heygate]'s who stopped his allowance, cut him out of their wills and said they never wanted to see him again. . . . My horror and detestation of the basement boy are unqualified. . . .
>
> Can you suggest anything for me to do after Christmas for six months or so – preferably remunerative but that is not important – but essentially remote & unliterary?[19]

Waugh can have had little idea, writing this in the Royal George pub in Appledore, that profound changes in his life would defer that 'remote and unliterary' expedition for nearly a year.

17. 'Let the Marriage Ceremony . . .', *op. cit.*, 12.
18. 'Face to Face' interview, BBC TV, 26 June, 1960; BBCSL.
19. *Letters*, p. 38. 39. Heygate's parents did not disinherit him, but his uncle did.

*Vile Bodies* was probably finished by the end of September. He had hoped to head for Paris to stay with Bryan and Diana as soon as the last word was written but pressure of work enforced delay. He had very little money, probably less than none. The correspondence with Peters suddenly explodes with Waugh's suggestions for articles. He was keen to break into the Beverley Nichols and Godfrey Winn market of occasional journalism in the popular press. The *Mail* and the *Express* ran regular articles by 'personalities' commenting on the issues of the day. Despite his loathing for the papers and his disaffection for the cause, he remained eager to project himself as the arbiter of 'Youth'. There was money in it and he was spending fast.

Editors, however, were cautious. Waugh's hopes for serialising *Vile Bodies* in *Harper's Bazaar* foundered. All Peters could do was to sell a couple of chapters as short stories.[20] The *Mail* was sitting on the marriage article and refusing to pay until publication. Waugh's attempts to establish himself as a celebrity were failing. Odd pieces struggled into print but there was no breakthrough.

Towards the end of October he did get away to Paris but he neither stayed long nor in the Guinness's flat. He was still writing articles furiously on any subject he could think of. By early November he was back in England, staying with Alastair at Barford, still writing, still largely unsuccessful. 'By the way', he wrote to Peters in early November from Underhill, 'I am rather starving. Do you think that amiable Miss Reynolds would give me £50 or so in advance?'[21]

The cash was probably needed for his second trip to Paris. This time he moved in with Bryan and Diana at 12, Rue de Poitiers, an opulent apartment on two floors near the Seine. It was a delightful time. Nancy Mitford, Diana's sister, was there. Both she and Bryan were writing books. Waugh, too, was busy in the mornings, probably correcting proofs and knocking out more articles, possibly making a start on *Labels*. Diana rose towards lunchtime, now five months pregnant, large and lazy and beautiful. The afternoons would be spent at cinemas, dress shows, or the Musée Grevin. In the evenings they would often dine in, an excellent cook being attached to the household. Waugh relished female companionship. He loved Nancy scarcely less than Diana. It was a fortnight in paradise.

Back in London with Christmas approaching, much refreshed, he settled into the Spread Eagle at Thame for a final burst of article-writing before the publication of *Vile Bodies* in January. 'I am so delighted to hear of your creating a scene at a nightclub with the Heygates', he wrote to Henry Yorke:

20. 'The Hire-Purchase Marriage, an Inconsequent Version of the Love-in-a-Cottage Myth', *HB* (London), December 1929, 22–3, 98, 101, a version of Chapter V of *Vile Bodies;* 'The Tutor's Tale: Miss Runcible's Sunday Morning, An Episode in the History of the Bright Young People', *The New Decameron, Sixth Day*, ed. Vivienne Dayrell [Mrs Graham Greene] (Oxford, Basil Blackwell, 1929), pp. 165–71.
21. *Letters*, p. 48; *Catalogue*, E119, p. 89. Joyce Reynolds was the editor at *Harper's*.

I have decided that I have gone on for too long in that fog of sentimentality & I am going to stop hiding away from everyone. I was getting into a sort of Charly Chaplinish Pagliacci attitude to myself as the man with a tragedy in his life and a tender smile for children. So all that must stop and one conclusion I am coming to is that I do not like Evelyn & that really Heygate is about her cup of tea.

That novel about Vile Bodies is being printed off and I will send a copy as soon as I get them dreading your verdict very much. . . .[22]

He need not have worried. That Christmas was a turning-point.

*

A passage from *A Handful of Dust* (1934) describing Tony Last's feelings on the desertion of his wife perhaps best sums up Waugh's state of mind during that terrible summer. For a month Tony 'had lived in a world suddenly bereft of order; it was as though the whole reasonable and decent constitution of things, the sum of all he had experienced or learned to expect, were an inconspicuous, inconsiderable object mislaid somewhere on the dressing table; no outrageous circumstance in which he found himself, no new, mad thing brought to his notice, could add a jot to the all-encompassing chaos that shrieked about his ears.'[23] In later years he remembered with relish an invitation to his solicitor's house during 1929, probably during the divorce proceedings. Waugh was bruised and embittered and still shy of public engagements. It was effectively an invitation to an alternative world where the 'reasonable and decent constitution of things' was re-established.

Haynes had introduced Waugh to the artistic hero of his adolescence, Sir Max Beerbohm. At the same dinner were two other famous Catholics – Hilaire Belloc and Maurice Baring. Confronted by such august company Waugh had felt timorous and over-awed, spoke little and left for his club 'slightly drunk but slightly crestfallen'. Meeting Beerbohm in the foyer the next day the great man mistook him for someone else. His crest fallen further, Waugh sweated his sorrows out in the Hammam Baths. That evening a note arrived at the club from Sir Max:

> . . . Max Beerbohm was growing old, he said, and his memory played tricks with him. Once in his own youth he had been mistaken by an elder for someone else and the smart troubled him still. He reminded me that he knew my father well and had seconded him in days before I was born for this very club. He said that he had read my novel with pleasure. He was on his way back to Italy. Only that prevented him from seeking a further meeting with me.

22. *Letters*, p. 41.
23. *A Handful of Dust*, pp. 137–8.

It was an enchanting document. More exciting still was the thought that, seeing my distress, he had taken the trouble to identify me and make amends.

Good manners were not much respected in the late twenties; not at any rate in the particular rowdy little set which I mainly frequented. They were regarded as the low tricks of the ingratiating underdog, of the climber. The test of a young man's worth was the insolence which he could carry off without mishap. Social outrages were the substance of our anecdotes. And here from a remote and much better world came the voice of courtesy. The lesson of the master.[24]

It was this 'remote and better world' which Waugh now sought. Loyalty was to him a deep and abiding principle of behaviour, supplying the necessary 'illusion of permanence'. His mood of 'censorious detachment' was no longer 'mild' and amused by the anarchy of his generation. It might seem that he had unqualified sympathy for the Bright Young People in *Vile Bodies* or, later, for the sulky insolence of Basil Seal in *Black Mischief* (1932). Certainly many contemporary reviewers thought so. In fact, it is not this straightforward. His delight in 'social outrage' had largely been destroyed by the events of 1929.

Alec Waugh remembered that Christmas with pleasure. It was to be the last such family gathering at Underhill. Evelyn was correcting the final proofs of his novel. Alec read them and felt sure of its success. He was also about to release a book, *The Coloured Countries*, a travelogue, and was to sail for East Africa in February. The atmosphere in the house was, for once, easy. Arthur had resigned through ill health from the managing directorship of Chapman's (though he stayed on as Chairman). His asthma had made the daily journey to town an excruciating ordeal during winter. Catherine and Alec were relieved that he had relinquished his arduous post; Evelyn was in expectant mood and happy in the company of the Guinnesses and Yorkes. Late on Christmas Day he turned up at Buckingham Street where Bryan and Diana presented him with a gold pocket watch which he cherished for many years. In his relative poverty, he had no suitable gift for them – until January. He told them that on Christmas Eve he had attended a High Anglican Midnight Mass with Tom Driberg. But Waugh still was not a Christian.

24. 'The Lesson of the Master', *ST*, 27 May, 1956, 75; re-printed *Atlantic*, September 1956, as 'Max Beerbohm. A Lesson In Manners'; *EAR*, pp. 515–18. Waugh states there that the incident 'must have been in the spring of 1929' but he is surely antedating it by a few months. In the spring of 1929 Waugh was married and living in Canonbury Square. The article refers to Haynes's having 'acted for me . . . in a single, disagreeable piece of legal business', a clear reference to the divorce proceedings which began in September. His way of life also appears to be that of a bachelor: he stays the night at his club; he is invited to partner Haynes's youngest daughter. All the internal evidence points to the later date – probably September-December 1929.

'I was not one of the young men to whom invitation cards came in great profusion', he noted of his life at this period, 'I was the author of one light novel and a heavy biography. . . .'[25] In *Labels*, the book which he was shortly to begin, he recorded an incident in Paris when 'a beautiful and splendidly dressed Englishwoman' had mistaken him for his brother. Waugh had been introduced to a glittering company as a 'genius': 'I suppose real novelists get used to this kind of thing. It was new to me and very nice. I had only written two very slim books and still regarded myself less as a writer than an out-of-work private schoolmaster.'[26] The self-effacement of his literary persona does not quite square with his thrusting ambition and self-advertisement. But there was a genuine artistic modesty which never left him. He had never wanted to be a writer and still hankered after the world of the artist-craftsman. Amid the sheafs of articles Peters was receiving from him were drawings for the fashionable magazines. All this changed on 14th January, 1930, when *Vile Bodies* was released, just three days before Waugh was granted a decree *nisi*.

*

*Vile Bodies* was an instant success and secured Waugh's position as a prominent young writer, although more reviewers expressed displeasure than with *Decline and Fall*. Ralph Straus began his eulogy with 'Adjectives fail me. . . . It is a masterpiece of inconsequence';[27] V. S. Pritchett admitted: 'I laughed till I was driven out of the room'.[28] But Arnold Bennett was disappointed after the promise of *Decline and Fall*. He found the book structurally incoherent: 'the lack of a well-laid plot has resulted in a large number of pages which demand a certain obstinate and sustained effort of will for their perusal'.[29] Most liked it, but the older generation found the experimental structure and apparent cynicism little to their taste. St John Ervine called it 'appalling . . . a hateful book'.[30] Frank Swinnerton thought it 'bogus'.[31] Edward Shanks saw it as 'less of a novel than a revue between covers'.[32] But the coverage was wide and reviewers of senior status – L. P. Hartley, Gerald Gould, Richard Adlington, S. P. B. Mais and Rebecca West – noticed the novel. Evelyn Waugh had arrived.

Several remarked, rather perceptively, on the inconsistency of tone and drew attention to the author's occasional lapses into lugubrious moralising. Two selected the same passage for criticism. The central figures, Adam and Nina,

25. *Ibid.*, *EAR*, p. 516.
26. *Labels*, pp. 26–7.
27. *Bystander*, 15 January, 1930, 140; *CH*, pp. 95–6.
28. *Spectator*, 18 January, 1930, 99; *CH*, p. 97.
29. *ES*, 30 January, 1930, 9; *CH*, pp. 99–100.
30. *DE*, 30 January, 1930, 6.
31. *EN*, 7 February, 1930, 8.
32. *NS*, 8 February, 1930, 57; *CH*, p. 100.

indulge unsuccessfully in extra-marital sex. This merely gives the girl 'a pain'. For pleasure, she says, she would sooner go to the dentist's. A little later they begin quarrelling and, quite against his normal practice, Waugh allows an intrusive narrator to step in. 'The truth is', he remarks, 'that, like so many people of their age and class, Adam and Nina were suffering from being sophisticated about sex before they were at all widely experienced.'[33] Had the novelist's objectivity here fallen foul of the desire to discuss a personal problem in the guise of a universal principle? Dudley Carew wrote to the present author: 'I think it quite possible that sexual inexperience had something to do with the break-up [of Waugh's first marriage]. I do not think that people younger than ourselves realise how different our outlook and experience were then. We might appear sophisticated to a degree but in reality we were extremely innocent and in a curious way, we liked it that way.'[34] Be that as it may, the book remains an intensely personal document. Waugh in later years tended to agree with the adverse comments. His brief preface to the volume in the 1965 Uniform Edition apologises for the transition from gaiety to bitterness. It was occasioned, he says, by a sharp disturbance in his private life. The passage quoted no longer appears in the text.

Set against the misgivings of the elderly *littérateurs* there was a roar of approval from younger writers and the gossip columns. This would not necessarily have pleased Waugh. Too often his novel was lauded for the wrong reasons: because it was a sparkling evocation of the party world of the Bright Young Things; because it was a riotously funny piece of escapism: because it was 'naughty'. Clearly, in the second half of the book Waugh intended the humour to gall rather than to titillate: he was trying, perhaps with rather too heavy a hand, to make the distinction between harmless misbehaviour and self-destructive hedonism. Ralph Straus's comments in *The Bystander* were typical of this sort of misrepresentative praise: 'its improprieties', he said, 'are so deliciously subtle that I confidently expect even the late Home Secretary to succumb to its blandishments'. Having asserted that it was 'one of the drollest and most entertaining affairs that ever strayed into print', Straus was forced, rather hopelessly, to admit: 'The trouble is to know what to say about it. You cannot be given an outline of the plot, for the simple reason that there is none.'[35] It was to become the recurrent problem for the hack critics oblivious of the consistent nature of Waugh's abstract literary aims. Of the contemporary reviewers, only Rebecca West succeeded in penetrating the facade.

Miss West had been an ardent admirer of Waugh since *Rossetti*. By 1930 they shared several friends. On the night his divorce came through Waugh attended a dinner until the small hours with her, Harold Acton, Hamish Erskine and

---

33. *Vile Bodies*, 1st ed., p. 95.
34. Unpublished ALS letter from Dudley Carew, March 1979.
35. *Bystander, op. cit.*; *CH*, p. 95.

Nancy Mitford.[36] Possibly it was at that gathering at the Blue Lantern that Waugh and she discussed the novel in detail. Certainly her discussion of it in February's *Fortnightly Review* closely resembles Waugh's own analyses of his experiments which were to appear later in the year. 'In the monosyllabic conversations of [Adam and Nina]', she says, 'Mr Waugh has done something as technically astonishing as the dialogues in Mr Ernest Hemingway's *Farewell to Arms*, so cunningly does he persuade the barest formula to carry a weight of intense emotion.'

More importantly, she places Waugh in a tradition. '*Vile Bodies* has, indeed, apart from its success in being really funny, a very considerable value as a further stage in the contemporary literature of disillusionment. That may be said to have started with T. S. Eliot's *The Waste Land*. . . .' Next in this line of development comes Huxley. Above both, with certain qualifications, she places Waugh as the first accurately to define a pervasive distaste amongst intelligent youth for the 'overdrinking and underthinking' post-war world in which ruin represented the *status quo*. 'The exuberance of Mr Waugh's work, its indomitable creativeness, is the best proof that the movement is over.'[37]

The comments were, perhaps, over-generous, at least as far as this novel was concerned. Edward Shanks's remark in the *New Statesman* that 'He makes one feel that he had light-heartedly flung a handful of dried peas into the face of the world – and that some of the peas are soft'[38] has some truth in it. To some extent Waugh flounders between imitations of various successful contemporary styles – the ironical golf club slang of Wodehouse, the mannered ruthlessness of 'Saki', the mock-Thackerayan syntax of Michael Arlen; above all, the economy and 'indifference' of Firbank. But through all this there does percolate an unmistakably new voice, slicing through sentimentality. *Vile Bodies* is, after all, an unfair example of Waugh's capacity to organise his material. When one considers the extreme emotional pressure under which the second half of it was composed, the wonder is that it was written at all.

Of one thing, at any rate, we can be certain: Rebecca West's advocacy of Waugh as a major author had little or nothing to do with his novel's success. Indeed, Waugh himself must have been pleasantly surprised to find that seven impressions had sold in as many weeks. *Vile Bodies* was a runaway best-seller. By October, the eleventh impression was in the press and Waugh, almost like a character from his own fantastical fiction, was secure in his position as a celebrity. In all, the book sold perhaps 22,000 hardback copies in Britain during the 'thirties and as many again in America, Europe and Australasia.[39] But with an advance to

36. *DS*, 17 January, 1930, 5.
37. 'A Study in Disillusionment', The Fortnightly Library, *FR*, February 1930, 273–4; *CH*, pp. 106–8.
38. *NS*, 8 February, 1930, 572; *CH*, pp. 100–2.
39. This, of course, excludes further re-prints in the Uniform Edition and paperback.

work off against only a small percentage of the seven-and-sixpence per copy, the income it provided was little more than a comfortable living wage for the next year. The real benefits came from the re-issuing of *Decline and Fall* and the journalistic commissions which flowed into Peters's office. It was a strange irony: Waugh had been trying for months to project himself as a spokesman for modern youth. Now, when he felt least in sympathy with the cause, he found himself elected their leader. A brief discussion of the novel's thematic refrains will perhaps help to explain the phenomenon.

*

Adam Fenwick-Symes, a mild-mannered young author, returns from Paris with his recently-completed memoirs in typescript. On the boat we are introduced to many recurring characters: the omniscient Jesuit, Father Rothschild; Mrs Melrose Ape, a profiteering evangelist with a troop of working-class adolescent girls who form part of her 'act' and are known solely by their symbolic *noms de théâtre* – Faith, Charity, Fortitude, Humility, Prudence, Divine Discontent, Mercy, Justice, Creative Endeavour and, the only one to emerge as an individual, Chastity ('Hope' is noticeably lacking – it is this which Mrs Ape fatuously promises her audience); Miss Runcible and Miles Malpractice, leading lights of the Bright Young People; Walter Outrage, 'last week's Prime Minister', whose sexual tastes are predominantly 'Oriental'; Lady Fanny Throbbing and her sister Mrs Kitty Blackwater, selfish and scandal-mongering gentlewomen of uncertain age who had been *risqué débutantes* in the age of 'Souls', the naughty 'nineties. In addition there are two sets of 'extras': half-educated, hearty bores – a journalist who tells smutty stories and sits in the smoking-room with some card-playing travelling salesmen; and the Captain and Chief Officer.

The list alone conveys the idea that Waugh is presenting us with a cross-section of contemporary British society. The ship rolls and pitches; nausea attacks and people pretend not to feel sick. The weather is dark and tempestuous. Throughout the novel, save for the penultimate Christmas scene, Waugh conveys an impression of lowering gloom by soaking his characters with persistent rainfall.

The crowded vessel, it seems, is a symbolic Ship of State and the majority of its frivolous passengers are deranged by its upheavals. 1929–30 was a period of profound political and social unrest. In May 1929 women over twenty-one had at last been given the vote. The Depression was biting hard and the 'Flapper's Election' had resulted in a Labour government under Ramsay Macdonald. To Waugh and his upper-class friends, the signs were ominous. After taking tea with Macdonald on the terrace of the House of Commons during July 1930, Waugh described him as 'a nasty and inadequate man'.[40] On the other hand, the Defence of the Realm Act, enforcing rigid publishing and drinking restrictions, was

40. *Diaries*, 15 July, 1930, p. 322.

persistently outraged by the smart set in their illegal nightclubs. The confiscation of Adam's book by customs officials was probably a dig at Sir William Joynson Hicks's rigorous enforcement of the Defence of the Realm Act. Hicks (later Lord Brentford and known in the popular press as 'Jix') was an evangelist and teetotaller. As a vigilant Conservative Home Secretary (1924–9) in the administration toppled by Macdonald he became a figure of fun to Waugh's contemporaries. Neither the Conservative nor the Labour Party offered them a coherent manifesto.

Only two sections of Waugh's fictional community remain undisturbed: Father Rothschild, to whom 'no passage was worse than any other. He thought of the sufferings of the saints, the mutability of human nature, the Four Last Things, and between whiles repeated snatches of the penitential psalms';[41] and the crew. The captain nonchalantly remarks as the ferry plunges and rears that it looks as though they may get some heavy weather and a bit of a sea if the wind gets up. The overriding impression of the novel is of a comi-tragic failure of communication between all levels of society.

From this brilliant collective image of a disoriented and egocentric world Waugh whirls the characters off at Dover and into their various, separate and superficial lives in England. The satirical vignettes of each layer of social life are strung together, rather slackly on occasions, by the thread of Adam's fortunes. He is engaged to Nina Blount, the daughter of a delightfully eccentric Colonel. The loss of Adam's book, though, renders him penniless and the engagement is postponed.

And so it continues. Adam, quite unable to pay the bill, stays at 'Shepheard's Hotel'.[42] There he wins a thousand pounds in a drunken gamble and gives it to a 'Major', equally drunk, to put on a horse. The man leaves and Adam's marital prospects revive and decline arbitrarily for the rest of the novel, with the brief, hallucinatory, appearances and disappearances of this unidentified figure who technically (the horse won) owes him thirty-five thousand pounds. The suicidal naïveté of the Bright Young Things prevents any of them from spotting the drunken Major as an obvious confidence trickster.

Bored with these fluctuations, Nina marries Ginger Littlejohn, for money rather than love. She is easily persuaded back into an adulterous relationship with Adam, but even this is casual and passionless. The one scene of their brief, mutual contentment is depicted with magnificent ironical reserve. Her husband is called up by his regiment soon after the wedding. They were expected at Colonel

---

41. *Vile Bodies*, p. 15.
42. The proprietress, Lottie Crump, is a direct portrait of Rosa Lewis. Waugh was probably introduced to her Cavendish Hotel by David Plunket Greene. Anthony Powell also frequented the place. It was an elegant establishment where bills were infrequent but large and no questions were asked about lady guests. After the publication of *Vile Bodies* Miss Lewis refused to allow Waugh inside again, furious at the accurate caricature.

Blount's country house,[43] Nina's childhood home, for Christmas. Adam takes Ginger's place and identity. The scene is delicately set as the traditional manorial yuletide, with its routine of gifts, sherry in the servants' hall and carol singers. But in Waugh's hands this apparent evocation of the solid and continuous becomes pastiche. Festive Dickensian camaraderie had no place in his sceptical vision. The clean expanse of shadowless snow is not perfect but scarred by 'tiny broad arrows stamped by the hungry birds'.[44] Shades of the prison house.

Nina and Adam's happiness is mocked as radically sentimental ('Later they put some crumbs of their bread and butter on the windowsill and a robin redbreast came to eat them. The whole day was like that.')[45] Their simplicity and innocence are reviewed as decadence and ignorance. It was no accident that Waugh chose Christmas for this important scene. The Rector, with his gruff isolationist approach, is ill-prepared for fused lights. Colonel Blount shows his flickering, slipping, tedious home-made film in which the defenders of non-conformism begin by galloping backwards down the drive. Above all, Nina and Adam commit adultery on a day which enshrines in the Christian calendar the purity of the Incarnation. Where there should be harmony, discord reigns. Yet no-one registers the incongruity. There is a vague sense of *malaise*, of sickness, but each has only a partial, egocentric, vision of the collective tragedy, the relentless decline into barbarism.

After Christmas, the Second World War is declared. The final chapter, entitled 'Happy Ending', leaves us in little doubt as to Waugh's opinion of his characters. Adam sits on a splintered tree-stump amid a landscape of unrelieved desolation in 'the biggest battlefield in the history of the world'.[46] He reads a letter from Nina. She is back with her husband, although pregnant by Adam and untroubled apart from pangs of morning sickness. Through the mist struggles a grotesque, gas-masked figure carrying a liquid fire projector. Adam raises his leprosy-germ bomb but soon recognises the man. It is the drunken Major.

They are face to face at last. The debt, the deferred expectation, is now unpayable; the pound is worthless and anyway there is nothing left to buy. Both are lost. Adam cannot even remonstrate; the Major is now a Colonel. He is looking for his car which contains champagne he had earlier looted from a bombed out RAF mess. When they find the vehicle they also discover something the Colonel had forgotten. Sitting in the back is the bedraggled figure of Chastity, long since detached from Mrs Ape's troop and now a vagrant prostitute. The scene closes with the Colonel seducing her on the seat beside Adam. Too

43. Doubting Hall or, as a taxi driver names it, 'Doubting 'All', perhaps here parodying the Puritan Bunyan's Doubting Castle in *Pilgrim's Progress*.
44. *Vile Bodies*, p. 201.
45. *Ibid.*, p. 213.
46. *Ibid.*, p. 220.

exhausted for embarrassment, our hero sinks into a deep slumber. 'And presently,' Waugh concludes, 'like a circling typhoon, the sounds of battle began to return.'

The prostitution of Chastity had resulted from Margot Metroland's offer of a job with her South American 'entertainment' firm. Margot re-appears, as vital as ever, but distinctly more sinister than as the representative of a brashly modern 'life force' in the earlier novel. Waugh's disclamatory 'Author's Note' (not re-printed in paperback) states that: *'Vile Bodies* is in no sense a sequel to *Decline and Fall*, though many of the same characters appear in both. I think that some of the minor motives will be clearer to those who have read my first book. . . .'[47]

Indeed they are. Several delicate Firbankian touches would be lost without this historical knowledge. There are frequent allusions to Miles Malpractice's homosexuality and one particularly poignant scene where Maltravers (Lord Metroland) returns home to find Alastair Trumpington's hat on the hall table. Maltravers seems rather unwilling to meet the young man 'on the stairs'. His stepson swears drunkenly at him for no apparent reason. Maltravers potters into the study where, surrounded by massive works of reference, he smokes a cigar to relieve his mind of the fears about 'radical instability' suggested by Father Rothschild. Having heard the front door open and close behind Trumpington he 'rose and went quietly upstairs, leaving his cigar smouldering in the ash-tray, filling the study with fragrant smoke'.[48] Nothing more is said. It would be an incomprehensible sequence but for the fact that, from *Decline and Fall*, we have already learned that Alastair is Margot's lover. Metroland's complaisance represents, in Waugh's eyes, foolish compliance with the forces of anarchy.

This seems to be an essential difference between the two novels. Where *Decline and Fall* expressed a perverse delight in the 'dynamic' (often criminal) forces of society which refused to be smothered by 'matter', *Vile Bodies* rejects them as dangerous. The vision remains anarchic, the world's absurdity remains a source of humour, but the laughter now derives from mockery. There is no still point on the wheel of life such as Silenus suggested; the individual is not even given the choice of stepping aside from it as Pennyfeather does. Everyone is trapped in the vortex.

The nearest we come to spiritual quietude is Father Rothschild with his contemplation on the Four Last Things and, later, his analysis of the 'radical instability' undermining society. He asks Metroland and the Prime Minister:

> 'Don't you think . . . that perhaps it is all in some way historical? I don't think people ever *want* to lose their faith either in religion or anything else. I know very few young people, but it seems to me that they are all possessed with an almost fatal hunger for permanence. I think all these divorces show that. People aren't content just to muddle along nowadays. . . . And this word "bogus" they all use. . . . They won't

47. *Ibid.*, 1st ed., p. ix.
48. *Ibid.*, p. 135.

make the best of a bad job nowadays. My private schoolmaster used to say, "if a thing's worth doing at all, it's worth doing well". My church has taught that in different words for several centuries. But these young people have got hold of another end of the stick. . . . "They say, 'If a thing's not worth doing well, it's not worth doing at all." It makes everything very difficult for them.[49]

Some commentators have interpreted this passage as the key to the novel, the authorial voice of a writer who himself turned to Catholicism a few months later. In fact, when he did adopt the religion, Waugh looked back with shame on his characterisation of Rothschild. As he told Freeman, he was merely employing a fictional stereotype, the 'sly Jesuit'. He did not share the priest's compassion for the nihilism of the younger generation.

Rothschild is the only person to foresee the imminent war. He is alone in his omniscience, abjuring the partial, self-destructive views of his contemporaries. But at the same time he is lampooned for his love of intrigue (the false beard), his worldliness, and the logical inconsistencies of his argument (a 'hunger for permanence' is scarcely illustrated by the increasing number of divorces). Waugh had neither accepted nor fully understood Catholicism at this stage. He was simply presenting a more mature version of the philosophy of *The Balance*. Circumstance controls and circumstance is the inadvertent product of collective action. His considerable sympathy for 'the mystical habit of mind' still did not allow of a spiritual dimension beyond the vortex which ultimately contextualised its absurdity.

The fact remains, nevertheless, that Waugh did choose a Catholic for the most nearly admirable figure and he did root the irony of his splendid penultimate scene in the idea that it was taking place at Christmas. Acceptance of the Faith was some months hence. But there is no doubt that he was increasingly intrigued by its possibilities. The ideas of Bergson and Spengler, so ingeniously worked into *Decline and Fall*, were no longer adequate to satisfy his own 'hunger for permanence'. In *Vile Bodies* the same Spenglerian terminology of 'being' and 'becoming', the same preoccupation with 'the question of identity' recur, but in qualified form:

The truth is that motor cars offer a very happy illustration of the metaphysical distinction between 'being' and 'becoming'. Some cars, mere vehicles with no purpose above bare locomotion . . . are bought all screwed up and numbered and painted, and there they stay through various declensions of ownership . . . still maintaining their essential identity to the scrap heap.

49. *Ibid.*, p. 132.

Racing cars, he suggests, are different. They are:

> vital creations of metal who exist solely for their own propulsion through
> space. . . . These are in perpetual flux; a vortex of combining and
> disintegrating units; like the confluence of traffic at some spot where
> many roads meet, streams of mechanism come together, mingle and
> separate again.[50]

It seems significant that this ability to maintain a vital, individual identity is no
longer (Rothschild excepted) accorded to the characters in his novel, but to the
machines which destroy them. Agatha Runcible is allowed into the pits at the
motor races because she is given an arm-band stating that she is 'spare driver'.
When the 'speed king' is injured and drops out she takes his place without demur.
'It's on my arm', she insists drunkenly, and careers off round the track, eventually
leaving it altogether to smash into the Market cross (another Christian symbol?)
of a village fifteen miles away. Her very name had a special significance for
Waugh. Richard Pares, in his amusing parodies of scholarship at Oxford, had
suggested that Lear's word 'runcible' meant 'about to crash' or 'liable to crash'.[51]

Throughout the novel, the characters' lack of qualitative standards reduces
them, despite their superficial superiority to bourgeois conformism, to an anonymous, pullulating mass of bodies. Descriptions of restless crowds recur in Waugh's
early fiction, epitomising the essentially barbaric nature of human kind, so uncertainly suppressed by a veneer of civilization. At any moment, he obliquely suggests,
savagery can erupt to overpower the finer instincts.

The savage frivolity of London's party-going, drink-sodden wealthy young
people provided an ideal vehicle for this image: "Oh Nina," Adam feebly protests,
"*what a lot of parties.*" ' And Waugh's narrator adds:

> (. . . Masked parties, Savage parties, . . . Wild West parties, Russian
> parties, Circus parties, parties where one has to dress as somebody else,
> almost naked parties in St John's Wood, parties in flats and studios and
> houses and ships and hotels and night clubs, in windmills and swim-
> ming-baths, tea parties at school where one ate muffins and meringues
> and tinned crab, parties at Oxford where one drank brown sherry and
> smoked Turkish cigarettes, dull dances in London and comic dances
> in Scotland and disgusting dances in Paris – all that succession and
> repetition of massed humanity. . . . Those vile bodies. . . .)[52]

This quotation is now the most famous passage of the novel. It appears nowhere

50. *Ibid.*, p. 161.
51. 'A Disquisition on the Word "Runcible" in Edward Lear', *Cherwell*, 2 February, 1924,
    44, 46.
52. *Vile Bodies*, p. 123.

in the body of the manuscript, but is a later insertion, possibly written in his darkest mood. The passage reflects Waugh's own history of attempted escapism. The literary subject which he discovered after his wife's defection was the individual's need to break from the crowd and to assert his continuity with something more permanent. What ultimately renders *Vile Bodies* such a depressing book is Waugh's refusal to suggest any possibility of permanence.

The title is obliquely Biblical. The Burial Service in the Book of Common Prayer refers to 'The Lord Jesus Christ who shall change our vile body, that it may be likened unto his glorious body . . .'.[53] But Waugh was not offering the possibility of redemption through Christianity. As his article on marriage suggested, the most he hoped for in the latter part of 1929 was the 'illusion of permanence'. The novel is more a manifesto of disillusionment, hilariously funny but bitter. At every opportunity he weaves funereal touches into its fabric, dark abstract metaphors of imminent collapse. Machinery breaks down; the inheritor of titles bestowed on his forebears for vigorous defence of the Realm ingloriously gasses himself in a bed-sitting room after being expelled from a party; gossip takes on the status of truth; under leaden skies, the chief preoccupation of the majority of characters is the aversion of nausea. And always there is the crowd, the threatening, faceless mass, ever ready to absorb and destroy the individual. 'A torrential flow of wet and hungry motor enthusiasts', Waugh wrote of the races, 'swept and eddied about the revolving doors.'[54] Even the humour tastes of ashes.

Most of the comic effects derive from the dialogue. Waugh took infinite pains to attain the *mots justes* in whatever slang he was imitating. Many of his typescript corrections concerned this struggle to attain precisely the right 'pitch'. His ear for idiom was perhaps his greatest asset as a humorous writer. The experienced reader can not only distinguish between unattributed speakers, but he can tell immediately what Waugh wants us to think of the characters by the way he makes them speak. They are condemned both by their actions and by their vocal contributions to the dereliction of language. A vast range of debased speech is drawn on from the journalist's 'That's rich, eh?' (after an appalling joke about a woman with worms) to the mumbling clubman vagaries of the Prime Minister. Dialogue usually reflects imprecision of thought. Its chummy familiarity, Waugh implies, is designed to conceal isolation and self-interest. Characters of all classes unconsciously mock themselves and those who suffer most from this literary device are the Bright Young People.

In the Jebb interview Waugh said: 'I popularised a fashionable language, like the beatnik writers today [1962], and the book caught on.' This was the paradox of *Vile Bodies'* success. The 'sick-making', 'unpolicemanlike' vocabulary Waugh

53. A quotation from the Authorised Version of St Paul's Epistle to the Philippians.
54. *Vile Bodies*, p. 177.

had picked up from the Guinness set, in which context it was mildly amusing, but he transformed it in the novel into an example of the 'overdrinking ... underthinking' mind. The public relished it and before long a whole list of similar compound adjectives had found their way into the language. In attempting to undermine the glamorous image of his young characters he had inadvertently enhanced their image as an object of fashionable imitation. The element of *roman à clef* was supposed to be strong.[55] People bought the book as an adjunct to their romantic absorption in gossip columns.

There could have been no finer example of one of the novel's themes: the ease with which the public can be duped into slavish conformism. Mr Chatterbox sends his readers off in droves to buy black suede shoes for evening dress and to dine in dilapidated cafeterias on the Underground. Waugh himself caused a similar phenomenon. And the imitation did not end with the catch-phrases. The Prime Minister's daughter, Isabel MacDonald, followed Miss Mouse in holding a 'bottle party' at 10 Downing Street in March (the bottles filled with tea and lemonade). An anonymous hostess was reported in April to be 'negotiating for the hire of an airship in which she will give a dance up in the clouds'.[56] Waugh hated the parties but did not object to the publicity. The enormous sale of *Vile Bodies* brought him money, and wealth alone allowed separation from the masses. Never again, he hoped, would he be forced to live according to their rules. The fear of absorption into their schools, offices or bourgeois conventions had been a perpetual source of depression since Oxford. His common sense had been temporarily eclipsed by Evelyn Gardner. Now, he thought, he knew better. It was more sensible to carve out an individual path and to walk it alone. Watertight compartments were once again the order of the day.

*

After Waugh's death the complete contents of his library were auctioned and bought by the University of Texas at Austin. Waugh was a scrupulous bibliographer and it is a well-ordered collection. From his earliest days as a novelist he had had his manuscripts bound by Maltby of Oxford. He wrote in longhand on foolscap sheets of lined exercise paper. Each tall volume has its title stamped in gold leaf on a leather spine. Only two of his novels' manuscripts are missing: *Put Out More Flags* (1942) and *Vile Bodies*. The university does hold a fifty-three page typescript of the early chapters of *Vile Bodies*, corrected in Waugh's hand, but this had been acquired elsewhere. It was not part of the library. In 1984 the manuscript, until then presumed by scholars to be lost, was traced to the library of

55. Only a few minor characters were the result of direct portraiture: Aimée Semple Mac-Pherson as Mrs Melrose Ape; Rosa Lewis as Lottie Crump; Lord Kinross as Balcairn; Elizabeth Ponsonby as Agatha Runcible. Waugh borrowed the name of Archie Schwert, Miss Lewis's *major domo*, for an unpleasant young American.
56. *SD*, 27 April, 1930, 4.

Jonathan Guinness. On 4th January, 1930, Waugh had given it to Guinness's parents. It is inscribed to:

> Dear Bryan and Diana,
>   I am afraid that this will never be of the smallest value but I thought that, as it is your book, you might be amused to have it (as a very much belated Christmas present.)
> Best love from<br>Evelyn.

At Christie's in 1984, the manuscript was sold for £55,000. Its discovery provided the missing piece of a bibliographical puzzle but it also threw an interesting light on Waugh's life in 1929 and suggested an alternative account of the composition of the novel to that provided by Christopher Sykes.

It was noted earlier that Waugh made many detailed corrections to his typescripts using these as rough drafts, and that he would normally post his manuscript to the typist. On receiving the typescript he would correct one copy and send it to Peters to hawk among magazine editors. In 1929, before his wife's defection, it seems that he was sending sections of the *Vile Bodies* manuscript to her. She passed them on to the typist who returned the typescript to Waugh. He then corrected it and sent it to Peters and kept a clean carbon copy for reference.

The Austin typescript is the only one relating to the pre-war novels to have survived. It has, therefore, a high curiosity value for here one can see Waugh at work on his rough draft. One would expect the corrections to agree with the first edition in all but minor instances. They don't. Extraordinarily, many phrases deleted and replaced by others appear unaltered in the printed text: the inked-in corrections have often been ignored. It is clear that this was not the copy sent to the printer. Why? The answer was provided by the discovery of the manuscript.

Christopher Sykes states in his biography that the 'dark element' in *Vile Bodies* in no way 'reflects Evelyn's desolation at the breakdown of his marriage. It is an untenable view as the book was nearly finished when the breakdown occurred, and there is no change of mood from the beginning to the end.'[57] Waugh, though, told Jebb: 'I was in the middle of *Vile Bodies* when she left me'[58] and his memory was more accurate than Sykes's guesswork. Waugh *was* in the middle of it and the bibliographical evidence suggests that the Austin typescript was the section completed before his wife's desertion. On returning to the novel it seems that he completed it and then corrected the entire work as a piece, using the clean carbon of the early chapters. This would explain how deleted original readings found their way back into the text and why 'there is no change of mood from beginning to end'. In fact, the decision to ignore the first corrections could represent

57. Sykes, p. 98.
58. *Writers*, p. 108.

entirely the reverse of Sykes's assumption: a conscious desire to give the novel a consistently 'darker ' tone.

The mood of the typescript is noticeably lighter. It is prefaced, for example, by the amiable epigraph:

> BRIGHT YOUNG PEOPLE AND OTHERS KINDLY NOTE THAT ALL CHARACTERS ARE WHOLLY IMAGINARY (AND YOU GET FAR TOO MUCH PUBLICITY ALREADY WHOEVER YOU ARE)

This has been replaced in the printed text by the two mordant quotations from *Through the Looking Glass*. There are references to fashionable cockney chatter in a 'stage direction' style, reminiscent of *The Balance*, which uniformly disappear. Generally, Waugh's pleasure in the anarchic younger set and his quiet pride in being its literary representative are obliterated. The pagination of the manuscript suggests two larger blocks of composition and we can with some degree of certainty point to the very page at which Waugh broke off: almost exactly in the middle, at the end of Chapter Six.

With this specific reference in mind it is easy to see in the original where the 'darker' tone begins. Chapter Seven opens with the introduction of 'Ginger' Littlejohn who is to encourage Nina's callous infidelity. Certain passages take on an acerbic flavour in the light of what we can now see as recent events in Waugh's life. Heygate (the 'Basement Boy' of the *Letters*) worked for the BBC. On only the third page of this new section of manuscript we find a disparaging remark about 'cocktail parties given in basement flats by spotty announcers from the BBC'.[59] From this point Nina fades into the background, Adam's mythical fortune recedes beyond reach in the hands of the drunken Major and the remarks about marriage seem poignantly to reflect the author's wounded pride.

The economy of the telephone conversations, for example, in which Nina states her desire to marry Littlejohn[60] appears as a terse reflection of Waugh's own situation. Adam's ' "I don't want ever to see you again" ' was precisely Waugh's reaction to She-Evelyn's desertion. When we find early in this section ' "... I don't know if it sounds absurd," said Adam, "but I do feel that a marriage ought to *go on* – for quite a long time, I mean. D'you feel that too, at all?" ' and Nina replied: ' "Yes, it's one of the things about a marriage" '[61] it is impossible to avoid the conclusion that Waugh was using the book to bite back. If his ex-wife read it on publication, she was surely hurt by this acid private joke. What began as a light-hearted satire of the Bright Young Things becomes, in its entirety, a brutal castigation of them. It is, of course, an amusing book but the humour no

59. *Vile Bodies*, p. 111.
60. *Ibid.*, pp. 183–4.
61. *Ibid.*, p. 123; MS (second section), p. 9.

longer releases us into fantasy as in *Decline and Fall:* it teeters on the brink of hysteria.

*

Perhaps because he had changed course in the middle of it, and certainly because his personal troubles had made imaginative work irksome, he was thoroughly dissatisfied with the novel. 'It was a bad book, I think,' he told Jebb, 'not so carefully constructed as the first. Separate scenes tended to go on far too long – the conversation in the train between those two women, the film shows with the dotty father. . . . It was secondhand too. I cribbed much of the scene at the customs from Firbank.'[62]

Firbank was a profound literary influence on Waugh. At Oxford, as we have seen, Harold Acton had introduced him to the man's works and conducted a vigorous defence of the novelist as a master of 'the eloquence of indifference'. Firbank wrote of the *fin de siècle* upper classes despoiled by a misdirected romantic sensibility: decadent, languorous, inhabiting a patchwork world of unrealisable dreams. In many respects he was, for Acton, the prose equivalent of Chekhov as the chronicler of polite *ennui*. His immediate descendant in the English novel was William Gerhardi whose 'Russian' novel, *Futility* (1922), was a significant influence on Waugh. ('As no doubt you realised', he wrote to Gerhardi in 1949, 'I learned a great deal of my trade from your own novels.')[63] Chekhov, Firbank and Gerhardi all took as their subject an examination of the myths of persistently deferred expectation; none seriously constructed 'plots'. Their characters are effete and eccentric, superficially grand, yet rendered powerless by vanity. The titles of Firbank's first three novels were *Vainglory* (1915), *Inclinations* (1916) and *Caprice* (1917). Artificiality was Firbank's stock in trade.

In the late 'twenties Firbank was becoming popular again. Anthony Powell was responsible for Duckworth's producing a new collected edition and it sold well. The novelist was something of a hero with Waugh's Oxford generation. Powell, Betjeman, Yorke, Acton and the Sitwells all admired him. Waugh's appreciation was strong but qualified. There was a certain effeminacy and adolescent cynicism about Firbank which he had outgrown by 1929. It was as a technician, a revolutionary in literary method, that Waugh revered him.

Waugh is rarely accredited with the conscious artistry of writers like Joyce or Virginia Woolf. His statements about falling unwillingly into literature and his near-masochistic modesty have deluded many critics into believing that he was a lightweight. Nothing could be further from the truth. In happier days, early in 1929, he had written a brief but brilliant essay on Firbank for *Life and Letters* and in it we see the complexity of his views on contemporary literary composition:

62. *Writers*, pp. 108–9.
63. Unpublished ALS to William Gerhardi, 10 May, 1949, from Piers Court; *Catalogue* E70.

> [Firbank] is the first quite modern writer to solve for himself . . . the
> aesthetic problem of representation in fiction; to achieve, that is to say,
> a new, balanced interrelation of subject and form. Nineteenth-century
> novelists achieved a balance only by complete submission to the idea of
> the succession of events in an arbitrarily limited period of time. Just as
> in painting until the last generation the aesthetically significant activity
> of the artist had always to be occasioned by anecdote and representation,
> so the novelist was fettered by the chain of cause and effect. Almost all
> the important novels of this century have been experiments in making
> an art form out of this raw material of narration. It is a problem capable
> of many solutions, of which Firbank discovered one that was peculiarly
> appropriate and delicate.[64]

In 1962 Waugh said to Jebb: 'Experiment? God forbid! Look at the results of
experimentation in the case of a writer like Joyce. He started off writing very well,
then you can watch him going mad with vanity. He ends up a lunatic.'[65] At the
beginning of his career, though, Waugh was intrigued by similar technical innovation and his essay goes on to explain why he considered Firbank so important:

> His later novels are almost wholly devoid of any attributions of cause
> to effect; there is the barest minimum of direct description; his compo-
> sitions are built up, intricately and with a balanced alternation of the
> wildest extravagance and the most austere economy, with conversational
> *nuances*. They may be compared to cinema films in which the relation
> of caption to photograph is directly reversed; occasionally a brief, visual
> image flashes out to illumine and explain the flickering succession of
> spoken words.[66]

Firbank, he notes, satirises the same social *milieu* as Wilde; 'but Wilde was at
heart radically sentimental. His wit is ornamental; Firbank's is structural. . . . It
is very rarely that Firbank "makes a joke".'[67] A certain critical vocabulary, indica-
tive of Waugh's scale of aesthetic judgement, becomes apparent. The art he
appreciates is scrupulously structured, subordinating its component parts to the
whole, it works by *nuance* and allusion rather than statement and discussion, it is
unsentimental and opposed to decadent posturing for effect.

The essay was written just before he and his wife had set off for the Mediterranean. In more sceptical mood after she had left him, his infatuation with Firbank
had diminished to admiration. But the aesthetic principles remained unchanged.
Review work in 1930 saw him repeating the same ideas: 'It is told . . .', he says
of W. R. Burnett's *Iron Man*,

64. 'Ronald Firbank', *L & L*, March 1929, 191–6; *EAR*, pp. 56–9.
65. *Writers*, pp. 110–11.
66. 'Ronald Firbank', *op. cit.*, 194; *EAR*, pp. 57–8.
67. *Ibid.*, 192; *EAR*, pp. 56–7.

in what I am sure is going to become more and more the manner for the fiction of the next twenty years. There are practically no descriptive passages except purely technical ones. The character, narrative and atmosphere are all built up and implicit in the dialogue, which is written in a vivid slang, with numerous recurring phrases running through as a refrain. Ronald Firbank began to discover this technique, but his eccentricity and a certain dead, 'ninetyish' fatuity frustrated him. I made some experiments in this direction in the telephone conversations in *Vile Bodies*. Mr Ernest Hemingway used it brilliantly in *The Sun Also Rises*. It has not yet been perfected but I think it is going to develop into an important method.[68]

The remarks display a combination of arrogance and modesty which became typical of his later critical writing. In a discussion of someone else's work in 1930 he would blithely introduce his own name as a means of self-advertisement. Later that year he even had the effrontery to review his own new book, *Labels*. But this was, as far as he was concerned, merely a light-hearted exercise in good business sense. The artistic modesty is there for all that. He disparaged *Labels* in his comparison with the other book he reviewed. The connections he saw between *Vile Bodies*, Firbank and Hemingway are hinted at timorously. He only mentions the telephone sequences although it is plain from his analysis of Firbank's technique that the whole of *Vile Bodies* is constructed on similar principles. 'The character, narrative and atmosphere are all built up and implied in the dialogue. . . .' Nothing could better describe the arresting style of Waugh's early novels.

Before leaving the subject, it is worth mentioning that both the manuscript of *Decline and Fall* and the typescript of *Vile Bodies* offer evidence to support the idea that Waugh wrote with these distinct aesthetic concepts in mind. There are many examples but two will suffice. In *Decline and Fall* the slow demise, off-stage, of little Lord Tangent (shot in the foot by Prendergast) provides one of the richest, oblique pieces of black comedy in the novel. Yet it did not form part of Waugh's initial concept of the book. The brief sentences describing the relentless decomposition of the infant aristocrat are squeezed into the margins as decorative afterthoughts – a distinct echo of Firbank's 'structural' humour. Firbank, he had said, 'very rarely . . . "makes a joke" '.[69] Waugh followed his master in this too. The typescript of *Vile Bodies* includes a funny story told by the journalist in the first scene aboard the cross-Channel steamer. It was not the author's joke and was intended as a reflection on the man's intellectual poverty. Nevertheless, it is cut from the printed text.

\*

68. 'The Books You Read', *Graphic*, 12 July, 1930, 75; review of W. R. Burnett, *Iron Man* (Heinemann, 1930).
69. 'Ronald Firbank', *op. cit.*, 192; *EAR*, p. 57.

On the day of his divorce, Waugh published an essay on *Tess of the D'Urbervilles* in the *Evening Standard*. The 1929 essay had listed experimental authors developing Firbank's technique: Osbert Sitwell, Carl van Vechten, Acton, Gerhardi and Hemingway. Waugh nowhere mentioned his own work. With the success of *Vile Bodies*, however, he came quickly to regard (and project) himself as one of their number. There is a new air of authority about the *Standard* article. 'Conscientious novelists today', he states, 'direct their efforts mainly towards economy, selection and accuracy; they attempt a literal transcription of dialogue, choosing each extract only for its significance in the structure of their story; they convey their narrative, atmosphere and characterization by means of innuendo rather than description.' But *Tess* is condemned as a 'bad book, not merely an old-fashioned one'.[70]

Part of the significance of his remarks springs from the fact that the series, 'Searchlight on a Classic', had been inaugurated by Arnold Bennett with an appreciation of *Westward Ho!*. Waugh was publicly disassociating himself from the old guard and later in the year was to criticise Bennett's *Imperial Palace* for excessive length and incoherent structure. More interesting, though, is the way the attack on Hardy reveals social attitudes which were to remain with Waugh for life. There is a neurotic defence of upper-class morality, an unmistakable distaste for 'the spread of representative government and popular education' and the suggestion that one aspect of Hardy's failure was his ignorance of 'religious psychology and ecclesiastical teaching'.[71]

He does not condemn all Hardy's novels on these grounds. What sometimes attracts Waugh to Hardy's work is 'the structural magnificence of his plots and the solidity and continuity of the life he reveals'. What outrages him in *Tess* is the 'sexual' interest, the sentimental absorption in romantic intrigue and, above all, the implicit concept of tragedy:

> . . . the most repellent thing about this ponderous work is the immaturity of its philosophic basis. Compared with the inevitable tragedy and fine gloom of *Jude the Obscure*, the spiritual temper of *Tess* is like the vexation over a lost collar-stud. In such moments of everyday life, and throughout early adolescence, one is apt to give way to the sort of pessimism which ascribes the incongruities of life to malignancy in some higher power. Heaven forbid that I blame anyone for gloom. I yield to none, as they say, in misanthropy and pessimism. The trouble about the pessimism of *Tess* is that it is bogus. If the constitution of the universe is malignant, then malignant ceases to have any meaning. True tragedy consists in taking some theme in daily life, suffering, waste, decay, cruelty, death, separation, that seems in conflict with the benevolent organisation of the universe, and by making an artistic and significant form out of the

70. ' "Tess" as a Modern Sees It', *ES*, 17 January, 1930, 7.
71. *Ibid.*, 7.

chaos to reconcile it with the universe. That is why it is so much more pretentious to write books about sad and cruel people than about odd and amusing ones. Hardy, at the time he wrote *Tess*, had not grasped any genuine philosophic aspect of life, and for this reason failed to make the miserable people in his story the victims of inevitable tragedy.[72]

Certain themes stand out: 'pessimism', 'misanthropy', 'inevitable tragedy', 'the benevolent organisation of the universe'. The piece reflects the analysis in *Rossetti* of the difference between the romantic and mystical approach and it represents an apologia for the new, apparently frivolous, school of novelists. There is an assumption of ultimate order. Art, he suggests, should be the reflection of this order, not an image of the chaos (human behaviour, the endless contradictions of the rational mind) which masks it. Tragedy devolves from man, not the universe he inhabits. If tragedy is 'inevitable' then the 'fate' which grips the characters in a work of fiction must be the result of internal rather than external pressures; it must result from the immediate situation observed. This, it must be added, is a popular mis-reading of Hardy, who did not believe in a malignant 'fate' at all. Waugh's reaction against the idea nevertheless remains fundamental to any understanding of his own position as a writer.

Waugh's misanthropy, his disbelief in 'progress' as represented by social reform or freedom from traditional codes of behaviour, is clearly reflected in the relentless disintegration of *Vile Bodies*. The novel conveys a sense of man's permanent aesthetic exile in megalopolitan society. As such, Waugh had been compared with 'Absurdist' authors who present a similar, existentialist view of disorientation. To the absurdist there is a poignant beauty in acceptance, a cultured indifference.[73] Waugh seems to share this indifference. He has been attacked for lack of compassion, for the 'cruelty' of his vision. But there is an essential distinction between him and Sartre and Camus. Waugh was no absurdist. He was not indifferent. He was angry. He could see no logic or hope for the future in human behaviour but that was because it was in conflict with the 'benevolent constitution of the universe'.

Clearly Waugh considered himself to have grasped a 'genuine philosophic aspect of life' in this, although it is difficult to know exactly what he meant. The writings of Bergson and Spengler which had earlier absorbed him supported the idea that history was 'cyclical' rather than linear; that man lived in a 'time-mind' continuum in which past and future interpenetrated. Einstein's Theory of

72. *Ibid.*, 7.
73. 'L'une des conclusions de la pensée absurde', Camus noted in a letter (September 1956), 'est l'indifférence, le renoncement total, la nostalgie de l'immobilité'. Cf. Yvon Tosser, *Le Sens de l'absurde dans l'oeuvre d'Evelyn Waugh* (Reproduction des Thèses, Université de Lille III, 1977), p. 274, n. 27.

Relativity[74] appeared to lend the authority of scientific accuracy to such propositions. Theoretically, time could be slowed down or accelerated. The apparent limitations of the physical world, its cause and effect logic, had been overthrown as partial and 'relative'. The factual observations on which the rationalists and atheists based their assumptions could thus be criticised as obviously inadequate. It was in this mood of philosophical uncertainty but profound disaffection with humanist logic-chopping, that *Vile Bodies* was completed.

*

'Something remote and unliterary' had to be postponed. If he were to capitalise on his fame, he needed to produce that travel book as soon as possible. 1930 saw the inauguration of a way of life which was to remain unchanged for over six years: ' . . . no possessions, no home, sometimes extravagant & luxurious, sometimes lying low & working hard'.[75] The faun-like, fantastical creature of Oxford, the manic depressive, the artist-craftsman and the bright young husband had all taken their turn as a dominant identity. Deprived of the exclusive intimacy he coveted, he accepted his fate as a writer.

Much of the next three months was spent with the Guinnesses – in Ireland, in London, at Pool Place in Sussex. Diana was in the final months of her pregnancy; Waugh was often at her side to lighten the boredom. All this time he was writing *Labels*, presumably using as a rough framework the many articles (few had been published) written during his wife's near-fatal illness and his diary, destroyed when it had fulfilled its function. He was in high spirits and, for the most part, *Labels* reflects this. But it was a difficult book to write. Posting part of it to Peters, he remarked on his distaste for the work. It dealt, after all, with his honeymoon cruise.

By 19th February he had completed 30,000 words. By early April it was finished. Diana's baby, Jonathan Guinness, was born in March. The birth marked the end of Waugh's intimacy with her. 'Fortune', he says at the end of the book, 'is the least capricious of deities, and arranges things on the just and rigid system that no one shall be very happy for very long.'[76] In context it was a wry comment on his return to England and to the betrayal that lay ahead. He perhaps also sensed that Jonathan's birth would lose him another friend. In fact, he gained one. Waugh and Randolph Churchill were the godparents. According to Lady Diana, they met for the first time over the font.[77]

On 5th July Waugh recorded in his diary:

Bryan and I went on to Pool place. Nancy and Diana arrived later. Also

74. First proposed 1905.
75. *Letters*, p. 110.
76. *Labels*, p. 206.
77. Diana Mitford Mosley, *A Life of Contrasts, op. cit.*, p. 78.

Michael [Rosse], Patrick [Balfour] and [Henry] Lamb. Later Pansy [Lamb]. Still later Rupert Bowles. Diana and I quarrelled at luncheon. We bathed. Diana and I quarrelled at dinner and after dinner.

Next day I decided to leave. Quarrelled with Diana again and left. . . .[78]

They would encounter one another on the social circuit over the coming months but he was clearly avoiding her. She could not understand why his affection had cooled and was deeply hurt: 'I missed Evelyn badly and could not think what to do to get him back. It was through him that we made friends with the Lambs, who were to come and stay with us in Ireland; Lamb was to paint our portraits. I begged Evelyn to come too but he said no, certainly not. From then on he bestowed his incomparable companionship on others. I had to be content with the dedication of two books: *Vile Bodies* and *Labels*.'[79]

Thirty-six years later the mystery was solved when Waugh, a month before his death, wrote to explain:

You ask why our friendship petered out. The explanation is very discreditable to me. Pure jealousy. You (and Bryan) were immensely kind to me at a time when I greatly needed kindness, after my desertion by my first wife. I was infatuated with you. Not of course that I aspired to your bed but I wanted you to myself as especial confidante and comrade. After Jonathan's birth you began to enlarge your circle. I felt lower in your affections than Harold Acton and Robert Byron and I couldn't compete or take a humbler place. That is the sad and sordid truth.[80]

When *Labels* was complete, he escaped to France.

Alec had left for Africa in February as planned. Arrived in Mombasa, he had received a cable giving him the good news that his *Coloured Countries* (*Hot Countries* in the USA) was the American Literary Guild choice for May. This promised substantial financial reward and necessitated his being in the States for its release. So he returned to France to be within reach of daily cables and Evelyn joined him there in mid-April.

They had only five days of each other's company, at the Welcome Hotel, Villefranche, but they were a significant five days. The sun shone, the food and wine were good; they took long walks in the hills. Evelyn brandished a sword stick in a sailors' bar and bought novelties in a 'practical joke' shop in Nice which they would demonstrate to the waitresses at the hotel. Both were in good humour. But it was another turning-point. Alec's trans-Atlantic trip changed his life. From

78. *Diaries*, 5 July, 1930, p. 320.
79. Diana Mitford Mosley, *A Life of Contrasts, op. cit.*, p. 79.
80. *Letters*, p. 638.

that time he felt greater identification with American culture and transferred his metropolitian base from London to New York. In a little over two months Evelyn began a course of Catholic instruction.

When *Vile Bodies* had appeared, Arnold Bennett had compared it unfavourably with *Coloured Countries*. Alec, Bennett thought, had the weightier and more sympathetic mind. From *Labels* onward, it became clear that Evelyn was indisputably the finer writer. Alec never resented this and, to his credit, always praised his younger brother's work to the detriment of his own. But it was a change and Evelyn's adoption of Catholicism set the seal on their estrangement. They left the Welcome together and shared a taxi to the station. Alec was heading for Paris, Evelyn for Monte Carlo. 'There was no station bar', Alec wrote, 'where we could pour a final libation to our fortunes. I crossed to the southern platform; and we sat by our suitcases in the sun, facing each other with the tracks between us, waiting for our different trains to take us on our different roads.'[81]

The account of that holiday in Alec's *Early Years* (1962) had been decorously brief. After his brother's death, Alec revealed that Evelyn had had a romantic assignation in Monte Carlo. It is impossible at this distance to be certain who the girl was but the *Diaries* suggest that during the early summer he was involved in a lighthearted affair with Audrey Lucas. It was comforting after the embarrassments and rejections of the past year to present himself as a man of the world.

81.  *MBE*, p. 198.

# VII

## *Christianity and Chaos: 1930*

On 19th May, a few weeks after his return to England, Waugh resumed his diary. Instead of the inconsequential notes of 1928, storing magpie nests of gossip or personal history, we have a more methodical record. It has suddenly become a professional writer's *aide-mémoire* – where he went, what he did, whom he met – but largely without interpretative comment. The entries are bland and abrasive, reflecting the mind of a man who expects little but pain from life and is rather proud of his scepticism. Making money has now taken on prime importance. 'Peters made Dixon[1] pay £30. That brings my regular income temporarily up to about £2,500 a year. I feel rather elated about it.'[2] Shortly afterwards he wrote in Carl van Vechten's autograph book: ' "To Carl v. V. the playboy of the western world, who shares with the present Lord Rosslyn the distinction of being the one man of letters who is also a man of the world, in sincere admiration from E. W." '[3] E. W. was determined to be the third.

His life had utterly changed. From relative obscurity at Christmas he had found himself in January the most widely discussed young author. Society hostesses – Lady Cunard and Lady Colefax, for instance – courted him; newspaper editors plied him with commissions. The £30 extorted from the *Mail* was a weekly payment for a series of thirteen light pieces, barely more than 800 words each. The terms were extraordinarily generous. An average wage in 1930 would have been about £5 a week. It was a period of world-wide economic recession and massive unemployment. Goods and labour were cheap. Waugh became wealthy at a time when the purchasing power of his money was artificially increased. But, as he told Freeman, he never saved a penny. Indulgence in luxuries again rapidly developed into habit. Throughout 1930 he was constantly requesting cheques from Peters to reduce an overdraft.

At the beginning of June he began a second weekly journalistic assignment. In addition to the *Mail* series, Peters had secured him a regular review page in the *Graphic*, a glossy society magazine. The *Mail* series was what Waugh would have

---

1. Assistant Editor of the *DM*.
2. *Diaries*, 20 May, 1930, p. 309.
3. *Ibid.*, 25 June, 1930, p. 317. Van Vechten was a popular American *avant-garde* writer; author of *Nigger-Heaven* (1926) and *Parties* (1930), both 'Jazz Age' novels.

described as a 'money for jam job': half a day's work or less. But the *Graphic* reviews represented conscientious literary criticism. There were between four and six books to cover each week and he read most of them. Both series ran simultaneously for three months. During this period he also contributed a piece on Norman Douglas to the *Week-End Review*, his second article on marriage to *John Bull*,[4] another attacking the decadence of the 'nineties[5] and a fourth on his brother for the American *Bookman*.[6]

The *Diaries* for these months scarcely suggest such intense literary activity. The most he usually records is 'Worked' and occasionally the subject of the article. In fact, during those three months he wrote something in the region of thirty articles and saw the serialisation of sections of *Labels* through the press for the *Fortnightly Review* and the *Architectural Review*. Waugh had an enormous capacity for industry when the mood took him. He carved through this schedule with such peremptory brilliance that the work seems barely to have impinged upon that other important aspect of his self-reclamation: the campaign to establish himself in society.

'Campaign' is not too strong a word. He went out of his way to meet as many prominent and prospectively prominent figures as possible. He sought out Edith Sitwell dispensing buns and strong tea at her Bayswater flat; he met Christopher Sykes and cemented relations with Cyril Connolly; he kept up with Betjeman, van Vechten and Rebecca West and found himself now closer than ever to his old friends Henry Yorke, Harold Acton and Robert Byron. He maintained his intimacy with the Guinnesses and Mitfords and accepted almost daily invitations to lunch with titles.

The literary cocktail party, then at the height of its vogue, facilitated many introductions to both the literary and aristocratic worlds. Waugh was determined to capitalise on his fame. Being seen in the right places was one aspect of his tenacious determination never to be poor or obscure again. 'Went to see Frank Dobson's "Truth" ', he noted in his diary. 'Very fine torso but rather boring head and legs. I gave a guinea towards the fund to purchase it for the nation, partly because I think it will be a good thing for the nation to have it, partly because people will see my name on the subscription list and say "That young man is making good use of his money" and so buy more books and speak of them more tolerantly.'[7] A similar remark appears in *Labels*:

4. 'Tell the Truth about Marriage', *JB*, 23 August, 1930, 7; *EAR*, pp. 94–6.
5. 'Let Us Return to the Nineties but Not to Oscar Wilde', *HB*, November 1930, 50, 51, 98; *EAR*, pp. 122–5.
6. *Bookman*, June 1930, 299–301.
7. *Diaries*, 30 May, 1930, p. 312. Frank Dobson was a celebrated contemporary painter and sculptor. He painted the backcloth for Edith Sitwell's and William Walton's *Façade*. His 'Truth' was a headless and limbless torso.

One of the arts of successful authorship is in preventing the reading public from forgetting one's name in between the time when they are reading one's books. . . . Now, even if you are very industrious, you cannot rely on writing more than two books a year. . . . So you have to spend half of your leisure in writing articles for the papers; the editors buy these because people read your books, and people read your books because they see your articles in the papers. . . . The rest of your leisure you have to spend in doing things which other people will think interesting.[8]

Waugh's discussion of the mechanics of popular literary success was disarmingly frank. His non-fiction offered a refreshing combination of worldliness and apparent naïveté, which claimed a wide audience. He both made light of his talents and exploited the media.

At this stage, Christopher Sykes has remarked, Waugh could be an embarrassing companion, an awkward élitist who would ponderously drop names 'No-one', Waugh wrote in the *Mail*, 'has a keener appreciation than myself of the high spiritual and moral qualities of the very rich. I delight in their society whenever I get the chance. One can be fairly certain that anyone who lives in Park Lane, or Grosvenor Square, or Carlton House Terrace is one of these enviable and laudable people.'[9] Outrageous generalisation was his journalistic stock in trade.

One must take care, though, not to accept Waugh's yellow press statements at face-value. In his more serious work for the *Graphic* he explained: 'The average sophisticated novelist sits down to earn his [money] from the penny daily in a mood of apology. He hopes that his friends will not see his article, and he puts in several sly allusions to any who do that his tongue is in his cheek. He tries to secure the rewards of popular acclamation while remaining aloof from popular sympathy.'[10] The distinction usefully describes the difference between his two styles of journalism. More than this, the styles themselves reflect the division in his mind: on the one hand there is the serious artist; on the other, the assiduous opportunist driven by a fear of failure to excesses of vindictive snobbery.

It would be wholly inaccurate to characterise Waugh as a brilliant and scheming snob. In his more abrasive comments about social distinction there is often an element of self-mockery. His books pilloried no section of the community more aggressively than the rich. Keeping ahead of and keeping apart from the crowd, he realised, were often contradictory aims. Certainly he envied the life that wealth could provide. He rarely admired the use it was put to. He sat among the duchesses 'battered with fine diamonds'[11] as a rather lonely literary lion attempting

8. *Labels*, pp. 9–10.
9. 'Address Snobbery', *DM*, 12 July, 1930, 8.
10. 'The Books You Read', *Graphic*, 31 May, 1930, 476.
11. *Diaries*, 23 June, 1930, p. 317.

to consolidate a career. In fact, the only diary entries to reveal enthusiasm are those describing aesthetic excitement – a visit to Serzincote[12] with Betjeman and Frank Pakenham; another to Henry Yorke's Birmingham factory. 'I was chiefly impressed by the manual dexterity of the workers', he remarked. 'Nothing in the least like mass labour or mechanization – pure arts and crafts. The brass casting peculiarly beautiful: green molten metal from a red cauldron.'[13]

\*

In this conflict between artistic sincerity and panache, the former consistently proved the stronger influence. Nothing emphasised this more than *Labels* when it appeared in September. Reviews were largely favourable. The *Bystander*'s Ralph Straus found it 'piquant, entertaining and . . . pleasantly outspoken'.[14] Harold Nicolson detected a distinctly modern, 'post-war' consciousness, with Waugh as its freshest representative: 'He has all the scepticism of . . . Huxley and none of his despair.'[15] Only Edgar Holt in the *Bookman* considered *Labels* 'devoid of original thought or material', 'a farago of longitude and platitude'.[16] Waugh was established. With Nicolson's review even Bloomsbury was beginning to take notice. *Labels* immediately ran to a second impression, unusual for a travel book and, though its reign as a best-seller was brief, Duckworth's must by now have been bitterly regretting the loss of the option on his fiction.

Waugh thought very little of *Labels*. With typical modesty he dismissed it later in life as a collection of occasional essays 'bundled together' (he told Jebb)[17] for money and publicity. But the complaints by Holt that Waugh was only following that old beaten (and dead-beat) track of the Grand Tour were ill-founded. Waugh usually provides a perceptive commentary on the familiar sights and the odd and amusing are brilliantly worked up into high comedy. The delighted reviewers, though, in relishing this aspect, seem largely to have missed the book's point. Only the *New Statesman* noted (with disappointment at his turning from 'gay, holiday observations') 'a serious consideration of the aesthetic beauties'.[18] A large part of the book concerns Waugh's attempt to rationalise that powerful sense of artistic excitement with which he returned from Europe.

Much of the tone of *Labels* has been lost through Waugh's editing in *When the*

---

12. Col. Dugdale's country house near Oxford. Sir John Betjeman refers to it in *Summoned By Bells*.
13. *Diaries*, 23 June, 1930, p. 317. Yorke's family firm, Pontifex, made toilet ceramics and fittings. In 1930 he was learning the business on the factory floor. His novel *Living* (1929) describes his experiences there. Later, when Yorke came to manage the company, Waugh dubbed him 'the Lavatory King'.
14. *Bystander*, 1 October, 1930, 48.
15. *DE*, 3 October, 1930, 8; *CH*, pp. 116–17.
16. *Bookman;* November 1930, 140.
17. *Writers*, p. 108.
18. Unsigned review, *NS*, 18 October, 1930, 58; *CH*, pp. 115–16.

*Going Was Good* (1946), barely fifty pages remaining of the original two hundred. This contraction disguises the playful irreverence of the whole. It represented, in fact, an excellent example of that 'polite and highly attractive scepticism'[19] which he was to reject as a characteristic of Protestant humanism a month after his travelogue appeared. And as such, it provides a fascinating 'period piece': the only complete work written after the breakdown of his marriage and before his reception into the Church. The invention of Geoffrey and Juliet allows him to describe himself as a bachelor. The American title was *A Bachelor Abroad*. But inevitably, a certain bitterness percolates through this device. Their 'marked solicitude for one another's comfort'[20] is amusingly described and stresses his dissociation from such sentimentality.

In this semi-fictional travelogue Waugh presents himself both as the *ingénu* and as the man of the world. In the first role he is the innocent abroad, puzzled and intrigued by the intimacies of the honeymooners and the stampede of Middle-West schoolteachers craving 'uplift' from antiquity. In the second he is the wise (and unshockable) young judge of 'civilisation'. It is this pose as *naif* which allows him to write freshly of a well-beaten track. But it is clearly a pugnacious ironical device. To base a travel book on the experience of a common tourist route was in itself a gesture of impertinence.

Beneath this mock-modesty we are aware of a mind ruthlessly accurate in its observations. As we progress, we find that the book develops into a comparison of the 'Southern', Mediterranean cultures he visits with the 'Northern' civilisation he has left behind in the grip of a paralysing winter. This is a theme apparent in the travel writings of D. H. Lawrence and Norman Douglas. Waugh develops it in a quite different fashion. Unlike his predecessors he does not value primitivism. It is a book largely about the nature and value of 'civilisation'.

No religious preconceptions colour Waugh's judgement at this stage. There are, indeed, flippant references to religious conversion and the Holy Family as troglodytes. But the discontent with the 'narrow, scrambling, specialised life'[21] of Northern Europe, and the author's affinity with the warm south are perfectly clear:

> There was one sight . . . which was unforgettable – that of Paris lying in a pool of stagnant smoke. . . . This exaggerated sombreness and squalor, called up (particularly to me, who had lately been sick) all the hatred and weariness which the modern megalopolitan sometimes feels towards his own civilisation.[22]

19. See p. 230.
20. *Labels*, p. 29.
21. *Rossetti*, p. 13; cf. p. 140 above.
22. *Labels*, p. 14.

We are drawn with the author to examine a Mediterranean alternative and to delight in the baroque.

This alternative is not, however, one which Waugh has at this stage decided to accept. He derives, or pretends to derive, a certain *frisson* from uncertainty. The ingenuity of the pose of naïvety is an aspect of his desire to impress us as a man of the world. At one stage he concentrates on a malicious taxi-driver in Haifa who 'had no religious beliefs . . . no home and no nationality . . . an orphan brought up by the Near East Relief Fund':

> Did he like his present job? What else was there to do in a stinking place like the Holy Land? His immediate ambition was to get a job as a steward in a ship; not a stinking little ship, but one full of rich people like the *Stella Polaris*. I liked this man.[23]

The final expression of relish in this perverse product of a sterile culture is, significantly, cut from *When the Going Was Good*, as are similar references throughout.

The fascination of such characters is reiterated in *Labels* and it represents what Nicolson had noted as a sceptical post-war consciousness. *Goodbye to All That* is mentioned with respect. As they pass the Dardanelles an 'American lady' enquires sentimentally if he cannot ' "just see the quin-quē-remes . . . From distant Ophir . . . with a cargo of ivory, sandalwood, cedarwood, and sweet white wine" ':

> I could not, but with a little more imagination I think I might easily have seen troopships, full of young Australians, going to their death with bare knees.[24]

Masefield and the heroics of the Georgians are irrevocably rejected but, as yet, there was nothing to replace them.

His article, 'The War and the Younger Generation', had been written during the cruise and posted home. In it Waugh had stated: 'the restraint of a traditional culture tempers and directs creative impulses. Freedom produces sterility. There is nothing left for the younger generation to rebel against, except the widest conceptions of mere decency.' [25] In the early months of 1930 he seems still to have been uncertain which 'traditional culture' should command his allegiance; indeed, whether such allegiance were any longer possible.

*Labels* demonstrates his sampling of various civilisations: France, Italy, Greece, the Holy Land, Egypt, Crete, North Africa. He assesses a civilisation by its art rather than its politics. The emphasis in aesthetic judgement is on control,

---

23. *Ibid.*, pp. 63–4.
24. *Ibid.*, p. 139. Waugh's comment is again cut from *When the Going Was Good*.
25. *Spectator*, 13 April, 1929; *EAR*, p. 62.

temperance and discretion in design. Imperial Rome with its strident chauvinism, its glorification of wealth and power, turns opulence to decadence, 'discreet ornament'[26] to flamboyant decoration. This echoes the distinction made in the Firbank essay: Firbank is baroque; Wilde 'rococo'. In the former nothing is irrelevant, everything is structurally interrelated; in the latter all is garish decoration, exhibitionism. It is the difference noted in that essay between wit and epigram, between aesthetic modesty and egotism.

This distinction between design and decoration was not just an abstract point of aesthetic discussion: it became fundamental to his developing sympathy for Catholicism. What attracted him to the faith was its structural solidity. Waugh rejects the 'barbarities of Minoan culture',[27] the 'vulgarity of Persian workmanship'[28] and much Mohammedan art:

> The period of Arab supremacy in Egypt coincides almost exactly with the dominion of Latin Christianity in England; during those centuries when the Christian artists were carving the stalls of our cathedrals and parish churches, these little jigsaw puzzles were being fitted together beyond the frontiers, by artificers whose artistic development seems to have been arrested at kindergarten stage, when design meant metrical symmetry and imagination the endless alternative, repetition and regrouping of the same invariable elements.[29]

Waugh was beginning to find himself, as he wrote *Labels*, struggling with a consciousness divided between conservative/Catholic/Mediterranean aesthetic tastes and the essentially anarchic view of religious and political convention which had coloured *Vile Bodies*.

'We, who have grown up in ... a mature culture, have to some extent, an instinctive discrimination of the genuine from the spurious in our own civilisation.'[30] Although neither Christian nor patriot at the time he wrote this, Waugh still valued what he termed an Englishman's 'sense of period';[31] 'a certain uncon-

---

26. *Labels*, p. 107.
27. *Ibid.*, p. 136.
28. *Ibid.*, p. 141.
29. *Ibid.*, p. 110. In this Waugh was suggesting an alternative, specifically English, approach to that of his contemporaries (Robert Byron in particular) whose travel writings offered the 're-discovery' of Eastern and South American cultures. Minoan and African art (as well as that of ancient Egypt – which Waugh admired) had directly affected contemporary interior design, painting and sculpture. It seems that Waugh found Byron's early approach 'picturesque'. China and Byzantium are mentioned with reverence, perhaps because they were the specialist fields of Acton and Byron respectively. But *Labels* contains what can only be a parody of Byron's sentimental description (in *Europe Through the Looking Glass* [1926]) of Stromboli. Cf. Waugh's description of Etna, *Labels*, p. 169.
30. *Ibid.*, p. 111.
31. *Ibid.*, p. 40.

taminated glory in the fact of race'.[32] But the problem of squaring the English gentleman's quiet confidence in the superiority of his aesthetic judgement with his own loathing for contemporary Northern culture remained insurmountable. Instead of offering us an escape from the 'hatred and weariness which the modern megalopolitan sometimes feels towards his own civilisation', the narrative voice constantly reminds us of a boredom and scepticism which finds relief only in great art or by reporting the inept and grotesque in humorous understatement. A book which began as an escape from the north, ends with its narrator's melancholy gratitude at his re-absorption by it; an idiosyncratic account concludes on the final irony of condemning introversion and isolation as essentially sterile:

> It seems to me that there is this fatal deficiency about all those exiles, of infinitely admirable capabilities, who . . . have made their home outside the country of their birth; it is the same deficiency one finds in those who indulge their consciences with sectarian religious beliefs, or adopt eccentrically hygienic habits of life, or practise curious, newly-classified vices; a deficiency in that whole cycle of rich experience which lies outside personal peculiarities and individual emotion.[33]

The paradox that this represents – a sense of aesthetic exile which refuses the consolation of exile – was one only resolved by Waugh's adoption of Catholicism and, moreover, of Catholicism as a faith which could be regarded as continuously 'English'. This spiritual leap assimilated his straining towards the mystical habit of mind, the exuberance of the Mediterranean, the structural coherence of the baroque. It also isolated the pinched and parsimonious culture of 'Northern' life as something specifically 'Protestant'. The Protestants became in his view the ultimate introverts, fashioning a God to justify human behaviour. From the time he became a Catholic Waugh no longer felt the intellectual burden of humanism.

*

A sophisticated cultural perspective, Waugh felt, was the ultimate defence against artistic vanity. But *Labels* spares no sympathy for the pitiable gangs of Americans scavenging Europe for historical significance. Those 'bruised and upbraided by the thundering surf of education'[34] have no hope of sharing with the author the insights revealed over dinner with Osbert and Sacheverell Sitwell at the British Embassy in Constantinople. Culture, he believed, could be neither taught nor bought. As we have seen (p. 176), although he had felt uncomfortable at that

32. *Ibid.*, p. 205.
33. *Ibid.*, pp. 205–6.
34. *Ibid.*, p. 105.

luncheon,[35] *Labels* presents it as a gathering of an intimate *élite*. There were awkward distinctions to be made for a *parvenu*.

Invariably the two questions of class and Christianity began to find their way into his discussion of 'culture'. In his remarks about 'little jigsaw puzzles being fitted together beyond the frontiers' we can begin to see the basis for his growing disaffection for modern art and, implicitly, a gesture towards the concept of the 'Catholic city'. It was not their attack on representational form which caused him to desert Picasso and Joyce. It was their apparently spiritless toying with 'little jigsaw puzzles', a denial of form in his view, in favour of pattern which resulted in 'metrical symmetry' rather than 'design'. *Labels* condemns a Cocteau wire sculpture as 'the apotheosis of bogosity'.[36] Waugh's article on the 'nineties, written in August 1930, states: 'If one had learned the jargon there was quite a lot one could say about the painting of ten years ago – "recession", "plane", "significance" etc., but before a painting by M. Picasso in his latest manner the most glib tongue is compelled to silence.'[37]

He had not abandoned modernism but he was beginning to be baffled by and impatient with it. The same article vilifies Cocteau as a 'man in Paris . . . whose whole life is occupied in trying to be modern' and Waugh is equally critical of 'the people in Bloomsbury with the same idea'. Of the latter he remarks: ' . . . whether because they started later or work less feverishly, I do not know – these poor Britons have never quite caught up.' His attitude to Bloomsbury was ambivalent. As we have seen, he admired *Orlando* but disliked *Mrs Dalloway*. *Labels* speaks of Roger Fry as a cultured and articulate critic. The book was partly written in the company of Henry Lamb, a painter intimate with the Bloomsburies. Diana Guinness was a close friend of Lytton Strachey and must have talked about him to Waugh. Nevertheless, there was something unsatisfactory about it all. Waugh's attacks centred on the self-consciousness, the artistic vanity of those modernists who set themselves up as a separate and superior force to traditional culture. His admiration for T. S. Eliot remained constant.

Waugh's attitudes were, and remained, those of the artist-craftsman. Writer, painter, printer, carpenter – the object of all their labours was to produce useful, pleasurable, well-wrought objects. Nothing, as far as he could see, distinguished their essential function. A writer's business was not to confess or to proselytise or to render the states of heightened consciousness of sensitive introverts; it was

35. Unpublished ALS, nd, to Harold Acton from Venice: 'We saw Osbert and Sachie and Georgia Sitwell at Constantinople but only for a brief and rather uneasy luncheon party at the Embassy.' The Waughs had arrived ten minutes late and the ambassador, assuming that one of the women guests was Evelyn Waugh, spoke to her about *Decline and Fall*. Cf. *Letters*, p. 34.
36. *Ibid.*, p. 20.
37. 'Let Us Return to the Nineties but Not to Oscar Wilde', *HB*, November 1930, 51; *EAR*, pp. 122–5.

to entertain and to inform. His criticism in the reviews of 1930 attacks the various guises of intellectual self-indulgence. He loathed the clumsy imposition of symbolism and allegory, the use of fiction as philosophical argument. Lawrence's essential defect, Waugh thought, was reflected in his rambling prose. He was presumptuously taking too much upon himself in attempting to explain the innumerable crossed connections of human motivation. The too-frequent result was a lamentable subjective emphasis on sex, patched together with home-knitted psychoanalysis.

The authors Waugh revered in those reviews are now largely neglected: Ivy Compton-Burnett, Henry Green, Osbert Sitwell, Norman Douglas. Of his favourite contemporary writers, only Hemingway has remained in the front rank. 'I have just read *Brothers and Sisters* through twice', he wrote to Acton in January 1930, 'and think it magnificently humorous and well managed. Do try it again & tell me what you think.'[38] Clearly Acton did not share this high opinion for Ivy Compton-Burnett any more than had Leonard Woolf who had rejected the novel for the Hogarth Press.

Waugh was distressed when his artistic judgement failed to concur with Acton's. Acton had done more than anyone to form Waugh's taste. The 'homage and affection' with which *Decline and Fall* was dedicated were sincerely felt. He was delighted when Acton wrote to him enthusiastically about *Vile Bodies*. But during 1930 Waugh became aware of his increasing isolation from this dearest friend of his undergraduate days. 'I spent a great deal of the day reading Harold's *History of the Later Medici*', he noted in May. 'It is most unsatisfactory and I am afraid will do him no more good than his novel – full of pompous little clichés and involved, illiterate, passages. Now and again a characteristic gay flash but deadly dull for the most part.'[39]

Henry Green's work seems to have been another area of disagreement for them. *Living* was published in 1929. 'I hope you are not really angry with me for admiring Henry's book', Waugh wrote to Acton at the time.[40] The novel was poorly reviewed and sold badly. Evelyn, on returning from his honeymoon and perhaps sensing Green's depression, loyally wrote a detailed letter of critical adulation and offered to try to publish a complimentary review. 'I want very much to say in print how enormously I admire it.'[41] Though unsuccessful in his approach to editors in 1929, he did not let the matter rest. In 1930 he had his own review page in the *Graphic* and gave over the entire space to a retrospective review of *Living* entitled 'A Neglected Masterpiece':

Technically, *Living* is without exception the most interesting book I

38. *Letters*, p. 49.
39. *Diaries*, 28 May, 1930, p. 311.
40. *Letters*, p. 51.
41. *Ibid.*, pp. 35–6.

have read. Those who are troubled with school-ma'am minds will be continually shocked by the diction and construction. . . . These are the very opposite of slovenly writing. The effects which Mr Green wishes to make and the information he wishes to give are so accurately and subtly conceived that it becomes necessary to take language one step further than its grammatical limits allow. The more I read it the more I appreciate the structural necessity of all the features which at first disconcerted me. There are no unrelated bits such as one finds in most books. . . . Modern novelists taught by Mr James Joyce are at last realizing the importance of re-echoing and remodifying the same themes. . . . I see in *Living* very much the same technical apparatus at work as in many of Mr T. S. Eliot's poems – particularly in the narrative passages of *The Waste Land* and the two *Fragments of an Agon*.[42]

In the summer of 1930 Waugh had abandoned neither Joyce nor experimentation. The *Diaries* reveal him perusing Stewart Gilbert's 'very interesting treatise on . . . *Ulysses*'[43] while correcting the proofs of *Labels*. But his interest probably derived more from respect for reputation than personal enthusiasm. Waugh had set a determined course to establish himself as a 'sophisticated' writer. He did not want to appear reactionary. Above all, he wanted to maintain his position as a controversial literary figure. Priestly's *Angel Pavement* (1930) was loudly praised as a crushing indictment of middle-class inadequacy.

*

The correspondence and *Diaries* for 1930 reveal a bewildering succession of addresses. He had money but chose not to buy property. He shifted from house to house, rarely remaining anywhere for more than a few days. Week-ends would be spent country-house visiting; longer stays were with Pansy and Henry Lamb (who had also married in 1928) at Coombe Bissett (near Salisbury), the Guinnesses and Pakenhams in Ireland, the Sitwells at Renishaw. Whenever possible, he would 'borrow' his friends' homes while they were away. Peters had to chase him the length and breadth of the kingdom with urgent business letters.

During this period, and for the next few years, his only fixed home was that embarrassing establishment, 145 North End Road. He had a room there but never stayed long. Relations between himself and his father had improved considerably during the brief months of the marriage. The letters from Egypt are intimately humorous. Arthur Waugh had been dubbed 'Chapman and Hall' in

---

42. 'The Books You Read. A Neglected Masterpiece', *Graphic*, 14 June, 1930, 588; *EAR*, pp. 80–2.
43. *Diaries*, 31 May, 1930, p. 313.

the days when his son's respect for him had all but disappeared. In 1929 he could address him as 'Chapman' and share the joke. Since the separation this warmth had cooled.

His parents had been distraught at the catastrophe and generous with sympathy. Waugh, straitened by his frigid self-sufficiency, had refused to discuss the matter. Their constant pleas for reconciliation had seemed to him almost indelicate, a banal misinterpretation of facts he could not decently explain. Both Arthur and Catherine had been fond of She-Evelyn. Waugh wanted to erase all memory. He could not return to the domestic security of his home as a relief from his unhappiness. Perhaps that would have constituted an additional affront to his manhood. Instead he used the place as a hotel and *poste-restante*. He would arrive at Hampstead, aware of parental concern at his unsettled life but, unable or unwilling to confide, leave again quickly with a change of clothes and books. In June he took over Richard and Liza Greene's flat in Holland Park for three weeks while they were away on holiday. In July on their return, he joined the Savile Club to provide another bolt-hole in London.

Relationships with women were equally unsatisfactory. He had returned to the orbit of the Plunket Greenes. Olivia again became a valued confidante. But she was too frequently drunk or Charleston-crazy, and David now seemed pompous. Neither fitted happily into the *coterie* of his smarter friends. He began a half-hearted *affaire* with Audrey Lucas.[44] She was devoted to him but the depth of her affection, it seems, was not reciprocated. Whenever she is mentioned in the *Diaries* it is casually, as though he is describing an acquaintance rather than a lover: 'Audrey cocktail party . . . A. affectionate' (22nd May); 'Audrey says she thinks she is going to have a baby. I don't care either way really so long as it is a boy' (29th May); 'Went to Audrey's and brought her to tea with my parents' (1st June); 'Audrey felt ill all the week and we left on Monday' (6th June); '[Audrey] says she is not going to have a baby so all that is bogus. . . . Then I went to a party at Audrey's. . . . I waited for hours to sleep with Audrey but she was too tired' (19th June); 'Audrey dined with me' (25th June); 'Audrey came to dinner' (26th June). All the time he found himself drawn towards Teresa (Baby) Jungman, one of the more dynamic members of the younger set. His passion for this intelligent and beautiful girl was to torture him for several years. As with Olivia, though, Teresa appears to have found him physically unattractive. A brief entry in his diary hints at his lack of success: 'Saw Baby in the distance v. thick with Tom Mitford.'[45] And there was an additional complication. She, like Olivia, was a devout Catholic. As far as she was concerned, Waugh was still married; a physical relationship was out of the question.

Despite his fame, then, Waugh felt as uncertain as ever in his private life. For

44. The daughter of E. V. Lucas, the *littérateur* and friend of Arthur and Alec Waugh.
45. *Diaries*, 17 July, 1930, p. 322.

those beyond the circle of intimates he created an image of himself as the brash, divorced man-about-town. But he was fundamentally melancholy. Waugh hungered for absolute standards although he often failed to emulate them himself. The modern megalopolitan existed on a diet of compromise. This, he came to believe, persistently eroded the values of a civilisation which had been laboriously constructed over the centuries of Christian dominion. *Decline and Fall* had been something of a joke both as title and novel, expressing his own 'mildly censorious detachment'. Detachment was less easy after the experiences of the last year. He felt himself and the society he inhabited to be caught in a downward spiral. There seemed no escape from this decline. What he required was something to place it in a larger perspective. He campaigned for the 'structural and essential'[46] in art and against the 'slightly drugged repose'[47] of fashionable aestheticism. But there was a nagging frustration in not being able to apply these aesthetic principles to daily existence.

Back with Gwen and Olivia he was returned to the potent atmosphere of their mystical approach. Some of his closer friends were also Catholics – Acton, Alastair, Christopher Hollis, Douglas Woodruff, Frank Pakenham (later Lord Longford); Billy Clonmore, Driberg and Betjeman were ardently High Church. It became apparent to Waugh that religion need not necessarily represent the abnegation of intellect or submission to bourgeois compromise. Cautiously, during the spring and early summer, he began to read works of apologetics.

By the time *Labels* was going to press he had already come to regret its flippancy on religious matters. An author's note was added. 'So far as this book contains any serious opinions', it read, 'they are those of the dates with which it deals, eighteen months ago. Since then my views on several subjects, particularly on Roman Catholicism, have developed and changed in many ways.' On 2nd July he noted in his diary: 'To tea at Alexander Square with Olivia. I said would she please find a Jesuit to instruct me.'[48]

This is the first mention of serious religious investigation. But it was no hasty decision. *Pinfold* later confirmed that: 'He had been received into the Church – "conversion" suggests an event more sudden and emotional than his calm acceptance of the propositions of his faith – in early manhood ... when many Englishmen of humane education were falling into communism.'[49]. Olivia had found him Fr Martin D'Arcy at Farm Street and Waugh's attitude to his instruction is widely recorded, in several places by the priest himself. D'Arcy had never met a candidate like him before:

Few [converts] can have been so matter of fact as Evelyn Waugh. As

46. *Labels*, p. 175.
47. 'Let Us Return to the Nineties ... , ' *op. cit.*, 98.
48. *Diaries*, 2 July, 1930, p. 319.
49. *The Ordeal of Gilbert Pinfold*, p. 13.

he said himself: 'On firm intellectual conviction but with little emotion I was admitted to the Church.' All converts have to listen while the teaching of the Church is explained to them – first to make sure that they do in fact know the essentials of the faith and secondly to save future misunderstandings, for it can easily happen that mere likings or impressions, which fade, may have hidden disagreements with undiscovered doctrines. Another writer came to me at the same time ... and tested what was being told him by how far it corresponded with his experience. With such a criterion, it was no wonder that he did not persevere. Evelyn, on the other hand, never spoke of experience or feelings. He had come to learn and understand what he believed to be God's revelation, and this made talking with him an interesting discussion based primarily on reason.[50]

Waugh's childhood religiosity, he admitted in 1949, had been dangerously sentimental. 'The appeal then was part hereditary and part aesthetic.' His family was riddled with clergymen; the Church of England, resplendent with costume, ceremony, and much of the finest medieval architecture in Europe, used 'a liturgy composed in the heyday of English prose style'.[51] Religious feeling and aesthetic excitement had been indivisible in his boyhood. Catholicism, he always insisted, exerted an entirely different appeal.

In accepting its tenets he was effectively debarring himself from something he needed and desired – a secure marriage, a home and family. The Church did not recognise divorce. At the time, he told Greenidge that he had adopted the faith to prevent the foolishness of ever wanting to re-marry. But this seems to have been nothing more than a bitter, defensive joke at his own expense. He was, despite his numerous friends, a lonely man. So far as he knew, he was condemning himself to this condition in perpetuity. The decision represented a massive sacrifice for absolute standards. But the world was 'unintelligible and unendurable without God'.[52] There was no room for compromise.

'I reverence the Catholic Church', he told Jebb, 'because it is true, not because it is established or an institution.'[53] This was no mere debating point. Once the theological justification of Christ's divinity had been established to his satisfaction, there was no option but to accept Catholicism. It seemed common sense to him that other sects and schisms could be true only in so far as they approximated to the original institution. Religion, as he told Freeman, was not 'a sort of lucky dip which you get something out of.... It's hard without using pietistic language to explain, but it's simply admitting the existence of God or dependence on God –

50. Fr Martin D'Arcy SJ, 'The Religion of Evelyn Waugh', *EWAHW*, p. 64.
51. 'Come Inside', *The Road to Damascus*, ed. John O'Brien (New York, Doubleday, 1949), pp. 17–21; *EAR*, pp. 366–8.
52. *Ibid.*, *EAR*, p. 367.
53. *Writers*, p. 112.

your contact with God – the fact that everything in the world that's good depends on Him. It isn't a sort of added amenity to the Welfare State that you say well, to all this, having made a good income, now I'll have a little icing on top, of religion. It's the essence of the whole thing.'[54] The theme is constantly repeated in Waugh's post-war fiction. ' "Do you agree," ' Crouchback earnestly asks of the Anglican chaplain in *Men At Arms*, ' "that the supernatural Order is not something added to the Natural Order, like music or painting, to make everyday life more tolerable? It *is* everyday life. The supernatural is real; what we call 'real' is a mere shadow, a passing fancy. Don't you agree, Padre?" ' The Anglican, of course, replies with one of Waugh's famous non-committal phrases: ' "Up to a point." '[55]

*

Waugh was received into the Church on 29th September, 1930. It was a quiet ceremony, his only guest being Tom Driberg. Driberg, according to Christopher Sykes, was both baffled and flattered by the invitation. He assumed that he had been asked in his capacity as a gossip columnist. Perhaps having him there saved Waugh writing letters of explanation to his friends. Perhaps, even in this most sacred of moments, Waugh wished to keep himself in the public eye. Perhaps it was simply that, having confessed his loss of faith to Driberg at Lancing, Waugh needed his presence as a form of penance. Driberg, at least, did his duty and published the news in the *Express*.

The account does more than any commentary to capture Waugh's matter-of-fact coolness. Driberg describes a café crowd in Coventry Street after they had attended a performance of P. G. Wodehouse's *Leave it to Psmith*:

> Here, too, were Lady Ravensdale, lately back from Russia, but wearing an exquisitely capitalist evening dress; and Miss Tallulah Bankhead, who was with the Hon David Herbert; and Marquis de Casa Maury; and, watching critically from the balcony, Mr Evelyn Waugh who had earlier in the evening been received into the Roman Catholic Church.[56]

Waugh now disliked the parties, balls and dances that Diana Guinness and so many of his friends relished. He preferred a small, private dinner where the

54. 'Face to Face', *op. cit.*, BBCSL.
55. *Men At Arms*, p. 77.
56. *DE*, 1 October, 1930, 15. The *Bystander* noted: 'The brilliant young author' is 'the latest man of letters to be received into the Catholic Church. Other well-known literary people who have gone over to Rome include Sheila Kaye-Smith, Compton MacKenzie, Alfred Noyes, Father Ronald Knox and G. K. Chesterton' (8 October, 1930, 101). The grouping was inept. It implies a landslide of conversions which did not occur. No-one included in this list belonged to Waugh's generation although several of his contemporaries had, in fact, 'gone over': Greene, Sykes, Hollis, Pakenham, with Clonmore and Penelope Betjeman to follow.

conversation was good, or a stool in a pub. He had earned his place amongst this scintillating company and was proud of his celebrity. But if he was with them, he was not of them, separated now by that invisible wall of belief.

Shortly after his reception he published an article in the *Express* explaining his decision. Here he contemptuously rejected the three 'popular errors that reappear with depressing regularity in any discussion about a convert...'. These are: ' "The Jesuits have got hold of him", "He is captivated by the ritual", "He wants to have his mind made up for him" '. He dismisses the Jesuits' reputation as intriguers, believes the aesthetic appeal of Anglicanism to be greater, and asserts that 'the Roman system can and does form the basis of the most vigorous intellectual activity'. The problems involved are more fundamental:

> It seems to me that in the present phase of European history the essential issue is no longer between Catholicism, on one side, and Protestantism, on the other, but between Christianity and Chaos. It is much the same situation as existed in the early Middle Ages.... In the eighteenth and nineteenth centuries the choice before any educated European was between Christianity, in whatever form it was presented to him ... and ... a polite and highly attractive scepticism. So great, indeed, was the inherited, subconscious power of Christianity that it was nearly two centuries before the real nature of this loss of faith became apparent. Today we can see it on all sides as the active negation of all that Western culture has stood for. Civilization – and by this I do not mean talking cinemas and tinned food, nor even surgery and hygienic houses, but the whole moral and artistic organization of Europe – has not in itself the power of survival. It came into being through Christianity, and without it has no significance or power to command allegiance.... It is no longer possible, as it was in the time of Gibbon, to accept the benefits of civilisation and at the same time deny the supernatural basis on which it rests.... Christianity ... is in greater need of combative strength than it has been for centuries.[57]

Decline and fall were no longer the subject for jokes. Taking this as the basis for his argument he went on to say that because 'Christianity exists in its most complete and vital form in the Roman Catholic Church', this can be the only effective bastion against 'disorder from outside'. Catholicism is more 'complete and vital' to him because its teaching is 'coherent and consistent' and 'universal', because its clergymen represent 'competent organisation and discipline'.[58]

These ideas were not original. Chesterton and Belloc had crusaded for the concept of *Romanitas* in an earlier generation. The symbolism of the Catholic City beyond whose frontiers lies chaos is common to this debate as is the notion

57. 'Converted to Rome ...', *DE*, 20 October, 1930, 10; *EAR*, pp. 103–5.
58. *Ibid.*, 10.

that no country could consider itself civilized unless it had been conquered by Rome. In the early 'thirties it was, outside France, an eccentric thesis. By 1936, with the rise of Franco and Mussolini as defendants of Catholic culture against the Communists, it had gained popularity in some quarters while remaining generally unfashionable in literary circles.

Waugh's spiritual and political beliefs, then, do seem ultimately to have been influenced by aesthetic enthusiasm but not in the way most critics have supposed. His interest focused not on the appeal of the ritual but on the defence of the artistic sensibility against 'the ideal of a materialistic mechanized State, already existent in Russia and rapidly spreading south and west'.[59] The Catholic hierarchy might well have been suspicious of so pragmatic a belief in the supernatural. We cannot maintain civilisation without Christianity, he seems to say, therefore we should choose the most competently organised system of Christian philosophy. It comes awkwardly close to accepting civilisation as the justification of his faith. Towards the end of his life he noted in his diary: 'When I first came into the Church I was drawn, not by splendid ceremonies but by the spectacle of the priest as craftsman. He had an important job to do which none but he was qualified for. He and his apprentice stumped up to the altar with their tools and set to work without a glance to those behind them, still less with any intention to make a personal impression on them.'[60] Arts and crafts again.

The priest and the artist-craftsman, Waugh believed, were engaged on similar tasks. Their business was the organisation and elucidation of the disparate fragments of daily existence within a wider perspective. But for all that, the act of faith, that leap beyond the fallible intellect, was undeniable and recognised by Waugh as a fundamental precept of his new philosophy. A man of his acute intellect could never desert logical analysis. He merely re-directed it from the natural to the supernatural. From this point the supernatural became his new reality and he delighted in the scope this provided for anti-rationalist argument.

Life on earth could now quite happily be reviewed as an empty charade. All forms of humanism which attempted to rationalise it were equally absurd. 'Modernist' writers and painters, psychoanalysts and economists were, in his opinion, pretending to plumb the depths of reality in isolated ponds. Even those artists who ultimately concluded that the world's absurdity was itself the only consistent truth he saw as misguided. '[Picasso's] devotees', he wrote in 1945, 'tell me he communicates chaos and despair and these are not the messages of art. Art is ennobling and purgative. Chaos and despair are brilliantly conveyed by any issue of the *Daily Mirror*.'[61]

59. *Ibid.*, 10.
60. *Diaries*, Easter, 1964, pp. 792–3.
61. ALS, 27 December, 1945, to Robin Campbell, the painter, whom Waugh had met during service training at Largs in the last war. This is another version of the one (presumably re-drafted) which appears in *Letters*, pp. 214–16.

Waugh's altered perspective is immediately apparent in his review work of 1930. The quarterly contracts with the *Graphic* and *Mail* came to an end in August. A second series in the *Graphic* coincided almost exactly with his formal reception into the Church. In these articles he is kinder to the second-rate, more sober in the expression of his aesthetic tastes, less willing to laud the experimentalists. Reviewing Rose Macaulay's *Staying with Relations* he laments her failure to maintain the theme which interested him most. 'She seems', he says, 'to have begun with the situation of an oddly assorted household, living in an odd manner, intending to trace out their various sophisticated relationships and the influence upon them of the surrounding barbarity and chaos.'[62] For Waugh now, the anarchy threatening to destroy 'the whole moral and artistic organisation of Europe' had become an obsessive subject.

Earlier in the year, as a newly-established author, he had been unwilling to lambast the literary hierarchy. Joyce, Lawrence and Huxley, authors he soon came to detest, were dealt with generously. He could comment then on Lawrence's being 'at war with civilization' and let it pass.[63] After September 1930 any such ideas would have provoked a pungent riposte. But, allowing for this, his views on the aesthetics of novel-writing remained unchanged. It was better to deal with 'odd and amusing' characters than 'sad and cruel' ones; fiction should amuse rather than instruct. Above all, the principles of selection and structural arrangement should be maintained. It was this delight in skilful construction which gave him a lifelong delight in detective fiction and the work of P. G. Wodehouse.

Waugh's adoption of Catholicism virtually completed the development of his aesthetic. It altered very little during the rest of his life, with only one other significant change of tack in 1939. By September 1930 he had at last come to terms with life and with life as a writer. He had his subject and felt confident in his use of the technical apparatus to express it. But his religious opinions irrevocably altered his perspective.

The Church welcomed him to a community of faith but 'coming inside' meant leaving outside most of his family and many of his friends. It deepened his estrangement from Arthur and Alec whose rag-bag of Anglicanism he now found despicable. Casual sexual relations took on the more sinister proportions of Mortal Sin. The opportunities for pleasure were (technically at least) severely restricted. Self-pity and asceticism, though, rarely troubled him. The increasing obsession with luxurious living was a temporal recompense for the demands of his spiritual commitment. Cigars, fine wines and dinners at the Ritz were legitimate excesses condemned only by the religious Puritans or the new puritans of the Left. Temperance was an admirable virtue but it concerned the spirit rather than the

62. 'The Books You Read', *Graphic*, 27 September, 1930, 509.
63. 'The Books You Read', *Graphic*, 31 May, 1930, 476; review of D. H. Lawrence, *Assorted Articles* (Secker, 1930); *EAR*, pp. 70–1.

liver. Moreover, it concerned only the individual and his relationship with God. The theological imperative to save his own soul relieved him from concern for others' opinions or welfare.

Such deprivations as there were affected him little in comparison with the things which he could now joyfully shun. Faith offered release more than it demanded sacrifice. 'I can perfectly well understand how people get driven insane by their fear of crowds', he had written in August. His religion allowed, even demanded, separation from that multitude of interchangeable forms which had so nearly driven him mad. 'They are all there, the same inevitable faces; they provoke no glimmer of attraction or curiosity; you see them under different hats and over different clothes; sometimes their hair has been bleached with peroxide or their skin blackened with the sun; you scan them variously disposed and regrouped, but they are always there whatever you are doing, bobbing and grimacing in the background.'[64]

This recurrent image of the world as a bodiless harlequinade had nothing to do with snobbery. Waugh's terror of the loss of individual identity was instinct in him and permeated his art from beginning to end. His view of the charade had changed in only one respect since writing *The Balance* – he was no longer a part of it. He was up in the balcony critically observing the various patterns of failure. Sometimes it amused, sometimes it disgusted him, but, in the end, none of it mattered.

In September 1930 Waugh was still only twenty-six. He maintained a boyish appearance. He was a sprightly companion. But he was now a very serious young man with the philosophical resignation of one many years his senior. Already he had begun to adopt something of that persona which was to harden during the rest of his life into the eccentric don and testy colonel. So absolute were his religious beliefs and so violent his 'disgusto' that life often became, by definition, a waste of time. Having finished *Labels* and with no inclination to write another novel he looked round for something 'amusing' to fill the time, something to get him out of the country before winter set in again.

During August Waugh had paid his first extended visit to the Sitwells' country seat, Renishaw Hall in Derbyshire. 'Sachie liked talking about sex. Osbert very shy. Edith wholly ignorant', he noted in his diary.[65] But he really liked them all and discovered a household of delicious eccentricity. Robert Byron had travelled down with him. William Walton (the composer), Harold Monro, Francis Birrell and Arthur Waley were there. Almost everyone, though, with the exception of Sacheverell and his beautiful wife Georgia, was of an older generation.

Waugh was intrigued by the company but a little unsure of himself. He knew none of them well except Byron who secluded himself in his bedroom for the

64. 'The Old Familiar Faces', *DM*, 2 August, 1930, 8.
65. *Diaries*, 23 August, 1930, p. 327.

best part of each day. Lady Ankaret Jackson arrived and, unable to bear Osbert's reading aloud to the company, would interrupt or make dismissive remarks about Catholic *parvenus*. ' "I can't see any point in being a Catholic" ', Waugh records her as saying, ' "unless one belongs to an old Catholic family. Now when I stay at Arundel I feel very Catholic . . . " '[66] Having completed his period of instruction and prepared himself to enter the Church next month, Waugh's awkwardness in this secretive household can hardly have been relieved by such remarks. He 'summoned' Alastair Graham, and his loyal old friend and ex-lover promptly arrived.

They stayed on for ten more days. Alastair and his colleague Mark Ogilvie-Grant were shortly to follow their ambassador, Sir Percy Lorraine, to his new post in Cairo. It was a brief spell during which Waugh could relish the company of the man to whom he had once been passionately devoted, a last savouring of that Oxford intimacy before everything irrevocably changed. From Renishaw they moved on together to Eire and Pakenham Hall at Westmeath. The atmosphere there was a little easier. Frank Pakenham and his future wife, Elizabeth Harman, were there with John Betjeman. It was much more the sort of ebullient country house party Waugh was used to and, in this company, there was no need to apologise for his nascent Catholicism. Betjeman and Pakenham's elder brother, Edward, spent much time at the organ roaring out Victorian hymns.[67]

They were sitting in the library one day, talking of foreign travel, when Abyssinia came into the conversation. It was in the news because its ruler, Ras Tafari, was shortly to crown himself as Emperor Haile Selassie. Alastair contributed some information about Abyssinian politics. Others chipped in with hearsay about the national Church which had, they believed, canonised Pontius Pilate and consecrated bishops by spitting on their heads. Various obscure reference volumes were pulled from the shelves. The legitimate heir to the throne, one said, was imprisoned in the mountains. Polygamy and drunkenness, apparently, abounded.

This amateurish research was a game to absorb a dull afternoon. The more fantastic the picture they could paint of the country, the better the entertainment. But Waugh was genuinely fascinated. Here at last was the opportunity to do that something 'remote and unliterary' which he had mentioned to Henry Yorke a year earlier. He wrote to Peters immediately: 'I want very much to go to Abyssinia. . . . Could you get a paper to send me as a special correspondent. If needs be I could pay ½ my expenses. I think I am going anyway.'[68] The last sentence reveals his determination. A fortnight later he was back in London for his reception into the Catholic Church and, before Peters could arrange any financial support, had booked his passage for Djibouti.

66. *Ibid.*, p. 328.
67. Interview with Lady Penelope Betjeman, 29 March, 1984.
68. *Letters*, pp. 49–50.

Several papers were approached unsuccessfully to try to secure him a post as correspondent. It began to occur to Waugh that, without credentials, he might be debarred from the official ceremonies. He was quite prepared to pay for the trip, caring nothing whether he bankrupted himself in the process. But the problem of securing that *laissez-passer* was beginning to appear insurmountable.

Two days later, immediately after his reception, he had a stroke of good fortune. Travelling on a train to Gloucestershire he met Douglas Woodruff. Waugh was on his way to visit a mutual friend, Christopher Hollis, at Stoneyhurst, the Catholic public school at which he taught. Hollis had invited Waugh down for a retreat. Fr D'Arcy had kindly looked up some Catholic friends for Waugh to help him through this difficult time and Hollis and Woodruff were chief among them, having known him at Oxford. Both had been down to visit him in early August when he had taken over the Lambs' cottage in Coombe Bissett.[69]

The connection with Woodruff proved extremely useful. He was now on the staff of *The Times*. When Waugh mentioned the visit to Abyssinia Woodruff suggested that his Foreign Editor might be interested to employ a correspondent.

After his week-end Waugh went to see the man. A brief interview secured the commission and the bright young novelist emerged into Printing House Square a fully accredited journalist for the first time. All travelling and accommodation expenses for the period of the Coronation were to be paid by the paper. He was issued with a *laissez-passer* for the ten days of the celebrations. Five days later he was aboard the *Azay-le-Rideau* at Marseilles bound for Africa.

69. Just before their arrival Audrey Lucas had spent a few days there and seems to have been peremptorily removed in order to avoid embarrassment with his sterner friends. Hollis, according to Waugh, was easily shocked by his irreverence about a Catholic newspaper. Cf. *Diaries*, 9 August, 1930, p. 325.

# VIII
# *A Bachelor Abroad: 1930–1931*

'I can scarcely imagine any more romantic mission than to attend the coronation of the Emperor of Ethiopia, Conquering Lion of Judah, King of Kings, direct descendant of King Solomon and the Queen of Sheba. . . . It was only through renewed contemplation of my luggage labels that I was able to remind myself that I had, in fact, embarked on what should prove one of the really amusing journeys left in the world.'[1] Thus Waugh writing up the romance of the jungle only to debunk it later.

In fact, the voyage from Marseilles to Djibouti proved singularly dull. The *Azay-le-Rideau* was a *Messageries Maritimes* ship of the B class, crowded with French colonial visitors *en route* with their children to the Middle East, Africa and India. Two foreign legations, the Polish and the Dutch, were aboard for the entire trip. Two more, the French and the Eygptian, joined the ship at Suez. The crowd buzzed with gossip and Abyssinian politics in a comfortable bourgeois atmosphere and children screamed about the decks. 'For one blessed day', Waugh wrote, 'between Malta and Port Said we ran into fairly heavy weather, and all these beastly little boys and girls were dispatched to their cabins.'[2] By day there were competitive deck games; by night, dancing till the small hours to a quartet in alpaca dinner jackets. Waugh, unamused, sat critically to one side. This stage of the journey was redolent with painful memory. Describing Port Said in his diary he merely noted: 'All my acquaintances had gone.'[3] In 1929 he had docked there aboard the luxurious *Stella Polaris* with his young wife near death to spend two months fretting over her recovery. Now he was a bachelor abroad: brusque, detached.

Throughout his writings about this expedition there is a distinct air of misogyny, a fierce defence of the bachelor existence. Women are seen generally to lower the standard of conversation, their children to interrupt the contemplative life. There is also a mild sense of persecution – as though the world were out to cheat him and he was determined to cheat it first. He thought the Port Said officials

1. *Graphic*, 22 November, 1930, 350.
2. *Ibid.*, 350.
3. *Diaries*, 10 October–26 October, 1930, p. 330.

'noticeably less polite than eighteen months ago'[4] after a wrangle with the customs. The diaries reflect a man intolerant of what he termed the 'second rate'. Meeting an English mother and daughter on board, he thought at first that the girl might prove interesting. But no: 'Both mindless. Daughter . . . very much pigmented – crimson toe nails, black rims to eyes – but not to attract males: simply child-imitation of smart people she saw at Cannes. . . .'[5] He was befriended by Charles Barton, brother of Sir Sidney (the Envoy Extraordinary and Minister Plenipotentiary to Abyssinia), clearly a useful contact for a journalist. Barton was a kindly old buffer. All Waugh could bring himself to say was: 'Retired banker [?] bore; slightly mercenary but well intentioned'.[6] One unusually frank entry reads: 'I become slightly hypocritical as soon as I am away from my own background, adopting an unfamiliar manner of speech and code of judgements.'[7] Humility did not come easily. The battle against misanthropy was strenuous and only kept alive by the small flame of charity kindled by his faith. If he could not like many of the human race he could, at least, reconstruct their actions in a hilarious private farce.

The *Azay-le-Rideau* docked at Djibouti in French Somaliland at dawn on Friday 24th October.[8] It had been a thirteen-day journey, latterly in intense heat. 'The night before [we docked] . . . there was a fancy-dress dance. Rising at six next day I found two grey-faced couples in extravagant paper hats still dancing on a deck which was being swabbed by a Chinese steward.'[9] Recording his experiences in his next book, *Remote People* (1931), Waugh began with this image, reducing the two couples to one, detailing their shabby appearance, making the man shorter than the woman 'by several inches'. 'Their feet moved slowly over the wet boards to the music of a portable gramophone: at intervals they stopped and unclasped each other, to re-wind the instrument and reverse the single record.'[10] It is a brilliant first page conveying simultaneously the shoddy hedonism of this damp couple and a sympathetic impression of their hopeless intimacy. It is an image of a dislocated society, beyond tradition and formal restraint, an image

4. *Ibid.*, p. 330.
5. *Ibid.*, p. 330.
6. *Ibid.*, p. 330.
7. *Ibid.*, p. 330.
8. There is some confusion over dating here. Waugh states in *Remote People* that he docked on 'October 19th' (p. 11). The MS of the diaries reads 'Djibouti arrived dawn Friday 19th'. Davie omits 'Friday' because Friday was not the 19th. *Remote People* records his cabling to *The Times* the arrival in Djibouti of the Polish, Dutch, French and Egyptian Legations who had travelled with him. *The Times* (27 October, 1930) reports this as occurring on 24 October. Waugh, then, must simply have been mistaken in *Remote People* (relying on his inaccurate diary) in stating that he arrived on 19th. It *was* a Friday, but Friday 24th.
9. *Graphic*, 22 November, 1930, 350.
10. *Remote People*, p. 11.

of western culture oddly transposed, incongruous, running down. During his visit this incongruity was to prove delightfully refreshing or dangerously anarchic as his light mood lived or died.

Djibouti was dismal and steamy. A warm rain poured steadily on Waugh and Barton as they disembarked to investigate the schedules for trains to the interior. Neither had thought to bring a mackintosh or umbrella. As they jogged disconsolately round the port, drenched and impatient in a decrepit horse cab, they were nowhere able to secure accurate information. Normally it was a three-day journey to Addis Ababa with overnight stops. To cope with the Coronation visitors, through-trains had been introduced which would complete the trip in thirty-six hours. One of these was taking four of the legations at eight that evening. Waugh and Barton clambered aboard and secured a first-class carriage to themselves.

The next day they clattered across country, stopping only for lunch and dinner. To Waugh's eye it was a dead panorama of 'monstrous plain scrubbed trees'.[11] That night, beyond Hawash, the line mounted steeply to fresher air. In the early morning the train stopped for the faintly ludicrous purpose of allowing the diplomats to don their official regalia. Resplendent in gold braid and ostrich feathers, they resumed their seats and an hour later, at 10.30 on 26th October, Waugh had his first sight of Addis Ababa. He was to return twice over the next six years.

Red carpet, a military band and a phalanx of Ras Tafari's crack regiment greeted him, or rather, the delegations. 'As the train stopped', Waugh recorded in *Remote People*, 'the general presented arms; the head chamberlain advanced in a blue satin cloak to greet the delegations. . . . It is my misfortune to be quite insensible to music, but I was told by all who heard them that the tunes played were, in practically all cases, easily recognisable.'[12] Throughout the book, beneath the guise of modest good manners, Waugh's mischievous humour is at the expense of the Abyssinians. The garish cloak and the phrase 'in practically all cases' intimate inappropriate imitation. But *Remote People*, and Waugh's African experience generally, are easily misinterpreted.

His impressions of the country vascillated between wild excitement and the deepest depression. Generally, *Remote People* is a sympathetic book which relishes the unpredictable nature of African affairs. He freely mocked what he termed in a magazine article 'Strenuous and successful efforts . . . by the police to clear the town of lepers, corpses, mutilated beggars, hyenas and other incumbrances which might give an impression of incomplete civilization'.[13] But 'complete' civilization was scarcely presented by the rabble of newsmen, sycophants and old colonials who had tumbled into Addis Ababa for a free trip. The distinction between

11. *Diaries*, 10 October–26 October, 1930, p. 331.
12. *Remote People*, p. 28.
13. *Graphic*, 20 December, 1930, 544; *EAR*, p. 117.

civilisation and barbarism could no longer for Waugh be satisfactorily comprehended by political or anthropological terms: it was essentially a religious question. The supernatural was now the 'real'.

*Remote People* was written from this new point of view. Much of the neurotic reaction to attacks on 'standards' had by 1931 dropped away. In his public writings, only the boredom remained of that darker side of his nature. His faith released in him an ability to revel in what he saw as the *Alice in Wonderland* absurdities of Abyssinia. For a brief period, despite his professional commitments as a journalist, travel became an escape into fantasy:

> . . . no catalogue of events can convey any real idea of these astounding days, of an atmosphere utterly unique, elusive, unforgettable. If in the foregoing pages I have seemed to give undue emphasis to the irregularity of the proceedings, to their unpunctuality, and their occasional failure, it is because this was an essential part of their character and charm. In Addis Ababa everything was haphazard and incongruous; one learned always to expect the unusual and yet was always surprised.[14]

It was more the Europeans in Addis who drove him to distraction. Charles Barton was met off the train by his brother's two daughters. Waugh was introduced. He took an instant dislike to them and almost everyone else in the British contingent. The girls fussed and gasped. Had he booked no accommodation? Every bed in the town was taken. What *would* he do? Waugh stepped calmly into a taxi, drove to the Hotel de France, and secured himself a room (albeit in an outbuilding). 'First introduction hysteria Legation', he noted in his diary.[15]

At the hotel he met one of his aristocratic London acquaintance, Baroness Irene Ravensdale. Writing to Henry Yorke on the day of the Coronation, 2nd November, he said, 'Irene Ravensdale and Charles Drage are the only possible people in the town'.[16] But, as Christopher Sykes suggested to the present author, one might suspect Waugh of wishing to impress Yorke. Great friend as he was, Yorke could afford to denigrate 'society' as he came from an ancient landed family (Hardwicke) and Waugh respected this privilege. Yorke was, by descent, 'in society' despite his socialism; Waugh, as the *parvenu*, felt constant pressure to maintain his place there.

The *Diaries* give an entirely different picture of the Baroness. Although pleased to be taken up by someone who would distinguish him socially from the crowd of newsmen, he found her schoolgirlish élitism unpalatable. He merely records her pronouncements without commentary, but there can be little doubt as to his feelings: ' "After all Evelyn, you may think it's nothing [a social snub] but I *am*

14. *Remote People*, p. 63.
15. *Diaries*, 10–26 October, 1930, p. 331.
16. *Letters*, p. 51.

Daddy's daughter. I *am* Baroness Ravensdale." '17 'Irene was put next to the Emperor [at a banquet] and was translated with excitement. Coming back, she said, "That has shown all those Bartons. I have come out on top. I am Baroness Ravensdale in my own right." ' 'I think I must be a prig', Waugh added to this record, 'people do shock me so.'18 The Baroness, it seems, fell short of Waugh's aristocratic ideal: the leisured, cultured intelligence which could remain undisturbed beneath a surface of perfect manners. Her egotism is presented as another aspect of European 'hysteria'. 'Got up 7, went to Catholic church', he noted in his diary the day after the Coronation, 'island sanity in raving town'.19 The only other person with whom Waugh spent any length of time was Professor Thomas Whittemore, a celebrated Byzantinist who had assisted in the restoration of the mosaics of St Sophia. Christopher Sykes defends him as a man 'of great learning' with 'delightful and unusual conversational powers', a 'theatrical manner' and 'deep tremulous voice'.20 Graham Greene met him during the war and gives a similar account in *In Search of a Character*: a gentle, particular, rather effeminate fellow. Bernard Berenson, though, and many scholars, according to Harold Acton, considered Whittemore 'a pious fraud'.21 Waugh tended to Acton's view. Most descriptions of the Professor suggest a strong similarity with Francis Crease. But Waugh's days of sympathy with this sort of character were over.

Throughout these writings there is an assumption that Catholicism provides an 'objective correlative' in matters religious. Ras Tafari was, after all, crowning himself 'Haile Selassie' ('The Power of the Trinity'). It must have appeared blasphemous to Waugh, and Whittemore with his amateur's enthusiasm for Coptic liturgy became the butt of the jokes regarding Abyssinian 'heresy'. 'Professor W.', as he is known in *Remote People*, accompanied Waugh and the Baroness to the Coronation. In the hushed atmosphere of the proceedings, the American persistently interrupted with stage whispers 'explaining' the ceremony but invariably providing misinformation. The serious attention he paid to the event was in itself ludicrous to Waugh who looked upon the whole business not so much as a sacred historical rite as an *ad hoc* invention spun out for the benefit of the international press.

They had been informed that the Emperor would arrive at 7.30 am and that they should be in their places an hour before. Having risen at 5.30 and dressed in morning coat and top hat by lamplight, Waugh was not in the best of tempers when the ceremony was still unfinished by noon. The only light relief was provided by the Abyssinian air force. Haile Selassie was due to proceed from the large marquee at 11.00. No-one had thought to inform the pilots that the Coronation was

17. *Diaries*, 3 November, 1930, p. 332.
18. *Ibid.*, 8 November, 1930, p. 334.
19. *Ibid.*, 3 November, 1930, p. 332.
20. Sykes, p. 110.
21. Harold Acton, *More Memoirs of an Aesthete* (Methuen, 1970), pp. 174–5.

running late. At 11.00 precisely three aeroplanes swooped low over the tent time and again, drowning the liturgy with thundering engines. Only at 12.30 were the guests released. Waugh was hot and irritable. Whittemore was getting on his nerves.

During the proceedings, when Whittemore had refrained from interruption, Waugh had been composing his despatch to *The Times*. There had been considerable consternation among the press corps about getting their cables off in time for the next day's papers. The press officer had been unable (or unwilling) to assure the journalists of seats in the pavilion until the early hours of the preceding day. Accordingly, the more hard-nosed contingent invented the details of the ceremony and wired them before the event. Waugh delighted in these splendidly inaccurate accounts when the London papers began to arrive in the following days. 'I had the fortune to be working for a paper which values the accuracy of its news before everything else,' he wrote. ' " . . . Getting in first with the news" and "giving the public what it wants", the two dominating principles of Fleet Street, are not always reconcilable.'[22] Even so, for those who more honestly waited, there was an additional problem. It was Sunday. The telegraph office was shut.

An interesting, and apparently anomalous, note appears in the diary two days later: 'Cable arrived from *Express:* "Coronation cable hopelessly late beaten every paper London." '[23] Douglas Woodruff thought that Waugh had had an exclusive contract with *The Times* and was astounded when this entry was pointed out.[24] Sure enough, in the *Daily Express* for 4th November an article appears from a 'Special Correspondent' entitled: 'Dancing Priests at Emperor of Abyssinia's Coronation. Airplane Escort for the "Lion of Judah" '. At the head of the column is '(Delayed in Transmission)' and the piece bears remarkable linguistic similarities to Waugh's other accounts.[25] Coincidence? Perhaps. But we know that Waugh had contacted Tom Driberg by letter to ask him for help with his Abyssinian trip and had invited him to his reception just before leaving. Did Driberg also mediate with the *Express* to help raise funds for his friend? If so, it would seem that Waugh broke his contract with *The Times*. We shall never know: the files of the *Express* do not reach back that far.[26]

22. *Remote People*, p. 51.
23. *Diaries*, 4 November, 1930, p. 333. The MS of the diaries reads 'express', not *'Express'*. It is just possible that Waugh was referring to an express cable from *The Times*, but this seems unlikely.
24. Interview with Douglas Woodruff, 16 June, 1976.
25. It includes the aerobatic interruption and 'one American woman in a tweed suit with a sun helmet decorated with a miniature Stars and Stripes' (*DE*, 4 November, p. 8). In *Remote People* we see: 'One lady had stuck an American flag in the top of her sun helmet' (p. 55).
26. Donat Gallagher, the leading authority on Waugh's journalism, states categorically that Waugh *did* write this article and four others (between 29 October and 6 November) for the *Express;* cf. *EAR*, p. 110.

Waugh's own duplicity did nothing to prevent his alarm at the antics of the popular press and cinema photographers. 'Here I knew most of the facts and people involved', he wrote, 'and in the light of this knowledge I found the Press reports shocking and depressing. After all, there really was something there to report that was quite new to the European public; a succession of events of startling spectacular character, a system of life, in a tangle of modernism and barbarity, European, African, and American, of definite, individual character. It seemed to me that here, at least, the truth was stranger than the newspaper reports.'[27]

The contrast between this enthusiasm and his letter to Yorke on the day of the Coronation is strange:

> Life here is inconceivable – quite enough to cure anyone of that English feeling that there is something attractive and amusing about disorder. This morning we spent in Church . . . with interminable Coptic liturgy being sung. . . . I have rarely seen anything so hysterical as the British legation all this last week – or so incompetent to cope with their duties. . . . I go to very stiff diplomatic parties where I am approached by colonial governors who invariably begin 'I say Waugh I hope you aren't going to say anything about that muddle this morning. . . .'[28]

Here the picture is of drab formality. It is essentially the same picture, viewed from a different angle. The excitement engendered by Abyssinia was perfectly genuine. But the pompous European contingent obscured the vitality of the scene with protocol and golf-club morality. It was the clash of cultures which fascinated Waugh, that incongruous meeting of opposites which supported his lifelong view that 'fact' was stranger than fiction.

To find more interesting material Waugh needed to escape Addis. A week of celebrations had followed the coronation.[29] It was all rather tedious. As a journalist Waugh was required to attend every function and the need to meet cable deadlines increased his irritation at Abyssinian inefficiency. As this week of legation parties, gossip and ostentatious hypocrisy proceeded, his spirits began to flag. His spare time had been spent visiting churches, picture dealers and the museum, but the artistic resources of Addis were quickly exhausted. He wanted to explore further. On the Sunday, most of the delegations left Addis and he was at last free of his daily commitment to *The Times*. A single task remained to complete his contract:

27. *Remote People*, p. 53.
28. *Letters*, p. 51.
29. A native feast ('gebbur') and wreath-laying on the Monday, a grand procession on the Tuesday, a race meeting on the Wednesday, a reception at the British Legation on the Thursday, a muster of troops on the Friday, public luncheon with the Emperor on the Saturday.

a lengthy article on Abyssinian politics, and he could take his time over this and post it home.[30]

As this dull week was drawing to its close one incident stood out for him. It seemed, he wrote, 'to embody the whole essence of modern Abyssinia'.[31] He had just returned from a British Legation reception on Thursday evening, slightly drunk and very bored:

> . . . I was living in a kind of annexe at the back of my hotel; a stockade separated it from one of the clusters of native huts. . . . It was a magnificent night with a full moon and large, brilliant stars.
>
> I stood for some time outside the door of my room, dressed in the absurd white tie and tall hat of civilization.
>
> In one of the huts on the other side of the stockade a native party was going on. The door was open and I could see the interior dimly lit by a tiny oil flame; ten or a dozen people squatted round the walls; one of them had a little wooden drum covered with cowhide. They were clapping their hands and singing a nasal, infinitely monotonous tune.
>
> I think they were all drunk. It was probably a wedding or funeral party. At intervals throughout the night I woke up and heard the same chant going on. It seemed to me typical of the whole week; on the one side the primitive song of unfathomable antiquity; on the other, the preposterously dressed European, with a stockade between them.[32]

Again he emphasises the stimulating incongruity of cultural conflict. But he in no way patronises the Abyssinians. Their 'song of unfathomable antiquity' seems to represent something at least as permanent and valuable as the absurd White Rabbit figure of Waugh in his evening clothes. Another, similar description in *Remote People* echoes the attraction he felt for their country: ' . . . every evening fell cool, limpid, charged with the smoke of the *tukal* fires, pulsing, like a live body, with the beat of the tom-toms that drummed incessantly somewhere out of sight among the eucalyptus-trees'.[33] In *Black Mischief* (1932), the novel deriving from this experience, this obscure and insistent drumming became an image of menacing barbarism. In 1931 it still represented the attraction of a 'life-force'.

\*

'It is very surprising to discover the importance which politics assume', Waugh wrote, 'the moment one begins to travel.'[34] The same could have been said of

30. 'Ethiopia Today', *The Times*, 22 December, 1930; *EAR*, pp. 119–22.
31. *Graphic*, 20 December, 1930, 544; *EAR*, pp. 118.
32. *Ibid.*, 544.
33. *Remote People*, p. 63.
34. *Ibid.*, p. 159.

religion as far as he was concerned. Just as 'political issues' outside England were 'implicit in everything',[35] so were religious ones.

Apart from an abortive attempt to photograph monkeys with Baroness Ravensdale, Waugh's first serious expedition from Addis was with Professor Whittemore. The American suggested a visit to the Coptic monastery at Debra Lebanos. It had been the centre of Abyssinian spiritual life for four centuries, the repository of relics, a place of pilgrimage. As a recent convert, Waugh was fascinated by theological questions. He was keen to observe this Eastern form of Christianity more closely. The monastery supposedly held a recently discovered version of Ecclesiastes. At six in the morning they set out in an American 'Rugby', the car packed tight with themselves, a bullet-headed Armenian chauffeur, a native boy who, uninvited, perched on the running board, and a large stock of provisions: coats, blankets, tins of petrol, beer from the hotel and a Fortnum and Mason hamper courtesy of Lady Ravensdale.

They did not get far. No sooner had the car begun to move than Whittemore wished to return to his hotel. They drove round. He disappeared and emerged carrying a dozen empty Vichy water bottles. Waugh's patience was strained. What were they for? To carry back holy water: presents for the notables in Addis and Cairo. Wouldn't Waugh's empty beer bottles do? No, Whittemore thought that rather indelicate. So, the bottles chinking and sliding beneath their feet, they jolted uncomfortably away, heading due north over the summit of Entoto.

It was rough country and a difficult, at times hazardous, journey. There was no clearly marked road beyond Entoto. As it turned out, the native boy proved essential when, as frequently happened, they lost their way. About two o'clock they came upon a deep ravine which they descended to reach the monastery: a cluster of huts, two store houses and a couple of churches. The telegraphese of the diary account makes hilarious reading at this point. Waugh, irritated throughout the journey by Whittemore's bottles, had become increasingly impatient with the man himself. As they crossed the plains he noted 'Whittemore bowing to cowherds'. Arrived at the monastery they were 'surrounded naked boys covered sores also baboons. W. still bowing. . . . Monk wrote on his hand fine script. W. pointed to letter like + and crossed himself. Monk mystified.'[36]

In direct proportion to Whittemore's stupefied reverence, it seems, Waugh's own interest in the monastery declined. *Remote People* includes an amusing description of the expedition in which Waugh casts himself as the man of the world, a disillusioned, no-nonsense empiricist confronting the American's watery piety. Waugh chiefly loathed Whittemore's religiosity, his desire sentimentally to submerge himself in his surroundings and to fabricate truth to conform with this sentimentality:

35. *Ibid.*, p. 159.
36. *Diaries*, 10 November, 1930, p. 335.

'Look,' he said, pointing to some columns of smoke that rose from the cliffs above us, 'the cells of the solitary anchorites.'

'Are you sure there are solitary anchorites here? I never heard of any.'

'It would be a good place for them,' he said wistfully.[37]

Belief was not emotional indulgence for Waugh but adherence to a corpus of established fact.

Waugh contrasts the confused mysteries Whittemore saw in Debra Lebanos with the 'classic basilica and open altar' of European Catholicism as a 'triumph of light over darkness'; 'theology' had become for him 'the science of simplification by which nebulous and elusive ideas are formalised and made intelligible and exact'.[38] For Waugh, both the priest and the artist-craftsman were engaged in the 'science of simplification'. 'That's what makes story-telling such an absorbing task,' he wrote in 1946, 'the attempt to reduce to order the anarchic raw materials of life.'[39] Aesthetic and religious judgement were often related in 1931. The ancient holy 'book' at Debra Lebanos turned out to be 'two pieces of board clumsily hinged together in the form of a diptych ... they were then opened revealing two coloured lithographs, apparently cut from a religious almanac printed in Germany some time towards the end of the last century ...'. Whittemore, of course, 'kissed them eagerly'.[40]

After the library came the holy spring and the burial ground. As evening drew on, the priests proved keenly hospitable and a monk showed them to their accommodation. The diary suggests that this was not entirely to Waugh's taste:

> Offered us hut full of goats hornets. Said preferred tent. accordingly pitched. floor hay covered rugs. Abuna [high priest] supervised preparations. Should he kill goat, sheep & calf? No. Honey. Sat in tent. native bread, beer, honey brought in beer held for our inspection. all disgusting. Abuna sat down. Feared going share dinner. At last left. Ate from hamper. Little lamp hung on tent pole. Abuna came say good night dusted Keatings off rugs. Monk with rifle slept outside. ghastly cold night. Little sleep. W. snored. Chauffeur took some honey & beer.[41]

*Remote People* (pp. 81–5) works this up into a fine vignette in a comedy of manners. They have to disguise their disgust at the native food from the benignly generous Abuna. A starving Whittemore pleads indigestion to buy time while the Fortnum

37. *Remote People*, p. 75.
38. *Ibid.*, p. 88.
39. 'Fan-Fare', *Life Magazine*, 8 April, 1946; *EAR*, p. 303; *CH*, p. 252.
40. *Remote People*, pp. 78–9.
41. *Diaries*, 10 November, 1930, p. 335; MS p. 7. The quotation uses the original punctuation.

and Mason's hamper sits untouchable in the tent. As the priest leaves they pounce on the tinned grouse and bottled lager. The chauffeur gobbles the honey and drinks the native beer. Settling for the night they dust their blankets with Keating's flea powder. The Abuna returns and angrily calls the guard to remove this dust as 'evidence of neglect'. Bidding goodnight, he leaves them to the cold and the fleas, contented in the knowledge that he has done everything possible for their comfort.

Their ordeal continued. After rising at dawn the hours dragged past with further inspection of what Waugh considered tawdry art work and false relics. At last they were shown the sanctuary: 'Holy of Holies contained fumed oak tabor, old clothes, dust, umbrellas, suitcase, teapot, slop pail, hopeless confusion. Small shrine, prettier tabor containing cross that fell from heaven.'[42] That cross, the ultimately absurd relic, found its way into *Black Mischief* and was to cause Waugh considerable embarrassment in Catholic circles over the next year. The remark about 'hopeless confusion' is also interesting. What appealed to Waugh about Roman Catholicism was its meticulous institutional organisation.

Waugh, like Graham Greene, saw the Church as an international family with Latin as its *lingua franca*. One could walk into a Catholic church anywhere in the world and feel immediately at home. Catholics, Waugh remarked in 'Converted to Rome', really *used* their churches: they were always open. There was no nonsense about bolting the doors between services or feeling them to be the personal province of a particular congregation. People of any nationality could drop in for prayer or confession wherever they were, whatever the time of day. They were functional places. So when Waugh records attending a Mass at the conclusion of his visit to Debra Lebanos and finding the service 'quite unintelligible',[43] this constitutes his severest criticism. The monastery becomes in the book an image of unenlightened Christianity, a dark and secret institution, the apotheosis of muddle.

Much later than planned they finally escaped at two o'clock. Whittemore's parting gesture was to throw a handful of small coins into the dust to enjoy the spectacle of the native boys scrambling for them. Waugh was disgusted by this but worse was to come. The car had to be extricated from the place where it had stuck on the precipitous approach path. It was three o'clock before they were on their way and by six it was dark.

The feeble lights of the Rugby scarcely penetrated the night. They persistently lost the road and twice nearly overturned. Whittemore began to panic. 'I have decided', he would pronounce at every hiatus, 'we stop here.' 'It's of no consequence', the chauffeur would reply and implacably drive on. Waugh liked this man, as he did the Armenian race in general. Nothing confronted Whittemore's

42. *Ibid.*, 11 November, 1930, pp. 335–6.
43. *Remote People*, p. 87.

frailty more successfully than that simple statement ' . . . ça n'a pas d'importance'.[44] It might have served as a motto for Waugh's idiosyncratic Catholicism: nothing temporal mattered much. He seems to have had small fear of death after his conversion but rather, to have relished the prospect as release from the absurdities of the human condition. The real business began beyond the grave.

Reaching the summit of Entoto the car ran out of petrol. Two minutes earlier and this would have been distinctly awkward, involving a hike of several miles down a precipitous track in the pitch dark. But they were in luck. The car was on the down-slope. Taking the brake off they free-wheeled a dangerous course into Addis, pulling up outside the Professor's hotel. Neither he nor Waugh had the energy to say goodnight. Silently gathering his bottles Whittemore gave a nod and disappeared inside, a shaken man. Waugh had already fallen asleep. A can of petrol was fetched and he was driven to the Hotel de France where the manager, clearly worried about him, was sitting up with a kettle of boiling water and some rum. It was past eleven o'clock. Insomnia was not a problem that night.

*

The next morning he did not rise till eleven and spent a lazy day recovering. Addis was emptying fast. It was time to think of moving on. His original plan had been to travel straight on to Zanzibar and he had booked his ticket in London. The *Messageries Maritimes* ran a fortnightly service between Djibouti and Zanzibar. He felt that he had not seen enough of Abyssinia but the interior of the country was not easily accessible and caravans and camping equipment were beyond his means. From this point the journey was at his own expense. A balance had to be struck between desirable and financially practicable excursions.

The problem was solved by the generous offer of the British Consul at Harar, a Mr Plowman. Why didn't Waugh break his journey to the coast by travelling via Harar? Plowman would supply ponies; there was accommodation at the consulate. Waugh was delighted with the idea. Richard Burton's *First Steps in Africa* suggested a glamorous image of the place. Harar was an Arab city-state, a focal point for caravans travelling between the coast and the highlands; it was renowned for the beauty of its women. Moreover, it had once been the home of Rimbaud in the days when the French poet was running guns to the old Emperor, Menelik.

Four days after his return from the monastery, at ten o'clock on the morning of 15th November, the last of the special trains steamed out of Addis with Waugh, Plowman and Irene Ravensdale aboard. The plan was to take the train as far as Dirre Dowa and then trek across country via Haramaya to Harar. It was a strange departure. No military band or display bid them farewell but the entire European population of Addis packed the platforms. Waugh's carriage was filled with small

44. *Ibid.*, p. 90.

bunches of flowers placed there by the servants of one of the British officials going home on leave.

At dawn they drew into Dirre Dowa, cold and sleepless, and breakfasted at Bollolakos's hotel. It was here that Waugh came to the horrific realisation that he was included in a family party: 'Lunched with Plowman's governess and odious children. Slept. Tea with Plowman's governess and odious children.'[45] It was too much for this prickly bachelor and the company at dinner did nothing to improve his humour. In addition to Plowman and the governess there was a Mr Hall, a half-caste German, brother of the man who had acted as the inefficient Press Officer in Addis. He appeared with his drab English wife and the manager of the local bank. *Remote People* describes this with wry irony as 'a pleasant little party'. Waugh found it nothing of the sort.[46] During the day he had written his last article for *The Times* and posted it. For the first time since his arrival in Africa he felt a free man. He had no intention of wasting potentially adventurous days bogged in polite domesticity. The ponies had failed to arrive from Harar and this provided him with the excuse he was looking for. Over dinner he informed them that he had better push on alone the next day.

Returning to his hotel that night he wrote two letters: one (unpublished) to Harold Acton and one to his parents. The first is exultant:

> Am just off on two days ride across country to pay homage to Rimbaud's house. Harar. Richard Burton also lived there for a little.
>      This is an amazing country. I am too intoxicated with it at present to be able to describe anything. . . .[47]

Here was Waugh in the role of literary adventurer (Rimbaud was one of Acton's artistic heroes). Addressing his parents he was more sober:

> I am stopping the night here – Dire-Daoua [sic] – on my way to Harar for a few days. I am not sorry to have left Addis. Irene Ravensdale left me this morning for Khartoum & I go on alone with two native servants. . . . You will see a railway marked there on the map but that is one of the many cartographical jokes of the country. When I get there

45. *Diaries*, 16 November, 1930, p. 336.
46. *Remote People*, p. 93. Waugh's English friends reading the book could not have mistaken his irony. He simply notes Mrs Hall's proud display of 'a large enamelled brooch made in commemoration of the opening of Epping Forest' (p. 94). The description appears in the guise of generous acclamation but there is no doubt as to its tone of mockery. The diary speaks more plainly. There Mrs Hall is an 'English old maid who fell in love with [Hall] when he was a prisoner of war' (p. 336). According to the diary her father was Lord Mayor of London; his demotion to alderman in *Remote People* was perhaps another subtle snub.
47. Unpublished ALS to [Sir] Harold Acton, nd [c. 17 November, 1930], Hotel de France notepaper but from Dirre Dowa.

I sleep three nights in a tent in the consulate garden. I leave here again 22nd sailing from Djibouti for Zanzibar. . . . How dutiful I am to tell you all this. I expect to be back about Jan. 10th. I will keep you informed of my movements. I have the plot of a first rate novel. . . . All this trip is interesting me enormously. I think it is money well spent. As a matter of fact, now I've left Addis it isn't costing me very much. My two servants together only cost me about seven shillings a week. I have collected a great many Abyssinian paintings of little merit.[48]

How strange this staccato message must have seemed to his parents reading it at the cold end of autumn in Golders Green. It described a world they had never properly shared: of romantic adventure, aristocratic connections, reckless expense. Perhaps the remark about money was inserted for his father's benefit. Evelyn's financial irresponsibility had always been an area of intractable difficulty between them. Arthur was a cautious man. *Vile Bodies* had been a tremendous success. But no-one knew better than Arthur how temporary such public adulation could be. Clearly Evelyn was dissipating his resources again. The African trip must have seemed to Waugh *père* a quite unnecessary extravagance.

Waugh set out 'early next morning riding a lethargic grey mule, accompanied by a mounted Abyssinian guide who spoke French, an aged groom . . . who attached himself to me against my express orders, and a Galla porter, of singularly villainous expression, to carry my luggage'.[49] There is something of Don Quixote in the image he creates here but this was just Waugh the self-publicist 'writing it up' again. It was a modest expedition, plodding quietly across grassy downs. The night was spent comfortably at the rest-house in Haramaya and there we begin to see another side of Waugh the traveller. Any notion of Waugh as a sneering, public-school imperialist would be entirely inaccurate. It was precisely that Northern European race snobbery which he despised. Frequently in his travels we find him consorting with a cosmopolitan gaggle of taxi-drivers, salesmen, local pilots, restaurateurs. With these people he could get drunk and go to brothels. They were his only reliable guides to the practical details of daily life in any country. His Haramaya acquaintance was of this category. Here he enjoyed a delightful evening with the Greek landlord and a French bank clerk. And it proved a significant encounter, slight as it appeared at the time. The Frenchman sowed the idea in Waugh's mind that he might alter his plans and return to Europe via the Congo Basin. The suggestion had struck a romantic chord. He was hooked.[50]

On the road he had passed Plowman's smart ponies. Had he waited for the

48. *Letters*, pp. 51–2.
49. *Remote People*, p. 94.
50. In *Remote People* (p. 100) Waugh transfers his first meeting with the Frenchman to Harar. The *Diaries* (p. 337) clearly state that he met him first in Haramaya.

consulate party to catch him up he could have entered the city in higher style. But no: 'I . . . want to make a humble entry into Harar', he scribbled in his diary that night.[51] He intended to relish his first experiences of the place privately. In this instance he coveted anonymity as traveller and observer.

Harar did not disappoint. Waugh found a medieval walled city apparently 'dying at its extremities' but, in the centre, 'full of vitality and animation'.[52] It was enchantingly estranged from the modern world. Harar seemed to exist outside history: no wheeled traffic, a leper colony, a shabby Catholic cathedral and an ancient priest who remembered Rimbaud. Waugh spent much of his time being introduced to traditional hospitality and, as this largely consisted of 'parties' – in celebration of the coronation and a local wedding – it provided a stimulating parallel to the smart London life of the author of *Vile Bodies*.

His host during those four intriguing days turned out to be one of the 'heroes' of *Remote People*, although one would never guess at the warmth of Waugh's feeling towards him from the diary: 'Armenian, fat, black skull-cap, seized my bridle. I came in and found the French bank clerk.'[53] In fact, these three consti- tuted a convivial trio racketing round the town, often worse the wear for drink.

The Armenian was a Mr Bergebedgian, proprietor of a seedy hotel, the Léon d'Or. Having grasped the bridle of Waugh's mule to secure his custom, he proceeded to claim his affection:

> During my brief visit I became genuinely attached to this man; he spoke a queer kind of French with remarkable volubility, and I found great delight in all his opinions; I do not think I have ever met a more tolerant man; he had no prejudice or scruples of race, creed, or morals of any kind whatever; there were in his mind none of those opaque patches of unconsidered principles, it was a single, translucent pool of placid doubt; whatever splashes of precept had disturbed its surface from time to time had left no ripple; reflections flitted to and fro and left it unchanged.[54]

In Bergebedgian's character he found 'a marked strain of timidity' and everywhere they went together 'he not only adapted, but completely transformed, his manners to the environment'. The man came to represent a certain ideal of gentleman- liness. Of the Armenians in general he wrote:

> A race of rare competence and the most delicate sensibility. They seem to me the only genuine 'men of the world'. I suppose everyone at times likes to picture himself as such a person. Sometimes, when I find that elusive ideal looming too attractively . . . I . . . realise that . . . I shall

51. *Diaries*, 17 November, 1930, p. 337.
52. *Remote People*, p. 99.
53. *Diaries*, 18 November, 1930, p. 337.
54. *Remote People*, p. 99.

never . . . become a 'hard-boiled man of the world' . . . ; that I shall always be ill at ease with nine out of every ten people I meet; that I shall always find something startling and rather abhorrent in the things most other people think worth doing, and something puzzling in their standards of importance; that I shall probably be increasingly . . . vulnerable to the inevitable minor disasters and injustices of life – then I comfort myself a little by thinking that, perhaps, if I were Armenian I should find things easier.[55]

This is tongue-in-cheek (and possibly teases Michael Arlen, the most famous literary Armenian and Waugh's direct rival in the 'Mayfair novel' market). But there can be no doubt that Waugh envied the *savoir faire* of those who could remain undisturbed by life's inconsistencies. We are reminded by this passage of his diary entry about Carl van Vechten and of the ideal suggested by Roxburgh in his schooldays. Money allowed Waugh to some extent to control his environment; Catholicism largely shielded him from the 'minor disasters and injustices of life'. He did not ultimately share Bergebedgian's untroubled scepticism. But he admired the sceptical, anti-humanist frame of mind with which the man shrugged off the absurdity of human behaviour. Above all, he admired Bergebedgian's manners, and an 'aristocratic' ideal begins to develop in Waugh's mind which, strangely, has small connection with many of the aristocrats of his acquaintance.

Waugh knew himself to be an intemperate man with an acute sense of his own vulnerability. He was capable of reacting violently to any potential 'attack'. Abroad, though, he was less susceptible to uncharitable behaviour. In the *Diaries* his persecution complex crops up occasionally in his battles with 'fraudulent' taxi-drivers and servants: 'small boys fanned us hoping tips'; 'taxi-driver charged 18 thalers. Wrangle. Lost'; 'My taxi-driver laughed when I asked for the *carte de tarif* so I paid him nothing at all'; 'Made porter do transit free', etc.[56] It was crucially important to his image of himself as a 'man of the world' not to be publicly cheated. But generally, Waugh abroad was a milder man at this time, appreciative of tolerance and generosity, appreciative particularly of hospitality. The acerbity and reaction which was to characterise so much of his writing in the later 'thirties had scarcely taken hold by 1931.

Harar was much more to his taste than the aggressively modern Addis. Steeped in ritual, decadent, slightly dangerous, it presented a culture wholly alien to his own and he relished it. The compressed annotation of the diaries can mislead us here. A couple of incidents might seem to reflect badly on the author. 'Saw leper colony. Very cordial priest doctor. Little huts (because it takes several lepers to make a complete man)'.[57] And, 'Went into houses, looked at larders and kitchens,

---

55. *Ibid.*, pp. 110–11.
56. *Diaries*, pp. 331, 332, 334 and 343 respectively.
57. *Ibid.*, 18 November, 1930, p. 337.

pinching girls and tasting food'.[58] These appear, respectively, to offer us a picture of Waugh the cheap joker and Waugh the native girls' burden. In fact, he was relating in telegraphese the words and actions of his two companions.[59] He was being shown the sights and he wanted to see the impoverished level of society before leaving his less reputable companions. Waugh's African experience was oddly mixed. On the 19th November, for example, he had wandered the streets with Bergebedgian examining brothels, the prison and a caged lion. After luncheon he had boarded his mule and set out for the Consulate. The morning had been characterised by those elements of danger and 'barbarity' which fascinated him; the afternoon spent at the Plowman's large, attractive house, comfortably reading Burton's *First Steps*. On the one hand we have the anonymous adventurer delighting in the experience of low life; on the other we have Waugh the gentleman traveller with his letters of introduction padding safely between the public school strongholds of legations and 'English Clubs'. He liked to slip from one world to the other.

Waugh left Harar with regret. But he had to push on if he were to make his connection with the steamer at Djibouti and this involved re-tracing his steps through Haramaya to Dirre Dowa to pick up the train to the coast. It was this journey which inaugurated the period described in *Remote People* as his 'First Nightmare': four days of crippling boredom. Waugh speaks of himself in the book as 'constitutionally a martyr to boredom' and admits that he travelled to escape 'the boredom of civilized life'. But the latter, he says, is 'trivial and terminable, a puny thing to be strangled between finger and thumb' compared with the boredom of the tropics. These days, he says, 'were as black and timeless as Damnation; a handful of fine ashes thrown into the eyes, a blanket over the face, a mass of soft clay knee-deep. My diary reminds me of my suffering in those very words. . . .'[60] Does it? Not in the manuscript at our disposal. Quite the reverse. Crushed by this stupefying *ennui* the author of the diary falters into brevity.

He arrived in Dirre Dowa, knees red raw from the mule-ride, to find that he had been misinformed about the train. It did not leave that night (Sunday). There was no connection until Tuesday morning and he would probably miss the steamer from Djibouti. Melancholia deepened to paranoia.

He was stuck in Mr Bollolokos's hotel with no-one to speak to and nothing to do. Dirre Dowa was a dead town, hot and dusty. There was neither book-shop nor newsagent. The bar was closed. He rooted out the only books in his luggage: three volumes of a pocket edition of Pope and a French dictionary. For an hour or so he sat reading his way assiduously through the juvenile poems. Then he wrote letters home offering Christmas greetings to anyone whose address he

---

58.  *Ibid.*, 19 November, 1930, p. 338.
59.  Cf. *Remote People*, p. 110.
60.  *Ibid.*, p. 116.

could remember. When this palled he tackled the dictionary. In the evening worse was to come: the Halls and the bank manager arrived for dinner.

Hall had clearly interpreted Waugh's good manners on their previous meeting as an overture of friendship. After an embarrassing dinner during which Waugh found him 'boastful and pro-English',[61] Hall dragged him back to his house and displayed his amateurish pastels of Ethiopian sunsets and a draped easel displaying a photograph of the Prince of Wales. He (Hall) was more an artist than a businessman, he explained, claiming fellow-feeling with the young novelist. Waugh's patience was tested to the limit by the need to counterfeit interest. His description of Hall in *Remote People* as 'most amiable' was his revenge: another joke emphasised by Hall's ludicrous aesthetic tastes. But one benefit emerged from the visit. Hall lent him four issues of *John O'London's Weekly*. 'That night under my mosquito curtain, I read three issues . . . straight through, word for word, from cover to cover.'[62]

The next morning, after breakfast, he read the fourth. The diary for that day simply records: 'Cashed cheques at bank. In the evening Charles Barton arrived with the ugliest Miss Barton.'[63] Waugh felt suddenly worse. Charles was the amicable elderly brother of the British Minister with whom Waugh had travelled to Addis; 'Miss Barton' was his niece, Esmé. On their earlier encounters Waugh had found the old fellow dull and the girl foolish. The Bartons were stopping over in Dirre Dowa, he on his way to visit the Plowmans in Harar, she *en route* for the coast and Europe. Not only would he be stuck with them at dinner; he would be forced to entertain this (in his view) extremely silly girl all the way to Djibouti.

The train left the next morning. Enduring Miss Barton was bad enough. But there was only one comfortable carriage and no sooner had they settled than they were asked to leave it. An Abyssinian princess was on her way to the coast to do some shopping. She required the carriage for her drunken servants. Waugh's temper rose several notches, his dignity affronted. As the train progressed, the heat and humidity increased. The countryside provided only a grim panorama of desolation. Miss Barton was a persistent irritant with her censorious remarks about mutual acquaintances he held dear. It was a miserable journey.

They had left at seven in the morning. At sunset they at last glimpsed the sea and, to Waugh's immense relief, his ship, the *General Voyson*, still anchored in the bay. Despite the two-day delay it seemed that the captain was waiting for the rail connection. Not a bit of it. As Waugh noted acerbicly in the diary, 'She sailed just as we arrived'.[64] Depressed and exhausted he made his way back to the Hotel des Arcades, briefly visited before with Charles Barton.

61. *Diaries*, 23 November, 1930, p. 339.
62. *Remote People*, p. 119.
63. *Diaries*, 24 November, p. 339.
64. *Ibid.*, 25 November, 1930, p. 339.

Here the nightmare continued. His original encounter with the manageress had been pleasant enough. Barton and he had arrived drenched; they had found nowhere else to stay. She had provided comfortable rooms in which to change and rest. They had not even needed to remain for the night. This time things were different. With Barton's chattering niece at his elbow, he was apparently marooned in Djibouti for an indefinite period until another ship should arrive. The manageress appears in *Remote People* as a Fate in a pink *peignoir*, bringing news of persistent delay. In fact it was only two days before the Italian *Somalia* docked. But it was a chasm of the blackest melancholia, etched deeply in his memory as a period of which, paradoxically, he could remember almost nothing. He was an impatient man who suffered torments of irritation during any sluggish passage of time.

The first day he had been woken at dawn and told the *Somalia* was in. It wasn't. He bought his ticket as soon as the office opened and waited. During the afternoon he traipsed round the stores with Miss Barton, gloomily inspecting gongs and kimonos. That night, probably to escape her, he fell in with three Americans, a Movietone News crew celebrating the completion of their coverage of the coronation. Waugh got drunk with them. Later they all reeled off to a brothel in the native quarter where, according to the diary, they 'saw a little dance'.[65] 'One of the most boring days of my life', Waugh noted sadly on his return.[66]

The next day was almost as bad. Again he was woken at dawn. The ship had docked and would sail almost immediately. He rushed downstairs with a hangover to discover an enormous bill ('largely the ugly Miss Barton's drinks', he believed).[67] But there was no time to haggle. He paid it, dashed to the quay, and clambered up the gangplank. The *Somalia* eventually put out at around six o'clock in the evening. The entire day was spent on board, moodily reading 'a singularly ill-informed account of Abyssinia'.[68] The steamer for Europe arrived and departed with Miss Barton on board. He watched it go, unable even to raise the enthusiasm to return to the shore.

The *Somalia* was a small ship carrying a few passengers and a cargo of animal skins. Waugh befriended a French bursaries agent and a newly-married Italian official and his pretty wife. Together they dined with the captain but it was a tedious trip and the prospect of Aden failed to raise his spirits. He expected to find 'a community, full of placid self-esteem . . . ; conversation full of dreary technical shop among the men and harsh little snobberies among the women'.[69] One of the more surprising discoveries of this expedition was the convivial nature

65. *Ibid.*, 26 November, 1930, p. 340.
66. *Ibid.*, 26 November, 1930, p. 340.
67. *Ibid.*, 27 November, 1930, p. 340.
68. *Remote People*, p. 122.
69. *Ibid.*, p. 127.

of the Aden community. There he found a society unpolluted by what Shaw termed 'the hideous boredom of the hearth'.

*

At 7.00 am the *Somalia* docked at Steamer Point. It presented a barren landscape in the early morning light: a parched, extinct volcano, ash, scrub vegetation, bungalows littering the hillside behind the hotels, the club and the mess. Waugh headed for the most expensive establishment, the Hotel de l'Europe, where he stayed for six days. He was not pleased with it. He found the food pallid; the shower was a cubicle with a slimy cement floor and a tin can suspended on a rope.

Sir Stewart Symes, a distant cousin, was the Resident (British political head) of Aden at the time. As soon as Waugh had washed and taken breakfast, he set out, to leave his card at the Residency. This was in the other town of the Settlement, Crater Town, a more inviting place altogether. Again it presented a fascinating conflict of cultures – Moslem, Christian, Hebrew; again there was something fantastical about the place. On three sides it was surrounded by cliffs, the fourth being the entrance to the harbour, now completely silted up. The decline in sea-traffic had caused a radical shift in the commercial and political balance of the area which intrigued Waugh. Its solid nineteenth-century architecture proclaimed it as an outpost of the British Empire. But the old trade route was blocked, the barracks stood empty, the benevolent Anglican Chaplain preached every Sunday in the cavernous Victorian Gothic garrison chapel to near-empty pews.

Waugh seems again to have developed two quite separate sets of acquaintances: the one for drinking and local information, the other for 'society' and political gossip. In the first category we find 'the Welsh skipper' and the various 'airmen' of the *Diaries;* in the second, Sir Stewart, Mr Champion (the Chief Political Officer) and M. Besse, a millionaire merchant of whom Waugh gives a tenderly comic portrait in *Remote People* under the *soubriquet* of M. Leblanc.

Sir Stewart had responded quickly, sending an invitation for dinner at the Residency. Waugh struck up new friendships abroad with astonishing alacrity. On his first day in Aden he had got drunk twice with different men before setting off for the dinner. There he found solid comforts: fine food and wine, Wagner playing on the gramophone in the half-light. He took to Symes and to Besse. The former was intimately involved in the political reorganisation of the area. A major conference of Arab leaders was due to take place in a little over a week. Over dinner Sir Stewart explained that he would be keen to have it advertised. Waugh was grateful for the story and he spent the next five days immersed in books, papers and maps trying to grasp the complex political situation. On the 2nd December he wired *The Times* asking if they would be interested. They were,

[ 255 ]

though the piece was not published until the following March.[70] The enormous labour expended here for such small profit demonstrates both his loyalty to Sir Stewart and the seriousness with which he undertook *The Times*'s commission. But, as usual, nothing was wasted. The research proved useful for the travel book he wrote on his return.

Besse was another character for Waugh's treasury of eccentrics. Immensely rich, tough and slightly decadent, he offered that odd combination of sceptic and sybarite Waugh relished. *Remote People* provides a hilarious description of Besse's inviting him for a 'little walk'. This entailed advanced rock-climbing without ropes and a hike across rough hills for several miles. 'Every detail of that expedition', he wrote, 'is kept fresh in my mind by recurrent nightmares.'[71] At last they arrived at their destination where M. Besse's servants awaited them. Waugh, his knees trembling from fatigue, his shoes worn through, giddy with heat and exhaustion, must have looked with some relief at the cool water, the change of clothes, the tea laid out on the beach, the bathing dresses and towels. It was a temporary respite. Sharks were common there, M. Besse informed him before swimming strongly out to sea. Only last month two boys had been devoured. He preferred not to swim at the club. They had a screen there to keep the sharks out. Nothing daunted, Waugh followed him into the water.

The image we have of Besse is not dissimilar to that of Mr Baldwin in *Scoop* (1938): 'M. Leblanc had laid out for him in the car a clean white suit, a shirt of green crêpe-de-Chine, a bow tie, silk socks, buckskin shoes, ivory hairbrushes, scent spray, and hair lotion. We ate banana sandwiches and drank very rich China tea.'[72] He was another version of that mythological man of the world: courageous, stoical, fastidious. Besse was a bachelor and Waugh was in a frame of mind to appreciate the possibilities of an equable single life. In Aden he had found a society of bachelors and was forced to revise his ideas about expatriate bureaucrats. 'I think there is nothing essentially ludicrous about English officials abroad', he wrote, 'it is the wives they marry that are so difficult.'[73] Aden presented no such problem. The card tables and club bar remained packed till midnight; no-one had a wife to return to; no children were in evidence. Nothing could have suited him better.

\*

After covering the conference of Arab chiefs in Lahej, he sailed from Aden on 10th December for Mombasa and Zanzibar, heading south down the east coast of Africa. The *Explorateur Grandidier* was comfortable, the sea was calm, the

70. *The Times*, 17 March, 1931.
71. *Remote People*, p. 143.
72. *Ibid.*, p. 143.
73. *Ibid.*, p. 136.

weather fresh and warm. He secured his usual crop of shipboard acquaintances and he was particularly lucky this time. A young agent for the Shell Oil Company (the 'Smith' of the *Diaries*) offered help with accommodation in Mombasa; a beautiful American girl, Kiki Preston, also disembarking there, later introduced him to the fashionable set in Kenya; a Turk, Mohammed Ekram Bey, kept him amused, at least during the voyage, with analyses of European history seen from the perspective of Mohammedan culture.

The voyage to Mombasa appears to have taken a couple of days. Waugh was not stopping there this time but heading further south immediately to double back in a little over a fortnight and re-join his new friends. After dining ashore with Smith he boarded the *Explorateur* again and set sail. This journey took him several hundred miles out of his way. Money was running short and he had had no mail for weeks. His mind, though, was set on two things: to sample the exoticism of Zanzibar and Dar-es-Salaam; and, on his return to Mombasa, to make his way across Kenya to Lake Victoria and to find a route home via the Congo Basin. He was to be disappointed on both counts.

December is not the best time to approach the Equator. The mild weather experienced on the first leg of his voyage rapidly changed. Zanzibar, which he reached at sunset on 16th December, was blistered and breathless in fierce tropical heat. For six days he stayed at the English Club. Regularly, soon after dawn, the heat would jerk him from sleep. Sitting in the club library most mornings, reading local history for his travel book, he found his concentration destroyed by enervation. Back in his room he tried everything from baths of cold water to sitting beneath a fan with his hair soaked in eau de quinine. In the library the fan scattered his papers. If he tried to smoke, the draught showered pipe ash down his clothes. He left sticky thumbprints on the books and his ink bled in the droplets of sweat falling onto the page. The windows stood open but it did no good. Whatever light breeze there was served only to fill the rooms with the reek of copra, cloves and rotten fruit. He would eat luncheon with difficulty and immediately go to bed. At two-forty every afternoon the breeze would drop and the heat suddenly rise, waking him again. Only the evenings were tolerable, when he dined on the relatively cool Club terrace. He was miserable.[74] And then there was Mohammed Ekram Bey. The man appears to have been a cultured Turk whose conversation Waugh had at first found stimulating. Bey was the only acquaintance to have stayed with him for the entire journey. He even seems to have entertained Waugh at his home in the country. But the fellow *would* keep calling and talking obsessively about women.

Women were once again a problem. The supposedly exotic Zanzibar offered nothing to him but omnipresent gabbling wives. After lunch with the Resident

---

74. Cf. *ibid.*, pp. 160–2.

he recorded: 'women were present so could not talk of anything interesting'.[75] Visiting the red-light district he had presumably hoped for more energetic engagement with the opposite sex. Burton was his Baedeker during this trip and Waugh had not so far been disappointed by the Victorian explorer's judgement. *First Steps* promised a brothel quarter renowned throughout Europe. No sooner had Waugh entered it, though, than he realised that things must have changed. The women ran away.

Waugh had presumably wished to discuss with the Resident in Zanzibar the subject on which he had so profitably questioned Sir Stewart in Aden: local politics. 'I think that, more than the climate, it is the absence of any kind of political issue which makes Zanzibar so depressing. There are no primary problems at all; such difficulties as there are, are mere matters of the suitable adjustment of routine. There are no perceptible tendencies among the people towards nationalisation or democracy.'[76] It might seem an oddly Orwellian remark coming from Waugh. It is, though, perfectly in keeping with the tendency of his thoughts at this time. Profoundly disaffected with his own culture, he had not yet rejected the ideology of democracy.

Discovering the lassitude of the ruling class males and what he took to be ignorance among the women, Waugh set about unearthing the 'primary problems' for himself. He disliked the influences of Protestant British Imperialism. 'In the last two decades of the nineteenth century', he wrote, 'zealous congregations all over the British Isles were organising bazaars and sewing-parties with the single object of stamping out Arabic culture in East Africa.'[77] He lamented the resultant domination by the Indians. 'The East African Indians are without roots or piety. . . . The Arabs are by nature a hospitable and generous race and are "gentlemen" in what seems to me the only definable sense, that they set a high value on leisure; deprived by the Pax Britannica of their traditional recreations, these qualities tend to degenerate into extravagance and laziness, as they do in any irresponsible aristocracy.'[78]

It is anybody's guess as to what Waugh meant by 'traditional recreations': slaving, opium smoking, polygamy? We can't tell. At any rate, he appears to be constructing an analogue with the 'irresponsible' aristocracy and commercial usurpers at home. His preference for Arab rather than Indian (Hindu) culture derives from the idea that the latter had usurped the established culture of the landed gentry. The unbusinesslike dilettantism of the Arabs, their warmth, hospitality and class assumptions appealed to him as a contrast with the Indians' devotion to commerce. Their obsession with 'trade' appalled.

75. *Diaries*, 22 December, 1930, p. 344.
76. *Remote People*, p. 165.
77. *Ibid.*, p. 166.
78. *Ibid.*, p. 167.

Waugh's racial assumptions in his public writings often fail to marry with the personal experience as recorded in letters and diaries. Grinding out the prose of these books he was led into facile generalisation on the topic of race by his (perfectly genuine) attempt to make political judgements on aesthetic and religious grounds. (The severe criticism of the Hindu culture, for instance, is based on the idea that it lacks 'roots or piety'.) But, whatever we think of the intrinsic merit of this thesis, one thing becomes clear: in 1931 his concept of a 'decent and valuable' culture was not restricted to either Christian or European ways of life.[79] Although his discussion is phrased in the hackneyed nineteenth-century terminology of 'gentlemanliness' versus 'trade', he uses this to attack the British colonial 'caste of just, soap-loving young men with Public School blazers'.[80] He sees these chattering nonentities as having replaced the 'cultured, rather decadent aristocracy of the Oman Arabs'[81] and it is this 'aristocratic' ambience that he relishes wherever he finds it and in whatever form. Ultimately, of course, Waugh had only one allegiance: to the Catholic Church, that 'island of sanity' in a mad world. Wherever he went he would drop into a church for Mass or private prayer. He was at home with co-religionists of whatever nationality. He felt no call to support the Protestant ethic of British colonialism.

Christmas was approaching but he made no arrangements to share the festivities. Waugh had developed a loathing for the Protestant, Northern European Christmas with its Germanic accessories of yule logs and fir trees. He despised its sentimentality and preferred to keep a critical distance from Dickensian family gatherings. He boarded a boat for Pemba, an island north of Zanzibar: 'Dined three tipsy bachelors', he recorded on 24th December, 'who fought over the distribution of Christmas presents to children'.[82] This image seemed more appropriate to the season.

Next day he returned to Zanzibar, expecting to spend Christmas Night alone. But the British community did not fail him. As he stepped off the boat he was greeted by an invitation to dinner by a local lawyer. Waugh attended Benediction at the Cathedral and went on to the meal and a party. He was happy enough, apart from one thing: 'Ekram Bey came after me again', he noted darkly in his diary.

He had wired for money and was waiting for the post to catch up with him. In two days both came through and with two hundred pounds in hand he could

79. Cf. *ibid.*, pp. 167–8: 'We came to establish a Christian civilisation and we have come very near to establishing a Hindu one. We found an existing culture which, in spite of its narrowness and inflexibility, was essentially decent and valuable; we have destroyed that – or, at least, attended at its destruction – and in its place fostered the growth of a mean and dirty culture. Perhaps it is not a matter for censure: but it is a matter for regret.'
80. *Ibid.*, p. 165.
81. *Ibid.*, p. 165.
82. *Diaries*, 26 December, 1930, p. 344; cf. also *Remote People*, pp. 170–1.

review with equanimity his adventurous return via the Congo Basin. The post seems to have disappointed: 'Mostly letters of congratulation or vilification about my having become a Papist. Religious controversy seems the occupation of the lowest minds these days.'[83] 'Many thanks for your letter', he wrote to James Sterne from the English Club, 'which I have just received together with three months accumulation of mail – most abusive postcards from Belfast or begging letters from Papists. . . . I am just off to the Congo. You ought to come to Africa and escape those dreary bohemians you affect.'[84]

By 29th December he was aboard another Italian ship, the *Mazzini*, putting out at last from Zanzibar. Black beetles plagued the cabins and expired in the baths, though this seems not to have bothered him. He was hot and impatient, but the prospect of heading north to cooler air and new experience was invigorating. He bought a couple of Edgar Wallace novels and, in the evening, settled contentedly to watch a silent Tarzan film on an ancient, clicking cinematograph.

The only port of call before Mombasa was Dar-es-Salaam, which they reached a few hours later and where they docked overnight. It was another town of exotic reputation which Waugh found unimpressive. The trip ashore, though, served a purpose, for it was there that he visited an 'agent' for the Belgian Congo. The man was helpful and encouraging. There was, he said, a cheap air service between Albertville and Bomba. Admittedly his timetable was two years out of date but he was confident that any changes would have been changes for the better. 'I', Waugh states wryly in *Remote People*, 'believed him'.[85]

A day later, New Year's Eve, they docked at Mombasa, an island connected by bridge to the mainland. His first experiences there put him in a foul mood. The Customs officers, 'a pair of chubby nonentities',[86] took an instant dislike to him. Perhaps he was high-handed; perhaps he had forgotten to bribe. Whatever the reason, the men refused to accept Waugh's passport and letters of introduction (to the Colonial Secretary and Apostolic Delegate) as adequate proof of his honesty. They demanded fifty of Waugh's precious two hundred pounds. It would be returned on his leaving the country. But, he protested, he would be leaving through Uganda. The money would be forwarded. He would have to wait for its arrival at the Ugandan border post, probably for a week. Waugh was indignant but protest only hardened official resolve. He travelled into town in a black rage, cashed a cheque, and brought back the money in East African currency. It was a bitter blow to dignity, equanimity and resources. But there was nothing to be done but to pay up. His luggage released, he entered Kenya 'fully resolved to add all I could to the already extensive body of abusive literature that had grown

83. *Ibid.*, 29 December, 1930, p. 345.
84. Unpublished ALS to James Sterne, nd [late December 1930], from the English Club, Zanzibar.
85. *Remote People*, p. 172.
86. *Ibid.*, p. 173.

up around that much misunderstood dependency'.[87] As the word 'misunderstood' intimates, Waugh found nothing to abuse. On the contrary, the climate, landscape and people of Kenya delighted him.

As the train mounted to fresher air between Mombasa and Nairobi, his temper cooled and his sharp, bachelor's sense of humour returned. In the restaurant car he sat opposite another British girl travelling towards marriage: 'She said she had been a clerk at Scotland Yard and that had coarsened her mind a lot, but she had worked in a bank in Dar-es-Salaam and that had refined it again.'[88] The relief from sweating was in itself an intense pleasure. In the morning he changed from white drill to grey flannel. He was happily resuming his English identity and it was in large part the curious atmosphere of a displaced Barsetshire which constituted Kenya's appeal. He had wired ahead to the exclusive Muthanga Club but found it full. It was Race Week. Torr's Hotel was an excellent substitute: large, modern and comfortable. He booked in and slept all afternoon.

Driving out to the Muthanga again the next day he found his friends from the *Explorateur Grandidier*, Kiki Preston among them. Her husband, Gerry, was there as were two London acquaintances, Raymond de Trafford and Gerard de Crespigny. De Trafford was a figure of romance whose recklessness clearly appealed to Waugh. In a letter to Lady Dorothy Lygon two years later Waugh described the man lovingly as 'v. nice but so BAD and he fights & fucks and gambles and gets DD [disgustingly drunk] all the time'.[89] If Waugh's diary offers an accurate description of his friend, he had clearly changed little during the interim. De Trafford's past was equally exotic and violent. Lunching in Paris in 1927 with the woman he was eventually to marry, Alice Silverthorne, he had suddenly told her he must leave. *En route* to the station she had bought a gun and shot him and then herself. Both were severely injured.[90] In Kenya he had set up as a farmer and converted a lorry with an apparatus to catch gorillas. The Berlin Zoo was apparently offering two thousand pounds a head for the beasts and he was determined to cash in on it.

De Trafford was thirty; de Crespigny was an elderly, exuberant General, in Kenya to shoot the rare Bongo. Kiki Preston Waugh consistently describes as 'lovely', an American dilettante beauty who rarely rose before lunchtime and who, quite suddenly during Waugh's visit, set off for a safari without her husband. She had something of the style of Diana Guinness. Waugh found them a deliciously eccentric breed of country squires and Bright Young Things incongruously trying to maintain country-house life in the Tropics. They were rich and easy-going. They drank copious quantities of gin and of champagne, gave elaborate dinner-

87. *Ibid.*, p. 175.
88. *Diaries*, 31 December, 1930, p. 345.
89. ALS to Lady Dorothy Lygon, nd [April 1932], from Easton Court Hotel, Chagford; *Letters*, p. 64.
90. Cf. *Letters*, p. 62, n. 10.

parties and yet were perfectly serious and industrious about the management of their enormous farms. The section of *Remote People* describing their Nairobi life reads like a chapter of *Vile Bodies*. But, as they explained, life in Kenya was not always like this. It was a period of protracted New Year festivities.

Waugh had arrived during the concluding three days of Race Week and slept for that period at Torr's. The days were largely spent getting drunk at the Muthanga and gambling on the horses but he made time on 3rd January to interview the militant Indian leaders of the community. As in Zanzibar, he found their political aggression unpleasant and ungentlemanly. In the diary he describes them as 'Stupid men'.[91] *Remote People* offers a more mildly mocking, and slightly dishonest, account of his feelings:

> Mr Varma is very pugnacious; he smokes cigars all the time; bangs the table and snorts. He says that colour prejudice in Kenya has come to such a pass that Indians are made to share the same waiting-rooms with natives. I detect an inconsistency in that argument, but think it best to say nothing for fear of a scene.[92]

In his book Waugh passes off his own prejudice on de Trafford, neatly avoiding responsibility for racism: 'Raymond finds me reading the pamphlets and remarks that he is all for the blacks, but Indians are more than he can stand; besides they spread jiggas and bubonic plague.'[93] Mr Varma's snarled grievances and demands for equitable treatment in a European society which he wished not to join seemed absurd to Waugh and an unnecessary attack on an essentially well-balanced society.

Waugh was quite simply in love with the country. Its splendid panoramas of receding hills, its temperate climate, its comfortable lakeside houses evoked an image of a lost England. There was a spaciousness and ease about this land which attracted him immediately: 'a quality about it which I have found nowhere else but Ireland, of warm loveliness, breadth and generosity'.[94] In this relaxed atmosphere his interest in politics declined, as it always did on his return to his native land. Aesthetic pleasure outweighed humanist argument. *Remote People* is in many ways a political book but he recognises, in his section on Kenya, that 'it is futile to attempt to impose any kind of theological consistency on politics, which are not an exact science but, by their nature, a series of makeshift, rule-of-thumb, practical devices for getting out of scrapes'.[95]

The 'scrapes' he discovered were those concerning the friction between the

91. *Diaries*, 3 January, 1931, p. 346.
92. *Remote People*, p. 177.
93. *Ibid.*, p. 177.
94. *Ibid.*, p. 178.
95. *Ibid.*, p. 180.

Europeans, Indians and African Nationalists. Adopting the tone of a mild-mannered, quizzical outsider, he devotes nearly twelve pages to the defence of white settlement. While strenuously condemning all proven injustice he neverthe-less concludes: 'It is just worth considering the possibility that there may be something valuable behind the indefensible and inexplicable assumption of superi-ority by the Anglo-Saxon race.'[96] There is little doubt that Waugh shared this assumption.

Waugh's position regarding Africa was ambiguous and confused in Kenya by the subjective appeal of the settlers as fellow victims of the megalopolitan culture of Northern Europe. He regarded them as

> ... perfectly normal, respectable Englishmen, out of sympathy with their own age, and for this reason linked to the artist in an unusual but very real way. One may regard them as quixotic in their attempt to recreate Barsetshire on the equator, but one cannot represent them as land-grabbers.[97]

This desire to defend his new friends by relating them to the situation of the alienated contemporary artist somewhat strains credulity as a general principle. But it was something sincerely felt by Waugh. Their attempt to 'perpetuate a habit of life traditional to them, which England had ceased to accommodate – the traditional life of the English squirearchy',[98] was of immediate contemporary relevance to him. Kenya represented a striking contrast to an England in which the 'squirearchy' was under attack from the Labour Party. 1931 saw a National Government formed under Ramsay MacDonald in a desperate attempt to control an unstable political situation. The Statute of Westminster gave independence to the Dominions. At home it was a period of financial depression. Revolution was in the air as the workers and unemployed took to the streets. In England Waugh saw nothing around him but change and decay. In Kenya, at least, a well-regulated society existed offering the possibility of individual action. He despised the agitators for rocking the boat.

For the twelve days after Race Week Waugh exchanged his role of adventurer for that of country-house visitor, working a dilatory westerly course towards the Ugandan frontier on the northern shore of Lake Victoria. The variety and comfort of these houses delighted him. The Prestons inhabited a luxurious bungalow whose lawn stretched down to Lake Naiwasha. A Moorish palace stood off in the distance. They took dinner on the lawn in pyjamas, bathed in the lake in the mornings, slept after luncheon. The Longs had a baronial mansion on a hill overlooking another lake clouded with flamingos. De Trafford was an odd, but

96.  *Ibid.*, p. 191.
97.  *Ibid.*, p. 183.
98.  *Ibid.*, pp. 182–3.

no less delightful host. Quite often he would be absent from the house and Waugh would sleep there alone. When de Trafford was at home Waugh was able to pursue a more reckless bachelor existence than during those polite visits to neighbours. They would usually get drunk together, at which point Waugh would talk unremittingly about the Church.[99] One night Raymond returned much inebriated with 'a sluttish girl. . . . He woke me up later in the night to tell me he had just rogered her and her mama too. Have missed boat at Kisumu again. Getting restless.'[100]

Waugh was travelling with a party of his Kenyan acquaintances. But the pleasures of their company and country were beginning to stale before a fortnight was up. They accompanied him to the Ugandan border where, on 21st January, he took a train to Kampala, alone again in alien territory. Travelphobia was beginning to grip him. He was keen to return to England as soon as possible and the object of his journey now was the most expeditious route to Albertville and the Belgian air service which was supposed to operate from there to Leopoldville. Kampala, however, provided the first of many delays. He was marooned there from Wednesday to Sunday waiting for a steamer to take him to Mwazana on the southern shores of Lake Victoria.

As Waugh's thirst for European civilisation grew, so did his Catholic consciousness. The empty hours in Kampala were filled touring fever wards, schools and a convent. The negress nuns of the latter particularly impressed him. Three of his four days there were spent roaring off on the pillion of an eccentric priest's motor-bicycle investigating the practical application of Catholic Christianity. 'Father J[anssen] had told me with relish of the ex-communication of CMS priests for fucking', he noted with equal relish.[101] The rivalry between the Church Missionary Society and the Catholic missions excited Waugh's schoolboyish loyalty to his faith. The Catholics he saw as selfless, cosmopolitan, aesthetically sensitive figures. Fr Janssen built most of his church with his own hands, deftly counterfeiting wood carving with cement. The CMS contingent is seen as worthy but literal-minded, doctrinaire, dull. Waugh liked the rough and ready pragmatism of Catholic religious practice among remote peoples ('Mass at Father Janssen's. Dog in church. Packed').[102] These small communities of the faithful fended off the vastness of 'gross jungle, bush, and forest, haunted by devils and the fear of darkness, where human life merges with the cruel, automatic life of the animals . . .'.[103] The romance of Africa was dying fast.

On the Sunday he boarded a comfortable cargo boat, the *Rusinga*, and sailed south. That night he slept badly: the engines thundered on the still waters of the

99. Cf. *Diaries*, 7 January, 1931, p. 347.
100. *Ibid.*, 14 January, 1931, p. 347. Davie omits the last two sentences.
101. *Diaries*, 22 January, 1931, p. 348.
102. *Ibid.*, 25 January, 1931, p. 348.
103. *Remote People*, p. 207.

lake. In all other respects he was reasonably contented. The efficiency of the officers and their scrupulously smart uniforms were a source of pleasure to him. He felt comfortable and the journey round Lake Victoria proved uneventful. He settled back to read a collection of detective stories. Worse things, he knew, lay ahead.

It took him eight days to reach Kigoma on Lake Tanganyika. There he learned that the *Duc de Brabant* was sailing across the lake for Albertville at six that evening. It seemed, on the face of it, a stroke of good fortune after the delays of the past week. As it turned out, this was the point at which the 'Second Nightmare' of the African expedition began. The shabby, wood-burning steamer possessed only two or three cabins and the lavatory was padlocked while they were in port. Waugh's suspicions were roused further by the captain's quarters: ornaments, curtains, pin cushions, and ' . . . every conceivable sort of cheap and unseamanlike knick-knack. Clearly there was a woman on board. I found her knitting on the shady side of the deck-house.'[104] The slovenliness of the *Duc de Brabant* was an unhappy contrast to the slick bachelor atmosphere exuded by the officers of the *Rusinga*. Asked about cabins, the woman said that her husband was asleep and must not be disturbed until five.

When the captain eventually emerged he confirmed Waugh's worst fears: 'No-one, looking at him', he wrote, 'would have connected him in any way with a ship; a very fat, very dirty man, a stained tunic open at his throat, unshaven, with a straggling moustache, crimson-faced, gummy-eyed, flat footed.'[105] Waugh asked about cabins again. It was now only an hour before the advertised time of departure. The captain wasn't concerned with cabins. He asked instead for a medical certificate. Waugh did not possess one. The captain was adamant: no-one could sail without a medical certificate. What did it have to certify? The captain didn't care. Waugh must go ashore and find a doctor.

Furious, he dashed down the gangplank and was directed, in turn, to a hospital two miles away, the doctor's house, and back to the waterfront. Each whistle from the boat startled him into another jog-trot as he pictured the steamer sailing out with his entire complement of luggage and credentials. He eventually discovered the doctor tinkering with a speed boat. There was no medical examination. Five shillings purchased a few lines on the back of an envelope stating that Waugh was free from infectious diseases and had been vaccinated. Grabbing the paper, he ran the last quarter of a mile along the dock to the boat and staggered aboard by ten past six. No-one seemed particularly bothered. The boat eventually sailed around midnight.

By then it was crowded with passengers and the cabins had been distributed to those with the foresight to bribe the captain. There appeared to be no seats

104.  *Ibid.*, p. 218.
105.  *Ibid.*, p. 218.

or deck chairs; the very benches at the tables were instantly claimed after a paltry meal. Waugh and half-a-dozen others were left standing. Worse still, among his unaccommodated companions there was an officiously polite young man in a neat, dark suit and bow tie who was a member of the Seventh Day Adventist mission. The account of him in *Remote People* is superbly restrained: 'I offered him a drink and he said, "Oh, no, thank you," in a tone which in four monosyllables contrived to express first surprise, then pain, then reproof, and finally forgiveness.'[106] The diary is more blunt: '. . . one bloody American who turned out to be a missionary'.[107] It must have been close to Waugh's idea of Purgatory: to be bored and exhausted after a bad meal on a shabby steamer in the middle of Lake Tanganyika with nowhere to rest, no light to read by, and accompanied by a religious maniac who was, to boot, an accountant. As it turned out, this humble teetotaller was not to be shaken off for twelve long days.

One thing, at least, was in Waugh's favour. It was a warm, moonlit night as they put out. *Remote People* states romantically that he laid his overcoat on the deck and used a canvas grip as a pillow. This plays up his discomfort. In fact (if the diary is to be believed) he found a deckchair and, by three in the morning, was just beginning to doze.

It was at this point that the air turned suddenly colder and the boat began to roll violently. A clap of thunder preceded a blast of wind. The chairs crashed over; rain sheeted down; the Europeans scuttled nervously to the saloon where they packed themselves tightly on the benches round the tables. As the storm increased so did the general air of hysteria. Lightning flashed continually. Water flooded and slopped over the floor as the wind shrieked and buffeted. There was no respite till dawn, whose light revealed ashen faces staring fixedly ahead at the wrecked saloon. Most of those wedged behind the tables had been sick. The floor and surfaces were rancid with vomit; the sodden room stank as they moved outside to the fresh air.

They were still some hours from Albertville. Progress was slow as they were towing a barge of (presumably nauseous) cattle. Even when they docked at ten in the morning Waugh could not disembark for another two hours: more customs (they had crossed from the British territory of Tanganyika to the Belgian Congo), more forms full of idiotic questions. But Waugh had learned his lesson at the first Kenyan frontier: this time he restrained his indignation and gave fictitiously definite plans for his proposed movements in the country. He was, he said, going direct to Matadi, though he had no secure intention of doing so. A certificate of entry was immediately issued.

Albertville was a small town in 1931. A single street of bungalows, offices and shops along the lake front formed its nucleus, the hills rising unobscured behind

106.  *Ibid.*, p. 221.
107.  *Diaries*, 2 February, 1931, p. 351.

it. As he stepped ashore the rain stopped, the sun blazed down and everything began to steam. There were two hotels, of which Waugh selected the Belgian 'Palace'. He bathed, shaved, slept and changed, and with a considerable sense of relief, set off to buy his air ticket home.

A few minutes later he discovered how hopelessly he had misplaced his optimism. No-one had heard of an air service to Leopoldville unless, possibly, there was one from Kabalo – over a hundred miles further west. Certainly there had never been one operating from Albertville. There were, in fact, only two alternatives open to him: either to take the train to Kabalo or to return by boat to Kigoma. Anything was preferable to the latter prospect. Waugh purchased a first class rail ticket to Bukama via Kabalo in the hope that he could somehow make a rail connection to the coast from there. He was depressed, the weather hot and stormy and money was running short. The extra expense on the ticket was necessity rather than luxury: the only means by which he could escape the company of the Seventh Day Adventist. A day later, just before sundown, they steamed into Kabalo, a small settlement on the upper reaches of the Lualaba, a headstream of the Congo. There is no evidence of Waugh's having read *Heart of Darkness*. Had he done so, he might have been better prepared. Kabalo was worse than he had expected.

It was literally the end of the line. There was no platform; a few trucks shunted into sidings, a pile of wood fuel and some corrugated iron sheds were the only indications that this was in fact a 'terminus'. It was the rainy season. Ahead of him stretched the swollen, brown Upper Congo with a few barges and a rusting paddle steamer moored to the bank. The settlement was surrounded by swampland; the only available hostelry, a decrepit canteen, was infested with clouds of mosquitoes. Waugh hired a boy to sit on his luggage and tramped off to this 'hotel' to enquire when the next aeroplane left for the coast. The question provoked only laughter. There were just three possible escape-routes from this dismal place: back along the railway to Albertville, or steamer passage up or down the river. The idea of merely retracing his steps was unacceptable. The choice lay between the two directions of the river traffic. Downstream would take him north, deep into the Congo Basin. Upstream led to Bakama where there was at least a rail service to Port Francqui and Elizabethville. From there he might possibly get a plane to Matadi or a rail connection to Portugese West Africa. It did not take him long to decide on the upstream route.

With temper and cash depleted, a stupendous, manic-depressive boredom was growing as each day passed in exhaustion and discomfort. The Conradian Congo voyage, so appealing when he was happily relaxed in Kenya, seemed now a disgusting prospect. He had had enough of Africa, and the news that the *Prince Leopold* was leaving at dawn for Bukama settled the matter. His mood lightened a little. It instantly darkened again upon hearing that the Seventh Day Adventist was to accompany him.

That evening the *Prince Leopold* docked, a hulking, run-down, three-decked paddle-steamer. Waugh instantly detected signs of feminine presence: the upper-deck was given over to the captain's married quarters ('one could only regard it as a floating house not as a ship').[108] But at first it did not seem too awful. The Europeans were accommodated on the middle deck, the native passengers on the lower. Waugh had a cabin to himself; there was an observation deck and a bathroom. True, the captain – a young, neurotic and distinctly shabby creature – did not promise well but there seemed no reason for Waugh to encounter him. He and the Adventist slept that night on board. When he woke the next morning they were already churning southward against a sluggish current. Looking out, he could see only green banks and palm trees under a leaden sky. The horrors of Kabalo were behind him and, for want of anything better to do, he settled down in his cabin to grind out the first two chapters of *Remote People*.

As the boat passed along the Lualaba Waugh could observe the native life and fauna of untamed Africa in a leisurely fashion not possible before. When they moored at the tiny Greek or Belgian trading stations the boat would attract the local population: 'Great shouting. Women long hair in series of tight braided strings; coloured handkerchiefs on heads. Passengers come on board carrying live fowls in circular, wicker crates; sugar cane etc., bananas. Push one another off plank. Washing at edge.'[109] It was cool and often rained. During a severe cloud-burst the boat would draw in to the shore and wait for the storm to pass. Other delays were occasioned by the captain's blood sport, firing a small-bore rifle at passing antelope. If he thought he had hit something, the boat would stop and the native passengers would plunge, 'with whoops and yodels' according to Waugh, into the high grass, only to be summoned back 'invariably empty-handed'[110] by a series of blasts upon the siren. These small distractions, though, did little to relieve Waugh's boredom. He was four days on the river in a terrain of largely featureless swamp. All too often for his liking he was driven to his writing table merely to keep his mind occupied.

On his last day aboard composition was severely interrupted. 'I was sitting in my cabin, engrossed in the affairs of Abyssinia, when the captain popped in and, with wild eye and confused speech, demanded to see the ticket for my motor bicycle.'[111] The incident gives rise in *Remote People* to a brilliantly comic scene. Waugh at first treated the enquiry politely. It was clearly a mistake. He had no motor-bicycle. The captain would not believe him. Tempers flared. The captain insisted. He would search his luggage (two suitcases and a small bag). Waugh

108. *Remote People*, p. 227.
109. *Diaries*, 5 February, 1931, p. 352.
110. *Remote People*, p. 228.
111. *Ibid.*, p. 228.

was instructed to move it for inspection. He refused. A boy was called and told to pull the suitcase from under the bunk:

> I pretended to be writing. I could hear the captain puffing just behind me (it was a very small cabin). 'Well,' I said, 'have you found a motor-bicycle?' 'Sir, that is my affair,' said the captain.[112]

But if the encounter was amusing in retrospect it was galling at the time. A few minutes after storming off, the captain returned, his fury unabated, insisting that Waugh pack his bags and get off the boat the instant they docked at Bukama. There was no hotel in the place. The arrangement had been that Waugh should sleep aboard the steamer for the night until his train should arrive. But the captain was adamant. Waugh must disembark immediately. 'In this way I found myself stranded on the wharf at Bukama with two days to wait for my train. A humiliating situation, embittered by the Seventh Day Adventist, who came after to offer his sympathy. "It doesn't do to argue," he said, "unless you understand the language." Damn him.'[113]

Worse was to come as Waugh's 'nightmare' proceeded. The diary records that Bukama was 'a fever swamp with two or three houses, mostly derelict – a bank and a Greek bar'.[114] Beside this, Kabalo appeared luxurious. The 'houses' were two ruined bungalows and an unfurnished Government rest-house more than partially reclaimed by the jungle. This filthy establishment was the only place in which to sleep. A road led up to the Katanga railway. Dumped ashore at three in the afternoon, he could discover nothing about rail connections. All he could elicit from the locals was the utter futility of his long-held dream of escaping by aeroplane. The station lay at a considerable distance from the landing point; the heat and humidity were intense. But no rest was possible: the immediate consideration was to seek information about trains. In the relative cool of the early evening Waugh picked up his bags and trudged up the hill.

The proprietor of the Greek bar spoke a few words of French. Shivering and grey-faced from a recent bout of fever, he told Waugh that there was a train due that night for Elizabethville. No-one knew when it might arrive but this was, nevertheless, a moderately bright prospect obviating, at least, the need to walk back to the river and sleep in the rest-house. He bought a ticket and sat down to wait.

After seventeen hours on a hard, narrow seat sharing a carriage with a plague of mosquitoes and two Greeks who ate oranges all night, Elizabethville came as an immense relief. On the afternoon of 9th February he booked into the Globe

---

112. *Ibid.*, p. 230.
113. *Ibid.*, p. 230.
114. *Diaries*, 7 February, 1931, p. 352.

Hotel: 'expensive but well managed'.[115] It was his first taste of cosmopolitan comfort since Kenya. The very taps in the bedroom were greeted with reverence:

> These stimulating re-encounters with luxury! How often in London, when satiety breeds scepticism, one has begun to wonder whether luxury is not a put-up job, whether one does not vulgarly confuse expense with excellence. Then, with one's palate refined by weeks of (comparative) privation, of nameless and dateless wines, cigars from Borneo or the Philippines, one meets again the good things of life and knows certainly that taste, at least in these physical matters, is a genuine and integral thing. Reconciliation.[116]

After a bath and a change of clothes he went straight to the Cook's agency to seek that mystical aeroplane passage. At last he found it – but too late. He had just £40 left. The fare for the plane to the coast was enormous – £100, equivalent to that charged by Imperial Airways for the entire journey from London to Cape Town – and the project was finally abandoned. The quickest escape turned out to be circuitous: another train for hundreds of miles through the Rhodesias to South Africa, and a boat from Cape Town.

It was a dreary prospect, adding yet another week to his incarceration in Africa. But the two days in the Elizabethville hotel at least allowed comfortable preparation for the long haul home. He found a bookshop and a cinema. There was a large, cool room in which he could continue writing *Remote People*. He boarded the train refreshed but clearly apprehensive: 'Worked well and drank well. Left Elizabethville at 10 o'clock in clean, new carriage. Found the American Seventh Day Adventist in the carriage.'[117]

He was six days on that train, three of them with his *bête noir* until that dull young man finally disembarked at Bulawayo to audit his accounts. The connection there took Waugh on to Mafeking, Victoria Falls and the Karoo desert. The journey was hot, crowded, dusty and dull. The splendours of the Falls seem not to have interested him. He saw himself as traveller rather than tourist and this last, relatively comfortable, section of line offered him nothing but boredom. As the desert flashed past his window he ignored it, his eyes firmly fixed on detective fiction to consume time.

At last, at 6.30 on the morning of 17th February, he reached Cape Town. Even this seemed melancholy: a nasty, greystone city with a depressing preponderance of late Victorian Gothic architecture, reminding him unpleasantly of Glasgow. He booked a third-class passage on a fast mail boat for £20 and by midday was aboard. For the next three weeks he shared a cabin with 'a delightful

115. *Ibid.*, 9 February, 1931, p. 352.
116. *Ibid.*, 9 February, 1931, pp. 352–3.
117. *Ibid.*, 11 February, 1931, p. 353.

man from North Devon who had been working on the railway' and 'a Jew boy from a shop'.[118]

The diary describes only the beginning of the voyage but it seems that, steaming back towards civilisation, he was perfectly contented. His one recorded complaint concerns the superabundance of children. The days, it seems, were idled away with reading, sports (boxing, according to *Remote People*) and card games until, on 10th March, they docked at Southampton. In all, the journey had cost him just short of £500 – a large sum to find from private resources.

118. *Remote People*, p. 234.

# IX
# *Man of the World: 1931–1932*

Very little is known of Waugh's movements over the next four months. At the end of the travel diary there is a twenty-month gap and no letters have come to light from 1931 dated before 6th June when an active correspondence with his agent resumes. It seems, from the concluding section of *Remote People*, that he returned to a large circle of friends in London and spent many hours in hotels and restaurants catching up on the gossip of the last six months.

That final chapter, 'Third Nightmare', offers an interesting corollary to his experiences abroad. He describes how he was taken to a new underground restaurant ('Malmaison'?), the fashionable venue of his smart friends. The service was poor, the food execrable and expensive, the wine acid. The place was shoddy, and solid with weak-minded hedonists:

> Next day the gossip writers would chronicle the young M.P.'s, peers, and financial magnates who were assembled in that rowdy cellar, hotter than Zanzibar, noisier than the market in Harar, more reckless of the decencies of hospitality than the taverns of Kabalo or Tabora. And a month later the wives of English officials would read about it, and stare across the jungle or desert or forest or golf links, and envy their sisters at home, and wish they had the money to marry rich men.
>
> Why go abroad?
> See England first.
> Just watch London knock spots off the Dark Continent.
> I paid the bill in yellow African gold. It seemed just tribute from the weaker races to their mentors.[1]

The irony of this brilliant last page points to an increased seriousness in Waugh's writing and thinking: the 'luxury' that represented reconciliation in Elizabethville was different in kind from this ruthless pleasure-seeking. There is nothing to choose here between the barbarians at home and those abroad. In no sense other than the financial were the African races any longer 'weaker' or the Europeans their 'mentors'. A trust had been betrayed: the sacred trust of the defence of Christian civilisation.

Seeking 'the decencies of hospitality' Waugh looked elsewhere. Doubtless he spent several drunken evenings in nightclubs but he was no longer a part of that

---

1. *Remote People*, p. 240.

*Vile Bodies* world, nor had he wanted to be since his reception. While in London he probably stayed at his parents' house in North End Road and at the Savile Club. He had returned with (at least) two chapters of *Remote People* written but the first indication of its completion is in a letter to Roughead (at A.D. Peters') on 6th June stating that he will send the book to the American publishers 'when he feels like it'. As subsequent correspondence shows, though, it was far from finished then. It was tedious work and he was easily distracted. The letter came from Rolls Park, Chigwell, Essex. It seems that Waugh spent a leisurely few months lying low, country-house visiting and making dilatory stabs at his travelogue. In early June he had taken his manuscript to France, intending to finish it in the Mediterranean sun.

Money appears not to have been a problem. *Vile Bodies* was still re-printing and probably bringing in around £75 per edition of 2,000 copies.[2] By June 1931 it was in its eleventh edition and *Decline and Fall*, riding on the back of that success, was in its sixth. In addition to this came the income from foreign rights, translations and journalism. Waugh's financial position was entirely transformed from its impecunious state of eighteen months earlier and it was this security which allowed him the luxury of spending over six months writing *Remote People*. Even so, as fast as the money came in, it went out again. The African trip had knocked a large hole in his resources and though he was not rich, he mixed almost exclusively with those who were.

From France he wrote to Henry Yorke:

> I have dragged Patrick [Balfour] away from Mount Parnasse and we are at present staying at the Welcome [Hotel] at Villefranche.
>
> I look forward so much to your coming to St Tropez. When you write for rooms do book one for me – a large one if possible. I hope those fine Misses Ruthven are coming too. The district is full of chums, Connolly, Aldous H., Eddie S[ackville]-West, Alex Waugh etc. I meant to do a lot of work but it is all very gay and we bathe a lot and get sleepy. . . .
>
> An awful man called Keith Winter has arrived. Also Godfrey Wynne [sic] also Tennyson Jesse – too literary by half.
>
> Will it make Dig [Yorke's wife] shy if I appear in fisherman's clothes.
>
> I have more scandal and baddish blood about Robert [Byron] in Paris.
>
> I have found out more very shady things about Maurice [Bowra]'s continental relaxation.[3]

2. Cf. William Hickey (Tom Driberg), 'These Names make News', *DE*, 3 September, 1934, 6: 'Waugh now writes one novel every two years. Each sells 15,000–20,000 copies and brings in about £1,000.' Although Driberg speaks here of Waugh's sales after *Black Mischief* and *A Handful of Dust*, it is unlikely that they would have increased considerably. The substantial increase in sales came with *Brideshead Revisited* in 1945.
3. *Letters*, pp. 55–6. Amory appears to have the three letters on p. 52, p. 55 and pp. 55–6 in the wrong order. They should be in reverse order, this being the first.

Again one suspects Waugh's desire to impress Yorke. The Misses Ruthven were a pair of beautiful 'Society' twins who had taken to show business and appeared in the halls as the 'Rolli Twins'. He didn't know them. Of the 'chums' mentioned, only Connolly, Bowra and Balfour were more than acquaintances, and of these only Balfour could be classed as a 'friend'. Keith Winter had to be put in his place because he had written a popular 'Oxford' novel, *Other Man's Saucer*, and could be seen as a rival. Godfrey Winn was an embarrassment because Waugh's name was often linked with his as a 'smart' young society author. Tennyson Jesse was a mere detective-story writer.

In fact, as his next letter to Yorke reveals, if he did find the company 'gay' it soon became oppressive and he escaped into the countryside to stay with the village curate in Cabris:

> ... I got claustrophobia in the Nina-Maugham milieu and so came here into the hills where I am living in great discomfort with a crazy priest. ... I am finishing a very dull travel book and shall soon begin work on a novel which is genuinely exciting for me.
>
> I know what you must feel about your office. I have a corresponding longing for some kind of routine in my life.[4]

The enthusiasm for novel writing and the need for routine are interesting revelations. *Remote People* was tedious work and he was desperate to complete it. The problem appears to have been achieving a satisfactory structure for what might otherwise have appeared a flat catalogue of events. In the first draft the book lacked coherence and lively pace. He posted the third chapter to Roughead around 11th June along with corrected versions of 'other chapters', promising to dispatch the remainder within a month. If the Americans were becoming impatient, he said, they would simply have to be more 'humble'. All editors requesting copy should be informed that he had been instructed to rest.

Rest and 'routine' were not easily secured. Bored into inertia, he compulsively moved on. By the 25th June he was back in England writing again, and promising to deliver the completed manuscript in a week. His agents were having it typed as it came in but Waugh was a difficult man to track down. It was no use posting the typescript back to him at the address of his last letter, he remarked in a scribble to Roughead, as he did not know where he would be.

Tracing the addresses on his correspondence with Peters' office offers some guide to his restless progress: North End Road; The Manor House, Gt Billing, Northampton; Le Canadel, France. Around 14th August we find him back in one of his favourite bolt-holes: the Abingdon Arms in Beckley, near Oxford. From there he posted the final pages of the book and promised the corrected

4. *Letters*, p. 55. See also above, p. 218, n. 13, and cf. *Letters*, p. 62.

page proofs for the American edition within a fortnight. By the 22nd the process was complete: the corrected typescript of chapters 9 and 10, the 'Third Nightmare' and three copies of the 'Second Nightmare' were in the post. It appears that the structural problems were resolved by the re-writing of those 'Nightmare' sections. At any rate, towards the end of August this seemingly interminable literary misery was off his hands. He could relax and turn his thoughts to a holiday in the country and his next novel. There was no doubt in his mind as to the potential quality of the latter. It was, he told Roughead, going to be a best-seller – so the Americans could stop fussing and wait on his pleasure.

In the meantime he wanted November publication for the travel book and pre-publication of serialised extracts in whichever magazine would buy them. Literary production moved more rapidly in the 'thirties than today. The book was out by 3rd November. But the negotiation and sale of serial rights for a series of articles to appear before this date was impossible on such a tight schedule. There is no reason to suppose that Peters would have been unsuccessful in selling the material. Both *Labels* and *Ninety-Two Days* (Waugh's third travel book in 1934) were serialised in this fashion. Waugh's insistence on publication within three months points rather to the decimation of his bank account. He had already told Peters in July that he was 'broke' and had requested a loan. A.D.P. seems always to have acceded to these demands, perhaps sensing that the odd cheque for thirty pounds was a small price to pay to maintain the loyalty of such a writer. Literary agents do not usually act as bankers for their clients.

One letter to Patrick Balfour (dated by Mark Amory as 12th July, 1931) perhaps suggests reasons for this financial collapse. He writes from his parents' house in North End Road, gossiping wildly through the metropolitan activities of his aristocratic and literary friends. The list of names is enormous (Amory needs thirty-one footnotes to explain the allusions) and Waugh was probably drunk after an evening out when he composed it.[5]

In many ways it suggests a vast, supportive circle of acquaintances about whom Waugh loved to gossip and make 'bad blood'. He, perhaps unconsciously, creates a picture of himself as a child of the gods intimate with the rich and famous. One needs only to recall some of the names – Frank Pakenham, John Betjeman, Hazel Lavery, Gerald Berners, Loraine Berry, Freddy Birkenhead, Diana Guinness, Anthony Powell – to realise that Waugh was persistently in the company of gilded youth and very much the smart man-about-town. He talks of returning to France shortly, of securing an invitation for Balfour to Pakenham Hall, of lunching with Fr D'Arcy at the Ritz and going to stay with Cecil Beaton in the country. In some ways, of course, he was merely doing a favour to a friend in providing Balfour with material for his *Daily Sketch* gossip column. The favour would be

5. *Letters*, pp. 52–4.

returned in kind by Balfour's publicity-mongering in the popular press. But there is, surely, more to the letter than this.

Seen from another angle, it appears a melancholy epistle. Waugh is clearly not happy ('It is very nasty in London') and the gossip he retails reads like a miserable catalogue of amatory frustrations and failures, jealousy and depression. True, he fictionalises for effect ('Robert is hated by D. Guinness now' was dismissed as playful misrepresentation by Lady Diana. She was on perfectly good terms with Byron.)[6] But beneath the teasing, there is a sense of Waugh's complex misery. He had many friends who admired his talent and relished his company, many indeed who were seriously concerned for his welfare. In this frenetic social world, though, he was one of the few who were 'alone': he had no lover nor any prospect of marriage, home or family. Heavy drinking and high expense, living beyond his emotional and financial means, provided the necessary stimuli to blunt the unhappiness resulting from the rootlessness of his existence. 'I pretend to have schemes up my sleeve but I haven't any really I just trust in GOD.' A little later he adds rather sadly like an overgrown undergraduate, ' . . . I was sick the other night'.

The modest suburban atmosphere of North End Road was a curious contrast to the letter Waugh wrote there. The regularity of his parents' ménage married awkwardly with his glamorous bachelor life. Underhill was no longer his home: merely another temporary resting place for a displaced person. Something deeply rooted in him nevertheless demanded a similar permanence and regularity. It was easy to be flattered into superficial contentment by living an aggressive and 'successful' life envied by the thousands of readers of the *Daily Sketch*. In this mood we find Waugh name-dropping, keen to be seen to move comfortably in aristocratic circles, fastidious over social distinctions. In many ways this was a perfectly honest aspiration towards excellence, an aspect of a scrupulous aesthetic sensibility. But there was, as we have seen, an element of neurotic pragmatism in this behaviour which his friends could find awkward: Waugh was caught between two social worlds. Having gate-crashed the Mayfair party, he was determined not to be thrown out.

Amongst this crowd there were particular friends, some of long standing – Patrick Balfour, Henry and Dig Yorke, Harold Acton, Robert Byron, John and Penelope Betjeman, Elizabeth Pakenham – but more who had been acquired since his success: Hazel Lavery, Maurice Bowra, Gerald Berners, Teresa Jungman, Arthur Baldwin and the Lygon family. Teresa ('Baby') Jungman was to present Waugh with severe emotional difficulties over the next two or three years. His feelings for the Lygon girls were more platonic and playfully paternal, they being some years younger than himself. He had known their brothers, Viscount Elmley and 'Hughie' at Oxford, and had first met the girls in the

6. Interview with Lady Diana Mosley, 1 October, 1983.

schoolroom. It was only after 1930 that he began regularly to visit their country house, Madresfield Court near Great Malvern. As with the Plunket Greenes, Waugh had fallen in love with a family. He probably wrote some of *Remote People* there and when it was finished decided to return to the area.

This time he did not stay at the house as the children were away helping Elmley campaign (successfully) as a Conservative candidate in a by-election. Waugh put up at the County Hotel in Malvern and was there for a specific purpose: a rigorous course of horsemanship at Captain Hance's Academy. By the summer of 1931 he and the family were on intimate terms. Each had a nickname. Lady Mary was 'Maimie' or 'Blondy'; Lady Dorothy was 'Coote' or 'Pollen'; Waugh was 'Boaz'. He wrote regularly to tell them of his adventures at the Academy and to pass on local gossip, using nursery language spiced with hints of sexual perversion as a lascivious uncle might address unsuspecting nieces. They were, of course, quite grown up by this time, Maimie in her twenty-first year and Coote in her nineteenth. Both drank and attended the London nightclub and restaurant circuit. But the 'I miss you both so much at school and in playtime' phraseology was often part of Waugh's teasingly aggressive patronage towards the opposite sex. Quite suddenly, in the same letter and with no noticeable shift of tone, he could say, 'It is what is called Masochism and if you ask Elmley and he thinks you are old enough he will explain what that means'.[7] The same mixture of mock patronage and overt sexual reference was used in letters to Penelope Betjeman. Such 'shocking' openness was an essential ingredient of his comic sense and the Lygon girls remembered him as a companion of ruthless honesty and indefatigable good humour. Most of their time at Madresfield was spent roaring with laughter.

One of these letters states that when asked why he was learning to ride he had replied that it was a prescribed cure for drink. Obviously that is another joke. He was engaged in this painful exercise (and one for which he had no natural aptitude) so that he might more successfully share the country pursuits at the grand houses he visited. It was a necessary social skill and he stuck to the task tenaciously for a week or more.

*

*Remote People* was published shortly afterwards on 3rd November, 1931, to mixed notices. Reviewers were quick to spot that the title was misleading: Waugh concentrates more on colonials than the indigenous population. The *TLS* thought that Africa had eluded him and that his light-hearted manner was not suited to his matter.[8] The *Observer*, after praising the book, noted that Waugh's knowledge of local affairs was 'necessarily external and trivial. . . . It follows that the

7.  *Letters*, pp. 56–7.
8.  *TLS*, 5 November, 1931, 864; *CH*, pp. 120–1.

"political" parts are the least readable.'[9] Rebecca West compared the volume unfavourably to Norman Douglas's *Summer Islands* and, while supporting Waugh's cause as a novelist, found both *Labels* and *Remote People* 'well beneath his proper form'.[10] When in January the latter appeared in America under the title *They Were Still Dancing*, the *New York Times Book Review* thought that Americans, Africans and Indians might be aggrieved by some of the racial assumptions.[11]

These reservations, though, were all balanced by praise for Waugh's wit and prose style and some expressed intense enthusiasm. Frank Swinnerton thought that 'the sincerity of this book, its candour and originality, the quality of its perception, and the engrossing interest of the narrative, cause me to regard it as the best possible book of travel I have read for years'.[12] Peter Fleming saw it as 'the very best sort of book about this journey'.[13] Where Rebecca West thought that Waugh had broken an 'iron law of literature' in discussing his own boredom, Fleming saw all travel as 'discomfort recollected in tranquillity' and felt that we should distrust those writers who ignored the tedium and fatigue of moving about the face of the globe. Waugh and Fleming saw themselves (along with Robert Byron) as representing a new breed of travel writer: young, abrasive, irreverent. Waugh's travel books did not sell as well as Fleming's. But *Remote People* served its purpose in paying for some of the journey and in keeping Waugh's name before the public while he finished his novel. The title dropped from Duckworth's list quickly and the book has been reprinted in its entirety only recently.

Two days after *Remote People* was published he was back in London and corresponding with the Lygon family again:

> Well this is the last time I shall write for days. I tell you why, you see I find suddenly there is no more money in my bank and about six tradesmen have written to say look here this bill is going too far what about it. So I went to my agent & said give me some money and he said well if it comes to that you owe *me* quite a bit one way and another. So I am broke. Well what I am going to do is to go to a boarding house called Easton Court Hotel, Chagford, Devon (where you must write to me) because Patrick Balfour lives there & I argue that if he can so can I because he is worse broke even than me. . . . I shall sit all day in my bedroom writing books, articles, short stories, reviews, plays, cinema scenarios etc. etc. until I have got a lot more money. So I shan't have time even to write anything I'm not paid for besides there is the expense of postage so you must [not] think it is lack of love if I don't write and

9. *Observer*, 22 November, 1931, 5.
10. *DT*, 4 December, 1931, 18.
11. *NYTBR*, 3 January, 1932, 8.
12. *EN*, 30 October, 1931, 11.
13. *Spectator*, 23 January, 1932, 118.

you must please go on writing to me because I shall need some uplifting of spirits.

I hope Lord E[lmley] will dress up as Father Xmas and go around putting oranges in stockings. May I bring fireworks. . . .[14]

The last reference is to Waugh's planning to spend Christmas at Madresfield. In the meantime he had to lie low and work hard.

\*

The Easton Court Hotel was an excellent retreat for Waugh's purpose. Alec had discovered the place and told Patrick Balfour who, as Evelyn's letter indicates, was already there writing his own book, *Society Racket: A Critical Survey of Modern Life* (1933). (Balfour's father, Lord Kinross, had paid his son's debts in return for his relinquishing the gossip column of the *Sketch*.) The hotel was a 'thatched fourteenth-century farmhouse with low, dark rooms and small windows'.[15] It was run by an amiable, middle-aged American lady, Mrs Carolyn Cobb, and her second husband, a young Englishman, Norman Webb, more on the lines of a country house than a hotel. Well-known by 1931 as a cheap and quiet place to write, there was a constant stream of 'artistic' guests and their lady friends. No one was harried about payment or mildly 'bohemian' behaviour; the atmosphere was friendly and discreet.

Writing to Lady Mary, Waugh distils the richest fantasy from this placid setting:

I think I will tell you about this hotel well it is very odd. Kept by a deserter from the Foreign Legion and an American lady named Mrs Postlethwaite Cobb who mixes menthol with her cigarettes. We drink rye whisky in her bed room and there are heaps of New York magazines & rather good, sophisticated food. I think it is a distributing centre for white slaves or cocaine or something like that. They never give one a bill. Mr B[alfour] hasn't had one since he came six weeks ago. And there are two odious dogs.[16]

Waugh hated dogs and all household pets. Patrick Balfour's 'poverty' (he was known as 'Pauper') had become part of their shared comic mythology. Norman Webb had been harmlessly tending distressed animals in Morocco when he had met Mrs Cobb, a wealthy divorcee. But if composing such letters and reading their replies raised his spirits, a postcard to Lady Mary suggests that his enforced seclusion more often produced melancholia:

Very depressed. Rain all day. No money. Can't write. Fire smokes.

14. *Letters*, pp. 58–9.
15. *Letters*, p. 45.
16. *Letters*, p. 60.

> Filthy beams, pewter, lustrewear and every antique horror. Patrick usually drunk. He left the tap of the beer barrel open last night and flooded the cellar. I ride a little horse called Evergreen. Looking forward to Yuletide.[17]

Hacking round the countryside (sometimes hunting) and drinking in the evenings with Balfour were his only relaxations from a rigorous work schedule.

The correspondence with Peters's office reveals the extent of Waugh's industry. The major project was his novel, the working title of which was 'Accession'. The first chapter was posted to London in mid-September and by 4th December the third was written and dispatched. In the meantime he had also written a review, an article and a short story and expressed himself willing to write more articles or a regular book page, preferably for a fashionable magazine like *Vogue*. Self-advertisement was clearly of crucial importance. 'Tell Lady Sibell to say that all the smart set are reading *Remote People* the brilliant book by that well known hunting gent E.W.', he instructed Lady Mary with tongue only partially in cheek.[18] Lady Sibell, her elder sister, wrote a gossip column for *Harper's Bazaar*.

The article written during the composition of *Black Mischief* was dashed off and described by him to Peters as 'ridiculous' but it is worth more than a casual glance as a barometer of his developing social attitudes. 'Why Glorify Youth?'[19] was published in *Women's Journal* and represents a retraction of his former (insincere) adoption of 'youth politics'. He is quite blunt: 'The Youth boom has been very convenient for young men like myself who have made a living out of it, but it seems to me time that criticism adopted some more significant standard.' The piece makes an interesting comparison with 'Too Young At Forty', and he refers directly to it:

> Three years ago I was asked for the first time to write an article for a London paper. The subject was 'Give Youth A Chance'. My heart sank, but I was in no position in those days to pick or choose . . . my way of earning a few guineas.
>
> I wrote the article, stuffing it with all the clichés I could remember and doing all I could by bombast and exaggeration to qualify it for the trade label of 'challenging'. I got my guineas and I was grateful, but all the time I reflected what a fatuous subject it all was. Now, three years later, I am invited to write on 'Why Glorify Youth?' – and it seems to me that this reversal of theme reveals a most salutary change of attitude, a cool wave of sanity that has swept public opinion during the intervening

17. *Letters*, p. 59.
18. *Letters*, p. 60.
19. 'Why Glorify Youth?', *Women's Journal*, March 1932, 18–19, 107; *EAR*, pp. 125–8.

time, washing away the picnic-litter of Youth-movement sentimentality.[20]

In many ways his statements here are equally ingenuous. Wanting a quick return and from a magazine he clearly despised, Waugh is just as much intent on producing a 'challenging' approach which will cast him in the role of iconoclast as he had been in 1929. There is no shortage of 'bombast' and 'exaggeration'. As commentary it is largely worthless; he could hardly have picked a worse moment, corresponding as it does with the rise of Fascism, to declare that 'Youth-movement sentimentality' had collapsed. If anything, it was gaining momentum and had continued to do so. It was at least partly the youth cult which swept Auden, Isherwood and the *New Signatures* poets to prominence later in the 'thirties.

As a personal statement, though, it is intriguing. There was a passage from *Black Mischief* much quoted by reviewers to indicate the shift in tone between Waugh's second and third novel: ' "D'you know, deep down in my heart I've got a tiny fear that Basil is going to turn serious on us, too!" '[21] Waugh's journalism was taking the same direction.

The 'roaring twenties', he says, are dead. Just as the 'greenery-yallery artiness of the 'nineties' did 'a valuable social service in finally breaking up British insular, bourgeois materialism', so the 'twenties ' – futile, obstreperous, anarchic, vulgar, call them what you will – broke up post-war Rupert Brooke magnificently-unprepared-for-the-long-bitterness-of-life sentimentality, and made Youth openly and ludicrously inglorious'. This is familiar ground, recalling his Lancing editorials. His universal object of attack is 'sentimentality' but this he now associates as a cast of mind with 'the muddle-headed, mist-haunted races of northern Europe'. Who but them, he asks, 'would ever commit the folly of glorifying incompleteness and immaturity? For what is Youth except a man or woman before it is ready or fit to be seen?' The 'typical Teutonic confusion of general value with sex-appeal' is something from which Waugh disassociates himself. He stands here for the rational, the mature, for tradition; a Catholic (southern) rather than Protestant (northern) culture.

The article is a neat rebuttal of those writers – Wyndham Lewis and Gilbert Frankau – who had missed the ingenuous elements of those earlier articles and associated Waugh unequivocally with 'youngergenerationconsciousness'. But it goes further in pretending to a powerful distaste for all young people, and young women in particular: 'Sex-appeal is made up of an infinite number of different stimuli, and in all but very few the woman of over thirty has the debutante hopelessly beaten.' 'The English debutante', he says, 'is fit only for the schoolroom.'[22] This was patently hypocritical. Waugh, only just twenty-eight when he

20. *Ibid.*, p. 126.
21. Evelyn Waugh, *Black Mischief*, p. 233.
22. 'Why Glorify Youth?', *op. cit.*, pp. 126–7.

wrote this, adopts the position of the man of the world no longer subject to the obsessive love of nubility. The avuncular tone of his letters to the Lygon girls might seem to support this but of course it does not. His patronage there is facetious and overtly sexual; he revelled in their youth and laughter and in being part of their 'nursery'. Equally, we might turn to those *tendresses* he developed in the early 'thirties with older women – Lady Diana Cooper, for instance – to see him apparently turning his back on the follies of young women. Here again, though, there is no simple equation. For the most part these were 'untouchable', other men's beautiful wives, and Waugh had certainly not reached the point where his religious conviction could allow him to accept celibacy.

It seems that immediately after his marriage had broken down and the success of *Vile Bodies* had sent him spinning, with cash in his pockets, towards Lady Cunard's salon, Waugh was prepared to indulge in whatever casual sex came his way. The most important of these lovers seems to have been Audrey Lucas. She had maintained a childhood passion for him and 'made declarations of love' in 1925 while Waugh was offering similar devotion to Olivia Plunket Greene.[23] Nothing had come of it and, rejected by Waugh, she had married Harold Scott, the co-proprietor of the Cave of Harmony nightclub with Elsa Lanchester. At the time Waugh had felt profoundly guilty, supposing that he might have encouraged an unsuitable match by his rejection.

We next hear of Audrey Lucas in the *Diaries* in May 1930 and the affair lasted until he left for Abyssinia. Waugh found the relationship oppressive, but not for theological reasons. The teachings of his Church did not prevent this adultery or other attempts at the same sin. Not only was he (doctrinally) still married, but so was Audrey, and it seems that he did not wish to remain faithful even to her. Penelope Betjeman was most alarmed when, both before and after her marriage, Waugh made advances to her. 'I remember being very shocked as he was a practising Roman Catholic. . . . He never attracted me in the very least.'[24] She added that she thought it probable that Waugh suffered from an inferiority complex about his sexual prowess. It seems that there was an unbridgeable gap between the women he now desired – elegant, aristocratic, strong-minded, witty – and those who were physically attracted to him. Perhaps he felt himself to be a particular victim of that Teutonic confusion between 'general value' and 'sex appeal'. Unrequited passion and betrayal had dogged all relationships with the women he had loved – Olivia, Evelyn and, most recently, Diana Guinness.

1930 found him involved in another tortured relationship, this time with Teresa ('Baby') Jungman. Teresa's father was Nico Jungman, a half-Dutch painter; her mother had divorced him and remarried Richard ('Dick') Guinness shortly after the war. During the 'twenties and 'thirties they maintained an elegant house in

23. *Diaries*, 6 January, 1925, p. 196.
24. Interview with Lady Penelope Betjeman, 29 March, 1984.

Great Cumberland Place and the mother entertained lavishly in Edwardian style. The daughters were rich and often preferred their own amusements. Penelope Betjeman has described Teresa as someone who had 'a tremendous success [in Society]. She was not the least intellectual . . . she was just the sort of girl that every man falls in love with . . . rather chocolate-box blonde.'[25] Miss Jungman and her sister, Zita, occur in Balfour's *Society Racket* along with Lady Eleonor Smith as being the Bright Young People, unconsciously, long before the phrase was coined. It was they who in 1924 (the year Waugh came down from Oxford, Wembley year) began the treasure hunt craze and the masquerade parties. Teresa was seventeen then. Six years later she remained the same effervescent, wealthy, pretty girl but there was a fundamental seriousness about her in 1930 which clearly appealed to Waugh and distinguished her from characters like Elizabeth Ponsonby. She was a devout Catholic.

Waugh was not alone in his pursuit of her. One senses from the 1930 diary that he was keenly interested in her shortly after disentangling himself from the Guinnesses and while still sleeping with Audrey Lucas. One entry – 'Baby anxious to be friendly and very sweet'[26] – suggests the difficulties he encountered. Teresa, like Diana, found Waugh a man much in need of consolation and an amusing companion. But his obsessive devotion, as it developed, required sexual contact, and this she was not prepared to grant. His unrequited love for her becomes a leit-motif of the diaries and letters until October 1933.

Tom Mitford was one of many other 'rivals', the chief of whom (in Waugh's eyes, at least) was Arthur ('Bloggs') Baldwin (Baldwin of Bewdley), the third Earl and son of the former Conservative Prime Minister. Teresa would stay at Madresfield, being a friend of the Lygon girls; Baldwin was a close neighbour. Their unsuccessful pursuit of the elusive Miss Jungman seems to have brought Waugh and Baldwin into an intimate, humorously aggressive relationship. Waugh wrote to him as 'Friskey' and signed himself 'Boaz', a superscription reserved for those dear to him. Many a night they sat up over the Madresfield *crème de menthe* swapping 'deep man-to-man intimacies'.[27] Teresa was doubtless the chief subject of these conversations.

It was with this confusion and frustration in his emotional life that Waugh sat down to write *Black Mischief*. He buried himself in Chagford from 7th November until mid-December, by which time he was back at his London club (Savile) with four chapters nearly completed, in addition to the 'youth' article and a short story, 'The Patriotic Honeymoon'. The latter he considered only mediocre but he thought the editor wouldn't notice. She (Joyce Reynolds) was only too happy to accept it and the story appeared in the next (January) number of *Harper's*. It was

25. Interview with Lady Penelope Betjeman.
26. *Diaries*, 26 May, 1930, p. 311.
27. *Letters*, p. 60.

never re-published. Waugh was concerned with only one thing: hard cash. He wanted advance payment and American publication. Somehow he had to keep himself financially afloat while he continued the novel and the correspondence with Peters suggests that he thought it would take much longer than either *Decline and Fall* or *Vile Bodies*. When, just before Christmas, his American publishers (Farrar and Rinehart) began to agitate for news of the book's content and progress, Waugh replied that they would have to remain calm; it would not be ready for some months and he did not yet know what it was about himself. In the meantime, he would be taking a ten-day break for Christmas at Madresfield.

'Mad', as it was known in Lygon parlance, was the closest thing Waugh had to a home during this period. It was an unusual country house in that it was occupied only by young people, their father, Lord Beauchamp, having suffered a series of malicious attacks and subsequent scandal in 1931 with the revelation of his homosexuality. He had exiled himself in Italy; Lady Beauchamp had retired to live with her brother.[28] This scenario, or elements of it, sank deeply into Waugh's consciousness to find fictional expression in 1944 with the alienated Lord Marchmain of *Brideshead Revisited*. Lady Mary Lygon thought that her brother Hughie's character might have suggested Sebastian Flyte as 'a younger son ... under the shadow of not having an inheritance'.[29] There were several men known to them in a similar position – Charlie Cavendish, John Fox-Strangeways, Desmond Parsons – but Hughie was the one Waugh knew best. Hughie drank, though not, according to his sister, to excess. His death was early and unexpected, but had nothing to do with dissipation. He fell over in Germany in 1936. Claud Cockburn thought there was a great deal of Alastair Graham in Sebastian.[30] All such search for 'originals' of Waugh's major characters ultimately proves fruitless. It was an abstract image of the Beauchamp family which he absorbed and used, not a documentary record of it.

Madresfield in 1931–2 was a household alive with gaiety and laughter. Architecturally it was nothing like Brideshead (a Palladian structure based more on Castle Howard); 'Mad' was principally red-brick Victorian, a moated country seat, its only resemblance to the fictional great house being the *art nouveau* decoration of the chapel. Waugh's interest in Madresfield was not so much architectural as social. It was a place in which he could relax and play the fool.

As Lady Dorothy records: 'I was keeping a diary remarkable only for its dullness and found the entries – until then confined to weather, dogs and horses – enlivened by statements of incest and immorality; an innocuous and amateurish water-colour of a cart-horse had a large penis painted in – it was like having

28. See Sykes, pp. 114–15.
29. Interview with Lady Mary Lygon, 21 July, 1976.
30. TLS, 30 July, 1976, from Claud Cockburn to Martin Stannard.

Puck as a member of the household.'[31] Madresfield was somewhere Waugh could be contentedly low-brow and un-literary. Underhill, by contrast, rendered him truculent and defensive. It was a house of embarrassment and of middle-class values he now found stultifying. Underhill was 'old' in the way that 'Mad' was 'young'. A constant stream of friends, ample supplies of drink and food, and excellent riding country gave it something of the atmosphere of a country club. Above all, there was no-one, no *ancien régime* to cast a disapproving eye.

Waugh wrote a considerable portion of *Black Mischief* there in the new year and Lady Dorothy's is one of the few accounts we have of his working routine in the 'thirties: 'He wrote slowly and reluctantly . . . groaning loudly as he shut himself away in what had been the day nursery for a few hours every day; sometimes we were pressed into service as models for the line drawings with which he illustrated it, but we hindered more than we helped and had no conscience about disturbing him and dragging him away to join in whatever was going on, or even just to chat while we stitched away at an enormous (and never finished) patchwork quilt.'[32] This is noticeably different from the image Waugh gives us in *A Little Learning* of the reverential hush that fell on Underhill while his father was 'composing' in the book room. Evelyn preferred the rough and tumble no-nonsense philistinism of these girls to the serious self-esteem of the Hampstead or the Maugham coterie. He didn't like writing.

The next six months, however, had to be dedicated to little else. Moving on to spend New Year with the Yorkes at Fulhampton he received a message from Peters indicating that Basil Dean was prepared to commission a film scenario. Dean was the founder and chairman of Ealing Studios and the proposal involved working with John Paddy Carstairs on a screen treatment of a Sapper novel. Waugh readily agreed, not with any enthusiasm for the project (according to Carstairs he did very little work for it) but because he considered it a 'money for jam' job which would finance the completion of the novel and give him a few weeks' smart life in London.

Rachael MacCarthy (Sir Desmond's daughter and later Lord David Cecil's wife) was hired as a secretary for the duration and dictating through her he wrote to 'Friskey' Baldwin on 14th January:

> What can I tell you? Well, I am living like a swell, in Albany, as it might be Lord Byron, Lord Macaulay, Lord Lytton, or any real slap up writer!
> . . . I have joined a rattling sporting chap, name of Dean, making Movie Pictures. I hope you will soon be seeing our work at the Astley Palace or the Stourport Empire.[33]

31. Lady Dorothy Lygon, 'Madresfield and Brideshead', *EWAHW*, p. 50.
32. *Ibid.*, p. 50.
33. *Letters*, pp. 60–1.

According to Carstairs, Waugh was revelling in his popularity. Work would rarely begin before three and end at six with Waugh, dapper and affable, setting off for yet another cocktail party and dinner.[34] It seems probable, though no diary exists for this period, that several of these appointments were with Miss Jungman. The 'completed' treatment was never filmed.

January and most of February thus frittered away, he returned to serious work. Again, he was constantly on the move. From the Spread Eagle at Thame he arranged to write two stories, one contributing to a *John Bull* series, 'The Seven Deadly Sins of Modern Life', the other a hilarious tale about film-making, 'This Quota Stuff: Positive Proof that the British Can Make Good Films'. The sin Waugh chose to lambast was 'tolerance'. By late March he was at Stoneyhurst College where, as the colophon testifies, he wrote some of *Black Mischief*, probably while there with Hollis on an Easter retreat. April found him back at Chagford, working on the incomplete film treatment, but mainly writing the novel. By May he had returned to Madresfield to complete it. Writing from there around 8th May he instructed Peters to tell the annoying Americans that the book was to be called *Black Mischief*, that it would be ready in three weeks and that he thought it very good.

During early 1932 one other fund-raising venture was on hand. In October 1931 Arthur Boscastle had dramatised *Vile Bodies* but this, rather daring, version had failed to secure a licence and received only twelve private performances at the Arts Theatre Club in Hampstead. Nothing daunted, Bradley had rewritten the play in a milder form which this time gained the approval of the Lord Chamberlain. Waugh disliked the new version and, it appears, cared less for Bradley. But it was another opportunity to advertise himself and a potential treasure trove. So he allowed Bradley to proceed and the play was produced at the Vaudeville Theatre where it opened on 15th April.

It was not a success. Waugh, despite his misgivings about its literary merit, perhaps looked to it to establish him in Teresa's eyes as a man of the world. 'Still, it makes me feel a social figure', he wrote half-seriously to Dorothy Lygon, 'which is good in my low spirits because no-one knows how despised I am in the theatre.'[35] On the opening night he had packed the Vaudeville with his titled friends: Mary Lygon, Hubert Duggan, Irene Ravensdale, Eleonor Smith, Billy Clonmore, Frank Pakenham, Raymond de Trafford, Hazel Lavery. If he expected this aristocratic assembly to add *éclat* and capture the headlines, he failed in this too. The play closed in six weeks.

The night after the opening he attended another theatre and wrote to Baldwin to tell him about it:

34. See Carstairs's account quoted by Sykes, pp. 117–18.
35. *Letters*, p. 62.

Dear Friskey,

Well I call that downright pally and no mistake. Did Little Miss Jungman send me a line of good wishes from Ireland? Not on your life. And did I look through a sheaf of telegrams with trembling hands looking for one loved name and was I surprised at its absence. I can't say I was. . . .

So Boaz is momentarily a social lion and Lady Cunard (whom God preserve) calls him Evelyn and makes him sit on her right hand at luncheon and dinner every day of the week but is his head turned by these favours. No he remains the same simple lad who bounced round the Malvern Academy on the broad back of Mater (God bless her).

Well at 3.30 today I take a train for Devon and shall be there for four weeks finishing off a book. Then heigh ho for Sunny Italy with a fine desperado called Raymond de Trafford. . . .

Teresa and me went to a very terrible thing called *Miracle*. Then she popped off to Ireland.[36]

The 'terrible thing called *Miracle*' was one of the more famous productions of the 'twenties, directed by Max Rinehardt and featuring the society-beauty-turned-actress, Lady Diana Cooper. Following years of success in America it was revived in England in April of 1932 and had opened just six days before *Vile Bodies*. Richard Guinness had paid three guineas a seat for Waugh and his step-daughter and neither the Guinnesses nor Teresa seem to have been best pleased to hear Waugh say how sickeningly boring and blasphemous he found the play.[37]

Can it have been after this production that Waugh met Lady Diana Cooper for the first time? Her account suggests that it was:

*The Miracle* always brought me good things in its train and one night after the performance it brought me Evelyn Waugh. There was a treasure hunt in full cry and the kill was to be at the Café de Paris at Bray. When we arrived the hunt was up but the merriment was still there and I knew then that I wanted to bind Evelyn to my heart with hoops of steel, should he let me.[38]

She remained a lifelong friend. Waugh became infatuated with her. In a sense, she filled the place left in Waugh's affections by Diana Guinness: she was an outstanding beauty, *chic*, witty, unbullyable with a tendency to fits of nervous depression which Waugh's abrasive humour was suited to curing. Both women moved easily in the *beau monde*; both were nordic blondes. It did a great deal for Waugh's self-esteem to be seen to be on confidential terms.

36. *Letters*, p. 63.
37. Cf. *Letters*, p. 62.
38. Diana Cooper, *The Light of the Common Day* (Rupert Hart-Davis, 1959), p. 112.

Unlike Diana Guinness, though, she was nine years older than Waugh and happily married. Duff Cooper and she had married in 1919 while Waugh was still at school; the year he went up to Oxford, 1922, she became one of the first debutantes to star in a successful film, *The Great Adventure*. A decade later she was the established celebrity, Waugh the relative *parvenu*. She was on terms of intimate friendship with Maurice Baring, Rex Whistler, Hilaire Belloc (who wrote sonnets to her), Lord Berners, and Conrad Russell. The last was a significant figure in a small Somerset village, Mells, that was shortly to play a crucial role in Waugh's life as a focal point of the West Country Catholic intelligentsia. Lady Diana introduced Evelyn both to an older generation of literary men and to the world of national politics. Duff had given up a Foreign Office career to stand for Parliament in 1924. By 1932 he was a rising star of the Conservative Party and became, in turn, Financial Secretary to the Treasury (1934), Minister of Information (1941–2) and Ambassador to France (1944–7). A former rake and gambler, he had to some extent settled down in the 'twenties to more sober ambitions and, in his spare time, was a writer of political history and memoirs. Despite Waugh's remark to Arthur Baldwin ('Good old Duff Cooper. There's a man for you. Him, and his pretty wife too. Man of Affairs. Man of Taste. . . .')[39] one senses that he found Diana's husband unenlivening company. He was forty-one, Waugh twenty-eight, when they first encountered one another.

Waugh's image of himself as a man of the world inured to pain, intolerant of sentimentality, a man of taste on equal terms with the significant writers and politicians of his age was fully developed by mid-1932, though it was not taken entirely seriously by men like Duff Cooper. It was a deliberately constructed persona; Waugh relished celebrity and the friends it brought. In worldly terms his progress was triumphant and he had laboured to achieve distinction. But beneath the image there was unmistakably a man whose modesty about his own talents was somehow offended by the adulation. Paddy Carstairs's remark about Waugh's bravado is telling: ' . . . as he moved off he always winked at me as if to say, "It's great to be lionised, but don't think for a moment that I'm taking it seriously" '.[40] It marries exactly with the tone of so many of his letters (' . . . I am living like a swell in Albany, as it might be Lord Byron . . . or any real slap up writer!') and his refusal to take seriously or exploit his public image in his private life. He rarely discussed his work with his friends, unless it were with someone who, like Henry Yorke or Nancy Mitford, was engaged in the same trade. His books, like Pinfold's, he thought 'quite external to himself' and 'better than many reputed works of genius' but he considered them ingenious rather than works of genius.

His latest, he was dispassionately convinced, would be a best-seller and Peters

39. *Letters*, p. 60.
40. See Sykes, p. 118.

had prepared the ground by selling the first chapter to Desmond MacCarthy's *Life and Letters* for pre-publication in March. By June, *Black Mischief* was complete and he set off for Venice with Raymond de Trafford, 'the gambler and lover'[41] he had met in Kenya. There was no post-natal depression or Lawrentian *Angst*. It was 'heigh ho for Sunny Italy', another job done.

\*

Venice in August and September of 1932 was hot and luxurious. In those days, before the industrialisation of the adjacent coastline and the deluge of package tours, the tourist industry, such as it was, catered for a handful of wealthy Europeans. The city was becoming fashionable as an alternative to the Côte d'Azure and Waugh was there for a holiday among his recently acquired society friends. He went out night-trawling for scampi with the Chioggia fishing fleet in the Adriatic, dined in palaces, chatted the night away in Florian's. They rarely retired before dawn and usually slept till luncheon.

It was only his second visit to the city, the first being a brief stop-over on the *Stella Polaris* during his honeymoon cruise. The circumstances of his return were radically different. Where in 1929, as an improvident young husband he had been regarded by She-Evelyn's family as a bad bet, here he was Evelyn Waugh, the young lion of the literary world, on easy terms with the aristocracy. He revelled in it; success was a form of revenge.

Waugh's idea of a holiday was not to bake himself on the Lido. Sunbathing seemed to him a particularly ludicrous modern development, the inanity and vanity of its devotees only equalled by their immodesty of dress. He did not stop working. Several letters were written to Peters during August from the Palazzo Brandolin, S. Barnaba, arranging new contracts for stories and articles. Two were planned but never written: one for *Harper's Bazaar* on 'Why the Royal Academy is Quite Right', the other for *Architectural Design and Construction*. In the end he settled for an easier option: a short 'letter' on Venice which Joyce Reynolds could print in *Harper's* (for eighteen guineas), and an agreement to write a Christmas story for her on his return.

In the 'letter' (published as 'Venetian Adventures'),[42] Waugh sets out an argument for preferring Venice to the French Riviera (where he had been the previous summer):

> I like the fact that [Venice] has a traditional culture against which many
> of our friends appear in an entirely new aspect. The French Riviera is
> the creation of its visitors – a barbarous strip of rocky shore on which
> foreign holidaymakers have perched hotels and bars and casinos. It has

41. *Letters*, p. 62.
42. *HB*, 7 (March 1932), 54, 86; reprinted in *EAR*, pp. 131–2.

no history or nationality. It is morally the property of the sun-bathers and baccarat players who frequent it. And they are amply justified in behaving exactly how they like, and dressing how they like.... The Lido is the foreigner's property. People can dress how they like there. But if they wish to sit at Florian's in the evening they must dress as the Venetians think suitable. Young Englishmen who attempt to appear like gross schoolboys in shorts and vests present a very vulgar spectacle indeed under Venetian eyes.[43]

Even in casual journalism the terms of his aesthetic and religious dialectic were hardening. The 'barbarous strip of rocky shore' is opposed to the 'traditional culture' of Venice. Where the term 'culture' would be misapplied to life in Cannes, in Venice the term has significance in that it relates to 'history' and 'nationality' (Cannes was created by and for the British). What might appear as dress snobbery is justified in these terms. Correct dress is a question of propriety, of adherence to a set of immemorial cultural standards. Disregard for standards of dress is equated with disregard for that delicate relationship at the basis of all civilised discourse: that between host and guest. It is not to British national etiquette that he appeals, but to what 'the Venetians think suitable'. The article is a fragmentary vision of those principles Waugh was so ferociously to defend in the later 'thirties: loyalty, courtesy, the rights to liberty, diversity and privacy. These could only be safeguarded against the barbarians by constant vigilance.

In Venice Waugh had a perfect, if temporary, analogue for his ideal society. He liked the 'compactness' of the city, hated the sprawl of the Riviera. 'Here there are only about forty English or Americans who know exactly what everyone is doing every minute of the day.... on the morning after a party I love to see the convergence of patinas, canoes and bathers, sometimes into a single Sargasso Sea of gossip, sometimes into rival camps with rare swimmers travelling between and fanning the dissension.' As his letters reveal, Waugh loved gossip and required his special correspondents to keep him drip-fed with the minutiae of his friends' lives. It was the fabric of fantasy, the expression of his love for or jealousy of them. He delighted in the sense of community it provided as much as in using it to make bad blood. Venice is seen as a homogeneous society of cultured visitors and local inhabitants beyond vulgarity: 'I like the evening carnival, when all the poorer Venetians decorate their boats with lanterns and flow in procession down the Grand Canal, not to collect money or to attract tourists, but simply because it is their idea of an agreeable evening.'

'As you know', he remarked in this public gossip, 'I am a confirmed heliophobe, and I like the fact that in Venice you can escape the sun in the cool depths of the churches and palaces.' In Italy he was beginning to discover a spiritual home.

43. *Ibid.*, p. 132.

It was, after all, the focus of Catholicism. Italy released in him a long-subdued romanticism. He was surrounded by beautiful women (Diana Cooper, Diana Abdy, Bridgit Parsons, Mary Lygon, Diana Guinness, Doris Castlerosse, Anne Armstrong-Jones, Tilly Losche); his aesthetic sense was glutted by the magnificence of Venice's architecture and painting; the food and wine were excellent. The visit did nothing but confirm his preference for the warm south and his loathing for the chilly, megalopolitan north. (He even pretends to prefer the smell of sewage in 'garlic-eating countries – compared with those of the north'.)[44]

The Marxist perspective on history which condemned such indulgence during a period of economic depression seemed to him perniciously puritanical. Alec Waugh once wrote: 'When I was young, we were taught history in terms of battles and betrayals; of treaties and capitulations, of crowns and dynasties. . . . We were taught to assess the power of Spain by the defeat of the Armada. We were never taught that for a century and a half the stupendous wealth of the New World was poured into the coffers of Seville, while the people of Spain starved.'[45] Alec felt the need to offer half an apology for the extravagance of his life in the 'thirties. Evelyn rarely apologised. But both maintained largely the same historical approach: the large-scale events from which 'world-pictures' were constructed were seen as largely irrelevant to the individual; 'history' was essentially individual experience and an accurate sense of this was only to be obtained by the close observation of individuals or small groups. Both relished being 'in the swim', associating with those who appeared to be 'making history', but neither believed that any theory of history could explain behaviour.

Evelyn's perspective on the past was in one respect radically different from his brother's. Where Alec was an agnostic, liberal-minded conservative, Evelyn was before everything a Roman Catholic. And as an English Roman Catholic he tended to view the Reformation as a watershed dividing British culture from its European heritage. When Christopher Sykes suggests that, 'In 1932 the Western world was still under the spell of the nineteenth-century vision and delusion of inevitable and humane progress' he is perfectly correct. But when he continues, 'Evelyn's conclusion [of *Black Mischief*] is in keeping with this accepted belief . . .'[46] he misleads us. A significant aspect of Waugh's new 'seriousness' was his rejection of such a perspective and his belief that, since the Reformation, northern Protestant culture had suffered relentless decline.

\*

Returned from Venice in early September, he went to stay at Pakenham Hall in County Meath and it was from there that he contacted Peters, agreeing to

44.   *Ibid.*, p. 131.
45.   Alec Waugh, *MBE*, p. 201.
46.   Sykes, p. 121.

broadcast his first radio talk. Written immediately after the completion of *Black Mischief* (and probably while he was correcting the proofs), the text provides a fascinating corollary to the implicit historical argument of the novel. The *Radio Times*, advertising the programme, firmly grasped the wrong end of the stick:

> The series 'To an Unnamed Listener' is to be continued Monday, Nov. 28, by Evelyn Waugh. Mr Waugh will talk to an Old Man. This should be entertaining. Mr Waugh's wit and impudence are well known. His novels . . . quickly established him as our brightest young satirist.[47]

The following week, Arthur Waugh was to address a 'Young Man' in the same series.[48] The (incorrect) assumption was that Evelyn would continue to support the line of 'youth politics'.

In *Black Mischief*, banners proclaiming: 'WOMEN OF TOMORROW DEMAND AN EMPTY CRADLE' and 'THROUGH STERILITY TO CULTURE' are trampled underfoot in the Debra Dowa riot. In the broadcast Waugh states:

> . . . particularly I should like to ask you [i.e. 'an old man'] what it must have felt like to live in an age of Progress. But that is now a word that must be dismissed from our conversation before anything of real interest can be said. I daresay this comes less easily to you than to me because belief in Progress – that is to say in a process of inarrestable, beneficial change, was an essential part, as I understand it, of your education. You were told that man was a perfectible being already well set on the last phase of his ascent from ape to angel, that he would yearly become healthier, wealthier and wiser until, somewhere about the period we are now living, he would have attained a condition of unimpaired knowledge and dignity and habitual, exactic self-esteem. . . .[49]

Waugh considers that it is only 'in freedom from this idea' that the young and the old can converse. If it were a valid theory, then: 'I should be the proud heir of the inheritance of Freud, Einstein and Lenin and you would be the poorer by forty-five years of rich experience which separate us.'

'Progress', the 'uplift' satirised in *Labels* and *Black Mischief*, is a meaningless concept to Waugh in that 'man's capacity for suffering keeps pretty regular pace with the discoveries that ameliorate it and that for every new thing found there is one good use and uncounted misuses'. He prefers the term 'change' and a

47. 'Radio Notes. Youth Crabs Age?', *Radio Times*, 18 November, 1932, 509.
48. When Waugh accepted the contract he did not know that his father was to 'reply' in a broadcast the following week. Several others had been approached first and Arthur Waugh accepted after their refusal, quite late in the negotiations.
49. HRC TS, pp. 1–2. Lacking BBCSL.

significant aspect of such change is the fact that 'the BBC think it worthwhile hiring a young man to lecture an old'. For 'vast periods of time' in the world's history, he says, the 'old men' have been regarded as 'the undisputed guardians of the depository of known law and practice':

> But in Europe in the last four centuries there seems to have been an increasing acceleration of history, bringing a new set of problems for each generation, until in this particular age we have reached the maximum pace and it seems as though history must slow down or disintegrate.[50]

Aware that 'every age tends to arrogate unique importance to itself', he goes on to explain why he thinks 'the present time unique'.

Waugh sees unemployment, especially among educated young men, as symbolic of a society courting its own destruction. The university men are described as 'that part of the community which is normally the guardian of its thought and culture':

> For you, at any rate, sir, and I to some extent, were schooled in the belief that the culture of an age was its glory and its justification. But in England culture never flourished on its own account: our system was economic at base.[51]

The real value of university education (the development of cultured sensibility) derived accidentally, he thought, as the by-product of an economic system guaranteeing jobs:

> When the direct aim [securing employment] is seen not to be fulfilled, I do not see how its secret and glorious aim will ever survive. One will expect, in that part of society which moulds the ideas, manners and art of its generation, psychological symptoms of futility, inferiority and a revolt from culture. . . . Uncertain of his economic future and his right to property, a young man today shrinks from the responsibility of marriage or else translates it into quite other terms and makes it a temporary emotional relationship instead of a permanent social one. Physical sterility, whether artificial or organic, results from sterility of spirit.[52]

The talk concludes with a specific reference to European expansion in Africa. 'It seemed', he says, speaking of the world of the old man's youth, 'to be a simple

50. *Ibid.*, p. 3.
51. *Ibid.*, p. 4.
52. *Ibid.*, p. 4.

law of nature that the European should occupy and direct the rest of the globe.'
But the situation had changed:

> I am perfectly confident that in my life-time, if I live as long as you,
> sir, that I shall see the beginning of a vast recession of the white races
> from all over the world – a withdrawal of the legions to defend what
> remains of European standards on European grounds. I am less confi-
> dent of how much will remain to be defended.[53]

The whole tone of the piece reverts to the earlier severity of the 1930 *Express*
article ('Converted to Rome') and contrasts noticeably with the milder political
and religious temper of *Remote People*.

The article usefully explains certain ambiguities in Waugh's cultural perspective
not always clear to the critics of his novels. Here we see him neither as 'youth
agitator' nor as philistine reactionary. He takes his place in that long debate about
'culture and society' which was revived in the nineteenth century by Arnold and
continued in the twentieth by Ford Madox Ford, Wyndham Lewis, Yeats and
Eliot. It is an argument which has run on unabated through Leavis and Raymond
Williams. Waugh is in Eliot's camp: in many ways the talk popularised (and
clarified) ideas later discussed in Eliot's *Notes Towards the Definition of Culture*
(1948). Waugh rejects the humanist assumptions about 'a process of inarrestable,
beneficial change' and, by implication, rejects both the politics of socialism based
on this assumption and the conventional 'cause-and-effect', linear concept of time
and 'history'. The sense of the 'increasing acceleration of history' is abstractly
conveyed in his writings by the frenetic pace of the characters' lives, spinning off
from traditional restraint towards an ultimate smash-up. In the early works this
is associated with cyclical imagery and with nausea: the wheel in Luna Park
(*Decline and Fall*), the aeroplane looping the loop (*Labels*), the race-track (*Vile
Bodies*).[54] Waugh, like Eliot and Yeats, had been interested in his pre-Catholic
days in cyclical theories of history and as his early premonitions of imminent
catastrophe hardened into certainty during the 'thirties, the cyclical imagery is
replaced by various visions of civilised man's confronting the barbarous darkness
of the jungle.

Waugh's attitude towards the victims of humanism is ambivalent. Yet the quality
which raises his novels above accusations of cruelty is his ability to project the
pathos inherent in the collective tragedy of the individual fools, fiddling complac-
ently before the fires of Rome. His mockery is not merely the product of disgust,

---

53. *Ibid.*, p. 5.
54. Cf. David Lodge, *Evelyn Waugh* (Columbia Essays on Modern Writers, 1972), p. 15; also
    Stephen Greenblatt, *Three Modern Satirists: Waugh, Orwell and Huxley* (New Haven, Yale
    University Press, 1965).

for there was always enshrined in Waugh's artistic sense an irrational love of the Great British Eccentric.

The English abroad, much as they often infuriated him in reality, provided a fictional mythology, a menagerie of harmless, essentially honourable, beings out of step with modern times and all the more engaging for being so. His exuberant review of J. R. Ackerley's *Hindoo Holiday* in April of 1932 notes: '... one sees personified a new idea about the British in India – not as vulgar, arrogant interlopers, not as heroic keepers of the King-Emperor's peace, not as liverish bores waiting for meagrely pensioned old age in Cheltenham, not as conquerors in any of the guises in which they have attracted satire, but as absurd, other-worldly, will-o'-the-wisps, floating in little misty companies about the landscape, futile, shy little creatures, half-friendly, half suspicious, lurking like gnomes in their own bad places, a damp Celtic breath in the powder-hot landscape of Asia'.[55] How better to describe Sir Sampson and Lady Courtenay in *Black Mischief?*

Waugh, of course, had a GBE in his immediate family: his father. At home, though, the GBE was a different matter and it is interesting to note that Waugh's piece on Ackerley appeared on the same page of the *Spectator* as his father's review of Q. D. Leavis's *Fiction and the Reading Public*. Evelyn always despised the Cambridge school of 'state-trained literary critics' as another manifestation of contemporary vulgarity. Arthur applauds Mrs Leavis's book as a condemnation of modern publishing practice. He abhors the 'hard-sell' of the contemporary book trade and the self-advertisement of authors: '... it is a truth', he says, 'known to ... every bookman of business, that the shouting has long since grown so loud that it no longer matters what is shouted'.[56] He laments the tendency towards pandering to, and developing, the 'herd instinct' and sees the recent founding of the Book Society as another symptom of the same disease. When *Black Mischief* was published by his own firm amid cannonades of publicity, it was immediately chosen by the Book Society as their 'Book of the Month' for October. Evelyn has recorded no objection to this lucrative contract.

In November 1932 Arthur was, indeed, an old man; Evelyn at twenty-nine, still relatively young. The emotional gap which had always existed between them yawned wider as the years passed. Alec has noted that they 'were constantly in conflict. They were irritated by each other. In my mother's opinion they were too like each other.'[57] It seems a reasonable deduction: both were themselves manifestations of the Great British Eccentric, Arthur a Dickensian, Evelyn a Wodehouse figure. Both possessed a deep romantic strain and were fiercely loyal. Both were exhibitionists and enjoyed entertaining their friends. Both, ironically, laid great store by 'traditional' values. But Arthur's wit was beneficent where

55. *Spectator*, 16 April, 1932, 562.
56. *Ibid.*, 562.
57. Alec Waugh, 'Arthur Waugh's Last Years' in *MBE*, p. 201.

Evelyn's was acerbic; Arthur's cast of mind was optimistic where Evelyn's was the reverse; Arthur was an Ibsenite humanist where his son felt no allegiance to the optimism of the Victorian sages. When this father and son met briefly at Underhill they had little to say to one another. In 1932 Arthur was sixty-six and approaching the last decade of his life. Chapman and Hall were in financial trouble, partly due to his unwillingness earlier to engage in the brasher techniques of post-war publishing practice. Semi-retired, he worked mostly from home as reader and adviser. Whenever Evelyn went 'home' in the 'thirties his father was there.

Alec's description of the man and the place perhaps gives us some idea of why Waugh found both uncongenial:

> In winter Underhill was a cold house. The wind blew straight under the front door into the hall. There was no central heating. The book-room was uncarpeted, and the French windows opened on to a veranda. There was a direct draught through the house. My father had grown corpulent. He should have dieted, but he had a Latin love of bread. Often after dinner he would be forced to stand up beside the mantel-piece struggling for breath. When he left the warmth of the book-room, the change of air struck chill upon his chest, and he would be convulsed with asthma.[58]

How different this was from Madresfield and Venice. The decorous world in which Evelyn now moved must have jarred in his mind with the decrepitude and parsimony of that ugly, chilly house in Golders Green. Underhill was a monument to Arthur's caution and frugality. Neither quality appealed to his youngest son as a personal merit. Whereas Arthur had broken his health travelling home on the tube each lunchtime to save money on his midday meal and only late in his career accepted an expense account for professional entertaining, Evelyn dined regularly in the Ritz, drove everywhere in taxis or hired limousines and blew hundreds of pounds of advance payment on exotic travels. They simply could not understand each other's attitude to life and, from 1930, the essential difference was religious. Wherever he found it, Waugh was profoundly impatient with liberal-humanist Protestantism or agnosticism. In many respects he had more sympathy with intelligent atheists and ruthless profiteers. At least they held to a consistent and unsentimental code of behaviour. In *Black Mischief* one senses a certain charm in Basil Seal and even Youkoumian, totally absent in the miserably put-upon William Bland. Bland, like Arthur, suffered from excessive tolerance.

While at work on the novel in March 1932, Waugh wrote his story for the *John Bull* series, eventually entitled 'The Seven Deadly Sins of Today'. His short advertisement for the tale appeared in April:

58. *Ibid.*, pp. 202–3.

Twenty-five years ago it was the fashion for those who considered themselves enlightened and progressive to cry out against intolerance as the one damning sin of their time.

The agitation was well-founded and it resulted in the elimination from our social system of many elements that are crude and unjust. But in the general revolution of opinion that has followed, has not more been lost than gained?

It is better to be narrow-minded than to have no mind, to hold limited and rigid principles than none at all.

That is the danger which faces so many people today – to have no considered opinions on any subject, to put up with what is wasteful and harmful with the excuse that there is 'good in everything' – which in most cases means inability to distinguish between good and bad.

There are still things which are worth fighting *against*.[59]

Waugh's approach is fundamentally aggressive. This 'preface' precisely describes his distaste for his father's benevolent optimism. The story which followed was entitled 'Too Much Tolerance'.

The tale (never re-published) was printed under the heading 'Real Life Stories' and is told in the first person. It describes his meeting (probably in Djibouti) with a whimsical, middle-aged liberal humanist who (like Arthur) has reacted against the strictures of a repressive Victorian childhood. He sees no fault in anyone but, as confidence grows between narrator and subject, a life of betrayal and humiliation is revealed. 'As I watched', it concludes, 'he finished his business and strode off towards the town – a jaunty, tragic little figure, cheated out of his patrimony by his partner, battened on by an obviously worthless son, deserted by his wife, an irrepressible, bewildered figure striding off under his bobbing topee, cheerfully battering his way into a whole continent of rapacious and ruthless jolly fellows.'[60] 'Jolly fellows', of course, is heavily ironical. The anti-hero of the story had been quite unable to discriminate between the various races and their internecine factions: ' "Can't understand what all the trouble's about. They're all jolly chaps when you get to know them." ' 'British officials, traders, Arabs, natives, Indian settlers – they were all to my new friend jolly good chaps.'[61]

As we have seen in *Remote People*, to Waugh there were fundamental racial distinctions to be made, particularly between the Arabs and the Indians. Africa was an analogue for the world at large. Rather than adopting his father's gently tolerant belief in the essential goodness of man, Waugh saw the world as largely populated by a rabble of potential or actual savages, 'rapacious', vigilant for the

59. *JB*, 2 April, 1932, 7.
60. 'Too Much Tolerance', *JB*, 21 May, 1932, 21, 24.
61. *Ibid.*, p. 21.

first signs of weakness to move in for the kill. This savagery was all the more dangerous when disguised beneath the trappings of civilization.

Waugh wrote several other short stories during or immediately after the composition of *Black Mischief* and all can be related to this theme, just as the theme itself becomes a structural *leit-motif* of the novel. 'The Patriotic Honeymoon', 'Bella Fleace Gave a Party', 'Cruise' and 'Incident in Azania' are light pieces written hastily for a quick cash return. But Waugh wrote nothing badly and all touch on serious themes: infidelity, death, the dereliction of the English language and the consequent, implicit inability of the characters to comprehend their own active cruelty. In Waugh's phrase, they 'have no mind'; beneath their complacent, dull surfaces, they are mad, bad and dangerous to know, insane with the vanity of benevolence, driven by malice, or simply effete. Violence and betrayal characterise their world.

Since She-Evelyn's desertion Waugh's temporal success and directory of smart friends had gone a long way towards repairing his damaged self-esteem. But there can be no doubt that his first wife's apparently casual betrayal left deep scars and his relationships with women since her departure had done little to raise the sex in his estimation. All the young women in these stories are of a type: well-bred and attractive but trivial and faithless. Prudence in *Black Mischief* was to continue the line; Brenda Last in *A Handful of Dust* (1934) and Prudence in *Scoop* (1938) were variations on the same theme.

\*

During the summer of 1932 Waugh was pursuing Teresa Jungman more hotly than ever – but without success. He was by then hopelessly infatuated and, as with Olivia earlier, suffering agonies of unrequited love. In an envelope marked 'Sentimental Friendships' Waugh kept among his private papers a few letters from those he had loved: Alastair Graham's, Harold Acton's and Teresa's amongst others. Three letters from her are contained in an envelope postmarked 2nd June, 1932, and describe the misery of that year for Waugh. The second (undated) reads:

> Darling Evelyn,
>     Don't be cross with me and keep ringing off all the time. You know how fond I am of you and that you were the first person I wanted to see when I was miserable. . . . But what do you expect me to do when you say that you might fall in love with me and that your intentions are evil. . . . I mean to try as hard as I possibly can not to behave badly. It wouldn't be very consistent of me to go on seeing you all the time, would it? . . . I am really very proud of you and should like to go on being your friend for the rest of our lives. . . . If you weren't married you see it would be different because I might or I might not want to

marry you but I wouldn't be sure. As things are, I *can't* be so unfair as to go on when I am quite determined about what I mean to do. . . .
Best love from
Teresa

The third (undated) letter continues the same theme, imploring him not to be 'bitter about it and not to behave as if we didn't perfectly understand each other and weren't very fond of each other *indeed* quite apart from anything else'. Again she insists: 'If only you would be less obstinate about having evil intentions we could perfectly well go on seeing each other like we used to.' The letter concludes:

> I am afraid that it is my fault that you are cross with me. Perhaps you feel that I made too much use of you during those weeks when I was sad. Forgive me if I did. It was only because I felt you were sympathetic and trusted you completely *not* only because you were a Catholic because after all there are a good many others who might have been able to produce kisses and advice for me.

We can only speculate as to the details of the story. Mrs Cuthbertson (as she became) pleaded failing memory and, very properly, did not wish to disinter any indignities which might reflect unfavourably on either Waugh or herself. In fact, nothing unsavoury emerges: quite the reverse. Waugh's affection was genuine and deep, as was hers. But there was a theological problem. Marriage to him was out of the question for her and a sexual relationship without marriage even further beyond the pale.

Michael Davie in his edition of the *Diaries* remarks that 'He would have liked to marry her, but by becoming a Catholic after divorcing his first wife he had, he thought, permanently debarred himself from marrying again. . . . The journey to Brazil on which he embarked in the winter of 1932 . . . contains a hint of penance.'[62] The implication is that he gave up the relationship because of his religion. Clearly this was not the case. Waugh wanted earnestly, if only technically, to commit adultery. There seemed no other alternative to a man who refused sexual abstinence. He had set in train the legal proceedings which might conclude with Rome annulling his first marriage. But a favourable outcome was unlikely. In the light of later evidence we know that he did not relinquish his pursuit of Teresa with a penitential flight to South America.

Her letters seem unequivocally to indicate the accusations Waugh was levelling at her on finding himself rebuffed: he thought he had been 'used', he thought that she had gone to him because he was a fellow-Catholic rather than because she cared for him in the way she professed. He was bitter and humiliated. He seems to have suspected that he was being rejected on sexual grounds under

62. *Diaries*, p. 354.

the guise of theological argument. The faithless and deceptive women of his contemporary fiction were perhaps his expression of disillusionment, tinged with playful revenge. Ironically, Miss Jungman, for all her adoption of modern manners, seems to have been exactly the reverse of those feckless characters: determined not to betray her faith, deeply injured by the thought that she might have misled Waugh, loyal to him but scrupulous in her moral judgements. It is a rather 'sad story' and this was not the end of it.

Since the summer he had turned his attentions elsewhere. He hoped that Teresa might change her mind if his marriage were annulled but in the meantime there were other distractions. Lady Hazel Lavery was the second wife of Sir John, the fashionable portrait painter. It seems that she was (unsuccessfully) pursuing him, possibly after a brief affair. (*Remote People* is dedicated to her.) His relationship with Lady Diana Cooper had advanced to (a quite asexual) intimacy by the autumn. He was planning his trip to British Guiana.

Between the submission of his novel in late May and his departure on 4th December he maintained a heavy work schedule. Waugh had established himself with *Remote People* as a serious travel writer and Peter Fleming, Literary Editor of the *Spectator*, had offered him a review of two travel books in April. With the novel out of the way and keen to build up cash reserves, he took on similar work for the paper on a more regular basis, contributing four more travel reviews and one of Violet Hunt's *The Wife of Rossetti*. There were proofs to correct, three of the four stories were written and the Christmas article for *Harper's*. In addition, he was treating the publication of *Black Mischief* with some ceremony. A great deal depended on it.

It was almost two years since *Vile Bodies* had appeared and despite the largely respectful reviews of *Remote People* the previous November, it had only remained in the list of best-sellers for a week. The production of *Black Mischief* had been held up by his various schemes to raise money and an innate dilettantism which allowed him only to work in short spells. There was no doubt in his own mind as to the quality of the novel and he was determined not to be rushed. He looked to it to maintain his reputation as an artist and to supply him with enough ancillary work to finance his continued travels. Waugh lived on a dangerous financial precipice in order to share the lives of those with inherited wealth. Were his popularity to cease and the newspaper and magazine commissions to dry up he would have found himself immediately bankrupt.

His correspondence with Peters at this time is largely concerned with tough financial wrangling: he will accept £25 for the *Spectator* reviews but wants £30 (about 17th November); he wants £100 advance from Duckworth's and will need another £100 shortly (about 16th November). He writes about his work as might a craftsman providing a skill for the going rate. But between the letters about terms and conditions we find others indicating Waugh's carelessness of expense on the careful production of his book.

*Black Mischief* was the first of his novels to be printed in two 'first editions' and this was to remain his practice for the rest of his life. For his closest friends there was a special, Morocco-bound, numbered and signed edition on large, rag-made mould paper. The considerable extra cost was deducted from his royalty account. He did not go to this expense because he was a snob trying to impress the well-connected. He did it because he loved books and had a bibliographer's delight in seeing work elegantly produced. Around 17th October we find him requesting twenty-five typed slips from Peters explaining that, in view of the Chapman and Hall special edition of *Black Mischief*, he cannot sign copies of the ordinary edition. A little later he asked Peters to write to his American agent, Carl Brandt, enquiring about the originals of the illustrations. He wanted them returned, particularly the 'one of Haile Selassie'. Waugh was building up an archive of his work which he stored at Underhill.

\*

The description of the illustration's subject seems particularly revealing in view of the fact that Waugh consistently denied that Selassie was the model for Seth. But we need not be decoyed by it into supposing the novel a *roman à clef* in any more serious sense than had been *Decline and Fall* or *Vile Bodies*. It is perfectly clear that Seth is not a direct portrait of Ras Tafari but, as usual, a composite figure derived from several 'originals' and from Waugh's own imaginative obsession with creating a central naïf for his 'thirties fiction. Selassie in Waugh's documentary writings appears as a tiny, enigmatic figure, silent, perhaps rather devious, but with an exotic and fascinating aura. None of that oriental *chic* surrounds Seth. A relative of the Emperor's who appears in *Remote People*, George Herui, seems in many ways closer to the fictional creation. Selassie was characterised in the eyes of the Western press as a distinctly African figure, proud of his heritage, the only independent native monarch of the Continent. He represented a curious combination of splendid medievalism and a vision of the new Africa after European withdrawal. The seniority of the delegates sent to the Coronation in 1930 and the recent entry of Abyssinia into the League of Nations signified the Western powers' willingness to re-think their attitudes to imperialism.

Waugh's novel presents a different view. The European powers are seen to be keen to exploit and are engaged in a network of codes and espionage. The Abyssinians are, for their part, equally prepared to take advantage of the Europeans and are rather better at the politics of exploitation. A recurring image in *Black Mischief* is the spy scuttling from the door. Seth, a solitary, abstracted figure, obsessed by humanist ideology, believes fervently in the concept of 'Progress'. He is a materialist divorced from the mystical roots of his culture. Early in the novel, without the intellectual support of an adequate religious faith, the world presents itself to his imagination as a miasma of treachery and fear:

Night and the fear of darkness. In his room at the top of the old fort
Seth lay awake and alone, his eyes wild with the inherited terror of the
jungle, desperate with the acquired loneliness of civilisation. Night was
alive with beasts and devils and spirits of dead enemies; before its power
Seth's ancestors had receded, slid away from its attack, abandoning in
retreat all the baggage of Individuality. . . .[63]

This was Waugh's view of a world unqualified by the concept of 'supernatural
reality'. To combat this horror Seth turns to the material expression of humanism:
to birth control, tractors, modern architecture, Shaw's and Priestley's writings.
His irresponsible snatching at anything representing the 'modern age' as a curative
for the immemorial sickness of Original Sin is seen to be patently absurd. Under
the guise of altruism his policies appear insanely egocentric and domineering.
They culminate with the ultimate carelessness for his people's welfare when he
prints millions in worthless Azanian currency to pay for his projects.

A similar egocentricity divorces all the characters from sensible communication
with each other. Sometimes this is presented as farcical. Sir Sampson dislikes
being interrupted with diplomatic business when more seriously engaged with his
inflatable rubber monster in the bath; M. Ballon sees Sir Sampson's incompetence
as part of a devious espionage plan and misinterprets a telegraphed chess move
and a strip of paper from a game of Consequences as coded signals. Sometimes
the tone changes sharply. Youkoumian ignores his wife as she struggles, bound
and helpless on the floor, and carelessly slumps into bed for a few hours' sleep.
He is anyone's man, as is Basil, for the right money. The virtues of loyalty,
honesty or courage form no part of Youkoumian's character. In the manuscript
he appears for many pages under the appellation 'Youkonmi'.

'Conning' or cheating lies at the very heart of this society. In the face of this,
Seth's liberal reform plan or the campaign for 'dumb chums' prosecuted by
Dame Mildred Porch and Miss Tin are quite simply irrelevant. Dame Mildred's
blinkered vision, harmless as it seems at first, is another aspect of pervasive
barbarism: *'Fed doggies in market-place. Children tried to take food from doggies. Greedy
little wretches. . . .'*[64] No distinction is made in her mind between the suffering of
children and those of dogs. Waugh, by implication, is as bitterly critical of the
Europeans' barbarism as he is of the Africans' more overt departure from civilised
standards. As he had said in 'Converted to Rome', 'civilisation' did not signify to
him improved hospitals or even talking cinemas and tinned food. Its true manifestation, he felt, was in the aesthetic impulse deriving directly from the spiritual
vision of Catholic Christianity. This concept of the 'civilised', at least in theory,
transcended all barriers of class, nationality and race, but not that of creed.
Civilisation and religion were interdependent in Waugh's mind.

63. *Black Mischief*, p. 26.
64. *Ibid.*, p. 157.

In 1932, although 'religion' only meant Christianity to him (and 'Christianity' only Catholicism), his aesthetic and cultural tastes were broad. As we have seen, he was prepared to accept many cultures not based on Christianity as 'decent and valuable'. *Black Mischief* offers us a fictional version of the culture-and-society debate conducted in *Remote People*. The novel begins with the Iago-figure of Ali who has whined and cheated and flattered his way into the position of Seth's Private Secretary. Now that the revolution threatens his gains he betrays his master and tries to steal the crown jewels. Ali, the epitome of selfish materialism, is noticeably an Indian. Set against this vainglorious commercial interloper and the others like him are the quiet and dignified Matodi Arabs. Their culture, it is true, has run to seed, their leisured and caste-structured society has become decadent, but they represent the indigenous aristocracy who personify the essential decency of a coherent aesthetic and religious system.

The novel concludes with what can only be seen as a pessimistic view of the future. Seth is dead, Prudence eaten, Basil returned to England a sadder and wiser man. Order has apparently been restored by bungalows-full of those 'jolly chaps' Waugh clearly found repulsive. The foolish Gilbertian lines wafting across the newly-ordered and apparently peaceful suburbs of Azania must surely be taken as presaging doom in their total irrelevance to the volcanic political situation. There is, as in *Remote People*, a distaste for the anaesthetic influence of British middle-class colonial administration, dulling the vibrant life of Matodi. The recurrent image is of 'the water lapping very gently on the wall'. In this new and dangerous environment 'The blank walls of the Arab tenements gave no sign of life';[65] the stabilising influence of the native aristocracy has been destroyed.

\*

When it was published on 1st October, no-one noticed Waugh's thematic subtlety and reviews of the book varied enormously. L. A. G. Strong in the *Spectator* thought that 'Mr Waugh's note deepens in this book' and found it 'amazingly well-written' and entirely original.[66] Howard Marshall in the *Telegraph* also detected the increased seriousness and saw the novel as 'a transitional stage in [Waugh's] work. ... there is an air of uncertainty about it which we did not find in his previous novels'.[67] Eric Linklater in the *Listener* gave it more serious attention, reviewing it alongside H. E. Bates's *The Fallow Land*, Harold Nicolson's *Public Faces* and Edwin Muir's *Poor Tom*. All he saw as novels coloured by Eliot's *Waste Land* vision of western society, an unsentimental pessimism. Linklater also admired Waugh's artistic control: 'His narrative is swift and picturesque, and his

65. *Ibid.*, p. 238.
66. *Spectator*, 1 October, 1932, 420.
67. *DT*, 4 October, 1932, 16; *CH*, p. 127.

cutting – if one may borrow a Hollywood term – is masterly. *Black Mischief*, indeed, shows an all-round growth of strength.'[68]

Earlier in his review, though, Linklater had noted that ' . . . Mr Waugh, by living rather on the plane of Restoration Comedy, permits his readers, if they prefer it, to take his criticism simply as a good joke'. And this was the nub of the unfavourable remarks. Geoffrey West in the *Bookman* felt that ' . . . the [Book] Society might have looked further and found better. Mr Waugh seems to suffer from his early illusion that the vapid fatuities of Ronald Firbank are funny, and in this as in his earlier books he mounte-Firbanks all too readily, to his own delight perhaps but to the reader's tedium. . . . I confess that I should have given it up long before page 120, where the fun really begins, had I not been paid to persevere.'[69] James Agate in the *Express* took a similar line: 'This book is an extravaganza . . . I assume that Mr Waugh's plan was to think of an island of cannibals to whose vile bodies he could add Lottie Crump's clientele out of an earlier novel. The book will be deemed wildly funny by the intelligentsia, and there is always a chance that it is too clever for me.'[70] Too clever also, it seems, for the anonymous *TLS* reviewer. The *Supplement* was consistently patronising about Waugh's early fiction and here, ostentatiously yawning, their critic saw *Black Mischief* as little more than an 'extravaganza written largely about, and presumably for, the bright young people' which was 'insubstantial for its length'.[71]

It was a mixed bag, but adverse criticism rarely bothered Waugh, especially when the level of intellectual engagement was so lamentably low. It must have irritated him still to be classed as a youth agitator. Most of the unfavourable notices could so easily have been contradicted. But he rarely chose to defend his work unless, as was shortly to happen, his good faith were impugned. Ernest Oldmeadow's attack in the *Tablet* some months later was to sting him into bitter response. In October 1932, however, he was perfectly content with the book's reception. The Book Society selection ensured a wide circulation and his novels after *Vile Bodies* always sold well whatever the critics said. He had secured a large English public and an American *coterie* The immediate future was financially secure and his main concern now was to raise enough cash to finance an excursion to South America.

The correspondence with A. D. Peters at this stage comes from a variety of addresses: Madresfield and Chagford in October and November, and in December from hotels in Manchester and Scotland. The West Country letters reveal him working hard at short stories and reviews in a last burst to accumulate money. The others were written as he followed Lady Diana Cooper round the

68. *Listener*, 19 October, 1932, 576; *CH*, pp. 129–30.
69. *Bookman*, November, 1932, 135; *CH*, pp. 131–2.
70. *DE*, 6 October, 1932, 6; *CH*, p. 128.
71. *TLS*, 13 October, 1932, 736.

kingdom. He continued to work, producing the 4,000 word tale 'Incident in Azania' at this time, but it was a period more dedicated to pleasure. Lady Diana and he had become fast friends and she was delighted to have his company to cheer her more sombre moods. She seems, though, to have mistaken his attitude to *The Miracle:* 'Undoubtedly he approved of the play', she told Christopher Sykes, 'for when I left for a long tour of acting in the provinces Evelyn came with me on and off for several weeks.' Earlier she had remarked of their first encounter: 'I suppose he'd been to the performance. I wondered if he approved of it. Many of his faith took a critical line though the morality pantomime had been overseen and regulated by the Fathers of Farm Street. He surely liked it or he would not have taken me to the Bray party.'[72]

There is a delightful naïveté about this. Waugh's letters, as we have seen, indicate that he found *The Miracle* artistically inept and theologically heretical: a 'terrible thing'. His motives for accompanying her had small connection with his appreciation of the play. He was, once again, hopelessly infatuated. They lived in the most luxurious hotels – the Midland in Manchester, the Central in Glasgow, the Caledonian in Edinburgh. In their free time they would hire cars and travel across country, exploring country houses. 'It was during these most happy days that I learned to know and understand him and to form an attachment deep enough to last unplumbed and unclouded till his death.'[73] 'Unclouded' is not a word to describe any of Waugh's intimate relationships.

There can be no doubt as to Waugh's continued affection for her, but at this point in his life he was not the happiest of men. When the diary begins again on 4th December he is two days out into the Atlantic and writing up an account of the week before his departure. 'Left Edinburgh', he wrote, 'after strained hour in Diana's dressing room . . .'.[74] What caused the awkwardness on this occasion we shall never know. Perhaps it was simply Waugh's misery at having to leave her. But 'strain' there certainly was in their relationship because of his irrational jealousy of Duff Cooper. Lady Diana's husband was a handsome fellow and a man of affairs. He had earlier in the year published his first book, a biography of Talleyrand, and was nervous of its reception. It met with some savage reviews. Waugh, on the other hand, was cock-sure about the quality of *Black Mischief* and by and large maintained his reputation with serious critics. Duff he considered an amiable but dull man whose superior 'sex-appeal' unfairly secured him the love of beautiful women. The remarks about his qualities in the letter to Baldwin have an edge of bitterness to them. He believed 'Sexy' Cooper (Waugh's *soubriquet*) to have a manifestly inferior mind and wit to his own. Waugh must have been somewhat disappointed to see Talleyrand lauded in the Press.

72. Cf. Sykes, pp. 124–5.
73. *Ibid.*, p. 125.
74. *Diaries*, 4 December, 1932, p. 35.

At the turn of the year he was, more often than not, melancholy. He used the week before departure for a valedictory tour of his friends and family, first to the Lygons and Captain Hance at Madresfield, next to London to stay with Henry and Dig Yorke and to see Teresa. Writing to Lady Mary and Lady Dorothy while sitting in the Ritz waiting for a 'young lady' to turn up he produced another of his breathless, fanciful epistles, elaborating the mythology of Captain Hance and detailing his aimless metropolitan existence:

> So then I thought I'd like some SOCIETY so I found out that there was a lady giving a dinner party and I rang her up and said may I come and she said well I don't much want you because the numbers would be wrong and anyway I don't much like you but I said 'Please let me come because my back is broken and I must have some SOCIETY' so she said well all right if you must so I came and I sat between the Ladies Birkenhead and Colefax and told them about the Captain (GBH) till they thought Golly what a dull young man so that was my SOCIETY.[75]

'GBH' stood for 'God Bless Him', a suffix usually appended to Hance's name in Waugh's letters to 'Blondy' and 'Pollen'. It might equally have been a pun on 'Grievous Bodily Harm'. Waugh's equestrian tuition caused him some physical suffering and he was at this time undergoing a course of electric shock treatment for a strained back. The letter is typical of those delightful scribblings to the Lygon girls in the 'thirties. The language of a brainless juvenile fitted with his fantasy of them as schoolgirls, but he also employs the device unsentimentally to denigrate himself through a stream of jokes '. . . I think Jackie is in love with me only I often think this about girls and it is hardly ever true so I daresay she isn't'.[76]

The 'young lady' for whom he was waiting was almost certainly Teresa. She arrived late and seems not to have inconvenienced herself unduly on Waugh's behalf during his last days in England, though he was clearly desperate to spend every available moment with her. The situation was perhaps complicated by Hazel Lavery's pursuit of him.

Arrived in London he 'Found several telephone messages from Hazel, and Hazel herself sitting in the vestibule of the Savile. She drove me to North End Road, where I collected clean clothes, and to a passport photographer's for photograph for Venezuelan visa.'[77] Perhaps Waugh had accepted her earlier advances. At this time she was ardent and he cool, vaguely embarrassed by it all. Her husband, the prominent society portraitist, was an Irishman risen to

75. *Letters*, p. 66.
76. *Ibid.*, p. 65.
77. *Diaries*, 4 December, 1932, p. 355.

Evelyn Waugh in Corfu, January 1927, returning from his unhappy visit to
Alastair Graham in Athens

Evelyn Waugh and his first wife, Evelyn Gardner. The original caption in
the *Sketch* read: 'The marriage of Mr Evelyn Waugh, son of Mr Arthur
Waugh, and brother of Mr Alec Waugh, the well-known novelist, to the
Hon. Evelyn Gardner, youngest daughter of the first Lord Burghclere,
and of Lady Burghclere, was solemnised last week at St Paul's, Portman
Square. Above we give an original and unusual portrait study of the bride
and bridegroom, in which they are shown reflected in a mirror'

The dining room at 17a Canonbury Square, Islington, Evelyn Waugh's first marital home. The photograph above the chest of drawers is the one by Olivia Wyndham reproduced opposite. The portraits of She-Evelyn and Evelyn Waugh are by Henry Lamb (both now lost)

The photograph taken during the fortnight's attempted reconciliation after She-Evelyn's confession of infidelity. The original caption read: 'The Hon. Mrs Evelyn Waugh and her husband attired for the "Tropical" party – which was hot in more ways than one – on board the *Friendship*. The author of *Decline and Fall* looks somewhat scared, although there were no fierce Zulus on board'

Evelyn Waugh in 1930 as the successful young
author of *Vile Bodies*; studio portrait by Madame
Yevonde, 1930

Evelyn and Alec Waugh in Villefranche sur Mer, Côte d'Azur, as
they appear on a postcard sent to their mother on 15th April, 1930.
After this their paths irrevocably divided

Evelyn Waugh in Kenya, 1931, on the journey written up as *Remote People*

A house party at the Sitwells' Renishaw Hall. Left to right: Tom Balston (of Duckworth's), Lady Ida, Georgia (Sacheverell Sitwell's wife), Bryan Guinness, Edith, Diana Guinness and Tom Driberg

Laura Herbert when Evelyn Waugh
was engaged to her, about 1936

Evelyn Waugh in his lion-skin coat,
Abyssinia, 1935. The photograph was sent
from Palestine on a postcard dated 4th
January, 1936, with the message 'Portrait
of the author disguised as a patriot'

Evelyn Waugh (seated) with
Penelope Betjeman, her
arab mare and Robert
Heber-Percy in Lord
Berners's drawing room,
about 1936

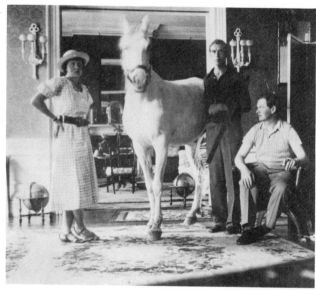

Wedding photograph of Evelyn
Waugh and Laura, 17th April,
1937

Lady Dorothy (left) and Lady
Mary Lygon arriving for the
wedding

Piers Court, near Dursley, Gloucestershire, Evelyn and Laura Waugh's first
permanent home, bought in 1937 for £3550

The dining room at Piers Court

international fame from humble origins, then in his vigorous old age. Lady Hazel, an American, was a volatile, gregarious beauty whom he had married as his second wife in 1910. She was sixteen years older than Waugh but thirty-one years younger than Sir John. In his autobiography, *The Life of a Painter*, the shortest chapter is about her and it tells us almost nothing. Clearly he was devoted to her to the end and, indeed, outlived her by six years. But his reticence seems to signify more than decent respect for their mutual intimacy.

Despite Hazel's attempts to please Waugh by being 'useful' on this occasion, he seems to have shaken her off fairly quickly. He stayed with the 'bright young Yorkes' and dined with Teresa at the Savoy Grill. 'Next day walked with Teresa in park and lunched with her and Ivan Davson at the Ritz. She sat quiet while he and I spread a map on the table and talked of Guiana. Dined with Henry and Dig – Teresa having gone to Northampton for a dance; later we went to Quaglino's.'[78] It is a restrained but unmistakably sad entry. He wanted Teresa to place him at the centre of her life. She kept her distance. Lieutenant-Colonel Ivan Davson was there for business purposes. He had commercial interests in British Guiana, was to travel there shortly after Waugh and had offered the use of his agent in Georgetown to secure Waugh accommodation. Davson's presence effectively precluded intimate conversation between Teresa and her suitor.

The following day Waugh went shopping with Dig as Teresa was unavailable, lunched with Teresa's mother, and had tea with Peter Fleming 'to talk of equipment for forests'.[79] Christopher Sykes says that there was no obvious reason for Waugh's selecting South America as the object of his next adventure. The 'obvious reason' was his fascination with Fleming's recent journey to Brazil as Special Correspondent for *The Times*. He had been reporting on an expedition to search for the explorer, Col. P. H. Fawcett, and Brazil was 'news'. South America was territory relatively untouched by the crowd of smart young men in the market for travel literature. Moreover, it was distant and potentially dangerous and Waugh felt the need for the stimulus of (what Graham Greene, quoting Browning, terms) 'the dangerous edge of things'.

On the voyage out Waugh dashed off an article attempting to explain his compulsive wanderlust:

> 1. It is essential for those who practise no regular profession to take long holidays from their own lives . . . men of leisure and writers are alike in this, that they never have a separation of interests. Their relationship with friends and relations and the routine of their day are invariable and interconnected. The more irritable have to get away or go off their heads.
>
> 2. Some measure of physical risk is as necessary to human well-being

78. *Ibid.*, p. 355.
79. *Ibid.*, p. 355.

as physical exercise. I do not mean acts of reckless heroism. . . . But everyone instinctively needs an element of danger and uncertainty in his life.[80]

The writing was slovenly but the sentiments genuinely felt. Waugh obviously classes himself among 'the more irritable' here and the central cause of his discontent was not far to seek. The diary account of his last full day in England speaks for itself:

Thursday last day. Shopped with Dig, lunched with my parents and packed. Am taking only suitcase and grip. A few tropical suits, camera, books, a pair of field boots and settler shirt and shorts . . . dinner Teresa at Quaglino's. . . . Friday. Mass at Spanish Place with Teresa and breakfast in Slip-In opposite where she gave me a gold St Christopher medal on a chain.

Down to the docks in Beatrice's [Teresa's mother's] car. Deadly lonely, cold, and slightly sick at parting. . . . Ship at first sight unattractive; like an Irish packet-boat. . . . Heating apparatus not working. Teresa drove off to lunch with Lady Astor in London. We sailed at about 2.30. Down the river in heavy rain and twilight. Heart of lead.[81]

80. 'Travel – And Escape From Your Friends', *DM*, 16 January, 1933; *EAR*, pp. 133–4.
81. *Diaries*, Sunday, 4 December, 1932, pp. 355–6.

# X

# *Turning Serious: 1932–1934*

The *S.S. Ingoma*, an ancient and lethargic cargo boat, slid out of Tilbury on 2nd December, 1932. Aboard were seventy-four bags of mail, two prize bulls, a racehorse, a pair of fox hounds and about twenty passengers including Mr Evelyn Waugh, Novelist. Only fourteen of these passengers were to travel all the way to Georgetown. British Guiana (now Guyana) was a little-known outpost of the Empire. The popular imagination, according to Waugh, frequently confused it with New Guinea. His knowledge of the country was little better. The coastal strip was well-mapped and its towns populated by decent chaps in topees. But the interior was often a cartographical mystery. On the voyage out Waugh suffered alternating panics as he feared that the trip might prove either suicidally dangerous or tediously uneventful. Both fears were justified.

Strong winds and heavy seas pitched the ship about for a week, preventing the passengers from emerging for any length of time on deck. Seasickness was rife. The ship creaked and crashed incessantly. Waugh, who began the journey in the slough of despond, sat in his cabin reading books on British Guiana and writing up his diary. Most of his fellow voyagers produced in him an overwhelming apathy. They were another dull collection of colonial wives and daughters, a female doctor, some planters returning to the West Indies, and a couple of 'old soaks' who were doing the round trip and rarely left the bar. Only three people appear to have engaged his imagination: a red-haired widow, Carson (an 'interesting young man from Fiji'), and someone called Willems. The widow had a noisy little girl, Carson disembarked at Antigua. That left only Willems, a 'melancholy young man – engineer, probably Portugese-Indian origin – who offered to help in journey up-country and knew a little about it'.[1] He wasn't much but he was better than nothing. Willem's parents had a timber business near Batika in the lower reaches of the Mazaruni. He was returning to prospect for gold.

By 8th December, beyond the Azores, the weather was warm and calm. The passengers came on deck and attempted unsuccessfully to engage Waugh in a variety of 'activities'. Where before he had been depressed and rendered near sleepless by the rolling of the ship, now he was 'incapacitated by a severe cold. I find it impossible to say anything in the dining-room, won't play deck games,

---

1. *Diaries*, 6 December, 1932, p. 356.

and I think that on the whole I must be giving the impression of a pretty dull young man – as indeed I feel.'[2] He sat to one side reading detective stories and philosophy. Van Dine's intriguing vocabulary in *Canary Murders* and Jacques Maritain's *Introduction to Philosophy* satisfied his two dominant intellectual interests: the English language and Catholic theology. But away from the misery of his relationship with Teresa and the temptations of city life his spirits were, at least, beginning to improve. 'I feel less tied to London than when I started', he recorded on the 11th, 'and have thrown off all the hesitations about the jungle which I felt driving down with Teresa. A certain inclination to take up being highbrow again.'[3] As relief from his unhappiness as social animal he could turn to the life of the mind and the soul.

In another week they had reached Antigua and Willems and he, as became their custom on these brief stop-overs in the West Indies, went architecture-hunting. Here Waugh admired the cathedral's pitch-pine interior, its 'sense of massiveness' and the elaborate marble tombs. In Barbados the government offices and St John's Church (both Gothic) caught his eye. He missed Grenada entirely, arriving at midnight and sailing before he rose. On 20th December they docked at Trinidad, but he found nothing of interest and his general impression of the place was that he didn't want to see it again.

There was a practical reason for Waugh's not giving the West Indies more serious consideration. In *Ninety-Two Days* (1934), the travelogue about this expedition, he explained:

> My brother Alec is also fond of travelling and like me, poor fish, he lives by writing books, so on one of our rare but agreeable meetings we made a compact each to keep off the other's territory; with a papal gesture he made me a present of the whole of Africa and a good slice of Asia in exchange for the Polynesian Islands, North America, and the West Indies. When he saw in a newspaper that I was going to Guiana he sent me a sharp note claiming that the West Indies included any places on the mainland of West Indian character – i.e. sugar estates, slaves, rum and pirates – and recommending British Honduras. We compromised by my promising to get up country as soon as I could and to pay as little attention as possible to what I passed on the way.[4]

This he duly did. But there was more to his evasion of the topic than this. Waugh judged a civilisation by its art and particularly by its architecture. Just as the raw concrete and *tukals* of Addis Ababa had signified to him a barbarian culture, so the mere smattering of fine workmanship in the West Indies failed to retrieve

2. *Ibid.*, 11 December, 1932, pp. 356–7.
3. *Ibid.*, 11 December, p. 357.
4. *Ninety-Two Days*, p. 21.

them from similar condemnation. He had no anthropological interest in the indigenous population and an irrational belief in the inferiority of negroid genes. The beaches and dinners and gin swizzles could occupy his attention for barely twenty-four hours at a time. Holiday resorts bored him. The two images from the islands which took seed in his mind relate to architecture. The marble tombs became part of the aesthetic argument of *Ninety-Two Days;* Gothic architecture is a dominant *leit-motif* of his next novel, *A Handful of Dust.*

\*

Waugh's first sight of British Guiana, on 23rd December, was of a 'misty palm-fringe through pouring rain and a few factory chimneys'.[5] Sailing down the estuary on the tide later that day, a closer inspection of Georgetown revealed further desolation: 'Dreary wind-swept wharfs; some corrugated iron roofs of ware-houses.'[6] True, the harbour had some picturesque elements: tropical vegetation, a pretty creek, rigged schooners rocking at anchor. But Waugh had little time for the picturesque. His travel book admits in a footnote that the melancholy picture he paints of the town is not literally accurate but a representation of a state of mind: 'Doubtless some local patriot will complain that I give a wrong impression; that there is a cricket club, a golf club, a promenade along the sea front and a spacious botanical garden. That is all true. I have nothing against the amenities of the place. Just the reverse, that it is disappointing to travel a long way and find at the end of one's journey, a well-laid-out garden city.'[7]

The hotel Davson's agent had booked for him met with equal disfavour: it was too polite an establishment, the best in town: clean, quiet and airy. What Waugh needed was a busy, more down-at-heel place with a bustling bar trade and 'elderly men talking stories until late into the night'.[8] The 'Sea-View' would not do. Instead he found the Hotel Tower, run by 'a dashing, handsome fellow with a military title, half Irish and half Portuguese, with a fine swagger and plenty of talk'.[9] This was more like it. On these premises he was more likely to glean the local information he needed. He was also more likely to find women and drinking partners. The next day he moved his belongings and felt moderately contented.

The first people he met, even before he had transferred his patronage, were two coloured reporters who came to the Sea-View to interview him. The visit signified no special accolade: every first class passenger was treated in similar fashion and his or her name dutifully recorded in the local papers. Nevertheless, having discovered a celebrity, both afforded Waugh a separate short column to announce his arrival.

5. *Diaries*, 23 December, 1932, p. 359.
6. *Ibid.*, p. 359.
7. *Ninety-Two Days*, p. 28.
8. *Ibid.*, p. 26.
9. *Ibid.*, p. 26.

Dull as their reports are, they offer an interesting reflection of our hero's public persona:

> Mr Waugh is on a two months' visit with the object of writing a book on his impression of British Guiana. He is particularly interested in Aboriginal Indian life and hopes to visit the Catholic missions. . . .
> On leaving British Guiana he will proceed to Surinam [Dutch Guiana] where he will spend another two months and make a study of the 'bush Negroes'.
> His itinerary includes the Venezuelan coast and Colombia. . . .[10]

The definite tone of Waugh's release is amusing. He now knew how to deal with reporters and customs officials. The slightest hesitation, he felt, rendered one suspect. In any case, he didn't care what he said to them. It would be bad public relations to admit that he didn't know what his next move would be. His statements represent, not a fixed itinerary, but a range of possibilities. In fact he never went to Surinam, Venezuela or Colombia, had no serious interest in Aboriginal Indian or bush-Negro life and ended up in Brazil. He also mis-calculated the length of his stay: the visit lasted three months.

*

Waugh disliked Georgetown; unlike Venice it was 'too diffuse'[11] and its architecture mainly of wood and cast iron. On his first day he trudged about the town bearing letters of introduction to the Bishop's residence, signing his name in the book at Government House. Various notes of welcome were waiting for him at the Sea-View including one from an elderly Mr Maggs who had been born in Midsomer Norton. Maggs he liked particularly as an English eccentric but it seemed a dull crop and Christmas, that most depressing season for Waugh, was almost upon him.

The Governor invited him to dinner the next day, Christmas Eve. Lord Denham was a frank and generous man. By a stroke of good fortune Waugh happened to remark on 'the futility of compulsory Kiswahili in East African schools and found it was a pet subject of his'.[12] His Excellency and Lady Denham took to him, offered help with his expedition and a further invitation to Christmas dinner. Most of Christmas Day, though, Waugh spent alone or in desultory conversation. Eventually he pottered off to see Maggs and finding him alone and disconsolate presented him with a copy of *Remote People*. It was an unhappy day and the evening party at Government House proved a miserable affair.

10. *Daily Chronicle* [Georgetown], 24 December, 1932, 4. I am indebted to Dr Donat Gallagher for retrieving this obscure article and for the information on Dr Roth.
11. *Diaries*, 23 December, 1932, p. 360.
12. *Ibid.*, 24 December, 1932, p. 360.

Having no dress clothes he had to manufacture a makeshift outfit from a white tie and mess jacket. Arrived, and feeling rather foolish, he found the valiant attempts at hospitality on the part of his host a melancholy spectacle. 'Rather a pathetic evening of the Denhams' charming attempts to be homely among childless officials; many jokes – imitation rolls which squeaked, a spoon which was hinged in the middle.'[13] It was all too decorous, sentimental and embarrassingly 'English'. Polite conversation with vicars and officials strained his patience. The only 'human moments' he could salvage were with a 'tall ginger-headed ADC and a pretty secretary'.[14]

On Boxing Day he wrote to Mary Lygon:

> So yesterday was Christmas and we had very far flung stuff – turkey and mince pies and paper hats at Government House and we drank to 'Absent Friends' and little Poll and Lady Sibell and Hughie and Lord Elmley and Mr and Mrs Arthur Waugh, and Mr and Mrs Alec Waugh and the Capt G.B.H. and Min and Jackie and Reggie and Barleet, and Diana and the Dutch girl and the tarts or pouncers and bubblesses and mannerlesses and Knatchie and Mr Conrad and Friskey . . . etc etc etc.
>     God how S[ad] . . .
>     Well I went as I tell you to G. House and it was very hot on account of the sun never setting and so the Governor said it is so hot on account of the sun never setting that I must go away for a little in my yacht and will you come too so I said yes so I am going.[15]

In this crazy register his mind flicks rapidly through his friends and family, though the memories probably failed to jerk a tear. The 'Dutch girl' (Teresa) occupied more of his thoughts than this letter suggests. But he would not repine.

The Governor's offer of a trip on his steam launch offered welcome relief from the Christmas spirit. Everyone, he wrote in *Ninety-Two Days*, 'has something to be melancholy about at Christmas, not on account of there being anything intrinsically depressing about the feast but because it is an anniversary too easily memorable; one can cast back one's mind and remember where one was, and in what company, every year from the present to one's childhood'.[16] If he could not escape

13. *Ibid.*, p. 360.
14. *Ibid.*, Christmas Day, 1932, p. 360.
15. *Letters*, pp. 67–8. Mr Hanson, Min, Jackie, Reggie and Barleet were friends in and around Captain Hance's riding academy. Diana was Diana Coventry; the 'pouncers' were Simon and Gloria Elwes; the 'bubblesses' Richard and Jean Norton; the 'mannerlesses' the Marquis of Dufferin and Ava and his wife Maureen (née Guinness); 'Knatchie' was (possibly) Lady Diana Cooper's friend and theatrical entrepreneur 'Kaetchen', Rudolf Kommer; Conrad was Conrad Russell; Friskey was Baldwin of Bewdley; Mrs Alec Waugh was Joan (née Churnside), an Australian whom Alec had married in October, 1932. The 'Dutch girl' was, of course, Teresa Jungman.
16. *Ninety-Two Days*, pp. 20–1.

the yule logs, snow-dusted robins and whisky punch, they at least appeared less disgustingly Teutonic in a displaced cultural context. He had watched with wry amusement as the *Ingoma* trans-shipped a cargo of holly at Antigua beneath a blazing sky.

During the day of that letter to Lady Mary, Waugh had been busy following his first lead:

> On Monday of last week I went to tea with the Willemses and met Dr Roth, an opinionated and rather disagreeable old man who said he was willing, if I paid his expenses, to take me to the only place where unsophisticated Indians are still to be found – in the head waters of the Essequibo. He estimated that this would take three months and £300. At first I was not attracted by the proposition, but later grew more enthusiastic and saw the possibility of a good book in it. Next day the Governor invited me to go to Mazaruni and throughout the trip, until the last evening, I became more determined to go with Dr Roth.[17]

No mention is made of Roth in *Ninety-Two Days* but he is an important figure.

Walter Edmund Roth (1861–1933) was a man of some eminence in anthropological circles. A biologist and surgeon, he had emigrated to Australia in 1887 where he eventually became Chief Protector of Aborigines. As an established expert on aboriginal culture he had moved to British Guiana in 1905 to take up the posts of medical officer, magistrate and Protector of Indians in the Pomeroon district. No-one knew more about the 'uncivilised' Indian in that area than he. But by the time Waugh encountered him he was an old man, seventy-two, and Waugh at twenty-nine came less and less to relish the idea of three months in his exclusive company. Roth had retired as Protector four years earlier and was in 1932 occupied as the Curator of Georgetown Museum and Government Archivist. Waugh's earlier visit to this 'dilapidated museum of faded photographs and badly stuffed fauna'[18] cannot have inspired confidence in its curator.

Nevertheless, setting off for his three-day cruise up the Mazaruni with Denham, Roth's proposal kept working in Waugh's mind. It was only the Governor's and his friends' earnest counsel that finally dissuaded him:

> Davies told me Roth irresponsible traveller; no sense of time or money; nearly kills himself whenever he goes up country through neglecting rudimentary precautions. He and H.E. and Woods all strongly advised against going with him.[19]

It was sound advice. Within a few months Roth was dead. On Waugh's return

17. *Diaries*, Sunday 1 January [retrospective account], 1933, p. 361.
18. *Ibid.*, Friday 23 December, 1932, p. 360.
19. *Ibid.*, Sunday 1 January, 1933, p. 361.

to Georgetown on 29th December, he went to the museum to inform the ancient that he had changed his mind. Roth didn't much care. He seems to have lost interest in the expedition himself. Waugh never saw him again. But the image of this elderly, opinionated, experienced bush man must have lodged in his imagination. Dr Messinger in *A Handful of Dust* bears a distinct resemblance to that 'irresponsible traveller'; Waugh's irrational determination to accompany him recalls Tony Last's equally foolish infatuation with his expedition.

On the Governor's advice, Waugh turned his attention to a Mr Haynes, a commissioner for the Rupunini district. Haynes appears as 'Mr Bain' in *Ninety-Two Days*, 'a middle-aged, emaciated man, creole with some Indian blood. Like everyone else in the colony he had at one time worked gold and diamonds; like most other people he had also been a surveyor, a soldier, a policeman and a magistrate; he had lately returned to the last avocation which included most of the other functions.'[20] At first sight Haynes appeared perfectly sane. He had, he said, a boat setting out up the Essequibo. Waugh could have a place in the boat as far as Kurupukari. The offer was eagerly accepted. It was a triumphantly simple arrangement which would send Waugh some one hundred-and-fifty miles into the interior with minimal effort.

Unfortunately complications arose. No sooner had Waugh fixed on his plan and ordered his stores than Haynes began to make re-adjustments. An hour rarely passed without some further alteration. Stores were ordered, countermanded, re-ordered. In the end Haynes said it would be impossible for them to go by boat at all if the provisions were to be transported. There was only one alternative. They should take the train along the coast to New Amsterdam. From there they could both travel up the cattle trail to Kurupukari by horse. Waugh was by this time irritated and impatient. These delays meant further wasted days in Georgetown. It was Friday 30th December; everything would shortly be closed until the following Tuesday. In glum mood he bought bush clothes, mosquito net, gun, hammock, rum, flour, sugar and a variety of tinned foods, and prepared himself to endure four more days of festivity and inaction.

New Year's Eve in the capital was celebrated with vigour. There were dances and parties everywhere but Waugh wanted none of it. Instead, he sought seclusion in a cinema. Returning to the Tower, the spectacle of numerous drunken Scotsmen in ungainly attitudes upon the floor and the incessant strains of the pipes and Harry Lauder drove him out again. He had been invited to a ball at the Georgetown Club, where he repaired for whisky and supper. Nothing satisfactory was to come of the evening: he consumed too much whisky, ate poisoned crab-back, and on his return, four drunken youths in fancy dress sang beneath his window till dawn. He rose at seven, nauseated and irascible, to attend Mass. As the day progressed in the dead town his illness worsened to a point at which

20. *Ninety-Two Days*, pp. 34–5.

he assumed he had contracted malaria. He retired to his bedroom, took an enormous dose of chlorodyne and slept for eleven hours: an inauspicious start to the New Year.

The next day he woke feeling better but the journey up-country, now only a day away, seemed 'fantastical and unsubstantial'.[21] He wrote to Peters assuring him that the travel articles he had promised for *The Passing Show* and the *Daily Mail* would be in his hands by 18th April. To his parents he sent a sober and dutiful note explaining that he was about to disappear beyond the reach of post-offices: 'So dont imagine that anything untoward has happened if you dont hear from me for two months or even longer. It is all perfectly safe & healthy.'[22] Such polite fictions did little to disguise from himself the fact that Haynes seemed unreliable and that accounts of the interior suggested innumerable hazards. His final sentence to his parents: 'I'll come home by All Fool's Day or thereabouts . . .',[23] has an air of self-mockery about it, as though the journey were sure to result in ignominious defeat. Few of the colonials strayed further inland than the tourist route to the Kaiteur Falls. Perhaps sensing disaster, Waugh determined to make the most of his last day. After the races and dinner, Willems and he took up with two policemen and set out to search for loose women. Even this proved fruitless.

After Mass again at 7.00 on the 3rd January Waugh spent an exhausting morning with final purchases and packing. He left his luggage in Willems's charge to be forwarded to London in the event of his not returning via Georgtown (or not returning at all) and by mid-afternoon he was on the train to New Amsterdam sitting opposite Haynes, worrying about his companion. As he turned the fellow over in his mind he appeared increasingly unsound.

*

Haynes was garrulous and asthmatic, given to interminable discourses on the Meaning of Life. Linguistic oddities and general eccentricity always fascinated Waugh and Haynes seemed a character of farce, plunging into subjects on which he had the most tenuous grasp in scarcely comprehensible English. In his stories he usually cut a heroic figure; Waugh consequently thought him a coward. Haynes had a store of tales recalling the tiniest signs of approbation offered him during an undistinguished career; this misplaced boasting caused Waugh to mark him down as one of life's failures. The man's moods veered unpredictably from histrionic self-confidence to melancholy. In his darker moments he would collapse, gasping with asthma, and sit for hours rocking back and forth in his hammock, his head between his knees.

21. *Ibid.*, p. 39.
22. *Letters*, p. 69.
23. *Ibid.*, p. 69.

In *Ninety-Two Days* Waugh presents himself as the beneficently-minded *naïf* confronted by this phenomenon. 'Many of his stories I found to strain the normal limits of credulity', he remarks innocently, ' – such as that he had a horse which swam underwater and a guide who employed a parrot to bring him information; the bird would fly on ahead, said Mr Bain, and coming back to its perch on the Indian's shoulder whisper in his ear what he had seen, who was on the road and where they could find water.'[24] Watching a ranting Jordanite street-preacher in New Amsterdam declaiming against white men Mr Haynes turned sadly away and remarked, ' "The black man got a very inferior complex" '.[25] On the paddle steamer up the Berbice River to Takama where they were to pick up their mounts, Haynes fell into animated conversation with a rancher concerning Rupunini horses. Waugh listened with trepidation. The warmest terms of commendation for these animals concerned the ferocity of their bucking and bolting. It seemed that all he had learnt at Captain Hance's would have small application here: ' "Yes, she *could rear*," said Mr Bain in wistful admiration, "it was lovely to see her." '[26]

Haynes's flamboyant discourse contained one further element particularly irritating to Waugh. The Governor had apparently placed the young novelist in the commissioner's charge with instructions to secure his safety. Waugh could scarcely move without Haynes immediately interfering. 'If I helped to saddle the placid pack ox he would cry out, "Stand back, be careful, or he will kick out your brains." If I picked up my own gun he would say, "Be careful, it will go off and shoot you." '[27] This was scarcely the companion for a writer who 'instinctively [needed] an element of uncertainty and danger in his life'.

The entire trip was, from the point of view of exciting exploration, a profound disappointment to Waugh. As he says of the first stage (Takama to Kurupukari): 'It would be tedious to record the daily details of the journey. . . . Mr Bain managed everything; I merely trotted beside him. . . .'[28] The story of *Ninety-Two Days* is one of boredom, privation, and persistently deferred expectation. It would be pointless to recapitulate it in detail. Travelling to Kurupukari they covered fifteen miles a day, first across parched savannah, then through the submarine twilight of the jungle. Waugh's dislike of the picturesque and ignorance of natural science rendered it all a dull spectacle with countless ants. He knew nothing and cared less about flora and fauna. It took six days. From Kurupukari he would be rid of Haynes and anticipated adventure, facing the bush alone save for his porters. It was not to be.

Arrived there, exhausted not by the journey but by Haynes's incessant clap-

24. *Ninety-Two Days*, p. 42.
25. *Ibid.*, p. 45.
26. *Ibid.*, p. 45.
27. *Ibid.*, pp. 46–7.
28. *Ibid.*, p. 54.

trap ('Haynes did not once stop talking. . . . "Look at Napoleon. He was a little corporal. But he wanted to marry a princess so he divorced his wife. The Bolsheviks will soon start that too" '),[29] there was no sign of the promised boat. For three days Waugh was stuck in the commissioner's residence (a rudimentary shelter) with Haynes expatiating and expectorating. There was nothing to do but wait. As soon as supper was finished, and Waugh had scribbled a brief entry in his diary, they retired to their hammocks to lie and listen. In the tumultuous silence of the jungle the screeches and chatterings of the bush were punctuated by the noise of falling timber and Haynes's wheezing. Although sleepless, Waugh was unwilling to encourage his companion in conversation. He had tried on one occasion to elicit some useful local information from the man:

> . . . 'Listen,' said Mr Bain one day, 'that is most interesting. It is what
> we call the "six o'clock beetle" because he always makes that noise at
> exactly six o'clock.'
> 'But it's now quarter past four.'
> 'Yes, that is what is so interesting.'[30]

He did not repeat the experiment.

By the third day they had run out of potatoes, sugar, rum, tobacco and tinned foods. Waugh smoked a pipe and needed alcohol. Haynes was driving him to distraction. On the previous day he had decided, very bravely, that, if the boat failed to arrive within twenty-four hours, he would set out alone without stores to search for help. That evening, however, the small craft was spotted chugging up the Essequibo.

There was another day's delay while Haynes sorted the mail for Bon Success. Waugh spent the dull hours reading Thomas Aquinas and itemising his provisions:

> Stores in hand are: one bag sugar; one bag flour; one bag potatoes and
> onions; lamp; oil; cooking pots; three rum (gave three Haynes); five tins
> tobacco; ten cakes common soap; two tins herrings; nine bully beef; one
> jam; one biscuit; two tea; two cocoa; twelve Milkmaid milk; six Nestlés
> milk; one Bovril; two pineapple; five fruit; four salmon; three sausage;
> four meat and veg; four butter; two tongues; six tomato soup.[31]

This was a far cry from the exoticism of Abyssinia with his Fortnum and Mason's hampers and smart friends. The list of stores emphasises his preparation for rough life.

The next day (15th January) he crossed the river, deeply grateful to have left

29. *Diaries*, 11 January, 1933, p. 364.
30. *Ninety-Two Days*, p. 58.
31. *Diaries*, 14 January, 1933, p. 365.

Haynes behind. He happily anticipated jogging off alone up the forest trail and feeling like an explorer for the first time in his life. His assistants (Price, a mulatto police sergeant, and Yetto, a negro porter who had been with the party since Takama) had been sent on ahead with supplies and pack horse. Waugh's immediate objective was the Jesuit mission at Bon Success on the Brazilian frontier. In his pocket he carried letters of introduction to the priests there from Frs Martin D'Arcy and Ned King. All seemed set, at last, for the real adventure to begin.

As the diary records, only vexation lay ahead:

> Set out after breakfast having sent Price and Yetto on at 10 am. Just as starting, boatman Duggin arrived with large tin of tinned foods saying pack horse had refused to start and had had to be lightened. Started in displeasure and one mile along trail found pack-horse tethered to tree, packs beside him. Price and Yetto chatting. They said pack-horse still refused to go. Took off another pile of stores. Set out and rode ahead. After ten miles found pack not following and turned back. Price and Yetto and horse at eight-mile point. Horse had lain down four times. Left packs; rode back telling Yetto to follow. . . . [32]

That evening found him, after a twenty-mile ride, back at Kurupukari, hailing across the darkening waters of the Essequibo for assistance from Haynes. It was not only frustrating but embarrassing. Haynes accepted his return with equanimity: 'He had never thought I would get far alone.'[33]

The next day he tried again. The pack horse was replaced by a donkey called Maria and an additional assistant, 'a vain young negro called Sinclair'.[34] Waugh loathed the latter and soon found that Price and Yetto held the young fellow in equal disdain. Yetto was much more to Waugh's taste: a muscular buccaneer who had made money and spent it. He prided himself on his strength and invited others to heap his pack. Sinclair mooned about, carrying only his personal belongings and, according to Waugh, 'malingering'. He was, nevertheless, a useful member of the party as he was the only one who knew how to cook.

The trail to Bon Success was a series of dismal stages from rest-house to rest-house, interspersed by slightly more luxurious accommodation in ranches along

32. *Ibid.*, 15 January, 1933, pp. 365–6. It is interesting to compare this diary entry with its reconstruction in *Ninety-Two Days*, pp. 69–70. In the travel book Waugh 'invents' conversation to embellish the comedy of frustration and distorts the facts very slightly to fabricate a more readable narrative. Instead of being met by Duggin at the outset, for instance, he pictures himself 'jogging happily up the trail' before encountering him, thus heightening the disappointment. He also adds a fulsome, and uncharacteristically sentimental, evocation of the beauty of the sunset which he says made a profound impression upon him. Not a word about this appears in the diary.
33. *Ninety-Two Days*, p. 70.
34. *Ibid.*, p. 70.

the route. The word 'resthouse' suggests something akin to a bed and breakfast establishment to the modern reader. In fact these places were scarcely more than sheds: rough timber frameworks with stinking and verminous thatched roofs under which travellers could sling a hammock for the night. The single tolerable aspect of the journey for Waugh was Yetto's history. During the first stage of the expedition from Tukama Haynes's unstaunchable chatter had prevented talk with any of the 'boys'. Now, in the evening, with rum and firelight, Waugh sat captivated by the negro's autobiography. Yetto had, it seems, once formed a part of the police guard of honour during a royal visit and had shaken hands with the Prince of Wales; he had been on adventures in Cuba; he had been unhappily married. Once as a 'pork-knocker' (diamond prospector) he had struck lucky, gone to Georgetown with $800 and spent it in six months. Most of that time had been passed in more or less continual sexual intercourse in a taxi driving round and round the town. Waugh liked this man.

It did not take Waugh long to discover that the local maps were unreliable and that places marked prominently as towns scarcely existed. Surama was a collection of a dozen or so huts; Annai was a single house and an outbuilding. It was a relief at Annai to be released from the claustrophobia of the forest and to find the savannah stretching before him, but the open country brought its own hazards: fierce heat and high winds during the day, penetrating cold at night. So windy was it that, if he wanted to light a pipe, he had to project his face into a boot. His horses were feeble and had to be changed twice. Having picked up a one-eyed chestnut stallion at Annai, Waugh found that he could not handle it. It stopped dead and refused to move. On further encouragement it reared, performed a back flip and very nearly rolled on him. The fall shook him badly and it was in this condition, his face skinned by the sun, exhausted, and suffering from delayed shock, that he arrived at Mr Christie's ranch.

\*

Mr Christie now has a firm place in literary history. In 1946 Waugh wrote an article explaining how this came to be: '*A Handful of Dust*', he remarked, ' . . . began at the end. I had written a short story about a man trapped in the jungle, ending his days reading Dickens aloud. The idea came quite naturally from the experience of visiting a lonely settler of that kind and reflecting how easily he could hold me prisoner. . . .'[35] That settler was Mr Christie and he was to prove an admirable addition to Waugh's 'treasury of eccentrics'.[36]

'Ranch' inadequately describes the huddle of huts Waugh discovered on the afternoon of 20th January. The place seemed deserted. Christie was an infamously

35. 'Fan-Fare', *Life* (International: Chicago), 8 April, 1946, 53–4, 56, 58, 60; *EAR*, pp. 300–4 and *CH*, pp. 248–53.
36. *Ninety-Two Days*, p. 234.

inhospitable figure in those parts and was known to be 'religious'. Waugh was anxious to meet him. He wandered curiously round the apparently deserted compound and then headed for the largest house. It was, he noted in *Ninety-Two Days*,

> ... only half built but there was another near it with dilapidated thatch, open at all sides, which was distinguishable from the others by a plank floor, raised a couple of feet from the earth. Here, reclining in a hammock and sipping cold water from the spout of a white enamelled tea pot was Mr Christie.
>
> He had a long white moustache and a white woolly head; his face was of the same sun-baked, fever-blanched colour as were most faces in the colony but of unmistakable negro structure.... I greeted him and asked where I could water my horse. He smiled in a dreamy, absent-minded manner and said, 'I was expecting you. I was warned in a vision of your approach.... I always know the character of my visitors by the visions I have of them. Sometimes I see a pig or a jackal; often a ravening tiger.'
>
> I could not resist asking, 'And how did you see me?'
>
> 'As a sweetly toned harmonium' said Mr Christie politely.[37]

Of all eccentrics Waugh particularly relished the religious maniac.[38] Christie was plain barmy and potentially dangerous. Waugh had no option other than to stay there the night, but we might suspect that he would have chosen to do so in any case. The man was a rich vein and Waugh tapped it assiduously:

> Questioned him about theology. 'Believe in Trinity. I couldn't live without them. But they are no mystery. It is all quite simple. It is in O[ld] T[estament] where – married his mother.'... He had been to see the 'elect'; found them few but hard to count as no bodies.[39]

The hyphen (a squiggled line in the manuscript) presumably represents the word 'God'. Even in this private account Waugh was not prepared to commit blasphemy to paper. But this did not prevent his delighting in the absurdity of Christie's Biblical misreadings. It was precisely this distinction in Waugh's mind, between blasphemy and the mockery of heresy, that Earnest Oldmeadow failed to observe in his review of *Black Mischief* which the novelist discovered on his return.

That night, after his bath, Waugh settled down to consume the best part of a bottle of rum mixed with limes, brown sugar and river water. Only in the morning

37. *Ibid.*, pp. 86–7.
38. The MS of *Decline and Fall* reveals that Waugh had at least three stabs at describing the religious maniac with whom Paul Pennyfeather is incarcerated, each version funnier than the last.
39. *Diaries*, 20 January, 1933, p. 367.

did he realise how much he had drunk. 'The sweet and splendid spirit, the exhaustion of the day, its heat, thirst, hunger and the effects of the fall, the fantastic conversations of Mr Christie, translated that evening and raised it a finger's breadth above reality.'[40]

\*

Two days later Waugh arrived at Bon Success bumping across the savannah in a Ford truck. It was the only motorised vehicle for hundreds of miles and he had found it the day before at one of the more civilised establishments of the interior, Mr Hart's ranch. Examining that house's odd 'library' (boxes of books ravaged by ants, which also found their way into *A Handful of Dust*) he had discovered Fr Carey-Elwes's diaries. They were reprinted in a mission magazine and he had spent a happy hour or two examining them.

Carey-Elwes had been another reason for Waugh's coming to British Guiana. As a relative of a friend of his, the painter Simon Elwes, Waugh had heard tales of this missionary at home. Apparently he had left the country suffering from a complete breakdown. Waugh had tried to cross-question Christie on the matter but had received only an insane story of Elwes having defiled a holy place by boiling a chicken. Elwes, he was delighted to discover, had also stayed with Christie and had left in his journal an account not dissimilar to Waugh's. Now, at last, he was approaching St Ignatius Mission, where he could hope to learn more of the Catholic work of the country from another sensible Jesuit, Fr Mather.

We have Mather's own affectionate description of Waugh's stay in a letter to F. J. Stopp. 'We had no comforts to offer', he wrote, 'only goodwill and that was enough to satisfy him. Friendship sprang up at once. . . .'[41] Waugh's opinion of the priest was equally generous:

> He was at work in his carpenter's shop when we arrived and came out to greet us, dusting the shavings off his khaki shirt and trousers, and presenting a complete antithesis of the 'wily Jesuit' of popular tradition. Like all his Society, Fr Mather is a self-effacing man and I think he would not relish any further personal description. He is a skilled and conscientious craftsman; everything he does from developing films to making saddles is done with patient accuracy.[42]

40. *Ninety-Two Days*, p. 88.
41. Unpublished ALS to Dr F. J. Stopp from H. C. Mather SJ, 5 July, 1954, from Main St Presbytery, Georgetown, British Guiana. Dr Stopp was compiling information for his book, *Evelyn Waugh. Portrait of an Artist* (Chapman and Hall, 1958). He did not use the letter but it is included in his papers, the F. J. Stopp Collection in CUL. Fr Mather transcribed extracts from his diaries. He left Takutu in 1943. Waugh's diaries and *Ninety-Two Days* suggest that he arrived at the Mission in a motor lorry; Mather's letter states: 'He arrived in a bullock-cart (about tea-time 4 pm, I think) after a tough journey.'
42. *Ninety-Two Days*, p. 101.

The mission seemed, by contrast with Christie and the general discomforts of British Guiana, a haven of order, craftsmanship and peaceful religious observance.

Waugh stayed there for nine days until 1st February, happily doing very little. It was a watershed in his journey. Yetto and Sinclair were sent back. Each morning he would hear Mass at seven with the farm hands (the mission was also a ranch) after which Fr Mather would retire to his workshop. Waugh read Cunninghame Graham on the Jesuits in Paraguay and relaxed in the slow, methodical life of this outpost of the Faith. In comparison with the missions he had visited in Uganda with their zealous congregations, nuns and children's choirs, he found St Ignatius distinctly refreshing. Here the life was starker but the pace more leisurely. Sugary churchiness and community spirit he always found difficult. Here he could idle the days away in congenial male company, chatting with Fr Mather, going for walks with him on the savannah, photographing an Indian village, visiting a local ranch and store. It was the happiest period of the entire expedition.

In this easy atmosphere he discussed the possibilities of extending his travels into Brazil. Manãos, deep in the Amazon Basin, had long been a city of romantic associations for the European imagination with its incongruous Opera House. Waugh decided to make this his objective, travelling via Boa Vista. Bon Success was on the Takutu River which here formed part of the border between the two countries. He hoped to canoe downstream to, and beyond, the confluence with the Rio Branco to Boa Vista. The Rio Branco led directly to Manãos.

Fr Mather dissuaded him from attempting the Takutu river journey. The water was low, it was dangerous; better to follow the trail beside the river. Waugh then discovered that it was possible to cut straight across country via Boa Vista. It was an arduous trek but it would save at least a week on the road. With silent misgivings David Max y Hung (Mather's *vaqueiro*) agreed to accompany him and in blinding heat they set off across the parched savannah, David's brother-in-law Chikino leading the way on a pack-horse.[43]

Those three days were the first period of real privation Waugh had experienced. His luggage was now reduced to a canvas grip and a rucksack. Provisions were kept to a minimum to hasten the transit, every ounce being calculated in terms of the energy required to shift it. It was the custom of the country to travel without water, partly to reduce load and partly because the land was usually well-supplied with streams. But January to April were the dry months. Stopping at noon on the second day they found that a long-anticipated creek was reduced to muddy puddles fit only for washing down the horses. That day they rode from dawn to sunset without a drink. For the most part they lived on *farine* (coarse flour) and *tasso* (dried beef). They were not in any serious danger. But the heat and thirst, the long hours in the saddle and the miseries of the diet, caused

43. Cf. *ibid.*, p. 116.

Waugh to fantasise about Boa Vista. It had, he says, ' . . . come to assume greater and greater importance to me'. Most people ' . . . had spoken of it as a town of dazzling attractions'.[44] The pain of those sixty miles was somewhat ameliorated by the promise of respite in civilised surroundings.

Fr Mather had packed him off with a letter of recommendation to the Benedictine Priory. On arrival, however, Waugh found only a single monk, whose spirit of hospitality was largely nullified by illness. The town itself was a 'ramshackle huddle of buildings'.[45] Never, it seemed, had a place been so inappropriately named. From the first Waugh felt uncomfortable there. It was shabby in a way that contrasted sharply with the ascetic and aesthetic order of Fr Mather's establishment. The Boundary Commission[46] had a boat heading for Manãos in six days. There was little to do but wait, an unwelcome guest of the lugubrious Brother Alcuin.

Part of Waugh's frustration was the result of his own ignorance. A German and a Swiss were also staying at the Priory. Waugh spoke no German and only schoolboy French. At mealtimes he found himself struggling between three languages and unendurably bored. 'Conversation difficult', he noted in his diary on the evening of the first day, 'particularly as German's English quite unintelligible. He is local planter. Walked up and down terrace after dinner until I insisted on sitting. Bed 8 o'clock. Took large dose of chlorodyne and slept heavily with vivid dreams.'[47]

Each day he attended Mass at seven and benediction twelve hours later. The time between was torture. He would explore the streets but could find nothing worthy of investigation. In *Ninety-Two Days* the place is characterised as something akin to a 'wild-west' frontier town. The people are seen as alternately idle and murderous:

> They are naturally homicidal by inclination, and every man, however poor, carries arms; only the universal apathy keeps them from frequent bloodshed. There were no shootings while I was there; in fact there had not been one for several months, but I lived all the time in an atmosphere that was novel to me, where murder was always in the air.[48]

This may have been true, but the diaries make no mention of it. In fact, he seems to have been merely bored. He would go out for a beer in the evenings with the German and a lonely storekeeper, retire early with chlorodyne and thankfully kill another day.

44. *Ibid.*, p. 116.
45. *Ibid.*, p. 116.
46. Fr Mather's letter notes that the British Guiana-Brazil Boundary Commission was 'in progress'.
47. *Diaries*, 4 February, 1933, p. 370.
48. *Ninety-Two Days*, p. 124.

The discovery of Dr Roth's bastard son working as a boatman and blacksmith did nothing to improve matters. He was the only English-speaking person there, a pallid, cadaverous youth who harboured only resentment towards his father and was a melancholy companion. He held out little hope of Waugh's obtaining a place in the Boundary Commission launch and he proved correct. On the day he made this miserable discovery Waugh entered in his diary: 'Six days of degrading boredom. Nothing to read but some lives of the Saints in French and Bossuet's sermons. The German's conversations unbearable. The priest confined to his room with fever.' The Commissioner was 'amiable but immovable. His boat was already full.'[49] It was a bitter disappointment.

There was talk of a cargo boat due in a few days' time. But Waugh had effectively given up all hope of reaching Manãos. The romance of the place had been dissipated by his incarceration in Boa Vista. On first arriving he had written a jocular letter to the Lygon girls:

> Well I have gone too far as usual & now I am in Brazil. Do come out & visit me. It is easy to find on account of it being the most vast of the republics of South America. . . . You go up the Amazon, easily recognisable on account of its being the largest river in the world, then right at Rio Negro. . . . The streets are entirely paved with gold which gives a very pretty effect especially towards sunset. But otherwise it is rather dull. . . .[50]

After a week of suspended animation he found his situation beyond a joke. Boredom had even driven him back to literary composition: 'Wrote a bad article yesterday but thought of plot for short story.'[51] The next day's entry (13th February) reveals that the story was finished. He was pleased with it but could not have guessed how its theme would nag at his imagination, eventually to generate his next novel. The story was 'The Man Who Liked Dickens'.

The subject of the article is less easily defined. Waugh posted his story to Peters from Boa Vista on 15th February saying that he enclosed 'one first-rate story and three second-rate articles'.[52] Two of the articles, he suggests, could go to the *Daily Mail* and the other was for the open market.[53] On his return to London Waugh was appalled to find that the *Mail* had re-titled a piece on the

49. *Diaries*, 10 February, 1933, p. 371. Davie reads 'four days'; MS reads 'six days'. The latter makes perfectly good sense as he had arrived in Boa Vista on 4 February.
50. *Letters*, pp. 69–70.
51. *Diaries*, 12 February, 1933, p. 371.
52. Unpublished ALS to A. D. Peters, 15 February, 1933, np [from Boa Vista]; HRC; *Catalogue*, E208, pp. 102–3.
53. The *Mail* bought 'The Shadow Land' and 'Brazilian Hospitality' and *NPMM* one entitled 'Debunking the Bush', later sold to Randolph Churchill's *Oxford and Cambridge Magazine*.

Rupunini District, 'My Escape From Mayfair'.[54] Nothing could have been further from his image of himself writing this hack-work in Boa Vista than that of the jaunty society author. He was profoundly depressed. Whatever the difficulties, he had to get out.

Escaping from Boa Vista, though, was far from straightforward. Having abandoned Manãos he had decided to return to British Guiana, if possible following a different route back to Georgetown. But where on British territory horses and supplies could be collected efficiently, in Brazil, linguistically marooned as he was between French, German and Portuguese, such arrangements were annoyingly protracted. It took three days to gather saddles and mounts and three attempts before he actually set out. The story of these frustrations Waugh transforms into a supreme comedy of manners in *Ninety-Two Days*.

A new Prior was due to arrive with some ceremony on the day of his first attempt. Waugh was sorry to miss him but he had to get down to the river and await his guide. Arrangements had been made for the man to conduct a second horse to the crossing there during the afternoon. Marco (the guide) failed to appear until nearly dark. It seemed that the horse had evaded capture for some time. Marco was keen to compensate for his tardiness by plunging straight into the dark water. But Waugh thought it too dangerous and, quite simply, too late to initiate a journey into strange territory.

There was no alternative but to return to the Priory where he discovered the Prior, newly installed and in mid-repast. He had been sent to tidy things up in this infamous district. Waugh burst in, wet to the knees and breathless, uncertain as to the etiquette of the situation. Should he interrupt to explain his return? Or should he slip quietly into his place at table and begin eating as though nothing had happened? Clearly some introduction was required. He interrupted. The Prior, he remarks in *Ninety-Two Days*, 'had already fixed me with a look of marked aversion'[55] but there was nothing for it. The explanation apparently did little to dispel suspicion. Waugh hastened to bed early, and rose at 5.30, keen to be gone before more awkward farewells. Once again the horse was mislaid and this time the canoe also had disappeared. He returned to the Priory for lunch, its spiritual leader now confirmed in his misgivings. The afternoon was spent waiting for *vaqueiros* to scour the countryside for the elusive quadruped. Eventually it was secured and another nag bought blind to serve as a pack animal. Everything at last seemed set fair for departure. But by then evening was again drawing in. Deeply embarrassed, Waugh returned to the Priory for dinner. 'Prior convinced', he scribbled in his diary that night, 'I am mad and undesirable'.[56]

On the third day he rose again and crossed the river in Roth's motor launch.

54. Cf. ALS to Henry Yorke from Grand Pump Room Hotel, Bath, May 1933; *Letters*, p. 71.
55. *Ninety-Two Days*, p. 143.
56. *Diaries*, 17 February, 1933, p. 372.

The pack horse was waiting on the other side. One look assured Waugh that this miserable beast was worth considerably less than the pound he had paid for it. No sooner had they started than it went lame. But he was not going to turn back again. 'Only possible get [horse] along with great cruelty but what else to do?'[57] Returning to the Priory a fourth time was out of the question. He pressed on into the wilderness hoping to change the animal at the first ranch.

During the second day they crossed the Takutu back into British territory and here their real troubles began. On the slimmest cartographical or topographical evidence he convinced himself that he could pinpoint his position. According to his calculations they were only four or five hours from the St Ignatius Mission and, as they were running short of food and water, he decided to change the itinerary and head straight for Fr Mather. He informed Marco (who understood only Portuguese) and rode on ahead on the best horse, confident that he would be dining with the priest that evening.

It was a particularly stupid move and one only attributable to Waugh's moods of astonishing arrogance. He describes Marco as his 'guide' in the diary but seems to have been incapable of allowing himself to be instructed. The language barrier was no problem; all he needed to have done was to have followed and he would have been led to safety. But no, Waugh had to be 'Bwana'. In his diaries and travel book he protects his self-esteem at this stage by dropping the pose of naïf and substituting that of competent leader. Anyone, he suggests, could have made his mistake. The maps were inaccurate and he had only a young man for a companion. Given the evidence at his disposal he had made a reasonable decision.

We might ask how, if he assumed that Marco did not know the way, he expected him to follow? If Marco did know the way, then why did he leave him behind? The charitable answer must be that Waugh had not the smallest inkling of his own geographical incompetence and had no doubt whatsoever that he was right.[58] This was the first time he had travelled 'alone' in poorly-charted country and he made a hopeless mess of it. In retrospect it appears that he could not even read a compass accurately.

As night began to fall that apparently indomitable self-confidence began to waver. He knew that he should by then have reached the Mission and the landscape which had at first appeared familiar now seemed strange. He was

57. *Ibid.*, 18 February, 1933, p. 373.
58. In *Ninety-Two Days* Waugh, perhaps unconsciously, suggests that he was only concerned with his own safety. After emphasising the harshness of the country and the dangers of losing one's way he remarks: 'Marco, who had everything with him including my hammock, was some miles behind. It is easy in that district to pass within a quarter of a mile of someone and not see him. Since I was off the trail there was no probability of his picking it up if I stopped to wait' (p. 151). The generous interpretation of this is that Marco knew the trail and would be safe.

exhausted, dehydrated and had eaten nothing for twenty-four hours. The horse could no longer support him and had to be led. He was lost and had abandoned his guide. Waugh knew that he could travel for hundreds of miles without meeting anyone but shy Indians who would scuttle away at his approach and who, if cornered, spoke only Macushi. The situation was desperate. Without water he would probably have been unable to keep moving for more than another day.

Fortunately, after dark, he benefited from a chance meeting, the odds against which he calculated to be 1:54,750,000.[59] He came upon an old Indian who spoke English, had surplus food in his hut and was planning to travel to Bon Success the next day. It was certainly an uncanny coincidence. Waugh later preferred to describe it as supernatural intervention. Sensing that he might be approaching death, he had remembered the St Christopher medal Teresa had given him and prayed for safe conduct. Immediately afterwards he had found the Indian. Convinced that his rescue was miraculous, Waugh sank into sleep, thankful that he was a Catholic.

Next day Fr Mather received a scribbled note brought by a Wapisiana Indian: ' . . . No luck at Boa Vista. Am at present stranded at Gore's ranch. . . .'[60] Mather had sought out David and sent him off immediately with a spare horse but Waugh and he must have crossed without seeing each other. Our hero had discovered Marco waiting calmly for him on the trail as the ancient Indian and his family guided Waugh towards Bon Success.

Marco's enthusiasm at their reunion had at first surprised and then pleased him. He admits in *Ninety-Two Days* that 'Up till then, for no very good reason, I had rather disliked the youth'.[61] Perhaps he felt a pang of remorse and embarrassment on discovering that his guide had known the route perfectly well. The party had continued round the Kanuku mountains and separated at Gore's ranch where the Indian was paid off in barter goods: red cotton, fish hooks, a knife, a necklace and a bright celluloid comb. Here Waugh lunched and wrote his note, but did not wait for assistance. He ploughed on, aching in every muscle, badly sunburned and irritable until, at two in the afternoon, Fr Mather saw him plodding up alone on his weary horse. Marco appears to have been left in Bon Success.

This time there were two priests in residence. Fr Keary, a tall, raw-boned Irishman, used the Mission as his base but spent most of his time servicing the Catholic community in a wide circuit of Indian villages. He was a silent, tough man, an ex-army chaplain with a bush of grizzled beard, radically different from Mather. Where Mather would gossip and bustle about indefatigably in Waugh's service, Keary kept his own counsel. And as it happened that only Keary could help Waugh in his proposed return journey, the man's reticence was to prove

59. *Ninety-Two Days*, p. 154.
60. ALS to F. J. Stopp; *op. cit.*
61. *Ninety-Two Days*, p. 154.

problematic. *Ninety-Two Days* is uniformly gracious towards him. The *Diaries*, in contrast, reveal that an unarticulated tension developed between these two abrasive personalities.

The return to St Ignatius effectively marks the end of Waugh's adventure, only one other place being worthy of note: Mr Winter's diamond mine. He had met Winter in Georgetown and struck up a friendship. The plan was to cross the mountains to Winter's camp, head on for the Kaiteur Falls and to continue down river to Georgetown. Fr Keary could not wait for him but set off for the Patamona country on 25th February, Waugh leaving eight days later with the intention of catching up with the priest on the trail.

There was no rush. Keary had plenty of clerical business which would delay his progress and Waugh needed respite before the long haul home. He sat and read, and slept a great deal. In the Mission library (perhaps that short story was already turning in his head) he found some copies of Dickens's novels. Arthur Waugh was an expert on Dickens, having edited the Nonesuch Edition for Chapman and Hall. In his younger son's imagination the novelist had formerly represented the fatuous optimism of Victorian humanism. Waugh associated Dickens with the 'old men' and their concepts of progress. And yet, in this timeless outpost of religion, apart from the social pressures of contemporary western life, he found himself avidly devouring the sentimentalities of *Dombey and Son*:

> The other pleasure [apart from bathing] I discovered, oddly enough, was reading: or rather re-discovered, for I seem to recall having experienced some pleasure in this occupation as a child. But never since; I have read numerous books for various reasons – to acquire information; out of politeness because I knew the author; I have dipped into most best-sellers to make up my mind whether they were justly or unjustly successful, and as soon as I knew, have put them aside; I have raced through detective stories because the problems they set leave an itch for completion . . .; I have read books because I was being paid to review them, but I have not for ten years read a book for the mere pleasure of the process. At Father Mather's, I began to read with this motive and by good chance the books he had were just those which were meant to be read in this way and when I left him I took away a copy of *Nicholas Nickleby* and read it with avid relish during the ensuing journey, bit by bit while the light lasted, grudging the night every hour of her splendour and the day its toil, which kept me from this new and exciting hobby.
>
> Alas [this pleasure has] eluded me since I came back to Europe . . . the rapture is gone. . . .[62]

62. *Ibid.*, pp. 160–1.

The statement makes the choice of Dickens as an instrument of torture for Tony Last all the more poignant. His readings to Mr Todd are painful to him (and to us) because they represent precisely the reverse of Waugh's experience here. By definition, the 'pleasure of the process' is out of the question and by implication (see Waugh's concluding remarks) that pure imaginative joy is alienated and destroyed among the barbarians of Europe as effectively as it is among the savages of the rain forest.

On his last day at the mission Waugh noted with gratitude his host's practical benevolence: 'Father Mather has done innumerable things for me, mending saddles, making a pack-saddle, measuring out farine, flour etc., making bags, cutting walking-sticks, packing films, mending watch-glass etc.'[63] The priest also taught him how to barter ('1 tin gunpowder equals 1 chicken')[64] and arranged for horses, a pack bullock and a Macushi guide, Eusebio. As a valedictory gesture Mather gave him a copy of *Martin Chuzzlewit* (not *Nicholas Nickleby*, it seems)[65] and an aneroid barometer. 'Mutual regrets at parting and good wishes', Mather wrote in his own diary.[66]

The aneroid was necessary for Waugh to record the ascent of the trail; the Dickens to allay boredom. Eusebio, pleasant as he was, promised little in the way of companionship. According to Waugh he would say 'Yes Father' to every enquiry. It looked as though it would be a tedious journey and indeed it was. Mather's letter is enthusiastic about the weather and topography: 'January to April are dry months – terrific breeze, beautiful weather – everything glorious. . . . Grand country – magnificent mountains – utterly different from the dismal muddy coast of B[ritish] Guiana.'[67] None of this inspired Waugh. His diary records a monotonous trek via local ranches towards the foothills of the mountains (where he again succeeded in losing his way by attempting a short cut). It is dreary reading reflecting his own disaffection with this dogged plodding across savannah, baked marshland, dry gullies and mountains.

The next fortnight was a purgatory of exhaustion and insects. Kabouri flies were his particular bane in the first week: small red creatures which could penetrate a mosquito net and left the skin smarting horribly. Then came the mosquitoes, fleas and djiggers (insects which burrowed through boots to the sole of the foot and laid eggs beneath the nails and skin). He muffled his hands in handkerchiefs and his head in a scarf but it did little good. The nights were biting cold. He slept with full kit over his pyjamas and shivered beneath the blanket.

63. *Diaries*, 4 March, 1933, p. 375.
64. *Ibid.*, p. 375.
65. The *Diaries* (4 March, 1933, p. 375) state that he 'Borrowed . . . *Chuzzlewit*', not *Nickleby*, on his departure.
66. ALS to F. J. Stopp; *op. cit.*
67. *Ibid.*

Four days out (9th March) he at last overtook Fr Keary in a village called Tipuru, a thousand feet above sea-level. The priest was about his business, instructing the Indians (in fluent Macushi). He took time off to try to secure Waugh a guide, porters and hunter for the next stage of the trail through the mountains. None could be found, 'so Father Keary kindly changed his plans and decided to start with me tomorrow'.[68] This, perhaps, was the root cause of the awkwardness between them. Keary had important business to attend to on his circuit. Waugh makes out in *Ninety-Two Days* that Keary was perfectly happy to alter course to accommodate him and doubtless the priest charitably wished to convey this impression. But his schedule was exhausting and exact. Under the circumstances he had small option other than to revise it and it cannot have pleased him to have had to do so because a smart young novelist had found himself in difficulties on what was, by all accounts, an expedition purely for personal pleasure and profit.

For ten more days they trudged upwards from village to village ('Father Keary baptised a child and married the parents')[69] largely in silence. Keary told his beads. Waugh counted the days and scratched himself raw. On the 12th March he recorded: 'Very bad night as moon kept *kabouras* [*sic*] awake – also great number of fleas, some mosquitoes, and old bites itching intolerably.'[70] Part of the divide that began to open between Keary and Waugh seems to have been caused by Waugh's inexperience at protracted rough-country transit. Keary was a sinewy, well-tested bushman. Although a generation older than Waugh, he pushed on methodically, so many miles a day, apparently impervious to exhaustion and bad weather. Waugh was relatively 'soft' and his masculine pride was probably irritated by this unfavourable comparison – all the more so because Keary would not speak. Waugh was simply not fit enough. Weight fell from him. Sleeping badly he woke exhausted and often damp. The impossibility of giving vent to his discomfort in the presence of a priest must have exacerbated the tension.

To be fair to Waugh, it was a tough schedule. He did well to keep up with Keary for as long as he did and his determination not to be a handicap says much for his tenacity. In the end it was simply bad luck which caused him to slow the party down. Djiggers had to be removed as soon as they were detected. Normally it was a painless process, picking them out with a pin. On the morning of 14th February, though, after having had six or seven extracted (*Ninety-Two Days* expands this to 'a dozen or more'),[71] he woke to find himself lame in both feet. It was a grave handicap. By then some two-and-a-half thousand feet up in the

68. *Diaries*, 9 March, 1933, p. 377.
69. *Ibid.*, 11 March, 1933, p. 378.
70. *Ibid.*, 12 March, 1933, p. 378.
71. *Ninety-Two Days*, p. 188.

mountains, most of the journey was on foot, leading the pack animals through a low-cut path in the forest.

He hobbled on between the two sticks Fr Mather had presented, taking frequent swigs of brandy. But a two nights' rest at Kurikabaru did little to help his injuries. His feet were badly bruised and though the pin-pricks in the soles had healed, a big toe was now infected. Even worse, provisions were running low. They were now still two days' normal travelling from Winter's camp. It was 'hunger rather than restored fitness that decided us on the march'.[72] The journey took five days and they were agony for Waugh.

His lameness necessitated the hiring of a small, plump stallion. ' . . . I set out the next morning, a relieved, if highly comic figure, riding bareback with Antonio [Keary's guide] leading the horse by his rope.'[73] Waugh tries to make light of it in *Ninety-Two Days* but he found the situation acutely undignified. Tortured by bites, hungry, lame and angry he was forced, because of the nature of the terrain, to keep hopping on and off his tiny steed. While he hung low over the neck to dodge overhanging branches, those pushed aside ahead of him whipped back painfully across his face. His poisoned toe would be regularly buffeted against tree trunks. And though the boot had been cut to ease the pressure, he could not support this persistent attack from the undergrowth for more than a few minutes at a time. Jumping down he would skip along until that, too, became unendurable. And so the process continued.

Inevitably his ill-temper began to find expression: 'the official map of the [Essequibo] river system was wildly inaccurate and, what with my complaints about the complexity of the geography, and my lameness, I must, I think, have proved a very tiresome travelling companion to Father Keary.'[74] There seems little doubt of that and, equally, that Keary's stoical silence became irksome for Waugh. The night before their arrival at Winter's completed his misery. The roof of their shelter collapsed in Waugh's section under torrential rain. Fr Keary helped him re-sling his hammock in the only unflooded corner and then retired to his own (dry) room. Waugh, soaked and sleepless, sat up all night in the steep U-bend of his immovable bed, head on knees, listening with uncharitable irritation to the priest's snores.

After this, the modest comforts of Winter's camp were positively luxurious. Winter was a vast improvement on Keary as a companion, 'full of good conversation'.[75] There was an enforced halt here for ten days while they waited for Winter's boat to return, but Waugh was happy to lay up for a while. He was stiff and sore and needed to allow his foot to heal. There was time to dawdle round

72. *Ibid.*, p. 190.
73. *Ibid.*, p. 193.
74. *Ibid.*, p. 192.
75. *Diaries*, 18 March, 1933, p. 381.

the diamond workings and to observe the social habits and language of the small Patamona Indian labour force. The only difficulty was that the camp had insufficient supplies to support Keary's retinue. The priest was forced to trek back to Kurikabaru (all uphill) the next day. 'There', Waugh says, 'he would probably be able to collect cassava and yams. It was not a very satisfactory prospect and I watched him go with concern – but there was no possible alternative.'[76] The *Diaries* are perhaps more honest. 'Father Keary went off at 9. Glad to see last of him. Spent restful day in hammock.'[77] Thus relieved, he divided *Chuzzlewit* in half with Winter and settled down to the last chapters unperturbed.

The remainder of Waugh's journey can be compressed into small space. Between 30th March and 4th April he travelled down through foothills and ruined plantations to the headwaters of the Essequibo and thus to the coast. For company he had two of Winter's negro workmen, Sobers and Gerry, and a small family of Patamona Indians (father, mother and son), though 'company' inadequately describes the latter as far as Waugh was concerned. Uniformly silent, they infuriated him by what he took to be their constitutional idleness and compounded their felony by bringing a dog. Waugh's attitude was simple: if they were to share in the expedition, they ought to share in the work. Taking a flat-bottomed boat downriver he was at one point so roused by their refusal to paddle the craft that he did so himself. (This merely resulted in severe muscular strain.) The Indians (who were there to act as porters for Winter's stores on the return journey, not as boatmen for Waugh) sat placidly unimpressed in the stern chewing odd morsels of repulsive food.

At the Kaiteur Falls Waugh left them behind with no compunction and no certainty that they could survive on the land. He saw their disinterest in visiting this spectacular landmark as symptomatic of a deeper malaise. It seems not to have occurred to him that as natives of the area they had probably seen the Falls a hundred times. On discovering that the only available boat was too small to accommodate everyone, he abandoned them.

Ironically, Kaiteur was less interesting to him for his own betrayal than for the story of another lost traveller. Carved on the wall of the rest-house he found 'Alfredo Sacremento, Author and Globe Trotter starved here'. Winter had already told the tale of this fellow who had scrounged his way into the interior and then found himself at the Falls without food or hope of escape for six months. Winter had discovered him ten days later and slowly nursed him back to health. As Waugh was setting off on the last stage of his journey, it seems that this story became part of that amalgam of images relating to isolation and desperation beyond the citadels of civilisation which was ultimately to find expression in *A Handful of Dust*.

76. *Ninety-Two Days*, p. 198.
77. *Diaries*, 19 March, 1933, p. 381.

Two days later he found himself crushed into a trailer beneath a tarpaulin with a group of coloured people. They were being towed by tractor between Rockstone and Wismar where Waugh's ship was docked. It was raining; he thought the blacks smelt; the transit took over four hours. When, at four in the morning, he was able to clamber up the gangplank, it was with considerable relief that he slung his hammock on board and snatched two hours' sleep in a cloud of mosquitoes. Longer rest was impossible. Early next day the grinding of machinery and babble of voices signalled imminent departure. He rose, went ashore to pay bills, and hurried back. At 8.30 they sailed. By early afternoon he was back in the colony's capital.

*

From the Hotel Tower he wrote to the Lygon girls:

> Well I am back in Georgetown & all the world is Highclere.[78] . . . The delight of these simple people at my return is very touching. A public holiday has been declared and all the men & women prostrate themselves in the dust & bring me their children to bless; great banners & bonfires decorate all the streets & several elderly niggers have already died of excitement. . . . I have got so thin on account of starvation that I have to put a cushion in my trousers to keep them up. . . . Will you lunch with me at 1.30 on May 7th . . .? . . . I have spent all my money on stuffed alligators for my god-children. Would you like one?
>
> I suppose that I shall not be able to understand any Madresfield jokes by the time I get home.[79]

Away from the tortures of rough life his spirits had immediately risen. Almost everything in this gloriously inconsequent letter is pure fantasy, probably a distortion of the town's mild preparations for Easter. But the baby alligators were real enough. He bought a box of them and encountered some difficulty in getting them through the Customs at Southampton who wished at first to tax them as 'furniture'.

Unable to secure direct passage, he boarded a smart Canadian ship sailing for Trinidad and spent Holy Week there, in the guest house of a small Benedictine monastery perched in the hills behind Port of Spain. Here, that irascible temper which in extreme conditions sometimes pushed him towards racism disappeared completely. Inspired by the sense of spiritual renovation which Easter now always

---

78. Lygon-Waugh slang for 'grand' or, more specifically (not as here), 'grand house'. 'Highclere Castle is the home of Lord Carnarvon. Lady Sibell Lygon had stayed there and referred to its splendour afterwards' (*Letters*, p. 71, n. 1). The name of the Herberts' Italian villa in Portofino was 'Altichiari', a direct translation of 'Highclere', but Waugh did not discover this correspondence until his first visit there in 1932.
79. *Letters*, p. 70.

brought him, he was for a time perfectly contented with his fellow men of whatever race or creed. On Good Friday, amid streams of Hindus, Protestants and Chinese as well as Catholics, he joined, as the solitary white man, a lengthy procession descending the hill and then climbing back up to the Church. Each carried a candle in a paper shade and Waugh was humble enough to share in this simple gesture of faith. As they reached the summit of the hill dawn was breaking and there was, he wrote, 'a feeling of New Year'.[80]

That annual regeneration was of profound spiritual significance to Waugh. But, in this case, there were also secular comforts to be anticipated. He was on course for civilisation: the Ritz, the Savile and Madresfield. There was also Teresa. How would she have responded to their separation? Above all, perhaps, he was, like Denis Barlow at the end of *The Loved One*, 'carrying back . . . the artist's load, a great, shapeless chunk of experience . . .'.[81] He did not know what he would do with the Gothic architecture, lost travellers, vampire bats and Dickens novels which were fermenting in his imagination. But he must have sensed that, once the slavery of writing his travel book was completed, something good would emerge from his journey.

*

On his return in early May Waugh went straight from London to Bath to recuperate among the civilised amenities of an unspoiled Regency town. From the Grand Pump Room Hotel he wrote to Henry Yorke:

> Just back after a journey of the greatest misery. So I came to Bath which was absolutely right and live in a suite of rooms overlooking a colonnade with servants as it might be a club and a decanter of Crofts 1907 always on my sideboard and am getting rid of some of the horrors of life in the forest. Soon I hope to feel up to London – on the 15th in fact when I shall arrive at the Savile & mean to stay intermittently until the end of July at least. I am longing to see you & Dig again. So much to discuss. Guinness – well it will keep. I've seen literally no one except my parents for a brief passage – five months mail to go through mostly Christmas cards. And press cuttings all requiring legal action. Heavy Catholic trouble. Income Tax, dentist and so on. Now Bath is most satisfactory.
>   Woodruff married.
>   Don't tell Hazel I am back. . . .
>   Do both write to me & tell me scandal.[82]

It appears that he still wished to keep Hazel Lavery at a distance. The 'Guinness'

80. *Ninety-Two Days*, p. 238.
81. Evelyn Waugh, *The Loved One* (1948), p. 127.
82. *Letters*, pp. 71–2.

news was the radically shocking information that Diana had left Bryan and was having an affair with Oswald Mosley. Waugh's finances were once again in a parlous condition (he always left Peters to sort out the necessary data for his income tax return). But the most important item here was the 'heavy Catholic trouble'. Theological disputes were not to Yorke's taste and Waugh didn't bother him with the details. There can be no doubt, though, that on his receipt of those press cuttings and letters from his Catholic friends, Waugh had felt enraged and indignant. For they revealed that, in his absence, the Editor of the *Tablet*, Ernest Oldmeadow, had published a virulent attack on *Black Mischief*.

The first volley had been fired in the issue for 7th January. Oldmeadow was sixty-three, a pedestrian *littérateur* who had turned out some dull novels and was conducting a campaign in support of the Pope's recent encyclical discouraging 'immodest' books. Unfortunately he was gifted neither with tact nor critical insight and what might have been a simple call to order became a vindictive accusation, as Waugh's friends not unreasonably saw it, of bad faith:

> A year or two ago, paragraphs appeared in various newspapers announcing that Mr Evelyn Waugh, a novelist, had been received into the Church. Whether Mr Waugh still considers himself a Catholic, *The Tablet* does not know; but, in case he is so regarded by booksellers, librarians and novel-readers in general, we hereby state that his latest novel would be a disgrace to anybody professing the Catholic name. We refuse to print its title or to mention its publishers. Indeed, this paragraph is not to be read as a review. We are mentioning Mr Waugh's work only because it would not be fair on *The Tablet*'s part to condemn coarseness and foulness in non-Catholic writers while glossing over equally outrageous lapses in those who are, or are supposed to be our co-religionists.[83]

The *Tablet* was an official organ of the Catholic faith. It was the personal property of the Cardinal Archbishop of Westminster and could be taken as representing his views. Moreover, it was the Catholic equivalent of the *New Statesman* or *Spectator*. To be pilloried in the *Tablet* carried the double penalty for Waugh of being rejected by his co-religionists on both theological and intellectual grounds.

It must have been gratifying (in retrospect) to notice how rapidly his supporters had sprung to his defence. There were twelve signatories of a letter of protest (dated 10th January) which Oldmeadow 'printed with shame' a fortnight later, foreseeing 'that its publication must lower more than one of [them] in public esteem'.[84] Tom Burns had organised it. Among those subscribed were three distinguished Jesuits (Frs D'Arcy, Martindale and Steuart), the Prior of Black-

83. *Tablet*, 7 January, 1933, 10.
84. *Ibid.*, 21 January, 1933, 10.

friars (Bede Jarrett OP), senior Catholic artists (D. B. Wyndham Lewis, Eric Gill) and several of the younger Catholic 'intelligentsia' who were personal friends of the accused (Christopher Hollis, Douglas Woodruff). Poor Oldmeadow was dumbfounded. As Editor he had doubtless believed his pontifical style to be perfectly in keeping with the authority vested in him. To find respected fathers of the Church calling his judgement into question was astounding. He attached considerable importance to being earnest, being Ernest and being Editor of the *Tablet*. Had he let the matter rest it might have sunk without trace. But his own pride was now at stake. Having made a fool of himself in public he next proceeded to try to convince his readers that his critics were, in fact, the fools.

A major controversy developed in the pages of the magazine and for several weeks the arguments raged back and forth under the heading (note that Oldmeadow steadfastly refused to mention the book's title) 'A Recent Novel'. It was a risible performance on Oldmeadow's part. In support of his case he quoted letters from, of all people, Marie Stopes and rather silly folk snorting about 'family values' from obscure provincial addresses. In support of Waugh's he was forced to quote logical and unpleasantly acute reproofs of his own stupidity. For those *contra*, their case was simple. Would the Editor of the *Tablet* be kind enough to cite the passages he found offensive? Wherein lay this 'coarseness and foulness' which had so enraged him?

Oldmeadow eventually attempted to terminate the dispute by printing a long editorial on 18th February recapitulating, with weary disdain, the entire discussion. But, as Tom Driberg's 'William Hickey' column revealed more than a year later, it did not rest there:

> Dispute went on. Eventually Waugh wrote pamphlet apologia in form of open letter to Cardinal himself. Influential priests induced him to withdraw it, on grounds that (a) more authoritative representations re. *Tablet* were being made to the Cardinal, (b) the Cardinal was seriously ill.
>
> Cardinal got well again. *Tablet* flourishes. But pamphlet wasn't published. Only about half a dozen copies of it exist.[85]

The Cardinal was Cardinal Bourne and it seems clear from Waugh's biography of Ronald Knox (1959) that he had scant respect for the prelate's mind. (Bourne is cast there in the role of a dull-witted philistine interrupting the glorious progress of one greater than himself.) Oldmeadow and Bourne were probably in perfect agreement about the indecency of Waugh's writings. Waugh had to tread carefully: in returning Oldmeadow's fire he ran the risk of hitting the Cardinal, and publicly to attack the most senior British Catholic dignitary could only be construed as

---

85. 'These Names Make News', *DE*, 10 September, 1934, 6.

impertinence and indiscipline on the part of a recent convert. And there was another aspect to be considered: Waugh's attempt to have his first marriage annulled was at this time being considered by the ecclesiastical courts. Cardinal Bourne was a crucial figure in the process.

The open letter was set up in print but, as Driberg says, never published. The manuscript, however, was bound and kept in Waugh's library (now in Texas) and contains a covering note from the Savile Club dated 'May 1933'. The fact of its being so carefully preserved (Waugh usually only had bound the manuscripts of his books) suggests that he regretted not one word of it. But his friends were doubtless wise to dissuade him from distribution. It seems that he came straight from London to Bath burning with indignation and, before writing a word of the articles he had promised Peters, sat down in his hotel room to compose his riposte.

Peters was clearly anxious that the *Passing Show* should have its copy as soon as possible, a loan from him (against future income from these articles) having partly financed the South American trip. To allay his agent's fears Waugh wrote from Bath (about 7th May, 1933) explaining that he had broken off writing the series to defend himself in the 'Open Letter' which he hoped to finish by the end of the week. But as he had only been there for some three days and as the first piece does not appear to have been dispatched until about 11th June, we may suspect a white lie here on Waugh's part. The need to write the series had been a Damoclean prospect for six months. On his return to Georgetown he had cabled Peters promising delivery of all six pieces by mid-May. Doubtless he expected to write them during the month at sea. He appears to have done nothing during the voyage other than to relax. Perhaps in Bath he began the first article and found it impossible to concentrate. It seems more likely that he concentrated all his energies on the open letter.

*

He was deeply shocked to be charged with blasphemy and obscenity. The invective of his 'Open Letter to H.E. the Cardinal Archbishop of Westminster' boils with a scarcely restrained rage at Oldmeadow's misrepresentations. Waugh attempts to circumvent the problem of potential insult to Bourne by couching the argument in the most decorous and archaic of epistolary styles, at times almost parodic in its stiffness, assuming a division between the Cardinal's views and those of his henchman. It reads like an elaborate summing-up of the case for the defence in a nineteenth-century courthouse: 'Your Eminence's patronage', he concludes, 'alone renders this base man considerable.' But no matter how strenuously he emphasised his wish to state his case 'with humility and restraint', it was undisguisedly a full-blooded assault. The failures of reason and sensitivity in Oldmeadow's literary criticism were obvious and were pointed out with merciless precision. But Waugh went further. He imputed moral failure on the Editor's part – malice and even frustrated lasciviousness which Waugh pretended to see as the only possible explanation for the man's inane literal-mindedness. The letter concludes with an elliptical, but unmistakable, suggestion that His Eminence should sack this ass forthwith.

It was too much. In retrospect the document makes amusing reading at Oldmeadow's expense (it first reached a wide audience with its publication in Mark Amory's edition of the *Letters* in 1980, pp. 72–8) but contemporaneously there might well have been a case for libel proceedings against Waugh. The bitterness of his invective moreover renders its author vaguely ludicrous. He had a case: he had been unfairly attacked by a fool and a bigot. But his profound sense of vulnerability prompts over-reaction as he swings right and left at an inadequate opponent. Oldmeadow had dug his own grave by becoming so profound an embarrassment to the majority of intelligent Catholics and it was better that, on this occasion, Waugh should bite his lip and allow the Editor to cast himself into oblivion. Unfortunately, this took some time and Waugh had to suffer the continuous calumny of the *Tablet*'s editorials until 1936. Then, at last, Oldmeadow was removed and replaced by a bright young man, Waugh's friend Douglas Woodruff. From that time, Waugh's books were uniformly applauded by the Catholic press.

In 1933, though, his position as a Catholic author, or rather, as an author who was a Catholic, was more delicate. Waugh never introduced serious theological discussion into his pre-war fiction and the letter elucidates his moral stance as a Christian writer. As Oldmeadow intimated in his initial statement, becoming a Catholic carried with it in the view of the Establishment of the Church a willingness on the part of an author to produce only 'temperate' works. The question at issue here was how one defined this temperance. In Oldmeadow's mind it signified an avoidance of all salacious subject-matter. The very mention of extramarital sex, birth control, or rape, or any levity regarding religious observance (of whatever denomination), was enough to plunge him into a paroxysm of disgust. To Waugh the 'question of modesty' was 'one of peculiar complexity': it did not relate to subject-matter but to language.

In a passage cut from the version in the *Letters* he presents himself in the now familiar role of skilled craftsman with a trade to pursue:

> My own trade is that of novelist... let me rather suppose that I sell wines and spirits. It is highly probable that in the course of my business I am providing the occasion for gluttony to some of my customers; should my wares fall into the hands of children they are likely to endanger their health but it is not taught by the Church that it is my duty to put up my shutters; still less that I must wrap up every bottle in a penny catechism or a tract from the Catholic Truth Society. But the Church does teach ... that a writer *is* culpable if his work becomes

an occasion for sin to his readers; he is at a disadvantage as compared with the wine merchant but it was with the understanding of that disadvantage that I became a Catholic. I am making no plea for free speech and nothing, apart from the original libel, has disgusted me more in the controversy than to find my case the subject of sympathetic comment in the rationalist press.[86]

The analogy with the wine merchant is mischievous (Oldmeadow used to be one) but his argument is straightforward: 'It is not required of me to prove that mine is an actively propagandist work';[87] Oldmeadow, he suggests, has confused fictional with documentary writing and entirely missed the ironical implications of the text. But:

> The question of modesty is one of peculiar complexity.... There are different standards of modesty in every period, and every country, and to individuals of different races, ages, classes and sexes. ... The author is reporting, say, the speech of a stoker... and is accordingly constrained to various often ingenious devices by which he can retain the flavour of the original while purging it of offence. Thus in reporting the conversation of General Connolly I had often to alter and re-edit what would have been his actual words.[88]

With regard to the scene in the hotel bedroom between Prudence and Basil he agrees that the impression he wished to convey 'was that the woman in question was the man's mistress. I do not write for children', he remarks, 'and I so phrased this statement, essential to the structure of my book, that it would only be intelligible to an adult reader.'[89]

All this was reasonable defence but the particular interest of the letter lies in the fact that Waugh felt himself driven to 'the slightly ludicrous position of reviewing my own book'.[90] He rarely revealed his artistic intentions, loathing the pretentiousness of authors who regularly paraded their 'seriousness' in this fashion. Here, however, in defending his good faith, he offers us a fascinating glimpse into that private conceptual world:

> The story deals with the conflict of civilisation with all its attendant and deplorable ills, and barbarism. The plan of my book throughout was to keep the darker aspects of barbarism continually and unobtrusively present, a black and mischievous background against which the civilised

86. MS of 'Open Letter', p. 2; HRC.
87. *Letters*, p. 74.
88. *Ibid.*, p. 75.
89. *Ibid.*, p. 76.
90. *Ibid.*, p. 77.

and semi-civilised characters performed their parts: I wished it to be like the continuous, remote throbbing of those hand drums, constantly audible, never visible, which every traveller in Africa will remember as one of his most haunting impressions. I introduced the cannibal theme in the first chapter and repeated it in another key in the incident of the soldiers eating their boots, thus hoping to prepare the reader for the sudden tragedy when barbarism at last emerges from the shadows and usurps the stage. It is not unlikely that I failed in this; that the transition was too rapid, the catastrophe too large. As I say, this opinion has been represented to me by many whom I respect, and if they are right, as they very well may be, I must plead guilty to an artistic mistake.[91]

We see here Waugh's aesthetic predilections as being radically different from those of his 'rationalist' or 'confessional' contemporaries. A novel was to him neither a political tract nor an explanation of personal motivation. It was an independent, internally coherent system, reflective of, but not controlled by, the 'reality' of daily life. The only grounds on which a book might be sensibly criticised were those of artistic ineptitude, failures in the coherence of the 'structure' or language. He explains his aesthetic intentions – to use the *leit-motif* of the conflict of barbarism and civilisation as a recurrent refrain – and effectively admits that the 'tragedy' of the cannibal scene was a weak element in the novel's construction. (Henry Yorke had written to him unhappy about this 'fantastic' element.) Waugh was quite prepared to accept criticism on artistic grounds. What he could not stomach was an attack on his character and good faith which assumed a fiction to represent a lucid exposition of its author's opinions. Such an approach was not only impertinent, it was intellectually obtuse.

His position here seems close to that of Wilde's in the 'Preface' (1890) to *The Picture of Dorian Gray:* 'There is no such thing as a moral or immoral book. Books are well written, or badly written. That is all.' But this would be to misrepresent Waugh. Even as an undergraduate he had despised the vanity of languor of Wilde, the 'greenery-yallery-Grosvenor-Gallery' decadence which he saw as effete. He perfectly accepted the moral responsibility of an author to his readers not to encourage sinful behaviour and would certainly have rejected Wilde's other precept in that Preface: 'No author has ethical sympathies.'[92]

Waugh's attitude, as usual, was brilliantly simple: while not wishing to distort his picture into a sentimental, anaesthetised world purged of base instincts he, at the same time, reserved the right to write of man's depravity in such a fashion as to make it unattractive. But his ultimate defence against accusations of obscenity was that his descriptions of such behaviour were only intelligible to adult readers.

91. *Ibid.*, p. 77.
92. 'The Preface', *The Picture of Dorian Gray* in *The Works of Oscar Wilde* (Collins, 1966 and 1970), p. 17.

In Waugh's eyes, Oldmeadow, in admitting to the effects of salacious stimulation, did nothing but condemn himself as one who relished such sensations.

The manuscript of *Black Mischief* reveals many re-written sheets which would seem to represent a severe re-ordering of certain pages or the sort of correction necessitated by this 'question of modesty'. Waugh was by 1932 a mature author, largely avoiding the cliquish camaraderie and scandalous innuendo of earlier manuscripts. But if there is a tiny element of dishonesty in his argument about the division between fiction and documentary writing, then it concerns the element of *roman à clef* in his novels.

He always maintained that his fiction was an imaginative amalgam of experience, various characters and events being compressed and refined to create something utterly different.[93] This is perfectly fair. But there is no doubt that he used his novels, as he used his letters, as a medium through which he could tease his friends and sting his enemies while staying on the safe side of libel. Poor Cruttwell's name appears again, this time attached to a parasitic diner-out. Cyril Connolly's surname graces the no-nonsense English General who is married to Black Bitch. (As Christopher Sykes points out, Connolly's wife in 1932 was of dark complexion.) Basil Seal incorporates recognisable aspects of Peter Rodd, the rakehell husband of Nancy Mitford. Abyssinia is clearly the model for Azania and the frontispiece drawing of Seth undeniably based on native portraits of the Emperor. Perhaps the most subtle piece of teasing concerns the characterisation of Prudence and the Sampson Courtenays. It seemed perfectly obvious to the Bartons that Waugh was ridiculing the household of the British Consulate and they were furious. When Waugh returned in 1935 as war correspondent for the *Daily Mail* they cold-shouldered him. Esme Barton, in particular, had not forgotten the insult of being characterised as Prudence. Waugh denied the charge but we can see from his account of her in the *Diaries* that he thought her a fool. One cannot escape the feeling that, however much he may have protested, many elements of Prudence's character bore a marked resemblance to Esme's.

None of this, however, seriously undermines Waugh's case. 'But look', he interrupted Jebb in 1962, 'I think that your questions are dealing too much with the creation of character and not enough with the technique of writing. I regard writing not as an investigation of character, but as an exercise in the use of language, and with this I am obsessed. I have no technical psychological interest. It is drama, speech and events that interest me.'[94] The same argument is implicit in his riposte to Oldmeadow.

*

93. Cf. *Ninety-Two Days*, p. 13: ' . . . the truth is that self-respecting writers do not "collect material" for their books, or rather that they do it all the time in living their lives. One does not travel, any more than one falls in love, to collect material. It is simply part of one's life.'
94. *Writers*, p. 110.

Having completed his 'Open Letter', Waugh returned to the Savile and sent the manuscript to the printers. There was now no avoiding those articles, and with that prospect as a preface to the even more deadly task of composing a travel book, he sat in the writing room of his club in the lowest of spirits. He was deeply in debt. The summer stretched ahead as a gloomy panorama of endless hack-work. He tried through Peters to secure a review page in the *Daily Telegraph;* he offered to write *A Boccaccio in Modern Dress* for Faber. Nothing came of either proposition. He negotiated for an article in the *Daily Express* ('Gold Getters in Guiana') which was probably never written and certainly not published. He agreed to write short stories and more articles for the *Passing Show* when the first series was complete. None of them appeared. In no market, it seems, was he able to secure a quick cash return. Quite simply, rushed and distracted as he was, he was for the first time in his life writing badly.

Editors began to complain. Waugh demanded such high fees (*Harper's* usually paid thirty guineas, *Vogue* twenty) that he trod a dangerous path between pricing himself out of the market and needing to produce work of a consistently high quality. This low ebb in his skill at hitting the light and sparkling tone necessary for the fashionable magazines lasted for two years and cost him dearly. Joyce Reynolds at *Harper's* remained loyal, but Elizabeth Penrose at *Vogue* found it difficult to use his material when she could acquire similar for almost half the price.

The *Passing Show* articles (travel sketches) took him a month. So poor were they that Donat Gallagher found himself unable to include even one in his *Essays, Articles and Reviews*. Waugh was enraged when a piece on boredom requested by *Vanity Fair* in July was refused in September. Even his fiction was suffering: the *Bystander* rejected the short story 'An Ill Wind'. It was never published and has so far proved untraceable. Perhaps he destroyed it.

Peters felt it necessary to apologise to aggrieved editors. 'Evelyn's work has not been up to much lately . . .', he explained in September and, during the next month, 'Evelyn has not been doing his best lately . . . he agrees it is time he pulled up his socks.'[95] Waugh replied resignedly to Peters's adjurations: 'You can't tell me a thing I don't know about the low quality of my journalism.'[96]

Of the journalism that *was* published during 1933 there were two rather silly pieces – one marking Wilberforce's centenary, suggesting that he might have been wrong to free the slaves;[97] the other on cocktail parties[98] – and a review,

---

95. The first remark is dated 21 September, 1933, the second 19 October, 1933; quoted by Donat Gallagher in his 'Introduction' to Section 3, 'Rough Life', *EAR*, p. 112.
96. *Catalogue*, E 228, p. 105; quoted J. D. MacNamara, 'Literary Agent A. D. Peters and Evelyn Waugh, 1928–1966: "Quantitative Judgements Don't Apply"' (PhD thesis, University of Texas at Austin, 1983), p. 100.
97. 'Was He Right To Free the Slaves?', *DE*, 15 July, 1933; *EAR*, pp. 135–6.
98. 'Cocktail Hour', *HB* (London), 9 November, 1933, 26, 87.

which is at least of biographical interest, of Peter Fleming's *Brazilian Adventure*. 'The Man Who Liked Dickens' had first been published during September in America (*Hearst's International*),[99] and two months later at home in *Nash's Pall Mall*.[100] Two further stories had reached the public during the year – 'Cruise'[101] and 'Bella Fleace Gave a Party',[102] both appearing in *Harper's* – but these had been written before his departure for British Guiana. From his return in May to the end of the year only one story was written and published (in the *Harper's* Christmas number): 'Out of Depth'.[103] This was partly due to the fact that the period between 12th October and 13th November was given over entirely to writing *Ninety-Two Days*. The book, though, had occupied only one month out of the seven and the remainder of the year had been singularly unproductive. Clearly something was wrong and Peters was worried.

A complex of issues oppressed Waugh. On 15th October, thirteen days before his birthday, he had written to Peters asking if any newspaper apart from the *Daily Mail* would be interested in publishing his thoughts on turning thirty. (They were not.) On that day he was at work on the opening pages of *Ninety-Two Days*. There he admits that it had been a 'crowded and fretful summer' and that his South American experience had never left his memory 'obtruding itself in a fragmentary way at incongruous moments'.[104] It seems that this journey and the drudgery of writing it up, coupled with the prospect of entering his thirties alone, had plunged him into melancholy.

Seclusion in a dark Victorian villa near Bognor did nothing to raise his spirits. While at work on the book there he had written to Mary Lygon mocking his misery:

> ... I wrote and wrote for 3 days and once I went to Chichester in a bus hoping to find a Cinema but there wasn't one.... Yesterday I couldn't stand the disillusion, death, bitterness any more so I went to see a Mr Plunket Greene.... I will see you on Wednesday when the sun has passed its zenith. In the evening, unless shes dutch I shall be with Miss J[ungman]. can't help loving that girl.[105]

David Plunket Greene was still music master at Lancing. Waugh must indeed

---

 99. 'The Man Who Liked Dickens', *Hearst's International* combined with *Cosmopolitan*, September 1933, 54–7, 127–30.
100. 'The Man Who Liked Dickens', *NPMM*, 92 (November, 1933), 18–21, 80, 82–3.
101. *HB* (London), February 1933, 12–13, 80.
102. *HB* (New York), March 1933, 36–7, 96–8.
103. 'Out of Depth – An Experiment Begun in Shaftesbury Avenue and Ended in Time', *HB* (London) 9 (December 1933), 46–8, 106.
104. *Ninety-Two Days*, p. 14.
105. Unpublished ALS to Lady Mary Lygon, nd [October/November 1933?], np [probably West House, Aldwick, Bognor]; cf. *Catalogue*, E230, p. 106 where he writes to Peters from this address, the Sussex house of Diana and Duff Cooper.

have been desperate to return there. But Teresa was the root cause of his depression. Her warm friendship was restrained by her continued unwillingness to enter into a sexual relationship with him. The nullity hearings dragged on. If the result were favourable, he intended to propose to her but there seemed little hope of either problem resolving itself to his satisfaction.

It was a period of considerable anxiety and one in which he appears to have associated himself with the recurrent figure of the lost man. Both 'The Man Who Liked Dickens' and 'Out of Depth' centre on this image. The first effectively represents the scenes of Tony Last's imprisonment by Mr Todd (only the names and other minor details being altered) and will be best dealt with later in the context of *A Handful of Dust*. 'Out of Depth', now out of print, merits close examination here as a reflection of his mood. It is a substantial piece, subtitled 'An Experiment Begun in Shaftesbury Avenue and Ended in Time'.[106]

*

He wrote it in July 1933, immediately after finishing the *Passing Show* series, 'I Step Off the Map' (a running title which possibly had more than literal significance). The story concerns a forty-three-year-old American, Rip Van Winkle. Born a Catholic he has become a fashionable, cosmopolitan agnostic. Like Waugh, he had 'reached the age when he disliked meeting new people'. Unlike Waugh, though, he has lived immune from questions about 'time and matter and spirit'. Taking dinner at Margot Metroland's he meets a Mr Jagger ('Kakophilos' in the revised 1936 text) who speaks in 'a thin Cockney voice'. The man is introduced as a magician and appears to be fraudulent (his accent slips from sonorous, 'poetic' intonation to shrill East End vocables).

Jagger is cold, rude and threatening. Later in the evening when Alastair Trumpington and Rip return to the man's flat, he parades in a 'crimson robe embroidered with gold symbols and a comical crimson hat', garments which provoke unrestrained hilarity in the two drunken *boulevardiers*. Jagger asks them which period of history they would choose to visit were it possible for them to become time-travellers. Alastair randomly selects the age of Ethelred the Unready and Rip, with equal facetiousness, states that, being an American, he 'would sooner go forward – say five hundred years'. Leaving the man's house in search of more drink, they turn a corner and drive broadside into a mail van 'thundering down Shaftesbury Avenue at forty-five miles an hour'.

106. 'Out of Depth' was reprinted with substantial revisions in Waugh's collection, *Mr Loveday's Little Outing and Other Sad Stories* (Chapman and Hall, 1936), pp. 121–38, and in Charles A. Bradey (ed.), *A Catholic Reader* (Buffalo, NY, Desmond and Stapleton, 1947) with a commentary by Brady, pp. 78–9. Waugh did not include it in Penguin Books' *Work Suspended and Other Stories* (Harmondsworth, 1943), nor has it appeared in subsequent Penguin editions with this title. Quotations are from the *Mr Loveday* text unless otherwise stated.

Rip awakens in the same place but in the twenty-fifth century. All signs of 'civilisation' have disappeared. The tube station is a flooded hole in the ground. Symbolically, Eros (the Greek god of Love) is missing from its pedestal in what was Piccadilly Circus. No buildings exist other than fifty or so huts on stilts to raise them above the tidal floods and mud flats of the Thames. The night is characterised by a penetrating silence. Darkness and chaos rule. The people of this 'Lunnon' are savages, shy and ignorant, their aesthetic sensibility and language decayed: 'They spoke slowly in the sing-song tones of an unlettered race who depend on an oral tradition for the preservation of their lore'. In his incongruous evening suit, Rip appears first as an object of mystery.

Silently the savages surround him and begin 'to finger his outlandish garments, tapping his crumpled shirt with their horny nails and plucking at his studs and buttons'. Their curiosity is soon supplanted by suspicion: gently they place him under guard, feeding him as the days pass on 'fish, coarse bread and heavy, viscous beer', squatting on their haunches to discuss him in unintelligible patois. Rip closes his eyes and says to himself, ' "I am in London, in nineteen-thirty-three, staying at the Ritz Hotel. I drank too much at Margot's. Have to go carefully in future. Nothing really wrong. I am in the Ritz in nineteen-thirty-three." ' Forcing his 'will towards sanity', he is at last convinced of the truth of his proposition. But when he opens his eyes again he sees ' . . . early morning on the river, a cluster of wattle huts, a circle of barbarous faces'.

'Lunnon', the surrounding villages, and by implication the world, are ruled by negroes, some of whom arrive in a launch to barter goods. The Londoners spend their time raking the debris of their civilisation in a form of crude archaeology. In return for 'pieces of machinery and ornament, china and glass and carved stonework' the black overlords (dressed smartly in vaguely fascist uniforms of leather and fur) provide 'bales of thick cloth, cooking utensils, fish hooks, knife-blades and axe-heads'. Once discovered, Rip is taken by the leader on a 'phantas-magoric' journey down river. ' "This is not a dream," ' he says to himself. ' "It is simply that I have gone mad." Then more blackness and wilderness.' Something, however, saves his sanity:

> And then later – how much later he could not tell – something that was new and yet ageless. The word 'Mission' painted on a board: a black man dressed as a Dominican friar . . . and a growing clearness. Rip knew that out of strangeness, there had come into being something familiar; a shape in chaos. . . . Something was being done that Rip knew; something that twenty-five centuries had not altered; of his own childhood which had survived the age of the world. In a log-built church at the coast town he was squatting among a native congregation . . . ; all round him dishevelled white men were staring ahead with vague, uncomprehending eyes, to the end of the room where two candles burned. The priest turned towards them his bland, black face.

'Ite, missa est.'[107]

The tale ends with Rip, back in the twentieth century, coming round in hospital. Talking to the priest at his bedside, he asks the cleric how he (the priest) came to be there. Sir Alastair apparently had asked for him. Alastair wasn't a Catholic but he had suffered a disturbing dream about the Middle Ages and had felt the need for a priest. Learning that Rip was in the same establishment, the priest had come along to see how he was. ' "Father," ' Rip replies in the last line, ' "I want to make a confession . . . I have experimented in black art." '

In some ways it is a simple fable, dexterously told. Waugh himself presumably considered it slight as he refused to have it reprinted. In one sense it is a Christmas story reaffirming the continuity and lucidity of Catholic teaching. Rip's return to the Church from the apathetic sleep of agnosticism signals his unconscious recognition of the link between civilisation and faith. The horror he experiences, though, is not unlike that of Conrad's Marlow in *Heart of Darkness:* 'And this, also [London], has been one of the dark places of the earth.'[108] As has been said, there is no evidence of Waugh's having read this work. Unlike Graham Greene, Waugh found Conrad an unsympathetic writer. But the comparison remains useful both for the similarities and differences it throws up.

The second half of Waugh's tale is strongly reminiscent of Marlow's voyage on the Congo, even to the 'phantasmagoric journey downstream' and Rip having his head measured with callipers. Both works suggest the temporary nature of civilisation. 'The dreams of men, the seed of commonwealths, the germs of empires'[109] are powerful emblems of man's attempts to impose idealisms upon chaos. To both Waugh and Conrad, this materialist idealism is delusory. Both refute nineteenth-century concepts of progress and question the validity of seeing history as a linear sequence of cause and effect. Yet there is an obvious point at which they part company. Where Conrad suggests that chaos and darkness must inevitably reclaim all attempts at control, Waugh remains a stolid, fundamentalist theologian. The artefacts and culture of a civilisation may decay but the Faith, that island of sanity in a raving world, will survive.

The story is of particular interest from a biographical point of view in that it represents Waugh's first overtly apologetic work of fiction. From this, one inevitably looks forward to *Brideshead Revisited* (1945) and what renders this tale even more peculiar is that there was a twelve-year gap before Waugh's defence of his faith finds its way back into his fiction. His 'Open Letter' had stressed the idea that he was not, as a writer who was a Catholic, required to produced overtly propagandist art. Suddenly, only two months later, he did precisely that.

107. 'Out of Depth', *Mr Loveday's* . . ., pp. 136–7.
108. Joseph Conrad, *Heart of Darkness* (first published 1902; reprinted Harmondsworth, Penguin Books, 1973 and 1976), p. 7.
109. *Ibid.*, p. 7.

It seems clear that, foolish as they were, Oldmeadow's attacks had had their effect. Nothing stung Waugh more sharply than the imputation of bad faith and he began at this point to consider seriously the use of his pen to assist the Church militant. At first sight the description of the negroes' dominance in the twenty-fifth century might appear as a reactionary gesture on Waugh's part. This, the tale seems to suggest, will be the inevitable and ghastly result of our not defending our civilisation. But the story is profoundly ambiguous on this point. It is a negro priest and a negro congregation who maintain the faith; the governing class appears to be tough but fair-minded. It is they who value the shards of the lost culture, not the white Londoners. The emphasis seems rather to be on the arbitrary nature of political power when set against the permanent values of the Church, the delicacy of the fabric of civilisation when set against the second law of thermodynamics. All social structures in Waugh's fictional world tend towards collapse. It is only through the most tenacious defence of civilised values that their decay may be arrested.

In the Preface to *When the Going was Good* (dated 1945) Waugh remarked:

> Had we [Waugh, Greene, Byron and Fleming] known, we might have lingered with 'Palinurus';[110] had we known that all that seeming-solid, patiently-built, gorgeously-ornamented structure of Western life was to melt overnight like an ice-castle, leaving only a puddle of mud; had we known that man was even then leaving his post. Instead we set off on our various stern roads; I to the Tropics and the Arctic, with the belief that barbarism was a dodo to be stalked with a pinch of salt. The route of *Remote People* was easy going; the *Ninety-Two Days* were more arduous. . . .[111]

Waugh was writing there in the full flood of his sentimental reaction to the disappointments and destruction of the Second World War. The implication is that he gadded round the world in the 'thirties oblivious of the imminent dissolution of that ' . . . gorgeously-ornamented structure of Western life'. 'Out of Depth' demonstrates emphatically that this nightmare was an obsessive concern as early as 1933. The missing Eros seems to suggest not only the absence of love and finer feeling. The monument has quite specific political connotations, being a memorial to the nineteenth-century philanthropist, Lord Shaftesbury. Waugh's story is a counterblast to Victorian humanism and its concepts of 'progress'.

The details of Rip's encounter with the savages, of course, suggest distinct parallels with Waugh's experiences in South America and the same anti-humanist argument structures much of his commentary in *Ninety-Two Days*. This new

---

110. A reference to Cyril Connolly's pseudonym for his book of pensées, *The Unquiet Grave*, which Waugh thought intellectually inept and fraught with humanist fallacy.
111. *When the Going was Good*, p. 10.

seriousness shifts his travel writing in another direction: the dilettantism, the 'polite and highly attractive scepticism' of *Labels* and *Remote People* are largely dropped. In their place we find Waugh's attempts to construct a literary symbolism from the events which relate to his conservative/Catholic view of history.

Throughout, he suggests that the last outposts of civilisation have been left behind in Europe. The churchyard in Antigua holds 'the memorials of a lost culture – the rococo marble tombs of forgotten sugar planters carved in England and imported by sailing ship in the golden days of West Indian prosperity'.[112] Beyond Barbados, he notes, the transparent blue of the Caribbean becomes clouded by torrents of mud spewing from the mouth of the Orinoco. As South America looms nearer, Waugh suggests that he is moving towards the heart of darkness. The facetiousness has gone from his humour; the sceptical objectivity of his earlier travel writing has been replaced by a set of rigid presuppositions about culture and anarchy.

*

It was in this frame of mind that he first attached himself to the Catholic community centering on Mells, near Frome, in Somerset. His Oxford friend, Christopher Hollis, lived nearby. But we may suspect that Diana Cooper had something to do with Waugh's suddenly increased interest in Mells. She knew Katharine Asquith (Lady Horner, daughter-in-law of the ex-Prime Minister) and it was probably through Lady Diana that an introduction to the Manor House was effected. Lady Horner, a Catholic convert, had inherited Mells Manor, and it was there, in 1949, that Monsignor Ronald Knox went to live. Another of Lady Diana's friends, Conrad Russell, occupied a cottage farm, 'Little Claveys', nearby.

An eccentric and confirmed bachelor, Russell was of noble birth and had quantities of disposable wealth to waste on presents for Lady Diana. But he preferred the humble life. His smallholding was a model of efficiency; he was a keen horticultural prize competitor; every morning he would deliver the milk to Mells Manor. A friend of many writers and aristocrats, and a man with a keen historical mind, he had nevertheless decided that neither authorship nor the *beau monde* was for him: 'I think being a novelist like Maurice Baring or Evelyn Waugh', he once wrote to Lady Diana, 'hardly a fit occupation for a man. Just scribbling. So I suppose it's got to be farming, sweat or no sweat.'[113] Nevertheless, Waugh and he liked each other. Russell's abrasive humour, his practical skills and no-nonsense intelligence exerted an immediate appeal. Towards the end of his life Russell became a Catholic.

Lady Horner was forty-eight in 1933 and a considerable figure in the grand world. Waugh was at first rather nervous of her and particularly of her opinion

---

112. *Ninety-Two Days*, p. 11.
113. Diana Cooper, *The Light of Common Day* (Rupert Hart-Davis, 1959), p. 130.

of his books. But it is evident from their correspondence (which dates from this year) that they soon became close friends. His first, rather touching letter displays an unusual timorousness after a week-end at Mells. How he would have cursed himself had he realised that he had mis-spelled her Christian name:

> Dear Catherine,
>     I sent off two books to you today Remoters and Blackers. Well I don't know what the effect will be. I don't think there's much to bring a blush in Remoters & yet I don't know – is it justified teleologically? As for Blackers there are bits in that to make your hair stand on end worse than [David] Garnett or Maugham. But what was I to do? There the books were and any minute you might come across them & the fat would be in the fire, cat out of the bag etc. So it seemed best to take a risk & send them on and perhaps the result will be no more lovely week-ends like the last.
>     Anyway I have had that, and it was the most enjoyable in years.
>     Diana [Cooper] just can't believe you like me.
>                                         Love from
>                                         Evelyn.[114]

One senses him here, half-expecting Oldmeadow's ghost to appear and ruin this latest feast. But Lady Horner, devout Catholic as she was, had an astute and sympathetic mind. She welcomed him back and they remained friends until his death.

Waugh's attachment to Mells, with its solid religious and temporal comforts, could not have come at a better time. He felt persecuted by some of his co-religionists, miserable over Teresa, and unhappy about the quality of his writing. The prospect of Mells as another escape hatch from the tyrannies of metropolitan life must have cheered him. But there was to be another meeting, in September of that year, which was to change his life even more dramatically. 'You will think me insane', he wrote to Nancy Mitford from Madresfield, 'when I tell you that I am just off for Hellenic Society Cruise. . . .'[115]

Mrs Rodd must indeed have thought Waugh crazed: Hellenic Society Cruises were scarcely 'his tea'. She perhaps imagined a ship packed with dons and 'uplifters' who would, in all probability, provoke only ill-temper in her friend. But he had his reasons, principal among which was the need to escape. It had been a bad summer spent mostly in London; he was feeling stale. Six weeks in the sunshine and damn the expense seemed a fine idea before settling to the composition of *Ninety-Two Days*, especially as the passenger list included many of his friends.

---

114. *Letters*, pp. 78–9.
115. Unpublished ALS to Nancy Mitford, nd [September 1933?], from Madresfield Court.

From the *Queen Mary*, he wrote to the Lygon girls in the highest of spirits:

> Darling Blondy and Poll,
>
> So I am in the sea of Marmora and it is very calm & warm and there are lots of new & old chums aboard and I have seen numbers of new & old places and am enjoying myself top-hole.
>
> I had only 2½ minutes in Venice so couldnt buy bad taste shoes but hope to do so on return journey.
>
> Alfred (brother of bald dago) has behaved very well so far except for once farting at Lady Lovat.
>
> Lady Lavery missed the ship and so did Mr Yorke but instead there came those decent Bobbities. The ship is full of people of high rank including two princesses of ROYAL BLOOD. There is not much rogering so far as I have seen and the food is appalling. . . .
>
> I went to Athens . . . now go on to Istanbul. . . . There is a decent cousin of Porchy called Gabriel Herbert. She got drunk on gin for the first time & is a little sheepish about it.
>
> Perhaps that handsome Dutch girl is staying with you. . . . Give her my love & a kiss on the arse and take one each for yourselves too.
>
> Bo[116]

As it turned out it was perhaps as well that Hazel Lavery missed the ship and that there was a deficiency of 'rogering'. Lady Horner was another passenger and Waugh spent much of his time with her. 'Alfred' was his close friend from Oxford, Alfred Duggan, at the time a confirmed dipsomaniac. According to Mr Sykes, part of Waugh's purpose in taking this trip was to reclaim the man from drink. After spending a week sightseeing with Lady Horner and her son in Ravenna and Bologna, Duggan and he moved on to stay with the Herberts in Portofino.

Gabriel Herbert was then a gauche twenty-two-year-old. Her family owned an elegant villa near Genoa where her mother, Mary, her brother, Auberon, and her two sisters, Bridget and Laura, were hosting a large house-party. Gabriel had invited Waugh and Duggan to join them, though they must have accepted with some trepidation. The Herbert girls were first cousins of Evelyn Gardner and the awkwardness of that divorce was legend in the family. They were all Catholic converts. Duggan could be a boisterous and facetious guest in his cups.

The visit was not without its difficulties. Christopher Sykes records Bridget's account of how Waugh and Duggan were pelted with buns by Mary Herbert for supposedly mocking Ireland, her native country, and then banished from the house for some hours. Duggan would search for strong drink under cover of darkness, closely followed by Waugh who would attempt dissuasion and return him to bed. But the arguments and embarrassments seem not to have been

---

116. *Letters*, p. 79. The 'Bobbities' were Viscount Cranborne (Conservative statesman) and his wife, née Elizabeth Cavendish. 'Porchy' was the fifth Lord Carnarvon.

serious. The atmosphere of the household was one of volatile good humour; sharp conversation in delightful surroundings.

Some of the company were not entirely to Waugh's taste, nor the exertion required for traversing the steep local terrain. But he liked the Herberts immediately: 'white mouse named Laura; fat girl full of sex-appeal named Bridget; ... very decent hostess'.[117] He could not have guessed that the 'white mouse', a quiet but determined eighteen-year-old debutante, was to alter the whole course of his life and work. The following week he was on the Rome Express heading back for London, his thoughts still obsessed with Teresa Jungman.

On his return in October, after a brief visit to Madresfield, he learnt that at last his nullity hearings were to come before the Ecclesiastical Court. This was the occasion of his last meeting with his first wife.

Among others, Waugh summoned Pansy Pakenham and She-Evelyn as witnesses. The women did not meet during the hearings but had been in contact since the separation. Lady Pansy had travelled down to the Heygates' cottage in Sussex to meet Heygate for the first time. Her friend's elopement with a complete stranger had been as much of a shock to Pansy as it had to Nancy Mitford, but, unlike Nancy, she remained loyal to both Evelyns.

Heygate she had found of a type with the sort of man Evelyn Gardner had always felt a weakness for, 'rather bounderish'[118] in manner. During the days when the two debutantes had lived together, Lady Pansy had witnessed two broken engagements with similarly unsuitable fellows. Lady Burghclere had crushed the first alliance and her daughter had left for Egypt, only to return on the boat committed to an even less desirable candidate. 'Lady B' was unapologetically mercenary in trying to arrange her daughters' marriages. (She almost prevented She-Evelyn's sister, Alathea, from pursuing her match with Geoffrey Fry until assured that Geoffrey would inherit millions from his family's chocolate firm.) In 1927, this daunting matriarch had 'allowed' her daughter to live independently because she thought Pansy would be a stabilising influence. Pansy now felt it a debt of honour to appear in these unpleasant proceedings: having got Waugh into this mess by supporting the match, she felt that it was the least she could do to help him get out of it.

To her credit She-Evelyn responded with equal loyalty: 'Evelyn gave me lunch near Westminster. As you can imagine, I was more than anxious that he should be able to marry again. He told me to say that I had refused to have children, where the Devil's Advocate would sit and where the priest who was on his side would be. It was very intimidating as there appeared to be many black-clothed priests sitting on each side of a long table. Otherwise the hangings in the room were red. I had not refused to have children, but we had agreed to wait until we

117. *Letters*, p. 80.
118. Interview with Lady Pansy Lamb, 24 January, 1986.

had an income which did not depend sometimes on others. I think Evelyn must have forgotten this. I didn't remind him. But my sister Mary had a letter from him, after an operation I had, saying how glad he was we could have children.'[119]

It seems doubtful that Waugh had forgotten his earnest desire for a fruitful marriage with her. But to admit to this would have been damning evidence against the granting of an annulment. He primed Lady Pansy in just the same way before she entered the courtroom. It was essential, he emphasised, that she state that the couple had wanted to remain childless, that the marriage had been entered into frivolously, that they did not foresee any permanent relationship. Lady Pansy complied with a clear conscience: there had scarcely been time, she remarked, for any other attitude to take root. No-one could blame Waugh for attempting to 'nobble' the witnesses on this fine point of Catholic law. He was in danger of being persecuted for the sincerity of his original intention. He had, moreover, found a girl he wanted to marry and, with the prospect of a successful outcome in the annulment hearings, he proposed to Teresa.

The letter Waugh wrote at this point to Lady Mary Lygon marks a nadir in his fortunes:

> God how sad not to see you and say thank you thank you for all your kind hospitality. It has been lovely staying with you. Thank you. Thank you.
>
> Just heard yesterday that my divorce comes on today so was elated and popped question to Dutch girl and got raspberry. So that is that, eh. Stiff upper lip and dropped cock. Now I must go. How sad, how sad. . . .
>
> Now I will go to Mells.[120]

It was with this rejection still stinging in his memory, and the embarrassment of the Court hearings, that he had travelled a week or so later to the deserted nurseries of the Duff Coopers' Bognor house to begin *Ninety-Two Days*. He was alone.

\*

As the opening words of the book testify, he had put off writing it for five months. It is an ill-structured work, ground out for money, amusing for the first half where his wry assessment of various companions reads more like a novel than a travelogue. The latter part, however, slavishly follows the diary, detailing the tedious stages of his return to Georgetown and making a few superficial comments on the insubstantial nature of anthropological generalisations popularised by 'Outlines' of culture. In *When the Going was Good* he significantly dropped the

119. ALS from Evelyn Nightingale, *op. cit.*
120. *Letters*, p. 81.

whole of Chapters VI–IX, being most of the second half of the book. Also cut were most of his own 'anthropological generalisations' and they are no great loss. There are the usual disparaging remarks about negroes. At one point he comments on expatriate Germans:

> I have encountered them, wistful and denationalised as Jews, in Abyssinia, Arabia and East Africa, and they make real to me some of the clap-trap of Nazi patriotism.[121]

His youthful interest in Fascism as an alternative political system was something he came to regret.

The book was finished in record time (one month) but clearly Waugh was dissatisfied. Writing to Peters on 13th November, 1933, he explained that the work was complete but short because he lacked material. Of the 192 photographs he had taken, scarcely fifty were of any use. And the dull collection of snap-shots Duckworth's reproduced reflects the disappointment of the journey as a whole. He had gone looking for adventure and discovered boredom and fatigue. Near the beginning he remarks:

> for myself and many better than me, there is a fascination in distant and barbarous places, and particularly in the borderlands of conflicting cultures and states of development, where ideas, uprooted from their traditions, become oddly changed in transplantation. It is there that I find the experiences vivid enough to demand translation into literary form.[122]

It was this approach which resulted in both the virtues and the failings of the travel books after *Labels*.

'Translation into literary form' did not simply mean 'writing it up' but imaginative reconstruction. When forced to settle for reportage, as he does for much of the second half of *Ninety-Two Days*, he is often dull. Joyce's and Orwell's gift for making the ordinary appear interesting was not part of Waugh's artistic talents. Instead, he prefered to reduce the extraordinary and exotic to the level of the mundane, to debunk the romance of the jungle. Perhaps the uneven quality of *Ninety-Two Days* can be directly related to the fact that he needed characters, 'unusual people', as he says in *Remote People*, who 'in retrospect become fabulous and fantastic'.[123] It is through these eccentrics, as a background to them, that Waugh best describes landscape and alien cultures. When during the next year he travelled to Spitzbergen and the frozen, almost uninhabited, wastes above the

---

121. *Ninety-Two Days*, p. 131.
122. *Ibid.*, p. 13.
123. *Remote People*, p. 115.

Arctic Circle, this proved to be the only one of his expeditions to remote lands during the 'thirties from which no travel book resulted.

The one priceless eccentric, Christie, struck deeply into his imagination and, in retrospect, we can detect other ideas which were to merge in his subconscious with this encounter: the imagery of Gothic architecture, the search for the city and, as a parallel theme to that of the lost man, the false leader. Reviewing Peter Fleming's *Brazilian Adventure* in August he admitted to an obsessive interest in Major Pingle, the original leader of Fleming's expedition: 'Where is Pingle now?' he asks. 'One cannot get as absorbed as I was in that preposterous character and then see him disappear without a hint of his destination.'[124] A few months earlier he had met Roth. Both must have provided material for the creation of Dr Messinger. *Ninety-Two Days* even suggests direct correspondences between the experiences of Tony Last and Waugh's in British Guiana:

> Already, in the few hours of my sojourn there, the Boa Vista of my imagination had come to grief. Gone, engulfed in earthquake, uprooted by a tornado and tossed sky-high like chaff in the wind, scorched up with brimstone like Gomorrah, toppled over with trumpets like Jericho, ploughed like Carthage, bought, demolished and transported brick by brick to another continent as though it had taken the fancy of Mr Hearst; tall Troy was down.[125]

A much-quoted passage from *A Handful of Dust* reads:

> A whole Gothic world had come to grief... there was no armour glittering through the forest glades, no embroidered feet on the green sward; the green and dappled unicorn had fled....[126]

It describes Last's sense of betrayal and dispossession.

It seems, then, that while the specific incidents of his journey failed to stimulate his creative powers, its general effect was profoundly significant to his increased moral seriousness as a writer. Forming a backdrop to his 'crowded and fretful summer' it began slowly to generate the imagery, used in his two short stories, of a civilisation decaying at its extremeties, of lost men and false leaders, of the Faith surviving in embattled outposts, of betrayal and the delusions of Victorian humanism.

During 1933 Waugh had suffered for his beliefs, both through Oldmeadow's attacks and through appearances before the Ecclesiastical Court to testify to the insincerity of his first marriage. 'The path of the convert in England', he remarked

124. 'Mr Fleming in Brazil', *Spectator*, 11 August, 1933, 195–6; *EAR*, pp. 136–8.
125. *Ninety-Two Days*, p. 120.
126. *A Handful of Dust*, p. 151.

tersely in his 'Open Letter', 'is not without its embarrassments.'[127] It cannot have been other than painful publicly to relive his wife's desertion. He had even been forced to meet her again: '. . . Over lunch, Waugh told his former wife that his father would never again receive her; but he added that his mother took a less censorious view and indeed held him partly responsible for the marriage's failure; she had told him that he had left his wife too much alone.'[128] It had been a miserable year and Teresa was as unwilling as ever to commit herself to him. The end result was that Waugh developed a powerful determination to re-establish the sincerity of his faith in the eyes of the Catholic hierarchy.

\*

With *Ninety-Two Days* completed he was once again restless and felt the need to be out of the country. Winter was setting in and his next novel beginning to take shape in his mind. He wanted to begin it somewhere in sunshine and solitude.

For this purpose he chose Fez in Morocco, probably on the recommendation of Norman Webb, co-proprietor of the Eastern Court Hotel. The animal welfare organisation for which Webb had worked was based there and doubtless the place had figured in many of their conversations during the regular 'cocktail hour' in Mrs Cobb's shabby bedroom-cum-office. Perhaps Waugh thought this Arab, medieval walled city might exert the same appeal as had Harar in Abyssinia. Christmas was probably spent at Madresfield. Immediately after, Diana Cooper had seen him off on the boat for Tangier. By early January he had reached Africa to find letters already awaiting him from the Lygons.

His reply offers the best description of those early days in Fez:

> It is a very decent town – with little streams running all though it & very old houses with walled gardens & shops selling some of the worst taste objects I ever saw. There are 100,000 Arabs and 30,000 Jews and about 3 white people. . . .
>
> I made friends with a froggy taxi driver . . . and he took me round the [red light] quarter. It was very gay and there were little Arab girls of fifteen & sixteen for ten francs each & a cup of mint tea. So I bought one but I didn't enjoy her very much because she had a skin like sandpaper and a huge stomach which didn't show until she took off her clothes & then it was too late.
>
> It is not at all hot in fact it is cold & there are no fires or hot water pipes in the hotel. But the wine is free & rather nasty & there is lots of food. I have begun the novel and it is excellent, first about sponger and then about some imaginary people who are happy to be married but not for long. . . .

127. Unpublished section of 'An Open Letter to H.E. The Cardinal Archbishop of Westminster', MS p. 1; HRC.
128. Davie in *Diaries*, p. 306.

There was a shameless blonde (English I think) in evening dress with a thing in her hair going round the brothels just as did Mme de Janzé and the tarts despised her terribly & made her pay double for her mint tea.

There is also a brothel full of white ladies very cleverly named Maison Blanche but they cost 30 francs each so I haven't bought any of them.

When I have finished this novel I think I will go to Jerusalem for a pilgrimage to become holy. . . .

No love to anyone except your dear selves.

Bo.[129]

In these curious circumstances and in melancholy mood *A Handful of Dust* got under way.

129. *Letters*, pp. 82–3. 'Sponger' was Murrough O'Brien (b. 1910), a major in the Irish Guards.

# XI

# *A Handful of Dust:*
# *January-August 1934*

... I was in Morocco, at a small French hotel outside the fortifications of Fez. I had been there for six weeks, doing little else but write. ... I was ... a serious writer. ... I took pains with my work and I found it excellent. Each of my seven books sold better than its predecessor. ... I never tried to sell my stories as serials; the delicate fibres of a story suffer when it is chopped up ... and never completely heal. ... To produce something, saleable in large quantities to the public, which had absolutely nothing of myself in it ... that was what I sought. ...

... Fez ... is a splendid compact city, and in early March, with flowers springing everywhere in the surrounding hills and in the untidy patios of the Arab houses, one of the most beautiful in the world. I liked the little hotel. It was cheap and rather chilly – an indispensable austerity. ... The clientele was exclusively French; the wives of civil servants and elderly couples of small means wintering in the sun. In the evening Spahi officers came to the bar to play bagatelle. I used to work on the verandah of my room, overlooking a ravine where Senegalese infantrymen were constantly washing their linen. My recreations were few and simple. Once a week after dinner I took the bus to the Moulay Abdullah [brothel]; once a week I dined at the Consulate. The consul allowed me to come to him for a bath. I used to walk up, under the walls, swinging my sponge-bag through the dusk. He, his wife and their governess were the only English people I met; the only people, indeed, with whom I did more than exchange bare civilities. Sometimes I visited the native cinema where old, silent films were shown in a babel of catcalls. On other evenings I took a dose of Dial [sleeping draught] and was asleep by half-past nine. In these circumstances the book progressed well.[1]

Thus John Plant, the hero of *Work Suspended* (1942); thus Waugh in January and February of 1934. In several respects Waugh's life was substantially dissimilar to Plant's: Waugh's father was still alive, though clearly in failing health; Plant wrote detective fiction; Waugh's time in Fez was also structured by religious observance, and his visits to the brothel were more frequent. But for the most part the opening

1. *Work Suspended*, pp. 107–9.

pages of his story appear to be a documentary account of his experience while at work on *A Handful of Dust*.[2]

His chief correspondents during this period of austerity were Mary Lygon and Katharine Asquith and for each there was a separate epistolary style. To Mary (in the throes of a tortured relationship with her lover) he could write as a fellow-sufferer: amusing, honest accounts of his sexual activities, the jubilant ferocity of his earlier letters still there but darkened a little by depression. Lady Mary was his particular *confidante* regarding the sad story of Teresa.

Katharine heard nothing of the Moulay Abdullah. To her he was respectful and a little cautious about her possible response to his book. In these letters he casts himself not in the role of buccaneer but of Catholic ascetic, the serious artist:

> Some French Franciscans have made a chapel a kilometre away so I haven't got away from that. . . .
>
> I peg away at the novel which seems to me faultless of its kind. Very difficult to write because for the first time I am trying to deal with normal people instead of eccentrics. Comic English character parts too easy when one gets to be thirty. . . .
>
> Reading the life of Charles de Foucauld – so thats edifying.[3]

The letters suggest that he particularly wanted this novel to be a 'good taste book', something to stem the flow of Oldmeadow's abuse. But the writing soon began to tug Waugh in another direction and he could see the comical impossibility of his producing anything of which Oldmeadow would approve:

> I am sorry to read of Lulu's death [a white pekinese belonging to Phillis de Janzé], the more so as I have just described him fully in my filthy novel and now that will be bad taste. I have written 18,500 words. It is excellent – very grim. About adultery so far. I am so afraid that Periwinkle [Lord Brownlow] will think it is about him – it isn't but bits of it are like.[4]

He was writing well and quickly. Yet even the realisation that he was probably at work on his finest book could not decoy his impatience for long. He scoured Dalroy's society column in the *Daily Sketch* to catch echoes of London gossip. It

2.  It is a dangerous practice to associate fiction with autobiography but there seems little doubt in this instance that Waugh was writing directly out of his experience in Fez while at work on *A Handful of Dust*. His letters confirm most of the 'geographical' details; the remarks about Plant's attitude to his work are reiterated in Waugh's, confessedly autobiographical, novel *The Ordeal of Gilbert Pinfold* (1957); the sales figures are confirmed by A. D. Peters's file. Cf. also *CH*, pp. 7–9 and No. 197, pp. 512–17.
3.  *Letters*, pp. 83–4.
4.  *Ibid.*, p. 84.

flattered his ego to feel privy to the domestic details of the aristocracy but perhaps the most significant element in his letters to Lady Mary is their persistent self-mockery: the half-serious presentation of himself as a loveless, down-at-heel adventurer running out of steam:

> The evenings are v. dull as there is nowhere to go or to talk to [*sic*] except froggy soldiers & they don't talk to me much so I go most evenings & take my coffee in a brothel where I have formed an attachment to a young lady called Fatima. She is not at all Dutch in her ways. She is brown in colour and her face is tatooed all over with blue patterns v. pretty but does not play the piano beautifully, she has a gold tooth she is very proud of but as we can't talk each other's language there is not much to do in between rogering. I gave Fatima that milk ring you gave me, so now if you are angry I shant be able to send it back & be forgiven. I don't think F. thinks much of it as her taste runs to gold and silver.[5]

The milk ring story was a good touch. Here was Waugh in his old Madresfield identity: the 'Puck' of the household, the Basil Seal figure careless of others' feelings, property or gifts. Like Seal he is self-consciously 'naughty' and seeks, in nursery language, the forgiveness of the stern sister, the sanctuary of the nursery chair.

No playful sexual innuendo found its way into his letters to Katharine Asquith. To her he spoke not of reading Dalroy but de Foucauld, not of society gossip but of her son's success in winning a Balliol scholarship from a Catholic school (Ampleforth), not of travelling to Marrakesh in search of entertainment but of going to Jerusalem for Easter (he never got there). As his work progressed he felt increasingly anxious as to her reaction to the subject matter:

> The novel drags on at 10,000 words a week. I have just killed a little boy at a lawn meet and made his mother commit adultery and his father get drunk so perhaps you won't like it after all.[6]

The week's break from his work (Marrakesh, Casa Blanca, Rabat, probably in early February) enabled him to return to his desk refreshed. By 10th February he could write to Peters saying that 45,000 words had been completed and dispatched to the typist. He was uncertain what might occur in the second half[7] and equally uncertain as to whether serialisation would be possible. Peters seems to have been keen on the idea as a means of raising extra revenue. But Waugh, like John Plant, still felt that 'the delicate fibres of a story suffer when it is

5.  *Ibid.*, p. 84.
6.  *Ibid.*, p. 85.
7.  Probably the section that now begins *'Chapter IV. English Gothic – II'*, p. 126.

chopped up'. Of all aesthetic principles, he held most strongly to the belief that the art of the novelist lay in his ability to conceive and complete a structure. He thought that the first section might stand on its own – and indeed it would have done. (It concluded with the now famous lines 'He had got into the habit of loving and trusting Brenda.') But he was unwilling to write another 5,000 words to 'complete' the serialised version of the novel if publication could not be guaranteed in both America and Britain.

This haggling over serialisation continued for some months. In the meantime he plodded on with the documentation of Tony's life after receiving Brenda's letter. Returned from his holiday he wrote to Lady Mary saying that he hoped to be finished within three weeks. But the composition of the next section proved more difficult than he had anticipated. By the end of February he was back in England with a substantial portion of his novel still unwritten.

We can only guess at the reasons for this hiatus. Perhaps it was simply induced by boredom. It seems more likely, though, that it was something to do with the subject matter. There was a strong, if oblique, element of autobiography in this work. As he had said, it was the first time he had attempted to describe 'real people' rather than 'eccentrics'. More importantly, it was the first time he had explored in detail the delicate subject of a wife's infidelity. It is arguable that the nagging sorrow of Evelyn Gardner's behaviour had at last spilled over from his experience into his fiction in unusually intimate fashion.

Waugh's previous literary strategy for describing infidelity had been to discipline himself into adopting a cool and humorous detachment which obstructed the reader's serious engagement with the characters. Here he was trying something new. So veiled had his irony been in *Vile Bodies* and *Black Mischief* that his outrage at a culturally degraded society had been mistaken for an advocation of anarchy. This time, it seems, he wanted to write a novel which would unequivocally establish him as a writer in T. S. Eliot's camp, defending civilisation against the barbarians. The detachment remains but, as Brigid Brophy said when reviewing the novel in 1964: 'It is the most open of Waugh's books about having a tragic intention.'[8] He was dredging the memory of his personal agony more deeply than he had dared before.

What distinguishes *A Handful of Dust* from his earlier work is Waugh's ability both to mock and to sympathise with his second-rate protagonists. There can be no tragedy without sympathetic involvement and he goes out of his way to establish grounds for Brenda's dissatisfaction. Tony is a prig and a bore, an amiable half-baked schoolboy living in a world of arrested development. The focus of the tragedy has moved beyond questions of personal culpability (although this remains a crucial issue), to centre on a more abstract, deep-rooted sickness in 'civilised' man. It is a world of 'nobody's fault' in which the characters are subject to forces

8.  *NS*, 25 September, 1964, 450; *CH*, pp. 160–2.

beyond individual control. The only figures to escape this maelstrom of egotism are Mrs Rattery and the strange, reserved girl Tony meets on the ship to South America. In the manuscript the latter appears as 'Bernadette'. At the typescript stage he altered the name throughout to 'Thérèse', a clear indication, surely, that he had another 'original' in mind. The contrast between Brenda's promiscuity and Thérèse's virginal adherence to the letter of the Catholic creed seems to signal a conflict in Waugh's own mind between his need for a sexual relationship and his respect for Catholic values. The problem was irresoluble without re-marriage.

Any hopes for his future happiness, and they were few, hung in the balance. His encounters with prostitutes only irritated his wounded self-esteem. The glamorous public image of a boisterous and brilliant adventurer was a long way from the melancholy, *déraciné* figure, loveless despite many 'friends', whom he often felt himself to be. In truth he wanted only one thing beyond his art: a safe Catholic marriage, and it was precisely this which his religion might have withheld from him. The schizophrenic difference between his letters to Madresfield and Mells Manor was not the product of hypocrisy. Waugh was torn between a desire to immerse himself in the Catholic way of life, to settle down and become 'respectable', and a contradictory, self-defensive need to maintain, if refused this, at least the dilettante luxuries of the man of the world. These had begun to pall on turning thirty but it seemed that there might be no alternative.

It would not be surprising, then, if, having taken his story up to the point of Brenda's desertion, he had required a breathing-space. The subject-matter was cutting uncomfortably close to the bone and he had to maintain distance from his material in order to write well. (The manuscript shows clear signs of heavy re-writing and excision at this point.)[9] Back in England he isolated himself in the Easton Court Hotel but could not concentrate on the novel. He attempted editorial work and began planning his next book. Fiction was becoming both arduous and inadequate as a medium for his deepest beliefs. Writing to Peters from Chagford in late February, he had his mind occupied by many other projects than *A Handful of Dust*:

> I am back & this is my address until the novel is finished.
> I here return the dramatic version of *S. Blandish*[10] which I have kept too long. I don't see any possibilities in it.

9. This is an intriguing example of how deceptive the apparently 'clean' appearance of Waugh's early MSS can be. The first sheet of the new section is truncated and unusually free from alteration. This probably represents the rewriting of a heavily-corrected sheet; possibly several pages were boiled down into tighter form. It almost certainly signifies that Waugh's normal fluency was interrupted at this stage and that he found it difficult to begin the second section.

10. Enid Bagnold, *Serena Blandish or The Difficulty of Getting Married* by 'A Lady of Quality' (1924).

The name of the novel is A HANDFUL OF ASHES.

If you have your copy, could you send it to me here to put into order for book publication. I won't do anything about arranging it for serial until I hear from you. If those Americans wrongly called cosmopolitan take it there must be no monkeying with the text. The serial form, as I see it, would have an additional chapter of about 5,000 words, making 50,000 in all, at the end of the scene where Tony refuses to be divorced. The chapter will describe reconciliation. . . .

P.S. There was an article of mine about debunking the bush came out in December in a crook paper called *Oxford and Cambridge [Review]* and another in U.S.A. called, I think, *Virginia Quarterly*. If they have paid up could you let me have the cash, dough, tin, spondulicks, ready, oof, doings or whatever it is. Read *Decameron*[11] & see no possibility of modernisation. *V* sorry to have wasted so much of your time.

Want to write a 'Great Life' of Gregory the Great when novel is done. Perhaps you'd see what [Tom] Balston [of Duckworth's] will pay. Could you let me know how much advance I am likely to get on *Handful of Dust* & how soon? WHAT ABOUT THAT PORTRAIT OF EMPEROR OF ABYSSINIA MRS BRANDT STOLE.[12]

The letter is reproduced in full as it tells us so much about his working practice and the jocular relationship he had with Peters and Roughead. 'Mrs Brandt' was Carol, the wife of his American agent, Carl Brandt. The pursuit of the Haile Selassie portrait continued unabated for over a year until it was finally returned. The *Oxford and Cambridge* was not a 'crook paper' at all but one run by Randolph Churchill to whom Roughead had sold Waugh's article. His annoyance stemmed from the fact that they paid the agent only £7 after an oral promise of twenty guineas. Waugh wrote not for 'self-expression' but for money and he reacted strongly to those he believed to be trying to cheat him of his wages. As part of his elaborate network of private jokes with Peters he presented himself always as suspicious of 'literary people', a jobbing book-maker out to turn an honest shilling, proud of his craft but refusing entirely the priest-artist mantle of the Romantic heritage. He saw the willingness of gullible readers to confer near-divinity upon artists as yet another manifestation of the humanist fallacy.

The technical details are also interesting. Waugh happily committed his precious manuscripts to the post of any country he happened to be in. None of the pre-war material ever seems to have been mislaid. (In this instance, Waugh

11. Possibly a reference to Boccaccio but more probably to *The New Decameron* to which Waugh had contributed two stories: 'The Tutor's Tale: A House of Gentlefolks' (1927) and 'The Tutor's Tale: Miss Runcible's Sunday Morning' (1929). The *New Decameron* was an annual collection of stories published by Blackwell.
12. *Letters*, p. 87. Amory dates it 'March? 1934'. Peters's file suggests about 27 February, 1934; cf. *Catalogue*, E236, p. 107.

probably asked for Peters's copy as his own was lodged at his parents' house.) Coupled with Waugh's brash attitude to his 'takings' this comes as a charming and rather whimsical approach. To have travelled to Chagford without his copy of the first half of the novel was perhaps mere carelessness. More probably it bears witness to his supreme command of his material at the peak of his powers. In 1962 he told Julian Jebb: 'I used to be able to hold the whole of a book in my head.'[13] This was no idle boast.

Each of his novels took him longer to write. He could not, like his brother, sit down day after day at his desk until a book was finished. By the time Peters received the letter, Waugh had already been engaged on *A Handful of Dust* for three months. It seems to have taken another month to complete. Chapman's hurried the proofs through and by 12th April he had corrected half of them, though the title was still uncertain. 'A Handful of Ashes' and 'The Fourth Decade' were both considered but, as the post-script of his letter demonstrates, the eventual title had been in Waugh's mind throughout the later stages. The manuscript merely has 'Novel (as yet unnamed)' on the cover sheet.

*

On 15th April, 1934, *Ninety-Two Days* was published, just as he was completing *A Handful of Dust*. It was generally applauded. V. S. Pritchett in the *Christian Science Monitor* saw it as 'a deep improvement on *Labels* and the book on Abyssinia [*Remote People*] in which farce and satire had become *farouche* in order to conceal a sentimental *malaise*'. He saw Waugh as emerging from a Noel Cowardly phase and exchanging his 'little stock of sophistication for a pleasing collection of sympathies, prejudices, fusses, worries and patient determinations'.[14] Like Peter Fleming in the *Spectator*, Pritchett selected the Christie episode as outstanding. But Fleming, perhaps smarting a little from Waugh's qualified praise of *Brazilian Adventure*, was marginally less enthusiastic: 'Though the book is far from being dull – the digressions especially are often brilliant – it is as nearly dull as anything Mr Waugh can write. . . .' He had other quibbles: 'That element of suspense which to a certain extent enlivens all narratives of human endeavour is lacking . . .', and 'As for the photographs, they may, as the publishers claim, "be of great anthropological interest"; but not to anthropologists'.[15]

This was fair comment and there is no evidence of Waugh's taking exception to any of it. Indeed, he was probably pleasantly surprised by the eulogies which some heaped upon the book. Blair Niles, for instance, in the *New York Times Book Review*, linked Waugh's name with Lawrence, Douglas and Tomlinson as one of an élite who 'had led the way back to high travel writing standards', in

13. *Writers*, p. 109.
14. *CSM*, 25 April, 1934, 10; *CH*, pp. 144–6.
15. *Spectator*, 23 March, 1934, 474, 476; *CH*, pp. 143–4.

the tradition of Doughty. Niles saw *Ninety-Two Days* as a welcome relief from 'the distortion of truth and the tawdry self-exploitation of the travel books of the recent degenerate era'.[16]

Waugh's own opinion of his book was less generous. He was aware of its structural faults; it was too 'thin' and too short; it had been written hurriedly. His decision to scrap over a third of it in *When the Going was Good* is adequate testimony to his reservations. Reviewers were often able to praise from opposed standpoints. The *TLS*, usually patronising about his early novels, delighted here in Waugh's prejudices and boredom, seeing these as productive of a tone of voice, an attitude which 'invests him with personality, and renders his epithets ... a reliable medium for exchange into the reader's own mental currency'.[17] This was largely Pritchett's line. To others, like Gilbert Armitage in the *Bookman*, it was the travelogue's objectivity which appealed, 'the *absence* of prejudice'. Waugh is seen as 'the "pure" observer'. We might suspect Waugh to have been displeased with the ground for this argument. He had clearly wished to establish a consistent scale of value judgement in the book and Armitage, moreover, would not let the public forget Waugh's image (long since abandoned) of youth agitator. The direct comparison with Godfrey Winn must have rankled.[18]

\*

Just over a fortnight after the book's publication Waugh accepted an invitation to stay at Pixton Park, near Dulverton in Somerset. It was his first visit to the Herberts' elegant country house. No record of his stay there exists other than the address on a letter to Peters promising to deliver the serial ending before the end of the next week (he didn't). Early in 1935 he wrote to Mary Lygon saying: 'I have taken a *great* fancy to a young lady named Laura. What is she like? Well fair, very pretty, plays peggoty beautifully. We met on a house party in Somerset.'[19]Was it in April 1934 that he first struck up a friendship with Laura? The consensus of opinion suggests September. Obviously his first encounter with her (the 'white mouse') in Italy in 1933 had made little impression. We shall probably never know but it is interesting to speculate that he may have been attracted to her before completing *A Handful of Dust* and before setting out for Spitzbergen.

The latter trip, like so much in his life during the early 'thirties, came about by accident. After finishing his proofs and, eventually, providing the concluding chapter for the serial, he had spent two months country-house visiting and enjoying the London season. In early July, after tea at Gerald Berners', with the

16. *NYTBR*, 27 May, 1934, 12; *CH*, pp. 146–8.
17. Unsigned review, *TLS*, 15 March, 1934; *CH*, pp. 141–3.
18. *Bookman*, May 1934, 12.
19. *Letters*, p. 92.

Sitwells, and Dianas Cooper and Guinness, he found himself outside the house on a warm July evening and at a loose end. It is with the details of that day that the diary picks up again after a gap of over a year:

> ... so I walked across Belgrave Square to see if anyone was at home at Halkyn House [the Beauchamp town house]. Hugh [Lygon] was in the library drinking gin. I asked why he was in London and he said he was going to Spitzbergen on Saturday with Sandy Glen who had come over to Madresfield for the day at Sibell [Lygon]'s Chepstow Races Party. ... I said I would go to Spitzbergen too. Then I went back [to the Savile Club, Piccadilly] to dress. While I was in my bath Sandy Glen rang up and came to see me. We had some champagne while I dressed. He said it was all right my going to Spitzbergen with him. I gave him £25 for fares and he gave me a list of things I should need.[20]

Two months of circulating luxuriously in 'Society' had rendered him corpulent and lethargic. Much as he loved the company of the rich he was impatient for change. Hugh Lygon's expedition offered escape and, possibly, danger. July in London was uncomfortably hot for a confirmed heliophobe; Spitzbergen was above the Arctic Circle.

The trip had been organised by Glen as an exploratory mission for the Oxford University Arctic Expedition of 1935–6. He wanted to find out if the trappers had husky dogs to sell and if they were of the quality required for long journeys over the polar ice and across the islands to the east and north. Spitzbergen, an island about the size of Wales, touched on 81°N and was one of the northernmost landfalls usually accessible during the summer because the Gulf Stream kept its harbours relatively ice-free. It had been sparsely populated since the seventeenth century but with the discovery of coal in the nineteenth, it had become a small exporter of fuel. The Russians and the Norwegians both maintained mines there. In 1934, Glen's interest in the place was also academic. Twenty-two years old and still an undergraduate, he was some nine years the junior of Waugh and Hugh Lygon. Another object in mounting the expedition was to write up during the following term his scientific observations as a thesis on the central, coal-bearing block of the island.

Other explorers had less altruistic aims. Offering the only available winter harbour in four hundred miles of Arctic Ocean between Cape Norway and Russia, Spitzbergen's vital strategic importance had not escaped the attention of the German Navy, and, without realising it, Waugh met one of their advance guard during this journey. While he was idling across Belgrave Square from one aristocratic household to another, sinking champagne in his club and producing twenty-five pounds for another casual foreign excursion, Britain was in the grips of the

20. *Diaries*, 5 July, 1934, p. 386.

Depression and Hitler firmly established as the Chancellor of Germany. No echoes of these momentous historical issues intrude upon his private record.

He had only a few days to prepare. A visit to Lillywhite's secured skis, an ice-axe and a balaclava helmet. Then he dashed to Holborn to purchase a sleeping bag and a cape-groundsheet. That night he dined with his parents but he did not stay:

> Rang up the 43 and asked for Winnie. They said she had not yet arrived so I went to her flat. She put up a good show of being sorry for my departure.[21]

The 'Forty-Three' was the notorious night club run by Mrs Meyrick at 43 Gerard Street, described by Alec Waugh as 'half a speak-easy and half a brothel'.[22] It was much frequented by Waugh's contemporaries. The description of the 'Old Hundreth' in *A Handful of Dust* was modelled closely on it. Waugh used the place for late-night drinking and prostitutes. Winnie appears to have been his regular woman and he had already repaid her generosity by donating her name to the call-girl's child in his novel (and possibly by offering a direct portrait in Milly).

Drunken conversations with loose women were unpleasantly familiar to Waugh at this time. He was not proud of this aspect of his existence. The diary entry for the next day reveals the tension he felt:

> To Farm Street [Catholic Church] to confess Winnie. A few more purchases included birthday cake for Teresa. Waited at the Savile for parcels to arrive. . . . Tom [Balston] came too. We drank gin and waited for news from Lillywhite's. . . . Winnie sent me a telegram of good wishes. Nothing from Madresfield.[23]

He was still hoping that Teresa might change her mind and 'save' him. But no telegram came from her. He never forgot her birthday during the years of his infatuation. Some of the parcels included equipment for the expedition. Others were presents for Teresa which he arranged to have posted in relays on 9th July while he was away. The gifts did not carry his name: 'It is more fun for her that way.'[24]

*

He wrote that entry aboard the *Princess Ragnhild* two days out from Newcastle. The trip thus far had been a success. On the train from St Pancras, Waugh had

21. *Ibid.*, 6 July, 1934, p. 386.
22. Alec Waugh, *The Fatal Gift* (W. H. Allen, 1973; Book Club Edition, 1973), p. 16.
23. *Diaries*, 7 July, 1934, p. 387.
24. *Ibid.*, 9 July, 1934, p. 388.

introduced young Glen to black velvet and sitting in their shirtsleeves after a substantial meal, they had become comfortably inebriated on this and gin. The arrangements at Newcastle had gone smoothly. Glen's *laissez-passer* had allowed them and their equipment easy passage aboard and there they had discovered more drink and an amusing Norwegian alcoholic who paraded on the tables and smashed light bulbs with his head. Glen remembers the trip as 'a jolly, irresponsible six or seven weeks'.[25] Waugh recalled it less charitably as a 'Fiasco in the Arctic'.[26] Glen's impression was that they had never been in any serious danger. Waugh felt that it had been his closest encounter with death.

The slow voyage up the Norwegian coast, though, he found pleasant enough apart from a noisy, stuffy cabin and his perennial insomnia. They stopped off at Bergen, Molde, Kristiansund, Trondheim, Bodö and Tromso; Lygon and Waugh killing time with cards, Edgar Wallace, drink and a beard-growing competition. Glen was an indifferent card-player and remained clean-shaven. It seems that by the time they trans-shipped to the *Lyngen* at Tromso, Waugh had become disaffected with him. From this point the *Diaries* refer disparagingly to 'the leader' and Waugh's only account of the expedition presents Glen (unfairly) as a hopeless incompetent. Perhaps his youth and *gaucherie* had begun to irritate. Under these circumstances any small mistake was amplified into a stupendous blunder. Waugh appears to have wanted to set up an exclusive relationship between himself and Hugh. Sir Alexander remembers nothing of this. He found Waugh a difficult but delightful companion, unfit certainly, but brave and determined.

They were an odd group. Having slipped and cut his head badly during the voyage Waugh had bandaged it roughly and was pleased with the effect. His bloodstained headgear and black, patchy beard gave him, he thought, the air of a desperado: ' . . . we look very disreputable and the English passengers have ceased to make friendly advances'.[27] Hugh was a tall, muscular and gentle man, a former heavyweight boxer fond of serious drinking. Glen was equally athletic, but fresh and enthusiastic, with a genuine love of the north. Waugh was small, irascible and, at the outset, fat. Unfortunately for Waugh, who would dearly have loved to patronise Glen, the latter was the only one with any experience of the Arctic, having already visited Spitzbergen twice before. Much as Waugh came to resent it, there was no option but to accept this youth's leadership.

'At Tromso a series of old men became important in the leader's life', he remarked sceptically in his diary, and, aboard the *Lyngen:* 'The leader had warned us that this was to be the most disagreeable part of the expedition, but like most of his predictions – notably that Tromso was a cosmopolitan resort full of bars

25. Interview with Sir Alexander Glen, 26 September, 1983. All allusions to Sir Alexander's recollections refer to this interview unless otherwise stated.
26. Evelyn Waugh, 'The First Time I Went to the North. Fiasco in the Arctic' in Theodora Benson (ed.), *The First Time I* . . . (Chapman & Hall, 1935), pp. 149–62; *EAR*, pp. 144–9.
27. *Diaries*, 10, 11 and 12 July, 1934, p. 389.

and hotels – this proved wholly inaccurate.'[28] The 'old men' disparaged here had been with Amundsen to the South Pole. And though inaccessibility of hard drink in Norway was a particular deprivation for Waugh, he forgot to mention in his irritation that at almost every port they discovered superb clarets. As Sir Alexander remarked to the present writer, 'We must have drunk a hell of a lot of them, too'.

This last stage, from Tromso in northern Norway across the Arctic Sea to Spitzbergen, took four days. The ship rolled, the weather was overcast, Lygon and Glen were sick and Waugh's mood darkened. The one consolation was the unexpected warmth of an extraordinary Norwegian summer but it was this which was ultimately to bring them close to disaster. They landed at Longyear City on Advent Bay in the midnight sun of the small hours of 18th July. It was a dull and uncomfortable place and after their eleven days' voyage, Waugh was already beginning to regret his impulsive request in Halkyn House.

A wall of black rock streaked with snow circled the bay and was hung with low cloud. In this desolate place they secured an open boat and loaded it with their stores. Bruce City was their objective, 'sixty miles or so', Sir Alexander recalled gleefully. 'We rowed our own boat up there. She was a fairly heavy whale boat. . . . That was good fun.' We may suspect that Waugh did not find it so. Glen and Lygon took the oars; our hero sat disconsolately at the tiller.

At Bruce City they discovered four huts and a length of trolley rail at the foot of a glacier. They lugged the whaler up the rail to a high point on the beach and Waugh watched distraught as Glen generously distributed the last of their rum among the local assistants. The air was full of the cries of terns which swooped disconcertingly and plucked at their balaclavas. When going to fetch stream water, the only defence was to carry a tin can on a stick to act as a decoy. Waugh was fascinated by the effect of the cold, dry climate in arresting decay. Stores left by Glen's Oxford expedition the year before were in perfect condition; a water-colour drawing remained uninjured by twelve months in the open. But these small curiosities did little to lift Waugh's spirits. The expedition was clearly going to be arduous and he was in no physical condition for it. The diary breaks off abruptly with their arrival.

After a night in one of the huts they set out again late on their second evening, rowing across the fjord to another, smaller bay:

> Seals bobbed up in the water all round us; there were innumerable small icebergs, some white and fluffy, others deep green and blue like weathered copper, some opaque, some clear as glass, in preposterous shapes, with fragile, haphazard wings and feathers of ice, pierced by holes. The whole bay was filled with their music, sometimes a shrill

28. *Ibid.*, 14 July, 1934, pp. 389–90.

cricket-cry, sometimes a sharp, almost regular metallic ticking, some-times the low hum of a hive of bees ... sometimes a resonant boom, coming from the shore where another crag of ice broke away from the underhung [*sic*] glaciers. The fog cleared about midnight, the sun lay on the horizon and in the superb arctic light, that is both dawn and sunset, the ice face shone clear and blue to the white snow above it and the water was dense indigo.[29]

This evocative description is from Waugh's only published account, a short article, 'Fiasco in the Arctic'. It was written entirely from memory nearly a year later. Perhaps the intensity of this visual impression was so deeply scored in his mind because it was to be the last pleasurable aesthetic experience before five weeks of continuous discomfort.

His agony began on their disembarking. The area was totally uninhabited; one derelict hut provided them with a base camp where they could leave emergency supplies. But the first task was to move the bulk of the stores up to the ice beyond the glacier's terminal moraine. This was three miles away across a mosquito-infested valley of mud and sharp stone. The only option was to carry everything: two journeys a day for two days with 30–40 lb packs. On the second day a heavy rainstorm reduced the valley to a bog and they were forced to pick their way from boulder to boulder, heavy ration cases swinging on their backs. Then the whaler had again to be lugged up the beach, this time with block and tackle. That took a whole morning.

At last, on 22nd July, the sledge was loaded and they were ready to start. Glen's plan was to head north. There were no dogs. Waugh and Lygon strained at the ropes, their leader shoving from the rear. But they had reckoned without the thaw; the snow was soft and wet. After two hours of crippling exertion they sank exhausted, barely a hundred yards ahead. The whole expedition, Waugh felt, was like that. 'Lygon and Waugh', Glen remarked in his *Young Men in the Arctic* (1935), 'had never seen a glacier before, let alone taken part in a sledge journey, and they had pictured our travelling twenty miles or so a day over a crisp, smooth surface.'[30]

They made camp and the next morning had no alternative but to move the stores in two loads. Working ten-hour shifts for a week carrying half the provisions on their backs and then returning for the sledge, they were lucky to cover three miles a day. In the fluctuating temperature everything, including their bedding, became sodden with no means to dry it out. On two small primus stoves they boiled oatmeal and pemmican (concentrated meat, fat and albumen, high in nutrition and to Waugh, disgusting to the taste). Lygon and Glen ate heartily but

29. 'Fiasco in the Arctic', *op. cit.*, p. 155; *EAR*, p. 146.
30. A. R. Glen, *Young Men in the Arctic. The Oxford University Arctic Expedition* (Faber, 1935), p. 232.

Waugh 'could only look upon pemmican as medicine, and porridge in rather the same light as his skis'.[31] Glen describes Waugh as 'definitely unhappy' on his skis. He regarded all advice to relax while using them as contemptible: 'the skis were a painful necessity fixed rather inevitably to his feet, and he would not look upon them as anything but despicable athletic implements. [They] were utterly beyond his toleration. Lygon on the other hand was amazingly good.'[32] Among their stores they were lugging two seven-pound tins of margarine: 'G. assured us that we should have a craving for fat as soon as we were on the ice', Waugh noted angrily in his article. 'We did not find it so.'[33]

Glen's objective had been to climb the Martin Conway glacier and penetrate the northern district. Finding the glacier too severely crevassed they decided instead to turn west to Widje Bay. Here Glen hoped to find a trapper's hut used on his last expedition, and a boat. Waugh did not share his optimism. He 'proved himself an irrefutable prophet by consistently forecasting the worst. He had never expected we should find a way off the glacier, and the idea that a hut lay in any part of Widje Bay was quite absurd. . . . He freely confessed that his prophecies were founded purely on the method of complete pessimism.'[34]

They came to the mouth of the Mittag Leppler glacier which flows north into the bay. A series of small streams trickled from its base to the sea. Dense fog obscured the route ahead so they camped there to be ready a few hours later for an exploratory mission round the coast. When they woke, the fog had lifted to reveal a landscape of stunning beauty. This apparently innocuous scene was to become the setting for their accident. Next day they packed their bedding and a few rations into rucksacks, waded across the stream and set off. When they reached the hut Waugh was left to clean it while Lygon and Glen returned for the stores and the tent. Waugh completed his domestic duties and, already exhausted, lay down gratefully to sleep.

He had not been unconscious for long when Glen burst into the hut. In the few hours since crossing, the streams had turned to torrents. Both men had tried to cross to the sledge but only Lygon had succeeded. Drenched and unable to abide this condition, Lygon had then provided Glen with the amusing spectacle of 'an entirely naked man running along the side of a glacier six hundred miles from the North Pole'.[35] But the serious nature of the situation soon reasserted itself: it was clear that Lygon would never be able to return laden with stores unless Waugh and Glen gave immediate assistance.

Striding back to the glacier Waugh could hear the roar of the water half an hour before it came into sight. The various channels were enormously increased

31. *Ibid.*, p. 236.
32. *Ibid.*, pp. 235–6.
33. 'Fiasco in the Arctic', *op. cit.*, p. 157; *EAR*, p. 147.
34. 'Young Men in the Arctic', *op. cit.*, p. 241.
35. *Ibid.*, p. 243.

in size and depth; the water, chilled to freezing, thundered in a racing current. It contained substantial blocks of ice which continually threatened to knock them off their feet. The danger of being swept away was considerable. Glen and Waugh tied themselves together with some tarred twine they had found in the cabin:

> First one of us waded in, the other paying him out from the shallow water. Half-way across the stream came to our middles and it was impossible to stand without the support of the cord; when the first was in shallow water, he pulled the other across; the cold was so intense that we did not feel the ice-blocks that pounded against us. In this way we reached the final channel. Hugh was already in sight with a laden pack. We threw him the string on a ski-stick and managed to drag him across. Then we began the return journey. At the last channel, after G. had got across, the twine broke in several places. Hugh and I were swept down, tumbled over and over. I had time to form the clear impression that we were both done for, when I found myself rolling in shallow water and was able to crawl ashore.[36]

Lygon struggled out a few minutes later still carrying his pack and they staggered back to the hut. Numb with cold, soaked, their teeth chattering uncontrollably, they managed to gather driftwood for a fire and rubbed each other with sand to restore circulation.

It is at this point that Waugh's and Glen's accounts diverge. Sir Alexander saw the incident as severely unpleasant but not as a serious threat to life. Waugh emphasises their injuries and particularly that Hugh had bruised a knee so badly as to require four days' rest in the hut on starvation rations until he was fit to travel. Sir Alexander believes they set off shortly after a twenty-four-hour sleep. Waugh suggests that Glen wanted to sit tight and wait for the streams to subside:

> G. maintained a pathetic belief in the abatement of the flood, but Hugh and I knew that this was its normal condition and that we had found it passable on the first morning only by reason of some ice-block higher up, forming a momentary dam. G. wished to build a turf cabin and wait for another occurrence of the same kind. Hugh and I voted for the mountain journey. I did not think it would be successful, but it seemed preferable to waiting.[37]

If we are to believe Waugh, he had been led astray by another buffoon and, as in South America, the only solution had been to take matters into his own hands. His account concludes by marginalising Glen's importance and, by emphasising

36. 'Fiasco in the Arctic', *op. cit.*, p. 160; *EAR*, p. 148.
37. *Ibid.*, pp. 161–2; *EAR*, p.149.

the hazards and sheer good fortune of their successful return to base camp, Glen's claims to leadership.

This is unfair. The decision to take the mountain route was not arrived at in the teeth of Glen's opposition. The country they had to cross had been mapped by Glen's expedition twelve months before. The distance was no more than sixty miles, probably nearer thirty. Without ice axes and sleeping bags it required care, but promised no serious hazards. It was the sensible solution. In fact it was straightforward, if extended, hill-walking: round the shoulder of the western mountain block, over it into the adjacent valley system, then 'common sense, you know', as Sir Alexander remarked, 'took one good col' and climbed up to it. 'A few small crevasses, I remember, near the top. But nothing big ... six inches, tiny things.' On the other side of the col they discovered an enormous natural amphitheatre and, below them, the area for which they were heading. They found a snow bridge, crossed onto the glacier and walked back down to the coast.

The journey had involved two uncomfortable nights sleeping in the open in damp and windy weather (once on the col, once on a large tabular boulder), but they arrived in good shape. The last stretch, nevertheless, had been particularly exhausting. As the sun never set they had thought it best to keep moving ('night' is the best time to travel in those latitudes as the lower temperatures reduce water flow and harden the snow). They had been on their feet for over twenty-four hours when they at last came in sight of their base-camp hut. A shallow stream separated them from it. But with only a quarter of a mile to go Waugh and Lygon refused to take another step.

Glen's hunger drove him on and, alone in the hut, he lit a fire and cooked a meal. Looking back towards the stream he saw his companions slumped in the snow and, conscience pricking, searched for something he could take back to restore their spirits. There were only meagre supplies and any food would have to be thrown over the stream. So he used some flour to make two dozen scones and filled them with redcurrant jelly. Wrapping each one in paper he lobbed them over the twenty feet of water to Lygon and Waugh who dived about fielding his missiles. The two stragglers then lay down again for some hours before joining Glen in the hut. There they slept for another thirty-six hours and stayed for three days. With their strength revived for the return journey, the whaler was hauled down the beach and rowed back to the Norwegian coal mine.

On the voyage out Waugh had noted disparagingly in his diary a couple in green leather shorts aboard the *Princess Ragnhild*. He had taken no further notice of them. Returning to Advent Bay, Glen found them still camped on the shore and struck up an acquaintance. Waugh and Lygon caught the next collier to Bergen. Glen stayed on and travelled to Gray Hook on the north coast with the German couple in a Norwegian boat, before returning to Tromso to examine the Laplanders' dogs in Sweden and Finland.

For Glen this journey was to form the basis of a lifetime's friendship. Had

Waugh known it, he was sitting on a considerable 'scoop'. The young Germans were Herman Ritter and his wife Christine. They were on a mission for the German Navy, investigating the strategic importance of Spitzbergen. Ostensibly a trapper, Ritter's real business was to locate potential stations for U-boat refuelling. In 1939 his experience here allowed him to direct the capture of a whale factory in the Antarctic and, later, to command a German weather expedition to East Greenland. He was to be intimately involved in the massive Nazi war effort in the Arctic in the early years of the war but later defected to the Allies. By 1941, Glen himself was back in Spitzbergen as a naval officer helping to evacuate the Norwegian and Russian mines. In 1934 the island had seemed only a miserable wasteland to Waugh. Ritter's significance and the political movements of Europe went unnoticed.

*

Back in England by late August, he was greeted by advance copies of *A Handful of Dust*. One of these he sent to Tom Driberg whose 'William Hickey' column in the *Daily Express* provided useful free publicity:

> Here is my new novel. I hope you will like it. I think it is better than the others. At any rate the frontispiece might amuse you. I instructed the architect to design the worst possible eighteen-sixty and I think he has done well.
>
> Just back from Spitzbergen which was hell – a fiasco very narrowly retrieved from disaster.[38]

The frontispiece was of Hetton Abbey. The 'worst possible eighteen-sixty' refers to its inglorious Gothic architecture. Driberg might have found it amusing in that the style of the building was reminiscent of Lancing College.

The novel was published on 4th September but Waugh's *leit-motif* of 'English Gothic' was something the reviewers unfortunately ignored. 'Unfortunately' because it was seen by him as a fundamental structural motif. He was, however, inured by this time to the low level of contemporary criticism and the book's instant popular success must have assuaged the miseries of Spitzbergen. Within days of being released it was in its third impression. The Book Society again chose it for its 'Book of the Month', ensuring substantial revenue. His financial problems, at least, were solved for the immediate future.

*A Handful of Dust* is now widely regarded as Waugh's masterpiece. He was sure of its quality. Strangely, there was no plethora of jubilant criticism. Most praised it, but the extraordinary power of the work and its superiority to his early fiction were not widely recognised. The *TLS* again expressed a certain weariness

38. *Letters*, p. 88.

mixed this time with admiration for Waugh's technical expertise: 'Whether his study of futility is worth doing – and doing at such length – is a matter of opinion; but there can be nothing but praise for his consistency of outlook.'[39] Among the book's reviewers only William Plomer and Peter Quennell would rank as 'critics'. Where were the rest of Waugh's powerful literary backers?

The enigma is perhaps partly explained by the earlier serialisation of the novel in *Harper's Bazaar*. Readers in both England and America had been devouring it in five monthly instalments published under the title 'A Flat in London' with a different ending in which Tony returns from Brazil. Had the story become too well-known before the novel was published? Certainly it did not burst upon an eager public as had the earlier works. Christopher Sykes remembered meeting Cyril Connolly after he had read the first instalment. Connolly was distraught at what he took to be evidence of Waugh's failing powers. The book appeared then as a jolly country-house novel. Snobbery, Connolly thought, had ruined a great talent. He changed his mind later.

Only one reviewer attacked Waugh: Ernest Oldmeadow in the *Tablet*. Still smarting from the rebukes received in the *Black Mischief* debate, he was eager for revenge. A novel describing adultery, drunkenness and despair confirmed his sense of Waugh's unorthodoxy and he counselled 'his friends to spend no money and no time in acquiring and reading the book'.[40] He had hoped to see Mr Waugh 'turning over a completely new leaf' after the scandal of the previous year, but: 'He has not done so. His 1934 novel, although it is disfigured by coarse expressions, is free from the gross indecency and irreverence which made its forerunner abominable; but the forerunner has not been scratched by its owner. On the contrary, all unwithdrawn, unrevised and unrepented, it is loudly advertised in a whole page at the end of the new work.'[41] The Book Society's recommendations, he said, 'are a deplorable aiding and abetting of the men and women who have rapidly succeeded in fouling English literature. So we also have a Recommendation; namely that, unless and until a wholesome change takes place, the words 'Recommended by the Book Society' shall be regarded as what the Ministry of Agriculture calls a Notification of an Infected Area.'[42]

The rest of the review was equally poisonous: the novel is seen as only feebly satirical; its 'brutal finale' is 'sedulously and diabolically cruel'; any contempt expressed for the vicious is 'obscured by the snobbery ... with which he fondly contemplates them'; the fun made of the Reverend Tendril would, the Editor felt, be gratuitously distressing to 'our Anglican friends', and religion in general 'is treated as if it were no longer even a matter for enquiry'.[43]

39. *TLS*, 6 September, 1934, 602; *CH*, pp. 149–50.
40. *Tablet*, 8 September, 1934, 10; *CH*, pp. 150–3.
41. *Ibid.*; *CH*, p. 150.
42. *Ibid.*; *CH*, p. 151.
43. *Ibid.*; *CH*, pp. 151–2.

Counselling modesty, charity and reticence, Oldmeadow revealed nothing but his own uncharitable pride. The disastrous inadequacy of his interpretation ought to have rendered it merely risible. But there was no mistaking the seriousness of this attack. It was an editorial, as was the first, not merely a review. Waugh was enraged and, again, offended to have had his good faith publicly impugned by a leading Catholic periodical. Perhaps this review did more than anything to turn him firmly in the direction of writing overtly apologetic books. No other Catholic paper reviewed *A Handful of Dust* at the time of publication. It was an ominous silence.

On this occasion, however, Waugh did not remain silent. As a gossip columnist, Driberg was interested in his friend's row with Oldmeadow. As a friend he had refrained from printing anything without Waugh's permission. The 'Open Letter' remained unpublished, the accusations of unorthodoxy unrebuked. Waugh had had enough. He gave Driberg the story and it seems that the journalist requested something quotable about the latest confrontation. Waugh responded briefly but with undisguised contempt for his assailant:

> Enclosed statement re Meadow. If you think it worth printing to be used as it stands, fully, or not at all.
>
> Evelyn.

> TEXT
> Two aspects of 'Tablet' article.
> a) an unfavourable criticism.
> b) a moral lecture.
> The first is completely justifiable. A copy of my novel was sent to the 'Tablet' for review and the Editor is therefore entitled to give his opinion of its literary quality in any terms he thinks suitable.
> In the second aspect he is in the position of a valet masquerading in his master's clothes.
> Long employment by a prince of the Church has tempted him to ape his superiors, and, naturally enough, he gives an uncouth and impudent performance.[44]

In Waugh's defence, Peter Quennell in the *New Statesman* voiced the fears of many before the appearance of the novel: that *Black Mischief* had signalled a new 'solemnity' which threatened to spoil the 'exquisite comic equilibrium' of Waugh's early fiction. Quennell had felt that 'when the satirist gave way to the Catholic moralist' in these works, this 'detracted from the charm of otherwise extravagant

---

44. ALS to Tom Driberg, nd, from 14A Hampstead Lane, Highgate; reprinted *DE*, 11 September, 1934. Sykes (p. 123) mistakenly dates this 1932 and believes the comments to have been a reaction only to Oldmeadow's attack on *Black Mischief*. Following him I repeated the error in including the letter in the *Black Mischief* section of the *CH*, p. 140.

and light-hearted stories; in short, that his serious passages were out of tune'. Quennell, though, was delighted to find his fears unfounded and was shocked by the *Tablet*'s accusations. 'Cruel *A Handful of Dust* certainly is; a more "moral" book – though Mr Waugh is too intelligent a novelist to append any explicit moral message – has seldom come my way. I rise from Mr Waugh's new novel as from a reading of one of the sterner and more uncompromising Fathers, convinced that human life is a chaos of inclinations and appetites, and that few appetites are strong enough to be worth gratifying.'[45]

Plomer, too, saw Waugh as 'moved chiefly by a kind of fascinated disgust' and delighted in the novel's literary economy: 'There is no waste, no whimsy and no padding; the book holds the attention throughout and is of exactly the right length. I think it would be a mistake to regard Mr Waugh's more surprising situations as farcical or far-fetched; they are on the whole extremely realistic, and charged with the irony that belongs to the commonplace but is rarely perceived.'[46]

Henry Yorke would have disagreed. In a remarkably frank letter he told his friend that 'The book was entirely spoilt for me by the end':

> I don't think the Demerara trip is real at all, or rather I feel the end is so fantastic that it throws the rest out of proportion. Aren't you mixing two things together? The first part of the book is convincing, a real picture of people one has met and may at any moment meet again. . . . But then to let Tony be detained by some madman introduces an entirely fresh note and we are with phantasy with a ph at once. I was terrified towards the end thinking you would let him die of fever which to my mind would have been false but what you did to him was far worse. It seemed manufactured and not real.[47]

Yorke's terms of approbation reflect the social realist element of his own fiction. He was an *avant-garde* writer with left-wing sympathies, an empiricist. Waugh was none of these. Yorke's is the familiar argument about the imbalance between 'fantasy' and 'realism' hinted at by Quennell. But Waugh had an answer:

> Very many thanks for your letter of criticism. You must remember that to me the savages come into the category of 'people one has met and may at any moment meet again.' I think they appear false to you largely because you don't really believe they exist. The reason they didn't take the stores was not honesty in any Sunday School sense.[48] I think it is

45. *NS*, 15 September, 1934, 329; *CH*, pp. 154–7.
46. *Spectator*, 14 September, 1934, 374; *CH*, pp. 153–4.
47. *Letters*, pp. 88–9; Sykes, p. 142.
48. Yorke had complained: 'To tell you the truth I was furious that the natives did not steal all the stores. I can't and won't believe that natives are honest, it's too much.' Quoted *Letters*, p. 89.

that they couldn't do two things at once. Going home meant going complete with their belongings – an act of theft, though not at all repugnant, would have been a different kind of action – and they were impelled by the mechanical mouse simply to go home.

I think I agree that the Todd episode is fantastic. It is a 'conceit' in the Webster manner – wishing to bring Tony to a sad end I made it an elaborate & improbable one. I think the sentimental episode with Thérèse in the ship is probably a mistake. But the Amazon stuff had to be there. The scheme was a Gothic man in the hands of savages – first Mrs Beaver etc. then the real ones, finally the silver foxes at Hetton. All that quest for city seems to me justifiable symbolism.

Best love to you both.[49]

The issues raised by this letter offer us an unusual insight into Waugh's technique.

The 'conceit' of Tony's death is similar in form to that of Prudence's: a preconceived symbolic mechanism. The use of the phrase 'had to be there' and his rejection of certain incidents as superfluous again reflects his aesthetic obsession with a coherent structure in which the component parts should be mutually conducive to the effect of the whole. Most interesting, though, are his remarks on the *leit-motifs* of Gothicism and the City.

The latter is surely an ironic vision of the Catholic's allegiance to Rome and his spiritual odyssey towards the City of God. (The idea of the search for a lost city was probably prompted by Colonel Fawcett's quest in Fleming's *Brazilian Adventure*. The image had already been used in the 'Lunnon' of 'Out of Depth', and this story had been written shortly after reviewing Fleming's book.) Waugh's 'Fan-Fare' (1946) states that: '*A Handful of Dust* . . . dealt entirely with behaviour. It was humanist and contained all I had to say about humanism.'[50] His use of the term 'humanism' is eclectic. He seems to mean that vision of the world which places man, not God, at the centre of existence and which believes that 'knowledge', and thus 'progress', derive from the observation of behaviour. To Waugh this was egotism and heresy. He saw only the manifest and repeated failure of societies and individuals to control and improve their lives through rationalist 'uplift' and it was on these grounds that he rejected psychoanalysts, economists, politicians and fortune-tellers as fraudulent, substitute mystics. For a man with so strong a predisposition towards 'mystical habit of mind' he was remarkably intolerant of muddled thinking. He loathed emotive phrases and mystification. The validity of Catholic doctrine he saw as based on historical facts.

'I believe', he wrote in 1939, 'that man is, by nature, an exile and will never be self-sufficient or complete on this earth; that his chances of happiness and

49. *Letters*, p. 88. Amory reads 'fake' for 'false', 'own belongings' for 'belongings', '[motive]' for 'mouse' and 'a city' for 'city'.
50. 'Fan-Fare', *op. cit.*; *EAR*, pp. 300–4; *CH*, pp. 248–53.

virtue, here, remain more or less constant through the centuries and, generally speaking, are not much affected by ... political and economic conditions ...; that the anarchic elements in society are so strong that it is a whole-time task to keep the peace.'[51] When he says to Yorke: 'You must remember that to me the savages come into the category of "people one has met and may at any moment meet again" ', he does not simply mean that he has met South American Indians and that they did indeed behave like that. It is not so much a defence of verisimilitude as an allusion to his sceptical conservatism. The Indians are a metaphorical extension of man's essential savagery along with Mrs Beaver and the silver foxes. One might add that the book is filled with animals and animal images from Mrs Beaver gobbling her yoghurt to Jock Grant-Menzies' pigs and the parallel boar-hunt in the forest. The reader is never allowed to forget man's primal bestiality and the narrow borderline between wholeness and corruption, sanity and insanity. The vampire bats, as it were, hang constant and silent upon the mosquito netting waiting to suck the blood of any unwary traveller who for a moment relaxes his guard. Often with the lightest of touches – the game of animal snap after John Andrew's death, for instance – the *motif* is repeated.

When accused of distorting normality into fantasy Waugh would suggest that 'normality' was a fiction invented to disguise this essential savagery. His novel persistently suggests incongruities between various concepts of 'normal' behaviour: '("Sitting there clucking like a 'en," Albert reported, "and the little fellow lying dead upstairs").'[52] And: ' "There's a man who's eaten two breakfasts and tries to drown his little girl" .'[53] It documents nothing more assiduously than the inability to communicate or share experience. Like the neurotic lovers in Eliot's *The Waste Land*, the individual is locked in the prison of the self and the key thrown away. The gap between expression and meaning, between action and intention, is seen to yawn ever wider in those empty telephone conversations and, especially, in the exquisitely painful scene where Brenda misinterprets the death of her son for that of her lover and thanks God for her mistake.

God, of course, is the key that has been thrown away in this purely secular world. What Waugh offers us in *A Handful of Dust*, as in *Black Mischief*, is the humanist *reductio ad absurdum*, life without (or at least in ignorance of) God. The novel, as we have seen, 'began at the end' with 'The Man Who Liked Dickens':

> ... Then after the short story was published the idea kept working in my mind. I wanted to discover how the prisoner got there, and eventually

51. *Robbery Under Law. The Mexican Object Lesson*, p. 16; *EAR*, p. 161.
52. *A Handful of Dust*, p. 113.
53. *Ibid.*, p. 144.

the thing grew into a study of other sorts of savage at home and the civilized man's helpless plight among them.[54]

The theme of the threat to civilisation by 'anarchic elements' is familiar. There seems, though, to be a shift of emphasis here in the attribution of some kind of heroic status to the central figure. Brigid Brophy's remark about the book's 'tragic intention' appears to be supported by what Waugh told Yorke: that 'the scheme was a Gothic man in the hands of savages'. The obvious interpretation is to see Tony as the representative of high culture brutalised by barbarians and, undeniably, much of the book's emotional tension derives from the spectacle of Last's exploitation. The Gothic *motif*, however, offers a double irony and a rather different reading of Tony's character.

We might presume from the term 'Gothic man' that to Waugh the Gothic Revival represented a fascinating cultural regeneration, restoring the social ideal of chivalry and the aesthetic significance of architecture and decorative art. We know of his latter-day fascination with Victoriana and we are tempted to interpret Hetton Abbey, draughty and impractical as it is, as representing a vandalised ideal. But if this were so, why did he instruct the architect to design the '*worst possible* eighteen-sixty' [my italics]? One answer is suggested by the manuscript.

This demonstrates that the original 'scheme' was changed at its inception. In the Guide Book description of Hetton (p. 14) 'Hetton Castle' has been altered to 'Hetton Abbey', 'the Castle' to 'the house' and 'fine paintings' to 'good portraits'. Later, an important excision appears. The paragraph describing Hetton beginning: 'They saw it all: the shuttered drawing-room, like a school speech hall, the cloistral passages, the dark inner courtyard, . . .' (p. 35) was originally prefaced by:

> It was a huge building conceived in the late generation of the Gothic revival [*sic*] when the movement had lost its fantasy, and become structurally logical and stodgy.[55]

This was cut from the text, presumably at typescript stage. But as nothing is altered in the subsequent description, and as it perfectly concurs with his instructions to the 'architect', there is no reason to suppose that he had changed his mind. (He removed the passage, surely, because of its incongruously didactic tone. Many such revisions delete authorial intrusion. The description dictates the reader's

---

54. 'Fan-Fare', *op. cit.*; *EAR*, p. 303. Small changes were made to 'The Man Who Liked Dickens' (Last was 'Henty', Todd 'McMaster') but so skilful was Waugh's literary carpentry that he managed to join the novel to the tale almost without alteration. The bulk of the story's original typescript is incorporated into the MS, corresponding to the chapter 'Du Côté de Chez Todd'.
55. MS, p. 19.

opinion rather than allowing the image to speak for itself.) Quite clearly, the house and Tony's idealisation of it were intended to be second-rate.

During 1932 Waugh had briefly visited Spain and from Burgos had written to 'Bloggs' Baldwin:

> I haven't seen any serious Gothic for some time so I thought I would spend Lent among Spanish cathedrals. Avila seems to me by far the most lovely. . . . I will discover all Gothic as the Gothic revivalists did. I mean living in Northern Europe so much, one's palate gets debauched by so much imitation and reproduction Gothic, that it is an effort to understand it when one meets the real thing. It must have been better to come to it straight from a classical civilization. By the way, did Ruskin ever visit Spain?[56]

The *Diaries* reveal a similar preoccupation with the Gothic Revival. Later that year, on his way to British Guiana he had noted that St John's Church in Bridgetown, Barbados, was '1830 Gothic of the best pre-Ruskin posh [?] kind. Pink coral rock with pitch-pine roof and cedar pillars; tomb of Paleologus'.[57]

Waugh, then, did not have unqualified respect for the Revival. He saw it as dividing into two quite distinct periods: pre– and post-Ruskin (late eighteenth and early nineteenth century, and late nineteenth century). Hetton is placed firmly in the latter category of 'structurally logical and stodgy' architecture dispossessed of 'fantasy'.

Waugh's love of the early English Gothic Revival (and the real thing) is in keeping with his delight in Gaudi and *art nouveau* and has clear aesthetic connections with his earlier advocacy of the novels of Firbank. All represented art forms of cohesive structure, solid and well-wrought, objective and yet suffused with a lightness of touch, tinged with 'fantasy'. Tony's ideal represents not this but its opposite: the house is drab, impractical, 'stodgy', the product, like his bedroom, of arrested development. Hence the double irony: Waugh uses Tony as a foil to the barbarities of modern civilisation while refusing his ideology heroic status. He is lamentably weak, suffers from misplaced tolerance, and is a feeble shadow of the gentlemanliness he supposes himself to represent. It is a book which rages against betrayals of trust and qualitative value but its society has long since decayed beyond the point where any sensible attachment to these ideals is (or was ever) possible in secular terms. Ultimately, as Quennell suggests, it is a book about the vanity of human wishes or, as Rose Macaulay put it in 1946: '*A Handful of Dust* seems to reach the climax of Mr Waugh's view of life as the meaningless

---

56. Unpublished ALS to Hon. Windham Baldwin, nd [probably late March, 1932], from Hotel Infanta Isabel, Burgos.
57. *Diaries*, 17 December, 1932, p. 358.

jigging of barbarous nitwits. Pleasure, sympathetic or ironic, in their absurdities has vanished: disgust has set in. . . .'[58]

One final word about the manuscript of the novel: it further suggests both his technical obsession with 'structure' and his concern with being branded irreligious. The Gothic *leit-motif* of the chapter titles was a late revision. It first appears at the end of the very last section – 'English Gothic III' (MS, p. 112). Similarly, late revisions result in the references to Jock Menzies[59] as Brenda's former lover and an MP with special interests in pig farming. We see Waugh here meticulously embellishing his work, Jock's absurd remarks about swine suddenly becoming an important thematic parallel in the latter part of the book when his question in the House regarding the Basic Pig is cross-cut with the Amazonian boar-hunt. The 'Basic Pig', of course, could ultimately be seen as a veiled description of human nature.

Other corrections suggest his particular concern with the 'question of modesty' discussed in his Open Letter. He wanted it to be a 'good taste book' and to be accepted by Catholics as orthodox. Oldmeadow's attack on *Black Mischief* directly affected Waugh's style. In revising the typescript he altered the club where Tony meets Babs from a replica of Mrs Meyrick's speak-easy/brothel to a more vaguely described 'night club'. In his first draft the manuscript read: ' "That's always the trouble with people when they have affaires [*sic*]." ' The last clause was changed to ' " . . . when they start walking out" '. A more subtle revision concerns the way in which Waugh, wishing to convey the idea of Princess Abdul Akbar's sexual promiscuity, found himself, after a struggle, unable to state this directly. Instead, rather than abandon the idea, he used the word 'promiscuously' in an abstract adverbial sense to describe the furniture (bracketed words represent deletions):

> The Princess's single room was [heavy with perfume and] [perfumed oriental promiscuity] furnished [with typically eastern] promiscuously. . . .[60]

There are several other such examples of his scrupulousness. Under the circumstances, it is not difficult to understand his fury at Oldmeadow's 'moral lecture'.

It would seem from his correspondence with Peters's office that Waugh was already inclined towards overtly apologetic writing before the publication of *A Handful of Dust*. Oldmeadow's review settled the matter. Sir Alexander Glen remembers Waugh stating during their miserable final trek on Spitzbergen that 'In the unlikely event of your getting us back I shall join the Church of Rome'. Glen was surprised to learn (in 1983) that Waugh had been a Catholic since

58. 'The Best and the Worst II. Evelyn Waugh', *Horizon*, December 1946, 367; *CH*, p. 158.
59. 'Jock Menzies' only became 'Jock Grant-Menzies' at typescript revision stage.
60. MS, p. 55.

1930. Perhaps it was simply another joke at the young man's expense. But it may also have been an indication of the novelist's desire publicly to reaffirm his faith. The fiasco of Spitzbergen had, he believed, confronted him with death and emphasised suffering as a universal condition. On his return the determination to write a 'great life' of a major Catholic figure remained constant, though the subject had by then changed from Pope Gregory to Edmund Campion. At the end of August he wrote to Roughead explaining that he had privately signed a contract with Sheed and Ward, the Catholic publishers, and that the proceeds were to go to a Catholic charity. He was informing Roughead officially so that Peters would not think he (Waugh) was avoiding the firm's commission.[61]

A letter to Lady Mary reveals the background to this decision more fully:

> So I too am staying with my Boom [father]. At present it is all dignity & peace but I expect we shall soon have a quarrel & black each others eyes & tear our hair and flog each other with hunting crops like the lovely Lygon sisters.
>
> I am going to spend a very studious autumn writing the life of a dead beast [priest]. I think I shall stay here so that I shall not be tempted to the demon at the Savile and to go out with whores & make myself ill as I do if I am away from good parents.
>
> That good taste book I wrote about sponger [Murrough O'Brien] is being a success and wherever I go people shout Long Live Bo & throw garlands of flowers in my path and I have a brass band to play to me in my bath.
>
> My Alfred's [brother's] wife has just inherited a fortune and is looking for a Highclere [superlative house]. . . .
>
> I have got fat again. I wish you could have seen me at the N. Pole I had great sex appeal – thin as Bartleet.
>
> I have just had a letter asking for the Dutch rights of *Black Mischief*. What a difficult book it will be – bound upside down with the pages in wrong order & bits left out. . . .[62]

The last paragraph, of course, refers obliquely to Teresa Jungman. As an extension of this network of private jokes he dedicated the Dutch edition of *Black Mischief* to her.

The light-hearted tone here barely disguises Waugh's uncertainty. It was a period of great change for him. The letter was written from 14A Hampstead Lane, Highgate, his parents' new home. Underhill, for all its inadequacies, had at least carried associations of a happy childhood. Now even that was gone. This

---

61. Unpublished ALS to W. N. Roughead, nd [c. 30 August, 1934], from Savile Club; *Catalogue*, E245, pp. 108–9.
62. *Letters*, p. 89. Alec Waugh had married Joan Churnside in 1932; in 1934 she inherited a quarter of a million pounds.

maisonette could in no sense be regarded as 'home'. He was more rootless than ever and embarking upon a literary enterprise requiring, for the first time, considerable research. The critical acclaim for his novel is recorded in terms of self-mockery. His estimate of his 'sex appeal' appears to have been at a low ebb. Worldly success was increasingly becoming a temporary *frisson* rather than a permanent ambition. Quennell and the reviewers of *Black Mischief* were right: he had turned serious. An ascetic scepticism came to dominate his thoughts more powerfully than ever.

# XII

# *Catholic Apologist: 1934–1936*

The reasons for his choosing to write a biography of Campion are lucidly explained in Waugh's 1946 Preface to its second (American) edition. The lease of Oxford's Campion Hall (in St Giles) was running out and it was decided to re-build off St Aldate's. A fund was set up and Sir Edwin Lutyens secured as the architect:

> I wished to do something to mark my joy in the occasion and my gratitude to the then Master [Fr D'Arcy] to whom, under God, I owe my faith. The alternatives were either a drastic revision of Richard Simpson's excellent work, which had long been out of print and had been corrected in many particulars by subsequent research, or to attempt an entirely new book. I chose the latter. . . . [1]

There is certainly a 'hint of penance' about this. But other factors also influenced him: an increased political awareness, his developing relationship with Laura Herbert and, above all, his desire unequivocally to establish his religious orthodoxy.

The political aspect is plain in the Preface. This was not merely to be a biography of a 'dead beast', a historical work, but an analogue for current political trends. Eleven years after the book's publication the parallel seemed more apposite than ever:

> We have come much nearer to Campion since Simpson's day. He wrote in the [Victorian] flood-tide of toleration when Elizabeth's persecution seemed as remote as Diocletian's. We know that his [Campion's] age was a brief truce in an unending war. The Martyrdom of Father Pro in Mexico re-enacted Campion's in faithful detail. We are nearer to Campion than when I wrote of him. We have seen the Church drawn underground in country after country. In fragments and whispers we get news of other saints in the prison-camps of Eastern and Southern Europe, of cruelty and degradation more savage than anything in Tudor England, of the same, pure light shining in the darkness, uncomprehended. The

1. 'Preface', *Edmund Campion*, p. ix.

> haunted, trapped, murdered priest is our contemporary and Campion's voice sounds across the centuries as though he were walking at our elbow.[2]

Though written after the Second World War, this describes equally well his contemporary approach. The persecution of the Church by the socialist régime in Mexico was soon to catch his attention (as it did Graham Greene's). Italy was threatening to extend its empire into Abyssinia. In Africa he had taken a dilettante interest in local politics. In South America political issues had rarely seemed important. Up to this point he had often relished 'abroad' as an escape from the political consciousness of Europe. Suddenly, in a specifically religious context, world politics were beginning to force their way into his writing.

Coupled with this, and of even greater importance to him, was the influence of Laura Herbert. By late 1934 he seems to have established a firm friendship with her. But it was initially an awkward situation. Despite the glamour of his literary reputation and society friends, there still remained the problems of age, marital law, reputation and 'propinquity and property of blood'. He was thirty-one, she eighteen; he was, according to Catholic law, still married; he was known as an ageing *enfant terrible* with some rather dangerous friends; she was a first cousin of Evelyn Gardner.[3] 'I thought', said one of Laura's elderly female relations, 'we'd heard the last of that young man.'[4] Laura's mother, Mary Herbert (née Vesey, 1880–1970), seems not at first to have approved. She kept her young daughter under close surveillance. It was not that she disliked Waugh. The Portofino bun-fight doubtless remained a memory but she bore him no ill-will for that. Half-Irish, she had a tough, volatile character. It was simply that, as a sensible mother, she saw that relationships with similar impediments rarely avoided disaster.

Mary Herbert was, like Katharine Asquith, a Catholic convert. Her family was of Protestant Ascendancy background and Laura and her sisters, Bridget and Gabriel, had been brought up as Protestants. Their father, Aubrey Herbert, an eminent Orientalist and eccentric Conservative MP, had towards the end of his life considered becoming a Catholic but had died in 1923 before making up his mind. His wife's conversion occurred shortly after his death and her two daughters followed her into the Church. Only Auberon, just a year old when his father died, was brought up as a Catholic. Waugh felt strong comradeship with other converts. Fr Ronald Knox, whom he first befriended during the composition of *Campion*, was another, and Campion himself had trodden the path from the

---

2. *Ibid.*, p. x.
3. Aubrey Herbert, Laura's father, was the half-brother of Lord Carnarvon (of Tutankhamen fame). Lady Burghclere, Evelyn Gardner's mother, was Carnarvon's sister.
4. Quoted by Sykes, p. 151.

Church of England to Rome. As in *Rossetti*, there was a deep personal involvement with the subject of his biography.

*

Waugh's courtship of Laura progressed very slowly. Christopher Sykes's biography muddles the issues of this period by misdating the crucial letter in which Waugh proposed. It was not written in 1935 but 1936.[5] There also seems to be some confusion of order in the *Letters*. The first recorded correspondence from Waugh to Laura is dated '1934?' and reads:

> Darling Laura,
> I am sad and bored and need your company. If you have a spare evening between now and when you leave London, please come out with me. Any time will suit me as I have no engagements that I cannot gladly break.
> Ask your mother first and tell her I wanted you to ask.
> That is, supposing you want to come. Perhaps you don't.
> I don't know where I shall be in the autumn so it may be a long time before we meet. Please come. I will behave respectfully, I promise.
> Love,
> Evelyn.[6]

His uncertainty of her reaction would seem to support the early dating but the phrase 'I don't know where I shall be in the autumn' points to 1935 rather than 1934. During the autumn of 1934 he knew perfectly well where he would be: in London and various country houses writing *Campion*. A year later he was planning a second visit to Abyssinia. The concluding 'I will behave respectfully, I promise' is equally intriguing. Does this not suggest a record of 'disrespectful' behaviour? The letter was surely written in the summer of 1935 after he had known her for almost a year. She was a shy but determined young lady and, like Teresa Jungman, fiercely devout. Any sexual overtures by Waugh would have been strongly rebuked.

The importance of *Campion* to Waugh was thus heightened by his desire to impress Laura and her mother as a respectable co-religionist. As the letter to Mary Lygon implies, he was making a concerted effort in the autumn of 1934 to turn his back on the flesh-pots in order to apply himself to serious study. But he only remained in his father's house for September. By early October he had decamped with his manuscript to Chagford whence he was in easy reach of Mells and Pixton Park, Laura's home.

It was during this period that he first visited Pixton as a regular week-end

5. Cf. *Letters*, pp. 103–4; Amory correctly dates it as 'Spring 1936'.
6. *Ibid.*, pp. 91–2.

guest and quickly became infatuated with Laura. Early in 1935 he had written the letter (already quoted in part) from Mells Manor to Mary Lygon:

> I have taken a *great* fancy to a young lady named Laura. What is she like? Well fair, very pretty, plays pegotty beautifully. We met on a house party in Somerset. She has rather a long thin nose and skin as thin as bromo as she is very thin and might be dying of consumption to look at her and she has her hair in a little bun at the back of her neck but it is not very tidy and she is only 18 years old, virgin, Catholic, quiet & astute. So it is difficult. I have not made much progress as except to pinch her twice in a charade and lean against her thigh in pretending to help her at peggoty.[7]

Part of the 'difficulty' is pointed up in the previous paragraph:

> I feel sad at Hazel [Lavery] being dead on account of having been very Dutch to her and so I feel a shit. So to beat myself I am having mass said at 7.30 which means being called at 6.30 and driving 6 miles in the cold & dark.[8]

It was not just that Laura and her mother were cautious: Waugh, too, for all his enthusiasm, perhaps sensed a conflict within himself. In this letter he ranges from the melancholy roué lamenting the death of a former (adulterous?) lover to the passionate schoolboy celebrating his first girl. Laura released in him the suppressed romantic, long-hidden beneath his mask of the 'man of the world'. But, after Teresa, and an extensive history of amatory disillusionment, he trod carefully.

Laura potentially offered so much. Restless and homeless, Waugh found few objects of idealism towards which he could direct his finer feelings. But here suddenly was a girl 'virgin, Catholic, quiet and astute' who seemed to be attracted to him. He had assumed that he would probably never have children. Success with Laura would mean an end to the perpetual motion of his life, the childless, reckless days which had been distasteful for so long, the casual whores and buccaneering across remote territory. More than anything he wanted to belong to the community of the Faith in an ordinary, domestic sense. *Campion* was his testimony of good-will. Success with Laura, though, seemed as far away upon the book's completion as it had at the outset.

He took from September 1934 to May 1935 to write this brief biography, a long time by his standards, and it was work for which he was effectively not paid. All royalties were made over in perpetuity to Campion Hall, a fact which he did

---

7. *Ibid.*, p. 92.
8. *Ibid.*, p. 92.

not advertise, but he was determined, no matter how long it took, to produce something excellent. That he certainly did, but if it was a labour of love, it remained laborious. Scholarship irked him and considerable research was required to set the record straight.

For the background material alone he needed thoroughly to re-acquaint himself with Tudor history. Then there were the Vatican archives and the papers in the Public Record Office. Much of the leg-work had been done for him by one of the fathers at Farm Street who had died while working on the definitive biography. Waugh never aimed so high. But we must not be deceived, as were several contemporary reviewers, by the modesty of his Preface: 'There is a great need for a complete scholar's work on the subject. This is not it. All I have done is select the incidents which struck a novelist as important and relate them in a single narrative.'[9] This is precise but unnecessarily self-effacing.

He undertook the project with great seriousness. When Peters wrote to him at Chagford in October offering a lucrative contract with the *Strand* magazine for a series of short stories he turned it down. He could promise nothing until after December, he said, because he was at work on a 'pious book'. But he found it either impossible or uncongenial to devote his time entirely to the biography. Despite the success of *A Handful of Dust*, he was still short of money.

The correspondence with his agent runs on unabated during that autumn, often several letters a week. He was angling (unsuccessfully) for a book review page in the *Daily Telegraph*. Two short stories and a newspaper article were turned out when he could drag himself from his historical studies. He appears to have had another novel in mind (clearly not *Scoop* (1938), which he did not begin until 1936). The work on *Campion* produced in him an industrious and relatively stable frame of mind.

The two stories reflect an impish black humour, much lighter in tone than 'Out of Depth'. The first – 'Mr Cruttwell's Little Outing' – pleased him immensely, though Miss Reynolds at *Harper's* did not share his enthusiasm. It was intended for the Christmas issue and she found it too savage. Waugh, angered at her refusal, was tempted to tell her to go to hell. But he restrained himself as she was a good customer and instructed Peters to send the 'dog story' – 'On Guard', vastly inferior in his view – in its stead. Both tales contained elements of mischievous private joking. Cruttwell was again lampooned, this time as a homicidal maniac, having appeared earlier in the year as an ignominious osteopath in *A Handful of Dust*. The chief character of 'On Guard' was a dog not dissimilar to the Blenheim spaniel owned by Teresa Jungman. By implication its owner was affectionately mocked as frivolous and unfaithful.

Waugh was in good spirits, as indeed were many British subjects, despite the Depression, in November and December 1934. The country was gripped by

9. *Edmund Campion*, p. ix.

Royal Wedding Fever. Prince George, the Duke of Kent (fourth son of King George V), was celebrating his union with Princess Marina of Greece, to a tumultuous public reception. London was ablaze with lights and banners, solid with squealing crowds in Marina hats, while Waugh remained quietly at Chagford, plugging away at *Campion*. Asked to write about the festivities for the *Sunday Referee* he agreed but his heart was not in it. He depicts the quiet routine of South Devon as undisturbed by this cosmopolitan frenzy. Was this unpatriotic? he asks. Not at all. Many of the farmers in his local pub were tenants of the Duchy of Cornwall and felt a deep affection for the Royal Family. No, it was just that the celebrations seemed a vulgar (he avoids the word) interruption of what ought to have been an intimate ceremony: 'Could the marriage not have taken place at Windsor? In London the whole affair seemed to have become a competition among photographers and milliners.'[10]

It was a trivial piece but, in its biographical context, it offers an interesting gauge of his mood. The London he had always loved was disappearing – 'a place full of front doors, long, decent rows of them soberly painted, with bright brass handles' – beneath the onslaught of the Common Man. 'That is the town which we love, which has survived intact in spite of the orgies of flat building and advertisement.' But this temporary disruption of order is seen to intimate a more permanent dissolution. He suggests an image of himself as a displaced person, a cosmopolitan 'kindly tolerated' by the country folk, appreciative of their decent routine but restless to return to bricks and buses.

Like many writers in the mid-thirties, Waugh was beginning to ask how much longer London could survive as a repository of civilised values. In the next column to his article the *Referee*'s editorial reported that 'France has decided to test the sincerity of Hitler's peace talk'. Just below it, Bertrand Russell's Bloomsbury pacifism appealed to 'believers in reasonableness' to 'band themselves together against the forces of fanaticism' but was unable to 'have any certainty as to what is politically desirable.'[11] The old world was dying and Waugh chose to write of its demise in the deep seclusion of the English countryside and in allegorical form.

*

His biography attempts to undermine the heroic associations of the Tudor period. It opens not with the traditionally glamorous image of Elizabeth – strong, sharp and learned – but with her squatting hopelessly on the floor in the last hours of life. Round her neck is a 'magical' talisman intended to protect her from death. This pathetic image is used by Waugh as an emblem of the inevitable failure of humanism and heretical mysticism. His story concerns a man much tempted by

10. 'Did We Overdo It?', *SR*, 2 December, 1934, 12.
11. *Ibid.*

the vanities of rational analysis and worldly success among the Tudor world's 'new men'. Campion's ignominious death at the hands of the Elizabethan pragmatists is seen not as a defeat but as a triumph of eternal over temporal values.

From this gruesome image of the shrunken Queen, Waugh tracks back through her thoughts to Campion's story. He was a brilliant young Oxford tutor in the heyday of Elizabethan material success. Oxford before the Reformation is described as emerging from the Middle Ages 'into the spacious, luminous world of Catholic humanism'[12] thanks to the international intellectual connections of the religion. But this was a 'humanism' qualitatively different from that of the Court in Campion's day.

His college remained, according to Waugh, predominantly Catholic; its concern for the development of knowledge was firmly rooted in coherent religious belief. The University as a whole, though, was beginning to feel political pressures to conform to the demands of Protestant government and Campion, like Waugh, was caught between a desire to cut a dash in the world and his need to remain true to his faith. Waugh uses this scenario as a justification of the uncompromising orthodoxy of Catholicism. With the Reformation the Church which, while 'in undisputed authority . . . could afford to wink at a little speculative fancy in her philosophers, a pagan exuberance of taste in her artists', was now 'driven to defend the basis and essential structure of her faith'.[13] This is what the book is really about: that, thanks to Campion and his fellows, Catholicism had remained 'something historically and continuously English, seeking to recover only what had been taken from it by theft. . . .'[14]

The Protestant aggressors are depicted as dull-witted barbarians, sacking Duke Humphrey's library, smashing the great reredos of All Souls, lying, informing, reduced to torture where they were found intellectually deficient in debate. The Catholics are seen as sincere, zealous and cultured men. Campion's *History of Ireland* is taken as a demonstration that 'had . . . [he] . . . continued in the life he was then planning for himself, he would, almost certainly, have come down in history as one of the great masters of English prose'.[15]

It is his submerged Catholicism, however, that prevents Campion becoming a literary man. 'He fled and doubled from the conclusions of his reason'[16] but, unlike Tobie Matthew, could not compromise: 'ideas for him demanded communication'.[17] The Jesuits he later joined in Douai 'sought to present everything as having an immediate significance and intrinsic interest; they fostered competition and argument. . . . Wherever they went they encouraged oratory and

12. *Edmund Campion*, p. 13.
13. *Ibid.*, p. 14.
14. *Ibid.*, p. 54.
15. *Ibid.*, pp. 37–8.
16. *Ibid.*, p. 25.
17. *Ibid.*, p. 29.

acting; they paid particular attention to style of language and dexterity of wit.'[18] This perfectly describes Waugh's ideal intellectual atmosphere and illuminates his own aesthetic. He looked for these qualities in his friends; he attempted to emulate the virtues of clarity and 'dexterity of wit' in his writing. His developing antagonism towards the obscurities of modernism was based firmly upon the principle that 'ideas ... demanded communication'.

The ideas communicated here were crucial to him. There can be no doubt that *Campion* was an extremely important book to Waugh – perhaps the first to which he was wholly committed. He looked to it to establish his integrity among intelligent Catholics and it seems, from the biography's polemical nature, that he wanted at last to be accepted into the ranks of the popular apologists: Ronald Knox, G. K. Chesterton and Hilaire Belloc. Knox had earlier (1927) emphasised the rational basis of Catholicism; Chesterton was later (1937) to attempt historico-political generalisation in *The Crisis of Our Civilisation*. Waugh's perspective was essentially that of the aesthete, the man who fears the erosion of the artistic developments of Catholic Europe. His emphasis, as in the 1930 *Express* article, is on the vivacity and substance of an 'organic' and sensibly 'international' culture; his criticisms are levelled at the parochial bombast of the insular English consciousness that was generated by the Reformation. Those influences – i.e. eighteenth-century town architecture, late eighteenth– and early nineteenth-century Gothic, the Pre-Raphaelite movement – to which he allowed artistic viability were all derived from Catholic Europe. His early taste for baroque and his repugnance for the stiff-necked Georgian 'men of letters' become resolved into a coherent aesthetic directly dependent upon the historical perspectives of his religion.

While writing *Campion* he regularly reviewed travel books for the *Spectator*. Of Albert Gervais he wrote:

> Perhaps one of the book's chief charms is the Gallic integrity of the author. Anglo-Saxons, when they become attracted by an alien culture, seem always to contrast it favourably with their own. Dr Gervais ... never falls into the sentimental fallacy of denying his own standards. He regards the English with their boiled mutton and whiskey, the Americans with their playing cards piously numbered instead of marked in the traditional suits, as literally barbarians.[19]

In a later piece he writes of his friends Sacheverell and Osbert Sitwell:

> Mr Sacheverell Sitwell and his brother are two of the very few living

18. *Ibid.*, p. 74.
19. *Spectator*, 12 October, 1934, 538; review of Albert Gervais, *A Surgeon's China* (Hamilton, 1934).

Englishmen who can describe architecture; it is a very gracious gift, requiring a keen visual memory, discernment and enterprise in taste, a sense of social standards, delicate accuracy of expression, and, unobtrusive at the back, a full technical scholarship of date and name and material.[20]

Here we see Waugh's qualifications for a cultured man and it is noticeable how 'a sense of social standards' is increasingly bound up with aesthetic definition. It was this tendency – to make social judgements on aesthetic grounds – and the apparently imminent onslaught of communism, which led him during the late 'thirties into overly reactionary politics. In the Gervais review the term 'barbarians' is not directed towards the native population described but to the philistinism of Western Protestant civilisation. Campion, for all his humility, spent much of his time as 'hero' in England travelling between the grand houses of the aristocracy. While writing the biography, Waugh was doing precisely the same thing. The colophon reads: 'Mells-Belton-Newton Ferrers October 1934–May 1935'. These were the homes of, respectively, Lady Katharine Asquith, Lord Brownlow and Sir Robert Abdy. No mention is made of Highgate or Chagford.

The friendship with Sir Robert and his wife, Lady Diana, was relatively new and Waugh appreciated their warm hospitality. He must have relished the house's fine library and exquisite collection of eighteenth-century furniture. He certainly enjoyed the company of Lady Diana, whom he describes affectionately in his letters as 'my midget'. In October he was invited to Newton Ferrers (near Chagford) for his birthday. But he seems not to have exerted himself to impress them as a gentleman. Rather, in the company of the aristocracy, he preferred to act the *agent provocateur*. He loved to shock. A letter to Lady Mary Lygon dramatises one such scene with vicious humour:

> So yesterday talking of this & that what should I mention but fucking. Oh said Sir Robert in pain with crocodile tears coursing down cheeks, oh you have a *low* view of love. *I* am so high-minded I never think of a thing like fucking. To *me*, he said, love is a spiritual and aesthetic matter, the worship of beauty and noble soul. How much better I am than you, he said.
>
> Did I give him away & expose his great pouncing before Lady D.? No. Gentlemanly Bo was silent and bore these undeserved reproaches without a murmur.[21]

No matter how he struggled publicly to emulate Campion's asceticism and restraint, Waugh's volcanic temperament would constantly erupt. The letters to

---

20. *Spectator*, 7 December, 1934, 890; review of Sacheverell Sitwell, *Touching the Orient* (Duckworth, 1934); *EAR*, pp. 140–2.
21. *Letters*, p. 90.

Lady Mary were a necessary safety-valve. Sexual intercourse was never far from his mind in those days.

*

Christmas was probably spent at Mells Manor. The biography was far from finished after the four months he had set aside for it, Laura appears to have been unresponsive, and the new year opened before him promising little but boredom and frustration. Holidays from the book became more frequent; his obsession with Laura more importunate. There was a strong contrast between his letters to Lady Mary and those to Laura early in 1935. To the first he could scribble hilarious (drunken?) gibberish laced with obscenity:

> I missed that train so have to wait wait wait wait god it is sad Hugh D Makingtosh [i.e. boring], H. D. M. Hugh D Hugh D I think I am about to die I missed the train. What will Laura say? say? Hugh D. Makingtosh Grainger [Lady Mary's dog] is impuissant as the frogs . . . GRAINGER CAN'T FUCK.[22]

Presumably this was his comical way of sharing his baulked passion for Laura. 'Wait wait wait wait' must have seemed an apposite motto at this point and Waugh was an impatient man. 'Estranged is the word re M[iss] Herbert', he wrote to Katharine Asquith in June. 'High estimate of her character and charm undiminished but not able to see her without embarrassment.'[23]

Writing to Laura from Belton House in May, his tone was utterly different, cool and respectful:

> Darling Laura,
> Its discouraging that we never meet. I begin to despair of ever seeing you again.
> Best wishes for Academy exam. I am sure you will pass effortlessly. Don't believe that governess. . . .
> I'm pegging away at Campion. Hope to arrest him this afternoon and rack him before I leave. Then I will hang draw & quarter him at Mells.
>
> xxx
> Evelyn[24]

She was about to take the entrance exam for the Royal Academy of Dramatic Art. The Ecclesiastical Courts were still considering Waugh's nullity case. It

22. *Ibid.*, pp. 93–4.
23. *Ibid.*, p. 95.
24. *Ibid.*, p. 94.

seems that he and Laura had reached an *impasse*. There would be no point in taking things further until he had heard from Rome. Wait, wait, wait, wait.

*Campion* was at last finished in May. In the intervening months Waugh's correspondence with Peters indicates that he was eager to begin some new project. He instructed his agent to draw up a contract with Chapman's for a 70,000 word life of Mary Stuart. He arranged to work for RKO Pictures adapting *Sylvia Scarlet* for Katherine Hepburn. He accepted an offer to go to Hollywood and, on 27th April, before the biography was finished, agreed to leave within seven days if absolutely necessary.

Nothing came of any of these projects. Instead, he plodded on with his book, wrote two more articles and, in July, a short story, 'Winner Takes All'. The story was a competent piece, more urbane mockery of 'too much tolerance' in which a younger son is constantly pushed aside in favour of an elder brother. Ultimately the latter even deprives him of his wealthy Australian fiancée. Again there is that element of private joking for his friends and relatives, especially Alec's new wife. Again Cruttwell's name graces a miserable specimen: this time a blousy blonde from a motor works called Gladys. It was amusing but bland and mechanical. The savagely unsentimental tale was now an exhausted form for him. He wanted to turn his attention to something which might stimulate his creative powers into taking a new direction.

In February his first article of the new year had been 'Abyssinian Realities: We Can Applaud Italy', published in the *Evening Standard*. This was a pugnacious attack on the sentimentalists, the liberal humanists and romancers, who saw Abyssinia as a delightful backwater of colourful customs. The reality, he insisted, was different: 'Abyssinia is still a barbarous country . . . capriciously and violently governed . . . its own governmental machinery is not sufficient to cope with its own lawless elements'. He condemned the frequent slave raids by local potentates and emphasised that, even in terms of international law, Haile Selassie had no more right to govern than the Italians:

> The proper title of Abyssinia is the Ethiopian Empire. It was taken by conquest a generation ago. The Emperor Menelik succeeded to a small hill kingdom and made himself master of a vast population differing absolutely from himself and his own people in race, religion and history. It was taken bloodily and is held, so far as it is held at all, by force of arms.[25]

In 1935 western governments were anxious about Mussolini's imperial aspirations. An invasion seemed possible and, by July, imminent. Waugh's support for Il Duce was defiantly out of step with that of most other serious writers and thinkers of

25. *ES*, 13 February, 1935, 7; *EAR*, pp. 162–4.

the time (Ezra Pound is the notable exception and he was incarcerated for a decade in a mental home for his wartime broadcasts from Italy). But Waugh cared nothing for the current of popular opinion which condemned imperialism on humanist grounds.

Italian government in Abyssinia, he thought, 'would be for the benefit of the Ethiopian Empire and the rest of Africa'. His political naïvety, though, was demonstrated by his conclusion:

> It is an object which any patriotic European can applaud. Its accomplishment will be of service to the world and, fortunately, the world may be allowed to play the part of spectator. It will be the supreme trial of Mussolini's regime. We can, with a clear conscience, fold our hands and await the news on the wireless.[26]

Europe did not 'fold its hands'. The fascist invasion sparked off similar confrontations in the immediate future. In 1936 the Spanish Civil War began; in 1938 General Cardenas's socialist government took power and bloody retribution in Mexico; in 1939 Hitler invaded Poland. The assumption that the Abyssinian war could be isolated from political instability in Europe showed a singular lack of foresight on Waugh's part.

This is all the more extraordinary in that he had never shared the adulation for Hitler of his friends Diana Mosley and her sister Unity. Hitler had always appeared to him as a bullying, Anglo-Saxon philistine. Perhaps we forget too easily that in 1935 Mussolini was not in alliance with the Nazis. Hitler was seen by many, including Waugh, as their natural enemy. In Waugh's view it was Britain's failure to support Italy over Abyssinia which pushed the Italians towards political complicity with Germany. As Donat Gallagher has put it: 'Catholic conservatives saw the situation differently.... Italian military strength, which then looked formidable, seemed the only barrier preventing Nazi Germany's annexing Catholic Austria.'[27]

The *Standard* article and *Remote People* placed Waugh in the tiny minority of people who had any detailed knowledge of Abyssinia. As the political situation accelerated towards conflict publishers began to rush out ancient travel books containing the most tenuous references to the country and Waugh was both keen to cash in on this market and dismissive of others who tried. He wrote to Peters asking if they could sell off the second serial rights of *Black Mischief* to catch the mood of (and the money in) the crisis.

In July he received a book for review bearing the label 'LEARN FROM THIS BOOK SOMETHING ABOUT ABYSSINIA, HER PEOPLE, THEIR CUSTOMS AND LIFE THERE TODAY'. Unfortunately for the author,

26. *Ibid.*, p. 164.
27. 'Introduction. The Political Decade', *EAR*, p. 158.

Waugh could discover only seven pages to which the advertisement could possibly refer and he gleefully savaged the entire work. Doubtless it was poorly written. But the basis for Waugh's attack was hypocritical. Marcelle Prat described the country as barbarous. Waugh insisted that the outrages she purported to have witnessed were more probably the dull routine of peasant life or mere lies. He was eager to establish himself as an authority because, earlier in the month, he had asked Peters to find him a job as a war correspondent.

Waugh's unfashionable political attitude and complete inexperience in war reporting did not make this easy. But Peters was astute. He approached the *Daily Mail*, one of only two national newspapers to support Mussolini (the *Morning Post* was the other) and quickly secured an assignment, expenses paid. By the beginning of August Waugh had changed his mind about the proposed contract with Chapman's and substituted one with Longman's. Tom Burns was interested in publishing a book on Abyssinia, particularly one which would offer a Catholic perspective on the situation. Burns's friendship with Waugh secured the publisher no financial favours. Longmans had to out-bid Rich and Cowan and pay an enormous advance – £950. With this deposited in his bank and the liberal expense account of the *Mail* at his disposal, Waugh made his final preparations. 'There are few pleasures more complete, or to me more rare', he noted in the subsequent book, 'than that of shopping extravagantly at someone else's expense.'[28]

\*

On 7th August he set off, apparently having stayed up all night drinking at Mrs Meyrick's. At six in the morning he caught the Golden Arrow, 'half seen through the feverish twilight of . . . Gerard Street gin'.[29] The route was now familiar: train to Marseilles; a *Messageries Maritime* ship to Port Said and Djibouti.[30] It was a dull journey at first made more tedious by the company of another English war correspondent.

In *Waugh in Abyssinia* (1936) the man remains anonymous, described as 'a reporter from a Radical newpaper'[31] or 'the Radical'. He was Stewart Emeny, the representative of the *News Chronicle*, a paper stridently opposed to Italian intervention. In his book Waugh used Emeny, as he had Whittemore in *Remote People*, as the butt of his humour. 'I did not know it was possible', he wrote, 'for a human being to identify himself so precisely with the interests of his

28. *Waugh in Abyssinia*, p. 50.
29. *Ibid.*, p. 50.
30. Sykes and Amory mistakenly suggest that Waugh sailed from Liverpool. The error results from the misdating of a letter to Laura from the Adelphi Hotel, Liverpool; cf. Sykes, p. 153, and *Letters*, p. 95.
31. *Waugh in Abyssinia*, p. 52.

employers.'[32] Waugh certainly did not suffer from this loyalty, and his unwilling-ness to fabricate 'colourful' items led to difficulties and eventual dismissal.

Emeny was the worst possible companion for Waugh. Waugh saw himself as a bachelor fiercely intolerant of the 'familiar depressing spectacle of French colonial domesticity'[33] aboard the ship; Emeny appeared to him timid and unworldly. Waugh enjoyed teasing him. 'He is a married man', he wrote to Laura, 'and does not want much to be killed and has a gas mask and a helmet and a medicine chest twice the size of all my luggage and I have told him so often that he is going to certain death that I have begun to believe it myself.'[34]

Despite Emeny, though, the voyage out seemed to promise adventure. Abyssinia was 'news'. Waugh's boredom gave way to an exhilarating sense of gravitating towards a focal point of international conflict. At Port Said a man named Rickett joined the ship. He spoke openly of having a 'mission' but professed only to be bringing funds to the Coptic Church in Abyssinia. Long, coded telegrams were received which he passed off as messages from his huntsman. The man was clearly up to something and encouraged both Waugh and Emeny to suspect that they might be sitting on a scoop.

Waugh's rather amateurish fashion of dealing with it was immediately to contact, not his newspaper but a friend (and by letter rather than cable), Penelope Betjeman:

> Can you find out for me anything about a man who should be a neighbour of yours, named Rickets [sic]? He says he is master of the Craven & lives near Newbury. I want particularly to know how he earns his living, whether he is in the British Secret Service and whether he is connected with Vickers or Imperial Chemicals. Don't on any account mention my name in your enquiry. Be a good girl about this and I will reward you with a fine fuck when I get back.[35]

The concluding promise is, of course, a joke, and one which annoyed Mrs Betjeman, who disliked the schoolboy obscenities used by Waugh and her husband in those days. Indeed, the whole enquiry is faintly ludicrous, displaying a touching faith in the power of his coterie to command an infinite range of discreet infor-mation. Waugh seems often to have confused gossip with reliable confidences. Mrs Betjeman had never heard of Rickett.[36]

*

32. *Ibid.*, p. 52.
33. *Ibid.*, p. 51.
34. *Letters*, p. 96.
35. *Ibid.*, pp. 96–7.
36. Interview with Lady Penelope Betjeman, 29 March, 1984.

By 21st August Waugh was back in the tin and tarmac of Addis. The two hotels were packed with about fifty journalists and various other dogs of war: cinema newsreel photographers, armament touts, soldiers of fortune. Patrick Balfour had preceded him as correspondent for the *Evening Standard* and they and some other English journalists set up at a comfortable *pension*, the Deutsches Haus, run by an amiable German couple.

Waugh soon discovered himself to be on a fool's errand. His first days in Addis set the tone for the following months of frustration. He had arrived with a heavy cold and mild dysentry and taken to his bed for two days. The *Mail* was unsympathetic: they wanted immediate copy. Pestered by a stream of cables into staggering onto the streets, Waugh set off angrily in search of something he was sure he could not find: hard news.

There were particular obstructions. 'I am universally regarded as an Italian spy', he wrote to Laura:

> In fact my name is mud all round – with the Legation because of a novel I wrote which they think was about them (it wasn't) with the Ethiopians because of the *Mail*'s policy, with the other journalists because I'm not really a journalist and it is black leg labour. Fortunately an old chum name of Balfour is here and that makes all the difference in the world.
> Nothing could be less romantic than my circumstances at present. . . . There is no news and no possibility of getting any, and my idiot editor keeps cabling me to know exactly what arrangements I am making for cabling news in the event of the destruction of all means of communication.[37]

That last joke at his sub-editor's expense is typical of Waugh's approach. (The cable read: 'What alternative means of communication in event breakdown?',[38] a reasonable request.) The ungentlemanly scramble for any scrap of information or 'colour' was profoundly distasteful to Waugh. Lord Kinross's (Patrick Balfour's) impression was that his friend cared nothing for his paper or for his reputation as a journalist.[39] With Balfour and Charles Milnes-Gaskell (another Englishman who 'had come out primarily in search of amusement'),[40] Waugh mischievously enjoyed the *gaucherie* of his colleagues, inventing a fantasy world for them to inhabit. The whole atmosphere of the expedition until Balfour left the country was that of a public-school prank.

Addis was daily becoming less endurable as train-loads of press-men spilled

37. *Letters*, p. 97.
38. *Waugh in Abyssinia*, p. 74.
39. Interview with Lord Kinross, 13 May, 1976.
40. *Waugh in Abyssinia*, p. 88.

into the capital. For the reasons outlined in the letter, news was difficult to procure and the correspondents were subject to the perpetual evasions of the Press Bureau. If there were to be an invasion, most thought that it would come from the south. Accordingly, in an attempt to reconnoitre the ground which this advance might cover, Waugh and Balfour set off for Harar and Jijiga, taking the train back down the line to Dirre Dowa. There Milnes-Gaskell joined them and the school party was complete.

Harar held a special place in Waugh's affections as a haven of ancient and delicate Moslem custom, a sharp contrast in its architecture and religious observance to what he saw as the general barbarism of Abyssinian life. He proclaimed Harar's virtues loudly to his companions, only to be disappointed on arrival. In the five years since the coronation Harar had been defiled with modern concrete; the disruption of its cultural coherence was symbolised for him by breaches in its walls. Abyssinians – generally described as idle and boastful in Waugh's writings – had flooded the town in preparation for war, displacing the native Hararis. There seemed to be no interest in religion any longer. A drunken police chief, his nostrils stuffed with leaves to alleviate a cold, seemed better to typify the place now than the 'light-hearted girls dancing formal and intricate figures'[41] at the wedding-party in 1930.

But there were consolations, chief among which were the delicious eccentricities of the spies Balfour and he engaged there while waiting for permission to move on to Jijiga. Waugh's was an Afghan, Wazir Ali Beg, a serious fellow with a good command of English and a nose for scandal. On their first meeting – 26th August – Beg supplied him with crucial information about Italian troop movements in Eritrea. Waugh promptly cabled the news back to London and, a week or so later, on 3rd September, it was published and immediately denied. Nothing more was said until, a month later, verification of this report resulted in general mobilisation and hastened the outbreak of hostilities. The neglect of his story is mentioned dispassionately in *Waugh in Abyssinia*. It was for Waugh the first of a series of missed or misconstrued 'scoops' and he affected complacency at the stupidity of his employers. But much as he despised the press corps, he dearly wanted to beat them at their own game.

Beg was found to be sharing his 'exclusive' information with other correspondents and was sacked. Balfour hung onto his spy, a character of unmistakable criminal tendency named Halifa and dubbed 'Mata Hari'. Waugh and Balfour were constantly providing allowances on his salary to buy him out of jail. He would disappear at night and return in the morning, in undaunted good spirits, plastered with mud. Pugnacious and thoroughly unreliable, he was always lying and looking for fights. He acted the part of the spy with Victorian theatrical relish. They loved him.

41. *Ibid.*, p. 90.

Best of all were his news bulletins:

> *Somalie Merchant Mahmood Warofaih* made trench in his garden and put his money, few day repeat to see his money and not found, at once come mad.[42]

When the authorities began to clamp down on spies, Mata Hari suggested that he and Balfour should communicate in code. He presented the idea in the following message:

> *Pantomime* as at present time very dangrouse as many Ethupian ettectives in the town and outside and *urgently* to *pantomime* and if you made the pantomime if you wants me to daily write to send you in pantomime for the words.[43]

Then there was Balfour's servant. Each correspondent had a spy, an interpreter and a servant. Balfour's arrived in Harar stiff with dope (he had been chewing khat all the way from Dirre Dowa) and obsessed with the idea that he was the Belgian Minister. All this was great fun but there was serious business on hand as well.

*

They took a coffee lorry to Jijiga where Mata Hari produced a second scoop:

> He came to our room in a kind of ecstasy, almost speechless with secrecy. He could not say it aloud, but must whisper it to each of us in turn. Count Drogafoi, the French Consul, had been thrown into prison.[44]

Many such tales had turned out to be invention. This one was true. Drogafoi was a Count Maurice de Roquefeuil de Bousquet. He mined mica near Jijiga and the day before their arrival an ancient Somali woman had been arrested on leaving his house, on her way to the Italian consulate in Harar. When she was searched, a film tube was found in her armpit. It contained pictures of lorries and five pages describing the defences of Jijiga. Waugh and Balfour believed themselves at last to have discovered something approaching the 'colourful' material their papers sought. It was a first class spy story. There was, as Waugh wryly remarked, 'even an imprisoned "bride" '.[45] No other journalists had access

42. Patrick Balfour, 'Fiasco in Addis Ababa' in Lasdislas Farago (ed.), *Abyssinian Stop Press* (Robert Hale, 1936).
43. *Ibid.*, p. 64.
44. *Waugh in Abyssinia*, p. 101.
45. *Ibid.*, p. 106.

to the news. They gleefully typed out their reports, engaged a car to rush these to the nearest wireless station, in British Somaliland (Hargeisa, about a hundred miles away), and sat back contented with their work.

The next day they accidentally bumped into Wehib Pasha, a mysterious Turk who had left Addis secretly and was clearly disconcerted to be found in Jijiga. (Waugh puts it beautifully in his travel book: 'His disgust at seeing us was highly gratifying.')[46] With Mata Hari's help they discovered that he was about to head south the next day with a massive labour gang and a train of lorries to dig a series of lion pits. These were to act as a defensive line against tanks. Another scoop. They decided to cable it from Harar.

That was on 30th August. When they returned to Harar the next day Waugh received a cable from the *Mail*. He had expected congratulations. Instead, it said: 'What do you know Anglo-American oil concession?'[47] Several others followed quickly, all demanding similar information: 'Badly left oil concession suggest you return Addis immediately.'[48] Neither Balfour nor Waugh had the smallest idea of the meaning of these messages. Clearly something had occurred in Addis but it was impossible to learn anything in Harar. Only one thing seemed embarrassingly certain: their Count Drogafoi and Wehib Pasha stories were worthless in the light of this (as yet unidentified) news from the capital.

Embarrassment was heightened by unavoidable delays in returning. The only available transport was a two-day train from Dirre Dowa where they at last heard that the news from Addis centred on Rickett. He had been promising something dramatic to Waugh and Emeny before Waugh's departure for Harar. But there had seemed no reason why the man should not have been subject to the inevitable delays and diversions of Abyssinian politics. A few days' absence, Waugh thought, could make no difference. He could not have been more wrong. The Rickett scandal was the single biggest scoop of the war and, much to Waugh's chagrin, it went to the old contemptibles Sir Percival Phillips of the *Daily Telegraph*, Mills of Associated Press and, worst of all, Emeny and the *News Chronicle*. Waugh had his revenge on all three in the books that were to follow.

They eventually reached Addis four days after the story had broken. On 29th August Emeny had been woken at four in the morning by someone hammering on the bedroom door. It was Rickett. Emeny was scarcely awake. ' "It's signed and sealed," gasped Rickett. "Lend me an electric torch." ' Too sleepy to care, Emeny passed over the torch and returned to bed. In the morning he discovered Rickett hastily packing for Europe and learned from him that he had secured an enormous mineral concession from the Emperor.[49] Rickett had given the entire

---

46. *Ibid.*, p. 107.
47. *Ibid.*, p. 109.
48. *Ibid.*, p. 109.
49. Stewart Emeny in *Abyssinian Stop Press*, *op. cit.*

text of the agreement to Mills and Phillips which they had cabled back *verbatim* at enormous expense. Phillips filled five columns in the *Telegraph* at half-a-crown a word.

Rickett was the English negotiator for an American oil firm. First reports described this inaccurately as an 'Anglo-American' company. As such, the concession represented a considerable embarrassment to the British Government for it came at precisely the time when Anthony Eden was moralising to the world about Italy's imperialist policies. It appeared that, with delicate negotiations continuing in Geneva to try to avert conflict through the League of Nations, Britain was covertly securing her own financial interests. The involvement of the United States presented another complication. If large American interests were involved in the country this suggested firstly that they recognised its sovereignty and right to grant such concessions, and, secondly, that they would wish to help defend them against any Italian attempt at expropriation. Haile Selassie had, it seemed, pulled off an ingenious piece of economic diplomacy which would commit Britain and America to more than merely vocal defence of his country. Small wonder Rickett was excited.

Small wonder, also, that the *Mail* was enraged at finding its Special Correspondent *incommunicado* for four days during the crisis. It was particularly galling for them in that Phillips had left the *Mail* after a quarrel with Lord Rothermere. They had had to supplement the Drogafoi and troop movements cables with Reuter's reports. By the time Waugh had returned to Addis the Rickett story was dead. Unwilling to be hoodwinked into political complicity, the State Department of the US Government had repudiated the concession and Britain had denied all knowledge of the deal.

For Sir Sidney Barton, the British Minister in Addis, it had come as the last of a series of embarrassments. Waugh's *Black Mischief* was widely supposed to caricature his family; his eldest daughter, Marion, was married to a member of the Italian Legation, Muzi Falconi, who had unsuccessfully attempted suicide three days earlier. Now this. Rickett had not confided in Barton and the Minister suddenly found himself at the centre of an international political scandal. It was indeed like something from the pages of *Black Mischief*.

Waugh did not accept reprimand easily. His horror of being publicly rebuked prompted the usual retaliation. 'The journalists are lousy competitive hysterical lying', he wrote to Katharine Asquith:

> It makes me unhappy to be one of them but that will soon be O.K. as the *Daily Mail* don't like the messages I send them and I don't like what they send me but I don't want to chuck them on account of honour because they have given me this holiday at great expense and would be left in soup if I stopped sending even my unsatisfactory messages; they

don't want to sack me for identical reason. So it is deadlock and we telegraph abuse at 4 and something a word.[50]

This did not prevent his trying to cancel his contract. 'By the same mail as this', he wrote to Peters, 'I am sending in my resignation to the mail [*sic*]. It wasn't possible for me to work with them they have all the wrong ideas.'[51] It seems that for most of a very dull September he continued to try to get out and the paper continued to try to replace him. Later in the month he wrote to Laura:

> It is not proving so easy to leave the *Mail* as they have made themselves so unpopular by abusing the Abyssinians that they cant get a visa for another chap to come in. They sent a chap but he is stuck at Djibouti and that is no place to be stuck in . . . and this particular chap has gone bats on account of the heat and thinks he is a lepper. So I cant very well leave them flat without anyone here at all and it looks as if i shall die in harness as they say. I am sure you will sympathise because you are lazy too. . . . [52]

The picture he paints is of the man of honour remaining at his post, despite hardship, until relief should arrive. The truth was rather different.

The *Mail* certainly sent a replacement, W. F. ('Binks') Hartin, and in the meantime begged Waugh not to desert them: that much is accurate. What is omitted from these letters is the fact that once Hartin had arrived in Djibouti the Abyssinian authorities would not admit him until Waugh had left. One *Daily Mail* correspondent was quite enough. Much of the 'abuse' of the Abyssinians carried by the paper had, after all, come from Waugh. He, however, in typically casual fashion, decided to remain where he was at the end of September because it appeared that war was imminent. It was Hartin who suffered, as the letter suggests. Marooned in Djibouti by Waugh's intransigence, he succumbed to the heat and contracted dysentery. According to Sir William Deedes, it was only Waugh's whim to hear the bells of Bethlehem over Christmas that resolved the *impasse* and released Hartin for immediate admission.[53]

Waugh's studied dilettantism appears as a form of avenging snub to the vulgar demands of his employers. Where in 1930 he had been mildly amused by the antics of the international press, in 1935 he considered the majority of his colleagues to be offensive and dangerous. He loathed the intrusive tactics of

---

50. *Letters*, p. 98. The expense of the cables is inflated for comic effect: it was half a crown a word.
51. Unpublished ALS to A. D. Peters, nd [early September 1935], np; *Catalogue*, E274, p. 113.
52. *Letters*, p. 100.
53. The Hartin story and many of the details of Waugh's domestic life in Abyssinia come from an interview with Sir William Deedes, Spring 1976.

American journalists who hunted out (or manufactured) 'impertinent personal details'.[54] In his letters to Katharine Asquith he tries to except himself from such corrupt practice:

> ... Don't believe anything sent from here. Tough American correspondents are aghast at the lies everyone sends. . . . I hope you don't see the Mail. I got a batch the other day and was appalled at the way everything I wrote had been mangled. Every joke cut[55] – half the cables misconstrued well one must expect that too but do tell any friends that read the Mail that nothing there is as I wrote it. . . . [56]

Oldmeadow was continuing his offensive against Waugh in the *Tablet*, this time complaining about the uncharitable nature of Waugh's reports from Abyssinia. Waugh was obviously nervous about his reputation in Catholic circles because of the delicate situation with Laura and the annulment. In June, before he had left, the diocesan tribunal had found in favour of his case but there was still the formality of its being argued in Rome. *Campion* was due to be published at the end of September and he hoped that this overtly apologetic work might assist his case. But Oldmeadow's vendetta was a profound embarrassment and Laura's mother remained dubious about the unorthodox figure Waugh cut in the world. In writing to Laura he would often make special mention of her family: 'PS it is odd that i dont say more about love to your mother and gabriel etc. that is to be taken for granted. it is very sincere love so please tell them.'[57]

Waugh's reports for the *Mail* were often late and unsuited to the paper's policy. As Sir William Deedes saw it: 'There was always a certain cross-purposes between what Waugh thought was worth pursuing and what the *Daily Mail* thought was news. As one who was living with Evelyn Waugh, one enjoyed the fun.' After breakfast each day Waugh would light a small cigar with the cables from his irate sub-editor. During that September of enforced inactivity, effectively confined to Addis, the journalists sought a variety of distractions to amuse themselves while they waited. Waugh taught Deedes and Emeny to ride, an essential skill in a country with only a rudimentary system of metalled roads. Each morning he would school the two younger men rather sternly in the finer points of Captain Hance's instruction. Most evenings they would get drunk.

54. *Waugh in Abyssinia*, p. 116.
55. Not all the jokes were cut. Cf. Waugh's de Roquefeuil report, *DM*, 2 September, 1935, 7: 'The Count settled in Jijiga three years ago. . . . His manner of life excited suspicions, as he had many servants, entertained guests of all races, and seldom went out except to Mass on Sunday.' This perfectly describes Waugh's concept of a decent and gentlemanly life.
56. Unpublished TLS to Katharine Asquith, nd [September 1935], np; second sheet of typescript.
57. *Letters*, p. 100.

Addis supported two 'night clubs': the *Select* and the *Perroquet*. Each had a 'cinema', bars and an almost exclusively male clientele. Each was equally dismal but they were the only places of amusement, apart from Tedj houses with their Abyssinian prostitutes (the Deutsches Haus was the immediate neighbour of one). Deedes had arrived as a cub reporter for the *Morning Post* a fortnight after Waugh and was introduced to the night-life by him. In the *Perroquet* one evening Esme Barton discovered the novelist. She had, in a sense, survived the three years since the publication of *Black Mischief* as the living model of Prudence. Waugh was not her favourite man. She concluded their discussion by dashing a glass of champagne in his face but Waugh took no offence. He laughed uproariously.

When the night-clubs palled, there was gambling. Waugh loved crosswords and cards and he befriended an American journalist with whom he played poker. H. R. Knickerbocker was an international press celebrity. He had reached Addis on 11th September as the 'Hearst Star' of Hearst International News. A man of great splendour, Knickerbocker was always paid in gold. (He later secured fame by staying at the Savoy Hotel and submitting his expense account: 'To entertaining generals, etc.: $10,000'.) Waugh fascinated him and an aggressive relationship developed. During a poker school in the early hours of one morning Knickerbocker, not entirely sober, declared that the two outstanding contemporary English novelists were Aldous Huxley and Evelyn Waugh. Rather than accept this as a compliment Waugh, probably even less sober, was enraged at his name being coupled with Huxley's and further infuriated at being placed second. 'If Knickerbocker is going to make a statement like that', he shouted, 'it should be Evelyn Waugh and Aldous Huxley, not Aldous Huxley and Evelyn Waugh.' Nothing could settle the matter but a fight. Outside the bungalow Knickerbocker handed his thick-lensed glasses to Deedes, thus rendering himself almost blind, and the two scuffled in the dust. It ended inconclusively but honour was apparently satisfied.

The incident serves to illustrate the atmosphere of aimless frustration in which the journalists, hampered by obstructive officials, spent the early months of the war: drinking, playing cards, rushing to investigate the prolific rumours of the capital and reports from their spies. (None of the correspondents saw the fighting they had come to report before Christmas.) It also serves as an illustration of the conflicting roles in which Waugh could appear when abroad: as the experienced traveller, hard-drinking, pugnacious, courageous; as the displaced London clubman; as the fractious child. Deedes remembers being impressed by Waugh's efficiency and expertise regarding supplies and equipment. (Deedes's own kit, which weighed a quarter of a ton and included two enormous zinc-lined trunks, snake-proof boots and a stupendous range of clothing and medicines was later parodied in William Boot's in *Scoop*.) Waugh knew how to maximise the small comforts of rough living. He was precise (and accurate) in his requisitioning for complex journeys. He appeared to many as the man of the world he had striven to become.

That toughness earned him some respect. His mockery of his colleagues, though, and pro-Italian sympathies largely isolated him. *Black Mischief* had damaged his credibility as an impartial observer of African affairs and set up a particular antagonism with the British Legation. He received no confidences from the Bartons or the Abyssinian authorities. Instead, he turned to the Italian Minister, Count Vinci, a man whose political (and social) position was decidedly awkward. Italy had stated her intention of invading the country but war had not yet been declared. As the representative of an aggressive Fascist state, Vinci found himself effectively, though not officially, *persona non grata*. The fittings and furniture of the Italian consulate had been packed in preparation for the inevitable withdrawal. Then nothing had happened. The Geneva talks pursued a meaningless course, the Abyssinians drilled in every available public place with a lamentable shortage of modern weaponry, and Vinci waited for the word from Il Duce.

It was the manner in which Vinci waited that engaged Waugh's sympathies: the man had style and strength. He 'had little of the manner of a professional diplomat', Waugh wrote later. 'He was stocky, cheerful, courageous, friendly and slightly mischievous; he seemed thoroughly to enjoy his precarious position. He rode out daily into the town, alone or in the company of a single groom. His enemies said that he was seeking to provoke an "incident".'[58] Waugh was being ingenuous here. Later in the same book and in his letter to Laura about Falconi he admits that the provocation of an 'incident' was precisely Vinci's intention. The lack of one had produced the political stalemate and the Abyssinians were scrupulously careful of the Count's welfare.

This was Vinci's trump card. He knew that for all their bluster and attempts to render his position ignominious, there was nothing the Abyssinians could do to him without plunging their country into war. Like Waugh, he had a sense of his own superiority in confronting a barbarous and ignorant people. So he played with them: a kind of Russian roulette, daring the authorities in ever more flagrant fashion to discipline him. Waugh delighted in Vinci's ease and good humour, his sense of the absurdity of the whole business, above all in his puckish courage. Vinci had even opened a small Fascist club in the bazaar quarter. Every day he and his First Secretary would repair there and make themselves available to any journalists who wanted to interview them. Very few, apart from Waugh and Balfour, attended these informal conferences.

Vinci necessarily became Waugh's chief source of reliable confidential news. But the Minister was discreet and devious. He gave little away. One senses that he played with the journalists as he played with the politicians. His recalcitrant behaviour, nevertheless, gave the correspondents something to write about during

58. *Waugh in Abyssinia*, p. 129.

that miserably damp September. Vinci had an elaborate network of minor agents all over the country in various consulates. On 7th September he applied for permission for consular staff to withdraw with safe conduct. The Abyssinians neither gave nor withheld permission, hoping to evade responsibility for the welfare of the Italians and insisting that they return via Addis rather than taking the shortest route to the nearest frontier. (This was to prevent them seeing any defences deployed near the borders.) The Count refused to instruct his agents' withdrawal until permission was given. The Abyssinians backed down a fortnight later. Trick one to Vinci.

Waugh found a fourth scoop here. Vinci, appreciating the *Mail*'s support, gave Waugh advance warning of his intention to withdraw his staff. Waugh immediately realised the significance of this: instructions must have come from Il Duce. Italy was preparing for military invasion as soon as the rainy season should finish in late September. After months of lethargic stasis this was the crucial signal all had been waiting for. Waugh hurried to the cable station with his 'exclusive', keen to repair the damage done by his absence during the Rickett affair. Certain that he had an even bigger story than that, he telegraphed it in Latin to avoid pilferage. In London the message proved incomprehensible. It was received as a joke and sharply rebuked. By the time the confusion was resolved, the news had become common property.

The festival of Maskal on 28th September marked, no doubt with ludicrous conflation as far as Waugh was concerned, both the end of the rainy season and the finding of the True Cross. There was a massive gathering of military, clergy and journalists. Haile Selassie stared out impassively over the multitudes, apparently unperturbed by the fact that the rainy season had not, in fact, stopped but was indulging in a final onslaught. The square was awash, priests huddled beneath canopies waiting for the ceremony to begin. All knew that this year the festival marked a more sinister date: the division between peace and war and the possible end to centuries of freedom from European domination. On 1st October Waugh telegraphed Peters: 'remaining mail'.[59] Two days later the Italians bombed Adowa in the north and the Abyssinians beat their great war drum in Addis. By 7th October the Italians had invaded from Eritrea and occupied Adowa and Adigrat. The war was at last in full swing and Waugh anticipated action. 'Binks' Hartin would have to wait.

\*

Vinci, with extraordinary bravado, also decided to wait. The commercial agent for Magalo was still on the road, making a dilatory course towards Addis collecting butterflies. Selassie was enraged. The Count went about his normal business.

59. Cable to 'Literistic' (A. D. Peters's office), 1 October, 1935, from Addis Ababa; *Catalogue*, E275, p. 113.

The authorities tried to force his hand. An elaborate departure ceremony was prepared at the station on 12th October. The entire press corps and the Abyssinian hierarchy were present. Vinci remained quietly in the Legation playing piquet. No entreaty could move him. There was no choice but to confine him elsewhere in the town under house arrest and to allow him to wait for his agent. Waugh found all this a delicious comedy: Vinci's refusal to be bustled out of the country by his future subjects struck, he thought, the right balance between dignified and mischievous behaviour.

There was little else to stimulate his novelist's imagination. All hopes of seeing action were soon dashed. Since the declaration of war, life in the capital had ground on unchanged. The fighting was hundreds of miles away and the authorities were not disposed to allow the correspondents anywhere near it in the foreseeable future. Waugh was again dogged by boredom.

He acquired a pet, a lion-skin coat and some obscene Abyssinian paintings to try to cheer himself. But the coat stank, the paintings were clumsy and the animal, as he remarked to Laura, was a failure:

> I had a baboon but he seemed incapable of affection and he kept me awake in the afternoons so I threw him away. I will try to bring you back some antilopes and ostriches.[60]

To Katharine Asquith he wrote:

> . . . it seems as though we shall all be recalled soon. Those censorship [sic] ludicrous daily propaganda communiqués, no other news, absolute impossibility of getting anywhere near the front and even the prospect of an air raid very slight. Nothing could be less heroic than our lives here. But now the rains are over we can ride in the mornings on weak little unschooled ponies then we sleep in the afternoons and get drunk in the evenings. But it is wonderful material for a novel and £25 a week are piling up in my bank and I am well used to being bored so it's OK really.[61]

He continued to try to make light of everything. After the bombing of Adowa the scandal story was that a hospital had been destroyed and an American nurse killed. Investigating this, he and Balfour decided there was no truth in it. Waugh cabled back 'Nurse unupblown'.[62]

Inertia, though, depressed him and the very nature of the war, which he believed the Italians could never win, seemed to promise nothing dramatic. 'The

---

60. *Letters*, p. 100.
61. Unpublished TLS, to Katharine Asquith, *op. cit.*, n. 56.
62. Cf. Sykes, pp. 155–6.

telephone to the north is cut', he says in a letter to Laura, 'and the only news we get comes on the wireless from europe [*sic*] via Eritrea':

> Noone is allowed to leave Addis so all those adventures I came for will not happen. Sad. Still all this will make a funny novel so it isn't wasted. The only trouble is that there is no chance of making a serious war book as I hoped. . . . You will have received a copy of *Campion* by now dont try and read it put it on the shelf and wait for the novel about journalists. all my love to you lovely poppet.[63]

The patronising tone of the penultimate sentence was a private joke between them. Douglas Woodruff remembered Waugh requiring Laura to 'say thank you to the kind gentleman' when given something.[64] It was Waugh's method of poking fun at the age gap. The implication that *Campion* would be too difficult or boring for her obviously bears small relation to his estimate of her intelligence. He particularly wanted her and her mother to read it to establish himself in their eyes as an orthodox Catholic. The noticeably more intimate tone (all the Abyssinian letters to Laura address her as 'darling') seems to have resulted from the favourable verdict of the diocesan tribunal. He was boiling up to a proposal and he was, at this time, encouraged in his hopes of appearing sufficiently respectable by the reviews of *Campion* that he was receiving. It had been published in his absence in late September.

'I am very excited about the reception of Campion', he wrote to Katharine Asquith. 'Just as a spinster with a first novel.'[65] Earlier he had asked her to get her friend Desmond MacCarthy to review the book. When he eventually did (on the radio in January 1936) it generated another controversy. At this time, though, everything was going well on the home front. The *Tablet* had, of course, ignored the biography. That was only to be expected. But Peter Quennell and Graham Greene had greeted it warmly in the *New Statesman* and *Spectator*. More importantly, the Farm Street Jesuits' journal, the *Month*, had responded with equal generosity. The *Tablet* was, in fact, the only serious Catholic journal not to notice the book. High praise had come from the rest. Over the next year *Commonweal*, *Blackfriars*, the *Catholic Historical Review*, *Catholic World*, *G. K.'s Weekly*, *Pax* – even the *Homiletic and Pastoral Review* and the *Irish Ecclesiastical Record* – all came down in favour of it. Waugh was delighted.

The excitement of what was happening in England seems only to have increased his boredom in Abyssinia. He pottered down the line to Harar again and back to Addis in the hopeless quest for news of military activity. Returned to the capital he decided that he would be better off camping in the Harar Consulate compound.

---

63. *Letters*, p. 100.
64. Interview with Douglas Woodruff, 16 June, 1976.
65. Unpublished TLS to Katharine Asquith, *op. cit.*, n. 56.

At least there he would be nearer any southern advance. But the whole business seemed futile. 'I am sick to death of the country and these lousy blackamoors', he wrote to Mary Lygon on 26th October, 'so I will soon come home. Perhaps in time for Xmas. Will you ask me to visit you at mad [Madresfield]? Pauper has gone away and I am lonely.'[66] Patrick Balfour's paper had posted him on to Arabia. Without his friend, the fantasy of Abyssinian life soon diminished for Waugh to dull incompetence and mendacity. Two days after writing this he celebrated a miserable thirty-second birthday.

Yet he refused to capitulate at this stage. Determined to see the fighting, he was delighted when, in early November, the Press Bureau issued travel permits for Dessye, the Emperor's northern headquarters. Waugh hired a lorry, ordered stores, and shared the cost with Deedes and Emeny who were to accompany him. They informed the Bureau that they would be leaving on 13th November and sat back to wait for confirmation. None came. This ingenious evasion – giving permission to travel but none to leave Addis – was enough to baulk the majority of correspondents but not Waugh. As at Lancing, he enjoyed leading boisterous excursions in defiance of authority. He had given notice of the date of their departure and he intended to stick to it.

Waugh, Deedes and Emeny consequently set off at nine in the morning concealed on the floor of their lorry amongst cases of stores, only to emerge when their servants gave the 'all clear' beyond the town. Six hours out they were stopped but allowed to continue. They travelled north until dusk, camped, and were on the move again at sunrise. But bluffing their way out of the first enquiry had done little good. Later that day, about a hundred miles from Addis, a one-eyed native chief, backed by a group of armed warriors, blocked the road. Barricades were built at both ends of the lorry and the journalists were held in a hut overnight.

The future, as Sir William remarked to the present author, 'seemed uncertain'. Deedes was only twenty-one and it was his first time in Africa. Emeny was of a nervous disposition. Waugh alone appears to have been fearless. They spent a sleepless night surrounded by native guards, unable to speak a word of their language and listening to the clicking of rifle bolts. Waugh was convinced that the protection of the Foreign Office would secure safe conduct. Sir William remembers being less certain. His worries were dispelled, though, by Waugh's insistence that they should all three play cut-throat bridge. Waugh and Emeny were accomplished players; three-handed bridge, at the best of times, is difficult and unsatisfactory; Deedes had no head for cards. Throughout the night his fear of imminent execution was displaced by Waugh's fury at his incompetence.

The next morning the barricade behind their *camion* was removed and they were escorted back to Addis to be greeted by the complaints of fellow journalists,

66. *Letters*, p. 101.

Abyssinian officials and the British Legation. The latter had instituted an official search. It was yet another embarrassment at Waugh's hands for Sir Sidney Barton.

*

On Waugh's return to Addis, he wrote to Joan, Alec's wife:

> It was delightful of you and Alec to cable the news of Cruttwell's ignominy. It has made my week. I needed cheering up as I have just returned from an unsuccessful attempt to get to the Front. . . . Really Cruttwell's failure is supremely comforting. It must be the first time in history that the official Conservative has bitched things so thoroughly.[67]

Poor Cruttwell had stood as Conservative candidate for the normally safe seat of Oxford University and had not only lost to a comic novelist (A. P. Herbert), but had lost his deposit. The news was nectar to Waugh in the desert of Abyssinian frustration. 1935 had been a good year for Cruttwell baiting. Some months earlier Cecil Hunt had written to Waugh asking for a contribution to his *Author-Biography*:

> A surprise came from Evelyn Waugh, who admitted that his favourite book was not published and that it might be years before it was completed. 'It is a memorial biography of C. R. M. F. Cruttwell, some-time Dean of Hertford College, Oxford, and my old history tutor. It is a labour of love to one whom, under God, I owe everything.'[68]

The final sentence parodies the compliment he paid to Fr D'Arcy in *Campion*. He had not seen Cruttwell for eleven years but Waugh never forgot an injury. No stone was left unthrown at the sometime Dean of Hertford College. In his present circumstances, malice spiced boredom: 'Everything is intolerably dull here', the letter continues. 'I long to get back. When I do I shall buy a house in the West and settle down.'

Settling down was clearly at the forefront of his mind. All his *confidantes* at this time received requests to find a house for him. A substantial change to his nomadic existence was envisaged, but he had only a vague idea of what might be suitable. 'When i get home', he had written to Laura, 'i shall buy a cottage':

> Please find me one. Dorset or Somerset near water sea or river long way main road but near main line station. . . . No pine trees. Sanitation light etc. no consideration . . . preferably thatch but no beams. Think

67. Unpublished ALS to Joan Waugh, 18 November [1935], from Addis Ababa.
68. Cecil Hunt, *Author-Biography* (Hutchinson, 1935), p. 216.

of Mr Beverley Nichols famous cottage and get the opposite. How about the Minehead district then you could come and visit me.[69]

He also asked Katharine Asquith to find him a cottage:

> Why not near Mells? Must be near water away from high road very quiet. A genuine cottage not a great house. Ready occupation my return at least. When I say ready occupation I mean ready to be knocked about and painted up. Three rooms in a farm would do well if the farmer wouldn't object to some very savage and obscene Abyssinian paintings I have bought.[70]

In the meantime, a last possible adventure presented itself. Shortly after their enforced return from the north, permission to leave Addis was finally granted.

On 19th November Waugh and Emeny set out again for Dessye which they reached in four days. Camped there, in a village of journalists' tents, he wrote to Penelope Betjeman:

> darling penelope ungrateful bitch I gave you a rare copy of my excellent book named E. Campion and not one word of thanks do I get.... I am celibate since Aug 1st on account of the altitude which reduces the carnal appetite, the great ugliness and disease of Abyssinian women, & my love for Miss L Herbert.... I am in a bitterly cold mountain with a boring hypochondriac socialist God I could kill him. The telegraph very sensibly refuses to accept press cables any more. I am a very bad journalist, well only a shit could be good on this particular job....[71]

The socialist was Emeny. In Emeny's account of the campaign no mention is made of Waugh on the journey to Dessye and none of their earlier abortive attempt to get to the Front. *Waugh in Abyssinia* quietly corrected these omissions which cast Emeny in the role of lone hero-adventurer. By late November Waugh could scarcely bear the man's company.

The camp at Dessye was the last straw. Nothing happened for a week (when the Emperor arrived to open a hospital) and then nothing happened again. Emeny wrote exuberantly of hikes in the mountains with fellow correspondents, boating and picnics at Christmas. Waugh's tastes could not stretch to this. He sat in his tent and wrote to his parents:

> ... It is deadly cold and dull. We came here in the hope of going to the front but cant even move out of town.

69. *Letters*, p. 100.
70. Unpublished TLS to Katherine Asquith, *op. cit.*, n. 56.
71. *Letters*, p. 102.

> We get absolutely no news from outside. The war may be over for
> all we know. So my opinion is worth less than anyones but I believe the
> Italians are beaten.[72]

The final statement emphasises how worthless his opinion was. But Waugh was
correct in his assumption that the terrain and guerrilla tactics would prove difficult
for the Italians. It was 5th May, 1936, six months later, before they entered Addis.
Even then they had secured only tenuous control of the country.

Three days after Waugh's letter to Highgate a cable came for him:

> Concerning [?] special war services regret fully obliged terminate our
> present agreement stop please therefore accepte [sic] this as stipulated
> fortnights notice stop sorry long delay in mails renders cut saunding
> [sic] cable unavoidable stop have much appreciated your work [?] our
> behalf writing – Cranfield daily mail.[73]

It was the sack. When the sub-editor's official letter of dismissal arrived it
contained a sentence which was to remain in Waugh's mind: 'From the beginning
it has proved a thoroughly disappointing war to us.'[74]

Cranfield's amicable tone was doubtless an attempt to placate his difficult
correspondent and get Hartin in, but he need not have bothered. Nothing better
suited Waugh's mood. He cabled his last piece: 'Emperor on Way to Front',
packed up, and very gratefully leaving Emeny behind, returned to Addis.

Addis was a moribund town with the press corps gone. On 5th December
Waugh telegraphed Peters requesting commissions to write a weekly article on
Abyssinia for the *Sunday Times*, the *Observer* or the *Spectator*. None wanted his
work. Quite apart from his (largely unjustified) reputation on Fleet Street as an
arrogant and unreliable reporter, Abyssinia was ceasing to be topical. As the
hostilities plodded their undramatic course, more and more papers began to
withdraw their correspondents during December. Waugh was able to indulge his
desire to hear the bells of Bethlehem with a clear conscience. He was missing
nothing. In Djibouti he found Sir Percival Phillips writing up the war from the
safety of his hotel bedroom with the assistance of a large scale map and flags on
pins. It was all good material for a novel and in the meantime he could relax. A
week later he was in the Holy Land.

*

72. *Ibid.*, p. 101.
73. The cable forms part of the specially-bound volume of *Waugh in Abyssinia* in Waugh's
     library [HRC]. The volume interpolates personal documents – travel permits, letters from
     his Afghan spy etc. – with the printed text. The first and last pages of the MS are bound
     in as endpapers.
74. Evelyn Waugh, 'The Disappointing War. 1.', *English Review*, August 1936, 114–23.

On 23rd December he wrote to Katharine Asquith from Jerusalem:

> Gradually getting the smell of the *Daily Mail* out of my whiskers. Spending four days penance for the shame of the last four months in intense discomfort at Franciscan Monastery. Moving to hotel on Xmas day. Tomorrow night at Bethlehem. I half hate Jerusalem. For me Christianity begins with the Counter-reformation & the Orientalism makes me itch. . . . The politics of Geneva, Rome, London, Paris horrify me. I have long ceased to be proud of being English – now we must cease to be proud of being European.[75]

This 'Orientalism' had prompted his distaste for the Abyssinian Coptic Church. Abyssinia had appeared to him as a vortex of all that was degenerate in western culture, including 'the politics of Rome'. In his next letter to Katharine, five days later, these feelings are resolved into a distinct withdrawal towards the core of his Faith:

> I wrote you a post card and said I half-hated Jerusalem. Well that is all over and I love it dearly.
>
> It has even made me love the Abyssinians a little to find them living in frightful squalor in a collection of huts *on the roof* of the Holy Sepulchre. Bits of meat lying about and dirty clothes and their pathetic éloingé black faces.
>
> It was decent to have Christmas without the Hitlerite adjuncts of yule logs and reindeer and Santa Claus and conifers. . . .
>
> I feel obliged to write a history of England and the Holy Places. You see St Helena, Baldwin, Lord Stratford de Redcliffe, General Gordon etc. all English.
>
> Off tomorrow to try to get to Petra. . . . After that Damascus. Then I don't know. I don't really want to return to Europe until I know one way or the other about my annulment and can arrange things accordingly.[76]

With the possibility of marriage and a more committed engagement with Catholic apologetics, the whole cast of his mind was changing.

Waugh returned to England during January 1936 via Rome where Lady Diana Cooper was staying with Gerald Berners and acting as British emissary to Il Duce. Christopher Sykes records how Waugh 'boldly applied through the Embassy for an interview'[77] with the Italian leader and was granted one on condition that he publish no account of it. He told Sykes that he had found Mussolini's personality most impressive after half-expecting him to be ridiculous. But this flirtation with

75. *Letters*, pp. 102–3.
76. *Ibid.*, p. 103.
77. Sykes, p. 158.

the self-dramatising bombast of Italian Fascism did not outlive the writing of his book on the Abyssinian war.

In London he discovered that *Campion* had spawned controversy. Desmond MacCarthy had reviewed the book favourably on the radio and the Protestant Truth Society was incensed that such a propagandist work should be accepted as accurate history. J. A. Kensit (Acting Honorary Secretary of the United Protestant Council) sent indignant letters, first to the Director General of the BBC suggesting that MacCarthy was 'an unfit person to review historical or biblio-graphical books' (MacCarthy's reading) and then to the *Listener* stating that MacCarthy (and, by implication, Waugh) had failed to take into account 'recently recovered Vatican documents at the Public Record Office'. MacCarthy was deeply shocked and resigned within a fortnight, unimpressed, as well he might have been, by the evidence of the PTS. (Kensit's published letter foolishly admits that one of these 'recently recovered' archives 'only came to light in 1886'.) Other letters flowed in; Kensit fired another broadside in the *Listener*. Waugh, distressed to see his friend attacked in this fashion, responded with devastating wit in a letter to the Editor:

> I have never (except with singular lack of success in the Final Schools at Oxford) sought reputation as a historical scholar; if I did so, I do not think ... Mr Kensit's opposition would seriously imperil it; I do not care a hoot that Mr Kensit thinks my life of Edmund Campion a 'second-hand hearsay romance of the novelist'. But it *is* important that readers of the 'Listener' ... should be left with the impression that new, damning evidence against Campion has lately come to light. ...
> I know all about the Cardinal of Como-Nuncio Sega correspondence. I did not mention it because it seemed to me irrelevant to the subject about which I was writing. It ... must be made clear that the division is not one between historians who wrote prior to the publication of the Sega correspondence and those who wrote after it, but between the United Protestant Council and the massed wisdom and knowledge of European scholarship. ... [78]

And so on for seven hundred words of closely-reasoned abuse.

It did not end there. Following this there were two letters (4th March and 1st April) from Fr Hicks, the Historiographer of the English Province, defending Waugh, and a final one from Kensit (18th March) hammering home the views of the UPC. The Editor then closed the discussion. It must have become tedious to his readers, unusual as it was in its subject, length and belligerence for the *Listener*.

Kensit, clearly aggrieved, would not let the matter rest. Under the imprint of

---

78. *Listener*, 26 February, 1936, 410–11; *CH*, pp. 172–3.

the PTS he produced a lengthy pamphlet in May 1937 entitled 'The Campion-Parsons Invasion Plot', reprinting the entire correspondence. Waugh always relished a *scandale:* 'épatez les bourgeois' might well have been his heraldic motto. But where in the past this delight in shocking the mild-mannered had led him into difficulties with his Church, here Waugh had the Jesuits on his side. Fr Hicks's letters set their stamp of approval on his orthodoxy. It was against this background that the favourable reviews of *Campion* in the more obscure and scholarly papers appeared. The controversy did more than anything to establish Waugh as a popular apologist and he loved every minute of it.

Waugh now had his Catholic enemies on the run. 8th February, 1936 was Oldmeadow's last stand in his three-year campaign against this 'mean writer'. On that date he published his last attack in the *Tablet*. The magazine changed hands in April, bought from the Archbishop of Westminster by a consortium of Catholic businessmen among whom were some of the novelist's closest allies. Their intention was to turn the paper from a parochial 'family' magazine into a Catholic competitor of the *Spectator*. Douglas Woodruff replaced Oldmeadow as Editor and Longmans (who had contracted Waugh's Abyssinia book) became the publisher. From this point, the paper sought to provide a serious counterblast to the agnostic/humanist/socialist press and it succeeded in immediately changing direction: Woodruff, Hollis, Waugh and Graham Greene all became reviewers. Authors like Waugh, who had previously been regarded as subversive, could now publicly be recognised as comrades in the struggle against the tide of left-wing ideology which swept along most of the intellectuals of the period. Connolly, Auden, Isherwood, Day-Lewis and Spender all came in for a sound spanking from Waugh in the review pages of the *Tablet* over the next three years.

With Woodruff's accession the magazine immediately advertised *Campion* and frequently referred to its merits. Waugh had spent a fortnight at Newton Ferrers and Chagford during late February and early March collecting and editing his book of short stories, *Mr Loveday's Little Outing and Other Sad Stories*. Nothing new had to be written for it and he was in high spirits. The book would bring in some cash for very little work, his relationship with Laura and her mother seemed to be progressing well and a clique of Catholic friends was about to take over a major periodical.

The only imminent unpleasantness was the writing of his 'serious war book'. There was a problem here in that he had seen no war. By the time he came to sit grudgingly at his desk in mid-April he had lost all enthusiasm for the subject.

# XIII
# *Marriage: 1936–1937*

During the composition of *Waugh in Abyssinia* Waugh wrote to Lady Acton: 'If the book bores its readers half as much as it is boring me to write it it will create a record in low sales for poor Mr Burns.'[1]

The letter is addressed from the 'Bridgewater Estate Office, Ellesmere, Salop'. Waugh had borrowed the place from Lord Brownlow in order to isolate himself for six weeks and, though the writing of the book was tedious, he turned it out rapidly once the first chapter, a historical résumé of the conflict, had been completed. He sent this to Peters on 10th May, by which time he had almost finished the second. A fortnight later 22,000 words, excluding Chapter 1, were complete and he was promising another 14,000 by the end of June. A difficulty had, however, presented itself during the writing. He had begun the work with the assumption that the Italians could never win. In early May, Haile Selassie had fled the country and the Fascists controlled the capital. He felt that he needed to return to Abyssinia in order to complete the book.

Two other significant events had occurred in this short period. During May he had heard that he was to be awarded the Hawthornden Prize for *Campion* and, probably shortly after, he wrote his now famous letter to Laura proposing marriage.

The Hawthornden, a major literary award for 'a work of imaginative literature by a British author under forty-one', gave him particular pleasure. Normally Waugh professed indifference towards such recognition. His work had been persistently ignored by Leavis's *Scrutiny*, Eliot's *Criterion* and most serious literary journals. He did not wish to be an 'intellectual' or to be the subject of debate for what he termed 'state-trained literary critics'. But *Campion* was different.

Henry Yorke wrote to him expressing the resentment that many of Waugh's friends and readers had felt at previous attempts to exclude him from the front rank of contemporary writing:

I saw Patrick [Balfour] last night who told me you had been given the

---

1. Unpublished ALS to Lady Daphne Acton, 27 April, 1936, from Bridgewater Estate Office, Ellesmere, Salop. Lady Acton married Lord Acton in 1931 and was a close friend of Ronald Knox.

Hawthornden prize for Campion. I would congratulate you on it if it were not for the fact that you are the outstanding writer of our generation and that recognition of this kind has been due to you for a long time. It may sound ungracious to put it in the way I have just done but I do feel hotly that there is not one book you have published which is not very far beyond the books they have given the prize for up till now. It takes time for outstanding work to get through their thick skulls.[2]

Waugh replied:

What a charming letter. Nothing could be less 'ungracious'.

I am very pleased indeed about the prize because, personally it takes the taste of the Daily Mail out of my tongue and generally which you won't sympathise with, because I am glad that a prize of that kind should go to a specifically Catholic book.[3]

His reputation had never been higher.

With this increased prestige and the fact that he was writing another 'specifically Catholic book' he felt relatively safe as a prospective son-in-law for Mary Herbert. He could scarcely have done more to establish himself in her eyes as one who had turned his back on the irresponsibilities of his youth. 'On m'a donné un prix qui s'appelle le "Hawthornden"', he wrote in a self-mockery to Mary Lygon, '... je suis bien content de cette affaire parce qu'il me fera beaucoup de bon avec Mde Herbert la mère de la jeune fille paresseuse au nez énorme'.[4] There had been delays in forwarding his annulment case to Rome but it was at this time being heard and a favourable result expected. Obviously his intention for some time had been to marry Laura. It was with a typical mixture of modesty and bravado that he proposed.

In asking for her hand there is a teasing casualness, as though the subject had not occurred to him before, and an unusual gentleness. The articulation of love was difficult to him. Laura had registered at RADA in May 1935 where she was, modestly and without much enthusiasm, trying to become an actress. The letter appears to have been written during the spring vacation of her first year. Isolated in Shropshire with Abyssinian politics, Waugh was thirsting for her company:

Sweetie. Another letter last night. It is noble of you. I wish I could show how grateful I am by writing six pages of vivid description on my last twenty-four hours. Well I don't think I can because you see I havent left my rooms. . . . I am pegging away at Abyssinina and the X words. . . .

2. ALS from Henry Yorke to Evelyn Waugh, nd [May/June 1936], np; quoted by Sykes, p. 152.
3. Unpublished ALS to Henry Yorke, nd [May/June 1936], np.
4. *Letters*, p. 106.

... Tell you what you might do while you are alone at Pixton. You might think about me a bit & whether, if those wop priests ever come to a decent decision, you could bear the idea of marrying me. Of course you haven't got to decide, but think about it. I can't advise you in my favour because I think it would be beastly for you, but think how nice it would be for me. I am restless & moody & misanthropic & lazy and have no money except what I can earn and if I got ill you would starve. In fact its a lousy proposition. On the other hand I think I could ... reform and become quite strict about not getting drunk and I am pretty sure I should be faithful. Also there is always a fair chance that there will be another bigger economic crash in which case if you had married a nobleman with a great house you might find yourself starving, while I am very clever and could probably earn a living of some sort somewhere. Also though you would be taking on an elderly buffer, I am one without fixed habits. You wouldn't find yourself confined to any particular place or group. Also I have practically no living relatives except one brother whom I scarcely know. You would not find yourself involved in a large family and all their rows. ... All these are very small advantages compared with the awfulness of my character. I have always tried to be nice to you and you may have got it into your head that I am nice really, but that is all rot. It is only to you & for you. I am jealous & impatient. ... You are a critical girl and I've no doubt you know ... all [my vices] and a great many I don't know myself. But the point I wanted to make is that if you marry most people, you are marrying a great number of objects & other people as well, well if you marry me there is nothing else involved. ... My only tie of any kind is my work. That means that for several months each year we shall have to separate or you would have to share some very lonely place with me. ... When I tell my friends that I am in love with a girl of 19 they looked shocked and say 'wretched child' but I don't look on you as very young even in your beauty and I don't think there is any sense in the line that you cannot possibly commit yourself to a decision that affects your whole life for years yet. But anyway there is no point in your deciding or even answering. I may never get free from your cousin Evelyn. Above all things, darling, don't fret at all. But just turn the matter over in your dear head. ... [5]

If Waugh was uncharitable, he was least charitable to himself. Vanity was not one of his vices. The uncertainty expressed here conflicts absolutely with the arrogant tone of the book he was writing and we must be careful to distinguish between the rhetoric of his public statements at this time and another register of (private) feeling altogether. The 'elderly buffer' who was making this proposal was only thirty-two. His public image of the hardened man of the world helped to disguise

5. *Ibid.*, pp. 103–4.

the self-destructive modesty revealed by this letter. It is written as from one child to another, desperate for intimacy, fearing failure.

*

The book was two-thirds completed when, after six weeks, he returned to his nomadic life. Week-ends were sometimes spent at Mells. There he might stay at the manor house or take rooms in a cottage in the village with a Mrs Long. Generally he preferred to remain in London, at the St James's Club, Piccadilly, whence he could visit Laura on her days off from the Academy.

Peters sold sections of the chapters of the book as they came in to another right-wing magazine which, like the *Tablet*, had recently been sharpened up: the *English Review*. For the previous seven years this had been edited by a prominent Roman Catholic, Douglas Jerrold. In 1936 it was re-organised with Derek Walker-Smith as Editor in the hope of providing a major organ of a committed but 'free' press, a 'mirror of informed and independent Conservative opinion', to use its own description. It set itself against the Beaverbrook and Rothermere organisations, the corporation press, and, as such, its general aims were perfectly in keeping with Waugh's. In the issues for August, September and October he published three long articles under the title 'The Disappointing War', and it was these sizeable pre-publication glimpses of the book (and others in the *Tablet* and *G. K.'s Weekly*) which helped disseminate the idea of his being an unrepentant Fascist sympathiser. The truth was much more complicated.

Waugh did not specifically select the *English Review* for his platform. Peters had tried to sell the chapters to the *Spectator* and to *Nash's Pall Mall Magazine*. The *Review*, perhaps, was the only magazine prepared to print articles supporting Mussolini. For Waugh's part, he would sell to the highest bidder. There is no doubt, though, that he energetically sought to consolidate his position as a right-wing Catholic apologist. He even went so far as to accept an invitation to speak to the Newman Society at Oxford on 7th June.

Public speaking was something he came to dislike after those boisterous and unsuccessful attempts at the Oxford Union as an undergraduate. He especially hated addressing 'societies'. This was his first such public act. Clearly he was making an effort for his faith. Perhaps it was a special favour to 'Trim', Lord Oxford, Lady Horner's son whom he had known for some time and who was in 1936 a Balliol History Scholar. It was 'Trim' who drove with him from London, an exuberant host in a white chef's cap. The young man had insisted on going via Farringdon to be introduced to the 'wicked Lord Berners' and so they arrived late.

It was a bad start. Fr Knox was agitated throughout by the delay; Waugh was equally distressed by the awfulness of his bedroom and dinner. With no time even for a cigar he was hustled into the lecture hall. Expecting to find a group of pie-faced undergraduates he discovered, to his horror, a phalanx of distinguished friends and guests: Lord 'Billy' Clonmore, the Woodruffs, the Actons and Sir Edwin Lutyens amongst others. He had no prepared text on his subject: 'The Abyssinian War'. After forty minutes of what he considered fumbling incompetence he sat down, lit a cigar, and felt better as questions were asked. The atmosphere lightened: 'I was admirable. Like a ventriloquist and his dummy. We kept that up for half an hour, wise crack back chat, & everyone laughed a lot & went away thinking the evening had been all right.'[6]

That was true of the Catholic guests who were intimately involved with the rebuilding of Campion Hall and who, a week or so later, were to gather in Oxford again for the official opening ceremony. Their attendance at the Newman was their homage to Campion's biographer and, more importantly, their public recognition of Waugh's eminence in the Catholic life of England. Woodruff wrote a complimentary account of the speech in the *Tablet* a week later. But not everyone was impressed. The *Cherwell*'s representative had been there. Where a generation earlier Waugh and Acton had used this undergraduate paper as the voice of their subversion, now the new young men saw Waugh as an oppressive agent of the Establishment. The subversive Oxonians of the 'thirties were Marxists and Waugh's account of the Abyssinian conflict seemed to the *Cherwell* to be frivolous and inaccurate. The humorous badinage at the end of his talk had struck a false note.[7]

In the space of two days in mid-June Waugh had been awarded the Hawthornden at the Aeolian Hall before several hundred people and attended the quieter but no less dignified dedication ceremony of Campion Hall. Among the guests at the latter were Fr Knox, 'Ned' Lutyens and Laura's mother. In early July *Mr Loveday* had appeared to favourable notices. Maurice Bowra in the *Spectator* had begun: 'Mr Waugh, like Mr Maugham, succeeds at every kind of writing he attempts' and must have delighted Waugh by emphasising that 'the criminal lunatic in the first [story] has had his name changed from Cruttwell to Loveday'.[8] Mr Waugh was on top but the Abyssinian book was in abeyance while he waited to see whether the Italians would grant him permission to return. He had applied to them in early June; it was 22nd July before they finally agreed to the proposition. In early July he appears to have gone to Ireland, possibly to visit the Pakenhams. On his return via Holyhead he found a cable waiting for him at his club. It confirmed the news for which he had waited so impatiently for over a year: 'Decision favourable. Godfrey.'[9] Archbishop Godfrey was informing him that Rome had agreed to annul the union with Evelyn Gardner.

Dawn was breaking as he read the telegram. Exhausted from his journey he

6. ALS to Katharine Asquith, *ibid.*, pp. 106–7.
7. Cf. *Cherwell*, 13 June, 1936, 164.
8. C. M. Bowra, *Spectator*, 10 July, 1936, 70; *CH*, pp. 182–4.
9. *Diaries*, 7 July, 1936, p. 391.

couldn't sleep but bathed, changed and waited for the earliest suitable hour to contact Laura. At 8.00 am he rang Bruton Street, her mother's London home, to discover that Laura had already gone to church. He hurried round to Farm Street where he found her and her mother in prayer. He knelt beside them. Nothing could be said until they had left the building. In the porch he told her: they were free to marry.

After a two-year gap Waugh resumed his diary with this dramatic incident, retailed in flat reportage: 'Walked back to Bruton Street to breakfast. Took Laura to her Academy, then bought her some handkerchiefs.'[10] The unemotional tone conceals his excitement. But there can be no doubt as to his mood. The time wasted while waiting for the Italians' decision could now be frittered in the most delightful fashion. He stayed at his club, dined with friends – Diana Cooper, Hubert Duggan, Maimie Lygon, Christopher Sykes, Nancy Mitford, the Yorkes – and spent every available moment with Laura. Having begun her second year at RADA by June 1936, she had a heavy acting schedule. Plays, or parts of plays, were put on every three or four days and there was little time to spare. On the day of Godfrey's telegram she was appearing in a mime as a factory girl.

The date of the engagement was, though, far from definite. Nine days later Waugh noted in his diary the hesitation still felt by Laura's mother: 'Went to tea at Bruton Street for interview with Mary who arrived late and agitated with Auberon [Laura's young brother] and headache. She says we must wait until October before being engaged and Christmas before being married.'[11] Speaking of this in a letter to Mary Lygon he said:

> I have got engaged to Miss L. Herbert. I don't think I ever told you about her. She is lazy with a long nose but otherwise jolly decent. When I say engaged Miss H. and the Pope and I and Gabriel have made up our minds but it is not to be announced until after Xmas because Gabriel is so busy selling a house and settling the civil war in Spain . . . and such things that she can't be bothered to pimp[12] for Laura for a bit. Also she is rather ashamed of me on account I move in a very undesirable set and it will take her some time to break the news gently to her high-born relations. So I shant be married for a long time. That is sad. Also Gabriel thinks it is wrong to fuck in Lent. So you must not tell people I am engaged or Driberg will put it in the papers. And dont tell pauper as he will spread foul lies about Miss H. in his unchivalrous way. And don't tell Capt. Hance or he will take Miss H. away from me on account of his superior sex appeal.[13]

10. *Ibid.*, 7 July, 1936, p. 391.
11. *Ibid.*, 16 July, 1936, p. 393.
12. 'To pimp': meaning unclear; probable sense: 'to act as chaperone/matron of honour/general factotum during the wedding preparations'.
13. *Letters*, p. 108.

The Spanish Civil War had begun earlier in the year and represented another site of conflict between Catholic conservatism and democratic socialism. Gabriel was later to go to Spain (as an auxiliary nurse for Franco's troops) and Waugh was tempted to join her. At its outset the fight between Franco's Nationalists and the Popular Front seemed a clear-cut ideological struggle. Waugh supported one side, Orwell (and most English writers) the other. Both were to modify their opinions.

During this lazy period in early July, while younger authors like Auden were ostensibly spending their time on 'the flat ephemeral pamphlet' Waugh produced his first review for the *Tablet*. Aldous Huxley's *Eyeless in Gaza* had just been published and Waugh, riding high on the tide of self-esteem, tore into it brilliantly under the title 'Blinding the Middle-Brow'. His one point of contact with the new school of Marxist writers was a shared objection to the obscurities of modernism. Huxley, Waugh suggests, 'in order to delay the middle-brow . . . has left things to the binder . . . to sew up the chapters in the wrong order'. He objects to the 'bourgeois and squeamish' nature of the characters, to the soft and shoddy ideas of the men and their 'obscure pathological derangements'. Only the women, in his view, 'sometimes come to life. Helen because she is unintellectual and has a sense of humour, her mother because she is at least a whole-hearted debauchee, are both real people.'[14]

The critical vocabulary here is a little flaccid: notions of the characters 'coming to life' and being 'real people' do not do justice to the sharpness of Waugh's powers of analysis. As he became a more practised reviewer in the following year such vagueness dropped away. In many ways this review offers a mixture of his earlier and later views. From the earlier we have the use of Bergsonian terminology: 'The men represent ideas . . . but the women represent matter . . .'. From the latter there is the general impetus towards what he was to term 'masculinity' and 'virility' in writing. The Huxley piece was a stab at an artistic enemy from the past. Lawrence, Joyce and Cocteau had been others. After this he sharpened his knife for the new generation of Marxist writers.

It was a luxurious period of constant entertainment: he dined at the Savoy and the Ritz, supped at the Café Royal, went on to the Manhattan and the Nest. During the day there was a strenuous round of luncheon parties. Now he was accepted as a prospective member of the Herbert family, much time was spent at Bruton Street, not entirely happily. Before leaving for Abyssinia he stayed several days at his parents' maisonette in Highgate. It was probably during this period that he introduced Laura to them. The atmosphere there appears to have been relaxed. Waugh slept well and for once there was no friction with his father.

---

14. 'Blinding the Middle-Brow', *Tablet*, 17 July, 1936, 84; review of Aldous Huxley, *Eyeless in Gaza* (Chatto & Windus, 1936).

But at no time was Waugh's impatience entirely quelled: 'Fury all day culminating waiters.'[15]

It was also a time of farewells: to Laura at Pixton, to his parents' house, and to an old near-mistress. At the Nest in the small hours of the day of his departure he discovered Olivia Plunket Greene, the girl with whom he had been in love while exiled as a schoolmaster in Wales. Now in her early thirties, she was an alcoholic. 'Drank with Olivia Greene', he scribbled in his diary, 'she very drunk. Put her to bed. Back to St James's very late and drunk.'[16] No other remark is offered but the spectacle clearly saddened him. Although he was conscientiously putting away childish things, he would never disown the friends of his youth.

*

'Awake early', he recorded later the same day, 'and still drunk; morning passed in trance. Got Rome Express at 2. Pleasant journey in empty sleeper. Sent perhaps indiscreet telegram to Laura.'[17] He was on his way at last but more difficulties than sobering up lay ahead, principal among which was money. The expense of recent months had been high. Marriage, house-purchase and a third trip to Abyssinia would somehow have to be financed from cash not as yet in his possession. He had always relished living on this knife-edge. 'So then I came to London', he had written to Katharine Asquith in June, 'saw my agent who dashed all hopes of solvency. Luncheon Laura. Now I must go & order a pressed duck for her dinner.'[18] Whatever else happened, it was crucially important that he should appear to Laura and her mother as a gentleman of means. To consider the cost of anything was merely vulgar.

On the train he read Peter Fleming's *News from Tartary* for review and, arrived in Rome, wrote the piece the next morning and posted it home. Then he set about getting the Italians to pay his expenses. Christopher Sykes implies that Waugh's Roman negotiations were concerned solely with securing a visa and that a further advance from Tom Burns had obviated all financial difficulty. Waugh's diary suggests otherwise: ' ... saw Ceralli who gave me visa ... but raised suspicion that the Italians expect me to pay for this trip myself.'[19] This was not a suspicion an overdrawn Waugh wished to encourage. After five days of haggling they 'gave in and agreed to pay my fare'.[20] By this time he had made his way to Assisi and was on the point of leaving for Naples to catch the *Leonardo da Vinci* to Djibouti. He would have gone without their help but it relieved some anxiety.

Financial support also signalled political approval of his mission. No British

15. *Diaries*, 21 July, 1936, p. 393.
16. *Ibid.*, 27 July, 1936, p. 395.
17. *Ibid.*, 29 July, 1936, p. 395.
18. *Letters*, p. 107.
19. *Diaries*, 31 July, 1936, p. 395.
20. *Ibid.*, 6 August, 1936, p. 396.

journalists were being allowed into Abyssinia so Waugh had the opportunity for an exclusive account in his book. He was keen to do the job well and struggled daily with Italian lessons. He was even more eager to use his experience as an extension of his quasi-Bellocian dialectic in defence of conservative Catholicism. Belloc's historical perspective relied on the notion that no country could be considered 'civilised' which had remained unconquered by Rome, an ingenious and absurd thesis which, at first sight, Waugh appears in his book to have accepted entire. This was not the case, but his enthusiastic desire to present a coherent argument sometimes led him to be his own worst advocate.

In fact, his mind at this time was dominated not by dreams of Roman conquest but by Laura. To some extent, of course, the two were conflated: Laura, Catholicism and Rome as the focus of his Faith all came into the same, *Romanitas*[21] category. Laura had released in him a sentimentality which clouded his normally brutal clarity of mind. The letters to her from Assisi are imbued with religious and amorous passion. He loved the town, with its bells and Giottos and the Church of St Francis opposite his hotel. 'Sweet poppet,' he wrote, 'it seems such a waste to see lovely things & not be with you. It is like being one-eyed & goggling out of focus. I miss you & need you all the time. Most of all when I'm happy.'[22] And: 'My darling ... I feel transported with the beauty of the night & wish you were here to share it. Assisi seems to be full of the Grace of God. ... '[23] In this frame of mind, it might not have been surprising had he wished to see that 'Grace of God' transferred to the political tenets of the State centred on the See of Peter. He was never that foolish. 'I am sick of Abyssinia and my book about it,' he wrote to Katharine Asquith at that time. 'It was fun being pro-Italian when it was an unpopular and (I thought) losing cause. I have little sympathy with these exultant fascists now.'[24]

After an eleven-day voyage in blistering heat, sharing a cabin with an Italian officer who slept in a hair net, Waugh arrived, exhausted, at Djibouti. One of the first people he met was Moriatis, the disreputable proprietor of *Le Select*. Expelled from Addis and deprived of his living, the man was a fountain of atrocity stories and predictions: Abyssinia was starving, the execution of the Abuna had been a ghastly miscalculation, Addis would be re-taken before Maskal in late September.

---

21. Cf. 'Understanding the Conservatives', *Commonweal*, 7 August, 1964, 547–8, where he speaks of '*Romanitas* – a civilisation formed by and activated by the Faith, a civilisation which some will recognise as the highest human achievement of history, but which all of us recognise is inessential to the Faith. ... The physical-psychological character of Rome, the City, reminds us everywhere of the Counter Reformation. ... It is true that in Northern Europe, in the lands of its origin, Protestantism is now so enfeebled as to be negligible. ... And Rome has always been the one citadel where the defence rallied and revictualled. ... '
22. *Letters*, p. 109.
23. *Ibid.*, p. 110.
24. *Ibid.*, p. 109.

Waugh was uncertain at this stage what to think. 'Truth appears to be', he noted laconically in his diary, 'Wops in jam.'[25] The extent of guerrilla activity was clearly causing them problems. All trains to the interior were heavily guarded with machine guns. Djibouti was packed with Italians who sat about 'like slightly bewildered cruise boat trippers'.[26]

At this stage Waugh's dominant impression was of disorder. The most alarming aspect of the situation (and one which is particularly apposite in the light of recent history) was that no crops had been planted and famine seemed inevitable. The Italians had no control over the road north to Dessye along which Waugh had travelled with Emeny. Marauding bands of *shiftas*, often the remnants of Selassie's battalions, would attack ruthlessly and then disappear into the hills. The 'victory', it turned out, meant control over a small collection of towns in the north adjacent to Eritrea (Adowa, Aksum, Makale) and over those served by the railway line from Djibouti to Addis. Other than that, the Italians could fly the length and breadth of the country dropping high explosive and poison gas, but they could move nowhere else by road without fear of attack. The difficulty of maintaining military dominance was exacerbated not only by ambushes on the roads but the scarcity of roads upon which to be ambushed. Most of the country was impenetrable to mechanised transport. Beyond Addis the country was a morass of mountains, bogs and bandits. The only immediate way to establish communications between north and south was by air and Addis had no airfield. 'Planes had to use Dirre Dowa, two days down the line from the capital.

Waugh set off for Dirre Dowa the next day. 'Shabby unshaven white soldiers all along line', [27] he noted in his diary, which account reveals an honest attempt to disinter the facts. His remarks about the general Italian soldiery are not complimentary. They seemed to him always to neglect elementary standards of dress and cleanliness: 'When taxed with filth the Italians say, "We are in Africa". Bad omen if they regard tropics as excuse for inferior hygiene. Reminded that they are the race who have inhabited and created the slums of the world.'[28] The British press had expressed outrage at the use of poison gas. It was a delicate subject but Waugh tackled it head-on by going to Harar and asking a series of blunt questions: 'Gas used four or five times on southern front . . . ; some blind brought back to hospital' is his unemotional record.[29] Another supposed atrocity was the bombing of civilians in Harar. 'Harar was entirely empty of troops at time of bombardment, but important supply centre and some arms found hidden there later by looters. When town first taken by Italians handed over to savage bands [?] who killed all Christians they found, including three priests within short

25.  *Diaries*, 18 August, 1936, p. 398.
26.  *Ibid.*, 18 August, p. 398.
27.  *Ibid.*, 19 August, 1936, p. 399.
28.  *Ibid.*, 31 August, 1936, p. 402.
29.  *Ibid.*, 20 August, 1936, p, 399.

distance British consulate.'[30] Thus far the case for the Italians was not looking good.

In 1930 he had visited the prison in Harar and found it a stinking den of tiny hutches whose inmates (mostly debtors) were shackled for years at a time. As such it became to Waugh a symbol of the country's degradation. In 1935 he had thought it quite in keeping with his image of the country that the Emperor should open a 'model prison' on European lines and then fail to ensure it was used. The press were shown round the new building; the criminals still found their way to the old. On his return in 1936 Waugh wanted to see what the Italians had made of the prison. His acerbic note, in the light of this history, suggests his deep suspicion: 'Tried to see jug but shown lions instead.'[31] If Mussolini's troops were to impress him as a civilising force, they would have to do better than that.

Two days later his train was pulling into Addis in pouring rain. The waterlogged military camps all along the line had seemed pathetic. He was met at the station by an officer and driven to the Hefts. Substantial changes had taken place there. The quiet Deutsches Haus which had formerly been a retreat for English correspondents was now the 'Pensione Germanica: Bar-Dancing'. Heft had gone into business in a big way with an English-speaking Italian. The entire downstairs living area had been converted into a flashy saloon and dance hall; a propeller studded with light bulbs added a shabby touch of cosmopolitan *chic*. Waugh had perhaps been anticipating the gentle domestic routine of the year before and was clearly disappointed. His old bedroom was now the dining room, and sitting in it, somewhat bewildered, that evening he was offered a meal which he could only describe in his diary as 'foul and minute'.[32]

Next morning a car and driver were supplied by the Italians and he toured the town. Disorder again seemed rife. There was no uniform rate of exchange; prices for some staple foodstuffs had increased ten times. Italian attempts to institute control seemed hopelessly impractical: notices everywhere proclaimed a list of fixed prices everywhere ignored; the shops had taken Italian names, and often displayed a photograph of Il Duce. These were cosmetic changes.

On his second day in Addis he attended a Fascist meeting in honour of the German Consul. The speeches in praise of Hitler failed to impress Waugh and must have roused his worst fears. Even Addis, it turned out, was not secure. Local groups of partisans conducted constant raids. He went to bed that night and rose the next morning to the sound of gunfire and fighter planes. 'I thought last night that I had never been in a city so full of unhappy people.'[33]

Two things occurred to change his mind: a visit to the Italian Viceroy later

30. *Ibid.*, 20 August, 1936, p. 399.
31. *Ibid.*, 21 August, 1936, p. 399.
32. *Ibid.*, 24 August, 1936, p. 400.
33. *Ibid.*, 27 August, 1936, p. 401.

that day and a tour of the northern sector organised by this frank, no-nonsense soldier. Marshal Graziani greeted him courteously and gave him twenty minutes. Waugh appreciated his brisk approach: 'No Fascist speeches about Roman civilisation and the wickedness of sanctions. He asked me where I had been, where I wanted to go, how much time I had.'[34] There was no secrecy and no bombast. Above all, Graziani showed no sign of panic in a town feverish with apprehension about a rising or attack.

The Viceroy offered a tour of the southern front with an armoured column. Rather ashamed of himself, Waugh declined. He was not afraid but his circumstances had changed. Time was short for the completion of his book and he needed the money to get married. He also needed to be alive for this purpose. His new responsibilities cheated him of the chance to see the fighting he had so eagerly sought on his last visit. 'Six months ago', he noted, 'it is [sic] the kind of thing I should have jumped at. Now I simply shirked it.'[35] Instead he accepted the offer of a plane journey to the north, an area entirely new to him. Two days later he was sitting in the gun-turret of a three-engine Caproni unable to see any of the countryside racing beneath him.

Most of the four hundred miles was covered in a day and by 11.30 on 30th August he was driving into Asmara. Here he was met by Signor Franchi, head of the Press Bureau who was to remain his guide for the succeeding days' investigations. Franchi admirably concealed his disappointment on meeting Waugh. From the indeterminate nature of the novelist's Christian name he had been expecting a woman. It was a bitter blow for an Italian in a land virtually devoid of European females. Waugh liked the man: a fat, obliging fellow who seemed prepared to arrange everything he wanted. But Waugh was bored and perhaps a little annoyed with himself at having to take the soft option. Without the stock of American fiction which he had borrowed in Addis, he would have been frantic. As usual, any delay threw him into a rage of frustration.

Franchi gave him a bungalow in Asmara, the town to be used as their base. Asmara was not in occupied territory at all, but in Eritrea which the Italians had governed long before the war. The house did not please – 'absolutely disgusting – no light or water. Bed full of fleas'[36] – but the excursions certainly did. Despite a heavy cold, Waugh was overwhelmed by the brilliance of Italian civil engineering: 'Road really magnificent being done in sections by various commercial concerns. Tarmac, concrete parapets, cuttings, graded, cambered, cuttings faced with stone, little beds of patterned pebbles. At 6.00 a.m. workmen going to work.'[37]

On this new road system he travelled first to Adowa and Aksum, then to

34. *Ibid.*, 27 August, 1936, p. 401.
35. *Ibid.*, 27 August, 1936, p. 401.
36. *Ibid.*, 31 August, 1936, p. 402.
37. *Ibid.*, 1 September, 1936, p. 403.

Adigrat and Makale. Both were substantial journeys. In all he covered some four hundred miles and the tone of the diary for this period is distinctly more enthusiastic. The great speed with which he was whisked from town to town clearly exhilarated him. Always 'the road' dominates the imagination: 'Road, where finished, magnificent: little gardens at corners with flowering cactus, trees; devices in pebbles; milestones carved with wolves, eagles and foxes.'[38] The language of approbation is that of the aesthete, not the engineer. The significance of this manifestation of civilisation is registered in its attention to detail and, by implication, the concern with craftsmanship. He had found what he had been looking for in the least likely of places.

After two more days of Asmaran tedium, scarcely enlivened by a visit to a brothel where eighty soldiers queued in the hallway for their ten minutes' relief, he was on his way home: Cairo – Tripoli – Ostia in three daily stages by Italian military aircraft. On 10th September he made the short journey from Ostia to Rome and breathed a sigh of relief. It is unlikely that he made use of the Asmara brothel. He was certainly looking for a similar establishment in Rome to complete a luxurious toilet and wash off the sweat of Africa. But it was not to be: 'Had intended to bathe, change, fuck and eat a luxurious dinner' he noted. 'Instead spent the evening driving to pay my debt to the English College in smuggled lire.'[39] Waugh was perhaps keen to make a donation to the College, registering his gratitude for some help with his annulment.

That evening, still celibate, he caught the Rome–Paris Express, stayed overnight at the Lotti and flew to Croydon the next morning. He was back in London in time for lunch with his parents on 12th September feeling refreshed and elated. The expedition had taken just six weeks and he had found the material necessary to complete his book. It was to be the last of those 'thirties adventures, alone in remote places, and he must have sensed that this would be the case. He let it go without regret.

*

The diary entry for the day of his return best suggests the direction in which his life was moving: 'Huge mail but no worries. Dined Buck's Burns: oysters grouse. Met Belloc after dinner. Heard of Hughie's death. Wired Mells.'[40] 'Burns' was Tom Burns of Longman Green, his publisher. Belloc was eager to make Waugh's acquaintance and enlist him among the contributors to the magazine he edited, G. K.'s Weekly. Hugh Lygon's early death was a profound shock. He had been ill for some time with an obscure disease. While travelling in Germany he had stepped out of a car, fallen downhill and hit his head. Some thought he had

38. *Ibid.*, 3 September, 1936, p. 403.
39. *Ibid.*, 10 September, 1936, p. 405.
40. *Ibid.*, 12 September, 1936, p. 405.

suffered sunstroke. No-one was certain what had happened. It was strange and disturbing news to lose a close friend of his youth and his ally in Spitzbergen in such arbitrary fashion. He wrote to Lady Mary immediately: 'It is the saddest news I ever heard. I shall miss him bitterly.' But there was no time to visit her in her distress: 'I go down to Mells for a fortnight to finish the book about Abyssinia. Will you write to me there. . . . I long to see you again in October.'[41] It was the end of an era.

Tom Burns had dined with him keen to hear news both of Abyssinia and of how Waugh envisaged the conclusion of his book. It seems that the bulk of *Waugh in Abyssinia* had already been set up in type and Longmans were agitating for its completion. They were probably fearful, and with some justification, of losing sales through the fading topicality of the Abyssinian crisis. The last significant development had been the Emperor's flight in May, four months earlier. No-one seemed especially interested in Abyssinia any longer; Spain had claimed the headlines. Waugh's intended title had been that used for his *English Review* articles: *The Disappointing War*. This was firmly squashed. It would be difficult enough to sell the book without such an invitation to bathos. Waugh, unhappy with the cheap pun of the substitute title, was to become irritated in the succeeding weeks by Longmans harrying him for copy. He would finish in his own good time. Burns, despite his friendship, must have had a delicate business on hand that evening when it came to the inevitable question of 'When do you think . . . ?'

The wire to Mells was to secure Waugh's room at Mrs Long's. Within two days of his return he was welcomed into the heart of the Catholic community centering on the Manor and anticipated two weeks' quiet labour to complete the remaining ten-thousand words. There were predictable distractions. On his first day he had to correct the proofs of an earlier section. He had agreed to write a review for the *Spectator* of Ladislas Farago's collection of British journalists' reminiscences, *Abyssinian Stop Press*. (This included Balfour's and Emeny's accounts and was thus 'essential reading'.) There was the usual round of dinners and visits with and to friends: Katharine, Christopher Hollis, Conrad Russell. Hollis he tended to find dull but the others, including the entire Asquith family, enchanted him. He was easily seduced into visits to Bath and Bristol during his stays there. At the week-ends he would return to London. All this he would have accounted for. What he did not expect was continued trouble with Laura's mother.

On his second day, as he would have been preparing to write, he found himself reading a letter from Laura saying that he 'might see her and that Mary is proposing further postponement of wedding'.[42] Unshaven, he rushed for the London train and spent the day at Bruton Street after picking Laura up from the

41. *Letters*, p. 110.
42. *Diaries*, 16 September, 1936, p. 406.

Academy. 'Decided nothing', he wrote in his diary, 'except to be civil'.[43] And being civil to Lady Herbert during these months was clearly strenuous. He liked her and she him but her attitude to the wedding plans infuriated him. There was no solution but to smile and to try to placate her. 'Worked myself into a rage with Mary last night and had to take dope [sleeping draught]', he wrote two days later at Mells. Then, the following morning: 'Rage justified by letter from Laura saying would I decide if I wanted to share London house with Mary. Mind boggled. In the afternoon went to see Nunney and Whatley [houses] which Katharine spoke of.'[44]

The prospect of spending his early married life cohabiting with an autocratic mother-in-law immediately drove him out in search of property. It was an occupation he came to relish. At this stage, though, it was yet another annoyance to drag him from his desk. Longmans wrote irate letters. Waugh replied haughtily. He still managed to complete the work by 2nd October, exactly as promised. Four days later Longmans rushed the final proofs to him in London. On 26th October, less than three weeks after he had corrected these, the book was published.

*

It was in this complex emotional atmosphere that those two (now infamous) final chapters were written: 'Addis Ababa During the First Days of the Italian Empire' and 'The Road'. Waugh had, in the rush, found no time to oversee the production of the jacket. When he saw it, he was appalled. 'Went to Longman Green to find they had composed a blurb giving exactly the impression of *W. in A.* which I had tried to suppress.'[45] It read (in part):

> He gives a vigorous and highly amusing description of the old regime, a chaos rendered comic by the enormous publicity given to it by the contending pressmen of the world. His recent visit enables him to give the British public the first picture of the achievements and difficulties of the new government.
>
> This book (as its title surely implies?) is not so much political as personal. Mr Waugh went to Addis Ababa as a war correspondent but failed to see very much of war. . . . He saw parades of warriors coming to do homage to the Emperor before going out to fight, parades of women (in high-heeled sandals and blue uniforms) going to fulfil their part as 'camp-followers,' the struggles of the journalists with the Abyssinian press-bureau, enthusiasm and then panic in the bazaars, the embarrassment of legations, the courage of certain journalists who, when an air-raid was expected, sat up all night playing stud poker in gas masks.

43. *Ibid.*, 16 September, 1936, p. 406.
44. *Ibid.*, 20 September and 21 September, 1936, p. 406.
45. *Ibid.*, 17 October, 1936, p. 409.

... Finally, he describes a recent return visit ... and the fruits of victory being 'enjoyed' by the conquerors: the inhabitants he suggests, as well as the Italian soldiers, must sigh for the good old days, comparatively so peaceful, of war-time.

Most reviews were unfavourably disposed towards Waugh's political bias. David Garnett in the *New Statesman* was his strongest assailant. Waugh's book suggests that, in supporting Abyssinia's membership of the League of Nations, the Italians had 'armed the Abyssinians against themselves' (the Italians). 'It does not cross his mind', Garnett remarks, 'that the covenant of the League ... was a binding document or that Italy was bound in honour to observe it. . . .' This was the chief complaint of the Liberal and left-wing Press. 'Mr Waugh', Garnett continues, 'says little about the Italian habit of persistently bombing Red Cross units.'[46] True, but Waugh had, in February that year, written at some length upon the subject.

Probably as a direct response to his interview with Mussolini, he had submitted 'Appendix VIII' to the 'Official Note' addressed by the Italian Government to the Secretary General of the League of Nations. The Italians wished to make the case that the Abyssinians plastered red crosses on any public building. Waugh's document concedes that there was no abuse of the sign in Addis but that it was a different matter in the provinces.[47] Perhaps it is just as well that Garnett remained ignorant of this appendix. Such open support of the Italians would only have confirmed his deepest misgivings. '[Waugh]', he concludes, 'does not tell us how many [natives] that "most amiable and sensible man, Graziani," is hanging and shooting every day.'[48]

The *TLS* found Waugh's approach generally ignorant or uncharitable. In 1946 Rose Macaulay, a Liberal friend, was moved to describe the work as 'a fascist tract'.[49] Inevitably it was the two concluding chapters upon which the discontented reviewers concentrated their attention. 'The Road' lauds the efficiency and fine workmanship of the invaders:

A main road in England is a foul and destructive thing, carrying the ravages of barbarism into a civilized land – noise, smell, abominable architecture and inglorious dangers. Here in Africa it brings order and fertility. . . . It is a tremendous work, broad, even, perdurable; a monument of organised labour.[50]

46. David Garnett, *New Statesman*, 7 November, 1936, 735; *CH*, pp. 188–90.
47. The text is reprinted in *EAR*, pp. 185–6.
48. Garnett, *op. cit.*, 735.
49. Rose Macaulay, 'The Best and the Worst. Evelyn Waugh. II', *Horizon*, December 1946, 370; *CH*, pp. 192–3.
50. *Waugh in Abyssinia*, p. 243.

This was not deliberately distorted propaganda. Waugh's diary reflects a genuine sense of the magnificence of the road. The problem for modern readers with this private record at our disposal is that it also notes many things which find no expression in the book.

*Waugh in Abyssinia*, for instance, makes great play of the fact that white men were labouring on the road, something previously unknown in East Africa. From this Waugh concludes that the Italians are culturally superior to their new subjects: 'to labour like a slave instead of sprawling idle like a master – was something wholly outside [the Abyssinians'] range of thought. It is the principle of the Italian occupation.'[51] This was absurd. His diary notes that the labourers were from imported 'commercial concerns' and were paid '£40 a day and most of their keep'.[52] £40 was approximately six times the average British working man's *weekly* wage in 1936. Italy was a poorer country. It was an immense financial inducement which Waugh quite simply ignores. The book presents their industry as a spontaneous expression of 'a new type of conquest' by a people intent on working in the colonised territory and 'treating an empire as a place to which things must be brought to be fertilised and cultivated and embellished instead of as a place from which things could be taken, to be denuded and depopulated. . . .'[53]

The idea was tempting. Most of the correspondents (including Emeny) saw idleness as an Abyssinian national characteristic. The brisk introduction of improvements was bound to appeal to Waugh. After floundering on ponies along dirt tracks during earlier visits, to be swept from town to town on the new roads seemed qualitative improvement. His book, though, while its reporting is scrupulously honest, constructs something akin to a fiction by editing the facts. He omits (or dismisses summarily) not only the massive payment of the workers but the inflation of food prices, the Italians' tenuous military control (which collapsed ingloriously before too long), the slovenliness of their soldiers, the bombing of civilians in Harar, and the use of poison gas. None of this suited his thesis so he chose either not to believe it or not to believe it important.

Transported on the tide of his own rhetoric Waugh argues in 'The Road' that this new kind of conquest is something quite distinct from English colonisation which 'has always been the expansion of the ruling class. . . . It has always been an aristocratic movement.'[54] Extraordinarily, he finds himself making a case for a democratic movement which he pretends is neither 'military' nor 'capitalistic'. Then, realising that he has boxed himself into a liberal ideological corner he has, rather desperately, to add that, although its interests are the spread of 'order and

---

51. *Ibid.*, p. 249.
52. *Diaries*, 1 September, 1936, p. 403. Even if the entry were a slip on Waugh's part for '£4.0' a day, the argument would still be valid: £24–£28 a week in 1936 was a very high wage.
53. *Waugh in Abyssinia*, pp. 248–9.
54. *Ibid.*, p. 249.

decency, education and medicine', it is not 'primarily a humane movement'.[55] He could not allow of that: that would lump Italian ideology together with the uplifters of Protestant humanism.

Determined to construct a cogent analysis, he blunders forward in magnificent prose, concluding with a crash of tympany:

> ... along the roads will pass the eagles of ancient Rome, as they came to our savage ancestors in France and Britain and Germany, bringing some rubbish and some mischief; ... but above all and beyond and entirely predominating, the inestimable gifts of fine workmanship and clear judgement – the two determining qualities of the human spirit, by which alone, under God, man grows and flourishes.[56]

The road by this stage has become a symbol neatly fitting the Bellocian view of Roman conquest. It was a symbol which his imagination failed to control, though the manuscript demonstrates his sense of its dangerous implications. (The phrase 'some rubbish and some mischief ... the inestimable gift of' is part of a large insertion attempting to balance the ideology and justify it on aesthetic grounds.) Ultimately it is plain that the views expressed are not those of a committed 'Fascist' but of a politically naïve aesthete. But this was not enough to save the book from condemnation. Peters found himself unable to sell it to the Americans. As Rose Macaulay put it, '*Campion* is ... mellowness itself compared with *Waugh in Abyssinia* ... a blast of triumph over Italian conquest of that land'.[57]

In one area, however, Waugh scored a palpable hit with this kind of writing. Certain Catholic papers greeted the book as sane and sensible. Count Michael de la Bedoyère, Editor of the *Catholic Herald*, picked up the last paragraph about the 'eagles of ancient Rome' and selectively misquoted it as 'Rome will bring to Abyssinia the inestimable gifts of fine workmanship and clear judgement'. This was a toned-down, de-militarised version suitable, perhaps, for the family reader to whom the Count sincerely recommended the book as 'unbiassed ... He never defends Italy's action',[58] an odd reading.

Such reviews nevertheless demonstrate that Waugh was not adopting an eccentric position in *Waugh in Abyssinia*. There was strong support for his ideas in the Catholic community. Finding their religion universally under threat from communist or socialist movements, large numbers of Catholics supported Franco and Mussolini as defenders of the Faith. Belloc's *G. K.'s Weekly* praised the book. The *Tablet* 'scooped' prepublication sections of the last two chapters, thus offering its stamp of approval. As a favour to Woodruff, Waugh had sold him the two

55. *Ibid.*, p. 250.
56. *Ibid.*, p. 253.
57. Rose Macaulay, *op. cit.*; CH, p. 192.
58. Count Michael de la Bedoyère, *C Her*, 31 October, 1936, 3; *CH*, pp. 185–8.

pieces cheaply. He cared nothing for the attacks in the 'rationalist' press, in fact rather courted them. The failure to secure American publication annoyed him only because he needed the money.

The strange thing about all this is that, read carefully, the bulk of *Waugh in Abyssinia* does not reflect the quasi-military enthusiasm of the concluding chapters. Even within those chapters we find him constantly qualifying his admiration for this brand of Fascism:

> Too often when talking to minor fascists one finds a fatal love of oratory. . . . I had been present when the German Consul-General paid a visit to the fascist head-quarters. The officer-in-charge – a blackshirt political boss from Milan – had straddled before us, thrown out his chin, flashed his gold teeth and addressed his audience of half a dozen upon the resurgence of Rome, the iniquity of sanctions and the spirit of civilisation and the Caesars, in a manner carefully modelled upon that of the Duce speaking from the balcony of the Palazzo Venezia. There was no nonsense of that kind about Graziani. He was like the traditional conception of an English admiral, frank, humorous and practical. . . . If he had to refuse anything he did so directly and gave his reasons. He did not touch on general politics or the ethics of conquest.[59]

The final rhetorical flourish on his book would seem, then, to convey entirely the wrong impression of Waugh's attitudes.

He was as little interested in the oratory, the gold teeth and bombast of the blackshirts, 'general politics' and 'the ethics of conquest' as Graziani. What he admired in Italian Fascism was its simplicity and honesty, its practical common sense. He had always felt an artistic predilection for the functional and a distaste for the sentimental preservation of artistically insignificant fragments of antiquity (arrow-heads and Tudor architecture). Abyssinian culture he believed to fall into the latter category as artistically insignificant. It had persistently, he thought, proved unreceptive to aesthetic stimulus:

> Of the gracious, intricate art of Morocco or the splendour of Benin, the Abyssinians knew nothing; nor of the dark, instinctive art of the negro. . . .
> In the Church alone his [the Abyssinian's] aesthetic feelings found expression. Compared with the manifestations of historic Christianity in any other part of the world, West or East, the decoration was shoddy, the ceremony slipshod, the scholarship meagre. . . . [60]

59. *Waugh in Abyssinia*, pp. 228–9.
60. *Ibid.*, pp. 64–5.

The expression of 'aesthetic feelings' and the disciplined structure of that expression were to Waugh the gauge of any civilisation's value. It is ultimately on artistic rather than political grounds that his book condemns the Abyssinians. They could only be improved by Italian influence. Alone they had 'produced so little'.[61] When later he acquired a house, his Abyssinian paintings were hung in the lavatory.

His arguments from art and his comments on Graziani are much more in keeping with that letter to Katharine Asquith which declaims against 'exultant fascists' and professes no interest in their cause. Editing *When the Going was Good* (1946) he clearly saw those concluding chapters as a mistake and omitted them entirely. He had foolishly attached himself to a public cause where normally he considered political involvement anathema to good writing. Why, then, did he do it? The next chapter will suggest the ways in which he distinguished between German and Italian Fascism but it is worthwhile pausing here to consider the curious circumstances of Waugh's life in late 1936 which seem to have led him temporarily into foolish overstatement.

*

Several elements have been noted already. The final chapters were written hurriedly and under extreme emotional pressure. Laura had released in him long-suppressed enthusiasms, a sentimental impulse. The passion of his love letters, one could argue, works its way detrimentally into his public writing. But there is, surely, something else. It seems that beneath the new assurance he felt in Laura's love there was a reciprocal uncertainty.

His temper was frayed by what he took to be Mary Herbert's delaying tactics and the inevitable drudgery of being engaged and organising the wedding. As we have seen, when proposing to Laura his remarks betrayed a range of personal misgivings. Another letter to her (from Assisi, 1936) reflects how he felt his life to be changing dramatically. The future seemed uncertain:

> You see, darling child, so often when people fall in love & want to be married, it is because they foresee a particular kind of life to which the other is necessary. But I don't feel that. Sometimes I think it would be lovely to lead the sort of life with you that I have led alone for the last ten years – no possessions, no home, sometimes extravagant and luxurious, sometimes lying low & working hard. At other times I picture a settled patriarchal life with a large household, rather ceremonious & rather frugal, and sometimes a minute house, and few friends, and little work & leisure & love.[62]

61. *Ibid.*, p. 64.
62. *Letters*, p. 110.

The tone of this letter is difficult to gauge.

On one level it is simply the rhetoric of love: 'I could lead any kind of life with you.' On another, it suggests that the radical alteration to his established bachelor existence had not been thought through. He had no idea what kind of life he might be living in a matter of months and whether or not he would, with his impatient nature, be able to cope with it. Finally there is perhaps a sense in which this apparently patrician stance of offering a variety of homes to his fiancée is in fact a nervous testing of the ground. He wants to discover which sort of life Laura and her family expect him to provide. Part of the difficulty about this marriage from Mary Herbert's point of view appears to have been precisely centred on this question of 'adequate provision' and it seems that she left Waugh in no doubt as to her intentions.

She did not wish to see her young daughter racketing round the danger zones of the world as the wife of an *agent provocateur*. Neither did she wish to see her in a cottage. It was awkward enough Waugh's being divorced and more so that he had been married to Laura's cousin. Mary Herbert wanted to be quite certain that there would be a proper establishment and a respectable life. It seems from the letters of the period that there was considerable family tension. 'Don't work too hard sweet child and let yourself get bothered by family confusions',[63] Waugh wrote to her in early November.

His endearments for her – 'child' or 'poppet' – usually emphasised her youth. She must sometimes have been irritated by the idea that two 'adults' (Waugh and her mother) were arguing over the most suitable arrangement for the minor in their middle. Laura was an obedient and demure young lady but she was also 'a critical girl', stubborn and single-minded. She would not be patronised. The decision to become Waugh's wife cannot have been easy: his assessment of his own character in that letter of proposal was accurate. Laura knew she was taking on a notoriously difficult man and that life with him would test her resilience to the limit. She was only nineteen and was progressing towards a career of her own. Marriage meant relinquishing that period of single, independent life. But she had immense admiration for his talent and, having agreed to devote her life to being the wife of a great writer, she wanted to move ahead directly and complete the business. The tensions that she was feeling would inevitably have been felt by Waugh.

The pressure on him to present a front of unblemished orthodoxy to Mary Herbert may well have pushed his writing of the final chapters of *Waugh in Abyssinia* towards extremes. That is not to say that he did not sincerely believe what he wrote: merely that he might have been transported by his enthusiasm to be associated with the Church Militant beyond his normal political scepticism. After the engagement had been formally announced to Laura's family at Christmas

63. Unpublished ALS to Laura Herbert, nd [6 November, 1936?], np [Chagford].

he wrote to Driberg offering him the 'scoop' for his column, a day ahead of *The Times:*

> In return, could you oblige me in one particular? I think that by now most people have forgotten or have never known that I was married before . . . it would be very painful both to me & my young lady to have it referred to (1) because in ecclesiastical circles they get embarrassed if annulments are given publicity (2) because my future wife is a near relative of my former wife's and there are numerous mutual aunts who would be upset. So may I rely on you not to bring the topic up?[64]

It was a matter of some delicacy and needed the tactful handling for which Waugh's temperament was not ideally suited.

Most of his other problems during this difficult period can be resolved under a single head: money. Waugh was keen to impress Laura not only as a co-religionist but also as a gentleman. With playful masochism he would draw attention to this most vulnerable aspect of his background, emphasising in his letters to her that he possessed nothing more than he could earn, that he was an artisan and not an aristocrat (like her) with a private income. But there can be no doubt that he was considerably worried, arguably for the first time, about ensuring a regular and high income. He had no savings. The failure to sell *Waugh in Abyssinia* to America was a serious financial blow. In all probability, when he embarked upon this business of settling down, he not only had no money with which to buy a house but was substantially in debt.

Nothing deterred, he set about trying to earn large sums quickly. He took on as much book reviewing as he could get, wrote a film 'treatment' for Alexander Korda and, most importantly, on 15th October, less than a fortnight after completing *Waugh in Abyssinia*, began a new novel. The diary notes the day: 'made a very good start with the first page of a novel describing Diana [Cooper]'s early morning'.[65] This was *Scoop* and he hoped to finish it quickly to provide the cash to set up house. The plan failed. *Scoop* was not published until May 1938, over a year after the marriage.

The delay is partly explained by a letter to Graham Greene: 'I am getting spliced and need as much money as I can get.'[66] During this period Peters was extraordinarily successful in securing work for Waugh. After much haggling over fees he was engaged in 1937 to write a weekly book review page for *Night and Day*, an English version of the *New Yorker*. Greene was the Editor and contributed film reviews. Between March and September 1937 Waugh's six occasional pieces for *Nash's Pall Mall Magazine* were published. Over the whole period of the

---

64. *Letters*, p. 112.
65. *Diaries*, 12 October–16 October, 1936, p. 409.
66. Unpublished ALS to Graham Greene, nd [1937?], from St James's Club, Piccadilly.

gestation of the novel he also wrote reviews for the *Tablet*, the *Spectator*, the *London Mercury* and the *Morning Post*. *Scoop* was begun with enthusiasm and at Waugh's old rapid pace. Two chapters were written and despatched to the typist by 29th October, 1936, only a fortnight later. He was unusually pleased with his progress: 'It is light and excellent', he wrote to Peters.[67] But by November this optimism was failing.

At first, secreted at Mells and travelling up to London to see Laura at week-ends, he had felt settled and had worked well. But Katharine Asquith had decamped to the metropolis for the winter at the end of October and the only acquaintances left in the neighbourhood were Hollis and Russell. Neither was an intimate friend. The constant separations from Laura and the difficulties of arranging the marriage distracted him. Returned from London on 6th November, he wrote to her immediately:

> So it was a fast train and I got here before dark. . . . I felt lonely and dispirited so I went to see Mr Hollis and then sat up until late reading a review book about a Portuguese. I didn't wake up till 11 so I felt grand. Wrote book review. So I have made five pounds today. If I did that every day I should make one thousand eight hundred and twenty five pounds a year and could afford to marry. After dinner I shall write for Belloc which is an act of charity and if I did that every day I might meet you in heaven.
>
> I have written for particulars about this house, not very far from here. . . . It looks quite decent. But am I getting folie de grandeur? I originally thought of a £2,000 vicarage. Now I seem to be setting myself up as a squire.[68]

Part of his uncertainty derived from the variety of possible social identities available to him. But, whichever one he chose, he would have to be able to pay for it, and the joke about his occasional five pounds points up at his own expense the problems involved in his temptations to 'folie de grandeur'.

The 'book about a Portuguese' was Elaine Sanceau's biography of Alfonso de Alburquerque, *Indies Adventure*.[69] Waugh was reviewing it for the *Morning Post*, one of four pieces written for this right-wing paper between October and December 1936. (The fourth, a review of Christmas books, was rejected by them and this appears to have concluded the arrangement.) Waugh's critical writings during the period 1936–9 will be dealt with together in the next chapter. It is worth noting here, though, that he selected his books largely to promote his

67. Unpublished ALS to A. D. Peters, 'received' 26 October, 1936, np [Mells]; *Catalogue*, E298, p. 117.
68. Unpublished ALS to Laura Herbert, nd [6 November, 1936?], np [Mells].
69. Elaine Sanceau, *Indies Adventure* (Blackie, 1936).

quasi-Bellocian views; Alburquerque is seen, as Waugh was beginning to see himself, as 'a man of the Crusades'.[70] In January of the new year he was trying to arrange a contract with Rich and Cowan for a book to be called *In the Steps of Caesar*. His intention was to blend Belloc's theory about the enduring nature of 'the Roman conquest' with his own anti-pacifism. 'I see a very good book *indeed* in this', he wrote to Peters. In the same letter he said that he was also considering a book on 'Saints or Renaissance explorers'.[71]

One is reminded of his letter to Katharine Asquith from the Holy Land, energetically committing himself to a 'history of England and the Holy Places'. None of them was written. The nearest he came to the completion of any of these projects was a historical novel, *Helena* (1950), and a small book of essays, *The Holy Places* (1952). Perhaps the reason for this was simply that in his heart he was convinced neither by Belloc nor his politics. During that week-end with Laura (noted above) he had met the ancient in his club: 'Painful evening with Belloc who wants free work for his paper and had persecution mania at Buck's.'[72] Christopher Sykes quotes Belloc as saying, after being introduced to Waugh, that he thought him 'possessed'. It is a colourful anecdote. But Waugh felt reciprocal unease. Belloc seemed to him a redundant eccentric to be humoured rather than admired. Working for *G. K.'s Weekly* was an act of piety.

These 'acts of piety', the largest of which was the donation of all income from *Campion* to Campion Hall, became a salient feature of his career from 1935 onwards. He was prepared to work for the *Tablet* for what he described to Graham Greene as 'joke wages'.[73] He would, later, work for the Jesuits' *Month* for nothing. This was all very well, and went some way towards satiating those periodic gusts of crusading spirit, but it did less than nothing to resolve his immediate financial crisis. The more he looked at houses, the more his aesthetic perfectionism pushed him towards expensive property. The prices climb as the letters progress. His inability immediately to pay for aesthetic excellence had never hampered him in the past and it did not curb his tastes now. But the strain of the house-hunting, reviewing, and Lady Herbert's continued vacillation, persistently eroded the time and emotional energy available for the novel and inevitably took its toll.

Alone in Mells before blank paper or a dreary review book, separated from Laura, his nerves began to fracture. He developed a skin disease on his fingers.

---

70. Evelyn Waugh, 'One of the Great Men of Portugal', *MP*, 24 November, 1936, 16.
71. Unpublished ALS to A. D. Peters, 26 January, 1937, from Pixton Park, Dulverton, Somerset; *Catalogue*, E305, p. 118.
72. *Diaries*, 4 November, 1936, p. 412.
73. Unpublished ALS to Graham Greene, nd [1937?] from St James's Club, Piccadilly: 'I am sure you will realise that the English New Yorker is a purely commercial proposition – not like the Tablet for which we are both willing to work for joke wages. . . .' The 'English New Yorker' was Greene's *Night and Day*. Greene was trying to persuade Waugh to contribute to it.

He slept badly. He caught a series of debilitating colds. 'Low spirited' recurs as a diary entry during November and December. Travelling to Oxford again on 8th November with Hollis to hear him lecture the Newman on Roosevelt's election, Waugh found his dejection unable to support the tedium of the occasion. Hollis, he thought, spoke poorly and, like a mischievous undergraduate again, Waugh began to heckle. The guests – Woodruff and Hugh Fraser were there – can hardly have approved. Waugh was not yet accustomed to maintaining the façade of distinguished public figure.

Progress with the novel, then, was arrested on two fronts: the desire to maintain prestige as an apologist drove him to accept most Catholic invitations; the need to make money quickly forced acceptance of any potentially lucrative contract, no matter how ludicrous. Into the latter category fell *Lovelies from America*. 'Went to London', he recorded on 20th November. 'Lunch with Laura Boulestin. Went to Korda's studio and was told plot of vulgar film about cabaret girls which he wants me to write. . . . Discussion with Mary [Herbert] about Spain made her violently abusive. Left early and had drink with Hubert [Duggan].'[74]

Doubtless Waugh was not in the best of tempers himself that night. The title of the film can scarcely have endeared the project to him. But the fee was high and he was in no position to refuse. Perhaps this affront to his dignity was partly the cause of his violent distaste for Korda. Waugh decided early that the man was intolerable and, much to Graham Greene's disgust, once publicly abused him. There was no way to dissuade Waugh from an irrational hatred once contracted; he clung to it like a fetish, burnishing it to shock or amuse his friends. The letters to A. D. Peters over the coming months cast Korda, quite unjustifiably, in the role of mendacious swindler.

By December Waugh had finished the first draught of his 'treatment' and was in the deepest depression. Laura was under considerable strain not only at home but also from her studies. Between 24th October and 17th December she had to appear in five plays. She was losing weight. In his diary for 21st November Waugh noted two occasions during that day on which she burst into tears. During a visit to try to placate one of her aunts at Tetton House (near Taunton) she fell ill and Waugh believed her to be suffering from malnutrition. Clearly she was in a state of extreme tension and Waugh did his best to console her despite personal melancholy over Korda and the baulked novel.

He stayed on at Tetton to nurse her, missing another day's work at Mells. His one delight, it seems, was to relish the biggest social scandal of the century then coming to its climax with the abdication. 'Conrad lunched with me on Sunday', he noted after completing his scenario, 'very happy with the crisis. Perry [Brownlow] is out with [Mrs] Simpson in Cannes. If it had not been for Simpson

---

74. *Diaries*, 20 November, 1936, p. 413.

this would have been a very bitter week.'[75] What particular pleasure did he and Russell derive from the event? It was not the romantic enthusiasm of the schoolgirl population or the impassioned horror of the nationalists. Perhaps it was simply that as a Catholic, Waugh thrilled to see the Head of the Church of England committing adultery.

The rest of December was spent house-hunting and socialising. He knew he would not be able to settle to the novel again until after Christmas. As soon as Laura had completed her term they left London together, first for Mells where for decency's sake Laura slept at the Hollis's and Waugh at Mrs Long's. The next day Hollis drove them up to Faringdon to look at three houses. John and Penelope Betjeman lived four miles away at Uffington. She had been hunting out property for Waugh and Laura and they spent an exhausting Saturday examining three possibilities. By this stage they had reached £5,000 as their upper limit. A visit to Gerald Berners and his companion Robert Heber-Percy concluded the day's travels.

The Sunday was equally busy: two houses to inspect followed by a dinner at the Betjemans attended by Waugh's old school friend Roger Fulford, Heber-Percy and John Sparrow. 'Laura v. flirtatious with R. H. P.', he recorded, tongue-in-cheek. 'Was bloody to her, she very nice to me owing to her feeling of guilt.'[76] It seems that Laura was learning to stand up for herself, doubtless encouraged by Waugh's friends who recognised only too well the need to combat his playful bullying. As Christopher Sykes has remarked, Laura and Evelyn may have appeared an odd couple at first: she rather introverted, confident but quiet; he boisterous and loquacious in the company of old acquaintances. 'She is thin and silent, long nose, no literary ambitions, temperate but not very industrious', was Waugh's description in a letter to his brother. 'I think she will suit me o.k. and I am very keen on her.'[77] It must have been difficult for her, twenty years old and modest by nature, to have been thrust into the volatile company she encountered that week-end. They were all a generation older than she, the men established figures in the arts or academic life, Penelope Betjeman a brisk, vivacious woman of sharp intelligence. But Laura survived it triumphantly. Waugh was always delighted when Laura liked his friends and there had been an unmistakably warm response from them to her: at last their spiky and brilliant friend had met his match. Laura, somehow, knew how to keep him in order.

If the visit was a social success, though, it failed in its primary business. Not one of the five houses was satisfactory. Laura's mother picked them up to drive them to Pixton for Christmas and they would have had to tell her the depressing

---

75. *Ibid.*, 4–8 December, 1936, p. 415.
76. *Ibid.*, 20 December, 1936, p. 416.
77. *Letters*, p. 111.

news that they still had nowhere to live. The next day they were out again scouring the neighbourhood of Pixton.

That excursion began badly but ended well: 'Saw two no-good houses then Piers Court, Stinchcombe. Absolutely first rate, delighted.'[78] This was the Gloucestershire house, now famous in Waugh parlance as 'Stinkers', which was to become their home for eighteen years. An extensive programme of alterations was undertaken over the next four months. When he sold it in 1955 he described it as 'occupying a lovely position overlooking the beautiful Berkely Vale . . . a fine example of an 18th-century Manor House . . . [with] an extremely fine façade'.[79] The property included a large garden and extensive grounds, a cottage and a farm. In all it covered forty-one acres. He put in an offer of £3,550 and had to wait through an uneasy Christmas and most of January before learning that it had been accepted.

*

Waugh did not take easily to large gatherings. This was his first Christmas at Pixton and it was important that he should make an effort to be amicable as a prospective member of the family. The engagement was unofficially confirmed; it was to be published in January. They had found a house. It should have been a happy time but, for all his efforts, Waugh's spirits rarely soared. There is, surely, a tinge of irony behind those terse 'family fun' notations in his diary. He was feeling ill and irritable: 'Family fun. No sleep' (23rd); 'Father D'Arcy came, very dotty . . . Felt very low . . .' (24th); 'Church again. Felt very ill. Family fun. Afternoon to Tetton to Christmas tea party of Howards. Nearly sick on the way home . . .' (Christmas Day); 'Hunted and galloped into two gateposts' (Boxing Day); 'More church. D'Arcy still here and dottier.'[80] It is a miserable record, not entirely explained by physical sickness.

As soon as the requirement to engage in 'family fun' was lifted, he felt better. On the 28th he resumed work on his novel and kept at it for four days. He seems to have been content to lock himself away. Korda wrote to say that he liked the film treatment. Waugh spent a pleasant day examining Piers Court with an architect, turned out with the stag hounds a couple of times, played bridge in the evenings. By 11th January he was back in London for the official announcement of the engagement in The Times on the 13th. Laura appears to have been upset by Driberg's publishing the news the day before.[81] Everything had, apart from this, been conducted in accordance with the strictest propriety. It was a social gaffe on Waugh's part but only he knew how important it was to his sales to keep William Hickey on his side.

78. Diaries, 21 December, 1936, p. 417.
79. Quoted Letters, p. 115, n. 1.
80. Diaries, 23–27 December, 1936, p. 417.
81. Cf. ibid., 12 January, 1937, p. 418: 'Driberg upset Laura re engagement. . . .'

With everything finally settled, Waugh visited Korda the next day. The film was accepted and a complete script contracted. This necessitated more wasted weeks away from his novel but the cash was irresistible. Four days later he heard that his offer on the house had been successful. He was now committed to financing it. By the end of January he was at the Easton Court Hotel labouring at the ridiculous film, now entitled *Lovelies over London*.

From January to March Waugh was based at Mrs Cobb's in a large, warm sitting room, lying low and working furiously: on the film, on the novel, and on anything else he could sell. The correspondence with Peters increased rapidly. There was the *Steps of Caesar* proposal, the Korda deal, the attempt to get *Scoop* serialised; there were the articles for *Nash's*, odd pieces for *Harper's*, and the Italian translation rights for *Waugh in Abyssinia*. The pace was frenetic. In addition to all this he became a director of Chapman and Hall. As the letters flew into Peters's office the neuroticism about Korda increased. Waugh had finished the second treatment by 9th February and expected instant payment. When he didn't get it he instructed Peters (who sensibly ignored the request) to sue.

Waugh's irritation was increased by the man Korda had sent down to Chagford to 'help'. The *Diaries* describe him, with the hindsight of Waugh's mounting fury, as 'a very brutish American called Kernell'.[82] Earlier, this mild-mannered and bewildered fellow was more generously dealt with. A letter to Laura describes the situation:

> Mr Colonel [*sic*] is very nice but absolutely useless. He has made absolutely no contribution to the film. Yesterday I sent him up to his room to think up some wisecracks and he turned up after 1½ hours and said, 'How would it be if all of the girls said to a policeman "I wish I had stilts, then I'd come up and see you sometime." ' His only use is that he makes someone to talk to about the film. I think he may have murdered the real Mr Colonel and come instead of him. I can't believe he was ever really in Hollywood.[83]

Later he wrote to her:

> Darling,
> So the treatment is nearly finished. Tomorrow I shall have Miss Hitchcock come out from Exeter to dictate it to her and bring it to London Thursday. . . . Korda says we can go right ahead with the scenario. I want to get it all done before the end of next week then I can get going on the novel, for which I am itching and full of ideas. Feeling very cheerful about all this.[84]

82. *Ibid.*, 4 February, 1937, p. 420; Davie reads 'Kerrell' for 'Kernell'.
83. Unpublished ALS to Laura Herbert, nd [early 1937], from Chagford.
84. Unpublished ALS to Laura Herbert, nd [early 1937], from Chagford.

But his high spirits did not last. The second treatment was unsatisfactory. Waugh admitted in another letter to Laura that he 'realised it was no good'. Nothing, though, would placate his fury with Korda and the hapless Kernell bore the brunt of it.

Waugh developed a twitch in his left eyelid and turned his bilious gaze on the wedding preparations. On becoming a director of Chapman's there had been a small ceremony and the presentation of 'an utterly worthless box of knives and forks'. The wedding invitations, he records, 'went out and have been almost universally refused. Presents have been mostly of poor quality. . . .'[85] None of this was true, of course, and neither did he believe it. It was his way of translating his frustration into the black comedy of his private record.

Most of the nuptial arrangements he left to Laura. Having abandoned RADA, she had time to spare. While Waugh was at Chagford she paid two visits to Paris for her *trousseau*. In London she organised everything with calm efficiency. 'Sorry to put all this on you', he wrote, 'but I really am very busy trying to get the film done and as it is correspondence takes ½ my morning.'[86]

He was working too hard, still apparently determined to finish the novel before the marriage in April. After submitting the 'third long treatment' to Korda he returned to *Scoop* 'which has good material but shaky structure'.[87] Peters received the beginning of a fourth chapter on 22nd February, the remainder of that and the fifth on 5th April. It was now clear, though, that the book could not be completed in time. When he realised this and heard nothing from Korda, a neuroticism exploded in his letters to Peters. He wanted to see Korda; he questioned Peters's charges and Longman's dealings. Everybody, it seemed, was out to cheat him.

*

As the wedding approached he put the novel aside altogether and turned his attention to writing the series of light pieces for *Nash's* (the 'money for jam' job secured the previous autumn). In one of these, 'Myself', he offers an amusing autobiographical sketch:

> . . . That is my trouble, an almost fanatical aversion to pens, ink or paper.
> I keep seeing books . . . about young men who have literary souls and are thwarted and even made to go into the family business and become mere money-makers and breeders of children instead of great writers. My plight is the exact opposite. I was driven to writing because

85. *Diaries*, 4 February, 1937, p. 420.
86. Unpublished ALS to Laura Herbert, nd [early 1937], from Chagford.
87. *Diaries*, 4 February, 1937, p. 420.

I found it was the only way a lazy and ill-educated man could make a decent living. . . .

Of course, in my case, writing happens to be the family business. . . . My father can claim to have more books dedicated to him than any living man.

My brother took to the trade without a moment's reluctance. . . . I held out until I was 24, swimming manfully against the tide; then I was sucked under. . . .

Dickens held it against his parents that they tried to force him into a blacking factory instead of letting him write. The last firm at which I solicited a job was engaged, among other things, in the manufacture of blacking. I pleaded desperately. If I wasn't employed there I should be driven to literature. But the manager was relentless. It was no use my thinking of blacking. That was not for the likes of me. I had better . . . settle down to the humble rut ordained for me. I must write a book.[88]

In most respects this is a perfectly honest account. Waugh had no time for the 'leisured littérateur' approach adopted by his father and brother. It seemed symbolic to him that during the previous autumn, in one of his brief visits to Highgate, he had set fire to the house and destroyed many of those signed and dedicated first editions, 'the carefully garnered fruits of a lifetime of literary friendships'.[89]

Writing to Laura at this time he says:

My papa wants to know what you'd like for a present. . . . My papa says will we come and choose a bit of silver from what he has left of his grandfather's, wrapped up in flannel under his bed. Also he will give us £25 to buy 'something definite and lasting – to remind you of me'. I think that's decent considering his reduced circumstances and the fact that he forked out handsomely for my mock marriage some years back.[90]

Laura constantly encouraged him to behave decently to his father. Evelyn could not escape an irrational distaste for Arthur's petit-bourgeois values. Although he was about to embark on a grand society wedding and set up in squirearchical style, Waugh's good fortune failed to elicit a reciprocal generosity towards those less comfortably situated. Just as he was unapologetic about destroying Arthur's books, so here he was ungrateful for his wedding present. Perhaps Waugh felt the need to apologise in advance to Laura for the moderation of the gift. Perhaps it was an inapt attempt at a joke at his own expense rather than at his father's. Whatever its intention, embarrassment about Arthur's 'reduced circumstances'

88. 'General Conversation: Myself', *NPMM*, March 1937, 10; *EAR*, pp. 190–2.
89. *Ibid.*, p. 190.
90. Unpublished ALS to Laura Herbert, nd [March 1937?], np [Chagford].

emerges. Waugh wrote many books; none was dedicated to Arthur. Arthur dedicated one of his few to Evelyn.

Waugh was a man of violently contradictory moods. He would often say and write what he would later regret but never publicly retract. It would be quite wrong, though, to suppose that he was in 1937 indulging in a long-cherished ambition to ape the aristocracy. Less than a year earlier he had been looking for three rooms in a farmhouse. He held aristocratic values to be important but, as we have seen, he also felt a strong attachment to vitality wherever he found it. It is probable that Mary Herbert suspected him of belonging to a rather undesirable set for her well-bred daughter. Laura herself had a strongly-developed sense of social distinction. There was perhaps an over-reaction on his part to prove his social and religious credentials. And yet there was always something unapologetically Golders Green about him. He liked pubs, he liked getting drunk, he loathed 'literary' society and he relished the 'common' pleasures.

In the same series of *Nash's* articles he applauds not grand opera or ballet, but the music hall. He delights in the engagement of the audience, the cat-calls, the coming and going to the bar, the crazy way in which 'mothers of twins, drunkards, unfaithful husbands, lunatics, illegitimate children are still thought funny' and not anaesthetised into the polite silence of statistical and sociological analysis:

> I love acrobats, particularly when things go wrong with them. I love the voluptuous contortionist who is thrown out of the window. I love whimsical, silent clowns and hoarse, octogenarian comedians. I love ventriloquists in particular with their unnatural rigidity of expression and their dummy's unnatural mobility; sometimes when I am low spirited I see in their endless losing battle of wits with the robot a symbol of our age. I love all feats of genuine dexterity and most feats of strength. I love the surrealist kind of humour invented in the first place by the clowns, which consists of successive entries bearing improbable objects. In fact, I love the Music Hall and glory in its resurrection.[91]

Can this be the same Waugh who deprecated his father's wedding gift? Certainly: it is the Waugh of Oxford and *Decline and Fall*. It is the Waugh who loved the Beggar's Opera, the silent cinema and Buster Keaton's long, impassive face. It is the Waugh who thought Charlie Chaplin a genius and relished the implacable pessimism of an Armenian hotelier. The passage reveals the same aesthetic predilections which led him to construct a new life on an 'aristocratic' model: dexterity and strength. The clown combined both qualities. To adopt this strangely settled life must have appeared at times 'surrealistic' to Waugh. His images of life here – as a ventriloquist at the mercy of his doll or as a series of clowns

---

91. 'General Conversation: Variety', *NPMM*, September 1937, 9.

entering with 'improbable objects' – was perhaps not so far from his mind as he prepared to change his own identity with his wedding.

*

The marriage took place on 17th April, 1937, at the Church of the Assumption, Warwick Street. Waugh recorded the event dispassionately in his diary:

> Early Mass: D'Arcy, with Laura and Herberts and Woodruffs. Breakfast St James's Douglas and F[rancis] Howard; Henry Y[orke] came later. Changed and pick-me-up at Parkins' and to church where got married to Laura. Reception Gloucester Gate. Bachelor gathering in bedroom: Henry, Francis, Douglas [Woodruff], [John] Sutro, Perry [Brownlow], Billy [Clonmore], Hubert [Duggan].[92]

He was surrounded by a selection of his more 'respectable' friends. Henry Yorke was his best man, though Alec attended the ceremony. Patrick Balfour had gone abroad suffering from unrequited love. Hughie was dead, Harold Acton in China, Waugh had fallen out with Robert Byron. Hamish Erskine had been struck from the guest list. Arthur and Catherine were there among a predominantly aristocratic congregation. It was a new beginning, dignified and gentlemanly, and Waugh looked to it to wash away the bitterness and discord of the last eight years. There was only one faintly ridiculous element to the proceedings: the bride was given away by her sixteen-year-old brother, Auberon, a moon-faced boy Waugh could never like. Later, Waugh and Laura drove to Clonboy, the house of Lady de Vesci, Laura's grandmother, to thank her for a magnificent wedding present – Piers Court. It was a grand gesture, which at a stroke relieved the couple of financial worries. Alec's wife paid for the honeymoon.

From Croydon they flew to Paris and dined on Laura's favourite dish – pressed duck. In the evening they caught the Rome Express. The next day the train chugged through the April sunlight along the rocky coast of the Bay of Genoa and deposited them at S. Margherita. A horse cab pulled them up to the Herbert's Portofino house where four years earlier Waugh had first caught a glimpse of his 'white mouse'. 'Lovely day,' he wrote in his diary that evening, 'lovely house, lovely wife, great happiness.'[93]

92. *Diaries*, 17 April, 1937, p. 422.
93. *Ibid.*, 18 April, 1937, p. 422.

# XIV
# A Call to the Orders: 1937–1939

The honeymoon was not a period of uninterrupted bliss. Waugh was ill on arrival with torpor and diarrhoea and the household régime did not suit his taste: the cooking was bad and the house devoid of alcohol. But they were both happy. The sun shone; they bathed from a motor boat and shopped in S. Margherita. Laura bought Waugh a St George's medal on the saint's day; Waugh bought brandy, strega and chianti and his health improved.

After seven days of this romantic seclusion they set off for Rome to spend Holy Week in more formal surroundings. Lord and Lady Howard repaid their call and took them on a motor tour to Lake Albano. Lady Howard's sister arranged for Laura and Waugh to attend a 'dais of public audience. . . . Pope very ill spoke French not about us.'[1] Waugh was becoming irritable. In Rome Laura and he appear to have had their first row: 'Laura very bad temper indeed. also I.'[2] The next day they moved on to Assisi, the town that had inspired those lyrical love letters of 1936. Then it had seemed 'full of the grace of God'. This time the diary records only brief, dyspeptic impressions; a bad room for the first night until they were moved on to the royal suite, mosquitoes everywhere. He got drunk at luncheon. The next day Laura was in tears.

In Florence forty-eight hours later the situation improved. Apart from the 'Filthy luncheon. Filthy dinner' of 5th May, they were enjoying themselves again. After the initial minor confrontations, both were learning compromise. He suffered a fancy-dress football match for her; she drank enough with him over dinner to render the purchase of a clockwork cat admirably logical. By 10th May they were back in Portofino in good spirits. Waugh had brought the manuscript of *Scoop* with him. Each day he bathed and wrote. 'Working fairly hard and fairly well', he noted after a week in the house.[3]

Concentration failed him in the following week: the house was invaded by uninvited guests; there were visits to be paid to the tenants. 'Wrote novel very badly all week', he recorded. By the end of May they were back in England and Waugh was feeling low. His book was far from complete and there was small

1. *Diaries*, Saturday [2 May, 1937], p. 423.
2. *Ibid.*, Friday [30 April, 1937], p. 423.
3. *Ibid.*, 10–16 May, 1937, p. 423.

prospect of his returning to serious work on it in the foreseeable future. The one consolation was that he had been out of London during the latest onslaught of Royal Family fever. In their absence the coronation of King George VI had flooded the capital with sightseers.

It was a profoundly unsettled time both for the nation and for Waugh. King George stuttered his way through his early broadcasts; the renovation of Piers Court kept Evelyn and Laura from their new home until August. In the meantime they took temporary accommodation at 21 Mulberry Walk, SW3. Expenses were high and, as long as they were living in London, Waugh could not resist the temptations of a social round which interrupted serious writing.

Peters and he travelled to Denham Studios for a conference with Korda but met only with frustration. Time was frittered away pleasurably at luncheons, cocktail and dinner parties. The two months treading water gave him the opportunity to carouse with his old metropolitan friends and also provided opportunity for visits to Highgate to see his mother. Perhaps he threw himself more vigorously into social activity by way of valediction to London and a way of life that he had supported for nearly eight years. He was happy to see it go but with it also went his youth. The new, more formal, life as a country gentleman was keenly anticipated but it had already revealed difficulties. He seems to have found some of Laura's family rather dull and a great deal of time had to be spent with them. He had, moreover, not the slightest interest in country life.

Quite apart from the social distractions of the metropolis there were two distinct occupations, noted in the last chapter, to keep him from *Scoop:* his need to raise money quickly and his desire to contribute to Catholic periodicals for little or no recompense. Establishing himself as a landed gentleman and becoming a prominent figure among the *literati* of the Church Militant were often mutually antagonistic aims. He struggled to ride these two horses for the rest of his life. Some, especially J. B. Priestley, later thought that these apparently conflicting forces had torn Waugh apart. But they were wrong. Nowhere is the cogency of his aesthetic and theological views more adequately expressed than in the reviews he was forced to write between 1936 and 1939.

He disliked writing literary criticism and had never before seriously engaged in it. The 1930 *Graphic* series provides interesting insights. It was, though, a society magazine: the tone was 'light'. Entering the critical arena in 1937 he faced more serious opposition than the *littérateurs* who had governed the journals seven years earlier. F. R. and Q. D. Leavis were now considerable figures representing the new criticism of Cambridge. C. S. Lewis was established in Oxford. Then there was a formidable array of younger neo-Marxist authors: W. H. Auden, Louis MacNeice, C. Day Lewis, Stephen Spender, Arthur Calder-Marshall. Cyril Connolly, Graham Greene and Christopher Isherwood, writers whom Waugh respected, tended towards the left in politics. Only a handful of established writers at that time were right-wing. To make a serious case he needed to think through his ideology and aesthetic more rigorously.

He made a shaky start. In 1937 Louis Aragon and Nancy Cunard sent a questionnaire to all leading authors asking: 'Are you for, or against, the legal government and the people of republican Spain? Are you for, or against, Franco and Fascism? For it is impossible any longer to take no side.' Only five out of 145 replies supported Franco and Waugh's was one of them:

> I know Spain only as a tourist and a reader of newspapers. I am no more impressed by the 'legality' of the Valencia government than are the English communists by the legality of the Crown, Lords and Commons. I believe it was a bad government, rapidly deteriorating. If I were a Spaniard I should be fighting for General Franco. As an Englishman I am not in the predicament of choosing between two evils. I am not a Fascist nor shall I ever become one unless it were the only alternative to Marxism. It is mischievous to suggest that such a choice is imminent.[4]

The response is intriguingly equivocal. Is it evasive? To one who had pointedly established himself as a 'conservative', basing his political argument on the defence of law and order, the Spanish Civil War posed an awkward political problem.

Franco was attempting to overthrow by force a democratically elected government. Perhaps ingenuously, perhaps foolishly, Waugh registered his disrespect for this socialist government by appealing to the tactics of Marxist revolution. No argument can lie there. He refuses to accept the responsibility of supporting one side or another on the rather silly grounds that he is English and not Spanish. It *appears* (between the lines) that he is a Fascist sympathiser while simultaneously offering a categorical denial of this. The popular impression of Waugh today would seem to be that he was, if not a signed up member of the British Union of Fascists, then a man whose whole political tendency was perfectly in keeping with its policies.[5] Nothing could be more wrong and it is worthwhile pausing to analyse the arguments of his journalism. Here we find him developing an idiosyncratic but perfectly logical political thesis directly related to his aesthetic principles.

Art and politics he always saw as mutually destructive. But in the late 'thirties it was impossible to escape political engagement. Somehow he had to find a way of explaining the irrelevance of the crucial issues of the day to good writing while at the same time accepting his responsibility as a public figure to meet the

---

4. Louis Aragon (ed.), *Authors Take Sides on the Spanish Civil War* (*Left Review*, 1937); *EAR*, p. 187.
5. Reviewing the *Diaries* Frederic Raphael said: 'Without [Waugh's] art, he would have emerged as merely the bellicose, vindictive and bullying clown he seemed to imagine impersonated all that was best in British life' (*ST*, 5 September, 1976, 27).

arguments of the powerful Marxist literary clique. His retirement to Piers Court in many ways signalled his desire to sequester himself from the desecrated modern world. As that world rushed headlong towards another cataclysm, he began to realise, as did Orwell, that such isolationism was no longer an option.

*

The reviews of this period are dominated by Waugh's concepts of 'civilisation' and 'culture'. In 1936 he had attacked Ray Strachey's *Our Freedom* in the *Morning Post:*

> It is not a question now of whether women may vote, own property and preach, but whether democratic institutions can work at all, whether private property shall exist for anyone, whether Christianity shall be tolerated.[6]

From 1936 onwards there is a note of urgency in his journalism, a feeling, constantly expressed, that 'the whole moral and artistic organisation of Europe'[7] is liable to imminent collapse. Seeing himself as a man of the Crusades Waugh laid siege to sceptical free-thinking. Aldous Huxley became a recurrent target: 'the Nineteenth-Century rationalist-liberal, partially awake to the full consequences of rationalism and liberalism, but stopping short of renunciation of the creed; a Matthew Arnold bewildered by modernity. . . '.[8] Waugh saw Huxley as a typical intellectual casualty of the humanist tradition of free thinking. In all, Waugh launched three attacks on him. One, 'Blinding the Middle-Brow', was noted in the last chapter. The third concluded his series of *Night and Day* reviews under the title 'More Barren Leaves'.

Analysing *Ends and Means* (essays), Waugh found it not only 'dull' but ephemeral. Unable to tolerate Huxley's constantly shifting attitudes, he condemns him as a writer without fixed standards. 'Like all thinking beings', Waugh concedes, 'he is in motion' but:

> in his particular case a painful motion, so burdened is his mind with superfluous luggage. Now and then he pauses to report progress. There is no reason to suppose that in ten years' time he will hold any of the opinions he holds today; that is one of the great embarrassments of lonely and individual thinkers. . . . Mr Huxley's exposition leads only to what Mr Huxley is thinking in 1937.[9]

6. 'Century and a Half of English Life', *MP*, 6 November, 1936, 16; review of Roy Strachey's *Our Freedom* (Hogarth Press, 1936).
7. Cf. 'Converted To Rome', *op. cit.*, p. 230 above.
8. 'A New Book By Aldous Huxley', *MP*, 15 December, 1936, 18; review of Aldous Huxley, *The Olive Tree* (Chatto & Windus, 1936).
9. 'More Barren Leaves', *ND* 23 December, 1937, 24; review of Aldous Huxley, *Ends and Means* (Chatto & Windus, 1937); *EAR*, pp. 213–14.

This is the point at which Waugh, in search of permanent standards, becomes impatient.

The earlier reviews had left it at that: a mocking, dismissive gesture. But by December 1937, with some thirty recent reviews under his belt, practised and polished in argument, he was prepared to confront Huxley's defective 'machinery of thought':

> 'The human mind', he says, 'has the invincible tendency to reduce the diverse to the identical. That which is given us, by our senses, is multitudinous and diverse. Our intellect which hungers and thirsts after explanation, attempts to reduce this diversity to identity. . . . We derive a deep satisfaction from any doctrine which reduces irrational multiplicity to rational and comprehensible unity. To this fundamental psychological fact is due the existence of science, of philosophy, of theology. If we were not always trying to reduce diversity to identity, we should find it almost impossible to think at all.'
>
> This seems to me to be the reverse of the truth. What our senses, unaided, perceive is far from multitudinous and diverse. We begin life in a world of practically uniform phenomena. A stretch of country to the Londoner, a street of houses to the Australian, a crowd of men and women to the book-worm, present no points of peculiarity; the trees and crops and lie of the land, the nature of the soil, require a long apprenticeship before they reveal their individual characters; a row of buildings may be a mere horizon of masonry or, to the instructed, an intricate narration of history. Men and women are only types – economic, psychological, what you will – until one knows them. The whole of thought and taste consists in distinguishing between similars. Mr Huxley carries his enthusiasm for reduction so far that he will claim identity between radically dissimilar things upon the strength of any common, or apparently common, feature. It is the old *Golden Bough* trouble at its worst.[10]

This is a crucially important statement to any understanding of Waugh's frame of mind in the late 'thirties.

'The whole of taste consists in distinguishing between similars' defines the basis of his aesthetic and, equally, suggests reasons for Waugh's support for the aristocracy and 'conservative' politics. Politics and aethetics became indivisible in his thinking at this stage. Politically he stood for liberty, diversity and privacy; as an artist he appreciated vitality, control, wit and fantasy in writers whose prime concern was not to contain their characters within a typology – 'economic, psychological – what you will' – but to release their irreducible individuality.

It was this predisposition for vitality and control which led him, during the

10. *Ibid.*, p. 213.

same period, to express admiration (separately) for both P. G. Wodehouse and Italian Fascism. 'Mr Wodehouse', he pleads, 'has been too little noticed as a serious artist'; he is, in Waugh's view, 'a neglected genius', 'a first-rate craftsman'. At first sight it might seem that Waugh was reaching the lunatic fringe. But he makes a case:

> His characters have always moved in a world entirely their own, happily segregated from any contact with reality. The plots have never been more than a stage-setting for his superb dialogue and narrative grace. . . . But most of all is Mr Wodehouse's art unique in the present age for the austerity with which he voluntarily limits his vision. There is no attempt to 'see his characters in the round'; he is wholly free from the reigning folly in which novelists believe that they are 'making their characters live' by portraying them in all their moods and frustrations. Mr Wodehouse's characters 'live' as the characters do in 'A Midsummer Night's Dream'.[11]

The review concludes with the idea that 'in the world of Mr Wodehouse's imagination they lead patterned lives comparable to the precise regularity of the great Diaghileff ballets. It is the apotheosis of the "Art for Art's Sake" ideal of the '90s.'

This belief in the self-contained and self-supporting world of a work of art, its fantasy a structured metaphor of reality but not an attempted imitation of it, remains the corner-stone of his aesthetic: pattern, control, limitation of vision, art for art's sake and not for sociology, psychology or modernistic bravado. And by the same token, Waugh believed that a human being had a right and a duty to preserve his individuality from forces attempting to absorb it and reduce it to type. Piers Court was to be Waugh's 'self-contained and self-supporting world'. If the future held only intolerance of democratic institutions, private property and Christianity, then this haven of personal control would perish and along with it would disappear the aesthetic significance of a writer like Wodehouse. This was the threat against which he was fighting.

The naturalist/realist assumptions of the socialist writers were directly equivalent in Waugh's mind to their political concept of the individual as a comprehensible entity whose significance lay primarily in his relation to the corporate body. Waugh was, in effect, re-iterating in other terms part of the argument of Virginia Woolf's essay, 'Modern Fiction', which attacked the 'materialism' of writers like Bennett, Galsworthy and Wells. Waugh also disliked Bennett and Wells and for more or less the same reason: the accretion of 'data' about a character's habitat or 'ideas' did not constitute a representation of his or her sense of 'reality' (nor

11. 'An English Humorist', *Tablet*, 17 October, 1936, 532–3; review of P. G. Wodehouse, *Laughing Gas* (Herbert Jenkins, 1936).

even of other characters' or the reader's sense of his or her 'reality'). But where for Woolf 'reality' was diffused between infinitely flexible individual perceptions, for Waugh such an attitude could lead only to the fallacies and despair of humanism.

Had it not been for his faith he, like Woolf, might well have committed suicide. As it was, an individual's 'significance' lay for him in his unique relation to God; 'supernatural reality' was the only true register of meaning. Temporal existence was thus released in his mind from the constraint of needing to 'make sense' and any writer who ignored the rich fantasy of daily existence was, to him, imposing a schema on the essentially formless nature of social intercourse. Waugh loathed 'symbolism' when it signalled the reduction of this anarchy to representative 'types'.

In these reviews Waugh sees the contemporary mind, influenced by writers like Huxley and Auden, as reductivist, dull and crisis-ridden. As a yardstick of excellence, he frequently refers to T. S. Eliot's *The Waste Land*. The poem's 'rhythmical grumbling' about the desecration of high culture had lodged in Waugh's mind since Harold Acton had chanted it through a megaphone from Meadow Building in 1924. Waugh was appalled at the socialist/humanist view of history. He saw no process of inarrestable, beneficial change nor a legacy of exploitation. Human suffering, he thought, was constant whatever the government or material circumstances of the individual: it was a spiritual, not a material question.

Again and again he rebuffs what he takes to be Marxist ideology: that the purpose of man's existence is to produce and consume more 'consumer goods'; that the answer to man's *Angst* lies in the redistribution of material things. In this respect he was antagonistic not only to the Socialists but to the Conservatives. Following the same argument, the acquisition and preservation of 'material things' for their own sake was equally absurd. In 1939 he applauded Wells's refusal 'to be misled by the preposterous distinctions of Left and Right, that make nonsense of contemporary politics'. But that was the limit of his praise. He was astounded by Wells's apparent ability, in his maturity, to maintain 'the exuberant and almost bumptious optimism of extreme youth' and felt that he had ignored the central question: that human kind was essentially not virtuous but vicious:

> The widely-accepted hypothesis of the Fall of Man and the Atonement
> – leaving aside the supernatural credentials on which they are held –
> did and still do explain the peculiar position of man in the universe.
> Remove them and, if you have a sanguine temperament, you must
> believe that only the most flimsy and artificial obstructions keep man
> from boundless physical well-being.[12]

12. 'Machiavelli and Utopia – Revised Version', *Spectator*, 10 February, 1939, 234; review of H. G. Wells, *The Holy Terror* (Michael Joseph, 1939); *EAR*, pp. 245–6.

Political optimism never influenced Waugh's opinions. He was again not offering here an alternative conservative ideology but an argument against materialism.

Another aspect of this argument can be seen in his review of Christopher Sykes's *Stranger Wonders* (a collection of short stories and sketches) and Robert Byron's travel book, *The Road to Oxiana*. The piece was entitled 'Civilisation and Culture'. Praising Sykes, he sees him in the 'art-for-art's-sake' tradition: 'In its precision and felicity and exquisite nicety of fancy', he says, ' "Invention" [one of the stories] is comparable to the best of Mr Beerbohm's work. It has that rare, supremely delightful, barely detectable unreality. . . .' But:

> . . . there is an essential difference between them which must be noted and can best be stated by saying that Mr Sykes is civilized and Mr Byron is cultured. Mr Sykes is at home in Europe. He sees England as any outlying province of a wide civilization; he is by education a member of Christendom. Mr Byron suffers from insularity run amok; he sees his home as a narrowly circumscribed, blessed plot beyond which lie vast tracts of alien territory, full of things for which he has no responsi- bility, to which he acknowledges no traditional tie, things to be visited and described and confidentially judged. So he admits no limits to his aesthetic curiosity and no standards of judgement but his personal reactions. It is a grave handicap, but Mr Byron's gusto is so powerful that the reader can only applaud. . . . [13]

Waugh suggests here that the English artist should be European rather than British in his tastes, morally responsible for, because tied to, the culture of Christendom, and aware of the dangers of egotistical self-expression. As we have seen, 'Christendom' is synonymous in his mind with Roman Catholicism. The fundamental cultural influence of Catholicism on European culture is thus re- stated: Sykes is a Catholic; Byron was noted for his virulent anti-Catholic polemic. Waugh seems to believe that the 'standards of judgement' he appeals to exist as universal principles.

He always liked to belong to exclusive clubs and cliques. In his Oxford days it was the Hypocrites and a collection of rumbustious young men subverting the dull 'Northern' intellectual atmosphere of the University. The description of Robert Byron's approach precisely denotes the 'polite and highly attractive scepti- cism' of *Labels*. With Waugh's reception into the Church that scepticism had been abandoned. After 1930 he saw himself as attached to the Church before his country. The Church, in one sense, was the biggest club of all and his leaning towards Italian Fascism was an expression of this belief in the universal values of his faith and the aesthetic order which had sprung from Catholic culture.

13. 'Civilization and Culture', *Spectator*, 2 July, 1937, 27–8; review of Christopher Sykes, *Stranger Wonders* (Longman, 1937) and Robert Byron, *The Road to Oxiana* (Macmillan, 1937); *EAR*, pp. 197–8.

In this respect it is interesting to see how he distinguished between German and Italian Fascism. On 5th March, 1938, the *New Statesman* published a letter by Waugh deriding the use by 'the pitiable stampede of "Left-Wing Intellectuals" ' of the word 'Fascist' as an all-purpose term of derogation: 'When rioters are imprisoned it is described as a "Fascist sentence"; the Means Test is Fascist; colonization is Fascist; patriotism is Fascist. . . . Is it too late to call for order?'

What apparently begins as a defence of Fascism, however, soon turns into the reverse:

> Only once was there anything like a Fascist movement in England; that was in 1926 when the middle class took over the public services; it now does not exist at all except as a form of anti-Semitism in the slums. Those of us who can afford to think without proclaiming ourselves 'intellectuals' do not want or expect a Fascist regime. But there is a highly nervous and vocal party who are busy creating a bogy; if they persist in throwing the epithet about it may begin to stick. They may one day find that there *is* a Fascist party which they have provoked . . . . it is because I believe we shall lose by such a development that I am addressing this through your columns.[14]

Waugh may have been naïve in lightly dismissing Mosley's BUF but his despite of them and their brand of Nazism is perfectly plain. Waugh felt so strongly on this matter of the 'crisis minded' creating a political horror which as yet remained still-born that he wrote to Peters urging him to find an editor willing to commission an article on the subject. Peters's enquiries were uniformly rebuffed but Waugh did not let the matter rest. He still had the review pages through which to voice his opinion. The unfortunate object of attack, nine months later, was his friend Cyril Connolly.

Connolly's analysis of contemporary literary techniques and social conditions, *Enemies of Promise* (1938), gave Waugh the opportunity to develop his theme. The review (in the *Tablet*) is in part an assault on what he believed to be the degraded state of contemporary literary criticism which ignored altogether 'the rare Art of Criticism'. Connolly, he remarks, is the 'only man under forty who shows any sign of reaching, or indeed, of seeking, this altitude. . . .'[15] Waugh dislikes the much-abused term 'creative', preferring 'architectural' as an adjective of commendation.

A 'writer' is distinguished from 'a clever and cultured man who can write' by 'an added energy and breadth of vision which enables him to conceive and

14. ' "Fascist" ', *Spectator*, 5 March, 1938, 365–6; *EAR*, pp. 222–3.
15. A view shared in 1936 by Orwell: 'Mr Cyril Connolly is almost the only reviewer in England who does not make me sick . . .'; *Collected Essays, Journalism and Letters*, Vol. 1 (Secker & Warburg, 1968; Harmondsworth, Penguin Books, 1970 and 1975), p. 254.

complete a structure'. Connolly's book he finds 'structurally jerry-built'. The method of practical criticism advocated in it, isolating passages like a wine-taster, is condemned because 'writing is an art which exists in a time sequence; each page is dependent on its predecessors and successors; a sentence which he admires may owe its significance to another fifty pages distant. I beg Mr Connolly to believe that even quite popular writers take great trouble sometimes in this matter.' The last sentence is surely a reference to Waugh's own work. The school of critics referred to is F. R. Leavis and Co., whom he later dubbed the 'Cambridge movement of criticism, with its horror of elegance and its members mutually encouraging uncouth writing'.[16]

The review progresses to a discussion of the artist's relation to society. Waugh finds no reason to doubt Connolly's belief in the value of art but is wary of 'the kind of art to which he inclines':

> ... there is a single common quality – the lack of masculinity. Petronius, Gide, Firbank, Wilde ... the names succeed one another ... all, or almost all, simpering and sidling across the stage with the gait of the great new British music hall joke. He loyally says all that he conscientiously can for the left-wing school of writers but he omits from his catalogue the name of Mr Calder-Marshall, whose faults are those of boisterousness and whose virtues virility and, unique among his fellows, enough self-sufficiency to be able to do his own work alone, without collaboration.

The terms of approval are interesting: 'masculinity', 'virility'; 'boisterousness', 'self-sufficiency'. The collaborative writings of Auden/Isherwood and Auden/MacNeice he found absurd. It seemed the height of intellectual depravity to him when it took two men to write a book. The emphasis on the ability of a single mind to 'conceive and complete a structure' points the contrast.

The review shifts from abstract aesthetics and concrete technical analysis to the nature of the artist and the fabric of the contemporary world which has frightened and depressed the artist in Connolly:

> He seems to have two peevish spirits whispering into either ear: one complaining that the bedroom in which he awakes is an ugly contrast to the splendid dining-room where he was entertained the previous evening; the other saying that the names have been made up for the firing squads; he must shoot first if he does not wish to be shot. And it is into the claws of this latter bogy that Mr Connolly finally surrenders himself; the cold, dank pit of politics into which all his young friends have gone tobogganing; the fear of Fascism, that is the fear of Hell to the new Quakers.

16. *Writers*, p. 113.

He hopes Connolly will 'escape from the café-chatter, meet some of the people, whom he now fears as traitors, who are engaged in the practical work of government and think out for himself what Fascism means':

> It is a growth of certain peculiar soils; principally it needs two things – a frightened middle class who see themselves in danger of extinction in a proletarian state, and some indignant patriots who believe that their country, through internal dissension, is being bullied by the rest of the world. . . . . It is quite certain that England would become Fascist before it became Communist; it is quite unlikely to become either; but if anything is calculated to provoke the development which none desire, and Mr Connolly dreads almost neurotically, it is the behaviour of his hysterical friends in the Communist Party.[17]

Waugh's position is considerably clarified by this: Fascism is 'a development which none desire' but which, in the Italian (and possibly Spanish) form, is a lesser evil than communism. Earlier in 1938 he had reviewed Beverley Nichols's *News from England* under the title 'The New Patriotism':

> He [Nichols] has never been shy of appearing foolish, and now he is not ashamed to admit deep personal admiration for Sir Oswald Mosley. He finds much to applaud in the Nazi State. (It is significant that he is led to the myths and youth-cult of Nazi Germany rather than to the more adult régime of Italy.)[18]

But why did Waugh consider Italian Fascism more 'adult'?

It seems largely to have been an emotional decision. Respect for the Fuehrer was impossible. As Hitler proved himself in Waugh's eyes a bully and a liar, a puerile fanatic, Mussolini began to stand out as a relatively temperate and cultured man. More importantly, Il Duce quite simply represented the country at the heart of Christendom. Rome signalled to Waugh fine architecture, painting and sculpture, the 'natural' expression of the incontrovertible truths of Catholicism. He liked the Italian people whom he saw as alternately dilettante and volatile, leisured, adaptable, cultivated, with a knowledge of good food and wine. He saw the educated classes, brought up in the shadow of Michelangelo and the Vatican, as natural gentlemen. It might remind us of his early delight in Rossetti's character and the distinction between 'Southern' and 'Northern' in his aesthetic vocabulary. The concept of *Romanitas* was at the heart of it.

Waugh's was an extraordinary cast of mind in the late 'thirties, quite unlike

17. 'Present Discontents', *Tablet*, 3 December, 1938, 743–4; review of Cyril Connolly, *The Enemies of Promise* (Routledge and Kegan Paul, 1938); *EAR*, pp. 238–41.
18. 'The New Patriotism', *Spectator*, 22 April, 1938, 714–15; review of Beverley Nichols, *News from England* (Jonathan Cape, 1938).

that of any other major writer. His attack on the 'left wing school of writers' was fierce. He loathed their political tendency towards collectivism, yet this never coloured his critical judgement.

Arthur Calder-Marshall, for instance, received three notices on Waugh's *Night and Day* page. Two were antagonistic; the third showered praise upon his book of short-stories, *A Date with a Duchess*:

> Mr Calder-Marshall's avowed aims, which he expanded at too great length in a book [*The Changing Scene*] recently reviewed on this page, strike at the whole integrity and decency of art. I approached this book prepared to see signs of deterioration, eager perhaps to point a moral against doctrinaire students. I find instead a book of fresh and vivid narratives, full of humour, penetration and acute observation. If this is Marxist fiction I have no quarrel with it.

The review was entitled 'Art from Anarchy' and concludes:

> It is the work of an anarchist, not a Marxist – and anarchy is the nearer to the right order, for something that has not developed may reach the right end, while something which has fully developed wrongly cannot. I do not think any artist, certainly no writer, can be a Marxist, for a writer's material must be the individual soul (which is the preconception of Christendom), while the Marxist can only think in classes and categories, and even in classes abhors variety. The disillusioned Marxist becomes a Fascist; the disillusioned anarchist, a Christian. A robust discontent, whether it be with joint stock banking or the World, Flesh and Devil, is good for a writer, and if that is all that Mr Calder-Marshall meant by his 'Left' politics, I am sorry I grumbled about them.[19]

Waugh was a 'disillusioned anarchist' and it was on this basis that he could claim affinity with a wide range of writers which, as a 'conservative', one might have suspected him of despising.

Hemingway and Isherwood are praised, though Waugh was ultimately disappointed by the embarrassingly confessional nature of *Lions and Shadows*.[20] He relished the pure prose of Malcolm Muggeridge's *In a Valley of this Restless Mind* (1938), while being unsympathetic to an intellectual temper he had once shared: 'that particularly English loneliness of a religiously-minded man suddenly made

19. 'Art from Anarchy', *ND*, 16 September, 1937, 25; review of Arthur Calder-Marshall, *A Date with a Duchess* (Cape, 1937); *EAR*, pp. 204–6.
20. 'Author in Search of a Formula', *Spectator*, 25 March, 1938, 538; review of Christopher Isherwood, *Lions and Shadows* (Hogarth Press, 1938): 'Those who know Mr Isherwood only as the part-author of *The Ascent of F6* will be agreeably surprised by the quality of his autobiography; those who know him only as the author of *Mr Norris Changes Trains*, slightly disappointed. . . .'

alive to the fact that he is outside Christendom'.[21] The first report from Mass Observation (*May the Twelfth*) is not condemned as an intrusion into private life but described as 'a new way of writing a thoroughly exciting book'.[22] Waugh disapproved of its sociological technique:

> ... the persistent denial of individuality to individuals. It is the basic assumption of all traditional Christian art and philosophy that every human being is possessed of free will, reason and personal desires. Mass-observation is based on the rudest of classifications – upper class, middle class, lower class; old, middle-aged, young. ... the observers are touchingly reliant on the value of rudimentary abstractions.[23]

But from a technical point of view, as a piece of writing, it remained intriguing. Moreover, it revealed a 'modern characteristic [that] is at the root of the whole movement: that is the distrust of democracy'.[24]

Waugh's distrust of democracy was profound and an image recurs in his reviews of the two Mass-Observation publications: 'Democracy to some people presents the spectacle of a robot for whom the manufacturer's book of instructions has got mislaid.'[25] It was this sense of a crisis-minded society whose democratic institutions had lost all relevance to the individual that drove Waugh further towards a preference for strong government and a hierarchical society. Those like Auden and Day Lewis who advocated the extension of democracy to the point of Communism were seen as socially irresponsible and intellectually blunted: '[Auden's] work is awkward and dull', he wrote of *Journey to a War*, 'but it is no fault of his that he has become a public bore.'[26]

As an alternative to this tedious nailing-down of issues and self-congratulatory political consciousness, Waugh wished to re-instate fantasy and escapism as literary qualities:

> A school of critics who see no reality except in the raw materials of civilization have popularised the jargon-word 'escapism' as a term to

21. 'Desert Islander', *Spectator*, 27 May, 1938, 978–9; review of Malcolm Muggeridge, *In a Valley of this Restless Mind* (Routledge, 1938); *EAR*, pp. 232–4.
22. 'The Habits of the English', *Spectator*, 15 April, 1938, 663–4; review of *First Year's Work, 1937–38, by Mass Observation* (Lindsay Drummond, 1938); *EAR*, pp. 226–8.
23. 'Strange Rites of the Islanders', *ND*, 14 October, 1937, 29–30; review of *May the Twelfth: Mass-Observation Day-Surveys* (Faber & Faber, 1937).
24. *Ibid.*, 29.
25. 'The Habits of the English', *op. cit.*, p. 226. 'Strange Rites of the Islanders' states: 'From the position of divinely inspired oracle, the lout with the ballot-paper has suddenly been deposed and his place taken by an automaton for whom the key has got into the wrong hands and the manufacturer's book of instructions mislaid.'
26. 'Mr Isherwood and Friend', *Spectator*, 24 March, 1939, 496–7; review of W. H. Auden and Christopher Isherwood, *Journey to a War* (Faber & Faber, 1939); *EAR*, pp. 251–2.

condemn all imaginative work; they hold that the only proper concern of man is buying, selling and manufacturing and the management of these activities in an equitable way; that anyone who interests himself in other things is trying to escape his obligations and his destiny. In consequence of this stultifying mis-use a useful word is in danger of being lost as soon as it was born. For 'escapism' does represent a reality and [Edward] Lear gives a classic example.[27]

This review of Lear's biography contains a distinctly personal note.

It seems that Waugh saw certain affinities between his own alienation and Lear's:

> He had immense gifts of social charm but he made and kept his new friends as an oddity, someone delicious but altogether singular whom they petted and cossetted and enjoyed but always as someone essentially different from themselves. . . . The friends liked him, lent him money, bought his pictures, asked him to stay . . . but they married and made careers for themselves and Lear was left constantly baffled and estranged. He was haunted, too, by a conviction . . . that he was physically unprepossessing . . . so he drifted in a wide and frivolous social life while he yearned for privacy and intimacy. . . . [28]

The passage could serve equally well as a description of Waugh's shiftless existence between 1929 and 1937. Marriage and the acquisition of property had failed to cure a sense of isolation from all but a few contemporaries. Fantasy and 'escapism' were dearly-prized evasions of melancholy mania and he valued those writers who provided them: Wodehouse, Beachcomber, Beerbohm, Ivy Compton-Burnett.

Waugh found himself 'baffled and estranged' in the face of a dominant materialism. As a man with a profoundly mystical habit of mind he could engage intimately only with co-religionists. Others he described as 'Protestants', 'heathens' or 'pagans'. His first review for *Night and Day* was of David Jones's *In Parenthesis*. Waugh found this long and complex poem about the author's experience of the Great War deeply moving. Not only was Jones (a Catholic) technically excellent in his writing ('seldom obscure and never esoteric') but he shared Waugh's world view:

> Mr Jones sees man in a dual role – as the individual soul, the exiled child of Eve living, in a parenthesis, a Platonic shadow-life, two-dimensional, the Hollow Man; and man as the heir of his ancestors, the link

27. 'A Victorian Escapist', *Spectator*, 6 May, 1938, 813; review of Angus Davidson, *Edward Lear* (John Murray, 1938); *EAR*, pp. 230–2.
28. *Ibid.*, p. 232.

in the continuous life-chain, the race unit. . . . the race-myth has been sloughed off, leaving only the stark alternatives of Heaven and Hell. That anyway is how I understand it.[29]

That anyway appears to be how Waugh saw his own predicament in 1937. If ever he had consoled himself with the material benefits of civilisation and 'race-myth' assumptions of cultural superiority, those consolations seemed increasingly ephemeral; Heaven and Hell loomed large in his imagination. He often found himself 'existing' not in this world but in anticipation of the next.

*

Between June and November 1937 the *Diaries* record only four days very briefly. In July, after the honeymoon, he had contacted his agents: 'The novel is to be entirely re-written. It will be ready in time for publication before Xmas. It will be called *Scoop*. That is all I can tell the yanks at present.'[30] He failed to meet even this deferred publication date.

By August he was installed at Piers Court. Once in his new home, he hoped to settle to the revision in businesslike fashion. But for the next six months there were further distractions. Apart from the requirement to read at least one book a week and write his *Night and Day* page, knocking out lucrative little articles for *Harper's* and *Vogue*, reading manuscripts and travelling to London for the board of Chapman and Hall, innumerable minor annoyances arose consequent upon setting up house. There was no mains electricity and the generator began to fail. A local carpenter spent some weeks completing the panelling and shelving of the library in which Waugh wrote. Workmen were everywhere in the house and grounds. As the inhabitants of one of the larger establishments in the district, decorum required Waugh and Laura to pay visits and to be visited. His planned régime of peaceful seclusion was constantly baulked by the invasion of neighbours: 'Two sets of callers, both with double-barrelled names', he noted darkly in November.[31]

Shortly after moving in he informed Peters: 'I have stopped work on the novel because I understood that there was no hope of serialisation. The book couldn't come out before Christmas, so there was no point in hurrying it.'[32] The new life was strange and confusing to him.

When the *Diaries* resume in November after a gap of five months, there are clear signs of strain, possibly of mental aberration:

29. 'A Mystic in the Trenches', *ND*, 1 July, 1937, 32–3; review of David Jones, *In Parenthesis* (Faber & Faber, 1937); *EAR*, pp. 195–6.
30. Unpublished ALS, about 7 July, 1937, to W. N. Roughead [at A. D. Peters & Co.] from 21, Mulberry Walk, SW3; *Catalogue*, E321, p. 121. Sykes implies that the revision only began in November (p. 176).
31. *Diaries*, 13 November, 1937, p. 425.
32. Unpublished ALS, nd, to A. D. Peters from Piers Court.

I have been surprised again and again lately by blanks and blurs in my memory, being reminded by Laura of quite recent events which delighted me and which I have now completely forgotten. I have therefore decided to try once more to keep a daily journal.[33]

Even in the daily entries which, for a brief period, follow this, it becomes clear that Waugh's thinking was muddled. He repeats, as new, information recorded a few days earlier.[34] On 12th November he travelled to London to speak on 'ideological writing' at the Sunday Times Book Fair:

Having an empty mind I drank two huge whiskies to stimulate it: paralysed it instead. Was led at last into a huge hall full of young women – 700 or more of them. . . . heard my voice like someone else's droning and stumbling; felt 'if only I could sit back and think of other things'; and realized that I must keep this thing in motion. At last, in an awful blank, . . . shut up sharp. . . . To bed early with headache.[35]

He was only just thirty-four at the time. Something was wrong. A week later he inexplicably hit himself in the face causing 'a nasty cut'.[36]

Christopher Sykes conveys an impression of a brisk and untroubled period in Waugh's life immediately after the honeymoon. He further states that Waugh recorded in his diary: 'Started work again on new novel' and supposes this to be *Work Suspended*. Here he is quite wrong. The entry referred to is misquoted; the word 'new' does not appear and the remark refers to Waugh's resuming *Scoop* during November. The mistake is particularly unfortunate. Not only does it lead us to antedate the initiation of *Work Suspended* by over a year[37] but it underrates the effort expended on *Scoop*. After appearing in his review work as the scourge of ideological writing, he was particularly keen to produce work which, in his own terms, would be immaculate.

One diary entry in particular suggests the flavour of this autumn and winter for Waugh:

The carpenter says he has now mended the light plant. . . . He has finished the shelves which look superb. I wrote my page for *Night and Day* and half my article for *Harper's Bazaar*. [Graham] Greene rang up to say that *Night and Day* was on its last legs; would I put them in touch with Evan Tredegar, whom I barely know, to help them raise capital. They must indeed be in a bad way. I moved two castor-oil plants and

33. *Diaries*, 12 November, 1937, p. 424.
34. Cf. *ibid.*, 18 November, 1937, and 25 November, 1937, p. 427 re Lord Tredegar.
35. *Ibid.*, 12 November, 1937, p. 425.
36. *Ibid.*, 19 November, 1937, p. 426.
37. The first reference in the *Diaries* to *Work Suspended* is 27 July, 1939, p. 433.

a holly and some berberis to the corner of the field-gate under the laburnum trees. The clearing of the slopes above the gates is having the best possible effect.[38]

Amid the frustrations of failing mechanisms and magazines, Waugh took genuine pleasure in his new identity as a landed gentleman. Before meeting Laura, he would not have known a berberis from a bamboo plant. The entries of the period are studded with the newly-acquired titles of shrubs and trees. With his digging and planting Waugh appears as an eighteenth-century man delighting in the fine aesthetic control of his environment. He would often spend hours labouring alone: 'As the men were away I had the run of my own tools and spent a happy day in the garden, where the new trees are in.'[39]

But it was not all felicitous gardening. His work on the grounds, if anything, was a necessary distraction from his confused state of mind. Waugh, slightly dazed by this sudden shift of environment and exhausted by hospitality, felt constantly annoyed by the dilatory progress of his novel and, as the remarks about *Night and Day* emphasise, money was still short. *Harper's'* reaction to his article on 'The new Palladian craze and its perils' plunged him into fury:

Miss Reynolds returned an article I had written her about architecture on the grounds that her paper stood for 'contemporary' design. I could have told her all about Corbusier fifteen years ago when she would not have known the name. Now that at last we are recovering from that swine-fever, the fashionable magazines take it up.[40]

Architecture had become an obsession shared with John Betjeman.

His journalism during this period often refers to the sack of London by functional architects. Otto Silenus in *Decline and Fall* had been used to poke fun at the fashionable Bauhaus influence. Now this was a serious matter:

A gallant, hopeless defence was made for [Reynold's house in Leicester Square] led by Lady Oxford and supported by an illustrious little company of connoisseurs, but all protests proved futile. The A.A. are going to smash it up, adding one more charge to the savage crime-sheet of the internal combustion engine. . . . The most mischievous feature of the new cad-architecture is its power with one beastly building to befoul a dozen fine ones.[41]

All around him, like Uncle Theodore in *Scoop*, he saw change and decay. More than ever he felt an aesthetic and political exile.

38. *Diaries*, 18 November, 1937, p. 426.
39. *Ibid.*, 14 November, 1937, p. 425.
40. *Ibid.*, 27 November, 1937, p. 428.
41. 'General Conversation. Cad Architecture', *NPMM*, June 1937, 8.

The article rejected by *Harper's* was later printed by *Country Life*, entitled 'A Call to the Orders'. Waugh saw himself as one of that 'illustrious little band of connoisseurs' struggling to arrest the rape of British culture:

> Even in London, that noble deer bayed and brought down and torn in pieces; the city of lamentations, ruled by Lilliputians and exploited by Yahoos[42] whose splendid streets, once one of the splendours of Europe, are now fit only to serve as the promenades of pet dogs or as vast ashtrays for the stubs of a million typists – even in London . . . a few buildings precariously survive in grace and decency.[43]

The allusions to *The Waste Land* are unmistakable; the prose is Augustan in its rhetoric; the orders appealed to are those of the 'system of artistic law'[44] followed by eighteenth-century architects.

According to this law the smallest decoration has its correct place; the proportions of a building followed a mathematically exact sequence resulting in perfect aesthetic equilibrium; the component parts did not draw attention to themselves but contributed humbly to the cumulative effect of the whole. In architectural terms, it is an exact equivalent of the rigorous structural principles on which Waugh constructed – and was constructing – a novel. As he reminded Connolly in his review, 'each page is dependent on its predecessors and successors'. Context was supremely important.

The *Country Life* article was a complaint against the imitation of odd bits of 'Georgian' decoration by contemporary architects. A frequent grumble in his reviews is that 'one of the greatest faults the novelist can commit' is to record 'conversations for their general instead of their particular interest; because the views expressed would be interesting in a magazine article on the subject, not because a certain character is moved to express them at a certain time'.[45] It is a clear example of what he meant by the literary artist's ability 'to conceive and complete a structure'. And it was precisely this attention to structural detail that was bothering him in late 1937 with his re-shaping of *Scoop*.

Christmas week was spent at Pixton; then they travelled to Mells to stay with Katharine Asquith. From here they went twice to London for board meetings and visits to a Dr Oxley. Laura was already six months pregnant. Work (and expense) on the house continued unabated. Mains electricity was to be connected by the end of March, just after the baby was due, at a cost of £120. *Night and*

---

42. Waugh originally wrote: 'ruled by hooligans and exploited by cads' but *CL*, fearing a legal suit, required the change. See *EAR*, p. 215, n. 1.
43. 'A Call to the Orders', *CL*, 26 February, 1938; *EAR*, pp. 215–18.
44. *Ibid.*, p. 217.
45. 'The Irish Bourgeoisie', *Spectator*, 29 April, 1938, 768; review of Kate O'Brien, *Pray for the Wanderer* (Heinemann, 1938); *EAR*, pp. 229–30.

*Day* folded after Graham Greene lost an expensive action brought by Shirley Temple against one of his film reviews. Waugh felt some bitterness at losing his main source of journalistic income and in the new year had to continue pressing Peters for any work he could get. 'Work on *Scoop* going slowly', he noted in January, 'with infinite interruptions and distractions.'[46]

*

Waugh's financial position was considerably more perilous than it appeared to outsiders. He seems to have arranged some of his review contracts privately through friends and then to have informed Peters of the deals later. This was certainly the case with *Night and Day* and the series which immediately followed it, from January to July 1938, in the *Spectator*. The review pages of the *Spectator* were edited in the 'thirties by a series of Waugh's cronies: Peter Fleming, Derek Verschoyle and Graham Greene. Verschoyle, an ex-pupil of Waugh's from Arnold House, remembered their time together with affection and respect. After the collapse of *Night and Day* he snapped up Waugh's suggestion and gave him a weekly column at five pounds.

As Waugh admitted in one piece, he rarely wanted to keep any of the books for his library. In fact, he could hardly afford to. They would be immediately parcelled up and sold, half-price, to a dealer. This brought in, on average, another two pounds a week. Seven pounds in 1938 would have been a middle class weekly wage. It just about kept Waugh in haircuts, drink and train fares. Other income, of course, resulted from odd articles, broadcasts and books.

All the novels remained in print and in late 1937 an edition of his Collected Works was launched by Chapman's. Was it Graham Greene who offered the anonymous free advertisement for this in *Night and Day?*

> EVELYN WAUGH'S NOVELS
> (Chapman & Hall, 5s. each)
> We have had collected editions of most of the contemporary bores from Lawrence downwards: here – in a thin, well-printed, thank-god-not-pocket edition – is an author we can read for amusement and not for exercise, somebody who isn't standard and isn't an ornament to *any* home.[47]

Waugh was delighted with the book-production and, careless of expense, issued simultaneously a select imprint of a dozen, signed copies morocco-bound, on large paper, half of which he gave to friends. The new series provided an injection of cash but not nearly enough. Only when Penguin Books began to publish a run of Waugh titles did he derive substantial income from earlier works.

46. *Diaries*, 10 January, 1938, p. 430.
47. *ND*, 16 December, 1937, 26.

Penguin opened shop in 1935. The first of his books to appear under their imprint was *Decline and Fall* in 1937. At sixpence a book the return was then modest. This mass-production technique enormously increased Waugh's audience and began to establish him as a genuinely 'popular' writer. The benefits of this, however, were not felt until the 'forties and 'fifties. In 1938 his major income from books still derived from first-edition sales at around 8s. 6d. a copy.

The revenue from casual (or even weekly) journalism was pin-money. Far more lucrative were the projects he most hated: film scripts. Not one of Waugh's scripts was used. Not a single contract for film-rights produced a film in his own lifetime. This didn't bother him; in fact it suited him admirably. It meant that he could take large down-payments without subscribing his name to an inferior work of art. Graham Greene has complained of the ways in which film contracts dispossess novelists of artistic control. Waugh never relinquished this power. His letters to Peters on this matter constantly insist that any additional dialogue must be written by him.

The option on *A Handful of Dust*, for instance, was held for fourteen years from 1950 to 1964 and sold and re-sold at various times for anything from $2,500 to $7,500. It provided a recurring income for no work other than correspondence with his agent. But, again, all that was in the future, after the *Brideshead* boom in American sales. No film-rights were sold before the war. In 1938 he was stuck with his pin-money and hardback sales. Even the income from the latter would have been severely depleted. Waugh had always lived on advances and over-draughts. Later there was the supplement of Laura's private income and the rents from the fields at Piers Court let to local farmers. (Laura ran a small-holding but did not need the entire acreage.) The expenses of the house and family, however, far outweighed these additional monies. Waugh, despite his public image, was probably worse off than when he was a bachelor.

It is no surprise, then, that he eagerly sought additional business. The Korda trail had gone cold but another, equally idiotic project presented itself: he set about rewriting Henry Bernstein's play *Le Venin*. The first act of this he returned to Peters in May with a note expressing hope that the project would go through. It didn't. Waugh had even lowered himself to appearing on the radio: once to be interviewed in late 1937; once in April 1938 to read 'On Guard'. He was still negotiating for the book on 'heroes', hoping, futilely, for a large advance. Times were bad.

On 6th April, 1938, Peters received a letter stating that, as it was the new tax year, he (Waugh) could not receive money again. There are several letters like this. Waugh used his agent as both banker and accountant. He fixed his income at an arbitrary figure (about £2,000), thus denying the Inland Revenue substantial gain. The rest he instructed Peters to stockpile until the new financial year. Peters then submitted a detailed account which Waugh could forward to the Revenue. Waugh was pragmatic: a writer might earn a small fortune in one year and then nothing for twelve months. It seemed iniquitous to lose a large slice of his money to the Revenue because every other year he was (technically) wealthy. By holding back payments and declaring them in the next year he could make the most of his tax allowance.

It was an ingenious system reliant entirely upon Peters's flexibility in business. Waugh was a hopeless businessman who thought himself rather astute. Peters was both astute and patient. He valued Waugh not only as a friend but as an artist and potentially his most valuable property. As such, he was prepared to look after Waugh's interests in a fashion far exceeding an agent's normal concern for his client. Waugh had an accountant (in Oxford). No doubt he tied up the loose ends and presented the final assessment. But the load fell most heavily upon Peters, who not only kept accounts but provided loans against future income. In keeping with this practice Waugh instructed the *Spectator* to send his cheques to his agent to hold until 5th April. As the years passed, the strategies for tax evasion became increasingly complicated.

Peters's worries were exacerbated by Waugh's desire to adopt an increasingly right-wing public position. As a friend he would have been delighted with the news that on 9th March Laura had given birth to a girl, Maria Theresa. (Waugh's note coolly describes the child as 'Laura's baby'.) As a businessman, Peters may well have been concerned that increasing family commitments and decreasing popular appeal were not mutually compatible elements in his client's life. But he had faith in Waugh and particularly in the new novel.

\*

That faith was justified when, on 7th May, *Scoop* was published. The reviewers were uniformly delighted with this extravaganza demolishing the pretensions of the popular press. In the 1946 essay which had condemned *Waugh in Abyssinia* as a 'Fascist tract' Rose Macaulay said: 'With it Mr Waugh re-entered his peculiar world; it was a relief to those of us who had begun to fear that we were losing him, that the wit was being slain by the propagandist and the partisan.'[48] This feeling was expressed by many. Here was Waugh back in his old form. 'I like Mr Waugh best', wrote Desmond Shawe-Taylor in the *New Statesman*, 'when he remains in his own territory, which I take to be the circles radiating outwards – not too far – from the lunch-table of Lady Metroland.'[49] Waugh would not have liked 'lunch'; neither did he accept this restriction of territory. And here was something else to bother Peters. No sooner had Waugh re-established himself as a popular humorist than he was preparing permanently to cast aside this reputation.

48. 'The Best and the Worst II. Evelyn Waugh', *Horizon*, December 1946, 370–1; *CH*, p. 202.
49. *NS*, 7 May, 1938, 795; *CH*, pp. 195–7.

Such limitation, to a form he knew he could execute with professional dexterity, was becoming irksome. *Scoop* had proved difficult to write and not only because of the interruptions to an established pattern of work. He was, like John Plant in *Work Suspended*, reaching a 'climacteric' in his career as a novelist. He thought *Scoop* 'light and excellent', but all the time he was thirsting for a new fictional form which could include the dimension of 'supernatural' reality. *Work Suspended*, written in 1939, was to mark the first tentative step towards a fuller prose style, although the transition was only completed with *Brideshead* (1945). *Scoop* was to prove almost the last in the sequence of anarchic fantasies which had so endeared Waugh to his large British audience and American *coterie*. Only *The Loved One* (1948) and *Basil Seal Rides Again* (1963) were to revert to the earlier style.

The *Scoop* reviews, generous as they were, can have done little to raise Waugh's estimation of contemporary criticism. Most simply giggled their way through plot recapitulation. The old problem of analysing Waugh's early work was raised yet again by John Brophy (Brigid Brophy's father) in the *Telegraph*: 'Mr Waugh is not a satirist', he wrote, 'for indignation founded on some belief is necessary to satire, and I have never been able from his books to discover what Mr Waugh believes in. His job is to provide laughter, and how well he does it.'[50] The inadequacy of such commentary reflects the fact that Brophy, and most critics in the 'thirties, still found it impossible to accept the idea of an author 'making a book' which (in Pinfold's words) was 'quite external to himself, to be used and judged by others'.

It might seem that Waugh's own remarks on satire in 'Fan-Fare' (1946) concur with Brophy's. But this is not the case. True, Waugh stated there that his writing was not satirical – but for different reasons:

> Satire is a matter of period. It flourishes in a stable society and presupposes homogeneous moral standards – the early Roman Empire and 18th Century Europe. It is aimed at inconsistency and hypocrisy. It exposes polite cruelty and folly by exaggerating them. It seeks to produce shame. All this has no place in the Century of the Common Man where vice no longer pays lip service to virtue. The artist's only service to the disintegrated society of today is to create little independent systems of order of his own.[51]

The emphasis here is not on his own, but his society's lack of values. We must remember also that this was written after the failure of his military ideals. In 1938, while profoundly pessimistic about the future, he still held to the fragile hope that the Church Militant might secure order.

50. *DT*, 13 May, 1938, 6; *CH*, pp. 198–9.
51. 'Fan-Fare', *Life* (International: Chicago), 8 April, 1946, 53–4, 56, 58, 60; *EAR*, p. 304; *CH*, p. 252.

There is no doubt that *Scoop* is aimed at 'inconsistency and hypocrisy'. His argument was that he did not believe that by exaggerating these he could hope to correct, let alone eradicate them; that they governed his society rather than being aberrations from an essential stability. His statement does less than justice to the serious threat Swift and Pope believed to be posed by their Yahoos and Belindas. It also omits to mention Original Sin: Waugh's argument had always been that man was innately vicious; that there had never been a period of relatively virtuous behaviour.

It is on these grounds that Waugh's vision is perfectly consistent and Brophy's point fails to convince. Brophy cannot accept Waugh as a satirist because he cannot see what the novelist 'believes in' in his work. It is perfectly plain that Waugh believes man to be innately corrupt and that he, by negative suggestion, states positively the higher values towards which human kind should aspire: loyalty, honesty, humility, patience. No matter how he tried later to wriggle free of the term, this novel is unmistakably a satire: a polished, cruelly objective, critical exercise. Perhaps it is this clinical objectivity which cools his humour and leaves the reader unmoved by the tragic implications. Brigid Brophy, reviewing the Uniform Edition in 1964, found *Scoop* 'a mere, though entertaining, after-flutter of the fine imaginative flight which had produced *Black Mischief*.[52] It remains, nevertheless, one of his most popular books.

Waugh made no extraordinary claims for it. His 1957 memorandum discussing a film scenario of *Scoop* states:

> This is a light satire of modern journalism, not a schoolboy's story of plot, counterplot, capture and escape. Such incidents as provoke this misconception are extraneous to the main theme which is to expose the pretensions of foreign correspondents, popularised in countless novels, plays, autobiographies and films, to be heroes, statesmen and diplomats.

The political details of the plot had no interest for him:

> No great pains need to be taken to make a plausible plot for the central section. The essentials are that a potentially serious situation is being treated frivolously, sensationally and dishonestly by the assembled Press. . . . Lightness must be preserved. The central section is not the climax of the story. The climax is the reception of Boot in London. . . . Boot should return home without ambition ever to go away again.[53]

There was no contradiction, even in 1957, in combining 'lightness' with scrupulous craftsmanship.

---

52. *NS*, 25 September, 1964, 450.
53. 'Memorandum for Messrs Endfield and Fisz', 12 April, 1957, p. 1; HRC.

Of all the pre-war manuscripts that of *Scoop* is the most heavily emended, and further revision is revealed by the substantial structural changes which appear when it is compared with the printed text. One aspect of these changes relates to the book's 'political' satire: he constantly struggles against his natural inclination to lampoon only the Left; the White Shirt movement is presented in equally ludicrous terms. The subject of John Brophy's complaint was in one sense a prime object of revision: Waugh strove to remove himself from the text, deliberately reducing all political manifestoes to risible self-contradiction. In his first draft he had explained the divisions in the ruling Jackson family with an extended anecdote about an argument over the brandy-butter one Christmas. The idea was presumably dropped, not because Waugh felt there to be any limit to politicians' absurdity, but because he had a strong sense of the limits to which he could push his readers' credulity.

If the book negates the validity of political argument, though, it remains in the widest sense 'political'; it reflects, albeit humorously, the chaos Waugh saw around him in 1938 in a world rent (in his view) by humanist fallacies. As a satire on journalism, indeed on the mass media in general, it remains a pungent and relevant document. The underlying notion of the absurdity of the rationalist viewpoint, implicit in the concept of a newspaper, that disparate events may be reported as reflecting an understandable 'whole', is another rendering of a continuous theme in Waugh's fiction. The world is not, he suggests, the composite of discernible facts Lord Copper would have us believe; without the dimension of 'spiritual' experience, human behaviour is manifestly bestial and unreasonable. 'There is almost every reason why Mr J. A. Spender should be a disillusioned and bitter man', Waugh had written during the composition of *Scoop*, 'he has given his life to daily journalism and to Liberal politics. . . . the daily press has sunk to a condition when it is a profession not only unsuitable to a gentleman but to an Englishman. . . .'[54]

In the same review Waugh had remarked that politics 'are getting into the hands of the toughs all over Europe, and knuckledusters and rubber truncheons are appearing even in England . . .'. It is this thuggery of competitive materialism which the press corps represents. There is no space in the world of Shumble, Whelper and Pigge for the lush places of individual fancy. Waugh was well aware of the significance of contemporary African political history. The African mandated territories, he wrote in November 1937, 'week by week occupy a more prominent and threatening place in world politics'.[55] He was not trivialising this. The setting for his novel was not an arbitrary result of a casual trip to Abyssinia.

54. 'An Old Liberal Says His Say', *ND*, 23 September, 1937, 24–5; review of J. A. Spender, *Men and Things* (Cassell, 1937).
55. 'All Memory Gone', *ND*, 4 November, 1937, 24–5; review of (among others) Patrick Balfour, *Lords of the Equator* (Hutchinson, 1937).

He saw the country as an axis of massive political change. But he was right; *Scoop* is not a political book in the sense that *Brave New World* is. It has no 'message'; Waugh's own political leanings are heavily disguised. It is, rather, a funny book about the World, the Flesh and the Devil.

Waugh worked on his manuscript like a cabinet-maker inserting inlay; Benito, Corker and Baldwin grew spontaneously from the narrative. Waugh then went through the text 'dropping in' short scenes to dovetail these characters into the entire structure. The 'lush place' *leit-motif* is the product of typescript revision; the scene cross-cutting to London is written on an insertion sheet at the back. These, and hundreds of other tiny modifications, represent the literary craftsman-ship in which he took such pride. The quality of a novel lay for him not in its 'argument' or in its analysis of human motivation but in its structural harmony. The book was intended to delight and to amuse the discriminating, not to educate or confess. But even Waugh was finding this pure aestheticism inadequate to confront the violence into which the western world was collapsing. Mrs Stitch was to be the last in that line of heroines stretching from Margot Beste-Chetwynde.

Waugh noted the type in a review: ' . . . straight from the 1920s – elusive, irresponsible, promiscuous, a little wistful, avaricious, delectable, ruthless – how often we have all read or written about such people.'[56] How better to describe Margot, Agatha and Brenda? With the possible exception of 'promiscuous', this also fits Mrs Stitch. Such women only emerge again in Waugh's fiction in a heavily modified form of the type. Lucy Simmonds, Aimée Thanatogonos, Virginia Troy – all suggest to us what they have or might have been in a different world. But the double-edged 'qualities' Waugh allowed Mrs Stitch become, in the Age of the Common Man, a list of demerits. In 1928 the whimsical, at least in his fiction, could withstand, even control, the onslaught of the philistine. As the last sentence of *Scoop* suggests in its mocking echo of William Boot's debased language, the régime of these will-o'-the-wisp figures is doomed: 'Outside the owls hunted maternal rodents and their furry brood.'

Waugh did not have far to look for the 'originals' of many of his owls. *Scoop* is unusual among the pre-war novels in containing a large number of recognisable portraits. Perhaps this in itself was a sign of flagging imagination. As we have seen, Waugh always prided himself on the construction of 'composite' figures. Here, though, Julia Stitch is recognisably Lady Diana Cooper, her husband (apart from his physical appearance), Duff Cooper; Lord Copper probably provoked Lord Beaverbrook's long-standing loathing of Waugh; Sir Percival Phillips and H. R. Knickerbocker cannot have been entirely delighted with Sir Jocelyn Hitch-cock and Wenlock Jakes. Only Lady Diana escapes the severest mockery.

There seems a certain bitterness in this. The portraits are no longer playful

---

56. 'Love Among the Underdogs', *ND*, 7 October, 1937, 29; review of Kenneth Allott and Stephen Tait, *The Rhubarb Tree* (Cressett Press, 1937).

jibes at friends but spiteful. 'Only a shit could be good at this job', he had written from Abyssinia, and he meant to revenge himself on all those shits who had dared to be better at the job than he. The fantasy of Abyssinia/Azania has been replaced by the *acidie* of Abyssinia/Ishmaelia. One of Waugh's late revisions was to change the names of the newspapers: the *Voice* and the *Daily Excess* become, respectively, the *Beast* and the *Brute*. The rain plummeting throughout the African scenes, crashing on tin roofs, bogging the roads, acts as a melancholy chorus. Beyond all this, beyond the law, arbiters of taste, elusive and intelligent, exist Julia Stitch and Mr Baldwin. But, mixed with Waugh's admiration for such figures, there was envy.

*

He craved the glamour and public influence of people like Diana Cooper and F. W. Rickett. He wished to belong to their club and, although many such invited him to their houses, a certain distance was always preserved. The sad truth was that in cultivating those who were unrepentant élitists, Waugh himself fell foul of their snobbery. He was entertaining, tough and extremely clever but he was not, and would never be, one of them. Duff Cooper thought him a bumptious *parvenu*. In a rage he once described Waugh to his face as 'a common little man . . . who happens to have written one or two moderately amusing novels'.[57]

Cooper, later Viscount Norwich, was the man of the world, the man of affairs Waugh had once so wanted to be: extravagant gambler, fornicator, husband of the most illustrious beauty of her generation, writer, and a star of the Conservative Party. For eighteen months from November 1935, he had been Secretary of State for War. Then he had been appointed First Lord of the Admiralty. As the friends of royalty, he and Diana had been invited to cruise with the King and Mrs Simpson aboard the *Nahlin* in August 1936 prior to the abdication crisis. Waugh only caught echoes of their gilt-edged gossip.

For some years Waugh had been known affectionately as Mr Wu among his upper-class friends. The name had derived from a Pekinese which would snap unexpectedly at ankles. Lady Diana's many slaves apart from Waugh included Rudolph Kommer – the impresario responsible for the *Miracle* – and Conrad Russell. Waugh was certain that Kommer and she had a physical relationship. In the early 'thirties Kommer was jealous of Waugh. Russell was offended that Waugh should have been promoted above himself in the amatory stakes: 'If [Kommer] has to be jealous of anyone it really might be me. It is galling to think that Wu is more dangerous than me.'[58] Few took Wu seriously as a prospective lover. There was always something awkward about him.

In later life Lady Diana described Waugh affectionately as 'the frog who people

57.   Philip Zeigler, *Diana Cooper* (Hamish Hamilton, 1980), p. 266.
58.   *Ibid.*, p. 162.

can't endure'. His gossiping knowingly about her supposed infidelities enraged her: 'How the hell can he tell if I am [unfaithful] or not? Just because I never responded to his dribbling, dwarfish little amorous *singeries*, he need not be so sure.'[59] Both she and Russell counted Waugh among their friends. Lady Diana was particularly fond of him. But there was a line Waugh could not cross. If he put on airs, pretended to sexual favour, assumed social equality, he was put in his place. He was, in their eyes, essentially a pet.

On 7th December, 1937, the day on which he wrote his last *Night and Day* review, he and Laura took a train to London. Lady Diana was holding court:

> Drank with Hubert [Duggan]. Lunched at Admiralty House – Diana, Duff, Venetia [Montagu] and Sir Cuthbert Headlam. . . . Diana spoke, as I thought, of a 'morning with the electric'; she said it was a play everyone was excited about and she made me feel like a bumpkin and wanted to. Got back a bit towards the end . . . Luncheon very nasty. House superb.[60]

The play was Eugene O'Neill's *Mourning Becomes Electra*. Waugh appears here as slightly deaf, dazed and astoundingly ignorant. The social game he loved was a form of Beggar Your Neighbour: the object was to embarrass by probing ignorance or guilt. Apart from Laura, his relationships with women tended to be aggressive. He liked beautiful, unbullyable, unpredictable women and as such had no objection to Lady Diana's tactics. Laura, quiet and astute, was utterly different. She must have been a trifle impatient with the glittering hostess who unmistakably enraptured her husband.

Laura, though, could be certain of Waugh's fidelity and Waugh knew perfectly well that Lady Diana, with her butterfly character, was wholly unsuited to his emotional needs. Waugh did not have Duff's *sang-froid*: he was impulsive and possessive. Diana regularly received men in her bedroom. The idea of Laura doing such a thing would have been unendurable. As a spectator only, Waugh found such extravagence amusing. Laura, like her sisters, was a no-nonsense countrywoman. A neighbour pictured her as never happier than when she had a sack on her back. Headscarves, gum boots and hard work were more her line.[61]

Lady Diana's 'style' was glamorous and effective. Lord Beaverbrook was another of the hopelessly infatuated. She, like Julia Stitch, believed herself to have significant influence in both Parliament and the Press. But, as Waugh surmised, the world in which such things were possible was dying. His visits to London were now those of a foreigner in alien territory. He liked to drop into the casino of its social life for the *frisson* of playing a hand in the sharp metropolitan

59. *Ibid.*, p. 160.
60. *Diaries*, p. 429.
61. Interview with Hon. Mrs G. Heathcoat-Amory, 26 November, 1976.

games. It topped up his sense of self-importance, renewed his membership of the club. But his real interests lay elsewhere: in Catholicism (Lady Diana was an unrepentant agnostic), in home and family.

\*

Seventeen days after the publication of *Scoop*, on 24th May, 1938, Waugh was on a train rattling across Europe. This was quite unlike any of his previous expeditions. He was not alone in search of adventure. He was part of a four-hundred-strong English and Irish Delegation headed by Cardinal Hinsley *en route* for Hungary. The Eucharistic Congress in Budapest was that year celebrating the ninth centenary of St Stephen, Hungary's patron saint. The Catholic Association had made all the arrangements for a 'package tour'. Waugh and his friend Fr Martindale were the Special Correspondents for the *Catholic Herald*, Martindale having gone on ahead to cover the entire Congress. It was a pilgrimage.

Waugh arrived on the 25th, exhausted by thirty-six hours' travelling but inspired by a sense of theological solidarity. The journey had been eventful. It seems that, prevented from crossing Germany, they had been diverted south through France and Austria. Many English and Irish pilgrims had cancelled their reservations because of a 'war-scare'. European hostilities did not begin with the bombing of Poland. In effect they had been inaugurated with Hitler's assumption of power in Austria, a quiet but no less insidious invasion. Powerful anti-semitic measures were in force. Throughout its passage through Austria, this trainload of benign Catholics was guarded by Nazi troops.

On arrival more evidence of oppression came to light. The German police had introduced a special visa for their countrymen wishing to travel to Hungary between 20th and 29th May. This effectively prevented anyone from Germany or Austria attending the Congress. The only people from the Teutonic countries whom Waugh could discover in Budapest were two tennis players competing in an early round of the Davis Cup.

It was a saddening spectacle to see the empty bishops' thrones and benches. Over a hundred thousand Austrians had made preparation to go. Waugh was deeply distressed at seeing Hungary's 'near neighbours abruptly and cruelly deprived of their primary human right of association in worship'.[62] It began to bring home to him the realities of Nazism and the imminence of Britain's confrontation with it:

> All over the world, men and women of every race and colour are looking to the Congress as a tangible sign of the Union of Christendom. Here, all too plainly, was another sign. At Budapest differences were being forgotten and ties strengthened; a few hours distant the conflict which

62. 'Impression of Splendour and Grace', *C Her*, 3 June, 1938, 1, 9; *EAR*, pp. 234–8.

dates from the fall of Adam still raged uncertainly. Europe was still divided. Here all was sunshine and warmth; there the sky was dark and a cold wind stirring. Who could say how long the good hours would last?[63]

For six days he gave himself up to the warmth of fraternity. There would be time enough for conflict in the years ahead.

Abroad in the company of fellow Catholics Waugh was a changed man. Fiercely competitive about social distinctions in England, in Hungary he was delighted to be absorbed into a corporate identity. Normally he loathed crowds; in Budapest he was swept along and jostled amid alien tongues. Rather than feeling intimidated by the tens of thousands there, he found himself wishing that their number were greater. He felt 'at home' in a way he rarely did in his native country:

> ... I do not think that anyone could have felt a stranger, for the atmosphere was permeated through and through with Catholicism, and that, I think, was the most valuable part of the pilgrimage – to be living for a few days entirely surrounded by people leading a specifically Catholic life. In England we are always in a minority, often a very small one. There is a danger that we look on ourselves as the exceptions, instead of in the true perspective of ourselves as normal and the irreligious as freaks.[64]

It was in this mood, elated by the community of faith, that he returned to England and determined to write a specifically 'political' book.

*

Just before leaving for Budapest Waugh had received a letter from Clive Pearson asking him to write a book on Mexico. Waugh knew neither his correspondent nor Mexico; but the offer was tempting. Pearson appears to have been willing to write a blank cheque. Waugh hesitated – but not for long. Accepting the contract entailed selling his skills for propaganda in advance of his findings. The positive gains were a free trip abroad for himself and Laura, the chance further to establish himself as a defender of the faith and a large cash payment. Budapest made up his mind. By early June he was instructing Roughead to negotiate insurance for the trip. An expense account of £800 promised three months of luxurious travel.

Clive Pearson represented the Cowdray Estate which had massive financial interests in Mexican oil. The socialist government under General Cardenas had expropriated the British oil industry with a promise, unlikely to be redeemed, of satisfactory compensation. Pearson looked to Waugh for a popular book to

63. *Ibid.*, p. 238.
64. *Ibid.*, p. 237.

advertise the injustice. Waugh was bored and frustrated at home. In the spring of 1938 Graham Greene had gone to Mexico to describe the persecution of Catholics and Waugh felt, if with some trepidation at this literary competition, that he was also needed to support the cause.

Greene's journey was highly productive. Two books derived directly from his Mexican experience: *The Lawless Roads* (1939) and *The Power and the Glory* (1940). Waugh's trip produced only a book which in future years he preferred to forget. On his return, Waugh reviewed Greene's work for the *Spectator:*

> I find it impossible to write of the *Lawless Roads* in any but personal terms, for I have been awaiting its publication with particular curiosity. It so happens that I arrived in Mexico last summer with ulterior literary motives a few weeks after Mr Greene had left with his notebooks full. There was an element of anxiety in the interest with which I began to read the report of so immediate a predecessor.[65]

The review is not at all unkind, as Christopher Sykes suggests (p. 188), but it is more of an advertisement for Waugh's opinions. Greene and he had taken different routes, under different circumstances and with different objectives. Waugh had made his first major excursion abroad with Laura; 'Mr Greene's was an heroic journey, mine was definitely homely. . . . Mr Greene's cinematographic shots', he remarks, ' . . . [are] all the more damning because they are not linked by any political thesis.'[66] This was not quite accurate. Greene's book leant sympathetically, if not dogmatically, to the left. And this was where they differed. Waugh was being employed to promote a 'political thesis' damning the Mexican government.

The trip took three months – August-October 1938 – and included Waugh's first visit to America. Laura and he arrived on the *Aquitania* to find New York broiled in a heat wave. With the temperature in the nineties, Waugh was in fractious mood. The prospect of a long train journey south to even hotter regions filled him with dread. Ignorant of the then luxurious accommodation of air-conditioned American trains, he decided instead to take the weekly steamer to Vera Cruz. 'New York was 93° and felt like 193°', he wrote to Henry Yorke, thanking him for help with travel arrangements. 'The *Sibony* was packed with jewesses. Your father is affectionately remembered by all the crew and stewards. . . .'[67] In addition to his letters of introduction from the influential Pearson clan, Waugh also carried others from Yorke's father, a director of the Mexican Railway (then a British-owned company). Waugh's note to Yorke was

65. 'The Waste Land', *Spectator*, 10 March, 1939, 413–14; review of Graham Greene, *The Lawless Roads* (Heinemann, 1939); *EAR*, pp. 248–50.
66. *Ibid.*, p. 250.
67. *Letters*, pp. 118–19; 'Silony' should read 'Sibony'.

written from the Hotel Ritz, Mexico City. Where Greene had travelled rough and alone, Waugh was cosseted throughout. Greene had investigated the rural south and covered the length and breadth of Mexico. Waugh was confined to the relatively prosperous central tableland and excursions from the capital.

The first page of his book, *Robbery Under Law: The Mexican Object Lesson* (1939), ingeniously tried to forestall criticism aimed at his limited understanding of the country: 'I do not see how it is possible to escape the imputation of presumption', he wrote. ' "The fellow mugs up a few facts in the London Library, comes out here for a week or two with a bare smattering of the language, hangs about bothering us all with a lot of questions, and then proceeds to make money by telling us all our own business." '68 He was there for two months rather than 'a week or two', but with this one exception the charge remains valid.

Waugh's smattering of the language was of the barest; his previous knowledge of Mexico negligible. The wonder is that he managed to absorb as much political history as he did in so short a time. The fact remains that his book often reconstructs the information at his disposal into a right-wing polemic. The present author's copy was owned by a British colonial who had lived in Mexico in 1901–2. His marginalia are interesting. Sometimes, it seems, Waugh hits off the character of the country accurately: 'Absolutely typical' is scrawled against Waugh's account of bartering with a recalcitrant dealer to smuggle a picture out of the country.69 On other occasions, though, the reader has marked errors: 'Not so in my time'. Waugh's geography even suffers from his desire to create literary effects. Mexico City, he wrote, 'lies in [Popocatapetl's] shadow and other travellers have felt, or professed to feel, the life of the place dominated by its vast and splendid bulk'.70 'Ridiculous!' comments the colonial. 'It is more than 50 miles away.'

Waugh makes no attempt to disguise his political disposition and one long passage must be quoted:

> Let me, then, warn the reader that I was a Conservative when I went to Mexico and that everything I saw there strengthened my opinions. I believe that man is, by nature, an exile and will never be self-sufficient or complete on this earth; that his chances of happiness and virtue, here, remain more or less constant through the centuries and, generally speaking, are not much affected by the political and economic conditions in which he lives; that the balance of good and ill tends to revert to a norm; that sudden changes of physical condition are usually ill, and are advocated by the wrong people for the wrong reasons; that the intellectual communists of today have personal, irrelevant grounds for their antagonism to society, which they are trying to exploit. I believe in

68. *Robbery Under Law*, p. 1.
69. *Ibid.*, p. 46.
70. *Ibid.*, p. 26.

government; that men cannot live together without rules but that these should be kept at the bare minimum of safety; that there is no form of government ordained from God as being better than any other; that the anarchic elements in society are so strong that it is a whole-time task to keep the peace. I believe that inequalities of wealth and position are inevitable and that it is therefore meaningless to discuss the advantages of their elimination; that men naturally arrange themselves in a system of classes; that such a system is necessary for any form of co-operative work, more particularly the work of keeping a nation together. I believe in nationality; not in terms of race or of divine commissions for world conquest, but simply this: mankind inevitably organizes itself into communities according to its geographical distribution; these communities by sharing a common history develop common characteristics and inspire a local loyalty; the individual family develops most happily and fully when it accepts these natural limits. I do not think that British prosperity must necessarily be inimical to anyone else, but if, on occcasions, it is, I want Britain to prosper and not her rivals. I believe that war and conquest are inevitable; that is how history has been made and that is how it will develop. I believe that Art is a natural function of man; it so happens that most of the greatest art has appeared under systems of political tyranny, but I do not think it has a connection with any particular system, least of all with representative government, as nowadays in England, America and France it seems popular to believe; artists have always spent some of their spare time in flattering the governments under whom they live, so it is natural that, at the moment, English, American and French artists should be volubly democratic.[71]

It is brilliantly written, its rhetorical structure echoing the Creed. But its propositions are again those of a pragmatic aesthete rather than those of the right-wing of the Conservative Party. One of his complaints against the Mexican government was that 'In practice, as in theory, the whole process conformed to the new, Nazi statecraft.'[72] By advocating 'conservatism' he did not mean to advance a system of political suppression or, in real terms, any specific movement. His 'manifesto' was prefaced by: 'Politics, everywhere destructive, have here [Mexico] dried up the place, frozen it, cracked and powdered it to dust. Is civilization, like a leper, beginning to rot at its extremities?'[73] Yet he insists that his is 'a political book; . . . The succeeding pages are notes on anarchy.'[74]

The idiosyncratic fashion in which Waugh employs the term 'political' is revealed by his complaint about the 'Left': 'Nowadays', he states, ' . . . Law is

71.  *Ibid.*, 'Introduction', pp. 16–17.
72.  *Ibid.*, p. 118.
73.  *Ibid.*, p. 3.
74.  *Ibid.*, pp. 1 and 3.

merely a formulation of the whims of the party in power.'[75] Politics, to Waugh, were only useful in so far as they maintained traditional moral and aesthetic standards. His horror of experimentation he saw as justified by the Mexican experiment in which, he believed, theft, murder and religious persecution had been legalised. It was a different case entirely from Abyssinia:

> If Mexico were a small, new country, just emerging from barbarism, house-proud of its little achievements . . . it would be ungenerous to wound the national pride and abuse hospitality by uncovering its failure. But it is nothing of the kind. It is a huge country with a long and proud history . . . ; it has been rich and cultured and orderly . . . ; now, every year, it is becoming hungrier, wickeder and more hopeless; . . . the jungle is closing in and the graves of the pioneers are lost in the undergrowth.[76]

The last image had been used before in *Ninety-Two Days* and implicitly in *A Handful of Dust*. Waugh cites Mexico's ancient universities, buildings and craftsmanship to support his case.

The particular horror of this leprous decay he saw, as in *Campion*, in aesthetic terms:

> So the great steal began and with it, inevitably, the campaign of justification, of slander; and with the guilt and the hate, the wanton destruction; the libraries thrown out into the gutters, the canvasses slit up, the statues piled up and burned in the plaza. . . . [77]

No account is taken of the Spanish exploitation of the Mexican peasantry, or the anger against centuries of social injustice which had exploded in the face of the Church. He relies for his argument on the rather naïve determinism of his manifesto. The universality of Catholicism had, in his view, bound the country together and made it a culturally important and politically powerful nation. With the persecution of the priesthood all the benefits of civilisation were disappearing, leaving the poor worse off than before, subject to the irrational greed of ignorant men. It was as simple as that. The 'object lesson' was that: 'There is no distress of theirs to which we might not be equally subject.'[78]

*Robbery Under Law* draws together those anti-rationalist theories which he had been developing during the 'thirties. 'We were educated', he says, 'in the assumption that things would not only remain satisfactory without our effort but with the very minimum of exertion on our part become unrecognizably better . . . ;

75. *Ibid.*, p. 85.
76. *Ibid.*, pp. 204–5.
77. *Ibid.*, pp. 213–14.
78. *Ibid.*, p. 277.

progress is still regarded as normal, decay as abnormal. The history of Mexico runs clean against these assumptions.'[79] It recalls the broadcast Waugh made in 1932: 'To an Unknown Old Man'. Material progress, if this meant the redistribution of wealth, signalled for Waugh the debasing of aesthetic sensibility; 'spiritual' progress he considered a philosophical absurdity beyond the framework of Christianity. 'Altruism', he states, 'does not flourish long without religion':

> A conservative is not merely an obstructionist. . . . He has positive work to do. . . . Civilisation has no force of its own beyond what is given it from within. It is under constant assault and it takes most of the energies of civilised man to keep it going at all. . . . Barbarism is never finally defeated; given propitious circumstances, men and women who seem quite orderly, will commit every conceivable atrocity. . . . [80]

Waugh's novels had returned persistently to this theme. With the hindsight of history, what appeared to some contemporaries as hyperbolic misanthropy can only be regarded as fair comment. Auschwitz and Belsen were yet to come.

Strangely, though, on the brink of war, he refused to believe that it would happen and, as we have seen, those who predicted catastrophe he accused of precipitating aggression. He was in Mexico during the September crisis when Chamberlain had returned from Munich with Hitler's worthless signature on a 'piece of paper'. The Mexican press told of children being sent from London, of trenches being dug in Hyde Park. It was all true. Waugh believed none of it, classifying the journalists' panic with the Americans' absurd belief, a few months later, that there had been a Martian invasion: the wireless was to blame, and the mass media in general. It was in their interest to manufacture a crisis.

*

By late October Waugh and Laura were back at Piers Court. The return journey had been dismal: Laura was in pain from a grumbling appendix; Waugh was gloomily confronting the prospect of writing his book. There was no possibility of lengthy deferral. Pearson was anxious to receive the manuscript. Waugh continued to review for the *Spectator* and *Tablet* and it was over the next six months that his pieces damning Connolly, Auden and Wells appeared. At least, Waugh hoped, he might make some badly-needed cash from occasional journalism. Mexico was topical. He immediately dispatched to Peters a synopsis for a series of articles for the *Daily Mail*.

But it was not to be. The *Mail*, it seems, no longer required Mr Waugh's

79. *Ibid.*, pp. 276–7.
80. *Ibid.*, pp. 278–9.

services. Only the *Tablet* would publish his Mexico material.[81] Instead he wrote a short story, 'An Englishman's Home', and an article for *Harper's Bazaar*, 'Well-Informed Circles . . . and How to Move in Them'.[82] Both dealt with subjects close to Waugh's heart. The story concerned the alienation of a 'new countryman' in an English village; the metropolitan Beverley Metcalfe makes the mistake of not buying the full acreage surrounding his property, thus exposing himself to exploitation by speculative builders. It satirises the ignorance and pallid rural romanticism of the new man, brutally exploited by the old hands.

The article offers the reverse vision: a tongue-in-cheek guide to metropolitan social gamesmanship. Both pieces are well-written but ultimately frivolous. Both reflect Waugh's obsession with creating a public image and defending it, by fair means or foul. 'To be well-informed in England', he says, ' . . . means to be in constant association with the Great.' He knew that, beyond the world of letters, he was largely excluded from the confidences of this company. It was important, though, to give the impression that this was not the case. 'An essential quality is resilience to public exposure.' If caught out over a matter of fact while pontificating at dinner the answer was simple: bluster your way out of it. 'Treat all discussion as though you were being heckled in a tough ward at an election.'[83]

The tone is facetious but the advice approximates his own social strategy. In the story there is a large distance between the sentimental Metcalfe and Waugh's own pragmatism. But he undoubtedly shared aspects of his character's dilemma. He too was having difficulty accommodating himself to the network of parochial politics and institutions which in its quiet fashion was intrusive, demanding and tedious. Like Metcalfe he was susceptible to violent shifts of mood if he thought someone was trying to get the better of him. Then: 'He was no longer the public-spirited countryman; he was cards-on-the-table-brass-tacks-and-treat-him-or-mind-your-step-Metcalfe, Metcalfe with his back up, fighting Metcalfe once again. Metcalfe who would cut off his nose any day to spite his face. . . .'[84] There is much of Waugh here – the character of his business correspondence. The single most obvious difference between himself and this ludicrous fiction was not that Metcalfe was essentially a materialist *parvenu* but that Waugh never made the mistake of considering himself a 'countryman'. He lived in Gloucestershire to be alone.

81. A series of four brief articles under the running title 'Religion in Mexico. Impressions of a Recent Visit': 'I. The Straight Fight', *Tablet*, 29 April, 1939, 543–4; 'II', *Tablet*, 6 May, 1939, 575–6; 'III', *Tablet*, 13 May, 1939, 606–7; 'IV', *Tablet*, 20 May, 1939, 638–9.
82. 'An Englishman's Home', *Work Suspended and Other Stories* (Chapman and Hall, 1943); reprinted Penguin Books with *Scott-King's Modern Europe* (1947) and *Basil Seal Rides Again* (1963) (Harmondsworth, 1967), pp. 43–62. 'Well-Informed Circles . . . and How to Move in Them', *HB*, 19 January, 1939; reprinted *Vogue* (New York), 1 April, 1939, 90–1, 127; *EAR*, pp. 241–4.
83. 'Well-Informed Circles', *EAR*, p. 244.
84. 'An Englishman's Home', *Work Suspended . . .*, *op. cit.*, p. 56.

The jokes in these two pieces were not far removed from self-criticism. Waugh, neurotically susceptible to public exposure (as opposed to public criticism), must have felt himself perilously close to it in the autumn of 1938. He was worried that no-one but the Catholic Press would publish his views on world affairs. Peters could not even sell the story for sufficient cash. Waugh knew that he was 'in trade': his product had to be marketable and it seemed that his very future as a man capable of earning his living by his pen might be at stake. He could continue to turn out novels in his old style but he was unhappy with it. The slick generalisations of his early travel books were wearing thin in the contemporary political climate. *Robbery Under Law*, when he settled to writing it in December, was significantly more serious in tone.

It was a depressing period for Waugh. Dennis Wheatley had secured the lucrative *Sunday Graphic* review page which Peters had tried to arrange for Waugh; money was short and Laura ill; there was a baby in the house. Whatever he wrote on Mexico could be edited by Pearson and indeed his proposed title, *Pickpocket Government*, was sternly vetoed. Waugh's letters to Peters haggle over small insurance claims for medical expenses and a lost hairbrush. Christmas in the taut formality of Pixton wasted more time. But by 20th January he had completed 40,000 words. It was dull work. 'Oh dear oh Mexico', he had scribbled to Betjeman in December, 'it is such a dry subject.'[85] By 24th January Laura was in a Bristol hospital for her appendectomy. He gratefully put the book aside for a week and moved to Clifton to be near her.

It was mid-April before the completed manuscript was in Pearson's hands and the four months of hard labour were complete. Chapman and Hall were to publish, not Duckworth's. (It is unclear whether Duckworth's contract had expired or they had refused the book.) Waugh probably sensed that it would not sell well. For all its propagandist gusto, it had been difficult and boring to write. It was pointedly anti-American and its pro-Catholic, pro-Franco stance was not calculated to appeal to the masses. He cared nothing for that other than from the financial point of view. But there were additional reasons for him to feel low-spirited.

His review work was a chore. He had nothing specific for his next literary project: he was still considering the book on 'heroes' and returned to work on Bernstein's play. Tom Burns wanted a book on the Jesuits' centenary in 1940 but it would have entailed a year's work and Waugh required an advance of a year's 'salary'. £2,000 was a figure wildly beyond the reach of Burns and Oates. Waugh fiddled about, uncertain where to turn. At one point he expressed himself willing to expand 'An Englishman's Home' to 20,000 words. After completing *Robbery* he knocked out another quick story, 'The Sympathetic Passenger'.[86] It

85. Unpublished ALS to [Sir] John Betjeman, 15 December [1938], from Piers Court.
86. 'The Sympathetic Passenger', *DM*, 4 May, 1939, 4.

might, he suggested, make a good comic film. It didn't and, in calmer mood, he later refused even to allow its republication. The tale is poor stuff: a cheap and abbreviated re-working of the Cruttwell/Loveday-escaped-lunatic theme. Cruttwell, in fact, had taken his valedictory bow in 'An Englishman's Home' as a dishonest treasurer for the Wolf Cubs of Much Malcock. An era in Waugh's professional life was drawing to a close.

Melancholy began to creep over him as he failed to find a way ahead. In every aspect of his literary life he seemed to be drying up, capable only of competent craftsmanship and the reiteration of old views. *Scoop* had taken far too long. His depression did not simply centre on the spectacle of a desecrated world. Certainly the despoliation of London and the encroachment of socialism appalled him as did the political thuggery of Europe. His journalism had constantly warned against precipitating military conflict. During these months, though, he was forced to accept the inevitability of the collision course on which Germany, Japan and Italy were set. Ultimately, he welcomed the war as an opportunity for action. It was stasis, inertia which confused him. Unlike Metcalfe he had no clear object of attack and he needed one. In his next work of fiction, *Work Suspended*, he touched on the subject:

> For the civilised man there are none of those swift transitions of joy and pain which possess the savage; words form slowly like pus about his hurts; there are no clean wounds for him; first a numbness, then a long festering, then a scar ever ready to re-open. Not until they have assumed the livery of defence can his emotions pass through the lines;.... [87]

That, it seems, was how Waugh felt. He appeared temporarily to have exhausted his resources and there was an element of desperation at the thought of another thirty years of novel-writing, with nothing new to say. The world had changed and his work had not changed with it.

*

Waugh's argument in *Robbery Under Law*, justified as it was in its critique of religious persecution, often relies on the cheapest form of polemic. He repeats atrocity stories while disclaiming responsibility for their authority, deliberately adding to the exaggeration. Unsupported generalisations masquerade as universal truths.[88] The text is laced with self-contradiction and what can only be construed as a willingness to indulge in hypocrisy. (Defending the petro-chemical industry

---

87. *Work Suspended* in *Work Suspended and Other Stories* (Harmondsworth, 1967), pp. 130–1.
88. Cf. *Robbery Under Law*, p. 62: 'Stories of this kind – many of them no doubt exaggerated – ...' is the escape clause allowing him to repeat the story. Cf. also pp. 72, 164, 194 and 259–60.

he argues *for* the convenience of the car-user[89] where in his other writings the automobile is seen as a principal rapist of Western civilisation. He speaks *against* elections[90] where earlier he had condemned Cardenas's régime as a one-party state.[91] The details of the book's thesis, despite its beautiful prose, do not bear close examination.

When it appeared at the end of June it met with conflicting responses. Harold Nicolson, a former admirer, thought it 'short but dull' and spoilt by anger, lacking the 'gay sparkle' of earlier work.[92] 'Mr Waugh's professional intuition', said the *TLS*, ' . . . is handicapped by the prejudices with which he approached the country.'[93] Even the Catholic *Dublin Review* disliked the '*simplisme*' of Waugh's judgements on 'the goodness or badness, the success or failure, of men's rationalization of their desires'.[94] But a surprising number found the book convincing. The *Spectator* thought it 'very brilliant, sad though its story is'.[95] The *Guardian* liked it, as did the *New York Times*.

Waugh had by this time quarrelled with his American publishers, Little Brown. Disappointed at the money they had offered, he had refused to correct the proofs or to have anything more to do with the US edition. It must have come as a pleasant surprise to find his attack on the States's 'Good Neighbour' policy with Mexico meeting a favourable response in the *New York Times*. R. L. Martin professed himself entirely convinced by the 'calm logic' of Waugh's argument, a view perhaps reflecting the nervousness of American conservatives at the proximity of Cardenas's socialist government.[96] By the time the US edition had been published, five months later, war had been declared in Europe.

After the war, Waugh came to regret this somewhat hysterical document. He omitted it entirely from *When the Going was Good*, saying in the Preface that he was 'content to leave [it] in oblivion, for it dealt little with travel and much with political questions. . . . So let it lie in its own dust.' It has not been forgotten. Anthony Quinton, reviewing the *Letters* in 1980, was clamouring for its republication.[97] It is still of interest to scholars as a 'period piece'. But it is perhaps best left in its dust. It was a mistake and Waugh knew it. He had let his guard drop. A radical change was needed.

---

89. *Ibid.*, p. 89.
90. *Ibid.*, p. 135.
91. *Ibid.*, p. 80.
92. Harold Nicolson, *DT*, 30 June, 1939, 9; *CH*, pp. 203–4.
93. *TLS*, 1 July, 1939, 382.
94. Gerald Vann, *DR*, June–December, 1939, 433–5; *CH*, pp. 208–9.
95. William Gower, *Spectator*, 21 July, 1939, 103.
96. R. L. Martin, *NYTBR*, 19 November, 1939, 9, 19; *CH*, pp. 205–8.
97. Anthony Quinton, *Listener*, 4 September, 1980, 307–8.

# XV

# *Work Suspended: June–November 1939*

With the publication of *Robbery Under Law* Waugh resumed his diary after a gap of eighteen months. There is an entry for almost every day from late June to December 1939. Perhaps he had been troubled again by the 'blanks and blurs' of memory which had annoyed him earlier. A more probable stimulus was the political turmoil of the country. He knew now that war was inevitable. When he came to write of it, the diary would be an *aide-mémoire*.

It provides a flat account of his now well-established routine as a country gentleman. He wrote an article on the subject, 'The New Rustics', for *Harper's Bazaar* (largely repeating the material of a piece for the *Spectator* a year earlier). Rural life, he says, has changed: the minor gentry has been squeezed out by the economic impossibility of running a thousand acres from the manor house; the farms have been sold off and partitioned. Three groups bought the smaller properties: 'retired' people, arty types or 'intellectuals', and genuine artists – writers or painters. A painter, he says, 'needs light and space for his work, a writer . . . silence. All need peace of mind. And these necessary things are not to be found in London.'[1]

The *Spectator* version (July 1938) had mentioned the discomforts of social re-adjustment: 'New questions of law and custom occur weekly and the newcomer runs the risk of rendering himself odious for officiousness or ridiculous for indulgence.'[2] A year later this fear of exposure had largely receded, but his search for silence was continually interrupted. Peace of mind was not easily obtained in the shadow of the war. Before long, evacuees began to haunt the streets of Stinchcombe, Waugh's village, and he watched them with pitiless horror. How soon, he wondered, would they invade his property?

A more immediate annoyance was the requirement to participate in ludicrous civil defence preparations:

> A misty moonlit night. Went out at two and found Mrs Baldwin and two farmers' boys at the Old Parsonage. Waited half an hour. Presently two special constables arrived, then some air-raid wardens, then Mrs

---

1. 'The New Rustics', *HB*, July 1939; *EAR*, pp. 256–9.
2. 'The New Countryman', *Spectator*, 8 July, 1938, 54–5.

Collins who attached labels to us specifying injuries. Then more officials gathered and presently someone let off a firework.[3]

Try as he might to reduce his life to 'Church and spade',[4] country house visits, and week-end parties for close friends, the war would not go away. When Diana Cooper and Conrad Russell arrived at the end of June, flushed with the excitement of the crisis, Waugh did not want to talk about it.

'There are few pleasures to touch those of embellishing a building', he wrote to Ann Fleming in 1959.[5] Twenty years earlier he was indulging in this pleasure heartily. Most days found him in his garden, not engaged with the suburban pursuit of growing flowers or laying out herbaceous borders but with large-scale 'architectural' revisions. As he dug paths, moved trees, re-aligned the lawns and tennis court he could clear his mind of other distractions. On his excursions from home he would constantly search for ornaments to his property. In London during late July he purchased 'three dilapidated copies of Halfpenny's and a fine copy . . . of Chamber's *Civil Architecture* . . .'[6] William Halfpenny was an eighteenth-century architectural designer.

But the distractions persistently returned. He was engaged in a dispute with the *Daily Mail* over a misrepresentative review of *Robbery Under Law* and involved with the internal wrangles of the board of Chapman and Hall. For the first month his diary is packed with the trivia of domestic routine and his irritable reactions to interference. No mention is made of any literary activity. 'Lady Featherstone Godley called this morning to ask where the first aid post was and complain of Lady Tubb's change of venue from boilerhouse to stable. Count D'Oyley rang up to ask us to weekend at Berkeley. Refused, controlling temptation to explain that I do not go visiting the immediate neighbours. . . .'[7] He had no time for parochial concerns. He wanted to be alone – and for an excellent reason. Since the publication of *Robbery* he had been intermittently engaged on a novel. It was to be unlike anything he had written and he was obsessed with it.

Quite suddenly in the diary we find him mentioning this work, not at its inception but after some weeks of laborious concentration:

> I have rewritten the first chapter of the novel about six times and at last got it into tolerable shape.[8]

Waugh's previous practice had been to send off sections to the typist as he

3. *Diaries*, 8 July, 1939, p. 432.
4. *Ibid.*, 6 August, 1939, p. 435.
5. *Letters*, p. 526.
6. *Diaries*, 28 July, 1939, pp. 433–4.
7. *Ibid.*, 8 July, 1939, p. 432.
8. *Ibid.*, 27 July, 1939, p. 433.

completed them and make many of his revisions to the typescript.[9] This meticulous attention to the manuscript was a radical departure. It was not merely structure which was bothering him here but his whole literary style.

Looking back in 1946 he remarked:

> When I gadded, among savages and people of fashion and politicians and crazy generals, it was because I enjoyed them. I have settled down now because I ceased to enjoy them and because I have found a much more abiding interest – the English Language. . . . I have never, until quite lately, enjoyed writing. . . . I wanted to be a man of the world and took to writing as I might have taken to archaeology or diplomacy . . . as a means of coming to terms with the world. Now I see it as an end in itself. Most European writers suffer a climacteric at the age of 40. Youthful volubility carries them so far. After that they either become prophets or hacks or aesthetes. . . . I am no prophet and, I hope, no hack. . . .
>
> The failure of modern novelists since and including James Joyce was one of presumption and exorbitance. They are not content with the artificial figures which hitherto passed so gracefully as men and women. They try to represent the whole human mind and soul and yet omit its determining character – that of being God's creature with a defined purpose.[10]

Waugh's artistic dilemma was complex and in 1939 he could not fully understand it himself. The overwhelming frustration was the difficulty of formulating a positive position as a novelist. Since 1931 his writings, working within a humanist framework, had described behaviour and asserted Catholic values by negative suggestion. But they seemed 'light' because they omitted 'the determining character' of the 'soul'. The climacteric which he describes as affecting European writers at the age of forty began for Waugh in the early years of his second marriage, 1937–9. It is this which is so carefully, if indirectly, analysed in *Work Suspended*.

*

*Work Suspended* is the most enigmatic of Waugh's writings. Its mockery of socialism and philistinism is quite in keeping with his role as the right-wing Catholic apologist defending 'civilisation' from the 'barbarians', but the emotional intensity of the work, expressed in a more conventional and committed prose style than that of the five early novels, is surprising. Although unfinished, *Work Suspended*

---

9. *Scoop* is a partial exception to this. He spent so long writing it, and was so dissatisfied with the structure of his first draft, that he made substantial revisions to the MS. Nevertheless, this MS revision was more of structure than of style.
10. 'Fan-Fare', *op. cit.*; *EAR*, pp. 301–2.

has an evasive cohesion, perhaps because the characterisation seems to be based on values and assumptions which derive from a private world beyond the text. It has the appearance of a longer novel from which many of the fictional linking devices have been cut and, to a certain extent, this was indeed the case.

The central figure, John Plant, is a fastidious and urbane thriller writer. He returns from Fez to England after his father is killed in a road accident by a travelling salesman called Atwater. The father, an artist, is luridly described as fulfilling the 'broken promise' of nineteenth-century subject painting. Plant himself discovers that he is undergoing a climacteric and cannot write. He becomes emotionally involved with Lucy, the pregnant wife of Roger Simmonds, an old Socialist friend. Plant decides to abandon his nomadic existence and settles in the country. Towards the end of the work, Humboldt's Gibbon (in the London Zoo) appears to have some symbolic relevance to this analysis of artistic and domestic transformation. The story concludes with the birth of Lucy's baby.

Waugh explains very little. Lucy is convincingly portrayed yet, ultimately, we must admit that we know almost nothing about her. Even when allowance is made for the narrating persona, Waugh appears to be laying his literary soul open in an entirely new fashion. True, the death of the old and the birth of a new, 'dark' age had been his subject since 1930, but this strange, incomplete tale alters his whole approach. What is the significance of these disparate figures? Why, when it is of such high quality, did he find himself unable to complete their history?

*Work Suspended* was embarked upon cautiously. It represented an innovation, a fictional approach which allowed of controlled sentimentality and sensuous description. For the first time, he introduced an intimate first-person 'voice', commenting extensively on the action. There can be no doubt that to Waugh this new 'novel' was the most important thing he had attempted since *A Handful of Dust*. But he did not quite know how to go about it. The anxious re-writing emphasises his struggle to transform his style. And there was another problem. It was to be his first novel to draw heavily on intimate autobiographical material. Perhaps for this reason and certainly because it represented a technical experiment progress was slow.

That first diary entry concerning the book appears at a moment of domestic crisis. Piers Court had been closed down for three weeks on 14th July and Waugh and Laura had left to stay with her family at Pixton Park only to find it crammed with guests and uninhabitable:

> After two weeks of Pixton life I leave for a few days' rest . . . various Amorys and Horners popping in and out, children all over the house, incessant rain, unpunctual, uneatable meals, incessant telephoning and changing of plans. . . . IRA bombs, surrender to Japanese, comic dependence on Russian negotiations fill newspapers.[11]

11. *Diaries*, 27 July, 1939, p. 433.

He was to grumble for the rest of his life about the inefficient social organisation of the Herbert family. He liked things to be exact. His own household ran like clockwork. If plans were made he insisted that they be properly executed. If a guest arrived late for a meal, or the meal were badly cooked, it could throw him into a paroxysm of rage. He could not bear to be part of a noisy, active household. This was an invasion of privacy. The precise regulation of his life had become an obsession. Escaping to London he relieved his frustration by seeking a lawyer to sue the *Mail*.

While there, he stayed at the St James's and in the evenings visited his parents at Highgate. Arthur Waugh was in 1939 truly an 'old man'. His chest troubled him. He pottered out every day to the cricket or to take the poodle for a walk. He had only four years to live. Having dedicated his life to Chapman and Hall he had been watching with sadness the demise of its fiction list during the 'thirties.

Part of Waugh's business in London had been to attend a board meeting at which more ungentlemanly subversion had taken place. He must have talked about it with his father. They shared a distaste for the new breed of publisher, keen for hard cash, expanding the range of 'technical' books. Waugh found the current list despicably second-rate but, like his father, remained loyal to the old firm. Perhaps he felt himself uneasily approaching Arthur's wistful longing for the easy give and take of a more leisured age. He said as much in his reviews. The novel he was writing concerned in part the destruction of gentility by materialists and philistines. He eventually called the first part 'My Father's House'. But if he admitted to such feelings in front of Arthur, their relationship remained distant and formal. 'Walked with my father in Kenwood', he noted, 'and attempted to undo the rather unamiable impression of my former two evenings.'[12]

Back at Piers Court in early August he began to despair of ever making a lasting impression on his house and grounds: 'the whole place looked as neglected as it did when we arrived two years ago.'[13] He settled into a steady routine, writing in the mornings, gardening in the afternoon, but the novel progressed only slowly. By the end of the month he was still tinkering with the first section. 'As in September of last year', he remarked, 'it is difficult to concentrate on work at the moment. I spent a restless day, but am maintaining our record as being the only English family to eschew the radio throughout the crisis. . . .'[14]

The news was bad but Waugh read *The Times* with something approaching exhilaration: 'Russia and Germany have agreed to neutrality pact so there seems no reason why war should be delayed.'[15] The Nazi-Soviet Pact clarified matters

12. *Ibid.*, 29 July, 1939, p. 434.
13. *Ibid.*, 4 August, 1939, p. 435.
14. *Ibid.*, 23 August, 1939, p. 437.
15. *Ibid.*, 22 August, 1939, p. 437.

for him: now he knew who the enemy were and they had plainly revealed their colours to the British public. It was time, in his view, to attack.

As he looked round his estate, though, his enthusiasm paled. His squirearchical seclusion had lasted for barely two years. Shortly all his efforts would be wrecked. 'Working in the afternoon in the garden . . . I thought: what is the good of all this? In a few months I shall be growing swedes and potatoes here and on the tennis court; or perhaps I shall be away and another two or three years of weeds will feed here. . . .'[16] All around he saw change and decay. On 25th August he began to apply for war work by writing to Basil Dufferin at the Ministry of Information.

Having decided to commit himself to the defence of his country, his mind cleared and the novel began to take shape:

> Worked well at novel. I have introduced the character who came here to beg, saying he was from the *New Statesman* and an authority on ballistics, as the driver who killed the father. I suspect he will assume a prominent place in the story.[17]

He did. Corker in *Scoop* had been a trial run. Characters like Atwater in fact assumed a prominent place in all his post-war novels. Blasé, half-educated, insensitive bores who converse only in slang become a recognisable type: Hooper, Apthorpe, Trimmer. These were for Waugh the human mass-produce of the Age of the Common Man. The choice of name was perhaps mischievous. A Donald Attwater had written one of the Catholic press's few unfavourable reviews of *Waugh in Abyssinia*.[18]

At this time Waugh was considering enlistment as a private:

> I have to consider thirty years of novel-writing ahead of me. Nothing would be more likely than work in a government office to finish me as a writer; nothing more likely to stimulate me than a complete change of habit. There is a symbolic difference between fighting as a soldier and serving as a civilian, even if the civilian is more valuable.[19]

He was rejected by the Ministry of Information two days later. Nevertheless, 'to please Laura rather than with any hope of result' he tried for another desk job, this time at the Foreign Office.[20] Again he was refused.

His brother Alec had been taken back into the army without hesitation. Waugh seemed always to be hearing of friends already in uniform. He wrote sheafs of

16. *Ibid.*, 24 August, 1939, p. 437.
17. *Ibid.*, 26 August, 1939, pp. 437–8.
18. *DR*, January–June 1937, 174–5.
19. *Diaries*, 27 August, 1939, p. 438.
20. *Ibid.*, 1 September, 1939, p. 438.

letters trying to pull strings with influential acquaintances: Bruce Lockhart, A. D. Peters (then in the Ministry of Information), Ian Hay, Ian Fleming. But no-one wanted him. His applications seemed uniformly to be blocked as he was shuffled sideways from department to department.

He had advertised to let the house and was impatient to make definite plans. Chamberlain declared war on 3rd September. Five days later Waugh bitterly remarked: 'It seems a very long time since the war began. No-one seems anxious to take this house or to employ me on National Service.'[21] His suspicions were well-founded. Few thought him suitable for positions of responsibility. It was galling to Waugh to find his influence with the 'Great' so small, to discover that his own view of himself as a man of the world was not shared by others. He was not blackballed but he was blocked. For some time he was refused admission to their club.

Waugh's frustration was intensely felt. The unwillingness to declare war on Russia seemed to him dishonourable. Piers Court was eventually let for the duration to Dominican teaching nuns and Waugh, Laura and their baby moved once again to Pixton. Before long, however, the strains of the overburdened household became too great. 'Work out of the question', he noted, 'as the evacuated children are now admitted to the garden at the back of the house under my windows.'[22] Unable to sleep, he took large doses of sleeping draught only to wake in a state of melancholy mania. On 23rd October he left for the Easton Court Hotel 'in the hope of getting my novel finished, or nearly finished, by the time I could take Laura from Pixton'.[23] Laura was then eight months pregnant with their second child.

At the hotel he began to work well: 'Wrote all the morning', he recorded after his first full day there. 'The second chapter taking shape and, more important, ideas springing.'[24] A new enthusiasm gripped him and continued to deprive him of sleep: 'I take the MS of my novel up to my bedroom for fear it should be burned in the night. It has in fact got to interest me so much that for the first time since the war began I have ceased to fret about not being on active service.'[25] But almost as soon as he had begun in earnest, two events prevented his bringing this exciting project to its conclusion: on 18th November Auberon was born and on 7th December Waugh was called up to join the Marines. The Army had not wanted him but the Navy was prepared to take a chance. Despite the interruptions he had managed to write over ten thousand words at the hotel.

*

21. *Ibid.*, 8 September 1939, p. 441.
22. *Ibid.*, 19 October, 1939, p. 447.
23. *Ibid.*, 23 October, 1939, p. 447.
24. *Ibid.*, 24 October, 1939, p. 447.
25. *Ibid.*, 'All Saints' [1 November], 1939, p. 448.

Waugh described Laura after the birth as 'happier than she is likely to be again', and 'drowsy and contented'.[26] It is, surely, no coincidence that the birth of Lucy's baby plays such a prominent part in the unfinished novel. Waugh was drawing, for the first time, on the experience of the immediate present. He was also dredging his intimate memory. Laura's pregnancy seems to have stirred the emotions felt a decade earlier for Diana Guinness (Diana Mosley since 1936). In 1929 he had described her during her first pregnancy as 'a huge vat of potentiality'. One of his last letters, as we have seen, explained to her his devotion and his jealousy: 'After Jonathan's birth you began to enlarge your circle ... and I couldn't compete or take a humbler place.' In 1939 she was embroiled in Mosley's BUF and its stand-up fights with the communists. By 1940 both she and Mosley were in prison. Waugh had not seen her for years and thoroughly disapproved of her politics. But, hearing of her distress, he sent her a present. It was *Work Suspended*.

Lucy is not a portrait of Lady Diana. After Waugh's death Laura wrote to her emphasising this. He had fretted over his last days thinking that Diana might have been offended. She was not. She recognised that it was a composite characterisation. In many ways Lucy was every woman Waugh had loved in the 'thirties. She is beautiful and pregnant like Diana Guinness, open and amiable like Teresa Jungman, astute and sensible like Laura. He did not want only to write about the collapse of civilisation. He wanted for once to write about love and about himself.

Various aspects of Waugh's personality and attitudes are distributed between John Plant and his father. In John we find the workmanlike approach to fiction, the growing consciousness of the evils of contemporary society, the older man with the young woman and the spiritual exile with a mild distrust of his contemporaries. In the father we see the immediate abandonment of popular causes, the aesthetic predilection for representational, communicative art, the abomination of the standards of his youth, the rejection of Clive Bell and Bloomsbury, and an almost perverse delight in formality: the 'huge grim and solitary jest'[27] (of his 'Academy' teas) at the expense of his friends and the contemporary artistic establishment.

The text we have today is radically different even from the one Waugh originally published in a limited edition of five hundred copies in 1942. In the version reprinted in *Work Suspended and Other Stories*, Waugh tinkered with the details of the narrative, transforming it from a personal document into a more soberly 'topical' allegory.[28]

---

26. *Ibid.*, 19 and 22 November, 1939, p. 450.
27. *Work Suspended*, p. 117.
28. Mr Plant's unfinished picture was originally dated 1932 and represented 'an old shipwright pondering on the idle dockyard where lay the great skeleton of the Cunarder that was later to be known as the Queen Mary. It was to have been called "Too Big?" ' (p. 22);

The 1942 text dealt in detail with John Plant's literary technique, emphasising his relish in 'Gothic enrichments' and 'the masked buttresses, false domes, superfluous columns, all the subterfuges of literary architecture and the plaster and gilt of its decoration'. A long and important passage was cut from 'Part Two' outlining the essential limitations of the novelist's aesthetic:

> The algebra of fiction must reduce its problems to symbols if they are to be soluble at all. . . . There is no place in literature for a live man, solid and active. At best the author may maintain a kind of Dickensian menagerie, where his characters live behind bars in darkness, to be liberated twice nightly under the arc lamps. . . . 'Are the lions really alive?' 'Yes, lovey.' 'Will they eat us up?' 'No lovey, the man won't let them' – that is all the reviewers mean as a rule when they talk of 'life'. The alternative, classical expedient is to take the whole man and reduce him to a manageable abstraction. . . . Beyond these limits lie only the real trouser buttons and crepe hair with which the futurists used to adorn their paintings. It is, anyway, in the classical way that I have striven to write, how else can I write of Lucy?[29]

Perhaps Waugh felt this to be too easily identifiable with himself, perhaps it was omitted on aesthetic grounds as being irrelevant to the structural coherence of the whole. At any rate, both Plant's and Waugh's aesthetic relied on the concept of art as artifice – it should have 'absolutely nothing of [himself] in it'[30] – and this was the paradox at the heart of both their climacterics: the problem of describing the subjective objectively.

The novel is not, then, as it now appears, simply a reaction to the war but a discussion of deep-rooted personal and artistic problems which the revisions disguise and objectify. (In the original text the war is not mentioned.) The distance and formality of the relationship between father and son is a reflection of Waugh's estrangement from Arthur. Mr Plant senior lives in 1932, like Waugh in 1939,

---

This became the 1939 painting 'Again?', of 'a one-armed veteran of the First World War meditating over a German helmet' (Penguin, p. 119). The father's anti-semitism is much less explicit in the later text. The phrase ' "I could tell they [the property developers] were Jews . . . by the smell of their notepaper" ' is omitted; 'Israelite' replaces 'Jew', and these attitudes are not quietly endorsed by the discovery that Mr Hardcastle is Jewish. John Plant is no longer approached by Mr Godley who fears blackmail over the father's 'restoration' work because the Jellabies have already attempted extortion; Roger Simmonds becomes a 'Socialist' rather than a Communist. The titles of the two parts are altered: 'My Father's House' becoming 'A Death', and 'Lucy Simmonds' 'A Birth'. The only substantial addition to the original is the 'Postscript' which moves the story forward to 1939; the other alterations to dates (and, for instance, to the description of Mr Plant's painting) were made to concur with this shift in historical perspective.
29. *Work Suspended* (Chapman & Hall, 1942), pp. 82–3.
30. *Ibid.* (Penguin), p. 108.

believing himself secure behind the 'massive defences of . . . "the border line of sanity" ',[31] yet obsessed by anti-semitism and the intrusion of gross modern architecture; 'the destruction of my father's house'[32] is clearly a major theme. The house becomes more an image of the aesthetic heritage of the English consciousness than a parental home. It is not a place of warmth and security; it has no intrinsic aesthetic merit. But it represents, with its Morris wallpapers and fabrics, the last flourish of a valuable line of English artistic development in which the virtues of honest craftsmanship were paramount.

The first part was originally entitled 'My Father's House', the second 'Lucy Simmonds'. These were altered to 'A Death' and 'A Birth'. The change draws greater attention to the central theme of decay and regeneration. The birth is the birth of the new age; what has died with the father can never be replaced by the son. In the first section Waugh speaks of 'the hide and seek with one's own personality'[33] and the exposing of 'the bare minimum of ourselves'[34] as characteristic of modern 'civilised' man. The violation of privacy becomes a subtle *leitmotif*. A high price is set on 'modesty' and it is this which is degraded by Atwater and the seedy world of pre-war Britain.

The strong autobiographical element in Waugh's description of Plant's experience in Fez was noted at the beginning of Chapter XI. In travelling home from Fez, Plant moves 'from spring into winter'.[35] With the death of his father, who had 'an historic position, for he completed a period of English painting', [36] Plant begins to realise the plight of 'civilised' man, a strange, hybrid and vulnerable creature:

> Not until they have assumed the livery of defence can his emotions pass through the lines. . . . Sabotage behind the lines, a blind raised and lowered at a lighted window, a wire cut, a bolt loosened, a file disordered – that is how civilised man is undone.[37]

The substantially altered prose style reveals Waugh's new commitment. There is a more passionate evocation and a desire to work through analysis rather than implication.

*Work Suspended* is essentially an exposition of John Plant's climacteric as a writer. No direct correspondence exists between Plant's and Waugh's novels other than their mutual delight in craftsmanship; no hint is given as to the outcome of

31.  *Ibid.*, p. 120.
32.  *Ibid.*, p. 121.
33.  *Ibid.*, p. 124.
34.  *Ibid.*, p. 125.
35.  *Ibid.*, p. 126.
36.  *Ibid.*, p. 130.
37.  *Ibid.*, p. 131.

Plant's problem. But it is, surely, a metaphor for Waugh's own. Like Plant, he had no idea where it would end. Both marriage and the certain prospect of socialist government represented an assault on his private world, the first willingly embraced, the second, he considered, attempting to subvert his individuality. Waugh only knew that, like his hero, he needed 'new worlds to conquer' and feared that he might mechanically be 'turning out year after year the kind of book [he knew he could] write well', 'becoming purely a technical expert'.[38]

The 'sense of homelessness'[39] becomes a companion theme to that of the invasion of privacy. Plant is driven to the seclusion of the countryside; he no longer belongs to the London of his youth. Waugh saw the condition of dispossession as symptomatic of a society which condemned private property and discouraged individualism. Roger Simmonds in *Work Suspended* writes a play called 'Internal Combustion'. The trouble with ideological drama, he explains, is that it is ' "too mechanical. I mean the characters are economic types, not individuals, and as long as they look and speak like individuals it is bad art . . . " '. Plant agrees, but not with Simmonds's resolution of the difficulty: ' "I've cut out human beings altogether." '[40] It is an absurd parody of Waugh's own concept of 'a manageable abstraction' and another dig at rationalist art. Simmonds's aesthetic is precisely the reverse of Waugh's. Politically, Waugh could not conceive of a free society without private property or with dialectical art.

Atwater thus becomes an important symbolic agent in the story. He lacks masculinity, is a scrounger, an uncultured and insensitive confidence trickster, whining about injustice, living by his wits. He is without the merest common decency and, in asking for the return of the money for the wreath, becomes a focus for the hideous paradoxes Waugh saw in liberal humanist politics: 'So I put a note in an envelope and sent it to the man who had killed my father.'[41] Civilisation has come to represent an exact inversion of traditional values. The manufacturer's book of instructions for the robot of Democracy has been lost.

There seems no choice but to comply with the 'exploiters' who turn out only to be represented by the struggling Mr Hardcastle, enmeshed in 'the kaleidoscopic changes of small finance'.[42] The Pre-Raphaelite ideal is destroyed as bulldozers effortlessly wreck the family home. But it is essentially an anonymous force at work. There is no discernible enemy to attack and this is precisely 'the plight of civilised man' and the significance of the imagery of espionage in the passage quoted above.

The second section of *Work Suspended* deals with the three things which occupied Waugh's own attention in 1939: the new country house, the new baby,

38. *Ibid.*, p. 132.
39. *Ibid.*, p. 133.
40. *Ibid.*, p. 134.
41. *Ibid.*, p. 141.
42. *Ibid.*, p. 143.

and (in the later version) the imminent war. The reasons for moving out of town are carefully analysed. Plant's friends encourage him for the selfish reason of having somewhere to visit at weekends. But there is a more serious argument. His generation, he says,

> ... professed a specialised enthusiasm for domestic architecture. It was one of the peculiarities of my generation, and there is no accounting for it. In youth we had pruned our aesthetic emotions hard back so that in many cases they had reverted to briar stock; we none of us wrote or read poetry or, if we did, it was of a kind which left unsatisfied those wistful, half-romantic, half-aesthetic, peculiarly British longings.... When the poetic mood was on us we turned to buildings, and gave them a place which our fathers accorded to Nature – to almost any buildings, but particularly those in the classical tradition, and, more particularly, in its decay.[43]

This is clearly autobiographical – Waugh even mentions the William Halfpenny works purchased during the composition of the novel.

There are many close parallels between Waugh's life and his hero's. Plant and his contemporaries 'defame' their own work as a gesture towards modesty. Lucy is a 'serious' and 'critical'[44] girl, in many respects like Laura. Plant, like Waugh, considers marriage 'an honourable profession'; he admires 'the Mediterranean respect for the permanence of the arrangement'.[45] It is the intimacy of this material which demands the new prose style and it noticeably strains under the pressure. In trying to describe the sensation of love Plant (or Waugh) ends by relinquishing the attempt, saying that it is 'beyond the proper scope of letters'.[46] Possibly the whole book is to some degree an abstract attempt to define the nature of his feelings for Laura and the way in which she had altered his life.

Lucy's social ease, her *savoir-faire*, is faultless, but not in any superficial metropolitan sense. She has solved the 'question of intrusion' in that she is impervious to insult and seems at home with everyone. Plant's initial feelings in her presence were that 'we had no separate or individual existence'.[47] She is an aristocrat and (unlike Laura) a socialist. Plant finds her provocative because he, the artist, wishes to 'assert ... [his] separate and individual existence'. Lucy's cool amiability represents 'a tiny disorder' in his life. He wishes to control 'the mirrored corridor

43. *Ibid.*, pp. 145–6.
44. *Ibid.*, pp. 150 and 151.
45. *Ibid.*, p. 151.
46. *Ibid.*, p. 152.
47. *Ibid.*, p. 155.

of cumulative emotion'.[48] The competitive parlour game of *'sauve qui peut'*[49] between himself and his contemporaries alarms her and results in her withdrawal from it. At first Plant sees this as priggishness. Later he appreciates her honesty and falls in love with her. But he feels too old to return wholeheartedly to her stage of innocent emotional exchange.

Into this complex, almost as a third party to the relationship, Waugh introduces Humboldt's Gibbon. It is an oddly ambivalent image. On the one hand it suggests the daemonically beautiful. Fierce, vital, grotesque, it is beyond the world of nannies' snobbery or Marxist dogma. It is perhaps a last image of the exotic and stimulating forces being obliterated in a world determined on a course of standardisation. But the animal's name offers another reference, now no longer humorous, to decline and fall and a monstrous atavism. Humboldt's Gibbon has no 'tricks', 'or, if he had, performed them alone, for his own satisfaction, after dark, ritualistically . . .'.[50] The ape suggests recession into primitivism. But simultaneously he is symbolic of primal individuality; like the 'real' artist, he is careless of the desire to impress. The hollow men surrounding Plant adopt convenient roles and he himself wants somewhere to hang his hats,[51] somewhere to house his partial social identities under one roof. The relationship with Lucy and the 'beauty' of Humboldt's Gibbon appear to offer some hope but, with the birth of the baby, sentimentality – the hackneyed slack emotions of maternity – intrudes; Lucy's clarity becomes clouded and she sinks back into the new age, her vocabulary reduced to 'sweet' and 'Kempy'.

Doubtless Waugh felt that the first edition did not make his points strongly enough when, in the revision, with the hindsight of the war, he added the 'Postscript'. In this the theme of the 'petrified egg' is reinforced by the image of the beavers in a concrete pool, which, with futile efforts, dam 'the ancestral stream'.[52] Traditional values, bulwarks against chaos (controls on the flood) are now without point. In his dedication to Alexander Woollcott, Waugh remarked: ' . . . even if I were again to have the leisure to finish it, the work would be vain, for the world in which and for which it was designed, has ceased to exist.' Plant's house is requisitioned, his father's house destroyed, Lucy lost for ever. The novel, like Waugh's own, remains 'a heap of neglected foolscap at the back of a drawer'.[53]

\*

48. *Ibid.*, p. 163. The relationship between Plant and Lucy is asexual. One Penguin edition called it 'a highly illicit love affair with his best friend's heavily pregnant wife'. In fact, it is taken for granted by Plant/Waugh that the pregnancy suspends sexual relations (cf. p. 163: ' . . . deprived of sex, as women are, by its fulfilment . . .').
49. *Ibid.*, p. 150.
50. *Ibid.*, p. 181.
51. Cf. *ibid.*, p. 133: 'My worries at this period became symbolised in a single problem; what to do with my hats.'
52. *Ibid.*, p. 193.
53. *Ibid.*, p. 194.

Before being called up Waugh wrote to John Betjeman enclosing 'the first chapter of a novel I have been writing and have discontinued. It would have been O.K.'[54] His later correspondence with Betjeman complains bitterly of the poet's desire to join a defensive regiment: 'The only way to bring this business to a happy conclusion is to kill a great number of Germans. If we go on thinking only of defence there will be nothing worth defending. Why do you prefer defence? I can't understand it.'[55] The discontinuation of the novel was symbolic. Its theme was, at least in part, an attempt to analyse why the civilised man's emotions must 'assume the livery of defence' before they can 'pass through the lines'. That shyness had been abandoned; an aggressive attitude was adopted after being so long submerged in an inability openly to wage war on the polite belief in progress. The problem had been the absence of a clearly-defined enemy. Now, as he expressed it (ironically) in *Men at Arms* (1952):

> . . . splendidly, everything had become clear. The enemy was plain in view, huge and hateful, all disguise cast off. It was the Modern Age in arms. Whatever the outcome there was a place for him in that battle.[56]

Guy Crouchback comes later to see this as an illusion but it fairly represents Waugh's own crusading spirit in 1939.

Ultimately, we can only guess at the real reasons for Waugh's inability to complete *Work Suspended*. His dedication to Woollcott represents only one aspect of the truth. But perhaps it was simply because he felt that he had failed to resolve the aesthetic problem of rendering the subjective objectively. 'Objectivity' in his post-war work relies on the assumption of a higher reality ultimately governing the action, where the 'determining character of the human soul' is 'that of being God's creature with a defined purpose'. No such dimension had been built into *Work Suspended* and Waugh may have decided that to continue his normal, externalised analysis of behaviour was meaningless; the negative assertion of order through an evocation of chaos now seemed inadequate. He had effected the stylistic but not the thematic transformation.

The novel thus became a curiosity to him, a museum piece made redundant by the fact that the characterisation failed to fit with the technical experiments. He would have needed completely to re-write the sections we have in order to include the dimension of 'supernatural' reality. Possibly, he was a little afraid of it. Although *Put Out More Flags* (1942) employs the fuller, more sensuous prose style, if anything it regresses towards the well-tried negative suggestion. Only with *Brideshead* did he take up the challenge he had set himself.

*

54. Unpublished ALS to [Sir] John Betjeman, nd [late November?], 1939, from Piers Court.
55. Unpublished ALS to [Sir] John Betjeman, nd [probably January, 1940], from Kingsdowne House Camp, Walmer.
56. *Men at Arms*, p. 5.

Six days after the birth of his son, Waugh was on the London train travelling up for his medical with the Marines. This time he was hopeful of a commission, but, at thirty-six, small, plump, myopic and unfit, he cannot have been certain of success. He had contingency plans for a civilian literary life. In September he had written to Peters saying that, if no-one wanted him for active service, he might go to the Faroe Islands to complete *Work Suspended*. Osbert Sitwell, David Cecil and he were negotiating with Chapman and Hall to found a monthly magazine, *Duration*. It came to nothing. Over dinner that evening Patrick Balfour informed him that the idea had already been up-staged by Cyril Connolly. Connolly's *Horizon* was to become a significant vehicle for Waugh's work. 'My Father's House' first appeared there in 1941; in 1948 an entire issue of the magazine was devoted to the first publication of *The Loved One*.

Balfour's news did not depress Waugh: he was already drunk on champagne. *Life Magazine* had unexpectedly commissioned two articles at $1,000 each and, after being prodded in various organs and cheating the optician, he had been accepted for the Marine Infantry. Waugh had been given a sealed envelope to take from the medical to the Admiralty interview. In the cab he had opened it and found that he had been pronounced unfit for active service. But it made no difference. The medical was obviously a formality: Winston Churchill and Brendan Bracken were backing his application. Duff Cooper had been First Lord until resigning over the Munich crisis. Fair means or foul: Waugh was both impervious to the indignity of benefiting by favouritism and ungrateful to his benefactors. Churchill and Bracken met with spiteful rebukes in the following years.

In high spirits, Waugh headed for a 'low joint', the Slip-In, where he found a character from his youth, Kathleen Meyrick. 'Ma' Meyrick was the infamous nightclub proprietress who had put one of her sons through Harrow and married her daughters into the peerage on the profits from illegal drinking establishments: the Forty-Three, the Silver Slipper, the Manhattan. Waugh sat down with her, a young man again, and drank three more bottles of champagne and one of brandy. About five in the morning he felt suddenly older and was sick.

'The subsequent hangover', he recorded, 'removed all illusions of heroism. I went to confession at Farm Street.'[57] Seeking a cure at the Ritz he met Randolph Churchill and Richard Plunket Greene; then Henry Yorke with whom he lunched. Yorke had preferred the Fire Brigade to the forces. Waugh was repelled by the idea. He looked to the Marines to supply those two virtues absent from his behaviour of the previous evening: dignity and discipline. 'A ghastly journey back, dark, cold, and feeling ill. I arrived to find Laura very much worse than I had left her, lachrymose and complaining of pleurisy.'[58]

57. *Diaries*, 26 November, 1939, p. 451.
58. *Ibid.*, 26 November, 1939, p. 451.

The next day, with Laura in the depths of post-natal depression, was Auberon's christening. Three of the godparents – Christopher Hollis, Frank Pakenham and Mary Lygon – failed to turn up, being cut off by the weather. Only Katharine Asquith got through. It was wet and cold and Waugh, miserable enough, felt it necessary to stay at Pixton to comfort his wife. Then, after so much delay, the Admiralty's letter arrived with inconvenient haste. He was to be in Chatham on 7th December, nine days after the christening.

This scarcely allowed time to order his affairs. (He had, for instance, no proper will providing for the two children.) He spent a full week alone with Laura, often in her room, writing letters, sharing meals and the crossword, watching her health improve. Both relished this as possibly the last intimate moment of their marriage.

Waugh's devotion to her is beyond question. Ultimately, though, he was irritated by such 'liverish inactivity'[59] and keen to be gone. He wanted to get on with the fighting. He was, in fact, anticipating a new love affair – with military tradition. 'The regular Marines are delightful people . . .', he noted on arrival at Chatham:

All the senior officers greeted us like embarrassed hosts with a flow of apology for the discomforts of our life. Something too of oriental courtesy . . . but, like oriental courtesy, based on great self-confidence. The barracks and mess are . . . extremely agreeable. I have a large bedroom, with a large fire and one-third of a derelict batman. The architecture of the square is charming and the mess full of trophies. . . . [60]

This was exactly what he had been looking for: power with grace. Waugh saw here only a fastidious, masculine tradition of selfless courage, culture opposing anarchy. In the Marines he believed he had found the courtesy and taste of the eighteenth-century gentleman surviving among its regular officers. He felt immediately at home. Many months were to pass before he could accept that this was yet another club which could dispense with his membership.

*

In 1930, as the agnostic author of *Vile Bodies*, embittered by his first wife's desertion, he had answered a questionnaire. It was a frivolous attempt to forecast the future and Waugh treated it as dismissively as it deserved. 'What', it asked, 'will be the religion of the future?' 'Christianity', Waugh had replied '(probably Roman Catholicism).' 'Can war be outlawed?' 'No!' 'If love dies, should marriage be dissolved?' 'No, why on earth should it be?' 'Should wives have a career?' 'No. Not because they are wives, but because they are women and therefore incompetent.' 'Are children necessary to a successful marriage?' 'Yes, dozens of them.' 'Shall chivalry continue?' 'I don't understand. (a) *Will* it in fact continue,

59. *Ibid.*, 28 November, 1939, p. 452.
60. *Ibid.*, 28 November, 1939, p. 453.

or *shall* it continue? (b) I don't know what chivalry is. Good manners? Superstitious respect for women? Boy-scoutism? Anyway I think it is high time it stopped whatever it is.'[61]

In 1939 he would have disclaimed his last reply. As he settled into the Marines he knew (or thought he knew) exactly what chivalry was.

61. Leonard Henslowe (ed.), *Things Have Changed* (Philip Allen & Co., 1930), pp. 70–1.

# Select Bibliography

[Place of publication is London unless otherwise stated.]

## 1. WORKS BY EVELYN WAUGH

*The World to Come: A Poem in Three Cantos* (privately printed, 1916).

*P. R. B. An Essay on the Pre-Raphaelite Brotherhood, 1847–1854* (privately printed, Alastair Graham, 1926).

'The Balance: A Yarn of the Good Old Days of Broad Trousers and High Necked Jumpers' in *Georgian Stories 1926*, ed. Alec Waugh (Chapman & Hall, 1926).

Preface to *Thirty-Four Decorative Designs by Francis Crease* (privately printed, Oxford, A. R. Mowbray & Co.; E. W.'s preface dated August 1927).

*Rossetti, His Life and Works* (Duckworth, 1928; New York, Dodd, Mead & Co., 1928). Reprinted Duckworth, 1975 with an Introduction by John Bryson.

*Decline and Fall, An Illustrated Novellette* (Chapman & Hall, 1928; New York, Doubleday, Doran 1929; New York, Farrar & Rinehart, 1929). Revised Uniform Edition (with Preface by E. W.), Chapman & Hall, 1962. Reprinted Harmondsworth, Penguin Books, 1937.

*Vile Bodies* (Chapman & Hall, 1930; New York, Cape, Smith, 1930). Revised Uniform Edition (with Preface by E. W.), Chapman & Hall, 1965. Reprinted Harmondsworth, Penguin Books, 1938.

*Labels, A Mediterranean Journal* (Duckworth, 1930); US edition: *A Bachelor Abroad, A Mediterranean Journal* (New York, Cape, Smith, 1930). Reprinted Duckworth, 1975 with an Introduction by Kingsley Amis; reprinted Harmondsworth, Penguin Travel Library, 1985.

*Remote People* (Duckworth, 1931); US edition: *They Were Still Dancing* (New York, Farrar & Rinehart, 1932). Reprinted Duckworth, 1986; reprinted Harmondsworth, Penguin Travel Library, 1985.

*Black Mischief* (Chapman & Hall, 1932; New York, Farrar & Rinehart, 1932). Revised Uniform Edition (with Preface by E. W.), Chapman & Hall, 1962. Reprinted Harmondsworth, Penguin Books, 1938.

*An Open Letter to H. E. the Cardinal Archbishop of Westminster* (privately printed but not distributed. Whitefriar's Press, 1933; first published in edited version, *Letters*, 1980).

*Ninety-Two Days, The Account of a Tropical Journey Through British Guiana and Part of Brazil* (Duckworth, 1934; New York, Farrar & Rinehart, 1934). Reprinted Harmondsworth, Penguin Travel Library, 1986.

## SELECT BIBLIOGRAPHY

*A Handful of Dust* (Chapman & Hall, 1934; New York, Farrar & Rinehart, 1934). Revised Uniform Edition (with Preface by E. W.), Chapman & Hall, 1964. Reprinted Harmondsworth, Penguin Books, 1951.

*Edmund Campion: Jesuit and Martyr* (Longman, 1935; New York, Sheed & Ward, 1935). 2nd revised edition (with Preface by E. W.), Boston, Little, Brown & Co., 1946; London, Hollis & Carter, 1947. Reprinted OUP, 1980.

*Mr Loveday's Little Outing and Other Sad Stories* (Chapman & Hall, 1936; Boston, Little, Brown, 1936).

*Waugh in Abyssinia* (Longman, Green & Co., 1936; New York, Longman, Green & Co., 1936). Reprinted Methuen, 1984 and Harmondsworth, Penguin Travel Library, 1985.

*Scoop: A Novel About Journalists* (Chapman & Hall, 1938; Boston, Little Brown, 1938). Revised Uniform Edition (with Preface by E. W.), Chapman & Hall, 1964. Reprinted Harmondsworth, Penguin Books, 1943.

*Robbery Under Law: The Mexican Object-Lesson* (Chapman & Hall, 1939); US edition: *Mexico: An Object-Lesson* (Boston, Little, Brown, 1939).

*My Father's House* [the first section of *Work Suspended*, later re-titled 'A Death' in the 1942 text; see below], *Horizon*, Vol. IV, No. 23 (November 1941), 329–341.

*Put Out More Flags* (Chapman & Hall, 1942; Boston, Little, Brown, 1942). Revised Uniform Edition (with Preface by E. W.), Chapman & Hall, 1967. Reprinted Harmondsworth, Penguin Books, 1943

*Work Suspended* [limited edition of 500 copies] (Chapman & Hall, 1942; reprinted in revised version *Work Suspended and Other Stories etc.* (1949, see below) and *Tactical Exercise* (1954, see below)). Reprinted Harmondsworth, Penguin Books, 1951 (see below).

*Brideshead Revisited: The Sacred and Profane Memories of Captain Charles Ryder* (Chapman & Hall, 1945; Boston, Little, Brown, 1945). Revised Uniform Edition (with Preface by E. W.), Chapman & Hall, 1960. Reprinted Harmondsworth, Penguin Books, 1951; revised edition, 1962.

*When the Going Was Good* (Duckworth, 1946; Boston, Little Brown, 1946). Reprinted Harmondsworth, Penguin Books, 1951.

*Scott-King's Modern Europe* (Chapman & Hall, 1947; Boston, Little, Brown, 1949). Reprinted in *Work Suspended and Other Stories*, Harmondsworth, Penguin Books, 1951.

*Wine In Peace and War* (privately printed, Saccone and Speed, Ltd, 1947).

*The Loved One* (Chapman & Hall, 1948; Boston, Little, Brown, 1948). Revised Uniform Edition (with Preface by E. W.), Chapman & Hall, 1965. Reprinted Harmondsworth, Penguin Books, 1951.

*Work Suspended and Other Stories Written Before the Second World War* (Chapman & Hall, 1949). Reprinted Harmondsworth, Penguin Books, 1951.

*Helena* (Chapman & Hall, 1950; Boston, Little, Brown, 1952). Reprinted Harmondsworth, Penguin Books, 1963.

*Men At Arms* (Chapman & Hall, 1952; Boston, Little, Brown, 1952. Reprinted Harmondsworth, Penguin Books, 1964.

*The Holy Places* (Queen Anne Press, 1952; New York, Queen Anne Press and British Book Center, 1953).

*Love Among the Ruins: A Romance of the New Future* (Chapman & Hall, 1953). Reprinted in *The Ordeal of Gilbert Pinfold*, Harmondsworth, Penguin Books, 1962.

*Tactical Exercise* [US edition of short stories] (Boston, Little, Brown, 1954). Eponymous story reprinted in *The Ordeal of Gilbert Pinfold*, Harmondsworth, Penguin Books, 1962.

*Officers and Gentlemen* (Chapman & Hall, 1955; Boston, Little, Brown, 1955). Reprinted Harmondsworth, Penguin Books, 1964.

*The Ordeal of Gilbert Pinfold* (Chapman & Hall, 1957; Boston, Little, Brown, 1957). Reprinted Harmondsworth, Penguin Books, 1962 with 'Tactical Exercise' and 'Love Among the Ruins'.

*The Life of the Right Reverend Ronald Knox* (Chapman & Hall, 1959); US edition: *Monsignor Ronald Knox* (Boston, Little, Brown, 1959).

*A Tourist In Africa* (Chapman & Hall, 1960; Boston, Little, Brown, 1960).

*Unconditional Surrender* (Chapman & Hall, 1961); US edition: *The End of the Battle* (Boston, Little, Brown, 1961). Reprinted Harmondsworth, Penguin Books, 1964.

*Basil Seal Rides Again or The Rake's Regress* (Chapman & Hall, 1963; Boston, Little, Brown, 1963). Reprinted in *Work Suspended and Other Stories*, Harmondsworth, Penguin Books, 1967.

*A Little Learning. The First Volume of an Autobiography* (Chapman & Hall, 1964; Boston, Little, Brown, 1964). Reprinted Harmondsworth, Penguin Books, 1983.

*Sword of Honour. A Final Version of the Novels: Men At Arms (1952), Officers and Gentlemen (1955), and Unconditional Surrender (1961)* (Chapman & Hall, 1965; Boston, Little, Brown, 1966). Reprinted Harmondsworth, Penguin Books, 1964 and 1984.


## 2. EVELYN WAUGH'S PRIVATE PAPERS AND JOURNALISM

| | |
|---|---|
| Amory, Mark (ed.), | *The Letters of Evelyn Waugh* (Weidenfeld and Nicolson, 1980). |
| Davie, Michael (ed.), | *The Diaries of Evelyn Waugh* (Weidenfeld and Nicolson, 1976). |
| Gallagher, Donat (ed.), | *The Essays, Articles and Reviews of Evelyn Waugh* (Methuen, 1983). |

## 3. MEMOIRS

| | |
|---|---|
| Acton, Harold, | *Memoirs of an Aesthete* (Methuen, 1948). *More Memoirs of an Aesthete* (Methuen, 1970). |
| Balfour, Patrick, | *Society Racket. A Critical Survey of Modern Social Life* (John Long, 1932). |

## SELECT BIBLIOGRAPHY

Beaton, Cecil,      *The Wandering Years. Diaires 1922–1934* (Weidenfeld & Nicolson, 1966).

Bowra, C. M.,      *Memories* (Weidenfeld & Nicolson, 1966).

Carew, Dudley,      *A Fragment of Friendship. Evelyn Waugh as a Young Man* (Everest Books, 1974).

Connolly, Cyril,      *Previous Convictions* (New York & Evanston, Harper & Row, 1963).

Cooper, Diana,      *The Light of Common Day* (Rupert Hart-Davis, 1959).

Cooper, Duff,      *Old Men Forget* (Rupert Hart-Davis, 1956).

Donaldson, Frances,      *Evelyn Waugh. Portrait of a Country Neighbour* (Weidenfeld & Nicolson, 1967).

Farago, Ladislas (ed.),      *Abyssinian Stop Press* (Robert Hale, 1936).

Glen, Alexander,      *Young Men in the Arctic. The Oxford University Arctic Expedition* (Faber & Faber, 1935).

Green, Henry,      *Pack My Bag: A Self-Portrait* (Hogarth Press, 1940).

Greene, Graham,      *Ways of Escape* (Bodley Head, 1980).

Greenidge, Terence,      *Degenerate Oxford?* (Chapman & Hall, 1930).

Hollis, Christopher,      *Along the Road to Frome* (Harrap, 1958).
*The Seven Ages* (Heinemann, 1974).
*Oxford in The Twenties: Recollections of Five Friends* (Heinemann, 1976),

Holman-Hunt, Diana,      *My Grandfather: His Wives and Loves* (Hamish Hamilton, 1969).

Holman Hunt, William,      *Pre-Raphaelitism and the Pre-Raphaelite Brotherhood* (Chapman & Hall, 1913).

Mosley, Diana Mitford,      *A Life of Contrasts* (Hamish Hamilton, 1977).
*Loved Ones* (Sidgwick & Jackson, 1985).

Pakenham, Frank,      *Born to Believe* (Cape, 1953).

Powell, Anthony,      *To Keep the Ball Rolling. Vol. 2: Messengers of Day* (Heinemann, 1978).

Pryce-Jones, David (ed.),      *Evelyn Waugh and His World* (Weidenfeld & Nicolson, 1973).

Rowse, A. L.,      *A Man of the Thirties* (Weidenfeld & Nicolson, 1979).
*Glimpses of the Great* (Methuen, 1985).

St John, John,      *To The War With Waugh* (Leo Cooper, 1973).

Sitwell, Osbert,      *Laughter in the Next Room* (Macmillan, 1949).

Sykes, Christopher,      *Four Studies in Loyalty* (Collins, 1946).
*Evelyn Waugh: A Biography* (Collins, 1975).

Waugh, Alec,      *The Early Years of Alec Waugh* (Cassell, 1962).

|  | *My Brother Evelyn and Other Profiles* (Cassell, 1967). |
|  | *The Fatal Gift* (W. H. Allen, 1973). |
|  | *A Year to Remember: A Reminiscence of 1931* (W. H. Allen, 1975). |
| Waugh, Arthur, | *A Hundred Years of Publishing* (Chapman & Hall, 1930). |
|  | *One Man's Road* (Chapman & Hall, 1931). |
| Wilson, Edmund, | *Classics and Commercials: A Literary Chronicle of the Forties* (W. H. Allen, 1951). |

## 4. CRITICAL WORKS

| Bradbury, Malcolm, | *Evelyn Waugh* (Oliver & Boyd, 1964), 'Writers & Critics' series. |
| Carens, James F., | *The Satiric Art of Evelyn Waugh* (Seattle & London, University of Washington Press, 1966). |
| Connolly, Cyril, | *Enemies of Promise* (Routledge, 1938). |
|  | *The Condemned Playground. Essays 1927–1944* (Routledge, 1945). |
| Cook, William J., Jr | *Masks, Modes and Morals: The Art of Evelyn Waugh* (Cranbury, N.J., Fairleigh Dickinson University Press, 1971). |
| Davis, Robert Murray, | *Evelyn Waugh, Writer* (Oklahoma, Pilgrim Books, 1981). |
| De Vitis, A. A., | *Roman Holiday. The Catholic Novels of Evelyn Waugh* (Vision Press, 1958). |
| Dyson, A. E., | 'Evelyn Waugh and the Mysteriously Disappearing Hero' in *The Crazy Fabric* (Macmillan, 1965). |
| Eagleton, Terry, | *Exiles and Emigrés* (Chatto & Windus, 1970). |
| Forster, E. M. | *Anonymity* (Hogarth Press, 1925), 'Hogarth Essays' series. |
| Fry, Roger, | *The Artist and Psycho-Analysis* (Hogarth Press, 1924). 'Hogarth Essays' series. |
|  | *Flemish Art: A Critical Survey* (Chatto & Windus, 1927). |
| Fussell, Paul, | *Abroad* (OUP, 1980). |
| Green, Martin, | *Children of the Sun. A Narrative of 'Decadence' in England After 1918* (Constable, 1977). |
| Greenblatt, Stephen Jay, | *Three Modern Satirists: Waugh, Orwell and Huxley* (Yale University Press, 1965). |
| Heath, Jeffrey, | *The Picturesque Prison* (Weidenfeld & Nicolson, 1982). |

## SELECT BIBLIOGRAPHY

Hollis, Christopher,  'Evelyn Waugh' (Longman's pamphlet for British Council, 1966). 'Writers and their Work' series.

Johnstone, Richard,  *The Will to Believe: Novelists of the Thirties* (OUP, 1982).

Kermode, Frank,  'Mr Waugh's Cities' in *Puzzles and Epiphanies: Essays and Reviews 1958–1961* (Routledge & Kegan Paul, 1962).

Linck, Charles E., Jr,  'The Development of Evelyn Waugh's Career: 1903–1939' (PhD thesis, University of Kansas, 1962).

Littlewood, Ian,  *The Writings of Evelyn Waugh* (Oxford, Basil Blackwell, 1983).

Lodge, David,  'Evelyn Waugh' (Columbia University Press, 1971), 'Columbia Essays on Modern Writers' series.

McDonnell, Jacqueline,  *Waugh on Women* (Duckworth, 1986).

McNamara, Jack Donald,  'Literary Agent A. D. Peters and Evelyn Waugh, 1928–1966: "Quantitative Judgments Don't Apply" ' (PhD thesis, University of Texas at Austin, 1983).

Myers, William,  'Evelyn Waugh' in *British Writers*, Volume 7 (Scribners, 1984), pp. 289–308.

O'Donnel, Donat,  *Maria Cross: Imaginative Patterns in a Group of Modern Catholic Writers* (New York, OUP, 1952).

O'Faolain, Sean,  *The Vanishing Hero: Studies in the Novelists of the Twenties* (Eyre & Spottiswoode, 1957).

Phillips, Gene, D.,  *Evelyn Waugh's Officers, Gentlemen and Rogues: The Fact Behind His Fiction* (Chicago, Nelson-Hall, 1975).

Spender, Stephen,  'The World of Evelyn Waugh' in *The Creative Element: A Study of Vision, Despair and Orthodoxy Among Some Modern Writers* (Hamish Hamilton, 1953).

Stannard, Martin (ed.),  *Evelyn Waugh: The Critical Heritage* (Routledge & Kegan Paul, 1984).

Stopp, Frederick J.,  *Evelyn Waugh, Portrait of the Artist* (Chapman & Hall, 1958).

Tosser, Yvon,  *Le Sens de l'Absurde Dans L'Oeuvre d'Evelyn Waugh* (Réproduction des Thèses, Université de Lille III, 1977).

Waley, Hubert,  'The Revival of Aesthetics' (Hogarth Press, 1926), 'Hogarth Essays' series.

## 5. INTERVIEWS WITH WAUGH

16 November, 1953:      Charles Wilmot, Jack Davies and Stephen Black for the 'Frankly Speaking' series, BBC Home Service: BBCSL

26 June, 1960:      John Freeman for the 'Face to Face' series, BBC TV; BBCSL.

April 1962:      Julian Jebb for the *Paris Review*; text in *Writers At Work. The Paris Review Interviews. Third Series* (Secker & Warburg, 1968), pp. 103–114.

16 February, 1964:      Elizabeth Jane Howard for the 'Monitor' series, BBC TV

## 6. CATALOGUES

Davis, Robert Murray,      A Catalogue of the Evelyn Waugh Collection at the Humanities Research Center, The University of Texas at Austin (New York, Whitston Publishing Co., 1981).

Davis, Robert Murray, Paul A. Doyle, Heinz Kosok, Charles E. Linck Jr.      Evelyn Waugh: A Checklist of Primary and Secondary Material (New York, Whitston Publishing Co., 1972).

# Index

## Works by Evelyn Waugh

The following section of the Index is divided thus:

## 5. FILM SCENARIOS

## 6. POETRY

## 7. SHORT FICTION

# 8. NON-FICTION

## 9. TRAVEL

# General Index